Digitalisation and Development

"India is undergoing rapid digitalization thanks to wide-spread diffusion of mobile phones across the country. While boosting India's economic growth, this process also exacerbates social challenges in terms of digital exclusion and inequalities. To understand the trade-offs between opportunities and challenges posed by digitalization, this book takes an expansive and multi-disciplinary perspective, combining insights from a variety of socio-economic dimensions. This offers an original and multifaceted view, which will be highly relevant for scholars, policy-makers, and practitioners interested in the current processes of digitalization and development."

—Professor Govindan Parayil, *Dean and Professor, University of South Florida, Tampa, USA*

"This work is a balanced and comprehensive survey and analysis of India's engagement with the ICT revolution including international comparisons. It is especially strong in mapping and assessing the channels of influence and the array of consequences from this engagement."

—Professor Edward Steinmueller, *R.M. Phillips Professor for the Economics of Innovation, Science Policy Research Unit, University of Sussex Brighton, UK*

"The digital economy is now the buzzword, but we know little about its developmental implications. This fine book addresses the gap in the literature, using India as a case-study."

—Professor Kunal Sen, *Director, UNU-WIDER, Helsinki, Finland*

Dibyendu Maiti · Fulvio Castellacci ·
Arne Melchior
Editors

Digitalisation and Development

Issues for India and Beyond

Springer

Editors
Dibyendu Maiti
Delhi School of Economics
Delhi, India

Arne Melchior
Senior Research Fellow
Norwegian Institute of International Affairs
Oslo, Norway

Fulvio Castellacci
Head of Department
Centre for Technology, Innovation
and Culture
Oslo, Norway

ISBN 978-981-13-9995-4 ISBN 978-981-13-9996-1 (eBook)
https://doi.org/10.1007/978-981-13-9996-1

This Springer imprint is published by the registered company Springer Nature Singapore Pte Ltd.
The registered company address is: 152 Beach Road, #21-01/04 Gateway East, Singapore 189721, Singapore

Acknowledgements

This edited volume collects some selected papers presented at the international conference on "ICTs, Digital Divide and Development" jointly organized by Delhi School of Economics, the TIK Centre for Technology, Innovation and Culture (University of Oslo) and the Norwegian Institute of International Affairs (NUPI) during 22–23 February 2018 in New Delhi. We acknowledge the financial support provided by the Research Council of Norway (SAMANSVAR research program; project grant no. 247921), which has made it possible to organize the event and edit the book, and also to finance a mobility grant to host Prof. Maiti at the University of Oslo during spring 2019 for the last phase and finalization of this book project, and earlier visits at NUPI for its preparation during summer in 2016 and 2017. Sincere thanks are also due to T. C. A. Anant, Aditya Bhattacharjea, Uday Bhanu Sinha, Anirban Kar and Mausumi Das, who volunteered to offer useful suggestions and comments for the revision of some chapters.

Contents

Editors and Contributors

About the Editors

Dibyendu Maiti is Associate Professor of Economics at Delhi School of Economics. Before joining at Delhi School, he worked at the University of the South Pacific (Fiji), Institute of Economic Growth, Centre for Studies in Social Sciences (Calcutta), the University of Manchester (UK). He held various research positions at Max Planck Institute of Economics (Jena, Germany), University of Nottingham, Chinese Academy of Social Sciences, University of Oslo, Norwegian Institute of International. He publishes articles in *Journal of Development Economics, Economic Modelling, Labour Economics, Journal of Productivity Analysis, Cambridge Journal of Economics, American Behavioural Scientists, Journal of International Trade and Economic Development* etc. He received the IDRC Indian Young Social Scientist Award 2009 and Global Development Network Award 2010. Currently, he is an associate editor of *Progress in Development Studies* (Sage) from 2018. He worked on research projects sponsored by ICSSR, WTO, ESRC, DFID and serves the national and international organisation as a consultant.

Fulvio Castellacci is Director of the TIK Centre for Technology, Innovation and Culture at the University of Oslo. He has a PhD in Innovation Studies (University of Oslo, 2004) and a PhD ("Dottorato di Ricerca") in Economics (University of Rome La Sapienza, 2005). He was Senior Research Fellow at the Norwegian Institute of International Affairs (NUPI) since 2007, and Head of Department of International Economics at NUPI between 2008 and 2014. Since 2014, he has been working as Director of the TIK Centre at the University of Oslo. His research interests are within the economics of innovation, and specifically on the patterns and socio-economic impacts of R&D and technological innovation at the firm, sector and country-levels of analysis. His research is published in major journals in this field, e.g. Research Policy, Industrial and Corporate Change, and World Development.

Arne Melchior is Senior Research Fellow at the Norwegian Institute of International Affairs (NUPI), Oslo, Norway, where he has headed the Research Group on International Economics and Trade for extended periods, and managed a large number of research projects focusing on international trade. He holds a PhD in international economics from the University of Oslo (1997) and a Certificate of Advanced European Studies at College of Europe, Belgium. His research focuses on international trade, trade policy and economic geography, with a large number of books, articles, policy-related and popular publications. Work in recent years includes studies of Russia, China, India and Western Europe and the use of large-scale numerical models. The book "Free Trade Agreements and Globalisation: In the Shadow of Brexit and Trump" (Palgrave Macmillan, 2018) uses a new model of the world economy in the analysis of world trade and trade agreements. Melchior also has extensive experience from university teaching as well as academic and popular presentations in Norway and abroad, as well as an early career dealing with international trade negotiations.

Contributors

Anubha Agarwal is a Ph.D. student at the University of Toronto. She has completed her B.A. Honors (Economics) from Shri Ram College of Commerce, University of Delhi, and M.A. Economics from Delhi School of Economics. She has worked as an assistant professor of Economics at St. Stephen's College, University of Delhi. She also worked at the Centre for Development Economics (Delhi School of Economics) as a research assistant in the project titled "ICT, Responsible Innovation and Wellbeing". She has also served at PwC-US Advisory in Bangalore as an associate in the analytics-embedded consulting space.

Poulomi Bhattacharya is a Ph.D. student in the Department of Economics at Jadavpur University, Kolkata, India. Her area of research interest is institutional economics and public economics.

Deb Kusum Das is with the Department of Economics, Ramjas College, University of Delhi. He holds a Ph.D. in Economics from the Delhi School of Economics. He is the co-winner of the IEDRA Award 2004 of EXIM Bank for his doctoral dissertation on "Some Aspects of Productivity Growth and Trade in Indian Industry". His research interests are empirical international trade, the economics of labour markets, economic growth and productivity. He is one of the co-researchers in the India KLEMS research project, which aims to create a productivity database for the Indian economy by industry. He is the editor of the book *Productivity Dynamics in Emerging and Industrialized Countries* economies (Routledge, Taylor & Francis, UK). He is the co-founder of the South Asian Economics Students' Meet (SAESM)—a platform for undergraduate students of the economics of South Asia. He is also associated with ICRIER as an external researcher.

Keshab Das is a professor at the Gujarat Institute of Development Research, Ahmedabad, India. He holds M.Phil. (Applied Economics), Ph.D. (Economics) degrees from the Jawaharlal Nehru University, New Delhi, and Bachelor's degree in Journalism and Mass Communication. He is a recipient of the VKRV Rao Prize in Social Sciences (Economics). He has been a visiting research fellow/faculty at the following: Punjabi University; Institute for Economic Research on Innovation, Tshwane University of Technology (South Africa), University of Insubria (Italy), Institute of Social Studies (the Netherlands); University of Manchester (UK), Institute of Developing Economies (Japan), Institute for Studies in Industrial Development (New Delhi), CNRS-REGARDS (France), Maison des Sciences de l'Homme (France); and Institute of Development Studies (UK). He had been empanelled as an Indian Council of Cultural Relations Chair Professor in Economics (2015–2016). He has worked on research assignments sponsored by various Indian Government Ministries; Planning Commission; ICSSR, New Delhi; Government of Gujarat; International Commission of Jurists; UNICEF; UNIDO; ILO; Ford Foundation; University of Sussex; French Ministry of Research; IWMI-Tata Water Policy Program; Swiss Agency for Development and Cooperation; Economic Research Institute for ASEAN and East Asia (ERIA), Bangkok; International Development Research Centre, Canada; National Agency for Research on AIDS and Viral Hepatitis (ANRS), Paris, France; Economic and Social Research Council, UK; Social Sciences and Humanities Research Council (Canada); and National Institute for the Humanities and Social Sciences (South Africa). He has authored, co-authored or edited eight books and wrote over ninety articles relating to his research and on policy issues in local and regional development; industrialization strategies; informal sector; MSMEs, industrial clusters and their global interface; innovation dynamics; labour; basic infrastructure; and politics of development.

Kushankur Dey is a faculty member of the Indian Institute of Management Bodh Gaya. Before joining IIM Bodh Gaya, he has held academic positions at Xavier University Bhubaneswar (School of Rural Management) and T. A. Pai Management Institute. He is Post-Doctoral Fellow of the Indian Institute of Management, Ahmedabad and holds a doctorate from the Institute of Rural Management Anand. Dey is a recipient of Reserve Bank of India Chair-Unit Fellowship at IRMA and ICAR Junior Research Fellowship to pursue fellow (doctoral) and postgraduate degrees, respectively. His research interests lie at agricultural value chain finance, agriculture insurance and risk management, price efficiency testing of agricultural commodities markets, organization and governance of farmer organizations. He has twenty-five odd articles, including research papers, teaching cases and book chapters, appeared in *Journal of Rural Studies*, *Economic and Political Weekly*, and *Journal of Agribusiness in Developing and Emerging Economies*, among others. In 2018, he served as a resource person for National Rural Livelihood program.

Abdul A. Erumban is a senior economist at the Conference Board, an assistant professor in the Department of Global Economics and Management of the University of Groningen and participant in the Groningen Growth and

Development Centre of the University. He has a Ph.D. from the University of Groningen and works on the fields of productivity, technological change, digital transformation and its impact, globalization, global value chains, international comparisons of economic development and structural change. He is also an external researcher in the India KLEMS research project and an active participant in the KLEMS initiatives (EU KLEMS, Asia KLEMS and World KLEMS). He has published articles in various academic and business journals, including *Journal of Economic Perspectives*, *Review of Income and Wealth*, *Industrial and Corporate Change*, *Journal of Comparative Economics* and *Journal of World Business*.

Nilabja Ghosh is a professor at the Institute of Economic Growth, Delhi. She works in the areas of agriculture, rural development, food and environment. She has been engaged in empirical studies using statistical and econometric methods.

Grace Kite is an economist and econometrician whose main research interest is in innovation and technology, particularly in developing countries. Her work touches on how economic growth and development is different in a modern economy where services rather than manufacturing are often the driving force, and low-cost labour cannot always substitute for technology. Grace also carries out empirical research on a consultancy basis for blue chip companies and NGOs. In this capacity, she regularly models firms' sales or other performance indicators and advises on strategy for growth, and she also evaluates the role of policy changes in driving human development outcomes.

Biswajit Mandal teaches Economics at Visva-Bharati University, Santiniketan, India. He worked at Balurghat College as Assistant Professor in Economics. He received National Scholarship from the Government of India and Junior Research Fellowship by the University Grants Commission. He has also received JSPS Fellowship to visit Kobe University, Japan. He visited the University at Albany-SUNY as C. V. Raman Fellow. He was also a visiting Professor at Soka University, Japan. He researches on International Trade, Development and Health Economics. *Review of Development Economics*, *International Journal of Economic Theory*, *Economics & Politics*, *Economic Modelling*, *International Review of Economics and Finance*, *International Economic Journal*, *Global Economy Journal*, *Eurasian Economic Review*, *Economics Bulletin*, etc. are among the journals that have published his research.

Susmita Mandal is an independent researcher. She has received a Ph.D. degree in Education from the University of the South Pacific, Fiji. She holds master degrees in Physics and psychology as well. She worked as an assistant teacher in a government school for more than nine years. Her research interests include understanding the role of technology on adjustment problem, cognitive behaviour and academic achievement of adolescent students. She publishes research articles in the *Journal of Advances in Education Research* and *Journal of Global Research in Education and Social Sciences.*

Per Botolf Maurseth is an associate professor at BI Norwegian Business School. He was a senior researcher at the Norwegian Institute of International Affairs (NUPI) in the period from 2001 to 2009. He holds a Dr. Polit degree from the University of Oslo (2001). Maurseth teaches international trade, microeconomics and development economics. His main research interests are economic growth, international trade, development economics, the economics of technology and regional economics. He has published in journals such as *Scandinavian Journal of Economics*, *Economics Letters*, *Europe-Asia Studies* and *Regional Studies*.

Satyendra Nath Mishra works at the School of Rural Management, Xavier University Bhubaneswar, India. His research interests lie in exploring how society works, the role of policy and institution and the limits of science and technology, with a focus on field-based exploration. His publications appeared in journals like *Current Science*, *Economic and Political Weekly*, *Agriculture and Food Security*, *International Journal of Rural Management*, *Journal of Rural Development*, and *Asian Journal of Management Cases*. He co-authored one book titled *Techno-economic Assessment of Bioenergy in India*. He had completed his Fellow Programme in Rural Management (FPRM) from the Institute of Rural Management, Anand, India, and was the recipient of RBI Chair Fellowship. He has done his M.Phil and M.Sc from the Indian Institute of Forest Management and TERI University, respectively.

Pratap C. Mohanty works as Assistant Professor at the Indian Institute of Technology Roorkee, India. He has been in teaching and research over 12 years in reputed organisations. Before here, he was in IIFT, New Delhi and Delhi University. He was a visiting professor to IIM Indore. He was engaged in training IPS and IRS probationers. He received a Ph.D. degree in the area of "diffusion of ICT in India". He has authored three books and several research papers in peer-reviewed journals. His major areas of research are ICT, information asymmetry in health care, gender issues and informal enterprises.

Vivekananda Mukherjee is Professor of Economics at Jadavpur University, Kolkata, India. He is a Ph.D. from Jadavpur University itself. His areas of research interest are applied microeconomics, institutional economics and public economics.

Chiranjib Neogi is a retired scientist from the Indian Statistical Institute, Kolkata, and now engaged as Guest Faculty of West Bengal State University. He has been working on the area of productivity and efficiency for many years and has published several research papers on this issue in the reputed journals. He has co-authored a book published *India's New Economy* from Palgrave, UK (jointly with Jati K. Sengupta, University of California, Santa Barbara) and co-edited a book on *Productivity and Efficiency* (jointly with Ranjan Ghosh, IIM Kolkata) from Macmillan, India. In 2017, he had co-edited another book *Women's Entrepreneurship and Microfinance* (jointly with A. Bhandari and S. Ghosh) from Springer. He has received D.K. Desai prize for an article written jointly with Nilabja Ghosh, published in the *Indian Journal of Agricultural Economics* in 1995. He was Visiting Research Fellow at the Institute of Developing Economies, Tokyo, Japan, in the year 1998–1999 and at the Korea Institute for International Economic Policy, Seoul, in 2009.

Alaka Shree Prasad holds an M.Phil. degree in Economics from Visva-Bharati University, Santiniketan, India. A part of her M.Phil. dissertation has been published as an article in an international journal. She is currently a Ph.D. scholar in the Department of Economics and Politics, Visva-Bharati University, under the supervision of Dr. Biswajit Mandal. Her area of research is international trade.

Mayanglambam Rajeshwor is a senior research analyst at the Institute of Economic Growth, Delhi. He is in the team of economists and statisticians involved in econometric crop forecasting in India.

Hastimal Sagara is an assistant professor of Economics at GLS University, Ahmedabad. He holds an M.A. (Economics) from Gujarat University. He did his doctoral thesis from the Indira Gandhi National Open University (IGNOU), New Delhi. He taught for more than 15 years at both undergraduate and postgraduate levels as well as various professional courses. He received a research project on "Evaluation of MGNREGS in Gujarat and Rajasthan" from the ICSSR, New Delhi. He received research award from the GLS University Management in 2015. He has authored more than ten books and published several research papers in edited volumes and journals. His areas of research include information technology, labour economics, development economics and environmental economics.

Prakash Singh is a Ph.D. in Economics from Delhi University. He was the recipient of ICSSR Institutional Doctoral Fellowship during his Ph.D. He is currently associated with the Centre for Development Economics, Delhi School of Economics. Previously, he has worked at the Centre for Regional Trade and Institute of Economic Growth. He has worked extensibly in financial development and its related areas. His additional research interests include regional growth, ICT, innovation and firm dynamics. He publishes in *Economic Bulletin*, *Journal of East Asian Economic Integration*, etc.

Nidhi Tewathia is an assistant professor in the Department of Economics, Gargi College, University of Delhi. She has also been the academic counsellor for Indira Gandhi National Open University. She has briefly taught at Guru Gobind Singh Indraprastha University. Her Ph.D. and past research work are related to residential electricity consumption. Presently, her specific research interests are ICT, digital divide in the context of social inequalities in India.

Sigrid Valberg is currently Higher Executive Officer at the Norwegian Ministry of Education and Research. She has previously worked as an intern with UN Women in Liberia, using ICT to improve women's economic empowerment. She has a master's degree in economics from the University of Oslo and did her work on ICT and gender equality in the labour market during an internship at the Norwegian Institute of International Affairs in Oslo, Norway.

Parmeet Kumar Vinit is Research Scholar at the University of Delhi. He was working as a research analyst in the team of econometric crop forecaster at the Institute of Economic Growth, Delhi.

Introduction

Digitalisation and Development: Issues for India and Beyond

Dibyendu Maiti, Fulvio Castellacci and Arne Melchior

Abstract Information and communication technologies (ICTs) provide new opportunities and new challenges for developing economies. ICT adoption, digitalization and automation provide formidable new opportunities in terms of increased efficiency and productivity, the creation of new services and occupations and increased connectivity among agents. However, the extent to which developing economies are able to reap these potential benefits is contingent on a set of other social, economic and institutional dimensions. While economic growth and rising productivity are the major expected outcomes of digitalization, digital divides and related forms of exclusion and inequalities are commonly observed too. India, one of the largest economies in the world, with a remarkable pace of ICT diffusion, represents a relevant case to investigate the impacts of digitalization on economic development. The present book collects a series of novel contributions on this theme, studying the Indian experience in an international cross-country perspective. This introductory chapter presents background information on the Indian case, introduces the main themes on the relationships between ICTs, socio-economic development and digital divides and provides a summary and road map to the chapters included in the book. On the whole, the main message of this book is that the impact of ICTs is contingent upon other assets, capabilities and institutional conditions. National policies should therefore not only promote digitalization as such but also ensure its co-evolution and complementarity with a variety of other country-specific factors.

D. Maiti (✉)
University of Delhi, New Delhi, India
e-mail: dibyendu@econdse.org

F. Castellacci (✉)
University of Oslo, Oslo, Norway
e-mail: fulvio.castellacci@tik.uio.no

A. Melchior (✉)
Norwegian Institute of International Affairs (NUPI), Oslo, Norway
e-mail: AM@nupi.no

D. Maiti et al. (eds.), *Digitalisation and Development*,
https://doi.org/10.1007/978-981-13-9996-1_1

1 Introduction[1]

Innovations in information and communication technologies (ICTs) have brought revolutionary changes not only on the economic front but also in the social and personal areas of human life. ICTs initially originated from the fast technological developments in the semiconductor industry, in the telecommunication sector and, more recently, in a wide range of new services linked to multimedia and the Internet (Dalum et al. 1999; Castellacci 2006). Key technological trajectories within ICTs are currently represented by automation and the Internet. The convergence of these technological advances may arguably constitute the rise of a new "technological paradigm" (Freeman and Louça 2001).

A technological paradigm is a set of interrelated and pervasive innovations that increases productivity in many sectors of the economy (Dosi 1988; Freeman et al. 1982). The new technological paradigm based on ICTs may have important economic effects on growth, wealth and welfare in the near future, and it may lead to radical changes in firms' production structure and organizations, in the patterns of consumption and in institutional settings. Innovation studies have extensively investigated the emergence and diffusion of ICTs and particularly focused on the pervasive economic effects that these general-purpose technologies have on different sectors of the economy (Castellacci 2006, 2008).

One major question that is often discussed in this field relates to the consequences that the diffusion of ICTs has for catching up and developing economies. Does the new technological paradigm based on ICTs create new windows of opportunity or further obstacles for catching-up countries? The answer to this question is a matter of considerable controversy in the literature on innovation and economic development, and it is rather difficult to discuss because of the fundamental elements of uncertainty, complexity and unpredictability that it entails. It is possible to identify, by and large, two different positions.

The first is a more optimistic stand, which stresses the new windows of opportunity opened up for developing economies by the creation and diffusion of the new information and communication technologies. This position is founded upon the old argument in the catching-up literature of the "penalty of taking the lead" (Veblen 1915). According to this, developing countries may exploit their backward position by imitating and implementing advanced foreign technologies created by the leader economies and by rapidly investing in the new technologies. In the new era, less developed economies are less committed to the mass production technological paradigm prevailing in previous decades (in terms of investments in physical capital, machineries and infrastructures) so that they may find it easier to make the jump into the new technological system based on ICTs.

The rapid catching-up process of Asian NICs (Newly Industrialized Countries, such as Korea, Singapore and Taiwan) in the last few decades shows that the opportunities opened up by the diffusion of the ICT-based paradigm can indeed be successfully exploited by catching-up countries, provided that the development strategy

[1] Some of the initial text in Sect. 1 is based upon Castellacci (2006).

that they pursue emphasizes the need to actively invest in the new technologies and in the related infrastructures and skills.

These successful cases, however, contrast with the general pattern of increasing disparities in income and technology levels that the world economy has experienced in the last few decades (Parayil 2005; Castellacci 2011). A large group of less developed economies, mostly in Africa, Asia and Latin America, have in fact been growing at a rather slow pace, and the technology and income gap has therefore significantly widened for many of them. Several countries have very low levels of technological capabilities, infrastructures and education and consequently find it hard to exploit their backwardness position by imitating ICT-related foreign advanced technologies.

There thus exists a second position in development research that is less optimistic with respects to the current and future prospects for innovation- and imitation-based growth. This is founded upon a strand of historically oriented studies on technological development, growth and catching up (Abramovitz 1986, 1994). Historical evidence indicates that economic development is far from being an automatic and easy process and that it is on the contrary very demanding and costly. This second stand therefore looks with greater concern at the social and institutional factors that may hamper the catching-up process. In this respect, it is argued that the new paradigm based on information and communication technologies is creating as many new obstacles for development as the opportunities it opens up. The process of creation of new technologies and its international diffusion is currently more difficult to exploit for catching-up countries, due to the greater requirement in terms of skills, competencies and capabilities that modern ICT-based global competition requires (Fagerberg and Godinho 2005). In particular, the international diffusion of technologies, which has been a major factor of catching up in previous decades, seems to have become more "difficult" and demanding over time (Fagerberg and Verspagen 2002).

The present book conceives these two arguments as largely complementary to each other, rather than opposite, as they look at different relevant aspects of the development process. By taking these two previous positions as a general starting point, the book investigates the new opportunities and further obstacles that the emergence of the new ICT-based technological paradigm creates for developing countries, particularly focusing on the case of India.

India, one of the largest economies in the world, with a remarkable pace of ICT diffusion, represents a relevant case to investigate the impacts of digitalization on economic development. Not only has India become the world's largest exporter of ICT-related services; the Indian Government has also made use of ICTs as a key policy strategy. For the sake of fast digitalization, the Indian government launched the important reform known as the "Digital India" project in July 2015. The project is having a total overlay of about 14 billion USD (or, Rupee 1 lakh crores) aimed at transforming the country into a knowledge economy by ensuring easy access to technology, infrastructure and government services to citizens. The Communications and IT Ministry sought to create business opportunities worth 1 trillion dollars through major impacts in IT/ITES, electronic, manufacturing and telecom sectors. The "Digital India" programme has sought to (i) provide high-speed Internet to common man, (ii) make all government services accessible to the population at large, and (iii) ensure digital empowerment of citizens. Besides, the "Aadhaar Scheme" was launched in January 2009 to integrate all citizens through the provision of biometric identification cards. Attempts were also made to provide direct benefits (like unemployment benefits, subsidies, public utilities, etc.) assisted by ICT in order to bypass intermediaries, avoid informality, detect cyber-crime, control border security and encourage online transactions so that the government could effectively pursue redistributive policies, preserve security and offer efficient public services delivery. Various other programmes have also been added to target and deliver specific programmes and group of people.

These recent development and policy efforts raise some important questions. First, to what extent does the access to ICT services enhance economic outcomes and performance in India? Second, how far has this reached across different social groups and regions of the country, and how has this affected economic and social inequalities in the country? Third, what is the success rate in terms of governance, control of corruption as well as contribution to social welfare and well-being? These issues are of crucial importance, and this book is set to investigate these questions by studying the Indian experience in a cross-country international perspective.

This introductory chapter is organized as follows. Sect. 2 provides background information on recent developments and economic patterns in India. Sect. 3 presents a brief overview of recent policy efforts and increasing trends towards the digitalization of the Indian economy, discussing why and how these are expected to affect economic growth, digital divides and social welfare in the future. Sect. 4 then summarises the themes and main results of the 14 studies collected in this book, and how these contribute to extant research and the policy debate on digitalization and development.

2 India's Growth, Development and Well-Being[2]

India has maintained a decent growth rate for the last two decades in spite of the global financial crisis. With an average Indian GDP growth rate about 7% in recent years, the current deceleration of growth in China has taken India from second tier to the top. The Indian growth rate was an impressive 8.2% in the first quarter of this financial year 2018 due to the strong performance of the manufacturing and agriculture sectors. This led to an increase in its lead over China to remain the fastest growing major economy of the world. According to a report by the Center for International Development at Harvard University, India, is expected to top the list of the fastest growing economies in the world for the coming decade, with a projected annual growth rate at 7.9%. Figure 1 shows India's impressive increase in GDP growth rate, surpassing Brazil and China.

Despite India's remarkable growth performance, there are also some painful realities in terms of economic development. According to the World Bank, still one out five Indians is poor. According to the latest official figures in 2012, the poverty rate is

[2]Some information for this section is drawn from Agrawal and Maiti (2019).

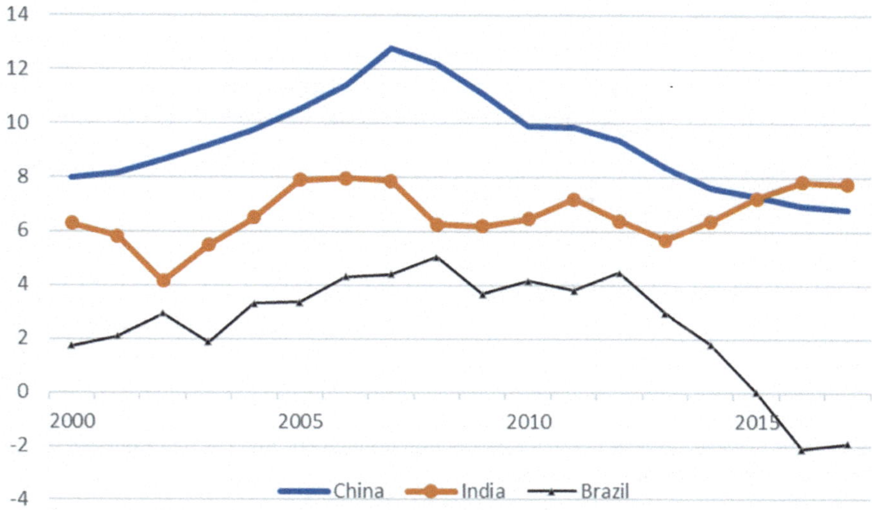

Fig. 1 GDP growth in India, China and Brazil, 2000–2017 (average of past 3 years). *Source* World Development Indicators, World Bank

14% in urban areas but 25% in rural areas. More than 60% of poverty is concentrated in seven states in the country. According to the recent Global Hunger Index Report 2012 by the International Food Research Institute, India ranks 97th in Global Hunger Index. This suggests that the benefits of economic growth have not been percolated equally to every stratum of the income distribution.

Gainful and decent employment is the single largest problem in the country. According to the latest National Sample Survey Organisation (NSSO) report, more than 80% of the working population is still in the informal and unorganized sector, without having any right to obtain social security benefits. Unemployment is still a major issue in rural and urban areas, especially for unskilled workers, and hence, the term "jobless growth" has been defined as India's growth story. The official unemployment rate was just below 5% in 2017, but a report by OECD found that over 30% of people aged 15–29 were not in employment, education or training. This is affected by high rates of illiteracy and poor infrastructures. Economic growth has not been uniform across all states and regions. Technological and corporate hubs like Delhi, Bangalore and Mumbai have attracted the maximum skilled and mobile workers leading to excessive urbanization and congestion, whereas other cities and rural areas have been lagging in employment generation and skill formation. Given the success of ICT in India, a key issue is how the ICT sector performs in terms of employment and wages. This book sheds light on the substantial job creation by the Indian ICT industries, but also the challenges ahead related to the fact that rapid technological changes also lead to higher demand for advanced skills.

For the labour market in India, the very low ratio of female-to-male labour force participation rate in India is also a serious concern. Especially in comparison with China and Brazil, gender inequality patterns show that women do not play yet a

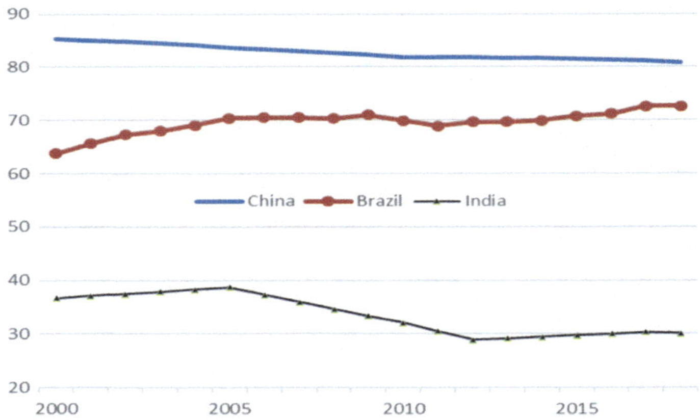

Fig. 2 Ratio of female-to-male labour force participation rate 2000–2018 (%, ILO estimate). *Source* World Development Indicators, World Bank

substantial role in the labour force as compared to men, and the ratio of female-to-male participation has even been declining (see Fig. 2). This can be taken to be a sign of low human progress in India despite healthy growth figures.

Increased female labour participation represents a significant development potential not only at the individual level but also for India as a whole, by tapping the huge unexploited potential among women. In the book, we also address how ICTs affect the labour participation of women.

Inequality pervades India not just at a geographical level, but also at an individual level. The remarkable economic growth has only to a limited extent been able to narrow the gap between the haves and the have-nots, as many of India's poor are yet to receive the fruits of India's economic growth. According to a recent report by Oxfam (cited in Business Today 2019, 30th January), India's richest 1% held 58% of the country's total wealth, which was higher than the global figure of about 50%. The wealth of this elite group increased by over about 293 billion USD (or, Rs. 20.9 lakh crore) during the period under review—an amount close to the total expenditure estimated in the Union Budget 2017. India's top 1% of the population now holds 73% of the wealth, while 67 crore citizens, comprising the country's poorest half, saw their wealth rise by just 1%. So, India's economic growth has not been pro-poor, and trickle-down economics has not played its role as expected. Hence, taking into account India's current position, it can be said that inequality is harming not only individuals but also adversely affect growth prospects and overall welfare. How do ICTs affect this pattern? This book sheds light on the exponential spread of ICT in India, partly also among the poor. Furthermore, ICTs are applied in public policies related to poverty, and some chapters address how these affect socio-economic outcomes and inequalities within the country.

India has also been plagued by corruption and a lack of transparency in institutions. One indicator of this is its score in the Corruption Perception Index. According to the World Governance Indicators, compiled by the World Bank, the figures on the control of corruption show a general improvement in both India and China in recent years, while Brazil shows opposite trend (Fig. 3). Still, corruption levels in China and India score well below the average. This has led to inefficient institutions that are unable to benefit the people to their full potential and are hampering India's image as a lucrative place for business. In turn, this has also affected economic activity and employment generation in India, again reinforcing inequality. Corruption also manifests itself as development fees, particularly when funds allocated to various social welfare and developmental programmes such as those earmarked for building roads/schools/expanding infrastructure for public distribution system (PDS) in villages are misused. There is ample anecdotal evidence to show how corruption in the PDS system leads to grains not reaching the actual beneficiaries due to leakages. There has been much debate and discussion on how these issues can be resolved, and one remedy that has found some support is to replace transfers in kind by transfers in cash. This is possible and plausible only when there are well-developed digital channels capable of transferring money to bank accounts seamlessly, thus stressing the importance of ICT for development and welfare enhancement. Has ICT effectively reduced corruption in India? Two chapters of this book investigate specifically this issue.

Moreover, India has not performed at satisfactory levels when it comes to life expectancy as compared to China and Brazil, two economies that are good comparison points as far as economic development and growth are concerned (see Fig. 4). Even though life expectancy at birth has increased, India is still lagging behind China and Brazil. It is hence relevant to ask whether India has succeeded in using ICT effi-

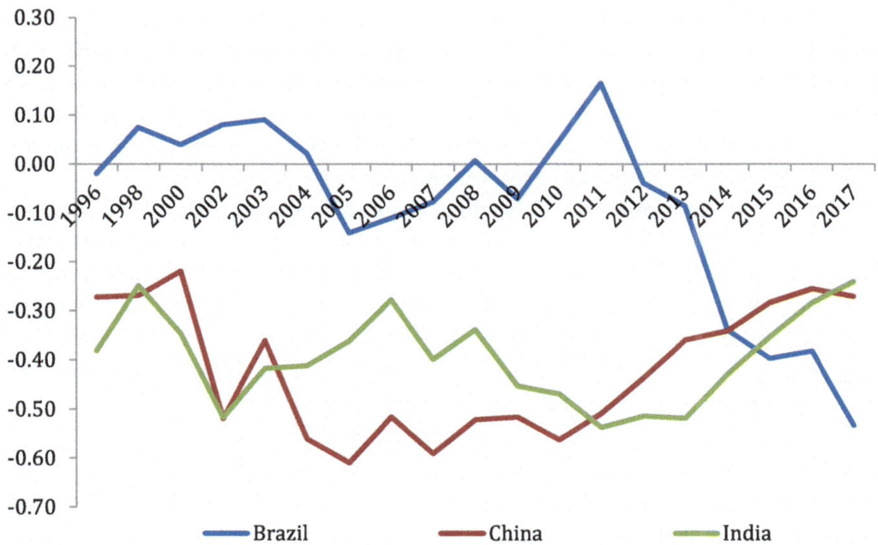

Fig. 3 Control of corruption index in major developing countries: 1996–2017. *Source* Wold Governance Indicators, World Bank

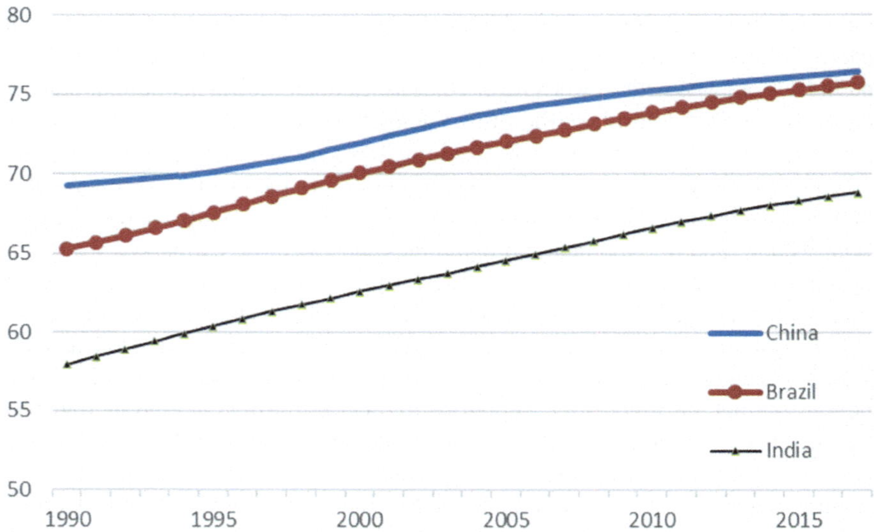

Fig. 4 Life expectancy at birth in India, China and Brazil, 1990–2016 (number of years). *Source* World Development Indicators, World Bank

ciently in order to provide better health services and governance to the benefits of its large population.

Therefore, it is evident that in spite of the spectacular growth experienced during the last two decades, the related benefits have not percolated to every section of the society in India. The majority of workers are engaged in the informal sector, there are less for formal jobs with growing the formal sector, inequality has increased sharply even though poverty has reduced to some extent, the rural sector is lagging behind, corruption and inefficiencies are crippling the public delivery of welfare programmes and so on. These have been perennial problems of the Indian economy since independence and thereby have remained binding constraints.

Aware of these problems, public authorities and policy makers have recently pointed to digitalization of the economy as an important strategy to address the twin challenges of economic growth and social inclusion. The implicit understanding is that a faster pace of adoption of ICTs will enhance productivity and economic efficiency, bring greater transparency in the delivery of public services and welfare programmes, reduce the level of corruption, integrate remote places with cities and towns and improve the level of democratic participation.

However, as noted in Sect. 1 above, research on digitalization and development points out that socio-economic benefits of ICT adoption are far from being automatic and do often depend on a set of economic, social and institutional dimensions that characterize each national economy. Hence, it is relevant to ask whether digitalization will be the right strategy to foster socio-economic development in India in the coming years, and what complementary factors and capabilities the Indian economy will have to focus on in order to magnify the benefits of ICTs and limit the related risks. This book focuses on three major themes that are crucial to address the question of digitalization and development in India: (1) economic impacts of ICTs; (2) digitalization and inequalities; (3) governance and users' well-being.

3 Digitalization and Development in India: Patterns and Questions

The ICT sector has been expanding rapidly in the last few years all over the world, as evident from its share of GDP and contribution to GDP capital (Fig. 5).

According to a recent report by the International Telecommunication Union, over 3 billion people are now online and ICT growth is buoyant across all countries. Latest data show that Internet use continues to grow steadily, at 6.6% globally in 2014 (3.3% in developed countries, 8.7% in the developing world). The number of Internet users in developing countries has doubled in five years (2009–2014), with two-thirds of all people online now living in the developing world.

More than 80% of the youth populations are online in 104 countries. In developed countries, 94% of young people aged 15–24 use the Internet compared with 67% in developing countries and only 30% in Least Developed Countries (LDCs). Out of the 830 million young people who are online, 320 million (39%) are in China and India (Fig. 6). Nearly 9 out of 10 young individuals not using the Internet live in Africa or Asia and the Pacific. This emphasizes the importance of ICT and the role it can play in affecting economic outcomes.

A report on the new digital economy and development, compiled by UNCTAD (2017), notes that it is not straightforward to measure the impact of ICT growth on development due to its rapidly changing nature and a complex web of areas

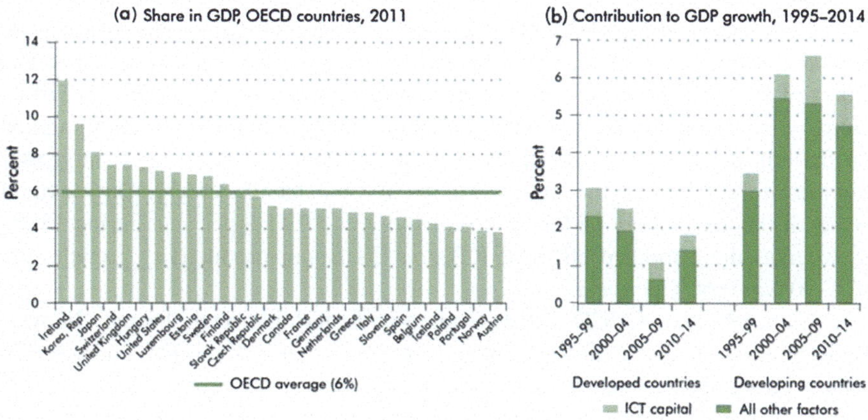

Fig. 5 ICT Sector as a share of GDP and contribution to GDP growth. *Source* ICT-centric economic growth, innovation and job creation, ITU

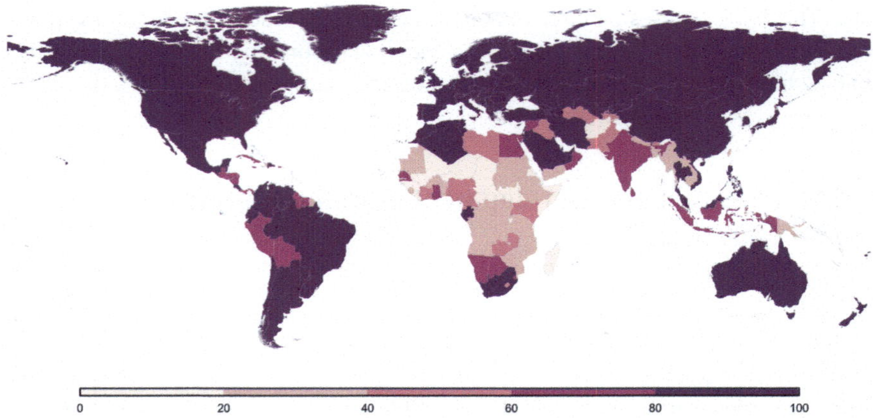

Fig. 6 Proportion of youth (15–24) using the Internet (2017*). *Source* International Telecommunications Union (ITU). *Note* *Estimates

that are impacted by growth in the ICT sector. Nonetheless, the study considers a diverse range of impact areas such as economic performance, employment, innovation (including research and development), privacy and security, education, health, citizen participation, individuals and communities and the environment. The book will focus on the following three related themes.

3.1 ICTs and Economic Performance

The exposure to ICT raises efficiency and productivity, saves time, reduces hardship, eliminates information distortions, improves communication and more so (Oulton 2012; Castellacci and Tveito 2018). As a result, ICT adoption has positively impacted on economic outcomes, like capital formation, exports and government accounts. The impact of ICTs has been viewed as a driving factor contributing to the GDP of an economy by raising the level of TFP and labour productivity. Crafts (2004) argued that the impact of ICTs on labour productivity in modern society has been greater than that of the steam engine appeared in the mid-nineteenth century. The maximal impact of this technology on labour productivity was 0.41% per year during 1850–70, whereas the estimated effect of ICTs on US labour productivity growth over 1974–90 was 0.68% per year.

A recent report by OECD (2018) focuses on fostering growth through digitization in South-east Asia, China and India. It indicates that ICT services embodied in manufacturing and services account for a considerable share of the value of exports from these Asian nations. According to a report by the World Bank Development Research Group, the Better Than Cash Alliance and the Bill & Melinda Gates Foundation to the G20 Global Partnership for Financial Inclusion, digitizing payments and remittances are vital to achieving G20 Goals, contributing to its core goal of achieving strong, sustainable and balanced growth. The report shows how the widespread adoption of digital payments in all their forms, including international and domestic remittances, can be instrumental in reaching the goals of G20. Digitization can help overcome the costs and physical barriers that have harmed valuable financial inclusion efforts, offer the opportunity to rapidly scale up access to financial services and promote women's economic empowerment by facilitating greater account ownership and asset accumulation.

Promoting digitalization has been the Indian government's focus for many years now. This includes attempts made to provide most services to every citizen on their web portals or electronically and make the transactions transparent and smooth. The Indian government launched the revolutionary reform "Digital India" in 2015, under which it envisioned increased Internet connectivity and making India a digitally empowered nation. This was also seen as being an engine propelling the growth of businesses, employment generation and increasing transparency in major sectors of the economy. Increased Internet penetration, improved telecom services, availability of skilled IT workers, start-ups providing ICT services and the government encouraging ICT through various schemes, operations and services are important factors fostering economic performance.

Access to ICT products by Indian citizens has grown substantially (Fig. 7). Internet, landline and mobile telephones are the major three types of products that are commonly used. Mobile use accelerated since early 2000s. However, in contrast to the growth of mobile/wireless telephone, the growth in usage of landline telephone has been falling for the same period. While mobile telephone subscribers register a substantial increase to 87.3 per 100 persons, landline connections drop from around 5 per persons in 2006 to 1.7 per 100 persons in 2017. The growth in the Internet and broadband connections has been modest. The growth of Internet subscribers has

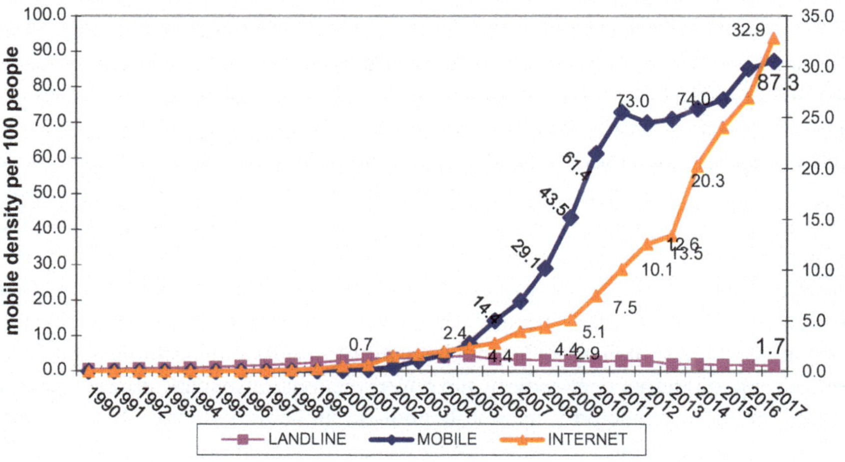

Fig. 7 Density of ICT products (per 100 persons) in India, 1990–2017. *Source* Mohanty (2019) and Annual Report, Telecom Authority of India (2018)

been slightly better since 1999. The density of Internet users reached 32.9 per 100 persons in 2017 from 4 per 100 persons in 2007, eight-time rise in the last ten years.

An even more recent trend relates to increasing patterns of automation, and the effects this may have by affecting labour wages and employment in developing economies. Further, digital communication technologies may also affect economic outcomes by enhancing business firms' productivity and their ability to participate in international trade. However, while these recent patterns foster expectations of strong economic benefits for developing economies, extant research has not yet provided analyses and evidence to corroborate these optimistic expectations. Have recent digitalization patterns experienced by the Indian business sector fostered economic growth, employment and international competitiveness of the Indian economy?

3.2 Digital Divide and Inequalities

Despite the government's efforts towards increasing ICT goods and services in the economy, there is a clear digital divide in the nation, as shown by data from the ICE 360° survey (2016), which gives insights into economic and social well-being of households, provides normative measures of social, political and financial inclusion and a degree of access to public goods, infrastructure and welfare measures.

A survey conducted by the People's Research on Indian Economy (PRICE 2016), covering 60,360 households and studying digital networking by deep diving into the Internet usage, its patterns, mode and purpose of their access, reveals that 10% (27 million) households reported having an Internet connection at their home. But, there were 22% (62 million) of Indian households where at least one member was accessing the Internet (either at work or home or elsewhere and either through a computer or mobile). It also showed that while every tenth underdeveloped rural household—including those in districts such as Kalahandi (Odisha) and Bastar (Chhattisgarh)—has access to the Internet, in the metros every second household has Internet access, hence giving evidence of the rural–urban differences in access to ICT goods. Additionally, the survey results showed that the level of education and Internet access are highly correlated since every second graduate household has at least one member who accesses the Internet versus every hundredth in the case of an illiterate household. The digital divide becomes more palpable between the rich and poor. Nearly 47% of rich households (top quintile) have at least one member with access to the Internet in contrast to only 4% of poor households (bottom quintile). This shows that even though efforts have been made to increase Internet connectivity by the Government in India, the impact has not been uniform across all sections of society.

In addition to Internet connectivity, the government has also made efforts towards increasing mobile connectivity, as mobile phones can be important tools especially in poorer areas where Internet use is not as widespread. However, a gap in the provision and use of ICT goods and services is visible even in terms of mobile phones. The 2017 global survey by the Pew Research Center shows that only one in four Indian adults report using the Internet or owning a smartphone. Despite the booming

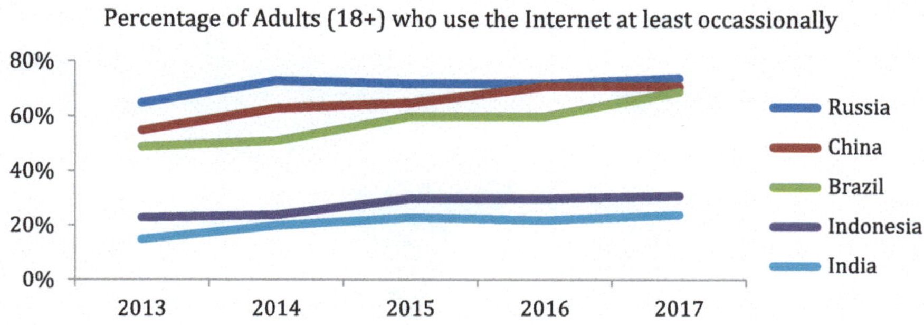

Fig. 8 Internet use in BRICs countries. *Source* Poushter et al. (2018)

economy, India's progress in smartphone penetration has been slow. In 12 of the 22 emerging and developing nations surveyed, fewer than 50% report owning a smartphone, and in India and Tanzania, less than one-quarter report owning smartphones, the lowest among the countries surveyed. This slow adoption of smartphones in India has hampered the growth of the Internet in the country since most Indians tend to access the Internet on their mobiles. In addition to the rural–urban, rich–poor and regional digital divide, India is also lagging in Internet usage (see Fig. 8) when a comparison is made with other emerging economies, as shown by the Poushter et al. (2018).

To bridge the digital divide, the central government has disbursed Rs. 34,000 crore to lay high-speed Internet in 150,000 villages by 2019, but only about 70,000 villages have been covered until now.

Even though there has been a major increase in the use of ICTs, this has not been uniform among genders. As Fig. 9 shows, the digital gender gap persists, as the proportion of men using the Internet is higher than the proportion of women using the Internet in two-thirds of the countries worldwide. The proportion of women using the Internet is 12% lower than the proportion of men using the Internet worldwide. While the gender gap has narrowed in most regions since 2013, it has widened in Africa. In Africa, the proportion of women using the Internet is 25% lower than the proportion of men using the Internet. In LDCs, only one out of seven women is using the Internet compared with one out of five men.

More than 70% population still live in rural India. There is increasing concern that the access to ICT is rising at much slower rate than that of urban area leading to a rising digital divide between urban–rural areas in India. Tele-density, which denotes the number of telephones per 100 populations, is an important indicator of telecom penetration in a country. Tele-density in India, which was 10.37% in 2001, sharply increased to 167.17% at the end of 2012 in the urban areas, followed by a decline to 154.18% in 2016 (Fig. 10). However, the tele-density was 0.93% in 2001 in rural areas, and this shows much lower than the urban share. But, the share has gradually raised to 51.26%. The gap of tele-density has increased ten times during the period, and this shows an increased digital divide in India.

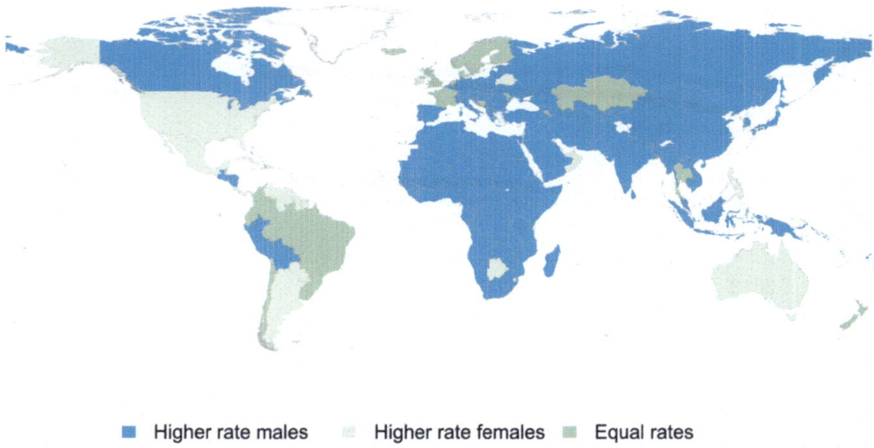

Fig. 9 Proportion of Individuals using the Internet, by gender (2017*). *Note* * Estimates. Proportions in this chart refer to the number of women/men using the Internet, as a percentage of the respective total female/male population

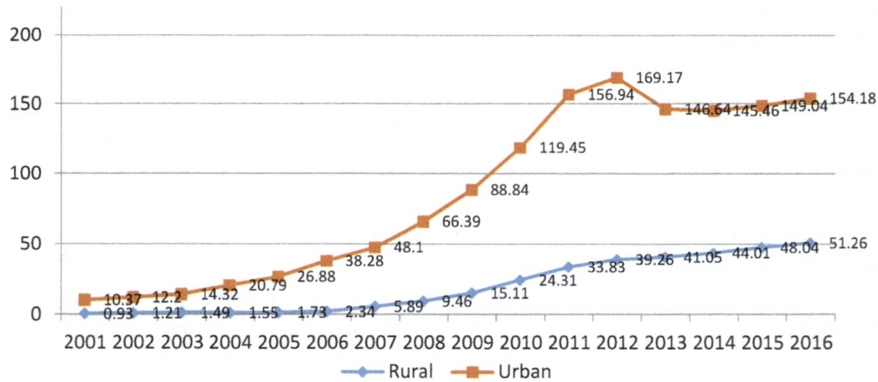

Fig. 10 Trends in tele-density in India during 2001–2016 (number per 100 populations). *Source* Annual Reports, Telecom Authority of India, 2018

Another current concern that will become increasingly important in coming years is that digitalization and automation of tasks may increase the skill gap in the labour market, and hence exacerbate wage and occupational differences between skilled and unskilled workers (Acemoglu and Restrepo 2018; Brambilla and Tortarolo 2018). Hence, there is the risk that increased firms' productivity enabled by ICTs will go hand in hand with an increasing skill gap and inequalities in the labour market, which is an issue of serious concern for a large population country such as India. On the whole, current digital divide patterns make it relevant to ask to what extent India will be able to close these divides in the coming years, and what the effects of these inequalities will be for Indian households and consumption patterns.

3.3 *ICTs, Governance and Users' Well-Being*

The impacts of ICTs on welfare go, however, much beyond than their effects on economic growth and income inequalities. ICT users and citizens can be affected in a number of ways by the increasing use of digital technologies. In particular, the socio-institutional environment that characterizes our society, such as governance structures, trust in other citizens, safety and security, is highly relevant for well-being (Dolan et al. 2008).[3] Helliwell (2006) point out that the ability of governments to provide a trustworthy environment is paramount for well-being, particularly in those countries with poor governance and low absolute income. Internet applications that improve in some way the socio-institutional environment can positively affect citizens' welfare. Therefore, if governments are committed to providing more online public services, this will likely increase well-being too.

There are three distinct channels mechanisms that are relevant here (Castellacci and Tveito 2018). First, moving certain public services online can save citizens' time and diminish the effort previously allocated to monotonous (and sometimes stressful) tasks. Second, through increased access to information, individuals can have better information about their society, increasing their sense of belonging to their community as well as their safety. For example, in India, citizens can register where they have been asked to bribe governmental officers, and their reports are sent to government officials and the media to increase transparency and the quality of life among citizens, who can learn where to go to avoid having to bribe someone (Ramanna and Tahilyani 2012). This can decrease the spread of bribery and corruption, increase trust and thus spur well-being. Third, digital communication tools enable more rapid and transparent interactions between citizens and public authorities, through, e.g. online portals for e-government services, or by improving civic engagement among citizens.

In the Indian context, the issue of arguably highest relevance is how ICTs can contribute to limit the extent of corruption and improve the country's governance quality. Existence of a parallel economy that thrives and flourishes on cash-based businesses and entities can be undermined through digitalization. Most of the individuals running the parallel economy do not have proper bank accounts and avoid paying taxes to the government. Digitalization initiatives like taxation being brought online and steps like demonetization can aid the government to weed out corruption from our system. If administered and implemented correctly and efficiently, these can be major game-changers. ICTs are supposed to help reduce the activities falling within the ambit of the informal sector and hence increase growth and development in India, which is why there has been a growing focus on these by the Indian government in the recent years.

An interesting example is the Aadhaar system, the world's most ambitious digital identity programme, which is becoming increasingly necessary for financial transactions and access to social welfare. The Aadhaar system has, however, also led to increased opportunities for corruption. Evidence from an arid village in Jharkhand

[3]These introductory paragraphs of Sect. 3.3 are based upon Castellacci and Tveito (2018).

shows the misery of families who were deprived of subsidized food from the vast public distribution system because their ration cards had not been linked to their biometric-based 12-digit personal identification numbers. Villagers travelling to the nearest town to submit the forms and papers necessary to get their ration cards linked to Aadhaar either had to shell out days of family earnings to bribe the government officers at the office or face rejection and the risk of having no food for many more days of the month.

Even though the government had made the linkage mandatory in order to avoid leakages and digitalize the process, it can be seen that a lot of people actually faced more hardships in getting access to food, hence hampering their well-being despite a well-functioning digital set-up. Similar issues have been faced by pensioners who are unable to get their pensions linked to Aadhaar. Many had to pay bribes to be eligible to receive their pensions and many genuine pensioners were excluded when 300,000 "fake" pensioners were removed from the list of beneficiaries (Biswas 2018). This happened due to mistakes made by data operators, resulting in discrepancies in name and age, highlighting the dangers of merely relying on the provision of ICT goods and services without ensuring a supporting institutional system to minimize risks associated with their provision.

These dangerous avenues that the increasing use of ICT has opened up need much more attention by policy makers. Various attempts have been made by the government to reduce informality and corruption through the adoption of ICT in its operations. But despite the many measures taken by the government to clean the system, India's ranking in the global Corruption Perceptions Index, released by Transparency International, slipped two places to the 81st mark in 2017 (Transparency International 2017). The report also termed India as one of the "worst offenders" in the Asia-Pacific region in terms of corruption and press freedom, attributes that are indicators of well-being. In 2016, it was ranked 79 among 176 countries in the index. In 2017, India's ranking stood at 81 with a score of 40 among 180 countries.

All the above evidences point towards weak institutions that are limiting otherwise positive prospects for the people. There is a dire need to shift the focus from a mere increase in the use of ICT goods and services to strengthening India's governance and institutional set-ups, to make them strong enough to provide the requisite support for ICT to affect well-being through the channels mentioned in extant research. Without the supporting background of a strong institutional framework, the evils of corruption, informality and mismanagement shall continue to negatively affect growth and well-being and prevent the positive effects of ICT from percolating to the whole economy.

4 This Book: Themes and Contributions

The present book is centred on the three major themes and questions outlined in the previous section. The book is therefore organized in three parts, one focusing on ICTs and economic outcomes, the second on digital divides and inequalities and the third on governance and users' well-being. The book collects on the whole 15 studies that present fresh empirical evidence and analyses on the issues raised earlier in this chapter. Before presenting these empirical contributions, though, the book includes a comprehensive survey of relevant literature on ICTs, economic growth and well-being.

Chapter "ICT, Growth and Happiness" (**Maurseth**) surveys extant research on ICT, growth and development in a cross-country comparative perspective. According to Maurseth, the diffusion of ICT typically follows an S-shaped development over time. This is also reflected in the sharply falling prices of computer equipment, where the so-called Moore's law—i.e. that real price for computers halves every 18 months—has been largely supported. According to Gordon (2016), the improvement in the performance/price ratio is unprecedented in history. The impact of ICT should also be enhanced by its nature as a general-purpose technology with widespread application, the public goods nature of some of its infrastructure (especially the Internet), and the special nature of digital products, that are often non-rival in the sense that they can be accessed by many users without affecting the utility of the others.

Given the fundamental impacts of the ICT revolution and its pervasive and observed impacts, we would expect ICT to be heavily reflected also in the statistics on growth and development. In this light, we expect that the diffusion of ICTs should have a clear impact on growth and productivity. In the light of existing research, however, this is surprisingly unclear. According to Chapter "ICT, Growth and Happiness", the macro-impact of ICT on productivity and economic growth is mixed, with an overall modest effect of ICT on growth so far. The spread of ICTs coincided with lower growth rates in industrial countries from the 1970s. Hence, the famous paradox of Solow (1987): "*You can see the computer age everywhere but in the productivity statistics*". Higher growth rates in the 1990s contributed to renewed optimism, but the positive impact of ICT was more visible in the USA than in Europe and Japan, and slower growth after the 1990s dampened the ICT optimism. Results from studies using macro-data are therefore mixed and divergent, some suggesting a positive impact of ICT on growth, others not. Adding new results from growth regressions, Chapter "ICT, Growth and Happiness" finds that the impact of Internet use on economic growth was positive before the year 2000, but for rich countries after 2000, the effect was even negative.

For development, a key issue is whether ICTs promote convergence and inequalities among countries. If high skill levels and sophisticated infrastructure are required to benefit from ICTs, rich countries may benefit more from ICTs so there may be economic divergence and a growing digital divide. On the other hand, if ICTs are non-rival and accessible for all with low thresholds, or if poor countries may "leapfrog" and drop expensive intermediate steps such as fixed telephone lines, the outcomes may be digital and economic convergence. According to Chapter "ICT, Growth and Happiness", results are also mixed in this respect. Some contributions find convergence, others divergence. According to Yousefi (2011), the observed growth impact of ICT is stronger for middle-income and rich countries, and several studies point to the importance of complementary assets such as literacy and education that are crucial for the "absorptive capacity" of countries with respect to ICT. Adding own results, Chapter "ICT, Growth and Happiness" lands on the positive side: while the Internet had a negative impact on growth in rich countries post-2000, there was a persistent positive effect in poor countries.

In the light of the diverging evidence based on macro-data, it is perhaps a consolation that studies at the firm level provide a more optimistic view, with stronger productivity effects of ICT. Chapter "ICT, Growth and Happiness" points out that firms that use ICT have higher growth in productivity than other firms and growth rates are often high in ICT producing industries. Some studies indicate that the direction of causality is an issue: ICT may enhance productivity and growth at the firm level, but ICT use may be endogenous so the causality may also run in the opposite direction.

For India, an important issue is also how ICTs relate to sectoral growth patterns. The so-called Baumol's disease predicts that ICTs are initially progressive but in the longer run related to stagnant industries or services sectors. In the light of India's services-driven growth, the long-run growth potential of services is a key issue. According to the survey in Chapter "ICT, Growth and Happiness", some contributions conclude that Baumol's disease has been cured, but others have found a higher growth potential on some manufacturing sectors than in services.

A reason behind the conflicting evidence on the impact of ICT may also be problems of measurement. ICTs are changing technologies and products so that standard metrics fail: counting the number of computers will not capture the immense change in their performance. These measurement problems apply to production as well as consumption and may be particularly important for ICT products. For consumption, an issue is how to measure well-being: do ICTs affect well-being beyond what can be captured by standard metrics such as income or income per capita? Chapter "ICT, Growth and Happiness" also surveys the literature on how ICTs affect measures of subjective well-being (Castellacci and Tveito 2018). Also here, there could be opposing forces at work. The Internet may be used for welfare-enhancing information and social interaction, but also create addiction and isolation for its users. There is generally a positive and logarithmic relationship between income levels and subjective well-being; hence, ICT may impact well-being indirectly via income. There is a fast-growing body of research based on person-level data, and the survey of recent contributions in Chapter "ICT, Growth and Happiness" indicates a mainly positive effect of ICTs on subjective well-being, however varying with individual or group characteristics such as age. There may also be saturation effects, by which ICT access is positive but with diminishing marginal returns, and even negative effects according to some studies.

Part I: ICTs and Economic Performance

In the light of the considerable measurement problems related to ICT, it is pertinent that Part I of the book, on ICTs and economic performance, starts with a chapter contributing significantly to the measurement of ICT effects in India. In the existing literature on ICT and growth, many empirical studies have relied on data for rich countries, and for the study of ICT and development, it is urgent to provide better data for developing country use of ICT. Chapter "ICT Investment and Economic Growth in India: An Industry Perspective" (**Erumban and Das**) maintains that the lack of accurate data on ICT use by industries is a major reason why knowledge on the impact of ICT on growth in India is still limited. Using various data sources and overcoming hurdles related to data availability, consistency and measurement, the authors estimate aggregate and sector-level ICT investments in India over time. This reveals that ICT investments have increased, but their share of GDP has declined, and India lags behind the more mature economies. The authors then extend the India KLEMS database to include ICT capital. KLEMS (capital-labour-energy-materials-services) is an international database built for the analysis of growth and sector-level productivity, with data that are comparable across countries. Using the new data, the authors find that the contribution from ICT investment to growth in India has increased marginally, but the manufacturing sectors lag behind the aggregate economy. The chapter suggests that complementary assets such as skill levels may explain this lag.

India is currently the largest exporter in the world of ICT-related services, but the industry is in constant change. According to Chapter "Technological Disruptions and the Indian IT Industry: Employment Concerns and Beyond" (**Sagara and Das**), the information technology (IT) industry in India currently employs 3.8 million people and contributes more than 9% to Indian GDP. Key segments of this industry are IT services and business process outsourcing (BPM), and the authors show that employment growth in these segments is strongly export-driven. A key issue in the chapter is how India will cope with the "Fourth Industrial Revolution"—including developments such as cloud computing, big data, Internet of things (IoTs), robotics and more. Based on a variety of sources, the chapter maps developments and industry perceptions in different technological fields and concludes there is a threat of technological disruption to the Indian IT industry. The change is likely to require considerable re-skilling and up-skilling in the industry, and the authors argue that a paradigm shift is needed for the industry to move up the value chain and maintain its leading role. The new developments represent opportunities as well as challenges. Innovation, improving IT infrastructure and removing legal and administrative bottlenecks are needed if the Indian IT sector is to sustain its leadership.

For ICT and development, a key issue is the speed of technology diffusion, as also addressed in Chapter "ICT, Growth and Happiness". In Chapter "IT Enabling Indian Firms: The Importance of IT Outsourcing Companies" (**Kite**), the role of information technology outsourcing (ITO) for technology diffusion is addressed. While previous literature has examined the role of ITO from rich countries, Kite presents new evidence based on a large data set for Indian firms, including their use of ITO. Kite finds that there is a strong positive impact of IT outsourcing on output and productivity and that the effect is bigger than the one achieved by IT investments alone. The analysis therefore also relates to Chapter "ICT Investment and Economic Growth in India: An Industry Perspective": IT investments are not enough—they have to be complemented by other assets such as skills, and ITO is one way for Indian firms to acquire these complementary assets. In addition to this evidence from a large firm-level data set, Chapter "IT Enabling Indian Firms: The Importance of IT Outsourcing Companies also presents qualitative evidence from interviews on the institutional characteristics of ITO. This evidence suggests that ITO companies are engaging in a conscious process of learning, and thereby facilitate technology diffusion into India, also by adapting foreign innovations to the local context.

ICT is not only transforming production and consumption, but also the networks and communication between producers, traders and consumers. ICT is thereby changing the world economy by reducing information and communication costs across borders. This is strongly evident in the evolution of global value chains, including business outsourcing and technology diffusion. Three other book chapters examine how ICT facilitates trade, internationally but also within India. According to the optimistic view supported by, e.g. the "flat earth" prediction of Friedman (2005), ICT should lead to the integration of markets and convergence of prices across cities, regions and countries. Also in this area, the research evidence is mixed since the role of distance and borders is persistent and not easily eliminated. Furthermore, there are also situations where low transaction costs promote spatial agglomeration so that spatial inequality may persist in spite of lower transaction costs. Nevertheless, there is growing evidence that ICT actually reduces the impact of borders and distance (see, e.g. Freund and Weinhold 2004; Lendle et al. 2016).

Based on the recent literature on trade with firm heterogeneity (e.g. Melitz 2003), ICTs could affect firms' export decisions by reducing entry barriers in the form of sunk export costs. ICTs could also affect export decisions directly through firm productivity if only the most productive firms export. Chapter "ICT, Access to Finance and Firm Exports: A Cross-Country Study" (**Singh and Maiti**) suggests that a third channel could potentially be ICTs' impact on access to finance, given that finance is important for covering the fixed costs of exporting. With this point of departure, the authors examine how ICT affects export decisions of individual firms across the world, using data from the World Bank Enterprise Survey. The conclusion is indeed affirmative: ICT is export promoting. Some evidence is also provided to the effect that ICT promotes the access to finance and thereby interacts with ICT in the determination of firm-level export decisions. The latter effect illustrates that ICT interacts with other assets or institutions, from strong complementarity in some cases to a secondary indirect effect as in this case.

With online communication around the clock, a new phenomenon in world trade is time zone trade; e.g. news and stock are monitored and traded around the clock, and when time is scarce, some tasks can be efficiently done by switching production between time zones. Time zone differences can be negative by making synchronization more difficult (when your business partner sleeps), but positive if there is something to gain from round-the-clock operation (named the continuity effect in the literature). Chapter "Time Zone Differences and Service Trade" (**Mandal and Prasad**) analyses the issue of time zone trade. According to their study, past evidence suggests that the continuity effect is on the whole stronger than the negative synchronization effect. Time zone trade is particularly relevant to India due to her large ICT-related services exports, and the fact that more than half of these exports are directed to the USA and Canada—i.e. several time zones away. In the chapter, the authors examine theoretically the potential impact of time zone trade. In their model, time zone trade increases production and the price of the traded services and raises the price of the factor used intensively in their production—and in particular skilled labour.

Focusing on the local level in India, Chapter "Towards One Agricultural Market in India: Does the ICT help?" (**Ghosh, Rajeshwor and Vinit**) examines whether ICT has led to integrated agricultural markets and reduced price dispersion across Indian regions. The Government of India and the regions have, jointly with producers, made large efforts to facilitate trade by new ICT infrastructure that improves price and market information and facilitates transactions in agricultural markets. The chapter presents a comprehensive overview of measures and institutions established for this purpose in recent years. Some ICT tools are linked to agriculture marketing reforms so an issue is whether markets are affected by market reforms or by ICT. The authors study empirically whether ICT and/or reforms have led to stronger market integration across Indian states. Examining the wholesale markets for pulses, the authors find some but not universal price convergence across states. Price convergence could also be affected by agricultural policies, particularly public procurement, but with the data at hand it is not possible to distinguish between the impact of ICT and the impact of policy measures.

Part II: Digital Divides and Inequalities

Since ICTs play a pivotal role in stimulating income through various channels, unequal access to ICTs goods and services across the economy may well be one of the factors contributing to rising inequalities. The widening accessibility of ICT goods and services is broadly defined as the *digital divide* in the literature. Part II of the book investigates whether ICTs contribute to convergence or, on the contrary, lead to a growing digital divide—between countries, regions and individuals within India.

Chapter "Digital Divide: How India and China Stack up" (**Tewathia**) investigates the pace and pattern of the digital divide in the largest and rapidly growing nations, India and China, using the ICT diffusion index (ICTDI) across regions. This chapter provides a descriptive empirical analysis for country-level comparison of major economic and information and communication technology indicators and their variation across Indian states and Chinese provinces. India is lagging far behind China with respect to all ICT indicators considered. On the one hand, Internet growth has recently been much faster in India than in China. On the other hand, some Indian states such as Kerala, Maharashtra, Karnataka and Tamil Nadu are more digitalised than others like Bihar, Chhattisgarh and Madhya Pradesh. Similarly, in China, the provinces in the eastern region like Beijing, Tianjin, Shanghai and Guangdong show higher ICT diffusion than the rest.

Using household survey data for India, Chapter "Is India Digitally Divided? Identifying the Determinants of ICT Diffusion at the Household level" (**Mohanty**) further shows that ICT access over time has been uneven. These patterns confirm the rising digital divide in India not only between regions but also across age groups, gender and castes. Using household data, the study uses probit regression and finds that caste, size of the household, occupation, marriage and location of the household significantly affect the intensity of use of ICT devices. The role of education is also important. The study also confirms the conclusion that place and inherent network effect, gender, education, age, occupation and caste are the dominant factors shaping ICT diffusion in India. The poor accessibility of ICT goods and services, specifically in rural areas, is the reason for the rising digital divide between rural and urban areas in India. Poor infrastructure and lack of ICTs supply, as well as less education, are the main reasons for the low accessibility in the rural areas. The chapter further emphasizes that not only the literacy rate but also poor writing and speaking skills remain the binding constraints for lower ICT access in the rural India.

Chapter "Effect of ICT on the Performance of Indian States in terms of Human Development Indices" (**Neogi**) makes a novel attempt to investigate the impacts of public ICT investments on human development across Indian states using data envelope analysis. The components of HDI have been taken as services produced by the state governments while some variables like tax collection of states, population, etc. are considered as inputs of the states. The differences in the capacity of states in utilization of grants and revenue of the states are important determinants in explaining the disparities among the states. Some of the states like Kerala, Maharashtra, Gujarat, Himachal Pradesh and Punjab are much better in term of human development indicators compared to the other states of India. The study outlines a ranking of Indian states in terms of efficiency using non-radial DEA, using as output variables some main socio-economic indicators and as inputs the revenue of the states, central governmental grants, roads and population of the states. A wide variation in the level of human development is observed across the states, and the revenue spending on the ICT sector explains a significant part of the variation. Taken together, the studies included in part II of this book indicate strongly that the digital divide is a key dimension that goes hand in hand with ICT diffusion in India.

Part III: ICTs, Governance and Users' Well-Being

Part III of the book collects contributions that investigate how ICTs' adoption affects users' well-being and welfare. As noted in Sect. 3, one of the relevant channels through which ICTs shape users' well-being relates to the effects of digital technologies on governance. Digital governance may in fact affect transparency and efficiency of public goods and services for households and citizens, as well as limit the extent of corruption.

Chapter "ICTs and Effectiveness of Governance: A Cross-Country Study" (**Agarwal and Maiti**) presents a cross-country empirical study of ICT adoption and the effectiveness of governance. The literature on digitalization and governance has until now mostly focused on the potential positive effects that ICT adoption may have on governance: With the ability of information storing and sharing, ICT innovation can improve governance by enriching the governmental information infrastructure, presenting opportunities for better decision making, encouraging pro-active government–citizen interaction and increasing public accountability. At the same time, however, ICTs also lead to potential risks for users such as cyber-crime, loss of privacy, unemployment and digital inequality. These risks put pressure on the ability of a state to govern effectively. On the whole, the resultant effect of ICTs on the effectiveness of governance is hard to predict on a priori ground, and it depends on the relative strength of the two forces. The chapter investigates this idea by using cross-country unbalanced panel data for the period from 1996 to 2017. The econometric results point out that the improvements in ICTs lead to a rise in the effectiveness of governance, but this positive effect largely depends on the efficacy of the judicial system and the rule of law in each country. In short, the presence of a better rule of law strengthens the favourable impacts of ICT on governance.

Chapter "Red Tape, Corruption and ICT" (**Bhattacharya and Mukherjee**) presents a study of the effects of ICTs on red tape and corruption. The work focuses on the idea that ICTs may reduce the length of red tape, and it analyses the desirability of introduction of ICTs from the stakeholders' perspective. The chapter presents a theoretical model in which the support for such a reform depends on the stakeholders' profile, the nature of the public goods and services, and the initial length of red tape. The main idea of the model is that, although all types of applicants pay speed money in the presence of red tape, it is not that everyone prefers a corrupt regime to an honest regime. The undeserving applicants do not typically complain about a corrupt regime. The deserving applicants, though, complain about corrupt regime in two types of situations: if the proportion of deserving applicants is high enough and if the proportion of deserving applicants is low but the length of the red tape is not long enough. In the presence of too long a red tape, no one complains about corruption. The introduction of ICTs, by shortening the length of red tape, may increase support for a honest regime if the red tape is not long enough and if the gap between the two types of applicants' pay-off is not large enough. The chapter also provides empirical evidence that illustrates the relevance of this model. The empirical analysis using cross-country data shows that ICT increases demand for an honest regime in general, but it reduces the demand for an honest regime and therefore implementation of further ICT reform in countries with longer red tapes. The results may provide an explanation as to why the introduction of ICTs in many high-corruption economies has not been as successful as previously expected.

While the previous two chapters investigate the theme of ICTs and governance in a cross-country international setting, Chapter "Role of Technology in Governance and Development: The Case of e-Uparjan in Madhya Pradesh" (**Pradesh and Mishra**) studies the same theme by focusing on the case of e-Uparjan in India. The e-Uparjan is a relevant case of digital inclusion and synchronization of activities of stakeholders like farmers, designate procurement agencies, technology providers, financial institutions and state administrative agencies. The chapter adopts a single case study approach to understand the technology-enabled procurement system at the micro-level. Field observations also expand the scope of understanding of the context and potential implications of the procurement system to associated stakeholders. The main idea of the study is that faster and real-time information flows along the decision nodes can plug in fund leakage, reduce transaction costs and mitigate rent-seeking behaviour of actors along the value chain. The chapter argues that adoption of ICTs can thus have potential to streamline procurement operations and secure farmers' pay-off in time-bound manner through direct benefit transfer under the price support scheme. The analysis shows that e-Uparjan appears indeed to have improved operational efficiency of collection, warehousing and optimizing transportation network for food grains procurement and distribution. The case of e-Uparjan is relevant because it offers fresh insights on social policy making as network processes that require an adequate understanding of social realities, seamless synchronization of involved stakeholders and aspects of public procurement policies.

As noted earlier in this chapter, India has very low female participation in the labour market, and an important issue is whether ICTs can improve this important social problem. Chapter "ICT, Gender, and the Labor Market: A Cross-Country Analysis" (**Valberg**) investigates the effects of ICTs on gender inequalities in the labour market. By increasing efficiency and access to information, lowering transaction costs and creating new jobs, ICTs have also changed the way we work. An aspect that has until now received only limited attention is that ICTs may potentially have beneficial effects on the labour market for women, which have traditionally been limited from working because of time and mobility constraints. A few previous studies on this topic have been conducted at the micro-level for selected countries, but few attempts have been made to systematically investigate the relationship between ICTs, female employment and development taking a cross-country international perspective. This chapter investigates whether ICTs have an impact on gender equality in the labour market, and it is among the first to investigate cross-country trends in this pattern. Using panel data analysis for 156 countries for the period 1991–2014, the work shows that ICTs contribute positively by narrowing the gender gap in labour market participation, mainly due to increased female labour force participation. However, the chapter also points out that the impact is lower in developing countries compared to advanced economies, suggesting that the adoption of digital technologies alone may not necessarily be an effective leapfrogging strategy for increasing female labour force participation in developing countries.

The final chapter shifts the focus to channels through which ICT use affects well-being and welfare at the individual level. Chapter "ICTs Exposure and Its Relationship with Academic Self-efficacy and Achievement of Adolescent students: The Field-level Study in India and Fiji" (**Mandal**) focuses on a topic of high current relevance: ICT use of adolescents and its effects on well-being. Specifically, the chapter focuses on whether and how ICT exposure affects adolescents' learning at school, by carrying out a novel data collection and empirical field-level study in India and Fiji. Nowadays, children and adolescents spend an increasing amount of time using digital devices such as video games, mobiles, computer and Internet, and doing so they often sacrifice learning and extracurricular activity. This may potentially have serious implications not only on their physical and mental health but also on academic aptitude. Extant literature records few studies in this area showing contentious results that encourage further research. The chapter investigates whether time devoted to ICTs adversely affects academic self-efficacy and achievement of adolescent students in two developing countries, India and Fiji. The study developed a structured questionnaire to capture relevant variables such as time spent using digital devices, academic self-efficacy and achievement and then used these variables in a quantitative analysis. A survey collected relevant information for these variables from 873 adolescent students of the tenth class from 16 schools selected in rural and urban areas in India and Fiji. Cronbach's alpha test was used as customary to assess the reliability of the instruments to justify the questions; and then principal component analysis (PCA) was employed to construct a suitable index of the socio-psychological variable academic self-efficacy. Statistical analyses (ANOVA and regression methods) were then used to establish various relationships among these variables. The empirical results suggest that ICTs exposure does on average improve academic self-efficacy and achievement of adolescent students. However, this is the case only for moderate exposure times and up to a certain daily limit (3 h per day); on the other hand, higher exposure times result in weaker learning effects at school. The results presented in this chapter contribute to the current important debate about well-being effects of the use of ICTs, and whether adolescents should use digital devices in a more cautious manner.

References

Abramovitz, M. (1986). Catching-up, forging ahead and falling behind. *Journal of Economic History, 46,* 385–406.

Abramovitz, M. (1994). The origins of the postwar catch-up and convergence boom. In J. Fagerberg, B. Verspagen, & N. von Tunzelmann (Eds.), *The dynamics of technology, trade and growth.* Aldershot: Edward Elgar

Acemoglu, D., & Restrepo, P. (2018). The race between man and machine: Implications of technology for growth, factor shares, and employment. *American Economic Review, 108*(6), 1488–1542.

Agarwal, A., & Maiti, D. (2019). Digitalization and development in India: Myths and realities. In D. Sanyal & S. Dutta (Eds.), Impact of digital technologies. Delhi: Kunal Publishers.

Biswas, S. (2018, June 27). Aadhaar: Is India's biometric ID scheme hurting the poor? *BBC News.* Retrieved from https://www.bbc.com/news/world-asia-india-43207964.

Brambilla, I. & Tortarolo, D. (2018). *Investment in ICT, productivity, and labor demand: the case of argentina,* Policy Research Working Papers, World Bank Groups, https://doi.org/10.1596/1813-9450-8325.

Business Today. (2019, January 30). Income inequality gets worse; India's top 1% bag 73% of the country's wealth, says Oxfam. Retrieved from https://www.businesstoday.in/current/economy-politics/oxfam-india-wealth-report-income-inequality-richests-poor/story/268541.html.

Castellacci, F. (2006). Innovation, diffusion and catching up in the fifth long wave. *Futures, 38*(7), 841–863.

Castellacci, F. (2008). Technological Paradigms, regimes and trajectories: Manufacturing and service industries in a new taxonomy of sectoral patterns of innovation. *Research Policy, 37*(6–7), 978–994.

Castellacci, F. (2011). Closing the technology gap? *Review of Development Economics, 15*(1),180–197.

Castellacci, F., & Tveito, V. (2018). Internet use and well-being: A survey and a theoretical framework. *Research Policy, 47*(1) 308–325.

Crafts, N. (2004). Steam as a general purpose technology: A growth accounting perspective. *The Economic Journal, 114*(495), 338–351.

Dalum, B., Freeman, C., Simonetti, R., Von Tunzelmann, N., & Verspagen, B. (1999). Europe and the information and communication technologies revolution. In J. Fagerberg, P. Guerrieri, & B. Verspagen (Eds.), *The economic challenge for Europe: Adapting to innovation-based growth.* Cheltenham: Edward Elgar.

Dolan, P., Peasgood, T., & White, M. (2008). Do we really know what makes us happy? A review of the economic literature on the factors associated with subjective well-being. *Journal of Economic Psychology, 29*(1), 94–122.

Dosi, G. (1988). Sources, procedures, and microeconomic effects of innovation. *Journal of Economic Literature, XXVI*, 1120–1171.

Fagerberg, J., & Verspagen, B. (2002). Technology-gaps, innovation-diffusion and transformation: an evolutionary interpretation. *Research Policy, 31,* 1291–1304.

Fagerberg, J., & Godinho, M. M. (2005). Innovation and catching-up. In J. Fagerberg, D. C. Mowery, & R. R. Nelson (Eds.), *The Oxford handbook of innovation*. Oxford: Oxford University Press.

Freeman, C., Clark, J., & Soete, L. (1982). *Unemployment and technical innovation*. London: Pinter.

Freeman, C., & Louça, F. (2001). *As time goes by: From the Industrial Revolutions to the Information Revolution*. Oxford: Oxford University Press.

Freund, C. L., & Weinhold, D. (2004). The effect of the Internet on international trade. *Journal of International Economics, 62*(1), 171–189.

Friedman, T. (2005). *The world is flat. A brief history of the globalized world in the 21st century*. Ferrar, Strauss and Giroux.

Gordon, R. J. (2016). *The rise and fall of american growth: The U.S. standard of living since the civil war*. Princeton: University Press.

Helliwell, J. F. (2006). Well-being, social capital and public policy: What's New? *The Economic Journal, 116*(510), C34–C45.

Lendle, A., Olarreaga, M., Schropp, S., & Vézina, P. (2016). There goes gravity: eBay and the death of distance. *The Economic Journal, 126*(591), 406–441.

Melitz, M. J. (2003). The impact of trade on intra-industry reallocations and aggregate industry productivity. *Econometrica,, 71*(6), 1695–1725.

Mohanty, P. (2019). Is India digitally divided? identifying the determinants of ICT diffusion at the household level, In D. Maiti, F. Castellacci, & A. Melchior (Eds.), *Digitalisation and development: issues for India and Beyond*, Springer (forthcoming).

OECD. (2018). Economic outlook for Southeast Asia, China and India 2018—Update: Promoting opportunities in E-commerce. Paris: OECD Publishing. https://doi.org/10.1787/9789264302990-en.

Parayil, G. (2005). The digital divide and increasing returns: Contradictions of informational capitalism. *The Information Society, 21,* 41–51.

Poushter, J., Bishop, C., & Chwe, H. (2018). Social media use continues to rise in developing countries but plateaus across developed ones. *Pew Research Center*: Global Attitudes Survey.

PRICE. (2016), 'Household Survey on India's Citizen Environment & Consumer Economy'. ICE 360° survey-2016. http://www.ice360.in/en/projects/what-are-ice-360-surveys/upcoming-survey-ice360o-2016.

Ramanna, K., & Tahilyani, R. (2012). I paid a bribe (dot) com. *Harvard Business School Case, 112*(078).

Solow, R. M. (1987). We'd better watch out. *New York Times Book Review, 36*.

Transparency International. (2017). Corruption perceptions index 2017, Berlin, Germany. https://www.transparency.org/news/feature/corruption_perceptions_index_2017.

Telecom Regulatory Authority of India (2018), Annual Report – 2017–18, Mahanagar Doorsanchar Bhawan, New Delhi https://main.trai.gov.in/sites/default/files/Annual_Report_21022019.pdf.

Veblen, T. (1915). *Imperial Germany and the industrial revolution*. New York: Macmillan.

Yousefi, A. (2011). The impact of information and communication technology on economic growth: Evidence from developed and developing countries. *Economics of Innovation and New Technology, 20*(6), 581–596.

ICT, Growth and Happiness

Per Botolf Maurseth

Abstract This chapter reviews two strands of literature. The first is on Information and Communication Technology (ICT) and growth. The increasing role of ICTs came together with stagnating growth rates in many countries. This has been denoted the Solow paradox. During the dot-com era from the mid-1990s, many believed that the paradox was solved. Growth rates increased, and the Internet became pervasive. The great recession has been followed by lower growth in Europe and the USA and a return of the Solow paradox. Evidence indicates that the share of Internet users in countries' populations had a positive effect on growth in the 1990s, but that this effect vanished for developed countries after 2000. The second strand of literature is a heterogeneous research tradition that relates ICT not to income and growth, but to human well-being. That literature indicates positive (as well as some negative) effects of ICT and the Internet on people's happiness. Some new evidence indicates that the share of Internet users in populations in a panel of countries is positively related to average happiness.

Keywords ICT · Internet · Economic growth · Happiness

1 Introduction

Information and communication technology (ICT) has always had major importance for human development. In all human history, ICT has, in some forms or others, had implications and consequences for economic, social and cultural interaction among humans. Collecting, producing, exchanging, storing, coding, adapting and using information has been important for mankind throughout history. Written and spoken language are *information* and *communication* technologies. Dudley (1999) traces the influence of communication technologies for economic growth over a

An earlier and preliminary version of this chapter was pre-published as a working paper, Maurseth (2017).

P. B. Maurseth (✉)
BI—Norwegian Business School, Oslo, Norway
e-mail: Per.B.Maurseth@bi.no

D. Maiti et al. (eds.), *Digitalisation and Development*,
https://doi.org/10.1007/978-981-13-9996-1_2

millennium. Modern ICTs are varieties of old and basic human technology. In this paper, the focus is on electronic and mostly digital technology for information and communication.

Modern ICT has gained increasing importance. The ICT industry is large and growing. ICT is being used in all types of economic activities, from simple traditional production to advanced, complicated and integrated production processes, via public and private planning and governance to household production and consumption for individuals. ICT is far-reaching and influences all types of human behaviour. While ICT became widespread in both production and consumption from the 1970s on, the internet sparked much more rapid and larger changes. Today, the internet has become omnipresent for most production processes and most people around the globe. ICT is a general-purpose technology (GPT) in the sense that it is used for many purposes, in many applications and that its use involves changes that have potential systemic effects.

There is an enormous literature on ICT and economic growth. This literature traces growth effects from the introduction and use of ICT among firms, case studies, effects of ICT in industries and studies at a macro level for single or many countries. Some findings in this literature are summarized in Sect. 2 below. The Solow paradox (high investments in ICT and stagnating growth rates) is an important issue in this literature. Even if growth effects from ICT (as measured by an increase in GDP) are hard to find, there is no doubt that ICT influences people's lives. One main interest in this paper is the relationship between ICT and human well-being or happiness. The use of well-being measures in economics is discussed in Sect. 3. Well-being relates to more than income. Well-being also depends on human sodality, environmental standards, democracy, health and security. In Sect. 4, the implications of ICT on happiness are discussed. Section 5 summarizes and concludes. In the next section, some characteristics of ICT are presented and discussed.

The topics discussed in this paper are many and involve important and complicated issues. This paper is not exhaustive neither in summaries of the literature nor in coverage of topics or mechanisms. Rather, the main purpose is to give a short overview of the impact of the ICT revolution (or evolution) for human well-being.

2 ICT—Conceptual Issues

There is no doubt that recent years have witnessed dramatic changes in the nature of the use of and the diffusion of ICT. These changes have happened very fast, and they represent *quantitative* and *qualitative* change. Historical comparisons do not overshadow the fact that recent changes in ICT have accelerated and become more pervasive recently. But rapid developments in ICT are not new.

Samuel Morse patented the electric telegraph in 1837 and developed the Morse alphabet. The telegraph was developed fast on both sides of the Atlantic, and these telegraph nets were connected with a trans-Atlantic cable in 1866. Obstfeld (1998), writing about international integration of capital markets, notes that (p. 11) "This communication advance in the era was perhaps more significant than anything that has been achieved since". Almost in the same period, telephones expanded rapidly, from its invention in 1876. Developments were fast, and by 1940, 40% of all American households had a telephone. In 1915 it took twenty-three minutes to connect telephones between New York and California. In 1951 it took eighteen seconds. In 2013, 91% of all American adults had a cell phone.[1]

The radio was developed at the beginning of the twentieth century after inventions inspired by Maxwell's theories of electromagnetism in the 1860s (see Freeman and Soete 1997). Developments, led by companies such as Marconi (UK), Telefunken (Germany) and RCA (USA), were rapid. Radio became important for communication as well as for mass consumption of news and entertainment. From radio technology, television developed. Based on ambitious R&D projects, RCA launched commercial television in 1939. In 1970, sales of colour TVs in the USA reached five million per annum. European and Japanese producers had followed. The introduction of television involved mass entertainment more than the radio did.

From the 1930s on, R&D was devoted to the development of the radar, which gained widespread use for military purposes in the Second World War (Freeman and Soete 1997). The invention of the radar later inspired the development of the laser which subsequently gained widespread use in the computer industry (and in particular for CDs) (see Scotchmer 2004, Chap. 5).

The developments of the computer are described in, e.g., Ruttan (2001). Its history dates back to long before World War II. IBM was founded in 1924. There was great optimism about the potential achievements of the new technology. In 1950, CEO of IBM, Thomas Watson Snr., claimed that the recently developed *Selective Sequence Electronic Calculator* (SSEC) was sufficient to "solve all the important scientific problems in the world involving scientific calculations". Due to this optimism about potential performance, there was pessimism about the commercial possibilities for computers. Because of the performance, there would not be a need for many computers; pessimists feared. It took decades before the use of computers become widespread. Life insurance companies bought the first commercially available computer, the UNIVAC 1, from 1954 onwards. But "Progress was slow because the initial computers did little more than juggle data read from punch cards and printed by punch-card printers" (Gordon 2016, p. 449).

Computers gained widespread use in larger corporations and public agencies before 1980. In addition, from about 1985, PCs became common for individual consumers. PCs became standard for writing, computations, accounting, design work and many other tasks during the 1980s. They were pervasive in business, public governments and households in the 1990s.

The diffusion of computers was closely related to Moore's law. Computers became more powerful and rapidly cheaper over time. Moore's law is the observation that computing capacity seems to double every 18th month (Gordon 2002; Aizcorbe and Kortum 2005). Gordon Moore observed in 1965 "that each new memory chip contained roughly twice as many transistors as the previous chip and was released

[1]Gordon (2016, p. 430).

within 18–24 months of its predecessor" (Jorgenson 2005, p. 748). In 2003, Moore continued being optimistic about future developments in ICT: "No exponential is forever, but we can delay forever" (Moore 2016). Gordon (2002, p. 51) writes that the cycle in which computers double their performance had shortened to 12 months in 1999, but that it has increased to almost six years after 2006 (Gordon 2016).

Caselli and Coleman (2001) study the diffusion of ICT equipment for a cross section of countries. The point of departure is that most countries have a relatively small ICT industry. Therefore, the use of ICT equipment is indicated by countries' imports of such goods. These are easily available data. In data for the period from 1970 to 1990, Caselli and Coleman find that imports of ICT equipment depend on countries' investment shares, the share of manufacturing in GDP, protection of intellectual property rights, level of education and imports of manufactured goods from OECD countries. Interestingly, similar variables also have explanatory power for GDP itself. This points in the direction that ICT is complementary to other growth-promoting variables.

Despite many past technological breakthroughs for ICT, many regard the introduction of PCs, the launch of the internet and the digitalization of many production and consumer processes as qualitatively different from previous advances. First, the size of the modern ICT industry is higher than before. Second, the use of ICT is more widespread than before. Third, complementarities, network effects and massive economies of scale have become more important than before. Use of the internet is now common for most people in rich countries, and access is becoming available throughout the world. This has come together with smartphones that enable the use of the internet everywhere people have access to mobile telephone subscription. The development has been fast and faster than the diffusion of previous technologies. Figure 1 graphs diffusion of the number of mobile phone subscribers and users of

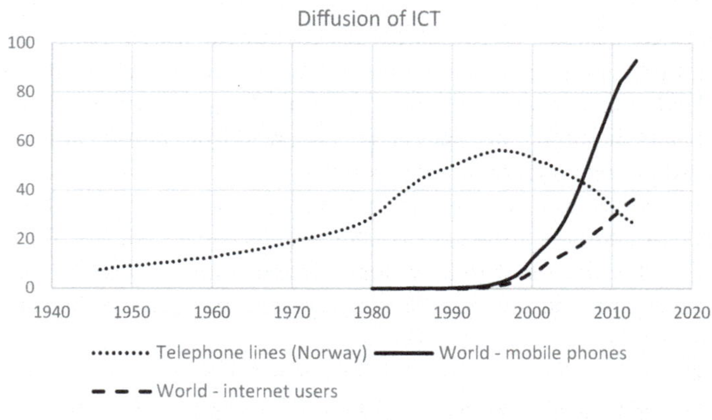

Fig. 1 Diffusion of ICT. *Note* Numbers are per 100 inhabitants. Number of internet users is the number who have used internet during the last 12 months. Telephone lines in 1997 in Norway are calculated as the average between 1996 and 1998 due to an unexplainable peak. *Source* World Development Indicators (2017) and Statistics Norway (2017)

the internet worldwide, and (for comparison) the number of standard telephone lines in Norway.

The graph illustrates three important aspects of the diffusion of internet technologies. The first is the typical S-shaped diffusion. At first, diffusion is slow. Thereafter it accelerates, and diffusion is fast. When the technology has matured, diffusion is slower, and it takes longer for latecomers to apply the technology. The graph shows that the S shape also was present for the diffusion of telephones (in Norway). Hall (2005) analyses the diffusion of many technologies. The S-shaped diffusion pattern is typical. Hall discusses heterogeneity among consumers and producers, learning effects and network effects as explanations. Technology is first adopted among those who need it the most. Thereafter consumers and producers who need it successively less start using the technology. If consumers' utility from the technology is normally distributed, the cumulative share of users over time will have the S shape. Similar effects come from learning. Users of technology learn from each other. If there are few users, learning is limited but increasing. When the technology is widely adopted, there are fewer left to learn. Also, network effects give similar diffusion patterns. Network effects denote that utility from being a network member increases with the number of network members. Therefore, the utility from adopting a technology increases with the number of other users. Stoneman and Battisti (2010), Geroski (2000) and Stoneman (2002) survey this literature.

The second aspect from the graph above is that diffusion of the internet has been fast (compared to diffusion of telephone lines in Norway but also compared to many other technologies).[2] In 2015, about 44% of the world's population were internet users.[3] In many countries, the share of internet users approaches 100%. In OECD countries, the number of internet users expanded from 60% in 2005 to 80% in 2013. In other countries, the share of internet users is on the steepest part of the S-curve. A reasonable prediction is, therefore, that the share of the world population that uses the internet will continue to increase fast in the years to come. Increasing internet use has benefited from the development of mobile infrastructure. Wireless broadband subscriptions in the OECD increased from 250 million to 850 million from 2008 to 2013. In sub-Saharan Africa, mobile broadband subscriptions grew from 14 million to 117 million between 2010 and 2013 (OECD 2014a). In addition, comes that broadband connection is becoming less costly. OECD (2014a) reports price developments. In most countries, price indexes for the broadband decrease. There is great variation in broadband prices between OECD countries, with prices being about three times higher in the USA than in South Korea (which is followed by Hungary, Slovakia, Israel and Denmark).

The last aspect of the graph is that internet substitutes for other technologies. Telephone lines reached a peak at almost 60 per 100 habitats in 1997. Thereafter the number of lines has decreased. The reason is the diffusion of cellular phones.

---

[2]Gordon (2016) describes diffusion of television in the USA, which was even faster than diffusion of mobile phones and the internet. In 1950, 9% of American households owned a TV set. In 1955, this number had increased to 65%.

[3]By 2017, therefore, probably most people in the world are internet users.

The fast growth and diffusion of ICT (and the internet in particular) are closely related to technological development in the ICT industry. Moore's law implies that real prices for computers halve every 18 months. There are also quality improvements in other dimensions. Broadband speeds increase and allow full internet services for cellular phone and tablet users.

Research on price developments in ICT is demanding. Computers today are radically different from computers, just 5 or 10 years ago. Computers today are even more different from those in the more distant past. Dale Jorgenson is a pioneer in calculating and estimating hedonic price indexes for (among other goods) computers.[4] Hedonic price indexes take into account nominal price changes as well as quality improvements for the goods in question. Jorgenson (2005) presents several results. Some of these are reported in Fig. 2. That figure shows hedonic price indexes for computers, software, telecommunication and ICT in aggregate. Also reported is the price index for GDP. The scale in the figure is in logs, and so that (log of) prices in 2000 are zero. Values below zero indicate lower prices than in 2000. Values above zero indicate prices higher than in 2000.

The striking fact evidenced by Fig. 2 is the dramatic decline in prices for computers. The decline has evolved in cycles. In the 1970s, it decelerated first and then accelerated. The price decline was slower during most of the 1980s. After 1995, price declines accelerated again. According to the figure, a computer was 1635 times more expensive in 1960 than in 2000 (in logs, 7.4). This corresponds to an annual price decline of 18%. Software, on the other hand, has had relatively stable prices. But compared to other goods and services (the price index for GDP), prices of ICT has decreased dramatically in the period described by Fig. 2.

Gordon (2016) compares real price declines for ICT goods with prices developments for other goods undergoing rapid technological change. He claims that large

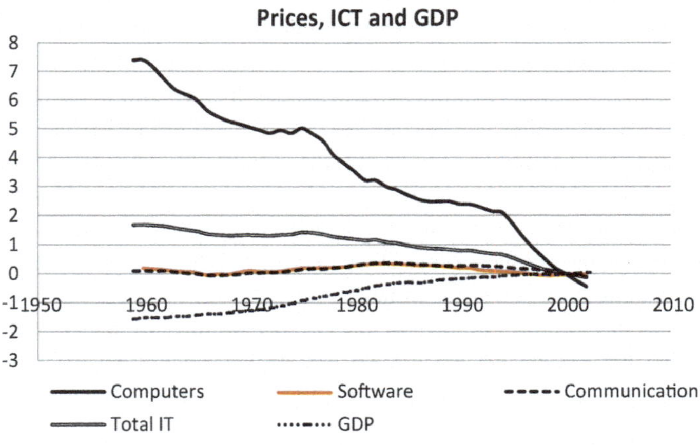

Fig. 2 Prices, ICT and GDP. *Source* Jorgenson (2005)

[4]For hedonic price indexes for computers, also see Chow (1967) and Berndt and Griliches (1993).

price declines have been frequent also for other goods. Gordon's estimates of price declines for TV sets in the period from 1952 to 1983 are 4.3% annually. Gordon notes that this estimate is "doubtless an understatement" (Gordon 2016, p. 423). After hedonic price indexes for TV sets were introduced in 1998, estimated price declines per year were 20.4%. Raff and Trajtenberg (1995) estimate hedonic price indexes for automobiles in the 1906–1940 period. They conclude that hedonic prices fell at an average annual rate of 5%. Gordon notes that previous underestimates of price declines also underestimated GDP *growth* more in the past than in the present. Still, Gordon concludes (p. 441):

> The improvement in the performance of computers relative to their price has been continuous and exponential since 1960, and the rate of improvement dwarfs any precedent in the history of technology.

Economists have since long agreed that technological change is the main source of economic growth.[5] Important in this respect is Solow (1957). Solow decomposed contributions to growth in the American economy in the period from 1909 to 1949 from investments and increasing employment. Solow's main idea was that with observable changes in production, in the use of capital and employment, one can estimate the contributions to growth from non-observable variables. These non-observable variables were denoted *total factor productivity* (TFP). Important and controversial assumptions in this *growth accounting* framework are that there is perfect competition (so that labour and capital are paid according to the value of their marginal productivities) and that there are constant returns to scale in production. Solow's main conclusion was that 87.5% of observed growth could not be explained by investments or use of labour. This part of the growth was, therefore, attributed to technological progress. Solow's study inspired many subsequent studies. These refined on methods and often decomposed growth into contributions from the capital, labour, human capital and technological change. Often, estimates of the contributions from technological change have been more modest, though still large, in more recent studies. An overview is provided in Barro and Sala-I-Martin (1995, Chap. 10), Jorgenson (2005).[6]

With pervasive adoption and use of ICT in almost all industries (in particular in rich countries), there was great optimism about growth potentials from this type of technology. Many believed that ICT could have far-reaching implications and change the entire economic system and also involve changes in social factors such as working and family life [see, e.g., presentation of the book by Helpman (1998)]. ICT was compared with previous technological shifts such as the industrial revolution, the steam engine, electricity, motors powered with electricity and the petrochemical industry. Such shifts have been identified as *technological paradigms* (Dosi 1988) or

---

[5]The agreement has weakened somewhat recently. In the wake of the literature about endogenous growth, technological change is the result of economic mechanisms and in need of explanation itself. As primary explanations for growth have *geography* and *institutions* emerged as candidates (see, e.g., Diamond 1997; Acemoglu et al. 2005 or Rodrik et al. 2004).

[6]Note that several contributions have relaxed the assumptions of constant returns to scale and perfect competition. See, e.g., Feenstra (2004, Chap. 10).

general-purpose technologies (GPTs). ICT has been characterized as a GPT. GPTs have received increasing attention in the literature on economic growth and technological change.

GPTs are characterized as being *general, having widespread use, stimulating further innovations and being complementary.*

GPTs are general in the sense that they have applications in many industries and for many purposes. This is the case for ICT. ICT is used in all industries and for many purposes. OECD (2014a) reports that 94% of enterprises in the OECD countries had a broadband connection and that 75% had a webpage. Use of ICT includes information flows management, accounting, planning, writing, copying and supply chain management. Use of ICT varies between countries and for different purposes. About 50% of all firms used e-purchase, while 20% conducted e-commerce sales in 2013.

ICT has indeed stimulated innovation. Moore's law exemplifies that the ICT industry is itself a highly innovative industry. ICT is used for countless purposes, and ICT is a major ingredient in all types of research and development (R&D). ICT has stimulated innovation in many industries. OECD (2014a) reports that ICT industries are the most R&D intensive. ICT is used for innovation purposes in most industries. Firm-level data indicates that innovating firms are more ICT intensive than other industries (OECD 2014a).

ICT is complementary to other types of technology. ICT is used for monitoring, planning, supervision and many other purposes in most industries. Evidence about complementarity abound. One example is that about 25% of patented inventions attributed to ICT-related technologies are also labelled under other technology classes.[7]

ICT is flexible. ICT can be used for many purposes and be adapted to special needs and requirements in different applications, in different industries and firms and for different persons.

There are many surveys and review articles about ICT as GPT. Examples are Bresnahan (2010), Jovanovic and Rousseau (2005), Bertschek (2003) and Rousseau (2008). In some of these, ICT is compared with previous GPTs. Many believe that the growth effects of ICT will be large. Others warn against effects for income distribution, employment and social life (see, e.g., Brynjolfsson and McAfee 2014 or Keen 2015). Gordon (2002, 2016) remains sceptical about growth potentials from ICT.

Cordona et al. (2013) relate GPT technologies to spillovers, where social returns from investments exceed private returns. If there are spillovers from ICT-producing industries to ICT-using industries and from ICT-using industries back to ICT-producing industries (vertical spillovers), growth may breed itself. Also, horizontal spillovers, either in ICT-producing industries or in ICT-using industries, may be growth promoting.

---

[7] In patent documents, patents are assigned a technology class (IPC). Patents are sometimes assigned to several IPC classes.

ICT also has other characteristics. In many instances, ICT has implied *path dependency*. Path dependency explains how history matters. One point of departure gives a different result than another point of departure. Often this results from high costs from changing direction. The best-known example is the QWERTY keyboard. It has been claimed that the QWERTY keyboard was introduced to reduce the speed with which people wrote on typewriters (David 1985). A too high speed made the typebars in old fashioned typewriters to "clash and jam together". David writes, (p. 333):

> From the inventor's trial-and-error rearrangements of the original model's alphabetical key ordering, in an effort to reduce the frequency of type bar clashes, there emerged a four-row, upper case keyboard approaching the modern QWERTY standard.

The standard was introduced for a completely different reason than what can be relevant today. Still, the keyboard is today's standard. David assumes that the reason is the costs of changing the established standard. David's argument has later been criticized (see Kay 2013 for an overview). Still, the case is an illustrating example of path dependency. Standards are chosen based on very different conditions from the conditions under which the standards get widespread use. Therefore, choice of standards can involve errors due to future changes and therefore impose high extra costs in the economy.

Whether path dependency is a major obstacle for change is an open question, however. There are many counter examples of rapid technological shifts in the use and production of ICT. The telex and the telefax are now outdated by scanning and email correspondence. So is the cassette (and the CD) format for storing and playing music. The video cassette is also out of use.

ICT is network technology. Utility (or productivity effects) from the use of ICT increases in the number of users. This is the case for telephone and the internet. If nobody else has a telephone, there is no need for it. Use of the internet is more useful when there are many internet pages. Information and *communication* technology implies human interaction. ICT involves interaction among human beings (and/or machines).

Since utility increases in the number of users, there are positive externalities from the use of ICT. But the marginal user pays a price that equals his marginal utility. Therefore, the market solution for ICT may involve too few users. It is easy to think of examples. Facebook groups for groups where some members are not Facebook users are imperfect. Since utility from networks increases in the number of users, the marginal social utility from an extra user is higher than the private marginal utility for this user. Scotchmer (2004) and Shy (2001) analyse network effects. They demonstrate that markets for network goods may have multiple equilibria. If everybody expects that use will be widespread, there will be many users. If everybody expects that use will be limited, there will be few users.[8]

---

[8]Network effects can be hard to identify. Brynjolfsson and Kemerer (1996) analyse the market for spreadsheets in the 1987–1991 period. They find that prices for spreadsheets depend on product characteristics, a time trend *and the accumulated* number of the particular spreadsheet sold. They find positive effects of the latter and interpret it a network effect. They acknowledge, however, that also strategic pricing may play a role.

Modern network-based ICT is different from traditional ICT in the sense that it is often multilateral. The telephone is bilateral while television and radio are unilateral. With modern ICT, there are not defined senders or receivers. Rather, all users are (potential) senders and receivers. And, different from telephone, but similar to old fashioned paper mail, ICT does not require that senders and receivers are active at the same time. ICT service production, therefore, differs from other types of service production (which are often characterized as requiring consumption and production at the same time and the same location, with haircutting being one example).

ICT depends on infrastructure investments. Infrastructure very often has *good public* characteristics. Once in place, marginal user costs are low or zero (in the absence of congestion effects). Infrastructure reduces transaction costs, which are important for well-functioning markets. Broadband investments have had priority in recent years.[9] Most OECD countries have reached high coverage of internet broadband. According to OECD (2014a), more than 70% of the population in the OECD countries has access to wireless broadband.

Quah (2003) emphasizes that the goods produced by ICT are *digital goods*. Such goods have five characteristics that distinguish them from other goods. Digital goods are *non-rival, infinitely expandable, discrete, non-spatial and recombinant*. Use of non-rival goods can increase infinitely without reducing consumption possibilities for existing users. Infinite expandable means that digital goods can be reproduced infinitely without changing the nature of the original. Copies are identical to the original. Digital goods are discrete in the sense that they cannot be partitioned into parts. Digital goods are non-spatial. They are everywhere and nowhere. For the production of digital goods, geographical market access is irrelevant. Therefore production can be located independently of market location. Quah argues that this facilitates clustering of the production of ICT goods. Since market access has no relevance, production can locate where it is most efficient. Digital goods are recombinant. They can be combined and re-combined in countless versions. Weitzmann (1998) has argued that knowledge and know-how can grow without limits because of unlimited possibilities for combining existing ideas in a model of economic growth. The number of websites grew from 18,500 globally in 1995 to more than 3,350,000 in 1998. Larry Page and Sergey Brin developed Google as a tool for handling this overload of information. The enormous amount of information also gave a name to Google, a misspelling of *googol*, the mathematical number 1.0×10^{100}, which denote an extremely large number (see Keen 2015).

The characteristics of digital goods make them well suited for knowledge sharing and diffusion. Innovating firms in the ICT industries report on collaboration in their innovative activities more often than firms in other industries (OECD 2014a). However, international collaboration in R&D has not increased much in any technology field (as measured by international co-invention as evidenced in patent documents).

Vannebar Bush (1945) contemplated about future for mankind after World War II. After five years of intense destruction, new efforts for human progress were called for. Scientists could now concentrate on constructive roles for building a better future.

[9]Broadband includes connections with data speed of 256 kbit/s or more (OECD 2014a).

The main challenge for scientists is that (p. 3) "There is a growing mountain of research. But there is increasing evidence that we are being bogged down today as specialization extends." But with new storage possibilities, existing knowledge could be made available (p. 8): "The *Encyclopedia Britannica* could be reduced to the volume of a matchbox." But also, data analyses needed to improve (p. 11):

> The advanced arithmetical machines in the future will be electrical in nature, and they will perform at 100 times present speeds, or more. Moreover, they will be far more versatile than present commercial machines, so they may readily be adapted for a wide variety of operations.

But the future has wider promises, for instance, the "memex" (pp. 18–19):

> Consider a future device for individual use, which is a sort of file and library. ... A memex is a device in which individual stores all his books, records and communications, and which is mechanized so that it may be consulted with exceeding speed and flexibility... It consists of a desk, ... On the top are slanting translucent screens, on which material can be projected for convenient reading. There are a keyboard, and sets of buttons and levers. ... Most of the memex contents are purchased on microfilm ready for insertion. Books of all sorts, pictures, current periodicals, newspapers, are thus obtained and dropped into place. Business correspondence takes the same path.

And (pp. 19–20):

> It affords an immediate step, ..., the basic idea of which is a provision whereby any item may be caused at will to select immediately and automatically another. This is the essential feature of the memex.

Bush concludes (p. 24):

> The applications of science have built a man well-equipped house and teaching him to live healthy therein. They have enabled him to throw masses of people against one another with cruel weapons. They may yet allow him truly to encompass the great record and to grow in the wisdom of race experience.

Vannebar Bush's ideas about the memex influenced generations of computer scientists, who drew inspiration from its vision of the future.

3 Growth Effects from ICT

3.1 Macrodata

Many have shared Vannebar Bush's optimism. The GPT characteristics of ICT could indicate growth-promoting effects. First, the ICT industry itself has grown large. Second, ICT is used in all industries. ICT is complementary to other types of technology and may enhance returns from investments in physical and human capital in many activities. ICT is network-based, and growth effects may be increasing in the number of users. ICT facilitates the reorganization of work life to enhance benefits from specialization. Digital goods are characterized by massive scale economies. Observed

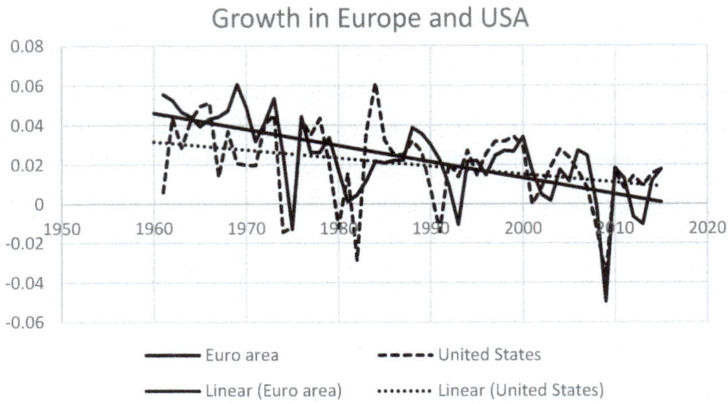

Fig. 3 Growth in Europe and USA. *Source* World Development Report (2016)

investments in ICT have been high. Most enterprises now use ICT for many purposes. Introductions of GPTs have previously resulted in high growth rates. Steam engines, the internal combustion engines, the steel industry and mass production are examples of GPTs that stimulated growth after their introduction.

Still, growth effects from ICT are debated among economists. One reason is the trends showed in Fig. 3. That figure graphs annual growth rates in the USA and Europe (EU member countries) in GDP per capita (in constant 2010 USD) in the period from 1960 to 2015. Along with the data are linear trend lines (from linear regressions).

The graph shows clear ups and downs in growth rates. The 1960s had high growth rates. In the 1970s, there was a recession in 1974–1975 and in the 1980s growth rates went from negative to very high. The great recession in 2008–2009 is visible in the graph. Over time, the picture is one of stagnating growth rates, however. This is so for the USA and Europe, and Japan as well. The trend lines are falling. European growth rates started higher than those in the USA but trended downwards over the period covered by the graph. This is the Solow paradox, which is the combination of high investments in ICT and at the same time, low growth rates in productivity (Solow 1987). Solow writes in his famous book review that:

> What this means is that they, like everyone else, are somewhat embarrassed by the fact that what everyone feels to have been a technological revolution, a drastic change in our productive lives, has been accompanied everywhere, including Japan, by a slowing down of productivity growth, not by a step up. You can see the computer age everywhere but in the productivity statistics.

Arguing along the same line, Dudley (1999, p. 596) writes:

> A paradoxical feature of the productivity-growth slowdown of the 1970s and 1980s is that it coincided with very rapid innovation in information technology.

Optimism substituted for pessimism in the 1990s. In that period, growth rates had increased in the USA, and there was much optimism about the dot-com economy.

It is shown in Fig. 3 that growth rates increased both in the American and in the European economies in the 1990s. The high growth rates in the 1990s were taken as evidence that the Solow paradox was solved. The interpretation was that "Computers are now everywhere in our productivity statistics" (Acemoglu et al. 2014). Cardona et al. (2013) notes that the higher growth rates in the USA in this period was taken as evidence of the GPT characteristics of ICT: efficiency gains from implementation of more productive ICT equipment were not limited to the ICT industry only, but created productivity growth also in other parts of the economy. For instance, Stiroh and Botsch (2007) find that growth effects spilled over from ICT-producing industries to industries that used ICT.

But thereafter, growth rates have decreased again. Whether this is permanent or transitory is a matter of debate. There has been a long debate among economists about the Solow paradox. In recent years, Jorgenson (2005) and Brynjolfsson and McAfee (2014) are examples from the optimist camp while Gordon (2016) and Acemoglu et al. (2014) are examples from the pessimist camp. Below is a discussion of recent contributions such as these. Triplett (1999) reviews the earlier debate.

Triplett proposed that computers constitute a too small share of the economy to generate large growth effects. Based on Oliner and Sichel (1994) and Jorgenson and Stiroh (1995), Triplett presents results from growth accounting, where contributions to growth from investments in ICT are estimated. Even if there are fast growth in the scale (and quality of) ICT investments, they still contribute little to overall productivity growth. In the 1980–1992 period, ICT investments contributed to about 15% of output growth while ICT equipment contributed with only 5% of total output growth in the 1990–1996 period. Some estimates indicate higher effects of ICT. But Triplett concludes that (p. 313): "Still, the share of computing equipment is too small for any reasonable return to computer investment to result in a large contribution to economic growth".

This is still relevant. You can see the computer everywhere. One reason is their costs, which have decreased dramatically. ICT industries lead in growth in labour productivity as compared to other industries (OECD 2014a). But the size of the ICT industry is limited. In Fig. 4, another measure of the importance of ICT is presented. That figure graphs the share of exports of ICT goods and ICT services in the world economy.[10]

The graph shows that trade in ICT represents a small part of the world economy. The graph also shows that such trade has been remarkably stable. Trade in ICT goods decreases somewhat. Trade in ICT service increases slightly. A similar graph for the OECD countries gives a similar picture. Trade in ICT is lower for the OECD countries than for the world economy, but with trade in ICT services representing a

[10]ICT service exports include computer and communications services (telecommunications and postal and courier services) and information services (computer data and news-related service transactions). ICT goods exports include computers and peripheral equipment, communication equipment, consumer electronic equipment, electronic components and other information and technology goods (miscellaneous). The definitions are explained in *World Development Indicators* (2017).

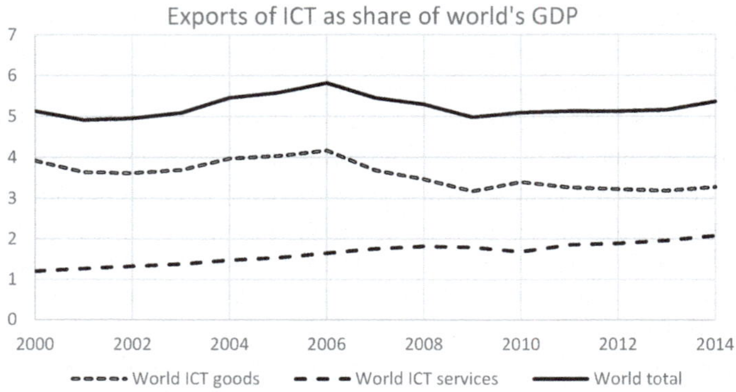

Fig. 4 Exports of ICT as share of world's GDP. *Source* World Development Report (2016)

larger share. Also, growth in trade in ICT services is higher for the OECD countries which are compared to total world trade.

In the OECD countries, the ICT industries account for about 6% of value added and 3.8% of employment (OECD 2014a). Investments in ICT goods as a share of GDP and as a share of gross fixed capital formation have decreased in the aftermath of the dot-com era at the end of the 1990s. ICT investments dropped from 3.2% of GDP in 2000 to 2.3% in 2012.

With the increasing use of ICT in all industries, it may be argued that the graph understates the importance of ICT in world trade. Still, the fact that the share of ICT trade in world trade is limited and stable demonstrates that growth effects from growth *within* the ICT industry might be limited. Since the ICT industry is of limited size, growth effects might be observed in ICT-*using* industries, rather than in ICT-*producing* industries. The large price declines of ICT (as evidenced in graph 2) also indicate that the use of ICT has become cheaper for all users.

Contributions from ICT to growth in non-ICT industries are hard to calculate. Jorgenson (2005), Jorgenson et al. (2008) and Jorgenson et al. (2014) are important contributions. Jorgenson with co-authors has contributed with several contributions from ICT on aggregate economic growth. Jorgenson (2005) decomposes contributions to growth from the use of labour, investments in non-ICT capital, growth in TFP outside the ICT industries, investments in ICT capital goods and growth in TFP within the ICT industry. The analyses indicate that both investments in ICT and TFP growth in the ICT industries explained a large and increasing share of aggregate growth in the USA in the 1980–2004 period.

European and Japanese economic developments have been weaker. This was so during the dot-com period from 1995 to 2001, but also later on. Some have suggested an "Atlantic divide" in the influence of ICT on economic growth. In Fig. 3, it is clear that European economic growth has been lower than in the USA from the 1990s onwards. While the dot-com era was visible in US productivity statistics, there were much weaker signs of ICT lead productivity growth among European countries. van Ark et al. (2008) analyse the weak European development. They argue that the

European slowdown is attributable to slower diffusion of the knowledge economy in Europe compared as to the USA. While Europe caught up with the USA in the post-war period, this convergence came to an end around 1990.[11] Using a similar type of growth accounting as used by Jorgenson, van Ark et al. estimate contributions to growth from the *knowledge economy*.[12] In the USA, total annual growth rates in the market economy were 3.7% in the 1995–2004 period. Of this, the knowledge economy contributed 2.6 percentage points. In Europe, on the other hand, total growth rates in output were 2.2% of which the knowledge economy contributed 1.1 percentage points. Even if the contribution from the knowledge economy varied between countries (in Finland, it contributed 3.4 percentage points), European performance was weak. Guerrieri et al. (2011) discuss why Europe has lower investments in ICT than the USA. They investigate how ICT investments depend on other variables. They argue that ICT investments depend on countries' industry composition, but also factors such as workers' competence and investments in R&D.

Cette et al. (2013) compare the contribution from ICT to growth in labour productivity in the USA, Canada, the Eurozone and the UK in the 1970–2013 period. They reach four main conclusions. First, ICT capital stock increased over a long period up until 2000 in all the four areas but then stabilized after 2000. Second, stabilization happened at different levels, with the USA ranking first and the Eurozone last. Third, the contribution from ICT to labour productivity growth rose in the 1994–2004 period compared to the 1974–1994 period. Fourth, after 2004, the contribution from ICT to labour productivity has fallen considerably. Draca et al. (2006) survey the literature. From their reading of the literature, they conclude that both in the USA and in the Europe, growth rates were higher in ICT-producing industries than in other industries. Only in the USA, however, they find growth stimulus from ICT in ICT-using industries.

Studying a longer period, Acemoglu et al. (2014) present evidence based on US manufacturing industries. They find little evidence of growth stimulus from ICT. There is labour productivity growth in ICT-intensive manufacturing, but the growth in labour productivity is driven by declining output combined with an *even more rapid* decline in employment.

Cardona et al. (2013) conclude that (p. 116) "In particular, during the period from 1995 to 2000, the US showed high investments in IT accompanied by productivity increases". For Europe, however, they write (p. 117): "Europe, on the other hand, shows lower productivity growth and ICT investments post 1995, while the differential to the US has increased throughout the early 2000s."

Evangelista et al. (2014) investigate the impact of ICT on European economic performance from a somewhat different angle. They make use of a more detailed database covering different indicators for ICT for EU member countries in the period from 2004 to 2009. From this database, they construct measures for ICT *infrastructure* (broadband, bandwidth, number of internet subscribers, internet access for

---

[11]Note that European and US trend growth rates intersect in the early 1990s in Fig. 3.

[12]They define the *knowledge economy* as changes in labour composition, ICT capital per hours worked and TFP.

households, etc.), ICT *usage* (number of people accessing the internet from home, number who accessed daily, ICT skills, etc.) and ICT *empowerment* (use of internet banking, extent of e-purchases, electronic job applications and use of the internet for health and education purposes). They regressed countries' labour productivity and GDP per capita growth rates on these as well as other variables (like investment shares, population and human capital). They found that only internet usage was significantly positively correlated with labour productivity and that only ICT empowerment was positively correlated with growth.

Yousefi (2011) analyses contributions from ICT investments for growth in a sample of both rich and poor countries. He finds that ICT investments have positive effects on growth in high-income and middle-income countries, but less so in low-income countries. Similar results are found in Papaioannou and Dimelis (2007).

Najarzadeh et al. (2014) find that internet use increases labour productivity in a panel data set with 108 countries in the period from 1995 to 2010. Results are significant at the 5% level in fixed effects and GMM versions, but not in the pooled data.

Choi and Yi (2009) study the impact of the share of internet users in the population for economic growth in a panel of countries for the 1990–2000 period. They base their study on data from *World Development Indicators*. From panel data growth regressions for countries covering both developed and developing countries (they use an unbalanced panel data set with a total of 1004 observations), they conclude that the internet significantly and positively increases countries' growth rates. They report results from (successively) pooled OLS, random effects panel models, individual fixed effect model; year fixed effects models and combinations of random effects and year fixed effects model. They also include auxiliary variables (investments share in GDP, government expenditure shares in GDP and inflation rates). The positive effects of the use of the internet are robust to model specification.

Maurseth (2018) investigates Choi and Yi's results. Maurseth reruns their regressions on updated data. Maurseth confirms the results from Choi and Yi for the 1990–2000 period. For the 1990–2015 period, however, the results for internet use are the *opposite* of those of Choi and Yi. The share on internet users in countries populations correlates negatively and significantly with countries growth rates.

Similar results are reported in Table 1. The results are based on data for the period from 1990 to 2015 from *World Development Report*. I have extrapolated some of the data for shares of internet users in the population. Data for many countries starts some years after 1990. When this is the case and the share of internet users in the first year was less than 1%, I inserted zero for the previous years. In other cases, I included the country observation for shorter periods (so that I obtained an unbalanced panel data set). When there were incomplete series, I included a constant trend in the share of internet users to fill in the data. This resulted in an unbalanced panel data set for 152 countries in the period from 1990 to 2015 and growth data from 1991 to 2015. In total, the data set contains 3396 observations. I report results first for the 1991 to 2000 period (similar to Choi and Yi) and thereafter for the 1990 to 2015 period and the 2001 to 2015 period.

Table 1 Regression results for yearly growth rates, 1990–2000

Variable	Choi and Yi (col. c)	Choi and Yi (col. e)	Fixed effects	Fixed effects	Fixed effects
Internet	0.053 (0.022)**	0.060 (0.214)***	0.036 (0.021)	0.051 (0.025)**	0.458 (0.664)
Investments	0.141 (0.022)***	0.174 (0.012)***	0.135 (0.022)***	0.155 (0.026)***	0.155 (0.026)***
Government	−0.423 (0.056)***	−0.142 (0.025)***	−0.383 (0.057)***	−0.362 (0.054)***	−0.363 (0.054)***
Inflation	−0.0004 (0.0002)**	−0.0008 (0.0002)***	−0.0004 (0.0002)***	−0.0002 (0.0002)	−0.0002 (0.0002)
Lagged GDP pc				−0.151 (0.012)	−0.152 (0.012)***
Interact					−0.039 (0.063)
Trade				0.044 (0.010)***	0.044 (0.010)***
Fixed effects	Yes	No (RE)	Yes	Yes	Yes
Year dummies	No	Yes	Yes	Yes	Yes
R^2	0.13	0.23	0.16	0.00	0.00
R^2 (within)	0.08	0.09	0.11	0.00	0.00
R^2 (between)	0.27	0.53	0.29	0.21	0.22
Countries	154	154	154	154	154
N	1 386	1 386	1 386	1 386	1 386

Note Standard errors in parenthesis. ***, ** and * denote significance at 1, 5 and 10% levels, respectively. RE denotes random effects GLS regression

The regression is with yearly growth rates in GDP per capita (in purchasing power parities) as the dependent variable. I include the same explanatory variables as Choi and Yi, e.g. the share of internet users in the population, investments shares in GDP, government expenditures as a share of GDP and the yearly increase in consumer prices.[13]

The first column in the table is for a fixed effect panel data model (similar to column c in Table 1 in Choi and Yi). The second column is for a random effects model with year dummies included (similar to column e in Table 1 in Choi and

[13]The share of internet users is measured as the share of the population that have used the internet during the last 12 months. Investments shares are gross fixed capital formation as share of GDP. Government expenditures are included. Choi and Li (2009, p. 40) expect this variable to negatively influence on growth since "the government distorts the private decisions". I expect its coefficient to be negative because government expenditures are often more stable than the more varying marked-based private sectors (and therefore serve as automatic stabilizers). High rates of inflation are known to retard growth. A priori, I don't have any expectations about the coefficient when inflation is low.

Yi). The third column reports results from a fixed effects model with year dummies included.

In the two last columns, I have included auxiliary variables. In the fourth column, I included lagged levels of (log of) GDP per capita to capture convergence and regression towards the mean.

In the last column, I also included an interaction term for GDP per capita and the share of internet users. It may be that the positive effects of the internet require a high level of income. In that case, the estimated coefficient is expected to be positive. In the opposite case, the growth effects of the internet are higher in low-income countries. Meijers (2014) propose that there are interaction effects between trade and use of the internet. I include trade openness as an explanatory variable (but interaction terms turned out to be insignificant).

The first two columns produce results that are qualitative similar to those of Choi and Yi. The share of internet users is significantly and positively correlated with growth in the 1990–2000 period. This is so in the fixed effect model as well as in the random effects model with year dummies included. The sizes of the coefficients are also very similar to those of Choi and Yi. A one per cent increase in the share of internet users in the population is associated with an increase in growth rates with 0.053–0.060 percentage points (0.049–0.057in Choi and Yi). The signs and significance of the other variables are in line with those of Choi and Yi.

The significant effect of the internet, however, does not survive the inclusion of both fixed effects and time dummies. In that case, the coefficient is positive but not significant.

Lagged (log of) GDP per capita in the regression has a negative though insignificant coefficient. Trade as a share of GDP is significantly and positively related to economic growth. This specification gives a positive and significant coefficient for the internet.

The results in the table, therefore, lend some support to Choi and Yi's findings. The internet seems to explain growth in the 1990s.

The last column reports result from a regression where also an interaction term between income and the share of internet users was included. That regression resulted in insignificant results for both the share of internet users and the interaction term. The other variables keep their sign and significance.

Table 2 reports similar results for the entire 1990–2015 period. The table indicates that the effect of the internet for the entire period is the opposite of those reported in Table 1. The share of internet users in the population correlates negatively and highly significantly with growth. This is so in all the regressions except for the last column. The last column is for a regression in which also the interaction term is included. This produces a positive and significant (at the 5% level) coefficient for the share of internet users and a negatively and significant coefficient for the interaction term. The conclusion is that for the entire period, the effect of the internet is positive, but that this effect is lower for richer countries.

In the period covered, the share of internet users increased in all countries. In rich countries, the share approached high levels. In poorer countries, the share increased to lower levels. The results are in accordance with three alternative interpretations.

Table 2 Regression results for yearly growth rates, 1990–2015

Variable	Choi and Yi (col. c)	Choi and Yi (col. e)	Fixed effects	Fixed effects	Fixed effects
Internet	−0.015 (0.004)***	−0.019 (0.473)***	−0.035 (0.006)***	−0.038 (0.062)***	0.116 (0.062)*
Investments	0.155 (0.011)***	0.159 (0.009)***	0.115 (0.010)***	0.103 (0.012)***	0.099 (0.011)***
Government	−0.184 (0.025)***	−0.078 (0.015)***	−0.129 (0.025)***	−0.168 (0.025)***	−0.171 (0.024)**
Inflation	−0.0006 (0.0001)**	−0.0006 (0.0001)***	−0.0006 (0.0001)***	−0.0006 (0.0001)***	−0.0006 (0.00021)***
Lagged GDP pc				−0.049 (0.004)***	−0.050 (0.004)***
Interact					−0.014** (0.008)
Trade				0.020 (0.004)***	0.021 (0.004)***
Fixed effects	Yes	No (RE)	Yes	Yes	Yes
Year Dummies	No	Yes	Yes	Yes	Yes
R^2	0.11	0.20	0.16	0.00	0.03
R^2 (within)	0.08	0.15	0.18	0.00	0.01
R^2 (between)	0.25	0.38	0.27	0.21	0.20
Countries	171	171	171	171	171
N	3781	3781	3781	3780	3780

Note Standard errors in parenthesis. ***, ** and * denote significance at 1, 5 and 10% levels, respectively. RE denotes random effects GLS regression

The first is that the internet is most productive in poorer countries. The second is that increase in the share of internet users is highest when it increases from lower levels. The latter interpretation is rejected in the data since separate regressions for countries with lower levels of internet users in 2001 did not changed the results, neither for the entire period nor for the period after 2001. The third interpretation is that the introduction of the internet resulted in level effects for income rather than growth effects.

The effect of the internet seems to change after 2000. This motivates a separate regression for the post-2000 period. Results from such regressions are reported in Table 3. Table 3 indicates that there were negative effects of the internet on economic growth in the post-2000 period. With the same model formulation as in Choi and Yi (2009), effects are strongly and significantly negative. In the post-2000 period, there were negative growth effects after the terror attacks in the USA in 2001 and during the great recession in 2008–2009. In the regressions, effects of these events are captured by the year dummies (to the extent that they influenced similarly on all

Table 3 Regression results for yearly growth rates, 2000–2015

Variable	Choi and Yi (col. c)	Choi and Yi (col. e)	Fixed effects	Fixed effects	Fixed effects
Internet	−0.050 (0.007)***	−0.019 (0.005)***	−0.055 (0.012)***	−0.043 (0.011)***	0.202 (0.080)**
Investments	0.143 (0.016)***	0.148 (0.013)***	0.138 (0.016)***	0.120 (0.016)***	0.116 (0.016)***
Government	−0.086 (0.034)**	−0.044 (0.0176)**	−0.020 (0.033)	−0.070 (0.0157)**	−0.074 (0313)**
Inflation	−0.0002 (0.0002)	−0.0003 (0.0002)	−0.0002 (0.0002)	0.0003 (0.0002)*	−0.0003 (0.0002)*
Lagged GDP pc				−0.116 (0.008)***	−0.119 (0.008)***
Interact					−0.024 (0.008)***
Trade				0.018 (0.005)***	0.020 (0.005)***
Fixed effects	Yes	No (RE)	Yes	Yes	Yes
Year dummies	No	Yes	Yes	Yes	Yes
R^2	0.07	0.17	0.15	0.01	0.01
R^2 (within)	0.06	0.16	0.16	0.00	0.00
R^2 (between)	0.16	0.24	0.15	0.26	0.26
Countries	171	171	171	171	
N	2 395	2 395	2 395	2 394	

Note Standard errors in parenthesis. ***, ** and * denote significance at 1, 5 and 10% levels, respectively. RE denotes random effects GLS regression

countries). Inclusion of a separate year-country dummy for these years and the USA did not alter the results.

Inclusion of the interaction term between the share of internet users in the population and income makes internet positive and significant (at the 5% level). The interaction term is negative and significant. This indicates that in the post-2000 period, the effect of the internet was positive for poor countries but negative for rich countries.

The regression results add to the many findings of small effects of ICT in aggregate data. The results indicate positive effects pre 2000, but negative effects for rich countries after 2000. The results indicate positive effects from the internet on growth in poorer countries, however.

Pradhan et al. (2013) investigate the impact of internet users on economic growth in *OECD* countries in the period from 1990 to 2010. They find close relationships, but they also find evidence of bidirectional causality. Economic growth explains an increase in the number of internet users, and the number of internet users explains economic growth. They conclude that (p. 1514): "these results reinforce the importance of economic growth for the continued development and use of internet in the economy".

Vu (2019) proposes that growth effects from the internet are decreasing in the number of internet users. Using the logarithm of the share of internet users in countries' populations, Vu finds positive effects of the internet for economic growth in some regressions. These results, however, are not robust to econometric specifications.

3.2 Disaggregated Data

The above studies are macrostudies. In macrostudies, an important challenge is to determine the direction of causality between variables. In microstudies, possibilities to check for the direction of causality are often better. Firm-level studies often find that large, profitable and productive firms are the ones that most often, earliest and to the largest extent use ICT. Doms et al. (1997) find that the most productive firms were more productive than others, both *before* and *after* their investments in ICT. McGuckin et al. (1998) report higher productivity in firms that use advanced technology. The study, however, indicates causality running in both directions; more productive firms more often use advanced technology, but productivity growth increases after investments in such technologies. In the survey by Cardona et al. (2013), the main conclusion is that microstudies do find growth effects for firms' productivities while macrostudies generally give support to higher growth effects from ICT in the USA than in Europe.

Brynjolfsson and Hitt review the literature on ICT and productivity as of 2000. They note the discrepancy between studies based on microdata and studies of aggregate productivity developments. Studies based on microlevel data often find positive relationships between productivity and investments in ICT. But such studies, both case studies and econometric studies, also reveal reasons why there are only weak relationships between productivity and ICT in studies on aggregate data.

Brynjolfsson and Hitt review several case studies of firms investing in ICT. They note that such investments often require large auxiliary investments in human capital, in business processes and work practices. If such investments do not occur, or if they fail, investments in ICT may give low, and even negative returns. ICT investments require an "all or nothing" attitude, according to Brynjolfsson and Hitt. Similarly, computer-based supply chains prove more efficient when supplemented with organizational investments.

In service industries, measurement challenges for productivity are often larger than manufacturing (see Sect. 4). Stiroh (1998) finds that many of the most computer-intensive industries are service industries. In many of them, non-computer input growth decreased with the increased use of ICT. ICT substituted for labour. But output growth increased less than before. Stiroh concludes that total factor productivity grew more slowly as ICT capital increased. Triplett (1999) proposes that the global economy has facilitated the outsourcing of many production processes. In developed countries, physical production and also many services are outsourced to low-wage countries. Often only headquarters with responsibility for design, marketing, distribution, coordination and R&D are left in high-wage countries. Headquarter production and headquarter productivity are hard to measure.

Brynjolfsson and Hitt review several studies based on firm-level data. Several of these indicate that firms that invest in ICT have higher productivity than other firms, also when other factors are controlled for. Studies based on firm-level data also report different results over time. Productivity effects of ICT were low in early studies. They cite Rauch (1987) who found that ICT investments increased in the 1977–89 period, but that output per worker did not increase. Studies from the 1990s reported positive effects, however. Brynjolfsson and Hitt (1995 and 1996) find significant and positive effects on firms' productivity levels from investments in ICT in a data set with more than 300 large firms in the 1988–1992 period. That study was based on panel data and included a variety of dummy variables for time, industry and firm. Later studies concentrated on productivity *growth* rather than levels. Brynjolfsson and Hitt (2003) find that productivity growth effects from ICT investments increase over time. There are lags between productivity effects and these investments.

Brynjolfsson and Hitt report studies that use Tobin's q to draw inferences about the impact of ICT investments on market value. Brynjolfsson and Yang (1998) found that while 1 USD investment in traditional physical capital increased firms' market value with about 1 USD, a 1 USD investment in ICT equipment increased firms' market value with 10 USD. They argue that, since the data is from the 1987 to 1994 period, this is not a consequence of the "dot.com bubble".

Brynjolfsson and Hitt note that firms that invest heavily in ICT are often smaller than other firms. Brynjolfsson et al. (1994) found that an increase in the level of ICT capital in an industry was associated with a decline in average firm size in that industry. They propose that ICT leads to a reduction in vertical integration. Brynjolfsson and Hitt also propose that firms that adopt decentralized work structures have higher returns from investments in ICT than other firms.

From the literature on ICT and growth reviewed above, there seems to be emerging agreement that growth effects from ICT have been limited in aggregate data. The growth revival in the USA in the 1995–2004 period has been attributed to ICT. Oliner and Sichel (2000) write that (p. 4) "we estimate that these developments (ICT investments and growth in the ICT industry) account for about two-thirds of the acceleration in labour productivity (…) in between the first and the second part of the 1990s". Apart from this, growth rates have been stagnating in the computer age. This is so for the USA, for Europe and Japan. Studies on disaggregate data, on the other hand, find growth effects. Firms that use ICT have higher growth in productivity than other firms and growth rates are often high in ICT-producing industries.

3.3 Unbalanced Growth and Baumol's Disease

Stagnating growth rates at the same time as massive investments in ICT was denoted the Solow paradox. Growth economics provide many potential explanations for stagnating growth, however. From the standard Solow model, growth is predicted to stagnate in the absence of technological progress. Due to decreasing returns from the capital, growth effects from savings decrease as capital intensity increases (see, e.g., Barro and Sala-I-Martin 1995). Slower technological progress may also reduce growth. If *research* and *development* face decreasing returns to scale, for instance, because researchers first research the simplest problems and thereafter increasingly complicated problems, technological progress may well stagnate even when endogenous growth mechanisms are present. Gordon (2016) discuss many reasons for stagnating growth. One is demographics and relates to the ageing population.

Another candidate for explaining stagnating growth rates is Baumol's hypothesis of unbalanced growth. If an economy consists of two industries, and there is high productivity growth in one industry and no productivity growth in the other, growth may stagnate over time. High growth rates in the progressive industry may result in decreasing prices for this industry's products. The relative prices for the other industry's products will therefore increase. Depending on demand elasticity, resources used for the stagnating industry may both increase, be constant or fall. In the first case, resources used in the stagnating industry may grow relative to the other industry. In this case, aggregate productivity growth will decrease over time and eventually cease. Baumol (1967) and Baumol et al. (1985) applied the above framework to study structural change in developed countries' economies. These countries witnessed higher growth in service industries than in manufacturing. Baumol hypothesized that the productivity growth potential in services was lower than in manufacturing. Baumol, therefore, predicted lower growth rates in productivity over time and increasing social problems, in particular in cities, which have particularly service-intensive economies. Baumol et al. (1985) added a third industry in a model of unbalanced growth, an "asymptotically stagnant" industry. This industry has one component with a high potential for productivity growth and one component with low potential. Such industries may first contribute much to aggregate productivity growth and thereafter less. The reason is that the unbalanced growth mechanism occurs in miniature within the asymptotically stagnant industry itself.

Baumol et al. hypothesized that the ICT industry belongs to the asymptotically stagnant industries. They observed that the costs of hardware decreased. These price decreases make the ICT industry initially progressive, stimulating aggregate growth in its infancy. But software production is more labour intensive. Therefore, the potential for productivity growth is lower in software production. Over time, therefore, software becomes a larger cost component in ICT industries. Growth stimuli from ICT, therefore, decrease over time. Figure 2 lends support to this hypothesis: while price declines for hardware have been very large, prices for software have been almost constant.

Nordhaus (2006) tests for the Baumol mechanism in economic growth. Nordhaus analyses growth in 67 American industries. In some of these, productivity growth is high. The fast-growing industries mainly belong to manufacturing. In other industries, productivity growth is low. These are mainly service industries. Nordhaus estimates the growth contributions from each industry to aggregate growth. Due to increasing costs and use of resources, growth contributions from the slow-growing industries become larger over time. This depresses aggregate growth.

Triplett and Bosworth (2003a, b) study the impact of ICT on growth in service industries in the 1973–2000 period. They argue that ICT contributed to high productivity growth in services after 1995. They conclude that "Baumol's disease has been cured". The results of Triplett and Bosworth do not necessarily contradict those of Nordhaus. Also, Nordhaus reports, but does not comment on, higher growth in the 1989–2001 period.

3.4 The Future

Many have argued that productivity growth effects from ICT have yet to come. As outlined above, ICT has GPT characteristics. There are network effects and complementarities, and there is a need for auxiliary investments, in physical and human capital, and, in particular in infrastructure.

As outlined above, broadband infrastructure has been high on the policy agenda in many countries, and access to broadband has increased in most countries in recent years. Broadband substituted for dial-up internet in the 1990s and the early 2000s and became more available ass time passed.

Ford et al. (2011) study broadband investments in OECD countries. They find that broadband coverage depends on price, GDP per capita, inequality (less inequality correlates positively with broadband coverage), level of education, the share of the population aged 65 or more, population density and the coverage of telephone lines. Ford and co-authors rank countries according to observed broadband coverage versus expected coverage. They conclude that Iceland, Belgium and Canada rank highest and Ireland, Greece and Slovakia lowest.

Koutroumpis (2009) estimates growth effects from broadband penetration for a sample of 22 OECD countries in the period from 2002 to 2006. Controlling for endogeneity with a instrument variable technique in which broadband demand is separated from the broadband supply, Koutroumpis concludes that broadband significantly increased GDP and that there are level effects in the sense that a broadband penetration over 30% gives the highest growth effects.

Greenstein and McDevitt (2011) find that the effects of broadband for consumers are limited. Their estimates show that returns to broadband investments were not higher than normal returns. The results are based on studies of revenues from sales of broadband. They also present estimates of consumer surplus from broadband. The results indicate that the broadband upgrade was equivalent to a price decline between 1.6 and 2.2% per year for internet access.

Czernich et al. (2011) study the relationship between broadband investments and growth in a cross section of countries. They use data from the OECD countries for the period from 1996 to 2007. They both include level effects of broadband investments (does GDP per capita increase as a function of broadband investments?) and growth effects (does broadband investments result in higher (permanent) growth rates?) An obvious problem is endogeneity. It might well be that richer and fast-growing countries invest more in broadband than other countries. Tranos and Mack (2016), for instance, find that sometimes firm-level growth explained broadband investments while causality goes in the other direction in other cases. To control this, Czernich and co-authors use the existing telephone and cable-TV extensiveness as instruments. Since telephone lines and cable-TV explains broadband investments but not subsequent growth, they claim that their instrument is valid. Their results are astonishing: introduction of broadband increases GDP per capita with 2.7–3.9%. 10% increase in broadband coverage increases the growth rate of GDP with 0.9–1.5 percentage points. These results contradict, for instance, Grimes et al. (2009) who obtain far more modest results. Based on firm-level regional data from New Zealand, they estimate productivity effects from different types of broadband coverage. They find that the existence of broadband increases productivity, but that this effect does not depend on broadband speed. They note, however, that the speed of broadband is a "moving target" so that the economic implications of broadband can change over time.

Bojnec and Fertő (2012) investigate the impact of broadband on economic growth in a panel data of OECD countries in the period from 1998 to 2009. They estimate growth (in GDP per capita) as a function of investments in physical capital, government expenditures and inflation and three alternative measures of broadband availability. The three measures are standard access lines per 100 inhabitants, access channels per 100 inhabitants and total broadband per 100 inhabitants. They find that the first two broadband access measures correlate positively to growth, while the last contributes negatively (and partly significantly so). Bjonec and Fertő do not, however, investigate whether the influence of broadband changes over time.

Majumdar (2010) argues that lower growth in the USA in the post-2000 period, in particular for ICT firms and users of ICT, was caused by lower investments in broadband in the USA as compared to other countries. Broadband has been more expensive and less available in the USA than in other countries, and the USA ranked as number 15 among OECD countries in broadband coverage in 2008. Majumdar finds that access to broadband for US firms positively and significantly correlated with the firm's revenue growth.

Studies on the economic effects of broadband indicate growth effects. As indicated above, however, broadband coverage is approaching 100% in many countries. Further growth effects, therefore, depend on whether broadband provision gives dynamic or static effects. If pessimists are correct, the main growth effects from ICT were observed in the USA in the dot-com period. Thereafter growth has decreased. Optimists claim that internet-based ICT has GPT characteristics that promise higher growth potentials in the future.

David (1990) compares the ICT revolution with the development of electricity. Because of, among other factors, network effects, it took time before the introduction of electricity increased productivity. David hypothesizes that it may be similar for the case of ICT. Bresnahan and Trajtenberg (1995) and Helpman and Trajentenberg (1998) construct growth models where there are substantial lags between investments and subsequent growth effects from the introduction of GPT.

Along the same lines, Dudley (1999) constructs a model of growth and communication technologies where there are growth cycles with three phases. GPTs (in communications technologies) occur exogenously. New GPTs have a wide potential for further growth since they open up opportunities for further innovation. New ideas are combined to spur further growth (in a recombinant manner), but with decreasing rates of success. Initially, the growth rate of productivity is low, since when the technology occurs, diffusion remains limited. But innovation is fast, and when the technology becomes more widely adopted, productivity growth accelerates. Even if the rate of productivity growth from new vintages of technology is decreasing, this effect is offset by the increase in the proportion of the population that is adopting the new technology. Growth subsequently decelerates as the number of new ideas to be crossed with old one falls. Growth rates become low when the technology has become widely diffused.

Brynjolfsson and Hitt (2000a) argue that auxiliary investments that are needed for ICT investments to be successful are often not counted correctly. For instance, they find that additional investments in human capital are often needed. Bresnahan, Brynjolfsson and Hitt (2000a), for instance, report results from a survey of firms. They found that investments in ICT are associated with an increased delegation at the workplace, higher levels of skills and education. They also found that these work practices are correlated with each other.

Akerman et al. (2015) study the effects of broadband on labour productivity and wages. Based on a public programme to support the rollout of broadband, they obtain exogenous variation in the availability of broadband firms. Their instrument allowed them to estimate the effects of broadband on worker productivity. The results indicate that broadband improves wages and productivity for high-skilled workers but has the opposite effects for low skilled workers.

The internet has expanded rapidly and has become pervasive, widespread and integrated into goods and service production. Smartphones have made the internet available for individuals everywhere. News production, banking and buying and selling are integrated into smartphone activities. The internet of things, where physical goods are online and communicate for the consumer, is becoming common.

E-commerce has become widespread. E-commerce denotes sales or purchases of goods and services conducted over computer networks by methods designed for this purpose (OECD 2014a, b). In OECD countries, 47% of consumers bought products online in 2014, up from 30% in 2007. The most common products purchased online are travel services, tickets for events, digital products and books. E-commerce is becoming more popular also for other product types, such as food and grocery products. The extent of e-commerce is likely to increase in the future. Einav et al. (2014) analyse the extensiveness and growth in the use of *mobile* e-commerce. They find that mobile e-commerce diffuses in the commonly S-shaped way and that diffusion is fast. They also argue that mobile e-commerce, at least partly, adds to regular e-commerce.

Recent developments in ICT and internet usage include growth of the *app*-economy. The app-economy, whereby individuals buy apps for fun and many other purposes, booms. The average smartphone user has 28 apps installed but uses on average 11 of these (OECD 2014b).

Machine-to-machine (M2M) communication accounts for increasing shares of mobile data traffic. M2M is predicted to expand in the future. For instance, in the automobile industries, M2M communication is now becoming widespread.

Big data analysis has become possible from the generation of large amounts of data from use of the internet. OECD (2014a) predicts a yearly growth in data traffic of 20%, from 70 exabytes (EB = 1 billion gigabytes) per month in 2014 to 120 EB in 2017. Big data analysis is used for many purposes, with marketing purposes as the main example (Gordon 2016). OECD (2014a) predicts that other applications will become more popular, like disaster management and applications in the health sector.

The ICT industry did quite well during the great depression. The major ICT firms (250, monitored by the OECD) did not report a decrease in their income or revenues during the crisis (OECD 2014a).

The ICT industry is populated by many new firms and firms that have higher survival rates than in other industries. In the 2009–2012 period, net business firm growth in the ICT industries was 4.5%, while the average was 1% in other industries (OECD 2014a). Gordon (2016), however, is sceptical about whether this will continue in the future. He reports that firm entry in the US economy is on the decline. Due to very low interest rates in the aftermath of the great recession, many investments have a low internal rate of return. With higher interest rates, many new firms may face challenges.

Gordon (2016) contemplates about likely developments in ICT industries in the future. He lists new medical advances, small robots and 3D printing, big data, artificial intelligence and driverless cars as the most likely areas of progress in the future. For different reasons, he predicts growth effects from each of these to be small. Progress in health is stagnating because most possible progress has already been achieved (compare the effects of reduced child mortality with cancer treatment of old patients). Robots and 3D printing can increase productivity, but Gordon thinks that (p. 596) "3D printing is not expected to have much effect on mass production and thus on how most U.S. consumer goods are produced". Even if big data has been available for some time, the lack of any productivity effects from them makes Gordon also pessimistic about their potential. For driverless cars, Gordon sees small potentials, for the reason that even if they can substitute for drivers at the highway, they cannot substitute for all the other man work involved in logistics and transportation.

Jorgenson et al. (2008, 2014) discuss future growth potentials in the aftermath of the great recession. Those studies incorporate projections of TFP growth for ICT-producing, ICT-using and non-ICT industries based on historic experiences. A base case is based on average contributions of TFP growth for the three sectors for the

1995–2010 period. For that base case, productivity growth is predicted to increase to about 0.6% per annum. This is higher than in the 1990–2010 period. Excluding the great recession from the historical data makes projected productivity growth reaching almost one per cent per annum. Jorgenson et al. (2014) conclude, however, that (p. 689):

> Negative productivity growth during the Great Recession is transitory, but productivity growth is unlikely to return to the high rates of the Investment Boom …

Despite Jorgenson's modest optimism, several authors are far less optimistic. Gordon (2010) argues that the dot-com era in the US economy was special. In Gordon (2016) growth projections for future growth in the US economy are presented. These are far less positive than those of Jorgenson. Using TFP growth rates from the *pre*-dot-com period as his base period, Gordon argues that future growth in production per capita will be very limited.

Projections for the future, therefore, differ among qualified economists. Whether ICT will spur fast growth or whether recent stagnation will continue is a matter of debate. Some are optimists. Brynjolfsson and McAfee (2014, p. 88) write:

> These and countless other innovations will add up over time, and they'll keep coming and keep adding up. Unlike some of our colleagues, we are confident that innovation and productivity will continue to grow at healthy rate in the future.

Gordon (2002) compares the promises of the computer with those of other important innovations during the twentieth century, like running indoor water, antibiotics, the internal combustion engine, the private car, air transport and many more and concludes that (p. 50):

> it is quite plausible that the greatest benefits of the computer lie a decade or more in the past, not in the future.

4 Happiness

There is no doubt that ICT and the internet have changed people's lives considerably. These changes are profound. They are important, even if macrodata does not reveal clear growth effects. How do ICT and the internet influence on people's well-being?

Economists have a well-established theoretical framework for analyses of welfare and happiness.[14] Individuals are assumed to be equipped with utility functions which measure their utility or welfare. Individuals are assumed to maximize their utility subject to budget constraints. From such maximization, economic behaviour is deduced. Typical results are demand functions and labour supply functions. For demand, utility maximization normally implies that demand falls with prices (except the theoretical artefact *Giffen* goods) and increases with income (except inferior

[14]For an introduction to consumer theory, see Kreps (1990) or Gravelle and Rees (1992).

goods). Standard assumptions about individuals' utility are that they enable the consumers to rank all goods (preferences are complete, negative transitive, reflexive, and characterized by no-satiation). Individuals are also expected to handle uncertainty (with the introduction of von Neumann–Morgenstern expected utility). When individuals are risk averse, they dislike the loss of a given amount of income more than they like a similar income gain. Therefore, individuals' utility increase with their income, but less than proportionally.

Based on consumer theory, economists have analysed economic behaviour based on what they observe that people do.

It is not straightforward to measure utility, however. For many purposes, it is not even important to measure utility. For deriving demand functions, any increasing function of a utility function will give the same results. All utility functions that give the same ranking of goods are equivalent to this perspective. This *ordinal* approach to utility is widespread.[15] Standard theory for introducing uncertainty in consumer theory restricts the class of utility functions to be unique up to a positive linear transformation (while ordinal utility functions are unique up to any positive monotonic transformation).

For measuring utility, one needs a scale. This is a cardinal utility. Cardinal utility measures are also used to compare utility (or welfare) between individuals and to aggregate welfare for groups of individuals. Within the ordinal utility framework, that does not make sense.

Economic theory favours Pareto improvements. Every change that makes some people better off without harming others should happen. In economic policy making, however, politicians need to weigh gains for some against losses for others. There are many criteria for doing so. One is to favour those changes that increase the pie. If the pie increases, the gains will be more than large enough to compensate those who lose. It is a political issue of whether there should be compensation. Cardinal welfare measures may help along the way.

In recent years, *happiness research* has become popular. Outstanding surveys are Frey and Stutzer (2002), Clark et al. (2008) and Stutzer and Frey (2012). Also related is Deaton (2013). The main objective is to measure utility.

Happiness research is based on individuals' subjective well-being. People are asked how happy they are. The results are used as measures of utility or well-being. The research agenda has been controversial. Frey and Stutzer write (p. 403):

> Standard economic theory employs an "objectivist" position based on observable choices made by individuals. ... Subjective experience (e.g. captured by surveys) is rejected as being "unscientific" because it is not objectively observable.

Peoples' answers in surveys are known to be unreliable. People misunderstand questions, they don't answer honestly, they do not take questions seriously, and they understand scales differently.

---

[15]The eminent Norwegian economist Asbjørn Rødseth writes (p. 46, my translations) "Most modern economists make use of such a utility notion (ordinal)" (Rødseth 1992). Gravelle and Rees writes (p. 182) "The utility function of consumer theory is an *ordinal* function ...".

For many purposes, however, Frey and Stutzer argue that subjective measures of well-being fruitfully complement standard theory. They can be used for policy evaluation. They can also be important for evaluating the quality of institutions, social capital and social trust. Effects of inequality is another topic that can be analysed with well-being measures.

Observed behaviour (as used in traditional standard economic theory) is an incomplete indicator for individual well-being. Subjective measures of well-being recognize that everybody has ideas about happiness. Subjective well-being measures, therefore, respect consumer sovereignty. Frey and Stutzer (2002, p. 405) conclude that "Measures of subjective well-being can thus serve as proxies for utility".

This point of view is critically discussed in Clark et al. (2008). They note that other individuals' perception of a person's well-being matches well with this person's reply. This is evidence that own evaluation of happiness reflects signals of happiness to the environment. Reported well-being from individuals correlates with income, marriage, job status, health and other variables that are usually interpreted as positive for well-being. They also discuss studies that have found that subjective well-being at a point of time predicts future behaviour in line with economic theory. Individuals choose to discontinue activities associated with low levels of well-being. Experiments also seem to support the hypothesis that well-being reflects utility in the sense that ordinal and cardinal measures generate similar results.

In line with the above, there are, by now, many data sources for happiness and well-being. Some of these also allow for international comparisons. The *Eurobarometer* Surveys conducted by the European Union is one. The *World Value Survey* (Inglehart et al. 2014) asks people: "All things considered, how satisfied are you with your life as a whole these days?"

Below I make use of data from the *World Happiness Report* 2016 (Helliwell et al. 2016) which contains data for several years for many countries about individuals' subjective well-being. Roughly 1000 individuals per year in more than 150 countries are asked (Helliwell et al. 2016, p. 9):

> Please imagine a ladder, with steps numbered by from 0 at the bottom to 10 at the top. The top of the ladder represents the best possible life for you, and the bottom of the ladder represents the worst possible life for you. On which step of the ladder would you say you personally feel you stand at this time?

The question is denoted the Cantril ladder question (Cantril 1965). Respondents are asked to evaluate their life satisfaction on one out of 11 steps. This normalizes answers. That normalization does not rule out typical problems from surveys. First, it is not clear that the 11 steps are understood equivalently among individuals. Is 11 obtainable? Is zero obtainable? What is the distance from three to five? Is the distance from three to five the same as the distance from five to seven? Or from seven to nine? Are there systematic differences between how people in different groups approach the scale? One finding, for instance, is that older people's happiness score is higher than younger people's (Frey and Stutzer 2002) in rich countries. Is this because older people are happier, or does it reflect that age influences how people react to questions about happiness? Further, it might well be that people in different countries deviate systematically in their life evaluations. It might also be that people do not give honest answers. Whether dishonesty in surveys are systematic or nor, is hard to answer.

Frey and Stutzer (2002) argue that many of the above problems can be overstated. For instance, happy people are rated as happy among those who know them. Di Tella and MacCulloch (2006) underline that many problems that arise in happiness surveys are *reduced* when it comes to comparing groups rather than individuals. Frey and Stutzer (2002, p. 408) conclude that:

> The existing research suggests that for many purposes, happiness or reported subjective well-being is a satisfactory empirical approximation to individual utility.

Similarly, Ferrer-i-Carbonell and Ramos (2014) conclude that (p. 1017):

> In short, there is now large evidence on the reliability of subjective well-being measures to be confident that we can measure an individual's well-being in a meaningful way.

Research on happiness has established a clear and significant relationship between income and happiness. Happiness is positively related to income. This result has been confirmed in several studies [see, e.g., Frey and Stutzer (2002) or Clark et al. (2008) for surveys or Easterlin (1974, 1995) or Deaton (2008)]. The finding that income is positively related to happiness is confirmed in micro studies as well as macrostudies and cross-country studies. Evidence also points in the direction of a causal relationship (so that income make people happier rather than happy people earning higher incomes). In microstudies, lottery winners reported higher well-being in the following year (Gardner and Oswald 2001).

But happiness does not increase linearly with income. The relationship is logarithmic. This is in line with diminishing marginal utility from income. Also, this finding is robust in the sense that it is found in micro studies as well as macrostudies and cross-country studies.

To discuss results already established in the literature, I have made use of data from the World Happiness Report. The data set is an unbalanced panel for average happiness scores (Cantril ladder) for up to 128 countries. The data also contains auxiliary variables (such as standard deviations in answers) as well as some other data (such as trust, Gini index and governance quality indicators).

The typical result of the relationship between happiness and income is shown in Fig. 5. That figure graphs average happiness scores (from the *World Happiness Report*) in 2014 for a sample of 144 countries and GDP per capita in constant purchasing power parity dollars. Data for GDP per capita is from *World Development Indicators*.

Using the log of GDP per capita instead of the absolute number produces Fig. 6. That figure suggests an almost linear relationship between happiness and (log of) income per capita. The implication is that a given percentage increase in income corresponds to the same absolute increase in happiness. The scatter plot does not form a straight line. But that is not to be expected. Apart from income, many other variables influence on happiness (e.g. health, democracy and climate). Still, the graph gives a clear impression that income is one main determinant for human happiness.

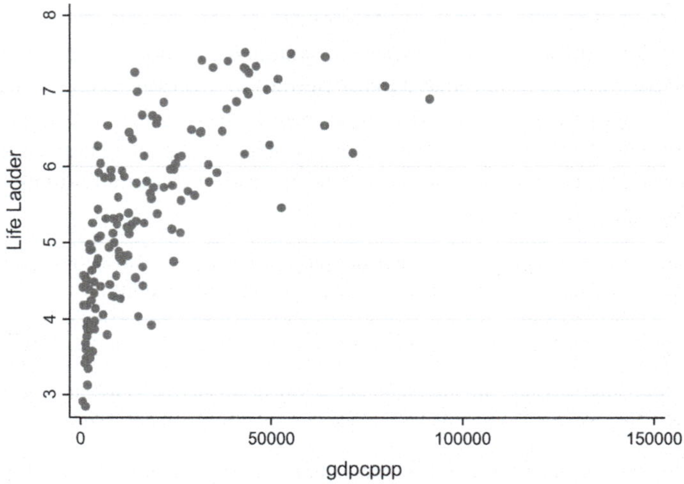

Fig. 5 Per capital GDP and average happiness in 2014. *Source* World Happiness Report (2016) and World Development Indicators (2017)

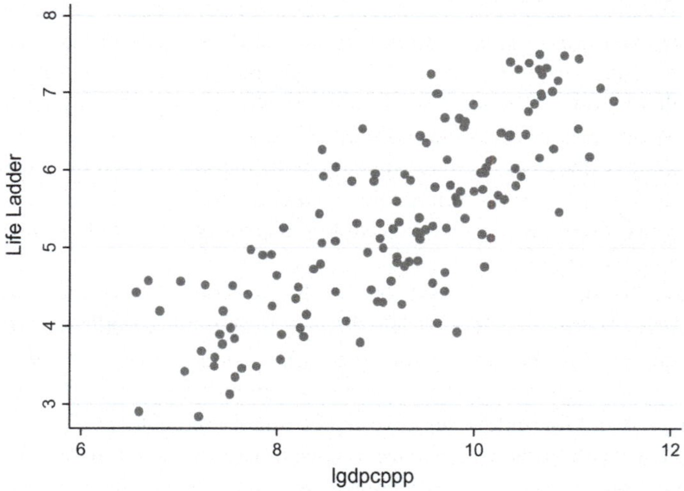

Fig. 6 Per capital GDP (in log) and average happiness in 2014. *Source* World Happiness Report (2016) and World Development Indicators (2017)

Note that the seemingly logarithmic relationship between happiness and income corresponds well with risk aversion and therefore decreasing marginal utility from income. An increase in income from a low level gives a larger increase in happiness than a similar increase in income from a high level.

Deaton (2008, p. 58) presents further evidence: the linear relationship between happiness and log of GDP per capita offers a reasonable fit for all countries, whether high-income or low-income. The result is striking. Many countries differ in income distribution. In a country with large income differences, many are poor while a few are rich. In countries with large income differences, therefore, one might expect some happy people and many unhappy people, and therefore less happiness on average. Still, the linear relationship seems to bear validity. A cross-country regression of happiness, log of GDP per capita and estimates of Gini coefficients give a *positive* albeit hardly significant result for the Gini coefficient. The sample size reduces to 61 with the inclusion of estimates of Gini coefficients.

Deaton regresses cross-country average happiness on other variables, such as health indicators. He includes life expectancy, infant mortality and child mortality. Neither of these turns out to be significant in regressions. Deaton adds HIV prevalence, which is also insignificant. Age, on the other hand, turns out to matter. Younger people are on average more happy than elderly, except for the richest countries in which old people are happier than younger ones. This finding does not necessarily contradict those reported by Frey and Stutzer (2002) since their study is based on data from developed countries.

A major finding from happiness research is that happiness scores *within* countries tend to stay quite constant despite growth in income over time. Easterlin (1974, updated in 1995) found that despite growing income over time in some countries, happiness stayed relatively constant. Easterlin (1995) reports such findings for Japan, the USA and several European countries. Later, many other studies have given similar results (for an overview, see Clark et al. 2008). Easterlin (1995) still finds a positive, cross-country relationship between happiness and income. For a sample of developed countries, he finds an almost linear relationship. Deaton (2008) finds, for a cross section of countries, that even if there is a positive relationship between happiness and log of GDP per capita, there is a negative relationship between happiness and growth.[16]

Two complementary explanations for the lack of a positive happiness–growth relationship have been proposed. First, what matters for people is not an income as such, but their relative income vis-à-vis others. Therefore, if income increases for everybody, average happiness does not necessarily increase. Clark et al. (2008) discuss implications for persons' utility functions from such explanations. They presume a utility function for individuals that depend on income (in a standard manner), but also on individuals' income relative to others (others refer to reference groups, and may be other people in the same country, or people with closer relationships to the individual). With this assumption, there are strong relationships between happi-

[16]Deaton (2008) regresses happiness on log of income in the same year as well as average yearly growth rates in for two alternative time periods.

ness and income for individuals at *a point of time*, but much weaker relationships for average relationships between happiness and income *over time*. Inclusion of income in other countries as reference incomes gives a positive relationship between happiness and income in cross sections of countries. With relative income as an argument in utility functions, average happiness will tend to decrease with unequal income distribution. Income growth for individuals has negative externalities for others.

Second, as people get richer, they get used to higher standards of living. Therefore, their aspirations increase in line with income, and the relationships between income and happiness over time get weaker than one would expect. In this case, short-run and long-run effects of growth in income on happiness differ. In the short run, happiness increases with income; in the long run, effects are lower.

Tsui (2014) investigates happiness in Taiwan. He includes income, average income and *expected* income in regressions on happiness together with other control variables. Expected income is estimated as the expected income given individual characteristics. The results indicate higher happiness with income and lower happiness with average income as well as expected income. Tsui interprets his result as support for both explanations (comparison with reference persons and aspirations) discussed above.

Some has claimed that there are strong relationships between happiness and income for low-income persons (and also in cross sections of countries), but that this relationship weakens as incomes grow. As Figs. 5 and 6 show, in a cross section of countries, average happiness seems to grow logarithmic with income. One reason for lower effects on happiness from income in aggregate data may be that for low-income countries, marginal utility from own (standard) consumption is high, while with higher incomes, the marginal utility from relative consumption (vis-à-vis others) increases. Therefore, the increase in average incomes may have larger effects in poor countries than in richer countries (where happiness depends more on being richer than reference persons).

An impression of developments in happiness across countries is given from Fig. 7. That figure shows average happiness scores in 2007 (horizontal axis) and 2015 (vertical axis).[17] The straight line shows what happiness would be if it were constant. In countries above the straight line, average happiness scores increase over time. In countries below, average happiness decreased over time.

Three conclusions are easily read from the figure. First, happiness is quite constant. Countries that scored high on happiness in 2007 tended to do so also in 2015. Second, it is not clear that the world is becoming happier. There are more countries above the straight line than below. But the average growth in happiness scores was 0.009 with a standard deviation of 0.57. Average happiness scores, therefore, were almost constant. Third, there is some convergence in happiness. From the graph, it seems that countries that ranked low in the graph in 2007 had higher growth in their average happiness scores than countries that ranked high. This is confirmed in a simple cross-country regression with change in happiness scores as dependent variable and level in happiness in 2007 as independent variable. The regression gives

[17]Data coverage increases much from 2006 (89 countries) to 2007 (102 countries).

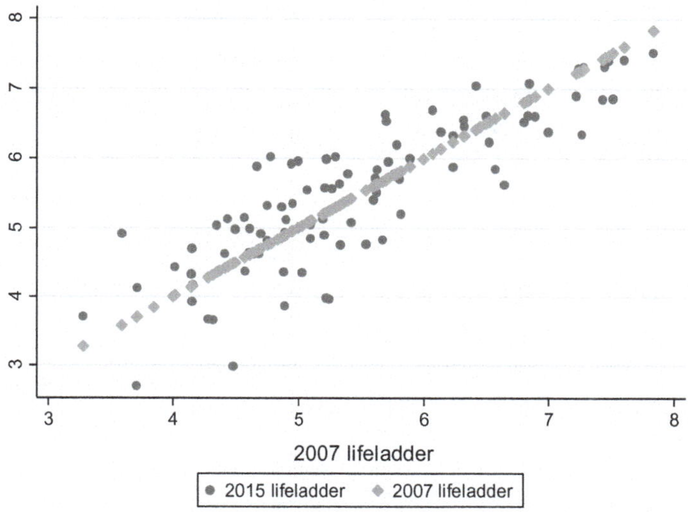

Fig. 7 Average happiness in 2015 against average happiness in 2007. *Source* World Happiness Report (2016)

a negative (−0.14) and significant (p-value 0.011) coefficient. A fixed effect panel data regression of growth in happiness versus initial happiness scores also gives a negative and significant coefficient.

As noted above, the main finding from happiness research is that, despite growing income, happiness stays constant over time. Still, happiness correlates positively with income. Expected results from a regression of happiness on income and growth in income would, therefore, be positive coefficients for income and insignificant coefficients for growth. Deaton (2008) found a negative and significant coefficient for growth.[18] In Table 4, regression results from an unbalanced panel regression for the period from 2005 to 2015 are presented. The first column is for a random effects model, and the second is for a fixed effects model.

The regression results indicate that both levels and growth rates in income influence average happiness scores positively and significantly. These results contradict those of Deaton (negative coefficients in growth). Deaton, however, reports results from regressions of happiness scores on income and growth rates lagged three years and average growth rates for over a decade in the past. Deaton's regressions are on a cross section of countries. In the above regressions, it is clear that between variations is far better explained between countries than within variations (compare the R^2s). The third column in the table results from a similar regression to that of Deaton. That is for happiness in 2015 regressed on income in 2015 as well as average annual growth rates in the period from 2005 to 2015. The results still contradict Deaton's. The regression gives a non-negative but insignificant coefficient for growth

[18]Note that a regression of happiness level on current income and previous income growth is indistinguishable from a regression on current and past income levels.

Table 4 Panel regression results for happiness

Variable	Random effects	Fixed effects	Cross-country
Income, current	0.74*** (0.039)	0.80*** (0.116)	0.77*** (0.049)
Growth in income (from previous year)	0.55** (0.269)	0.57** (0.271)	
Growth in income (2005–2015)			0.77 (2.922)
R^2 within R^2 between R^2 N	0.05 0.67 0.61 1216 159 countries	0.05 0.67 0.61 1216 159 countries	0.67 128

Note Standard errors in parenthesis. *, * and *** represent significance at 10, 5 and 1 percentage levels, respectively

rates. Splitting the sample in two at the median income does not change the results. The coefficients for growth rates are still insignificant. The coefficient for income is higher for the high-income countries than for the low-income countries. This is the Easterlin paradox: well-being is explained by income in the cross section, but growth in income does not lead to growth in happiness.

5 Happiness and ICT

The review of the literature on ICT and productivity above demonstrated contrasting views, although there seems to be increasing agreement that ICT contributed to high growth during the dot-com era, in particular, in the USA. Thereafter, growth rates in the USA and Europe have stagnated again, in particular during the great recession. Microstudies, on the other hand, have given higher estimates of the effects of ICT on productivity and growth.

Many have suggested that one reason for low reported productivity effects from ICT is measurement issues (see references above, such as Triplett (1999) or Brynjolfsson (1996)). Quality improvements in ICT have been enormous, as evidenced by Jorgenson (2005) and many more. And the use of ICT has become widespread, in production processes and for the consumer.

Some have argued that official national accounts underestimate the effects of ICT on welfare. One reason why macrostudies do not give larger productivity effects from ICT may be that price deflators fail to account fully for quality changes for consumer products. If quality increases while prices are constant and price deflators do not reflect the quality increase, quality improvements will be invisible in national accounts statistics. If quality improvements are constant over time and industries, the above concern will be equally important over time. Brynjolfsson and Hitt (2000a), however, argue that measurement problems are a particularly important problem for

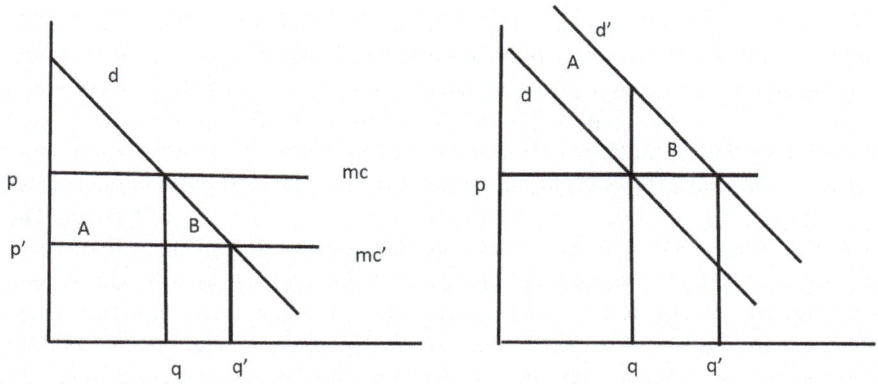

Fig. 8 Consumer surplus

ICT goods. For instance, in banking, official productivity statistics for the USA indicate a productivity increase of about 70% in the period from 1977 to 2000. According to Brynjolfsson and Hitt, this number massively underestimates productivity growth in this industry. For instance, in this period, the ATM was introduced everywhere. This had major benefits for consumers.

The essence of the argument is illustrated in Fig. 8 (left side).

That figure shows a market with a demand curve and a constant marginal cost curve. In a perfectly competitive market price is *p* (which equals presumed constant marginal costs, *mc*) and the good is purchased in quantity equal to *q*. The first graph illustrates the effects of a price decrease. Technological change reduces marginal costs. The new price is p', and the new quantity is q'. The change in consumer surplus is represented by the areas *A* and *B* in the left graph. The change consists of increased surplus for existing buyers and the surplus for new buyers. If the price change is due to quality improvements that are not properly measured (so that nominal price for a better good is the same as for the inferior good), only the quantity effect is measured. Brynjolfsson (1996) argue that this is often the case. As argued by Bresnahan (1986), the same reasoning also applies when upstream producers reduce the costs for downstream producers, and these costs reductions spill over to consumers. As seen from the graph, welfare effects from reduced prices will tend to be underestimated, in particular, if real price decrease is underestimated.

The graph to the right illustrates the possible effects of quality improvement with constant prices. In this case, consumers expand their demand towards the good in question. The welfare impact of the improved quality is given by the areas *A* and *B*. Also in this case, when physical quantities are accounted for, but not consumer surplus, national accounts will grossly underestimate welfare effects.

Hitt and Brynjolfsson (1996) estimate three different measures of the impacts of ICT. The first is productivity, the second is profitability, and the third is consumer surplus. The study is based on a panel of 370 US firms in the period from 1988 to 1992. They find that ICT capital has positive and significant effects on firms' productivity.

This is in line with other studies. They find no significant effect (but considerable variation) of ICT investments on firms' profitability. Hitt and Brynjolfsson argue that this indicates well-functioning markets and that lack of systematic effects on profits is well in line with profit maximization behaviour (the envelope theorem predicts zero effects). They find large effects of ICT on consumer surplus. Their estimation strategy is based on Bresnahan (1986) and consists in estimating the increase in the area under the demand curve but above the price line after price reductions on ICT goods. The method assumes that demand curves are constant over time. If demand increases over time, the method underestimates effects on consumer surplus from ICT. The method is used on firms buying ICT goods as intermediates. It is demonstrated in Bresnahan (1986) that in competitive markets, producers who purchase an intermediate good act as proxies for the ultimate consumers. In imperfectly competitive markets, there are additional gains from ICT. In a similar study, Brynjolfsson (1996) estimates that the contribution from ICT to consumer surplus represents approximately 0.3% of GDP in 1987 and that ICT investments generate about three times their cost in value for consumers. An industry decomposition of the method indicates that ICT increased consumer surplus the most in banking and finance. Notably, in the period under analysis, this industry had low measured productivity growth.

Similar concerns are relevant also to the treatment of new goods. Sales of new goods are measured in GDP as their sales value. This does not capture the consumer surplus of these goods.

Many new goods are introduced in the price indexes after a lag only. Often price declines are most rapid at the beginning of the life cycle of a product category. Official statistics will, therefore, be without price declines at the start of the life cycle. As for inaccurate price indexes, the treatment of new goods could well be a constant problem and not particularly relevant for ICT goods. This is the argument by Gordon (2002). He argues that ICT does not stand out as a special case when it comes to the impact of innovations. Rather, Gordon argues, electricity, indoor running water, health systems, new medications, private cars and public transport are examples of inventions that increased standards of living to a larger extent than what computers do.

Greenstein and McDevitt (2011) discuss the effects on consumer surplus from broadband upgrading. They find limited effects. They consider whether the data gives exact information. They write (p. 630):

> Consider YouTube, which is just over five years old, and the fourth most popular site on the Internet in the US. This site obviously benefits from widespread use of broadband. Have YouTube's economic gains been high? There is no way to tell because YouTube has never contributed a positive sum to measured GDP. According to financial analysis, Google has lost several hundred million dollars a year since it bought the site.

With underestimates of quality improvement and real price declines in the ICT industries and productivity effects from ICT in other industries, ICT may have important effects on people's lives even if the effects are not visible in economic statistics.

How does the internet influence on people's happiness? People around the globe use the internet daily, in work life and their personal life. They use the internet for direct and indirect benefits. The internet is used for entertainment, for searching and processing information and for storing information. The internet is used for transaction purposes. Internet is used for financial services.

Social media, from traditional emailing to social networking, have characteristics of relational goods (where utility increases when consumed together with friends or family members). Consumption of such goods can increase happiness (Gui and Stanca 2010). Others have proposed that the internet is a tool for sustaining and building social capital (Franzen 2010; Pénard and Poussing 2010).[19]

Kraut et al. (2001) find that internet use increases social interaction only in some strata of the population (people rich in social capital). For others, the use of the internet may increase isolation. Evidence indicates that this effect is present for TV viewers (Bruni and Stanca 2008). Frey et al. (2007) estimate the relationship between TV viewership and life satisfaction in a cross section of European countries. They find that heavy TV viewers report significantly lower life satisfaction. Lee et al. (2011) present evidence that only face-to-face communication has a positive effect on the perceived quality of life. Li and Chung (2006) argue that the internet may create addictive behaviour and be detrimental to mental health. Following up, Kraut et al. (1998), Kraut et al. (2001) study the impact of the use of the internet on psychological well-being. Kraut et al. (1998) found that heavy internet users became less socially involved and more lonely than light users. Kraut et al. (2001) find that these effects dissipate in a longitudinal study based on the original data. This study also made use of a larger data set with a control group. Also, for the larger data set, it was found that internet use had positive effects on communication, social involvement and well-being.

Elgin (2013) finds that use of the internet reduces the size of the shadow economy in a panel data with 152 countries in the period from 1999 to 2007, but more so in developing countries than in developed countries.

Bhuller et al. (2013) investigate the impact of the internet on sex crime. Using exogenous variation in broadband access in Norway, they estimate the effect of access to broadband internet on reports, charges and convictions of rape and other sex crimes. They suggest that the possible causality goes through broadband's effects on the consumption of pornography. They relate their findings to a broader literature on the effect of media. For instance, Besley and Burgess (2002) and Gentzkow (2006) provide evidence that media exposure affects political outcomes. On the other hand, Bellou (2015) finds that the internet (with the development of online dating services) has significantly increased marriage rates among youth (aged 21–30) in the USA.

Junco (2013) studies inequalities in Facebook use. Facebook is now established as a common platform for social networking. 92% of US college students used Facebook, with 58% using it several times a day. Still, there are differences along gender, racial and socio-economic lines. Junco finds that women used Facebook more

---

[19]The term *Social capital* is used with different definitions in social sciences. It can be used at group level as "informal values or norms shared among members of a group that permits them to co-operate with one another" (Fukuyama 1999). The term is also used as individual characteristics as "the number of trusting relationships and social ties in which she is involved and where she has access" (Laumann and Sandefur 1998). See the discussion in Pénard and Poussing 2010.

often than men. African Americans and students from lower socio-economic strata were less likely to use Facebook. Similar inequalities are present for ownership of cell phones, use of text messages and for knowledge about the internet. Similarly, college students whose parents had a college degree themselves were more likely to use Facebook than students whose parents that did not have a college degree.

Jin (2013) studies the relationship between loneliness and Facebook use. The data was collected among Facebook users and consisted of about 550 observations. Jin finds that loneliness was associated with fewer Facebook friends and less overlap between Facebook friends and real-life friends. Lonely people had lower satisfaction from Facebook use than people who were not lonely.

Lee et al. (2011) present results from a Chinese data set collected in four big cities (Wuhan, Beijing, Hong Kong and Taipei). The results indicate that internet use for personal communication does not predict people's quality of life, while face-to-face contact does. They even find, from regressions, that communicating with people on the internet hurts people's quality of life while face-to-face communication increases the quality of life. This study, however, is a cross-sectional study, and it does not control for other characteristics of internet users (such as income, education and gender).

Franzen (2010) reports results from a survey conducted twice on a sample of about 843 participants from Switzerland in 1998 and then in 2001. Franzen uses a difference in difference method to test the impact of internet use on participation in social activities and networks. Franzen does not find any significant effect of internet use. Franzen finds, however, that internet use substitutes for TV watching.

Pénard and Poussing (2010) use survey data from Luxembourg collected in 2002 with about 1500 individuals. They find that internet users more often are involved in organizations (civic and leisure) and declare higher levels of trust than do non-internet users. Internet users also have higher social abilities. Internet users have higher education and income than others. Use of the internet is complimentary with ICT equipment such as smartphone, GPS and DVD players, but substitutes for TV watching. Initial levels of social capital have a limited impact on internet use, but investments in social capital are positively correlated with internet use. Pénard and Poussing propose that since internet users build social capital internet use may increase inequalities in social capital. They also propose that, since social capital is positively associated with economic growth, the internet may increase an economy's growth potential. With internet access becoming a social norm, the necessity for it also increases. Internet may increase happiness through increasing opportunity costs: without internet access, people become increasingly socially excluded. With such an effect, the impact of the internet on happiness in time series may be small, but in cross-sectional data, the impact may be large.

Sun Lee and Chen (2017) find that digital competency can contribute to networking skills in a study using a data set consisting of about 600 college students in the southwest USA. The findings suggest that engagement in digital cultural production is more important for networking skills than being technologically competent.

Pénard et al. (2013) use a data set from Luxembourg from 2008 based on the *European Social Survey*. They find evidence that Internet users have higher life satisfaction than non-users. They do not find, however, that happiness depends on the extent of use of the internet among the users. They control for other socio-demographic variables, social capital, religious beliefs and income. They find evidence that the positive impact of internet use on well-being is higher for young people and people who are not satisfied with their income. They argue that some benefits of the internet are mediated through welfare effects. The internet helps people in consumer markets (online shopping), entertainment and to getter paid jobs. There are endogeneity issues in the data that are hard to handle without panel data.

BCS—The Chartered Institute for IT (2010) is a consultant report. The report discusses the impact of ICT and the internet in particular, on well-being. The report is based on international data as well as more detailed data from the UK. The analysis suggests that ICT has a direct positive impact on life satisfaction when controlling for income and other factor known to be important in determining well-being. The report suggests that ICT *reduces* inequality in the sense that gains are higher for people with lower incomes and fewer educational qualifications. For UK data, however, the report indicates the highest gains for middle-income groups. The report indicates that those who were recently connected to the internet experience the highest improvements in well-being. This is in line with the Easterlin paradox and may well be because people get used to using the internet (as they get used to higher incomes) or that happiness from using the internet depends on whether other people in one's reference group also use the internet.

The report rejects the assertion that ICT is linked to social isolation. Rather, the report suggests that ICT enhances social contact with friends and family. People's job satisfaction depended in their use of ICT. But changes in job satisfaction did not correlate systematically with use of ICT over income groups. People in the lowest income groups felt a larger increase in their job satisfaction as they started using ICT as compared to other income groups.

The international data indicates that several developing countries benefit greatly from ICT. Based on microdata from 39 countries with more than 30,000 individual observations, the report finds significant effects of access to the internet on individuals life satisfaction. With microdata, it is possible to control for the influence of other variables, such as gender, age, education, employment status, country effects and income. Adjusting for GDP and other variables, developing countries such as Zambia and Malawi outperforms many other countries in their use of ICT. Happiness depends on people's sense of freedom and being in control of one's life. ICT enhances these instruments for happiness. But even when controlling for this indirect effect, ICT has an independent positive effect on people's well-being. The report concludes that there is a significant positive correlation between IT access and use and reported life satisfaction.

Valberg (2017) studies the impact of ICT on gender equality in labour markets. The approach is a panel data regression of relative labour market participation among females and males in a data set containing many countries. Valberg concludes that (p. IV): "The most interesting contribution from this thesis is that ICTs impact in developing countries is almost non-existing and suggests that ICTs for female empowerment and employment might not, at least not alone, be a sufficient strategy for development".

Graham and Nikolova (2013) use data from the *Gallup World Poll*, which contains data from yearly interviews with representative samples of persons from about 140 countries. The data contains life evaluation scores (on an 11 point scale) as well as indicators for hedonic well-being (such as whether the respondent smiled yesterday, experienced stress yesterday and experienced anger yesterday). The data also contains many individual characteristics (e.g. age, gender, married, education and household income). In addition, the data contains information about access to ICT. The data contains information on whether the household had a landline telephone, cell phone, internet and TV. In total, the data contains about 300,000 observations for the period from 2009 to 2011. The results indicate positive and significant effects on happiness from access to each of the four IC technologies. Separate regressions for developed and developing countries indicate that access to TV and mobile phones was not important (insignificant) for people in developed countries but important in developing countries. In developed countries, people without TV and mobile phones have presumably chosen not to have these goods without serious budgetary restrictions. In all countries, however, access to the internet was important for well-being. To test for income sensitivity, Graham and Nikolova interacted income with internet and mobile phone access. The results indicate that both mobile phones and access to the internet increase well-being, but less so when income increases. They conclude that (p. 138): "technology access is positive for well-being around the world in general, but with diminishing marginal returns for those respondents who already have a great deal of access to these technologies".

Kavetsos and Koutroumpis (2011) use a pooled cross-sectional data set of European countries and study the impact of ICT on subjective well-being. Their study is based on the *Eurobarometer* 2005–2008. They find that access to ICT goods, such as mobile telephones, PCs or internet access correlates positively with higher levels of well-being. Similarly, living in a country with high proportions of mobile subscribers or internet users also improves subjective well-being scores. They argue that the latter finding indicates network effects from ICT. The utility derived from the internet, and mobile subscription increases with the number of other users.

Kavetsos and Koutroumpis note the cross-sectional correlation between income and happiness. This allows them to find the monetary equivalent of welfare effects from the internet. They report estimates of welfare effects from a 10 percentage point increase in penetration of ICT. They find that such an increase is equivalent with a 2.89 rise in real GDP per capita for broadband coverage and 2.36 from mobile network adoption. The results vary between European countries, with the lowest effects in the poorest countries. But in all countries, monetized happiness effects from broadband far exceed the expenditure on a broadband connection.

As described above, there is a clear correlation between measures of happiness and income levels in cross-country data. It is a general finding that also measures of health, income distribution and social security matters for life satisfaction, in addition to income levels (see, e.g., Helliwell et al. 2016).

The literature on ICT and happiness indicate that ICT has the potential for increasing life satisfaction. Evidence is mostly based on microdata or data limited to single country. An exception is, as described above, BCS—The Chartered Institute for IT (2010).

Here I make use of data from the *World Happiness Report*. I use country averages for happiness scores from that report to construct an unbalanced panel. I combine average happiness scores with auxiliary data from that database as well as data on GDP per capita (PPP adjusted), unemployment (ILO estimates) and the per cent of the population that use the internet from *World Development Indicators*. This gives an unbalanced data set for the period from 2005 to 2014 for 135 countries.

The idea is that use of the internet may influence on average happiness scores. The effects can be direct: People who use the internet gain utility from their use. The effects can also be indirect: People's utility increase from increased average internet use, for instance, because of network effects. Indirect gains may also come through other channels. For instance, information flows increase with the widespread use of the internet and some types of production may become more efficient (one example is banking services). There is also a third interpretation for potential effects of the internet on happiness. This is that the share of people using internet correlates with other variables that influence on happiness, such as ownership of a computer, a tablet or a smartphone.

In the period covered here, use of the internet increased over time. Figure 9 shows the average internet use globally and the (unweighted) average happiness scores for all countries. The average of internet users in the sample of countries increased from about 20% to almost 50%. Average happiness scores declined from 6.44 to 5.42 (on the scale ranging from 0 to 10).

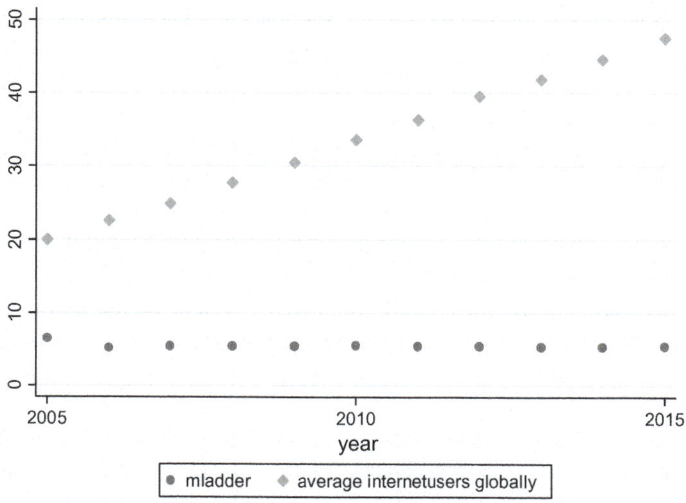

Fig. 9 Internet users and average happiness, 2005–2015. *Source* See text

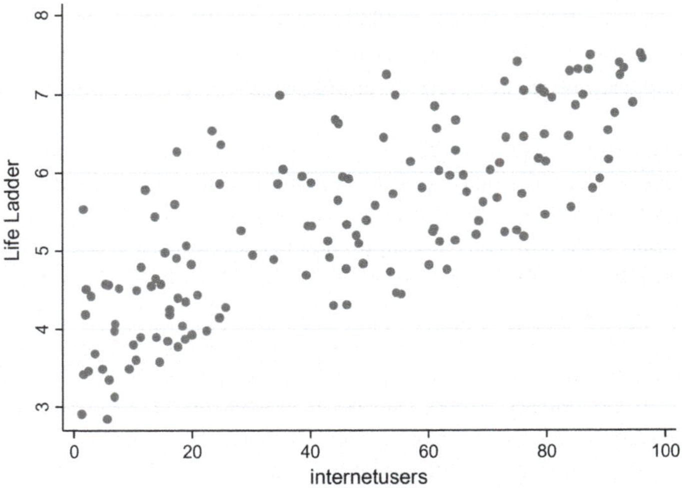

Fig. 10 Happiness and internet users. *Source* See text

In the cross section, there is a clear relationship between average life satisfaction and the proportion of internet users in the population. Figure 10 plots the relationship for 2014. The figure indicates a positive relationship. On the average, people are happier in countries where many are internet users.

The five countries that ranked lowest on average happiness scores in 2014 were Togo, Burundi, Afghanistan, Benin and Guinea. The five countries that ranked highest were Denmark, Switzerland, Norway, Israel and Finland. The five countries that have the largest negative changes in happiness scores in the period from 2005 to 2014 were Yemen, Ukraine, Ghana, Greece and Malawi. The five countries were average happiness scores increased the most were Sierra Leone, Moldova, Latvia, Nicaragua and Ecuador.

Variation in answers about happiness correlates with average levels in happiness. The countries that have the highest average scores on happiness are also the countries with the lowest standard deviations in people's answers about happiness. Figure 11 is a scatterplot of average happiness scores and standard deviation in 2014.[20]

The figure indicates a negative correlation between average happiness and variation in people's average answer (the correlation coefficient is −0.19). It indicates that it is hard to obtain high average happiness without allowing many to become happy. The outlier in the graph, with low average but little inequality in happiness, is the isolated country Bhutan (known for having pioneered *gross national happiness* as a policy target).

Determinants for happiness in international data have been discussed in the *World Happiness Report*. The 2016 issue presents typical results. Table 2.1 in that report reports regression results from regressions of happiness on the log of GDP per capita

[20] A plot of *relative* standard deviation shows an even closer relationship.

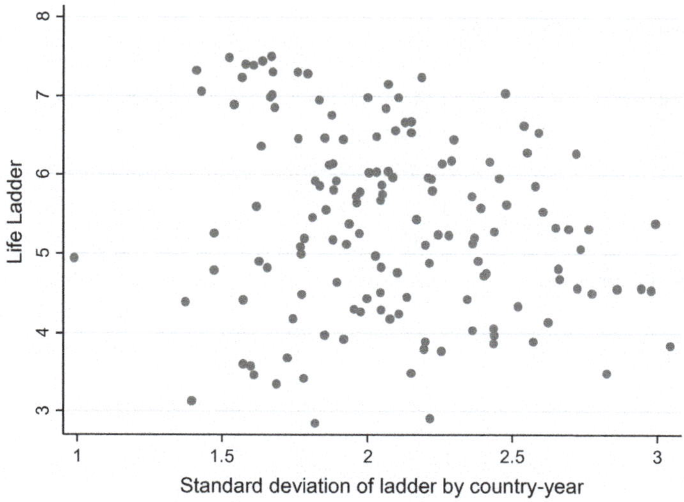

Fig. 11 Happiness and standard deviation in happiness. *Source* See text

and a set of other variables. The first is *social support*, which indicates whether people feel that they have someone to support them in times of trouble. The second is *healthy life expectancy at birth*. This variable is a constructed variable with data from the *World Health Organization* that captures both life expectancy at birth but also other health indicators. *Freedom to make life choices* are people's response to whether they feel free to do what they want with their life. *Generosity* indicates whether people donate to charity. Finally, *Perceptions of corruption* reflects whether people have the impression that the country they live in is corrupt (within the government or in business). The authors find that these variables significantly influence people's perceived happiness, all positively, except for perceived corruption (that influenced negatively). I have supplemented this data set with variables downloaded from the *World Development Indicators*.

Table 5 report two regression results. The regressions are for country averages in happiness on country averages in people's answers about *social support, health, freedom to make life choices, generosity* and *perceived corruption*. The first set is similar to the first column in Table 2.1 in Helliwell et al. (2016), included for comparison. The second set is when I also include the share of internet users in the population in the regressions. The regression is a pooled OLS that includes time dummies.

I also include unemployment rates (ILO estimates, taken from *World Development Report*). The reason for including unemployment rates is that unemployment is known to reduce people's happiness in microlevel studies (see, e.g., Frey and Stutzer 2002). Unemployment reduces happiness by far more than the estimated effect of the resulting income shortfall. The period covered by the data includes the Great Recession that resulted in increased unemployment in many countries. Inclusion of internet

Table 5 Regression results for happiness

Variable	Helliwell et al. (2016)	With internet
Ln (GDP per capita)	0.337 (0.091)***	0.287 (0.041)***
Social support	2.336 (0.205)***	1.952 (0.226)***
Health	0.030 (0.004)***	0.027 (0.004)***
Freedom	0.983 (0.154)***	0.804 (0.173)***
Generosity	0.867 (0.120)***	0.921 (0.134)***
Perceptions of corruption	−0.593 (0.112)***	−0.596 (0.124)***
Internet users		0.006 (0.002)***
Unemployment		−0.013 (0.004)***
Year fixed effect	Yes	Yes
Number of countries	153	135
N	1108	890
Adj. R^2	0.74	0.77

Note Standard errors in parenthesis. *** denotes significance at 1% level

users and unemployment rates reduces the sample from 1108 to 890 observations and from 153 countries to 135 countries.

The regressions confirm the findings by Helliwell et al. (2016) about determinants of average happiness in countries.

Also unemployment influences on happiness, significantly and with the expected sign. From the regression results, one cannot, however, know whether this reflects whether unemployed are more unhappy than others or whether times of unemployment also reduce employed people's happiness, for instance, due to job uncertainty, income uncertainty or effects via altruism.

The regression results indicate significant and positive effects of the internet on happiness. The coefficients of Helliwell et al.'s regressors keep their sign and significance when internet and unemployment are included in the regression.

The included variable is the share of internet users in the population. A 1 percentage point increase in the share of internet users increases happiness with 0.006 on the 0–10 scale for happiness. A ten percentage increase, therefore, implies a 0.06 increase in the scale. A rough calculation, therefore, implies that going from zero to full internet coverage implies a 0.6 increase on the happiness scale. According to the estimates, this corresponds to a 2% increase in GDP per capita.

The positive effect on the internet is for the share of internet users in the population. This effect has two alternative interpretations. The first is that as more people start using the internet, these people get happier. The other effect is the network effect. As more people start using the internet, existing internet users get happier. There is no way to distinguish between these two from the data. The may well co-exist. They may also co-exist in varying degrees. In countries where the use of the internet is widespread, the least motivated users are mobilized last. It may be that the network effects dominate when the internet is widespread while individual effects from personal use the internet are higher when the use of the internet is limited.

As noted above, the estimated impact of the share of internet users in the population may also reflect potential correlation with other variables, such as access to physical ICT goods. In line with Caselli and Coleman (2001), I also experimented with the inclusion of the share of ICT goods in imports to capture investments in ICT goods. Neither this variable nor the share of imports of ICT goods in *GDP* gave significant results. Exports of ICT goods did not significantly influence on countries happiness.[21]

Separate regressions for countries in which the share of internet users was below and above the median in 2005 (9.6%) indicate larger and more significant effects of internet users in the latter group than in the first.

Table 6 reports two other sets of regressions. These are for panel data regressions for the 2005–2014 period. The first set is for a random effects regression model, while the second is for fixed effect regressions.

The table demonstrates that the positive effect of the internet on happiness survives the most stringent test with the inclusion of fixed effects in a panel data regression (significant at 5% level).

Table 7 introduces distribution in happiness as a new explanatory variable. Figure 11 above demonstrated a negative relationship between average happiness and inequality in happiness.[22] The causality may run in both directions. Inequality may influence on average happiness if people dislike it (see Wilkinson and Pickett 2009 or Ferrer-i-Carbonell and Ramos 2014).

But if average happiness increases, inequality may decrease since unhappy people become happier. Since the Cantril ladder has an upper limit, this effect may be inherently present due to the nature of the data. Results in Table 7 should, therefore, be taken with a (larger) grain of salt than the other regression results.

Inclusion of inequality is relevant. Several studies have indicated that individuals in more unequal societies report on average, a lower score for happiness (Ferrer-i-Carbonell and Ramos 2014). The literature is not conclusive, however. Preferences for equality are higher in Western countries and higher in Europe than in the USA. In Europe, dislike for inequality also depends on the respondents' political preferences (on the left and right axes). Also perceived income mobility in society is believed to influence on people's preferences for inequality. Poor may dislike inequality if mobility is low, and rich may dislike inequality if mobility is high.

The table confirms the positive effect of the internet for happiness. The coefficient is positive and significant both in the random effects model and in the fixed effects

[21]Results were not significant. But the signs of the coefficient indicated that ICT imports increase happiness and that ICT export (as share of total exports) decreases happiness.

[22]I also experimented with using the Gini coefficient. Use of the Gini coeffcients produced qualitatively similar results, but reduced sample size and significance of several variables (internet users included). In fixed effects regressions, internet users were no longer significant. In pooled cross-country regressions, internet users significantly and positively correlate with average happiness scores.

Table 6 Regression results: Impact of internet on happiness

	Random effects		Fixed effects	
Variable	Helliwell et al. (2016)	With internet	Helliwell et al. (2016)	With internet
Ln(GDP per cap.)	0.494 (0.054)***	0.385 (0.064)***	1.047 (0.166)***	0.787 (0.219)***
Social support	1.530 (0.221)***	1.392 (0.239)***	1.260 (0.242)***	1.114 (0.267)***
Health	0.011 (0.007)	0.012 (0.008)	−0.030 (0.142)**	−0.021 (0.0167)
Freedom	0.963 (0.160)***	0.793 (0.179)***	0.842 (0.175)***	0.687 (0.197)***
Generosity	0.562 (0.141)***	0.478 (0.157)***	0.409 (0.159)***	0.315 (0.181)*
Perc. of corr.	−0.656 (0.159)***	−0.675 (0.169)***	−0.664 (0.195)***	−0.727 (0.218)***
Internet users		0.006 (0.002)***		0.005 (0.002)**
Unemployment		−0.019 (0.005)***		−0.021 (0.008)***
Year fixed effect	Yes	Yes	Yes	Yes
Number of countries	153	135	153	135
N	1108	890	1108	890
R^2	0.74	0.76	0.67	0.75
R^2 (within)	0.16	0.17	0.18	0.19
R^2 (between)	0.79	0.80	0.71	0.71

Note Standard errors in parenthesis. *** and ** denote significance at 1 and 5% levels, respectively

model. The coefficients are also quite stable (in the range from 0.004 to 0.006) independently of model version.[23]

Macrodata with average happiness scores in panels of countries, therefore, seems to support the findings in microstudies that access to the internet does increase people's happiness.

6 Summary and Conclusion

ICT has gained widespread use during the last generation. ICT facilitates and increases efficiency in collecting, producing, storing, coding, adapting, exchang-

[23]Using coefficient of variation (relative standard deviation) as a measure of inequality leaves several estimated coefficients insignficant, including internet users.

Table 7 Regression results: Impact of internet on happiness

	Random effects			Fixed effects
Variable	Helliwell et al. (2016)	With internet	Helliwell et al. (2016)	With internet
Ln(GDP per cap.)	0.495 (0.054)***	0.390 (0.064)***	1.093 (0.166)***	0.878 (0.220)***
Social support	1.466 (0.223)***	1.363 (0.240)***	1.156 (0.244)***	1.009 (0.268)***
Health	0.013 (0.007)*	0.014 (0.008)*	−0.022 (0.145)**	−0.013 (0.017)
Freedom	0.979 (0.160)***	0.812 (0.179)***	0.863 (0.174)***	0.712 (0.196)***
Generosity	0.5624 (0.141)***	0.487 (0.157)***	0.435 (0.159)***	0.340 (0.180)*
Perc. of corr.	−0.656 (0.159)***	−0.632 (0.170)***	−0.610 (0.195)***	−0.669 (0.218)***
Internet users		0.006 (0.002)***		0.004 (0.002)**
Unemployment		−0.018 (0.005)***		−0.018 (0.008)**
Inequality	−0.117 (0.052)**	−0.097 (0.061)	−0.157 (0.056)***	−0.201 (0.067)***
Year fixed effect	Yes	Yes	Yes	Yes
Number of countries	153	135	153	135
N	1108	890	1108	890
R^2	0.73	0.76	0.67	0.75
R^2 (within)	0.17	0.18	0.18	0.20
R^2 (between)	0.78	0.80	0.71	0.71

Note Standard errors in parenthesis. *** and ** denote significant at 1 and 5% levels, respectively. Inequality is measured as a country-wise standard deviation in happiness

ing and using information. ICT is now used in most production processes and also by consumers for many purposes. ICT is a general-purpose technology. It is complementary to other technologies. ICT industries have experienced very fast productivity growth, and prices on ICT goods have decreased. The internet has further increased the use of ICT. Network effects abound on the internet. Information is immediately accessible. Opportunities for combining information are unlimited. With the use of the internet, everybody is potentially both a sender and a receiver of information.

Many have been optimistic about potential growth stimuli from ICT and the internet. But widespread use of ICT came together with slowdown of growth. Long-run trends in growth rates are decreasing in OECD countries. It was argued that growth would accelerate when the new technology became widespread. Economic historians drew parallels to the introduction of electricity when growth increased first after massive use was established.

In the 1995–2005 period, growth rates increased. Many have attributed the higher growth rates to ICT and the internet. But after the great recession, growth rates have remained low.

Optimists about growth effects from ICT must now defend a more difficult case. If there is high growth potential from ICT and the internet, low growth must be explained by other reasons, such as Baumol's disease, macroeconomic policy, growth deceleration in other industries and demography. Whether ICT has the potential for accelerating growth, despite strong headwinds, is a matter of controversy.

Evidence presented in this paper indicates that in the post dot-com era, growth stagnated. The internet does not seem to have been able to accelerate it. For developed countries, growth correlates negatively with the share of internet users in the population. For developing countries, on the other hand, evidence suggests that there are positive effects of the internet on economic growth.

ICT is everywhere. It has transformed human life. Has it made us happier? Happiness scores are believed to reflect individuals' utility. Research on happiness indicates that people are happier if they are rich. This is in line with economic theory. But people do not get happier when their incomes increase. The Easterlin paradox has demonstrated that average happiness is constant despite increasing incomes. People get used to welfare, and they compare their situation with their reference groups.

Income buys happiness. But other variables matter too. Research indicates that happiness depends on health, freedom, having people you trust, unemployment and other factors. Does ICT matter as well?

Some findings were reviewed above. Microstudies seem to indicate positive effects on happiness from access to ICT goods and use of the internet. These effects are partly contradictory to findings of TV watching. Available data from the *World Happiness Report* indicates that average happiness scores in a panel of countries increase significantly from increasing shares of internet users in the population. These effects may reflect direct and indirect effects from more use of the internet or that the share of internet users correlates with other variables.

Acknowledgements I thank Arne Melchior, Jens C. Andvig, Hege Medin and Fulvio Castellacci for comments on a previous version of this paper. This paper was written with financial support from the project *Responsible Innovation and Happiness: A New Approach to the Effects of ICTs*, founded by the Norwegian Research Council.

References

Acemoglu, D., Autor, D., Dorn, D., Hanson, G. H., & Price, B. (2014). The return of the solow paradox? IT, productivity and employment in US manufacturing. *American Economic Review, 104*(5), 394–399.

Acemoglu, D., Johnson, S., & Robinson, J. A. (2005). Institutions as a fundamental cause of long run growth, Chap. 6. In P. Aghion, & S. N. Durlauf (Eds.), *Handbook of economic growth*. North Holland.

Aizcorbe,. A., & Kortum, S. (2005). Moore's law and the semiconductor industry: A vintage model. *Scandinavian Journal of Economics*, 603–630.

Akerman, A., Gaarder, I., & Mogstad, M. (2015). The skill complementarity of broadband Internet. *Quarterly Journal of Economics, 130*(4), 1781–1824.

Baumol, W. J. (1967). Macroeconomics of unbalanced growth: The anatomy of urban crisis. *American Economic Review, 57*(3), 415–426.

Baumol, W. J., Batey Blackman, S. A., & Wolf, E. N. (1985). Unbalanced growth revisited: Asymptotic stagnany and new evidence. *American Economic Review, 75*(4), 806–817.

BCS—The Chartered Institute for IT. (2010). *The information dividend: Why IT makes you happier*. Downloaded from http://www.bcs.org/upload/pdf/info-dividend-full-report.pdf.

Barro, R., & Sala-I-Martin, X. (1995). *Economic growth*. Mc Grawhill.

Bellou, A. (2015). The impact of internet diffusion on marriage rates: Evidence from the broadband market. *Journal of Population Economics, 47*, 265–297.

Berndt, E., & Griliches, Z. (1993). *Price indexes for microcomputers: An explorative study*. NBER Working Paper 3378.

Bertschek, I. (2003). Information technology and productivity gains and cost savings in companies. In D. C. Jones (Eds.), *The new economy* (pp 213–228). Elsevier.

Besley, T., & Burgess, R. (2002). The political economy of government responsiveness: Theory and evidence from India. *Quarterly Journal of Economics, 117*, 1415–1451.

Bhuller, M., Havens, T., Leucen, E., & Mogstad, M. (2013). Broadband Internet: An information superhighway to sex crime? *Review of Economic Studies, 80*, 1237–1266.

Bojnec, S., & Fertő, I. (2012). Broadband availability and economic growth. *Industrial Management and Data Systems, 112*(9), 1292–1306.

Bresnahan, T. (1986). Measuring the spillovers from technical advance: Mainframe computers in the financial services. *The American Economic Review, 76*(4), 742–755.

Bresnahan, T. (2010). General purpose technologies. In B. H. Hall & N. Rosenberg (Eds.), *Economics of innovation* (Vol. 2, pp. 761–791). North Holland: Handbooks. in economics.

Bresnahan, T., Brynjolfsson, E., & Hitt, L. (2002). IT, workplace organization and the demand for skilled labor: A firm-level analysis. *Quarterly Journal of Economics, 117*(1), 339–376.

Bresnahan, T., & Trajtenberg, M. (1995). General purpose technologies: Engines of growth. *Journal of Econometrics, 65*, 83–108.

Bruni, L., & Stanca, L. (2008). Watching alone: Relational goods, television and happiness. *Journal Economic Behaviour and Organization, 65*(3–4), 506–528.

Brynjolfsson, E. (1996). The contribution of information technology to consumer welfare. *Information Systems Research, 7*(3), 281–300.

Brynjolfsson, E., & Hitt, L. (1995). Information Technology as a factor of production: The role of differences among firms. *Economics of Innovation and New Technology, 3*(3-4), 183–200.

Brynjolfsson, E., & Hitt, L. (2000). Beyond computation: Information technology, organization transformation and business performance. *Journal of Economic Perspectives, 14*(4), 23–48.

Brynjolfsson, E., & Hitt, L. (2003). Computing productivity: Firm level evidence. *Quarterly Journal of Economics, 85*(4), 793–808.

Brynjolfsson, E., & Kemerer, C. F. (1996). Network externalities in microcomputer software: An econometric analysis of the spreadsheet market. *Management Science, 42*(12), 1627–1647.

Brynjolfsson, E., & McAfee, A. (2014). *The second machine age—Work, progress and prosperity in a time of brilliant technologies*. Norton.

Brynjolfsson, E., Malone, T., Gurbaxani, V., & Kambil, A. (1994). Does information technology lead to smaller firms? *Management Science, 40*(12), 1628–1644.

Brynjolfsson, E., & Yang, S. (1998). *The intangible benefits and costs of computer investments: Evidence from financial markets*. Downloaded from http://ebusiness.mit.edu/erik/ITQ.pdf.

Bush, V. (1945). As we may think. *The Atlantic*. July 1945 Issue. http://www.theatlantic.com/magazine/archive/1945/07/as-we-may-think/303881/.

Cantril, H. (1965). *The pattern of human concerns*. New Brunswick, NJ: Rutgers University Press.

Cardona, M., Kretschmer, T., & Strobel, T. (2013). ICT and productivity: Conclusions from the empirical literature. *Information Economics and Policy, 25,* 109–125.

Caselli, F., & Coleman, W. J. (2001). Cross-country technology diffusion: The case of computers. *American Economic Review* (Papers and Proceedings), 328–335.

Cette, G., Clerc, C., & Bresson, L. (2013). Contribution of ICT diffusion to labour productivity growth: The United States, Canada, the Eurozone, and the United Kingdom, 1970–2013. *International Productivity Monitor, 28,* 81–88.

Chow, G. C. (1967). Technological change and the demand for computers. *American Economic Review, 57*(7), 1117–1130.

Choi, C., & Yi, M. H. (2009). The effect of the Internet on economic growth: Evidence from cross-country panel data. *Economics Letters, 105,* 39–41.

Clark, A. E., Frijters, P., & Shields, M. A. (2008). Relative income, happiness, and utility: An explanation for the easterlin paradox and other puzzles. *Journal of Economic Literature, 46*(1), 95–144.

Czernich, N., Falck, O., Kretschmer, T., & Woessmann, L. (2011). Broadband infrastructure and economic growth. *Economic Journal*, 505–532.

David, P. A. (1985). Clio and the economics of QWERTY. *American Economic Review Papers and Proceedings, 75*(2), 332–337.

David, P. A. (1990). The dynamo and the computer: An historical perspective on the modern productivity paradox. *American Economic Review*: *Papers and Proceedings*, 355–361.

Deaton, A. (2008). Income, health, and well-being around the world: Evidence from the gallup world poll. *Journal of Economic Perspectives, 22*(3), 53–72.

Deaton, A. (2013). *The great escape—Health, wealth and the origins of inequality.* Princeton University Press.

Di Tella, F., & MacCulloch, R. (2006). Some uses of happiness data in economics. *Journal of Economic Perspectives, 20*(19), 25–46.

Diamond, J. (1997). *Guns, germs, and steel: The fates of human societies*. WW Norton.

Doms, M., Dunne, T., & Troske, K. R. (1997). Workers, wages and Technology. *Quarterly Journal of Economics*, 253–290.

Dosi, G. (1988). Sources, procedures, and microeconomic effects of innovation. *Journal of Economic Literature, 26,* 1120–1171.

Draca, M., Sadun, R., & Reenen, J. V. (2006). *Productivity and ICT: A review of the evidence*. CEP Discussion Paper 749.

Dudley, L. (1999). Communications and economics growth. *European Economic Review, 43,* 595–619.

Easterlin, R. A. (1974). Does economic growth improve the human lot? Some empirical evidence. In R. David & M. Reder (Eds.), *Nations and households in economic growth: Essays in honor of Moses Abramovitz* (pp. 89–125). Academic Press.

Easterlin, R. A. (1995). Will raising the income of all increase the happiness of all? *Journal of Economic Behavior & Organization, 27,* 35–47.

Einav, L., Levin, J., Popov, I., & Sundaresan, N. (2014). Growth, adoption, and use of mobile E-Commerce. *American Economic Review: Papers and Proceedings, 104*(5), 489–494.

Elgin, C. (2013). Internet usage and the shadow economy: Evidence from panel data. *Economic Systems, 37,* 111–121.

Evangelista, R., Guerrieri, P., & Meliciani, V. (2014). The economic impact of digital technologies in Europe. *Economics of Innovation and New Technology, 23*(8), 802–824.

Feenstra, R. C. (2004). *Advanced international trade—Theory and evidence*. Princeton University Press.

Ferrer-i-Carbonell, A., & Ramons, X. (2014). Inequality and happiness. *Journal of Economic Surveys, 28*(5), 1016–1027.

Ford, G. S., Koutsku, T. M., & Spiwak, L. W. (2011). The frontier of broadband adoption across the OECD. A comparison of performance. *International Economic Journal*, 111–123.
Franzen, A. (2010). Social capital and the Internet: Evidence from Swiss panel data. *Kyklos, 56*(3), 341–360.
Freeman, C., & Soete, L. (1997). *The economics of industrial innovation* (3rd ed.). Pinter.
Frey, B., Benesch, C., & STutzer, A. (2007). Does watching TV make us happy? *Journal of Economic Psychology, 28*(3), 283–313.
Frey, B. S., & Stutzer, A. (2002). What can economists learn from happiness research? *Journal of Economic Literature, XL,* 402–435.
Fukuyama, F. (1999). *The great disruption*. Touchstone. New York: Simon and Schuster.
Gardner, J., & Oswald, A. J. (2001). *Does money buy happiness? A longitudinal study using data on windfalls*. Warwick University. https://pdfs.semanticscholar.org/f47f/5af22e27756f6cc608b2f66074462137097b.pdf. (mimeo).
Gentzkow, M. (2006). Television and voter turnout. *Quarterly Journal of Economics, 121,* 795–813.
Geroski, P. (2000). Models of technology diffusion. *Research Policy, 29,* 603–625.
Gordon, R. (2002). Does the "New Economy" measure up to the great inventions of the past? *Journal of Economic Perspectives, 14*(4), 49–74.
Gordon, R. J. (2010) *Revisiting U.S. productivity growth over the past century with a view of the future*. NBER Working Paper No. 15834.
Gordon, R. (2016). *The rise and fall of American growth—The US standard of living since the civil war*. Princeton University Press.
Graham, C., & Nikolova, M. (2013). Does access to information technology make people happier? Insights from well-being surveys from around the world. *The Journal of Socio-Economics, 44,* 126–139.
Grimes, A., Ren, C., & Stevens, P. (2009). The need for speed: Impacts of Internet connectivity on firm productivity. *MOTU*. http://www.motu.org.nz/publications/detail/the_need_for_speed_impacts_of_internet_connectivity_on_firm_productivity.
Gravelle, H., & Rees, R. (1992). *Microeconomics*. Longman.
Greenstein, S., & McDevitt, R. C. (2011). The broadband bonus: Estimating broadband Internet's economic value. *Telecommunications Policy, 35,* 617–632.
Guerrieri, P., Luciani, M., & Meliciani, V. (2011). The determinants of investment in information and communication technologies. *Economics of Innovation and New Technology, 20*(4), 387–403.
Gui, B., & Stanca, L. (2010). Happiness and relational goods: Well-being and interpersonal relations in the economic sphere. *International Review of Economics, 57*(29), 105–118.
Hall, B. H. (2005). Innovation and diffusion. In Fagerberg, J, D., Mowery & R. R. Nelson (Eds.), *The oxford handbook of innovation* (pp. 459–484). Oxford University Press.
Helliwell, J., Layard, R., & Sachs, J. (Eds.) (2016). *World happiness report 2016 update* (Vol. 1), http://worldhappiness.report/ed/2016/.
Helpman, E. (1998). *General purpose technologies and economic growth*. MIT Press.
Helpman, E., & Trajtenberg, M. (1998). A time to sow and a time to reap: Growth based on general purpose technologies, Chap. 3. In E. Helpman (Ed.), *General purpse technologies and economic growth.* MIT Press.
Hitt, L. M., & Brynjolfsson, E. (1996). Poductivity, business profitability, and consumer surplus: Three different measures of information technology value. *MIS Quarterly, 20*(20), 121–142.
Inglehart, R., C. Haerpfer, A. Moreno, C. Welzel, K. Kizilova, J. Diez-Medrano, M. Lagos, P. Norris, E. Ponarin & B. Puranen et al. (eds.). 2014. World Values Survey: Round Six - Country-Pooled Datafile. Madrid: JD Systems Institute. Version: www.worldvaluessurvey.org/WVSDocumentationWV6.jsp.
Jorgenson, D. W. (2005). Accounting for growth in the information age, Chap. 10. In P. Aghion & S. N. Durlauf (Eds.), *Handbook of economic growth*. North Holland.
Jorgenson, D. W., & Stiroh, K. (1995). Computers and growth. *Economics of Innovation and New Technology, 3*(3-4), 295–303.

Jorgenson, D. W., Ho, M. S., & Stiroh, K. J. (2008). A retrospective look at the US productivity growth resurgence. *Journal of Economic Perspectives, 22*(1), 3–24.

Jorgenson, D. W. M., Ho, S., & Samuels, J. D. (2014). What will revive U.S. economic growth? Lessons from a prototype industry-level production account for the United States. *Journal of Policy Modelling, 36,* 674–691.

Jovanoc, B., & Rousseau, P. L. (2005). General purpose technologies. In P. Aghion & S. N. Durlauf (Eds.), *Handbook of economic growth* (Vol. 1A, pp. 1181–1224). North Holland.

Junco, R. (2013). Inequalities in Facebook use. *Computers in Human Behaviour, 29,* 2328–2336.

Kavetsos, G., & Koutroumpis, P. (2011). Technological affluence and subjective well-being. *Journal of Economic Psychology, 32*(5), 742–753.

Kay, N. M. (2013). Rerun the ape of history and QWERTY always wins. *Research Policy, 42,* 1175–1185.

Keen, A. (2015). *The Internet is not the answer*. Atlantic Books.

Koutroumpis, P. (2009). The economic impact of broadband on growth: A simultaneous approach. *Telecommunications Policy, 33,* 471–485.

Kraut, R., Patterson, M., Lundmark, V., Kiesler, S., Mukhopadhyay, T., & Scherlis, W. (1998). Internet paradox: A social technology that reduces involvement and psychological well-being? *American Psychologist, 53*(9), 1017–1032.

Kraut, R., Kiesler, S., Boneva, B., Cummings, J., Helgeson, V., & Crawford, A. (2001). *The Internet paradox revisited*. Carnegie Mellon University. https://pdfs.semanticscholar.org/fb6a/0d4c937b2494a9d298cac6fdfb1d0ede5ce2.pdf. (manuscript).

Kreps, D. M. (1990) *A course in microeconomic theory*. Harvester Wheatsheaf.

Laumann, E. O., & Sandefur, R. L. (1998). A paradigm for social capital. *Rationality and Society, 10,* 481–495.

Lee, P. S. N., Leung, L., Lo, V., Xiong, C., & Wu, T. (2011). Internet communication versus face-to-face interaction in quality of life. *Social Indicators Research, 100*(3), 375–389.

Li, S.-M., & Chung, T.-M. (2006). Internet function and internet addictive behaviour. *Computers in Human Behaviour, 22*(6), 1067–1071.

Jin, B. (2013). How lonely people use and perceive Facebook. *Computers in Human Behavior, 29,* 2463–2470.

Majumdar, S. (2010). Fiber in the backbone! The impact of broadband adoption in firm growth in network markets. *Economics of Innovation and New Technology, 19*(3), 283–293.

Maurseth, P. B. (2018). The effect of the Internet on economic growth: Counter-evidence from cross-country panel data. *Economics Letters, 172,* 74–77.

Maurseth, P. B. (2017). *ICT, growth and happiness*. NUPI Working Paper No. 876. https://www.nupi.no/nupi/Publikasjoner/CRIStin-Pub/ICT-growth-and-happiness.

McGuckin, R. H., Strietweiser, M., & Doms, M. (1998). The effect of technology use on productivity growth. *Economics of Innovation and New Technology*, 1–26.

Meijers, H. (2014). Does the internet generate economic growth, trade or both? *International Economics and Economic Policy, 11*(1), 137–163.

Moore, G. (2016) No exponential is forever. http://ethw.org/Archives:No_Exponential_is_Forever (downloaded, 12.27.2016).

Najarzadeh, R., Rahimzadeh, F., & Reed, M. (2014). Does the Internet increase labour productivity? Evidence from a cross-country dynamic panel. *Journal of Policy Modelling, 36,* 986–993.

Nordhaus, W. D. (2006). *Baumol's diseases: A macroeconomic perspective*. NBER Working Paper 12218.

Obstfeld, M. (1998). The global capital market: Benefactor of menace? *Journal of Economic Perspectives, 12*(4), 9–30.

OECD. (2014a). Investing in smart infrastructure. In *Measuring the digital economy: A new perspective*. OECD Publishing.

OECD. (2014b). *The app economy*. OECD Digital Economy Papers, http://www.oecd-ilibrary.org/science-and-technology/the-app-economy_5k3ttftlv95k-en.

Oliner, S. D., & Sichel, D. E. (1994). Computers and Growth revisited: How big is the puzzle? *Brookings Papers on Economic Activity, 2*, 273–317.
Oliner, S. D., & Sichel, D. E. (2000). The resurgence of growth in the late 1990s: Is information technology the story? *Journal of Economic Perspectives, 14*(4), 3–22.
Papaioannou, S. K., & Dimelis, S. P. (2007). Information technology as a factor of economic development: Evidence from developed and developing countries. *Economics of Innovation and New Technology*, 179–194.
Pénard, T., & Poussing, N. (2010). Internet use and social capital: The strength of virtual ties. *Journal of Economic Issues, 44*(3), 569–595.
Pénard, T., Poussing, N., & Suire, R. (2013). Does the Internet make people happier? *The Journal of Socio-Economics, 46,* 105–116.
Pradhan, R. P., Bele, S., & Pandey, S. (2013). Internet-growth nexus: Evidence from cross-country panel data. *Applied Economics Letters, 20*(16), 1511–1515.
Quah, D. (2003). Digital goods in the new economy. In D. C. Jones (Ed.), *The new economy*. Elsevier.
Raff, D. M. G., & Trajtenberg, M. (1995). *Quality-adjusted prices for the American automobile industry: 1906–1940*. NBER Working Paper No. 5035.
Rauch, S. S. (1987) America's technology dilemma: A profile of the information economy. *Morgan Stanley Special Economic Study.*
Rousseau, P. L. (2008). General purpose technologies. In S. N. Durlauf & L. E. Blume (Eds.), *Economic growth* (pp. 74–79). Palgrave Macmillan.
Rodrik, D., Subramanian, A., & Trebbi, R. (2004). Institutions rule: The primacy of institutions over geography and integration in economic development. *Journal of Economic Growth, 9,* 131–165.
Ruttan, V. W. (2001) *Technology, growth, and development*. Oxford University Press.
Rødseth, A. (1992) *Konsumentteori*. Universitetsforlaget.
Scotchmer, S. (2004) *Innovation and incentivs*. MIT Press.
Shy. O. (2001). *The economics of network industries*. Cambridge Massachusetts: MIT Press.
Solow, R. (1987). We'd better watch out. *New York Times,* book review section, 12. July.
Solow, R. M. (1957). Technical change and the aggregate production function. *Review of Economics and Statistics, 39*(30), 312–320.
Statistics Norway. (2017). *Statistikkbanken* http://ssb.no/teknologi-og-innovasjon.
Stiroh, K. J. (1998). Computers, productivity and input substitution. *Economic Inquiry, 36*(2), 175–191.
Stiroh, K. J., & Botsch, M. (2007). Information technology and productivity growth in the 2000s. *German Economic Review, 8*(2), 255–280.
Stoneman, P. (2002) *The economics of technology diffusion*. Blackwell.
Stoneman, P., & Battisti, G. (2010). The diffusion of new technology. In B. H. Hall & N. Rosenberg (Eds.), *Economics of innovation* (Vol. 2, pp. 733–769). North Holland: Handbooks in Economics.
Stutzer, A., & Frey, B. S. (2012). *Recent developments in the economics of happiness: A selective overview.* IZA DP No. 7078, IZA Germany.
SunLee, K., & Chen, W. (2017). A long shadow: Cultural capital, techno-capital and networking skills of college students. *Computers in Human Behavior,* (70), 67–73.
Tranos, E., & Mack, E. (2016). Broadband provision and knowledge intensive firms: A causal relationship. *Regional Studies, 50*(7), 1113–1126.
Triplett, J. E. (1999) The solow productivity paradox: What do computers do to productivity? *Canadian Journal of Economics*, 309–334.
Triplett, J. E., & Bosworth, B. P. (2003a, September). Productivity measurements issues in service industries: "Baumol's Disease" has been cured. *FBNY Economic Policy Review*, 23–33.
Triplett, J. E., & Bosworth, B. P. (2003b). "*Baumol's Disease*" *has been cured: IT and multifactor productivity in U.S. Services Industries.* Paper presented at 3rd ZEW Conference on: The Economics of Information and Communication Technologies, Mannheim, July 4–5, 2003.
Tsui, H.-C. (2014). What affects happiness: Absolute income, relative income or expected income? *Journal of Policy Modelling, 36,* 994–1007.

Uhlaner, C. J. (1989). Relational goods and participation: Incorporating sociability into a theory of rational action. *Public Choice, 62*(3), 253–285.

Valberg, S. (2017) *Information and communication technology and the global labour market: Do ICTs contribute to a more gender equal labour market.* Master thesis by the Department of Economics, University of Oslo.

van Ark, B., Mahony, M. O., & Timmer, M. P. (2008). Productivity gap between Europe and the United States: Trends and Causes. *Journal of Economic Perspectives, 22*(1), 25–44.

Vu, K. M. (2019). The internet-growth link: An examination of studies with conflicting results and new evidence on the network effect. *Telecommunications Policy, 43,* 474–483.

Weitzmann, M. (1998). Recombinant growth. *Quarterly Journal of Economics, 113*(2), 331–360.

Wilkinson, R., & Pickett, K. (2009). *The spirit level: Why greater equality makes societies stronger.* Bloomsbury Press.

World Development Indicators. (2017). http://databank.worldbank.org/data/reports.aspx?source=world-development-indicators.

World Happiness Report. (2016) http://worldhappiness.report/.

Yousefi, A. (2011). The impact of information and communication technology on economic growth: Evidence from developed and developing countries. *Economic of Innovation and New Technology,* 581–596.

ICTs and Economic Performance

ICT Investment and Economic Growth in India: An Industry Perspective

Abdul A. Erumban and Deb Kusum Das

Abstract The role of information and communication technologies (ICT) in driving economic growth has been well-established in the literature. By reducing communication and transaction costs, and improving the quality of capital, ICT helps firms improve their productivity and growth. Given her linguistic and engineering skills, India has been pioneering in ICT exports, in particular, the export of software services since the 1990s. However, there is hardly any attempt to understand how Indian industries have been taking advantage of the massive growth potential of ICT use in their production process, looking into the experiences of different industries. This has been primarily constrained by lack of adequate, disaggregated data on the ICT use by industries. While a few studies have attempted to understand the contribution of ICT to aggregate economic growth, the role of ICT at a detailed industry level is hardly studied in India. This paper is a first attempt to construct ICT investment series for the registered or organised segment of manufacturing industries in India, and one of the first few attempts that have made so far to build such ICT series for the aggregate Indian economy. The study extends the capital asset database in India KLEMS to include ICT investment, i.e. investment in hardware, software and communication equipment, in respect of different manufacturing industries. The paper also provides preliminary estimates of the contribution of ICT capital to growth in the aggregate economy and registered manufacturing sector.

Keywords India · Economic growth · Information technology · ICT · Organised manufacturing · Industry-wise investment · Aggregate economy

---

A. A. Erumban (✉)
Groningen Growth and Development Centre, University of Groningen, Groningen, The Netherlands
e-mail: abdul.erumban@conference-board.org

The Conference Board, Brussels, Belgium

D. K. Das (✉)
Department of Economics, Ramjas College, University of Delhi, Delhi, India
e-mail: dkd_ramjas@yahoo.com

D. Maiti et al. (eds.), *Digitalisation and Development*,
https://doi.org/10.1007/978-981-13-9996-1_3

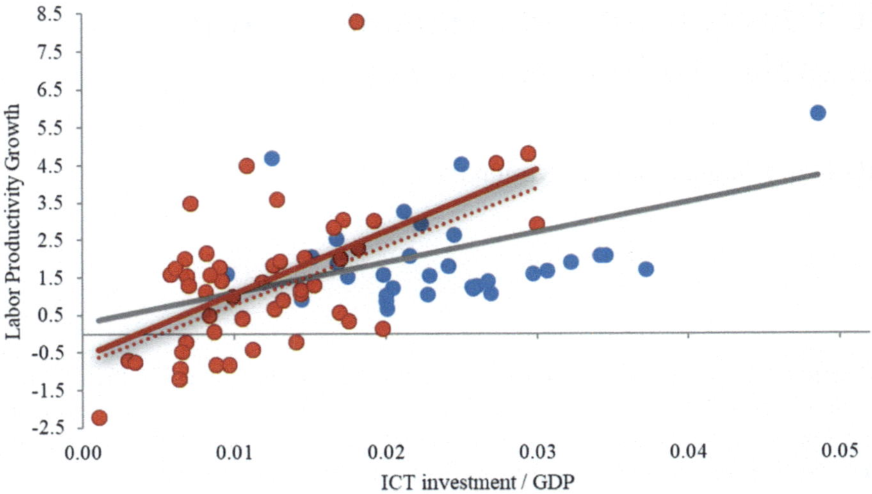

Fig. 1 Correlation between ICT investment and labour productivity growth, 1990–2015.
Note The red dots are emerging markets, and the blue dots are advanced economies. The solid grey line is the linear trend line for the entire 81 countries, and the solid red line is the linear trend line for emerging market economies only. The red dotted line is the trend line for emerging market economies only, but excluding outlier countries.
Source The Conference Board Total Economy Database, November 2016

1 Introduction

The role of information and communication technologies (ICT) in driving economic growth has been well established in the literature (see for instance Jorgenson et al. 2011; Inklaar et al. 2008; Jorgenson and Vu 2005; Jorgenson et al. 2005; van Ark et al. 2003; Jorgenson 2001).[1] By reducing communication and transaction costs, and improving the quality of capital, ICT helps firms improve their productivity and growth. In Fig. 1, we depict the ratio of ICT investment to GDP in 81 countries over the period 1990–2015 against labour productivity growth. It is quite evident that there is a positive correlation between the two. Even more important is that this correlation is stronger in the emerging market economies, and remains strong even if we exclude outlier countries. It is also evident that the emerging market economies are quite behind in ICT adoption, compared to most advanced economies. This

[1]For a while, productivity statistics failed to capture the effect of ICT, as the rapid declines in ICT prices and information on ICT investment were not fully captured in official data. In 1987 Robert Solow even remarked, "[Y]ou can see the computer age everywhere except in the productivity statistics", an observation which is often considered as 'IT productivity paradox". However, later studies which accounted for rapid declines in ICT prices using quality-adjusted hedonic prices observed significant contributions from ICT (see e.g. Jorgenson and Vu 2005). The debate on price is, however, far from settled. For instance, a recent study by Byrne and Corrado (2016), argues that the official US hedonic prices fail to capture the magnitude of price declines in ICT, and their alternative measures suggest even larger declines.

clearly suggests that these economies still have significant potential for improving their productivity growth by investing in ICT.

Given her linguistic and engineering skills, India has been pioneering in ICT exports, in particular, the export of software services since the 1990s. Taking its early bird advantage, India has maintained a relatively higher market presence in the software segment of the IT industry (Saith and Vijayabaskar 2005). However, there is hardly any attempt to understand how Indian industries have been taking advantage of the growth potential of ICT use in their production process. While a few studies have tried to understand the contribution of ICT to aggregate economic growth[2], the evidence on the ICT's impact on growth at the detailed industry level is even more limited. Available micro-level evidence based on plant or firm-level data is suggestive of a positive impact of ICT on growth and productivity in India's organised manufacturing sector. For instance, Sharma and Singh (2012), using ICT investment data from Annual Survey of Industries (ASI), observe that higher ICT capital stock is associated with higher levels of value-added. Similar conclusions have been made by Joseph and Abraham (2007), who observe a positive effect of ICT investment intensity on both labour productivity and TFP, even though the ICT intensity in the sector is low. Comparing firms in India and Brazil, Commander et al. (2011) suggest the importance of better infrastructure and labour market policy for higher rates of ICT adoption. These policies might be imperative for increasing the ICT intensity in India's manufacturing, which is arguably low, as is evidenced by previous studies. Kite (2012, 2013) observe positive ICT effects on productivity, and in particular, the use of outsourced ICT makes a larger contribution than in-house ICT.[3] A recent paper by Navyashree and Bhat (2016) analyses the ICT investments and its growth effects in small and medium firms in the food processing industry in India. Using Centre for Monitoring Indian Economy (CMIE)'s Prowess data, they demonstrate a positive impact of ICT use on the growth of small and medium enterprises. At a more aggregate level, Erumban and Das (2016) provide estimates of ICT contribution to growth for aggregate manufacturing. They use ASI and National Sample Survey Organization (NSSO) data on ICT investment, respectively, for registered and unregistered segments of the manufacturing sector. Their findings suggest a lower contribution of ICT to growth in the manufacturing, compared to the aggregate economy, thus implicitly suggesting a larger ICT contribution in the services sector.

Two recent studies looked at ICT in the Indian economy from a different perspective, which are Mitra et al. (2016) and Vashisht (2017). Mitra et al. (2016) look at the importance of ICT infrastructure for productivity growth in Indian manufacturing. While their study does not have any explicit measure of ICT capital (they have a measure of total capital stock based on CMIE's Prowess data, which is obtained using a perpetual inventory method assuming 7% depreciation rate), they evaluate the impact of ICT infrastructure on productivity, with the ICT infrastructure data being obtained

[2]See Erumban and Das (2016) for a most recent analysis of ICT's contribution to aggregate economy growth.

[3]ICT outsourcing in these studies is measured using data on expenditure on software and other professional services obtained from the Prowess database.

from World Bank's World Development Indicators. Vashisht (2017) looks at the job impact of technology, where ICT is considered as one of the major technologies. They find no evidence of technology destroying jobs; rather, their evidence is suggestive of it shifting jobs from intermediary skill to high skill jobs. While technology has led to an increase in capital intensity, it has not reduced aggregate employment in Indian manufacturing. They use ICT investment data reported in ASI—the same data as we use in this paper (see the discussion below)—in constructing ICT capital stock.

Thus, the detailed industry-level evidence on ICT's impact on economic growth in India is quite limited. The major reason for this, despite India being one of the major ICT service providers, is the lack of adequate, consistent data on the ICT use by industries. Since the onset of India KLEMS database, which provides detailed asset wise information on capital investment at the industry level, along with other indicators required to analyse sources of growth, it is now feasible to examine the sources of economic growth in India at a detailed industry level.[4] This study intends to extend the India KLEMS data to include ICT investment, i.e. investment in hardware, software and communication equipment. While the India KLEMS is an exhaustive database, covering all segments of the economy—be it organised or unorganised—due to data limitations, the current version of the paper will analyse the role of ICT in the organised manufacturing industries only, using detailed asset data from Annual Survey of Industries (ASI). Note that the India KLEMS data is fully benchmarked to National Accounts Statistics (NAS) data. The basic estimates of industry-wise ICT investment data in this paper are consistent with ASI and are subsequently benchmarked to NAS data to ensure consistency. A future extension may attempt to extend it to other India KLEMS industries, including services and unorganised manufacturing.

Following the economic liberalisation and large scale globalisation policies in the early 1990s, India has benefitted from the second unbundling of globalisation—the ICT revolution that has radically lowered transmission costs (see for instance Baldwin 2016). As Erumban and Das (2016) noted, Indian's English language ability, engineering and programming skills accompanied by lower labour cost helped the country catch-up quite fast, particularly in the software sector. Existing evidence suggests that the ICT revolution has helped several Indian firms introduce innovative entrepreneurship and governance model within the software sector (Arora and Athreye 2002). Going beyond the software producing sector, the use of ICT is expected to reduce communication and coordination costs in ICT using industries, and thereby help them improve their productivity. Following the previous literature, Erumban and Das (2016) summarises the channels through which ICT can contribute to economic growth, which includes: a production channel, in which ICT producing sectors benefit from rapid technological change in the sector; an investment channel, in which firms investing in ICT could enhance the contribution of capital to growth, and a productivity channel, in which firms using ICT could improve their

[4]KLEMS stands for capital, labour, energy, material and services. See Das et al. (2016) for a recent study that exploit this database to study sectoral productivity dynamics in Indian economy.

productivity.[5] To understand these channels better, we need to have industry-wise data on investment in ICT, along with output, employment and investment in other types of capital assets. While the India KLEMS provides all but the ICT, this paper is an attempt to fill this gap.

The remaining of the paper is presented in four sections. The second section discusses the methodology to estimate ICT investment for Indian economy. First, it discusses the approach to estimate ICT investment for the aggregate economy and the trends in estimated ICT investment series. Subsequently, it presents the approach used to derive a series on investment in ICT for the organised (registered) manufacturing industries covered by the ASI. The results are also discussed in the section. In Sect. 3, we discuss some practical aspects or issues that need to be tackled while incorporating the estimated series of ICT investment into India KLEMS growth accounting database. In Sect. 4, we provide some preliminary results on our estimation of the contribution of ICT capital to growth in the aggregate economy and registered manufacturing. In the latter case, following the India KLEMS practice, to keep full consistency with National Accounts (NAS) data, the obtained ICT series for ASI sector has been normalised to NAS aggregate Gross Fixed Capital Formation (GFCF) data. In Sect. 5, we provide a summary of the main findings, and in the last section, we discuss the way forward.

2 Estimating ICT Investment in Indian Economy

There is hardly any official data on complete ICT investment series, covering hardware, software and communication equipment, in India.[6] Therefore, it is essential to estimate a series of ICT investment, compiling various sources of information. We follow a three-step approach in estimating ICT investment for the Indian economy. First, we provide the investment in hardware, software and communication equipment in the aggregate economy, which is consistent with available data from the NAS. These estimates are obtained from Erumban and Das (2016), and hence the discussion of the methodology in the next section follows that paper. Then we estimate industry-wise investment for the organised manufacturing industries—i.e. 13 India KLEMS manufacturing industries. In the third step, we combine the two series, by which the manufacturing sector estimates are benchmarked to National Accounts data. In what follows, we discuss the approaches we follow to estimate aggregate economy series and organised manufacturing sector series separately.

[5] Also see van Ark et al. (2011).

[6] The text in this section on the methodological approach to measuring aggregate economy ICT investment heavily draws upon Erumban and Das (2016). This paper is an extension of Erumban and Das (2016) in that it adds ICT capital in detailed manufacturing sectors, though confined only to the registered segment.

2.1 Approach to Estimating Aggregate Economy ICT Investment

The available data on ICT investment in India include: software investment from NAS since 1999–00, ICT investment in organised manufacturing sectors since from ASI 1998, in unorganised manufacturing from NSSO 62nd round, firm-level data on gross fixed assets in hardware, software and communication equipment from CMIE's PROWESS (1989 onwards) and ICT spending by broad sectors of the economy since 2000 from World Information Technology and Services Alliance (WITSA)[7]. Erumban and Das (2016) make use of NAS, ASI and WITSA data, along with investment flows by commodities reported in Input–Output Tables to generate the ICT series for the aggregate economy (see the discussion below, drawn from Erumban and Das 2016).

Software Investment Erumban and Das (2016) consider the NAS data on software investment by different undertakings covering administrative departments, autonomous bodies, cooperatives, departmental enterprises, household sector, non-departmental enterprises, private corporate sector and public administration, as the benchmark series. This data is available since 1999.

The software series for years before 1999 has been extrapolated by applying software/hardware ratio to measured series of hardware investment. The measurement of hardware series is discussed below. Three alternative approaches to derive time series of software/hardware ratio have been attempted. They are: a constant software/hardware ratio from WITSA a linearly forecasted software/hardware ratio from WITSA; and a series of software/hardware ratio generated using the trend in software/hardware ratio in the United States (see Fig. 2 for the software/hardware ratio using these three approaches) obtained from the EU KLEMS database.[8] Although this is a rough assumption, Erumban and Das (2016) have argued that it is better than assuming a constant or linearly growing software/hardware ratio as the U.S., being the ICT leader, may provide a realistic picture of the required hardware/software ratio, particularly in the early years. Hence the third approach—the trend in U.S. software/hardware ratio has been used in the final estimation of ICT investment (Erumban and Das 2016).[9]

Hardware Investment While the National Accounts provides data on software investment, it does not provide investment in hardware and communication separately from total machinery investment. Following the suggestion of de Vries et al. (2010). Erumban and Das (2016) apply the software/hardware ratio from WITSA

[7]See http://www.witsa.org/.

[8]The 2011 version of the EU KLEMS data, has been used for this purpose see www.euklems.net.

[9]Note that the software investment data—be it directly from the NAS, or obtained using hardware/software ratio from WITSA or from the United States—does not capture pirated software used by companies, if any. While the use of such pirated software would indeed contribute to firm's output growth, it will never be reported by firms, and hence is hard to capture.

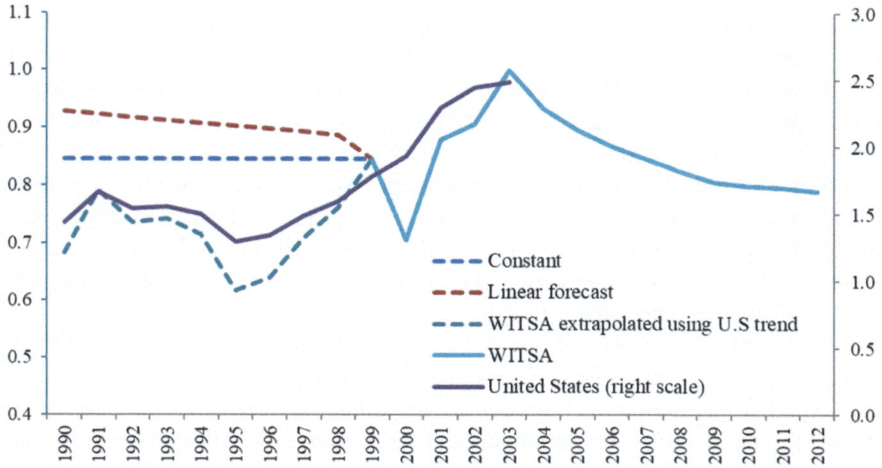

Fig. 2 Ratio of investment in software to hardware (current price), aggregate economy—the three approaches.
Note The solid blue line is the ratio of software/hardware spending in non-consumer segments, obtained from WITSA for the post-1999 period. This data has been applied to the NAS software investment series to estimate hardware investment for the post-1999 period. The U.S. ratio (the solid purple line) is plotted on the right-hand scale. The blue dotted line assumes a constant software/hardware ratio (based on WITSA) for all years, the red dotted line is a linear trend based on available data and the green dotted line is the trend in the U.S. ratio applied to 1999 software/hardware ratio in the Indian economy.
Source Authors' computations, using data from WITSA, EU KLEMS, NAS, and Input–Output Tables

ICT spending data (see the solid blue line in Fig. 2) to software series obtained from National Accounts for 1999–2011 period.

Hardware series for years before 1999, is obtained using the trends in the hardware investment series arrived at using a commodity flow approach (CFM)[10]. In the CFM approach, total economy investment in hardware and communication equipment are estimated using the information on the total domestic availability of these goods and its investment component. Using input–output tables, in combination with NAS and trade statistics the investment in ICT asset i is defined as:

$$\mathrm{GFCF}_{i,t} = \frac{\mathrm{GFCF}^{\mathrm{IO}}_{i,s}}{\left(Y^{\mathrm{IO}}_{i,s} + \mathrm{IM}^{\mathrm{IO}}_{i,s} - \mathrm{EX}^{\mathrm{IO}}_{i,s}\right)} \left(Y_{i,t} + \mathrm{IM}_{i,t} - \mathrm{EX}_{i,t}\right) \tag{1}$$

where $\mathrm{GFCF}_{i,t}$ is the current gross fixed capital formation, Y is gross domestic output, IM is imports and EX is exports—all for the aggregate economy. Superscript IO refers to input–output tables, i.e. for instance, $I^{\mathrm{IO}}_{i,s}$ indicates investment in asset type i (since we consider computer hardware and communication equipment, $i =$

[10]See de Vries et al. (2010) and Timmer and van Ark (2005) for a good description of the commodity flow approach, followed in Erumban and Das (2016).

1, 2, i.e. hardware and communication equipment) in year s (where s is the benchmark year for IO table) obtained from the input–output table. All other variables without the superscript IO are time-series data obtained from the NAS. Industry office equipment and machinery (sector 30 according to ISIC 3.1) is considered as computer hardware and industry radio, TV & communication equipment (sector 32) as communication equipment. In the absence of a strict concordance between ISIC 3.1 and India's input–output table classification, the Indian IO sector office computing and accounting machinery is considered as hardware, and communication equipment & electronic equipment including TV as communication equipment (see Table 1). This way, investment in hardware and communication equipment, along with total domestic output, imports and exports are constructed for six benchmark years, 1983, 1989, 1993, 1998, 2003 and 2007 from input–output tables published by the CSO. This information is used to compute the first part of Eq. (1). Then, using time-series data on gross output obtained from National Accounts and exports and imports obtained from United Nations (UN) Comtrade statistics (see Table 2 for the concordance between Comtrade and ICT assets), a series of hardware investment using Eq. (1) is consturcted (see Erumban and Das 2016). For years before 1983 (i.e. the first benchmark I-O table), the domestic availability ratios (see the first part of Eq. 1) are linearly interpolated till 1970. This long series of ICT investment is later used to estimate an initial capital stock for an early year (see Sect. 3.3).

To extrapolate hardware investment series backwards for years prior to 1999, apply the trend in the obtained CFM based hardware series is applied to 1999 hardware investment obtained using software/hardware ratio from WITSA and software data from NAS. Instead of taking the trend in the estimated hardware series, one could directly take the series generated using commodity flow approach for the entire period (i.e. before and after 1999). However, given that the industry concordances are not at the maximum precision for IO tables after 2003, that approach is not recommended (Erumban and Das 2016).

Communication Equipment For the communication equipment series, the series generated using the commodity flow approach, using data from the IO table, are taken

Table 1 Input–Output Table (IOT) and ICT asset concordance

Benchmark years	IOT sectors	ISIC industries	ICT asset
1983, 1989, 1993 and 1998	Office computing machines	30	Hardware
	Electronic equipment (incl. TV)	30	Hardware
	Communication equipment	32	Communication equipment
2003 and 2007	Electronic equipment (incl. TV)	30	Hardware
	Communication equipment	32	Communication equipment

Table 2 Comtrade and ICT asset concordance

HS revision	HS code	HS industry	ISIC industries	ICT asset
3 (1998 and after)	714	Office machines	30	Hardware
	724	Telecommunications apparatus	32	Communication equipment
1 (before 1998)	75	Office machines and automatic data-processing machines	30	Hardware
	76	Telecommunications and sound-recording and reproducing apparatus and equipment	32	Communication equipment

as such because the industry description was quite consistent and clear (see Table 1). Thus a complete series of ICT investment for the aggregate economy consisting of software, hardware, and communication equipment is generated. The results, which forms the basis of the growth accounting analysis presented in Erumban and Das (2016), are discussed in the next section presented in the next section. However, note that this approach allows to generate investment series only for the total economy, as an industry break-down is not possible with the input–output table.

2.1.1 Estimates of Aggregate Economy ICT Investment

This section presents the estimates of aggregate economy ICT investment—software, hardware and communication—using the methodology discussed in the previous section. This is also the underlying series used in the growth accounting analysis presented in Erumban and Das (2016). First, we provide the official software investment data as available from the NAS. It is evident from Fig. 3 that the nominal value of an investment in software has increased significantly over the period 1999–2000 to 2012–2013. It has increased from ₹14,175 crores to ₹107,166 crores (nearly eight times in 14 years). However, its relative size has remained by and large stable. As a percentage of total GFCF, software investment has declined from 2.9% in 1999–2000 to 2.3% in 2004–2005 (with almost all years seeing a decline) and then had a steady increase until reaching 3.5% in 2008–2009. Since 2008, it has been fluctuating, and it hovered around 3.3%.

In Fig. 4, we further provide the nominal value of total ICT investment by three asset types—software, hardware and communication equipment—along with the share of total ICT investment in aggregate gross value-added. Note that these numbers are obtained by using the methodology described in the previous section, except for the software investment for the period after 1999–2000, which are official NAS

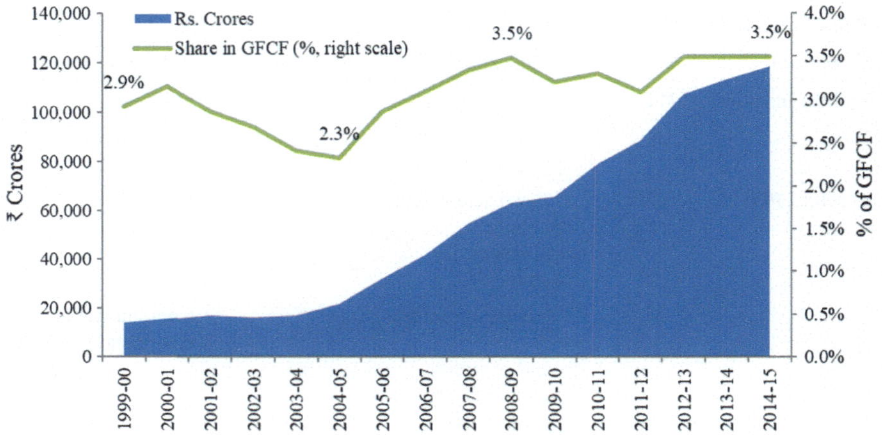

Fig. 3 Software investment (₹crores) and its share in total GFCF: Aggregate Economy. *Source* Authors' computations based on National Accounts Statistics

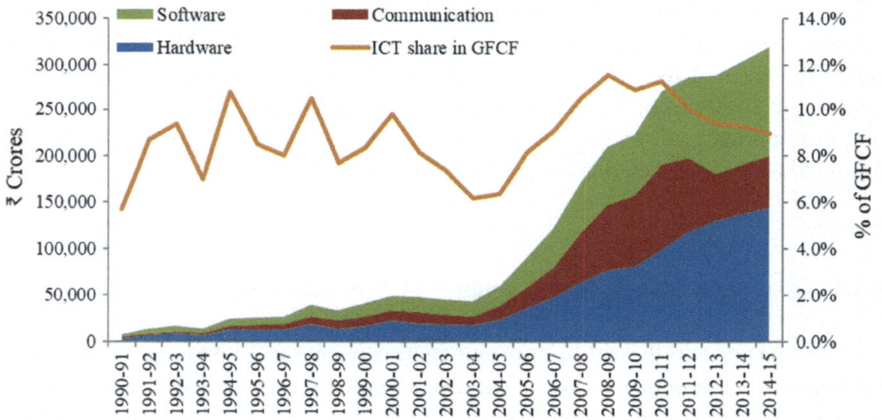

Fig. 4 ICT investment (₹ Crores) and its share in GFCF, Aggregate Economy. *Source* Authors' computations using data from National Accounts Statistics, WITSA and EU KLEMS (see text)

series. The figure suggests a significant increase in the total ICT investment over the years. It has increased from ₹7,995 crores in 1990–1991 to ₹40,475 crores in 1999–2000 (5 times in a decade). There has been a rapid increase after that, reaching ₹284,874 crores in 2012–2013. While the communication investment did see a remarkable increase during the 2004–2011 period, also the period of rapid expansion of mobile phones, it started declining since then. It increased from ₹14,267 crores in 2003–2004 to ₹79,362 crores in 2010–2011, but declined in the next two years, reaching ₹50,924 crores in 2012–2013. Hardware constitutes the largest chunk of ICT investment in India and has also been increasing over time; hardware investment increased from ₹23,265 crores in 2004–2005 to ₹130,723 crores in 2012–2013.

As is the case with software investment, the relative size of ICT investment in India, i.e. ICT investment as a proportion of GFCF has not increased significantly over the years. It has been quite volatile during the decade of 1990–2010, ranging from 5.7% in 1990–1991 to 10.8% in 1994–1995. In 2000–2001, it was 9.8%, and then started declining continuously, reaching 6.4% in 2004–2005. Though it increased since then until 2008–2009, reaching its peak at 11.6%, it declined since then and continued to decline until 2012–2013, reaching 9.3%, close to the share it attained in 1992–1993. Thus the relative importance of ICT investment in India has not increased significantly.

The distribution of ICT investment in terms of software, hardware and communication equipment during 1990–2011, is depicted in Fig. 5. Even though India's software sector has been dominating in its ICT exports (see Erumban and Das 2016), the share of software in aggregate economy ICT investment stayed at about 1/3rd on average since the 1990s. In general, hardware investment dominated, though its share has declined over time. In 1990–1991, communication equipment constituted about 1/4th of total ICT investment, which declined to less than 1/5th by the end of the 1990s. However, it did see an increasing trend since the 1990s, reaching its peak at 34% in 2010–2011, and since then it started declining, reaching 18% in the last year of the data. On average, during the 2008–2012 period, both software and communication equipment accounted for about 30% of total ICT investment each, whereas hardware accounted for nearly 40%.

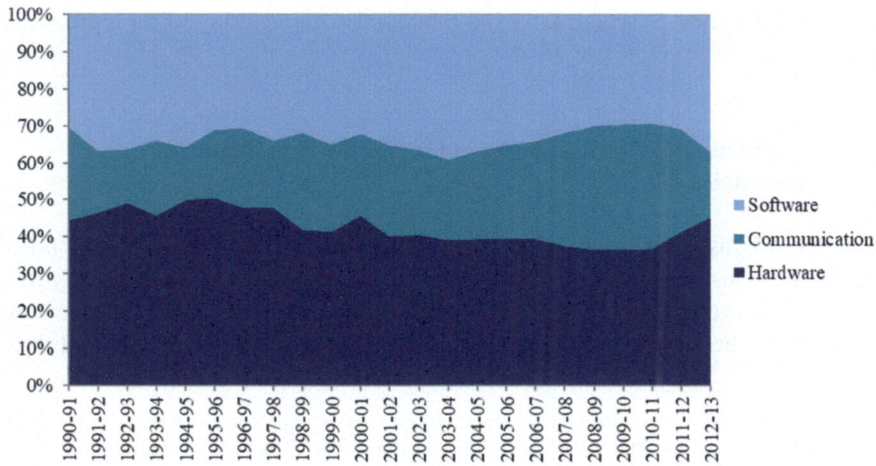

Fig. 5 Composition of ICT investment: shares of software, hardware and communication equipment in total ICT investment. *Source* Authors' computations using data from National Accounts Statistics, WITSA and EU KLEMS (see text)

2.2 Approach to Estimate ICT Investment in Organised Manufacturing

The construction of ICT series for KLEMS industries of the economy, which is the novelty of this paper, is even more challenging. Therefore, in the current version, we attempted this only for the industries in the organised (or formal) segment of the manufacturing sector. ASI schedule on fixed assets provides information on seven individual assets. These are land; building; plant & machinery; transport equipment; computer equipment including software; pollution control equipment and other assets. The data on computer equipment, including software, is available only since 1998–1999. This has been taken as the benchmark data for ICT investment in organised manufacturing.[11] We assume it to consist of the sum of hardware and software investment and exclude communication equipment. It appears that the communication equipment is still part of plant & machinery.[12] We impute GFCF from the fixed assets data using ASI tabulation procedure, i.e.

$$\mathrm{GFCF}_{i,t}^{j\_asi} = \mathrm{NVF}_{i,t}^{c,j\_asi} - \mathrm{NVF}_{i,t}^{o,j\_asi} + D_{i,t}^{j\_asi} - \mathrm{ADR}_{i,t}^{j\_asi} \quad (2)$$

where $\mathrm{GFCF}_{i,t}$ is the gross fixed capital formation, $\mathrm{NVF}_{i,t}^{c}$ is the net closing value of fixed assets, $\mathrm{NVF}_{i,t}^{o}$ is the net opening value of fixed assets, $D_{i,t}$ is the depreciation of asset i during the year, and $\mathrm{ADR}_{i,t}$ is the addition due to revaluation; all for ASI industry j, asset i ($i = 1$: ICT equipment)[13]and year t. A numeric example of this approach using the ASI schedule for food and food manufacturing sector is provided in Table 3.

2.2.1 Estimates of ICT Investment in Organised Manufacturing Industries

Note that ASI also provides data on actual additions of an asset during the year (also see Table 3). Instead of re-calculating GFCF using Eq. (2), one could directly use these series to represent an investment in ICT. In Fig. 6, we provide the estimates of ICT investment in the aggregate manufacturing sector, obtained from ASI data

[11]The ASI data on ICT investment has been used by previous studies, some of which are indicated earlier in this paper. For instance, Vashisth (2017) constructs ICT capital stock using ASI firm-level data on ICT investment and Joseph and Abraham (2007) make use of the ICT investment data from ASI at 3 digit level in their regression of labour productivity on ICT intensity. Sharma and Singh (2012), also uses investment in ICT from ASI, deflated using machinery and equipment prices. This paper makes a comprehensive attempt to compile the ASI data on ICT and construct measures of capital stock and capital services that are consistent with the approach followed in the India KLEMS database.

[12]Clearly, the ASI data underestimate the extent of ICT use in the organised manufacturing sector, as it only covers the hardware and software investments (also see Vashisht 2017).

[13]A similar approach is followed to obtain GFCF in all asset types in India KLEMS, while this paper deals only with the ICT.

Table 3 ASI fixed assets schedule—food and food manufacturing (ISIC 15) in 2007–2008 (all values in Rs. Lakhs)

	Types of assets	Gross value				Depreciation				Net value	
		Opening as on	Addition during the year		Deduction & adjustment during the year	Closing as on	Up to year beginning	Provided during the year	Up to year end	Opening as on	Closing as on
			Due to revaluation	Actual addition		(3+4+5−6)			(8+9)	(3−8)	(7−10)
1	2	3	4	5	6	7	8	9	10	11	12
1	Land	346,496	25,224	67,623	6,525	417,839	3,805	490	4,229	396,582	482,568
2	Building	1,427,116	15,543	250,910	11,518	1,651,114	399,857	81,554	459,616	1,249,114	1,424,485
3	Plant & machinery	5,181,320	24,921	1,118,921	68,849	6,157,510	2,285,977	392,100	2,607,042	3,251,903	3,951,832
4	Transport equipment	199,423	45	59,819	13,960	228,716	101,475	30,002	116,230	155,769	177,168
5	*Computer equipment including software*	*63,249*	*9*	*12,781*	*1,099*	*73,871*	*42,548*	*9,146*	*49,867*	*22,594*	*26,005*
6	Pollution control equipment	54,622	2	9,697	139	64,053	25,033	3,740	28,374	31,338	37,200
7	Others	475,123	1,657	82,990	11,080	539,896	248,120	41,657	280,660	257,574	294,437

(continued)

Table 3 (continued)

	Types of assets	Gross value				Depreciation				Net value	
		Opening as on	Addition during the year		Deduction & adjustment during the year	Closing as on	Up to year beginning	Provided during the year	Up to year end	Opening as on	Closing as on
			Due to revaluation	Actual addition		(3+4+5−6)			(8+9)	(3−8)	(7−10)
1	2	3	4	5	6	7	8	9	10	11	12
8	**Sub-total (2–7)**	**7,400,853**	**42,177**	**1,535,117**	**106,645**	**8,715,160**	**3,103,009**	**558,198**	**3,541,789**	**4,968,291**	**5,911,128**
9	Capital work in progress	474,152	0	302,488	328,053	434,456	299	215	722	498,310	439,788
10	**Total (1 + 8+9)**	**8,221,501**	**67,401**	**1,905,228**	**441,223**	**9,567,455**	**3,107,113**	**558,903**	**3,546,740**	**5,863,183**	**6,833,44**
	GFCF		**−R**					**+D**		**−O**	**+ C**

Note Estimated GFCF in ICT (12 − 11 + 9−4) = 26,005 − 22,594 + 9,146−9 = 12,548, and the estimated total GFCF in food and food manufacturing sector = 1,461,803. The reported ASI factory sector GFCF is 1,461,802

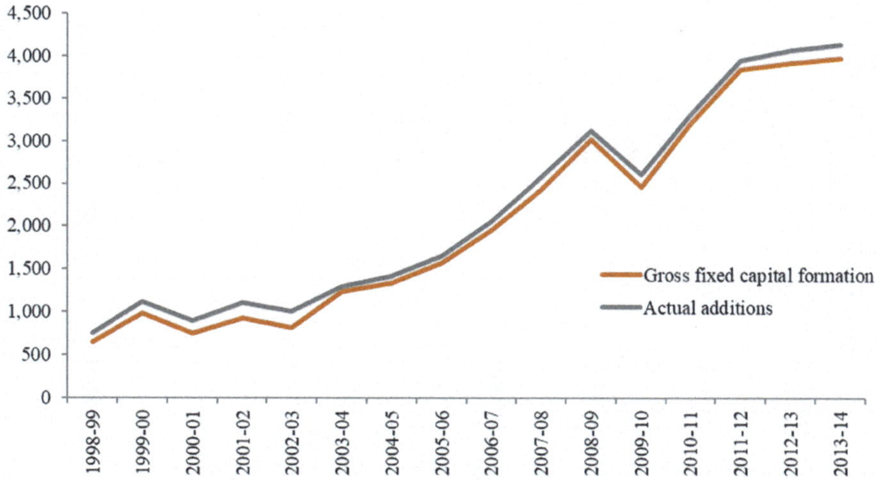

Fig. 6 ICT investment in the aggregate organised manufacturing sector (₹ Crores).
Note GFCF is Gross fixed capital formation in ICT, obtained using ASI tabulation procedure, i.e. actual additions to ICT assets—deductions during the year. Actual additions are as reported in ASI. The numbers in this chart are consistent with ASI data, but not with national accounts.
Source Authors' computations using data from the Annual Survey of Industries

using Eq. (2) along with the actual additions as reported in ASI. Barring some slight deviations, by and large, these two series are quite similar at the aggregate level. However, our preferred series is the measured GFCF series using Eq. (2), which is also consistent with ASI's own reported GFCF series for a total of all assets, as we have observed some notable differences between the two series across industries.

It is obvious from the figure that the absolute level of nominal investment in ICT in the aggregate organised manufacturing sector has increased over time. It increased continuously from about ₹650 crores in 1998–1999 to ₹3,122 crores in 2008–2009. After a decline in 2009–2010, it continued to increase again, reaching ₹4,144 crores in 2013–2014.

While the absolute level of ICT investment has increased over time, it has not increased at the same speed as the value-added in the sector. The investment to value-added ratio has been quite volatile and has declined over the years (Fig. 7). On average it was 0.5% for the entire period 1998–2013, with very little variation, ranging from 0.4% in 2000–2001 to 0.6% in 2003–2004. In the last year of the data, it was only 0.42% of the aggregate value-added. The pace of increases in ICT use in Indian manufacturing has been relatively slow compared to the pace of output expansion. Similar is the case, even if we compare the ICT share in total manufacturing investment, suggesting that other types of assets were growing even faster than ICT (Fig. 8).

Estimates of ICT investment are also made for 13 India KLEMS manufacturing sectors (see Table 4 for the list of these industries and their abbreviations used in the charts). As one would expect, more technology-intensive industries such as

Fig. 7 ICT investment/Value-added ratio: aggregate organised manufacturing sector (%). *Note* all numbers are consistent with ASI factory sector data, and not necessarily consistent with national accounts data.
Source Authors' computations using data from the Annual Survey of Industries

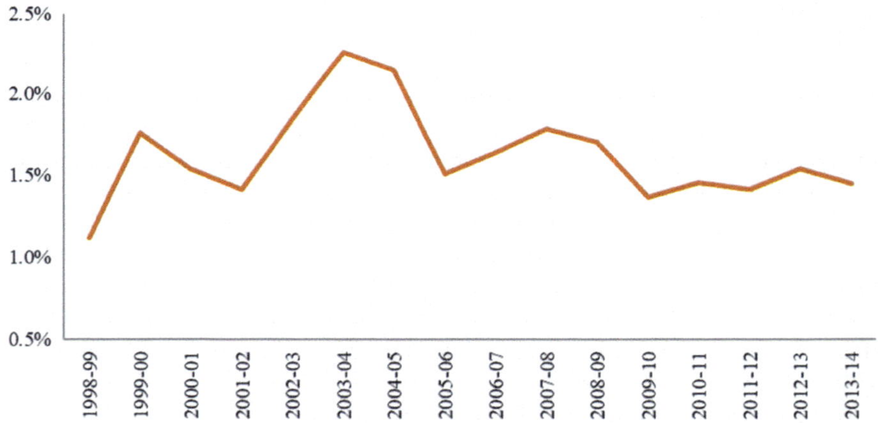

Fig. 8 Share of ICT investment in total GFCF: aggregate organised manufacturing sector (%). *Note* all numbers are consistent with ASI factory sector data, and not necessarily consistent with national accounts data.
Source Authors' computations using data from the Annual Survey of Industries

electrical & optical equipment manufacturing, transport equipment and machinery manufacturing industries absorb a major chunk of ICT investment within the organised manufacturing (Fig. 9). However, this composition was quite different in the early 1990s, compared to what it is in the recent years. In 1993–1994, 22% of total ICT investment was in chemicals, 18% in textiles and 9% in food products. All other industries had less than 5%, with wood products being the lowest and non-metallic mineral being the highest at 5%. The share of textiles, however, dropped substan-

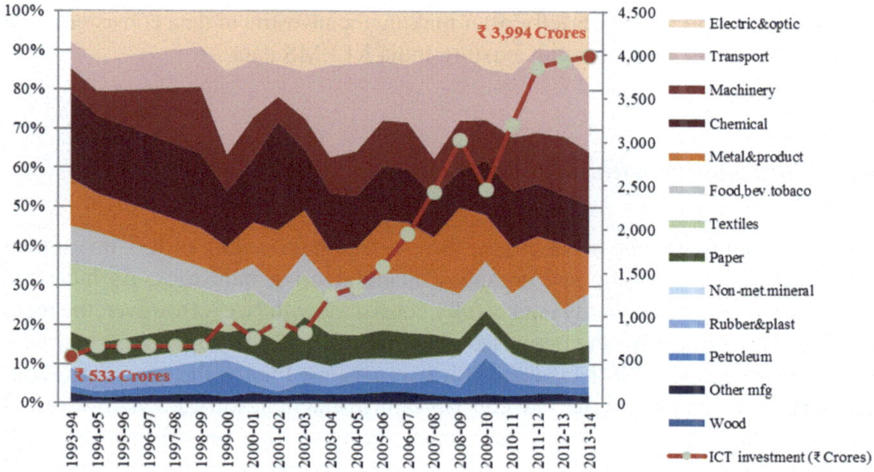

Fig. 9 Industry share in total ICT investment (%).
Note industries are ranked in order of their relative ICT investment size in 2013–2014. All numbers are consistent with ASI factory sector data, and not necessarily consistent with national accounts data.
Source Authors' computations using data from the Annual Survey of Industries

tially over the years, particularly until the mid-1990s, and is now 6%. The share of chemicals also declined by almost ten percentage point, reaching 13% in 2013–2014. The share of machinery, transport and electrical & optical equipment, on the other hand, increased respectively from 6 to 13%, from 7 to 17% and from 8 to 18%. Thus, together, these three industries constitute almost half of the total ICT investment in India's organised manufacturing sector in 2013–2014.

3 Extending India KLEMS Database to Include ICT Capital

In India KLEMS database, investment is used as an input to generate capital services that are ultimately used in a growth accounting analysis to estimate input and productivity contribution to output growth. In the case of ICT investment, it requires estimates of ICT capital stock—calculation of which requires nominal investment and ICT prices—and its rental prices or user cost. The approach to estimate rental prices are discussed extensively in Erumban (2008), and the specific context of India KLEMS database is described in the India KLEMS data manual and Erumban and Das (2016).[14] In this section, we discuss the approach to estimate ICT capital

[14]See the India KLEMS data manual available at: https://www.rbi.org.in/Scripts/PublicationReportDetails.aspx?UrlPage=&ID=855.

stock and rental prices very briefly, after making the investment data consistent with National Accounts, and thus with existing India KLEMS data.

3.1 Consistency with NAS

In the preceding sections, we discussed the estimation procedure of ICT investment for the aggregate economy and organised manufacturing industries. As indicated earlier, the aggregate economy data is fully consistent with NAS. However, the measured ICT investment for the organised manufacturing sector is not consistent with the aggregate economy ICT estimates for two reasons. Firstly, the aggregate economy series is a complete series that consists of investment in software, hardware and communication equipment, while the manufacturing series is only the sum of hardware and software investment (distribution of these two assets are not available), and does not include communication equipment. Secondly, all the series in the aggregate economy is benchmarked to available data on software investment from the NAS and is thus consistent with NAS. This is not the case with the manufacturing series, which is solely based on ASI data. It is to be noted that there is a significant difference between the organised sector capital formation as reported in ASI and the organised manufacturing GFCF data provided in the National Accounts. Therefore, while developing the asset-industry investment series for non—ICT assets (such as buildings, machinery and transport equipment), the India KLEMS has used the asset-industry distribution in the ASI data, keeping the NAS reported GFCF data as the benchmark series. This way, the India KLEMS data asset-industry investment in non-ICT assets is fully consistent with NAS data.

To ensure the NAS consistency, we assume the ICT investment to total GFCF ratio in the organised ASI manufacturing sector to the reported total GFCF data in the organised manufacturing sector in the National Accounts. More specifically:

$$\mathrm{GFCF}^{j}_{\mathrm{ICT},t} = \left[\mathrm{GFCF}^{j\_asi}_{\mathrm{ICT},t} / \mathrm{GFCF}^{j\_asi}_{t}\right]\mathrm{GFCF}^{j}_{t} \tag{3}$$

where $\mathrm{GFCF}^{j}_{\mathrm{ICT},t}$ is the gross fixed capital formation in ICT in industry j in year t, consistent with National Accounts, $\mathrm{GFCF}^{j\_asi}_{\mathrm{ICT},t}$ is the GFCF in ICT in ASI industry j, $\mathrm{GFCF}^{j\_asi}_{t}$ is the total GFCF (across all assets) in ASI industry j, and GFCF^{j}_{t} is the total GFCF across all assets in industry j, consistent with National Accounts. The obtained total ICT investment using (3) can then be split into software and hardware using the aggregate economy distribution of these two assets, as estimated in Sect. 2.1.1 i.e.

$$\mathrm{GFCF}^{j}_{i,t} = \mathrm{GFCF}^{j}_{\mathrm{ICT},t}\left[\frac{\mathrm{GFCF}_{i,t}}{\mathrm{GFCF}_{\mathrm{SOFT},t} + \mathrm{GFCF}_{\mathrm{HARD},t}]}\right] \tag{4}$$

where $GFCF^{j}_{i,t}$ is the GFCF in asset i (software and hardware) in industry j in year t, $GFCF^{j}_{ICT,t}$ is the GFCF in ICT (sum of software and hardware as obtained in 3) in industry j in year t and $GFCF_{i,t}$ is the GFCF in the aggregate economy.

The NAS consistent ICT investment series generated using the above approach appears to underestimate the total manufacturing ICT investment. As indicated in the previous section, National Accounts provides data on investment in software by various industries, which includes organised manufacturing as well. The total ICT investment (sum of hardware and software) generated using Eq. (3) is much lower than the total software investment reported in NAS. This is due to the differences in the way in which National Accounts and ASI compiles their GFCF data—while the former uses an institution approach making use of enterprise-level data, the latter is based on establishment approach. This remains a major issue and needs to be tackled in the future revisions of the data.[15] What is also less evident in the ASI data—which is based on the establishment approach—is how it treats ICT assets which are present at the headquarters of a firm and not in the factory surveyed. If these assets get distributed properly among the different factories the firms own, the difference between establishment and enterprise/institutional approach should be minimal, which is not the case here. A careful look at the distribution of these assets is required to understand this re-distribution issue.

3.2 *ICT Prices and Depreciation*

Price measurement for ICT assets has been an important research topic in the literature, as the quality of ICT capital goods has been rapidly increasing. The use of a single harmonised deflator across countries was widely advocated and used (Timmer and van Ark 2005; Schreyer 2002). We use a harmonisation procedure suggested by Schreyer (2002) where the US hedonic deflators[16] are adjusted for India's domestic inflation rates, i.e.

$$\Delta \ln P^{\mathrm{ICT}}_{\mathrm{IND}} = \Delta \ln P^{n-\mathrm{ICT}}_{\mathrm{IND}} + \Delta \ln P^{\mathrm{ICT}}_{\mathrm{US}} - \Delta \ln P^{n-\mathrm{ICT}}_{\mathrm{US}} \tag{5}$$

where $\Delta \ln P^{\mathrm{ICT}}_{i}$ is the growth rate of ICT prices in the country i (IND = India, US = United States) and $\Delta \ln P^{n-\mathrm{ICT}}_{i}$ is the growth rate of non-ICT prices in country i. Once a NAS consistent ICT series is developed (see the previous section), we use the harmonised ICT deflators to deflate the nominal ICT investments and thus obtain real ICT investment series.

[15] An alternative approach, which is not attempted in the paper yet, is outlined in Appendix 3.

[16] Our harmonised price deflators are based on the U.S. hedonic prices, which are constructed using a hedonic regression where prices of ICT equipment regressed on several characteristics, such as for instance processor speed, hardware size, memory etc.

For the depreciation rates, following the standard practice in the literature (see Jorgenson and Vu 2005), 31.5% for software and hardware and 11.5% for communication equipment are used (also see Erumban and Das 2016).

3.3 Capital Stock and the Contribution of ICT Capital to Growth

India KLEMS uses measures of capital services in its growth accounting analysis (see Das et al. 2016). This requires asset wise capital stock estimates. As is the case with all other assets (i.e. buildings, machinery, and transport equipment), we use a standard perpetual inventory method (PIM) to estimate ICT capital stock (see Erumban and Das 2016). Capital stock for a given ICT asset *i* can be obtained using the PIM as:

$$S_t^i = S_{t-1}^i \cdot \left(1 - \delta^i\right) + I_t^i \tag{6}$$

where $\boldsymbol{S_t^i}$ = capital stock in ICT asset *i* in year *t*, $\boldsymbol{\delta^i}$ = geometric depreciation rate of ICT asset *i* and $\boldsymbol{I_t^i}$ = real investment in ICT asset *i* (deflated using the harmonised price deflators). This requires an initial capital stock. Given that investing in ICT is relatively a new development, it is ideal to assume a zero initial stock for an early year, say 1970. Due to high depreciation rates of ICT assets, this assumption does not affect the growth rates for later years. As mentioned in Sect. 2, we have extended the ICT investment series for the aggregate economy until 1970, using a linearly extrapolated domestic availability ratio and the time-series of domestic availability of ICT assets, and these series can be used to obtain an initial stock for 1970.

For the manufacturing sector, given the short time-series we have, we approximated an initial capital stock using capital stock to investment ratio in the aggregate economy for 1992–93. Given that the initial capital stock is estimated crudely, the results on growth contribution will be reliable only after a few years, after allowing for the depreciation of a major part of first available investment data. Fortunately, given the high rate of depreciation, the effect of initial capital on estimated growth rate will vanish quite quickly.

The contribution of ICT capital to value-added growth is obtained as the product of ICT capital compensation share in nominal value-added and the growth rate of ICT capital stock.[17] The compensation share of ICT capital is estimated by multiplying the rental price of ICT capital with ICT capital stock, with the rental price being

[17]ICT income share is obtained using ICT rental prices, which are computed using internal rate of return, depreciation rate and ICT investment deflators (see Erumban and Das 2016 and Erumban 2008 for detailed discussion on the calculation of rental prices).

estimated using depreciation rate, an assumed external rate of return and investment prices, as spelt out in Das et al. (2016).[18]

4 Contribution of ICT to Economic Growth—Aggregate Economy and Organised Manufacturing

In Fig. 10, we provide the contribution of ICT to value-added growth in the aggregate economy from 1996 till 2011. The whole period is divided into three sub-periods, 1996–2000, 2001–2005 and 2007–2011. On the right-hand side of the figure, we have the value-added growth, and on the left-hand side, the contribution of ICT capital to value-added growth. Value-Added growth has increased over the years. However, the contribution of ICT capital has not increased by a similar magnitude. In the first period, out of more than 6% value-added growth, only less than one percentage point was due to ICT use (i.e. about 15% of total growth). This has declined to 0.6 percentage points in the second period, even when value-added growth increased to more than 6.5%, thus lowering the relative contribution to less than 10% of value-added growth. In the last period, however, there has been some improvement. When the value-added growth increased to 8.3%, the contribution of ICT increased to 1.4%, thus regaining its relative contribution to about 16%.

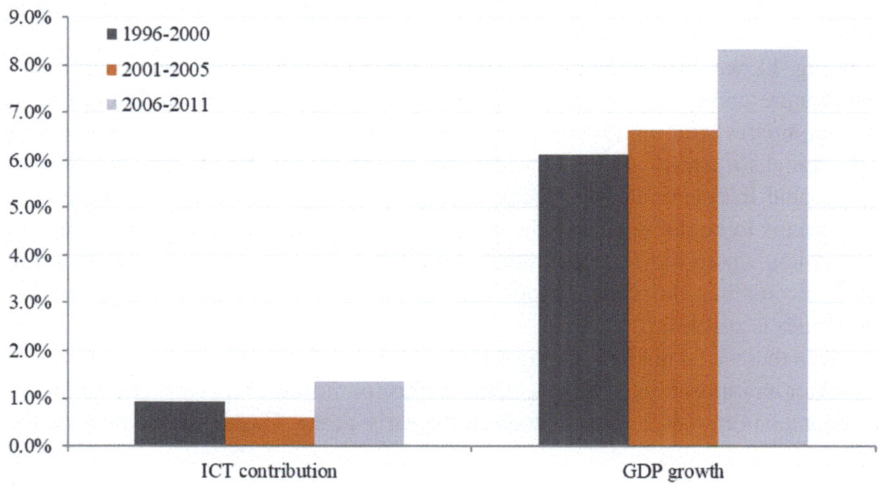

Fig. 10 Contribution of ICT (hardware, software and communication equipment) capital to value-added growth, Aggregate Economy. *Source* Authors' computations using data from NAS and Erumban and Das (2016)

[18]Also see the India KLEMS data manual, available at: https://www.rbi.org.in/Scripts/PublicationReportDetails.aspx?UrlPage=&ID=855.

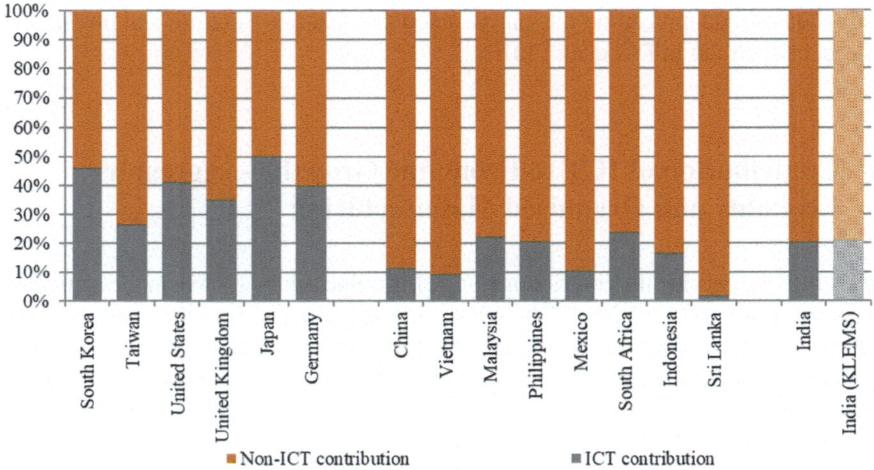

Fig. 11 Contributions of ICT (hardware, software and communication equipment) and non-ICT capital to GDP growth, Aggregate Economy. *Source* The Conference Board Total Economy Database, May 2016 and authors' computations using data from NAS

A comparison of our results with that of the Conference Board Total Economy Database (TED) suggests a similar trend in the contribution of ICT capital (Fig. 11). According to TED data, the relative contributions of ICT (relative to GDP growth) has declined from 18% during 1996–2000 to 9% during 2001–2005 and then increased to just above 1/5th of the GDP growth.[19]

In Fig. 11, we further compare our results for India with several other countries—both mature and emerging market economies—using the TED data. Interestingly, India compares well with other developing countries regarding the contribution of ICT capital to growth. If we consider the contributions of ICT capital and non-ICT capital to economic growth and assess the relative importance of these two, India seems to be doing well at the aggregate level. However, compared to mature economies, where the ICT revolution started even earlier than in most emerging market economies, the relative importance of ICT in India and other emerging market economies is still low.[20]

Given that we do not have a long series of ICT data for the organized manufacturing sector it is appropriate to focus on the results for most recent years, after allowing for depreciation of ICT capital stock in the early years. Therefore, we provide the

---

[19]Note that there are some differences between TED estimates and our estimates. The first is that in the TED output and GFCF data for the aggregate are converted to calendar year (using quarterly data) and the asset distribution is applied to those annual data to obtain asset wise data. Secondly, the price deflator for ICT used in the TED are based on a new alternative measures developed by Byrne and Corrado (2016), while the hedonic deflators used in our paper is based on official BEA ICT hedonics for U.S. Finally, the TED numbers are relative to 'GDP', whereas ours is relative to gross value-added.

[20]In an earlier study, Papaioannou and Dimelis (2007) suggest strong ICT effects on economic growth, with the effects being larger on developed economies than on developing economies.

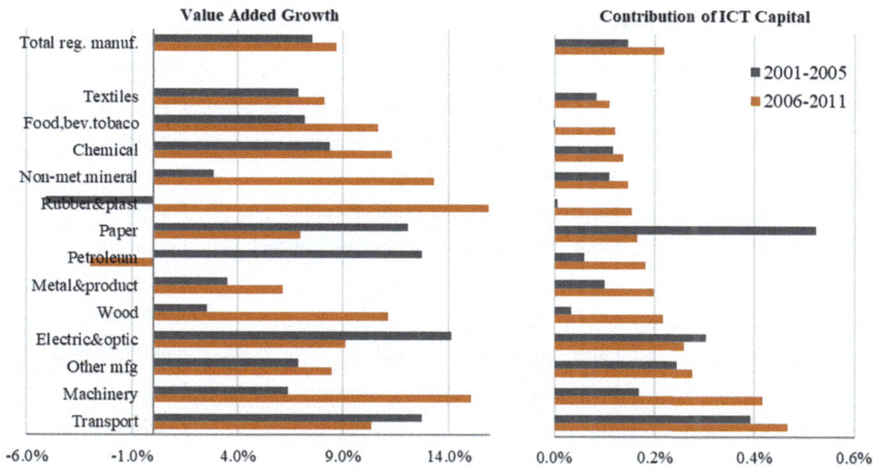

Fig. 12 Contribution of ICT (hardware and software only) capital to value-added growth, Registered Manufacturing Sector. *Note* The results in this chart are made consistent with national accounts data (see text). Detailed industry names are provided in Appendix Table 4. *Source* Authors' computations using data from ASI and NAS

results on the contribution of ICT capital to value-added growth in registered manufacturing only for the 2001–2011 period. On average, the contribution of ICT capital (excluding telecommunication equipment) in the registered manufacturing sector is about 0.2 percentage point over the period 2001–2011 (Fig. 12). There has been only a marginal increase from 2001–2005 period to the 2006–2011 period. Despite several industries witnessing improvement in ICT contribution, the drop in two major industries—paper, printing and publishing industry, and electrical and optical equipment manufacturing industries—has driven down the aggregate contribution. These two industries had the highest ICT contribution in the first period. In the case of paper and products, the faster growth of ICT might be due to the large presence of publishing industry (including media reproduction and newspaper), the share of which in the total value-added still relatively small, but is increasing. The electrical and optical equipment industry is an obvious candidate to have higher ICT investment, as it is globally an ICT intensive sector. Machinery and transport equipment sectors were the other two sectors with notable ICT contribution to value-added growth. While in both these sectors the contribution of ICT remained by and large the same, electrical and optical equipment sector and paper and publishing sector both witnessed significant declines in their ICT contribution.

There is significant variation across industries in ICT use. And overall there has been some improvement—11 out of 13 industries have witnessed an increased, albeit small in magnitude, in the absolute contribution of ICT to growth—leading to a minor increase in the contribution of ICT to growth in organised manufacturing. The performance of registered manufacturing, in terms of ICT use, seems to be quite negligible, when compared to the aggregate economy, implicitly indicating

Table 4 List of India KLEMS manufacturing industries

S. No.	ISIC codes	India KLEMS industries	Abbreviations
1	15t16	Food, beverages and tobacco	Food,bev.tobaco
2	17t19	Textiles, textile, leather and footwear	Textiles
3	20	Wood and of wood and cork	Wood
4	21t22	Pulp, paper, paper, printing and publishing	Paper
5	23	Coke, refined petroleum and nuclear fuel	Petroleum
6	24	Chemicals and chemical products	Chemical
7	25	Rubber and plastics	Rubber&plast
8	26	Other non-metallic mineral	Non-met.mineral
9	27t28	Basic metals and fabricated metal	Metal&product
10	29	Machinery, nec	Machinery
11	30t33	Electrical and optical equipment	Electric&optic
12	34t35	Transport equipment	Transport
13	36t37	Manufacturing nec; recycling	Other mfg

that perhaps it is the services sector of the economy that has been using the ICT more intensely. This, however, requires further extension of the data to include the service sector.

5 Main Findings

This paper made a first attempt to estimate ICT investment in the Indian economy—extending the estimates of Erumban and Das (2016) for the aggregate economy to individual manufacturing industries in the organised segment. The estimates suggest an increase in the nominal value of an investment in software, hardware and communication equipment in the aggregate economy over the last two decades. However, as a share in GDP, it has, in fact, declined. A similar pattern is observed in the case of the aggregate organised manufacturing sector as well, where we see the total ICT investment (sum of hardware and software) increases over the years, while its share in value-added and the total investment has been quite volatile with little increase.

Subsequently, the paper also provided some preliminary results on the contribution of ICT capital to value-added growth in the aggregate economy, and 13 India KLEMS manufacturing industries, in the organised segment of the economy. The results suggest that while there is some marginal increase in ICT use and its contribution to growth in Indian manufacturing, the sector still lags quite behind, particularly when compared to the aggregate economy. There is more potential for exploiting the benefits of ICT in the Indian economy, particularly in the manufacturing sector, which can help Indian firms to improve their competitiveness.

While many factors play a role here in making Indian industries' low ICT use, an important one is the role of complementary investment. To embrace ICT and digital technology fully into the production process, firms also need to invest in several complementary assets, including human capital, training, intangible assets, and organisational restructuring. For instance, a firm-level study by Bresnahan et al. (2002) suggests that the declines in ICT price lead to increased use of a complementary system. They observe a complementarity between skilled workers and ICT and suggest the importance of complementary organisational investment in raising the effects of ICT on labour demand. Such complementary investments, particularly those related to significant internal re-organisation within business organisations, are often a slow process and is often a function of culture as well. Therefore, even if the investment is made in information and communication assets, translating it into productivity requires such complementary investment. In the case of India, the low level of investment in ICT might itself is partly due to the low pace of such complementary assets. Even the invested assets may not be fully utilised and translated into growth, if not accompanied by required human capital and organisational investment—an aspect that cannot be captured by our growth accounting approach. The results in this paper are preliminary and require further scrutiny and revisions. Moreover, there is still substantial room for improving these estimates, as we are bound to make strong assumptions in the calculation procedure.

6 Way Forward

The estimates presented in this paper may be considered as preliminary, as it involves a significant amount of assumptions and imputations. In the process of constructing these estimates, we realise the estimates could be improved using more available information, and these will be explored in the subsequent works. For instance, instead of using trade data from UN Comtrade (see Sect. 2.1), we could exploit detailed data from WITS or Directorate General of Commercial Intelligence and Statistics (DGCSI). Also, given that most of the ICT investment goods are likely to be produced in the formal/organised segment of the manufacturing sector, instead of relying on NAS output data in constructing the domestic availability (see Sect. 2.1), one may consider using detailed output data from the ASI.

Since the commodity flow approach provides estimates of hardware and communication, it is logical to use this series on hardware for the entire period. However, the current version, we do not use the hardware estimates obtained from CFM for years after 1999, because of the inaccuracy in concordance between industry classification in input–output tables and our ICT definition. Future work may explore further possibilities of improving the commodity flow approach and rely fully on the IO based hardware series.

Also, for imputing missing data on hardware and software, we relied on hardware/software ratio from WITSA and the United States. An alternative option, which may be explored in the future versions, is to rely on the firm-level information on gross fixed assets in software and hardware from CMIE's Prowess data.

Finally, exploiting other available sources such as the Prowess and NSSO manufacturing surveys, estimates of ICT investment may be generated for other KLEMS industries, which include unorganised manufacturing and services industries. This would account for further heterogeneity across industries within the Indian economy. Indeed, such industry-level analysis would be insightful in obtaining a broad perspective on ICT's contribution to growth. Yet, one should not overlook the possibility that it can still mask several minute dynamics at the firm level. This is of particular importance when it comes to ICT's impact in a developing country like India, due to significant heterogeneity across firms in terms of their ICT use and exposure—depending upon for instance their export intensity, their target consumers, etc. In future work, one should complement industry analysis with detailed firm-level studies. While this paper is our first attempt to build an ICT investment series, and to quantify its contribution to growth in Indian industries, using a standard growth accounting approach, it does not end our quest to answer the question of ICT's role in India's growth. In the future, we aim to continue analysing the role of ICT using more comprehensive econometric tools, which would help us understand the intensity of ICT's effects more precisely.

Acknowledgements This paper draws heavily on the India KLEMS project funded by the Reserve Bank of India (RBI), housed in Centre for Development Economics (CDE), Delhi School of Economics. The authors are thankful to the RBI for financial support and the CDE for hosting the project. We are also grateful to many researchers who have contributed to the development of the KLEMS data and provided fruitful comments on this research. In particular, we wish to acknowledge K. L. Krishna, Bishwanath Goldar, Suresh Chand Aggarwal, and Pilu Chandra Das who contributed to an earlier version of this research, published as CDE Working paper # 284. The content of the working paper has been re-used with permission. Comments by participants of the India KLEMS Conference in December 2016, in particular, Ashok Jain, T. Rajeshwari, Rajiv Mehta and Satyananda Sahoo were quite beneficial to this work. Views expressed in this paper are those of the authors and do not reflect their respective institutions. The usual disclaimers apply.

Appendix 1

Another way of estimating NAS consistent ICT series for organised manufacturing is to consider the reported NAS software data as the benchmark, and obtain hardware as a residual. That is, for years for which the NAS software data is available (1998 onwards), consider the NAS data as the benchmark estimates for the aggregate registered manufacturing. Hardware investment for the first year of the data for which the software data is available in NAS can then be obtained using the aggregate economy software/hardware ratio. This way we can obtain the total investment in ICT for the first year as the sum of hardware and software. For all other years, the total ICT investment may be obtained by applying the growth rate of total ICT investment in ASI. The hardware series can then be calculated as the residual after subtracting the NAS reported software investment from this total. More formally,

$$\mathrm{GFCF}^{J}_{\mathrm{HARD},1998} = \frac{\mathrm{GFCF}^{J}_{\mathrm{SOFT},1998}}{\emptyset_{1998}}$$

where $\mathrm{GFCF}^{J}_{\mathrm{HARD},1998}$ is the GFCF in hardware in 1998 in total registered manufacturing sector, $\mathrm{GFCF}^{J}_{\mathrm{SOFT},1998}$ is the total registered manufacturing investment in software in 1998 and $\emptyset_{1998}$ is the software to hardware ratio for the aggregate economy in 1998. Subsequently, total ICT investment in total registered manufacturing sector may be obtained as:

$$\mathrm{GFCF}^{J}_{\mathrm{ICT},1998} = \mathrm{GFCF}^{J}_{\mathrm{SOFT},1998} + \mathrm{GFCF}^{J}_{\mathrm{HARD},1998}$$

And for $t > 1998$

$$\mathrm{GFCF}^{J}_{\mathrm{ICT},t} = \mathrm{GFCF}^{J}_{\mathrm{ICT},t-1}\left[\frac{\mathrm{GFCF}^{J\_asi}_{\mathrm{ICT},t}}{\mathrm{GFCF}^{J\_asi}_{\mathrm{ICT},t-1}}\right]$$

Since the software data is taken as such from National Accounts, the hardware can be obtained as a residual:

$$\mathrm{GFCF}^{J}_{\mathrm{HARD},t} = \mathrm{GFCF}^{J}_{\mathrm{ICT},t} - \mathrm{GFCF}^{J}_{\mathrm{SOFT},t}$$

While this is still a less perfect approach, the positive side of it is that it ensures complete consistency with NAS reported software data and the trend in aggregate ICT investment in ASI.

References

Arora, A., & Athreye, S. (2002). The software industry and India's economic development. *Information Economics and Policy, 14*(2), 253–273.

Byrne, D. & Corrado, C. (2016). ICT asset prices: Marshaling evidence into new measures. In *The Conference Board Economics Program Working Paper* #16–06.

Baldwin, R. (2016). *The great convergence*. Harvard University Press.

Bresnahan, T. F., Brynjolfsson, E., & Hitt, L. M. (2002). Information technology, workplace organization, and the demand for skilled labor: Firm-level evidence. *The Quarterly Journal of Economics, 117*(1), 339–376.

Central Statistical Organization, The Government of India, Annual Survey of Industries, various issues.

Central Statistical Organization, The Government of India, National Accounts Statistics, various issues.

Commander, S., Harrison, R., & Menezes-Filho, N. (2011). ICT and productivity in developing countries: New firm-level evidence from Brazil and India. *The Review of Economics and Statistics, 93*(2), 528–541.

Das, D. K., Erumban, A. A., Aggarwal, S., & Sengupta, S. (2016). Productivity growth in India under different Policy Regimes. In D. Jorgenson, M. P. Timmer, & K. Fukao (Eds.), *The world economy: Growth or stagnation?* Cambridge University Press.

De Vries, G. J., Mulder, N., Dal Borgo, M., & Hofman, A. A. (2010). ICT investment in Latin America: Does it matter for economic growth? In M. Cimoli, A. A. Hofman, & N. Mulder (Eds.), *Innovation and economic development: The impact of information and communication technologies in Latin America*. Northampton, Massachusetts: Edward Elgar.

Erumban, A. A., & Das, D. K. (2016). Information and communication technology and economic growth in India. *Telecommunications Policy, 40*(5), 412–431.

Erumban, A. A. (2008). Rental prices, rates of return, capital aggregation and productivity: Evidence from EU and US. *CESifo Economic Studies, 3*(54), 499–533.

Inklaar, R., Timmer, M. P., & van Ark, B. (2008). Market services productivity across Europe and the US. *Economic Policy, 25*(33), 139–194.

Jorgenson, D. W. (2001). Information technology and the US economy. *American Economic Review, 91*(1), 1–32.

Jorgenson, D. W., Ho, M. S., & Stiroh, K. J. (2005). *Information technology and the American growth resurgence*. Cambridge, Mass: The MIT Press.

Jorgenson, D. W., & Vu, K. (2005). Information technology and the world economy. *Scandinavian Journal of Economics, 107*(4), 631–650.

Joseph, K. J., & Abraham, V. (2007). *Information technology and productivity: Evidence from India's manufacturing sector*, Working Paper 389. Trivandrum, Kerala, India: Centre for Development Studies.

Jorgenson, D. W., Ho, M. S., & Samuels, J. D. (2011). Information technology and U.S. productivity growth: Evidence from a prototype industry production account. *Journal of Productivity Analysis, 36*(2), 159–175.

Kite, G. (2012). The impact of information technology outsourcing on productivity and output: New evidence from India. In International Conference on Applied Economics (pp. 239–248).

Kite, G. (2013). The role of information technology outsourcing on output, productivity and technical efficiency: Evidence from Indian firms. *Journal of European Economy, 12*(3), 260–285.

Mitra, A., Sharma, C., & Veganzones-Varoudakis, M. (2016). Infrastructure, ICT and firms's productivity and efficiency: An application to the Indian Manufacturing. In F. De Beule & K. Narayanan (Eds.), *Globalization of Indian Industries*, India Studies in Business and Economics. Singapore: Springer Science+Business Media.

Navyashree, G. R., & Bhat, S. (2016). *ICT investments and growth of small and medium firms: A study of food processing industry in India*. Paper presented at the Forum for Global Knowledge Sharing. Madras: Indian Institute of Technology. http://fgks.in/images/pdf/conf/2016/Navyashree.pdf.

Papaioannou, S. K., & Dimelis, S. P. (2007). Information technology as a factor of economic development: Evidence from developed and developing countries. *Economics of Innovation and New Technology, 16*(3), 179–194.

Saith, A., & Vijayabaskar, M. (2005). *ICTs and Indian economic development: Economy, work, regulation*. Sage Publications Pvt. Ltd.

Schreyer, P. (2002). Computer price indices and international growth comparisons. *Review of Income and Wealth, 48*(1), 15–31.

Sharma, S., & Singh, N. (2012). Information technology and productivity in Indian manufacturing. *India policy forum, 2012–13,* 189–238.

The Conference Board. (2016). *The Conference Board Total Economy Database*™, May 2016. https://www.conference-board.org/data/economydatabase/.

Timmer, M., & van Ark, B. (2005). Does information and communication technology drive EU-US productivity growth differentials? *Oxford Economic Papers, 57*(4), 693–716.

van Ark, B., Gupta, A., & Erumban, A. A. (2011). Measuring the contribution of ICT to economic growth. In B. van Ark (Ed.), *The linked world: How ICT is transforming societies, cultures, and economies*. Madrid: Ariel and Fundación Telefónica.

van Ark, B., Inklaar, R., & McGuckin, R. H. (2003). Changing gear: Productivity, ICT and service Industries in Europe and the United States. In J. F. Christensen & P. Maskell (Eds.), *The Industrial dynamics of the new digital economy*. London: Edward Elgar.

Vashisht, P. (2017). Destruction or polarization: Estimating the impact of technology on jobs in Indian manufacturing. *ICRIER working paper 334*.

Technological Disruptions and the Indian IT Industry: Employment Concerns and Beyond

Hastimal Sagara and Keshab Das

Abstract Internet of Things (IoT) industry is one of the most dynamic sectors in India. This US$ 150 billion-strong industry employs 3.8 million people and contributes more than 9% to Indian GDP. However, this largest private-sector employer has been experiencing stress due to fast-changing business models, increased competition from other countries, restrictive visa policies, upsurge in anti-outsourcing sentiments and, most importantly, technological disruptions. These disruptive technologies—captured in a moment in the history of technological transformations as the Fourth Industrial Revolution or *Industrie 4.0*—principally include such developments as cloud computing, big data and analytics, Internet of Things (IoTs), automation, robotics and blockchain. While *Industrie 4.0* has rendered conventional engineering expertise and low-end IT services redundant, it has the potential of creating new employment opportunities in a host of sectors including administration, banks, retail trade and online marketing. Disruptive technologies have a strong chance of transforming the nature and composition of the Indian IT industry in a big way, including endangering India's position as the software superpower in the world. Albeit, the Indian IT industry has historically proved itself to be extraordinarily resilient and fortified during turbulent shocks of the dotcom bubble, the sub-prime crisis and US visa restrictions. Based on secondary data, this paper aims at mapping the changing nature and composition of the Indian IT industry during recent years. It tries to identify contemporary challenges to employment and business opportunities in the Indian IT industry. The paper includes policy suggestions for enhancement of relevant technological and skill capabilities in the country.

Keywords IT industry · Fourth industrial revolution · Technological disruptions · Internet of Things · Robotics · Automation · India

JEL Codes F14 · J23 · J24 · L86 · O33

H. Sagara
GLS University, Ahmedabad, India

K. Das (✉)
Gujarat Institute of Development Research, Ahmedabad, India
e-mail: keshabdas@gmail.com

D. Maiti et al. (eds.), *Digitalisation and Development*,
https://doi.org/10.1007/978-981-13-9996-1_4

1 Introduction

Developing economies, including India, had been deeply influenced by the post-World War II industrialisation strategies that relied mostly on state-led approaches and, to promote import-substitution strategies, undermined the potential of export markets; this was the case at least till the early 1980s. The importance of participating in global markets—as could be facilitated through a lowering of tariffs and relaxing (or, getting rid of) domestic trade and industrial laws—towards promoting a competitive industrial system had come to dominate policy discourse by mid-1980s. During the subsequent years—till the early 2000s—"Governments still mattered but market forces were also critical, and exports were central to achieving scale. Import-competition was critical to ensuring market discipline" (Baldwin 2011: 2).

Experiences with global trade of some of the dynamic emerging economies, including India, appeared in line with what the new trade theory (based on monopolistic firm strategies to product differentiation to remain competitive), attributed to Dixit-Stiglitz model that was perfected in Krugman (1979) had envisaged (Ahmed 2012). However, the later approaches of the developing economies in dealing with 'liberalised' trade were increasingly focused on firm-level differences, especially when 'outsourcing' as an activity dominated trade clearly by the turn of the century (Melitz 2003; Antràs and Helpman 2004). The Indian IT sector rise may be best understood through the rise of what has come to be known as the 'new' new trade theory (NNTT) where the individual firm's strategic responses to challenges and opportunities of global market assume greater significance than the sector *per se*.

The information technology (IT) industry is one of the most accomplished and dynamic sectors in India that has been globally recognised. The industry's phenomenal and historic rise at the turn of the millennium following its unmatched solution to sort out what is termed the 'dotcom bubble' or 'millennium bug' remains a high point in India's technological supremacy in the sphere of the software. India is in the forefront of the rapidly evolving global IT-Business Process Outsourcing (BPO) or, as now known as the Business Process Management (BPM) market and is well established as a 'destination of choice'. It has grown into an over US$ 150 billion industry accounting for two-thirds of the total export of software in the world, and it has created direct employment to the tune of about 3.8 million and indirect employment around 10 million (NASSCOM 2017). Even as the industry could weather a steep fall during the sub-prime crisis in 2008–09, this sector is under stress as during recent times, due to a host of unforeseen obstacles like changing business models, increased competition from other countries, restrictive US and UK visa policies and technological disruptions. However, the most formidable of these is the technological disruptions which are impacting the industry in a big way.

The Fourth Industrial Revolution—also known as *Industrie 4.0*—includes developments in previously disjointed fields such as artificial intelligence and machine learning, robotics, nanotechnology, 3-D printing, and genetics and biotechnology (WEF 2016: 3). The inevitable acceleration of technology will 'disrupt', radically and fundamentally, global employment and the nature of work. For instance, robots can work continuously, as they become more flexible and easier to train for new tasks, they will become an increasingly attractive alternative to human workers, even when wages are low (Ford 2015: 9). Digital platforms and improvements in communication technologies have been squeezing transaction costs and information asymmetries (Productivity Commission 2016: 25). For instance, innovations in power storage battery and metering would disrupt the traditional models of power generation, transmission and monitoring.[1] Digital technologies offer greater scope for the market use of household assets, including labour (Productivity Commission 2016: 19). E-commerce has set in the fierce competition in the retail business (Kaur 2015). *Industrie 4.0* will transform labour markets in the next five years, leading to a net loss of over 5 million jobs in 15 major developed and emerging economies.[2]

With this backdrop, this paper attempts to identify the emerging services in the IT industry and tries to map new opportunities and challenges of the transformation from traditional low-end IT services of the back office and other repetitive tasks to high-end technical skilled-based ones. It tries to map the impact of technological disruptions on the IT industry in India. It is important to note that due to paucity of the relevant database on several dimensions of the impact of new technology, arguments and concluding statements have generally been drawn upon reports and newspaper articles published by responsible institutions. The remaining part of the paper is divided into four sections. Section 2 discusses the growth and composition of the IT Industry in India in recent decades. Section 3 deals with the present phase of transformation in the IT services through technological innovations like mobile applications, cloud computing and automation. Section 4 attempts to identify opportunities and challenges for the IT industry in India. Concluding observations and policy suggestions have been presented in Section 5.

2 Growth of the Indian IT Industry

Reasons behind the growth of the IT industry in India have varied over time. As summarised in Table 1, the 1980s witnessed cost arbitrage through software development and time and material (T and M) pricing as the prime reason behind the growth of the IT industry in India. During the 1990s through greater collaborative efforts, Indian IT firms contributed notably towards improving standards and productivity of western buyers even through non-critical functions. The period 2000–10

---

[1]An impression about the nature and impact of such technological disruption may be had from the following example. "The Tesla Powerwall home battery is a household technology enabled by Li-ion battery storage and has the potential to be highly disruptive. The Powerwall is a battery module that enables large amounts of electricity to be stored at the user's home. The battery can be charged using electricity from solar panels, or from the grid during non-peak energy use periods when rates are low. This stored electricity can then be used to power the home during peak hours" (Productivity Commission 2016: 208).

[2]https://www.weforum.org/press/2016/01/five-million-jobs-by-2020-the-real-challenge-of-the-fourth-industrial-revolution/ (Accessed June 5, 2018).

Table 1 Major factors responsible for the growth of the IT industry in India

Time	Major reason	Factors
1980–90	Cost arbitrage	Software development, T and M pricing
1990–2000	Collaboration	Improving standards and productivity through non-critical functions, project-based, fixed cost, T and M pricing
2000–10	Value addition	End-to-end services, non-linear growth, strategic partnerships, pay-as-you-use
2010–15	Enabling smart enterprise	Bimodel IT, digital BUs, automation platforms, IoT, smart tech, innovation, outcome-based risk-reward, start-up ecosystem

Source http://www.nasscom.in/impact-indias-growth

experienced value addition through a non-linear growth, end-to-end services and partnerships in the IT industry. In the current period, automation platforms, smart technology and innovations have emerged as dominant features.

The Indian IT industry grew at a snail's pace till the end of the previous century but, thereafter, a major shift upward was observed during 2000–15. The revenue shot up from around US$ 1 billion during 1980–90 to US$ 167 billion during 2015–18 (Fig. 1). The Indian IT industry was in a nascent stage during the 1980s with about 1000 firms employing a mere 0.06 million people. However, during 2010–15, there were more than 16,000 IT firms employing about four million people (Figs. 2 and 3). That the future of employment in the IT industry is quite uncertain may take exceptional turns have been a matter of emerging concerns. For instance, it is estimated that in the period up to 2022, around 75 million jobs across industries may be displaced by a shift in the division of labour between humans and machines, while 133 million new roles may emerge that are more adapted to the new division of labour between humans, machines and algorithms (WEF 2018: 10). For instance, around 20–33% out of the 1.5 million engineering graduates every year run the risk

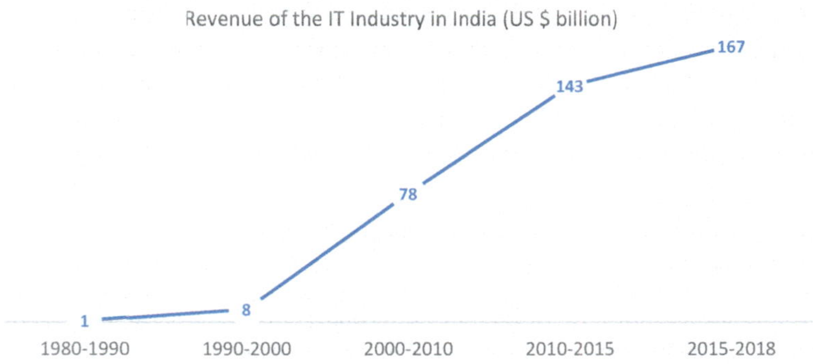

Fig. 1 Revenue from the IT industry in India. *Source* Drawn on data obtained from http://www.nasscom.in/impact-indias-growth

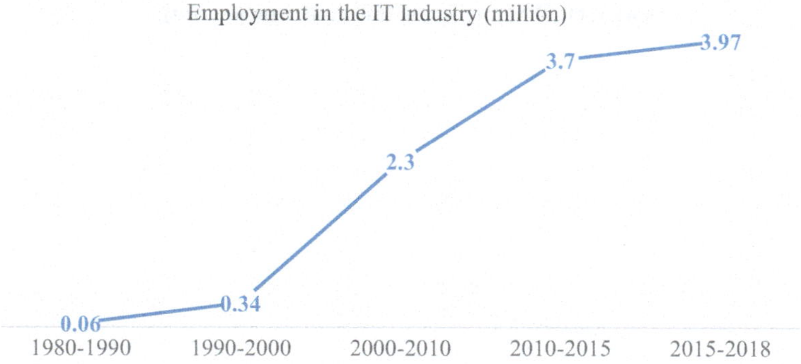

Fig. 2 Employment in the IT industry in India. *Source* Drawn on data obtained from http://www.nasscom.in/impact-indias-growth

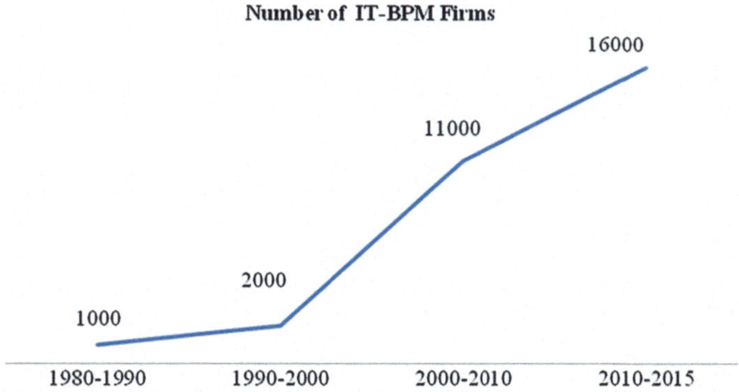

Fig. 3 Number of firms in the IT industry. *Source* Drawn on data obtained from http://www.nasscom.in/impact-indias-growth

of not getting a job at all in India due to sharp fall in the demand for IT-related jobs in India due to non-linear growth models of IT companies and a lesser number of men required to handle the same jobs as before due to a higher degree of automation[3]. This industry enjoys the distinction of being the single largest private-sector contributor to the GDP at 9.3% (Fig. 4). Even, IT exports rose at a CAGR of 12.9% from US$ 26 billion in the 2010s to US$ 117 billion in 2017 and its share was over 56% in total services exports from India (Fig. 5).

According to NASSCOM, the IT-BPM sector had generated revenue of US$ 150 billion and had made exports worth US$ 100 billion in 2017. Indian IT companies have set up over 600 delivery centres across the world and are engaged in providing services with their presence in over 200 cities across 78 countries and India continues

[3]https://dazeinfo.com/2014/10/28/1-5-million-engineering-pass-outs-india-every-year-fewer-getting-hired-trends/ (Accessed June 10, 2018)

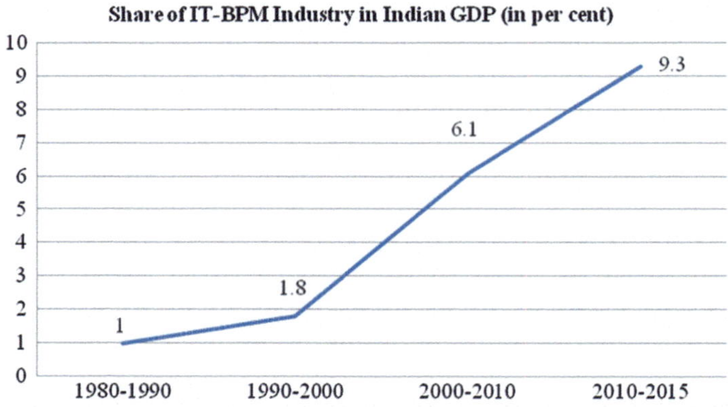

Fig. 4 Share of the IT industry in Indian GDP. *Source* Drawn on data obtained from http://www.nasscom.in/impact-indias-growth

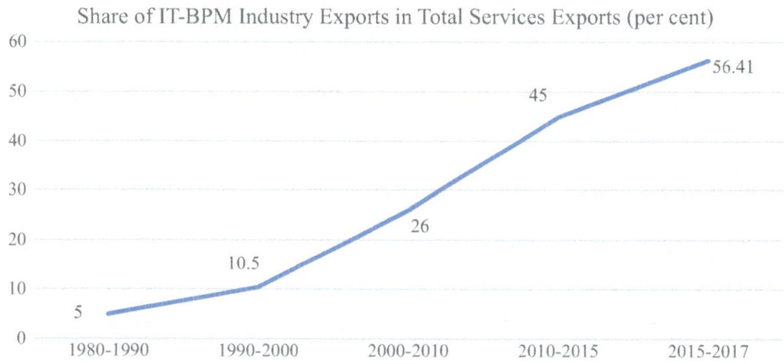

Fig. 5 Share of the IT industry in Indian services exports. *Source* Drawn on data obtained from http://www.nasscom.in/impact-indias-growth

to maintain a leadership position in the global sourcing arena accounting for almost 56% of the global market share in 2017.

Although India has had significant success in the IT services, it is yet to strike gold with IT products and intellectual property (Sadagopan 2012). Given that TCS, Infosys, Wipro and Genpact are renowned brands from India, there is no single IT product company yet like Microsoft, Facebook or Google. Bengaluru, Chennai, Mumbai and Hyderabad have earned their names as IT hubs, but the Silicon Valley of USA dominates in the field of IT innovations. Mani (2014) identifies three reasons for Indian IT firms not being able to break into the highly oligopolistic market of IT products. First, Indian IT firms did not have the domain expertise to create products. Second, they did not want to take risks. Third, India was not a big market for IT products in the past. Majority of the Indian IT firms operate on business-to-business (B2B) models, and not many have adopted the business-to-consumer (B2C) model.

Fig. 6 Export revenue from sub-sectors of the IT industry (2012–13). *Source* Drawn on data sourced from a report by India Brand Equity Foundation

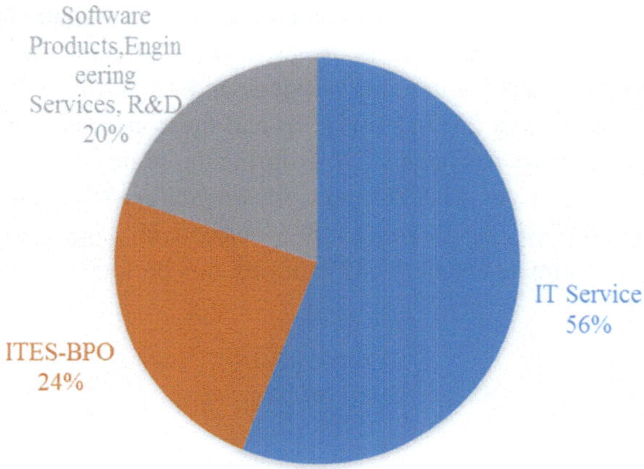

Fig. 7 Export revenue from sub-sectors of the IT industry (2017–18). *Source* Dawn on data sourced from https://meity.gov.in/content/performance-contribution-towards-exports-it-ites-industry

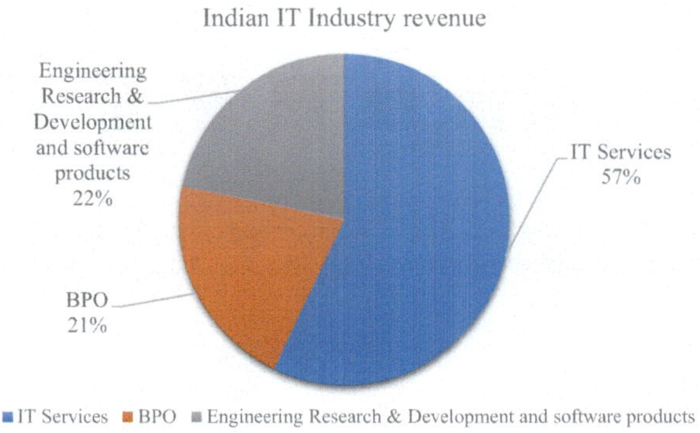

Hailed as a global giant, paradoxically, the Indian IT industry predominantly provides low-end IT services like BPO and IT software services. Figure 6 suggests that IT services and IT-BPO accounted for around 80% of the export earnings from this industry in 2012–13. As per Fig. 7, IT Services exports accounted for the largest share of 57% of about US$ 86.0 billion, Engineering R & D and software products has emerged as the second-largest segment with 21.8% share followed by BPO exports contributing 21.2%. Interestingly, while there is a continuous rise in the absolute value of the software product and engineering services, its relative share is just one-fifth of the total exports of this industry. In fact, from both the figures it is clear that the software products, engineering services, R and D that are categorised as high-end IT services had reported only a marginal rise from 20 to 22% during the five years between 2012–13 and 2017–18.

According to the *National Policy on Software Products*,[4] "The total revenue of the software product industry in India was US$ 6.1 billion, of which US$ 2 billion

[4]https://cis-india.org/internet-governance/files/national-policy-on-software-products.pdf (accessed June 10, 2018).

was from exports. However, comparing the Indian software product industry with its Western counterparts, it is still in its infancy" (p. 4). The IT services, software product and engineering services and IT-ITES-BPO have almost tripled between 2009–10 and 2018–19 (Fig. 8) and the compound annual growth rate (CAGR) for the industry has been 12.26% during the same period. The CAGR during 2013–2018 for IT services, IT-BPO and software product and engineering services were recorded as 10.07%, 9.19% and 13.09% respectively, and the CAGR for the entire industry was estimated to be 10.32% during this period (Fig. 9).

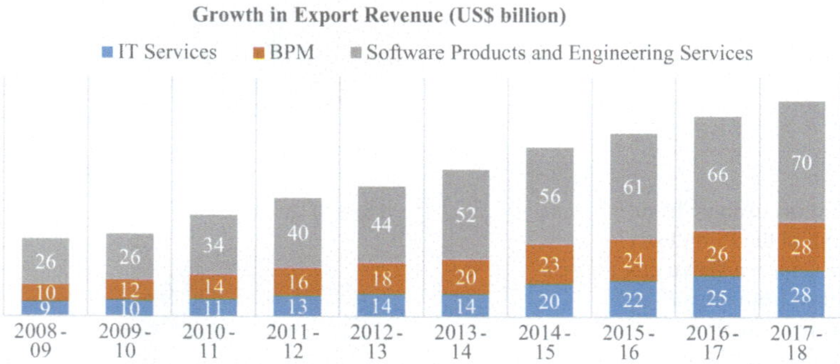

Fig. 8 Segment-wise export revenue trends in the IT industry. *Source* Drawn on data from https://www.ibef.org/uploads/industry/Infrographics/large/it-and-ite-nov-2018.pdf

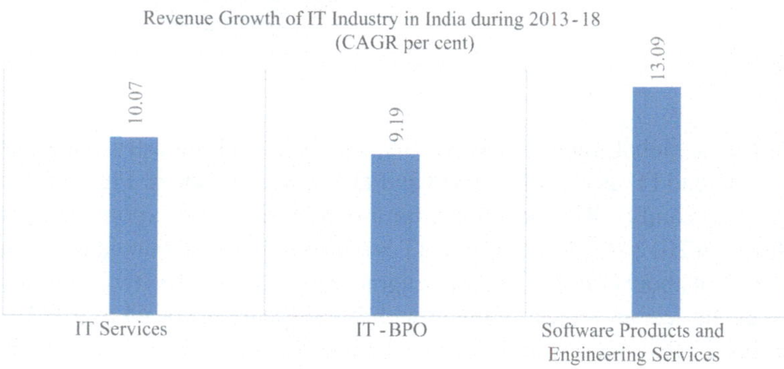

Fig. 9 CAGR of revenue of IT industry in India, 2013–18 (per cent). *Source* Drawn on data from http://deity.gov.in/content/performance-contribution-towards-exports-it-ITES-industry

3 Employment Implications

3.1 Data and Methodology

The empirical analyses relate to data on the IT sector and GDP Services for the years 1999–2017. As indicated earlier, the Indian IT industry had taken off since 1999 following the solution to the Y2K problem contributing significantly to the generation of employment, exports and GDP of India. Since the industry was typically dominated by low-end IT services, the introduction of 'disruptive' technologies like cloud, big data and analytics and automation in certain spheres has emerged as a challenge to the sustenance of existing jobs or creation of future jobs and obtaining orders from global buyers. Further, as IT-ITeS form an important component of the services sector, GDP Services is likely to be affected by technological disruptions. Hence, as shown in Table 2, variables such as employment, market size, exports and GDP Services have been included in the empirical analysis; all the values are in current prices.

Table 2 Aspects of growth of the IT industry in India, 1999–2017

Year	Employment in IT industry (million)	Market size of IT industry (US$ billion)	Total IT exports (US$ billion)	GDP services
1999–00	0.66	7.63	3.71	11198.5
2000–01	1.86	11.94	6.54	11799.8
2001–02	0.53	13.12	7.93	12,611.6
2002–03	0.68	15.42	9.86	13,490.4
2003–04	0.84	20.79	12.97	14,578.0
2004–05	1.06	28.18	18.05	15,762.6
2005–06	1.31	38.67	25.69	17,481.7
2006–07	1.62	49.58	33.22	19,239.7
2007–08	2.01	70.70	47.02	21,215.6
2008–09	2.21	73.40	50.41	23,332.5
2009–10	2.30	73.70	49.7	25,781.7
2010–11	2.54	74.00	59.0	28,273.8
2011–12	2.77	88.00	68.8	30,130.4
2012–13	2.77	101.00	76.5	32,009.5
2013–14	3.29	108.00	87.3	34,215.5
2014–15	3.52	118.00	97.8	37,269.6
2015–16	3.69	147.00	107.8	40,467.6
2016–17	3.86	143.00	117.0	43,469.1

Source For the IT sector data, NASSCOM and, for GDP Services data, *National Accounts Statistics*, Central Statistical Office. (Relevant years)

3.2 An Empirical Analysis

An attempt has been made through econometric analyses to establish the relationship between employment and growth of the IT industry, especially in terms of rising market demand, domestic as well as foreign. The massive rise in jobs in the IT sector in the country has often been cited as a high point in this sector's contribution to the economic progress of the country and also an acknowledgement of the quality of Indian IT-ITES personnel. The demand for labour in each industry is a derived demand. The size of the demand for the final product produced by the industry, hence, is a critical factor affecting the industry employment level. In the case of the Indian IT industry, the size of the market can be taken to be consisting of two components, namely, the domestic market (DM) and export market (EM). The growth of the Indian IT industry is historically driven by exports while the size of domestic IT market has been comparatively small. It is predicted that both these components of the IT market will favourably affect employment generation in the Indian IT industry.

In addition to the size of the market for IT, the employment level in the Indian IT industry can be expected to be related to the size of the services sector (SS). The growth of different areas of the services sector like finance, e-commerce, marketing, etc., has strong linkages with the IT industry. Higher the size of services sector greater is the employment level in the IT industry. Moreover, the global financial crisis may have affected the employment generation in the Indian IT industry. The period 2007–08 to 2009–10, during which the global financial sector had seen huge uncertainty had dragged the overall global growth. This shrinking global demand was likely to hurt the employment level in the Indian IT industry.

Keeping the above postulations, the study has used the following empirical framework to examine the determinants of employment in the Indian IT industry:

$$\mathrm{lnLAB}_t = \beta_0 + \beta_1 \mathrm{lnEM}_t + \beta_2 \mathrm{lnDM}_t + \beta_3 \mathrm{lnSS}_t + \beta_3 \mathrm{GF} + \varepsilon_t \quad (1)$$

where explanatory variables are as measured in Table 3 and ε_t is the random error term.

Equation 1 was estimated for the Indian IT industry for data concerning the period 1999–2000 to 2016–17. Given that issues of non-stationarity could arise only for a long period, and our study period is 18 years, the study has used the OLS method of estimation. The estimation results are presented in Table 4.

The initial problem faced by the study was that our sample suffered from strong multicollinearity as the mean value of variance inflating factor (VIF) for the independent variables was 22.47 while the condition number was 299. The VIF values for lnEM_t, lnSS_t and lnDM_t, respectively, stood at 45.14, 22.79 and 20.04.

To overcome the severity of this problem, the study preferred a modified Gram–Schmidt orthogonalisation procedure (Golub and Van Loan 1996) and created a new set of orthogonal for these three variables. In this successive orthogonalisation process, we have arranged lnEM_t, lnDM_t and lnSS_t by their theoretical importance in affecting employment. Industry output, namely, lnEM_t and lnDM_t are the most

Table 3 Description and measurement of variables

Variables	Symbols	Measurements
Dependent variable		
Labour	$\ln LAB_t$	Natural log of number of employment in Indian IT industry in the year t.
Independent variables		
Demand conditions		
Export market	$\ln EM_t$	Natural log of IT exports (US$ billion) from in year *t*
Domestic market	$\ln DM_t$	Natural log of domestic IT market size (US$ billion) in India in year *t*
Size of service sector		
Service sector	$\ln SS_t$	Natural log of the size of service sector in India (constant Indian Rs.) of in year *t*
Global financial crisis		
Global financial crisis dummy	GF_t	Takes unity value for years 2007–08 to 2009–10, zero otherwise

Table 4 Determinants of employment in the Indian IT industry

Dependent variable: natural log of no. of employment	
Independent variables	Coefficients (robust t-statistic)
$\ln EM_t$	0.554*** (5.608)
$\ln DM_t$	0.00,656 (0.126)
$\ln SS_t$	0.112*** (4.062)
GF_t	0.0406 (0.430)
Constant	14.38*** (190.7)
F (4, 13)	27.88
Prob > F	0.0000
Observations	18
R-squared	0.837

Note: Robust t-statistics in parentheses; ***$p < 0.01$, **$p < 0.05$, *$p < 0.1$; $\ln EM_t$, $\ln DM_t$ and $\ln SS_t$ are orthogonalised variables as described in the text

Table 5 Correlation coefficient between exports and employment by major IT segments, 1999–2016

Segment	Coefficient
IT services	0.977[a]
BPO/BPM	0.892[a]

Notes $N = 17$
[a]Correlation is significant at the 0.01 level (2-tailed)

important determinants compared to the size of the services sector in the economy. Re-calculation of the VIF on the new matrix of transformed explanatory variables reveals a mean VIF of 1.47 and a condition index of 2.67. The maximum VIF for individual explanatory variables is 1.93. This suggests that orthogonalisation of concerned explanatory variables has contained the severity of multicollinearity in the sample.

Within the Indian IT industry, the two segments that have grown notably since the late 1990s are i. the IT services and ii. The IT-BPO/BPM segment. These were also the segments where external demand had remained high, and the major share of jobs had been concentrated. To estimate the correlation coefficient between employment and exports by these segments, a bivariate Pearson correlation was run (on SPSS 16). The results have been presented in Table 5. It is obvious that the correlation between exports and employment in both segments has been strong and significant.

4 Emerging IT Services and New Technologies

Till around 2005, the Indian IT industry was largely dominated by call centres that focused on outsourcing services in business processes at costs considered low internationally. However, the industry has subsequently diversified in terms of IT services and the IT firms have grown into strategic business partners for their western clients. The number of BPO deals has been decreasing since 2013 with organisations typically looking for alternative options for cost reduction, such as greater use of shared service. It remains to be seen as to whether this points to a shrinking share of business process offshoring (KPMG 2016).

Key growth drivers for global businesses for technology and BPM spending in 2019, according to the NASSCOM's (2018–19: 12) *CEO Survey*, would be to digitise the core and build a truly digital organisation, build customer value through enhanced customer experience, unlock growth with new revenue opportunities, enhanced efficiency and modernisation and cost optimisation in their decreasing order. Digitizing business than just silos and enhanced customer experience are the top two spending areas for IT and BPM. However, cost optimisation was a much lower priority. Further, the top technology priorities for global businesses in 2019 were advanced analytics and AI, hybrid cloud, cybersecurity, devices and IoTs and blockchain. Advanced Analytics and AI are the top priorities for over 50% of the CEOs, and hybrid cloud and cybersecurity are witnessing increased spending (NASSCOM 2018–19: 12).

New IT services have emerged, and this industry has been adopting new business models over the last 15 years or so. The IT industry is a knowledge-based and services-centric sector and, hence, has been passing through a major technological transition. Such developments have posed a challenge before the Indian IT industry to assert its leadership position again. Constant innovations in Software Mobile Analytics Cloud (SMAC) technologies have been recognised as both a serious threat as well as a source of 'new' employment in the sector. Firms in India are exploring new opportunities in SMAC that have a tremendous potential to fulfil the demand not only in the so far untapped domestic market but also in other Asian and African countries. Newly set up firms during the last half a decade are attempting to exploit the SMAC technologies for their businesses in agriculture, healthcare and education.

4.1 Cloud Computing

Cloud computing is proving to be a breakthrough innovation as it offers benefits in terms of storing huge volumes of data with security with no investment in hardware. With the explosion of voice and visual data, it has become untenable for every organisation to cater to their requirements individually, thereby making the public cloud an attractive option to store important data (Cherian 2014). Most small businesses that have migrated to the cloud have reduced their cost of running applications as the cloud service provider has been investing in infrastructure and not the business firms. In the IT sphere, cloud computing includes Infrastructure-as-a-Service (IaaS), Platform-as-a-Service (PaaS) and Software-as-a-Service (SaaS) and provides a perfect platform on which unorganised data could be loaded, crunched and analysed (Sen 2015: 78–79). Cloud computing has opened up a whole world of possible industry disruptions allowing start-ups and SMEs to compete successfully with long-established enterprises (Bhattacharya 2016) and SaaS is the preferred model of over 50% of Indian product companies. Software and services revenue crossed US$ 150 billion during 2017–18 (NASSCOM 2018: 6). In India, 65% of large enterprises is making use of cloud technology, services and solutions as part of their IT infrastructure (Bhattacharya 2016).

Firms in the business of cloud computing possess sophisticated monitoring systems, multi-layered security safeguards and centralised management. Cloud-based applications, hosted by third-party vendors, have been helping replace the traditional warehouse management system that requires substantial investments in physical infrastructure and its maintenance and software licenses. People from across places could share/store data in the public domain of cloud services.

They are outsourcing IT software functions to distant data storage open doors to new security threats such as security breaches, data theft and service traffic hijacking. The risk in cloud computing is much more serious, particularly if it leads to a security breach or data loss by a bank or defence company or national security agency. The possible threats to cloud security identified by experts of the Cloud Security Alliance (CSA) are data breaches, data loss, account or service traffic hijacking, insecure interfaces, denial of services, malicious insiders, abuse of cloud services, insufficient due diligence and shared technology vulnerability[5]. There were more than 10,000 cases of cybercrime in India in 2016. India is ranked third after the United States and Japan among the countries most affected by online banking malware (Dawar and Lacy 2017).

India needs a large number of cybersecurity experts to protect firms from the increasing number of cyber frauds, cyberattacks and theft of sensitive information. Government departments like vigilance, police, intelligence and defence demand cybersecurity experts for their requirements. There is a whole range of demand arising from state agencies, corporate sector and even households and for investigation, surveillance and even spying.

4.2 Internet of Things (IoT) and Automation

IoT is a technology that connects devices such as mobile phones, digital watches, fitness bands and other digital machines through the internet, WiFi or GPS to share information among concerned persons. It allows physical objects to be sensed and controlled remotely across existing network infrastructure, creating opportunities for more direct integration between the physical world and computer-based systems and resulting in improved efficiency, accuracy and economic benefits (Modi 2015). Examples could include drone, driverless car and chatbot. According to World Bank estimates, automation threatens 69% of the jobs in India[6] but at the same time can potentially create numerous business opportunities to expand product and services offerings. It permits IT firms to harvest data on an unimaginable scale through devices that provide rich streams of data continuously. In the long run, the size of data generated will increase exponentially, creating new avenues for data managers, researchers and analysts to map consumer tastes and preferences to obtain business insights. As Shrikanth (2015: 12) predicted: "By 2020, there will be 50 billion networked devices and this level of connectivity will have profound social, political and economic consequences."

As per the *Business Process Management Report*, technology and automation are fast emerging as one of the key levers to create best-in-class business process management outcomes and Robotic Process Automation (RPA) is now emerging as an unassisted automation approach that offers high-value creation at relatively lower risk along with the opportunities of significant cost savings, better service delivery and manageability, and quicker time-to-value. The chatbots function as robotic customer service representatives for a host of companies such as taxi, e-commerce, news and weather and are increasingly being deployed globally and

[5]https://www.darkreading.com/vulnerabilities---threats/cloud-security-alliance-names-top-7-threats-to-the-cloud/d/d-id/1133074 (Accessed June 15, 2018).

[6]http://www.thehindu.com/business/Industry/Automation-threatens-69-jobs-in-India-World-Bank/article 15427 005.ece (Accessed June 5, 2018).

in India (Agrawal 2016a). The chatbots could spell the significant loss of revenue for BPOs along with leading to erosion of low-end repetitive jobs (Agrawal 2016b). Automation, with significant implications for employment in the Indian IT industry, is increasingly becoming a change enabler for Indian IT services. In 2018, an average of 71% of total task hours across the 12 industries covered in the report were performed by humans, compared to 29% by machines; but by 2022 this average is expected to have shifted to 58% task hours performed by humans and 42% by machines (WEF 2018: 10).

4.3 Big Data, Analytics and E-Commerce

Big data will enable implementing and monitoring several interconnected systems managing public amenities and services and features that will support 'smart' aspects of smart cities. Big data and analytics are going to play a pivotal role in checking illegal use of resources like water and electricity and would prevent various types of wastage. Improving citizen security, optimisation of water supply, and efficient power distribution are just a few examples of what big data could do to take the smart cities concept to the next level (Kiran 2015).

Big data and analytics are helping business firms to predict consumer tastes and preferences. The e-commerce industry has brought a mixed bag of opportunities and threats. While this sector has created new employment opportunities for a range of other sectors the challenges of predatory pricing, sale of poor quality products, delivery of wrong products and non-payment of claimed refunds remain some of its grey areas. Further, there have been cases of illegal trade and smuggling of endangered animals, their body parts and rare species of plants on e-commerce portals.

Cloud computing, e-commerce and domestic technology services grew at 43%, 17% and 10%, respectively, during 2017–18 (NASSCOM 2018: 5). The online business has been creating employment opportunities for transporters, courier and packaging companies. Having experienced cuts in their profit margins, even small retailers are increasingly going online. Smartphones have fuelled the growth of the e-commerce industry in India. Social media, particularly, Facebook and WhatsApp, have been extensively used in promoting online business in India. Although no country-level information is available yet, global estimates[7] suggest that these disruptive technologies are likely to have a trillion-dollar economic impact, viz., mobile technology (US$ 3.7–10.8 trillion), automation and robotics (US$ 5.2–6.7 trillion), IoT (US$ 2.7–6.2 trillion) and cloud computing (US$ 1.7–6.2 trillion) every year. These technologies can potentially be used in almost all sectors of the economy creating ample job opportunities for technicians, IT professionals and engineers. It is important to mention that 3D printing is another field that could potentially transform manufacturing in the entire world, including India. Although 3D printing is in

[7]Drawn on information obtained from McKinsey Global Institute (2013).

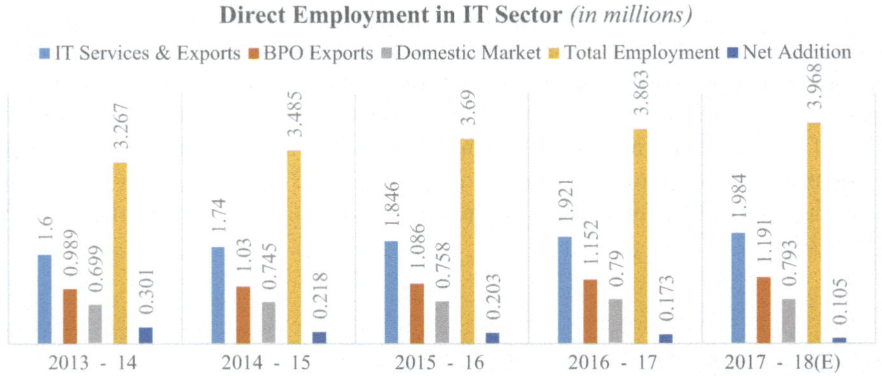

Fig. 10 Direct employment in the IT sector in India. *Source* Drawn on data sourced from https://meity.gov.in/content/employment

its nascent stage, it could create an economic impact of US$ 230–550 billion every year.

The IT industry is a major employer of the urban youth in India. As shown in Fig. 10, more and more jobs were created in this industry between 2012–13 and 2017–18. It is estimated that about 3.97 million people were employed in this sector in 2017–18. Within the IT industry, the sub-sectors, namely, export-driven IT services and BPO have the largest share in total employment. Domestic market of this industry had increased from 0.699 million to 0.793 million between 2012–13 and 2017–18. However, it makes just one-fifth of the total employment in the sector. Moreover, the net addition to the direct employment in 2017–18 is reduced to its one third in 2013–14.

In the changing context of the rise of disruptive technologies as a business driver, it is imperative that IT service providers not only reduce costs but deliver business outcomes in terms of value and impact (Nair 2015). The large IT corporate firms in India are increasingly becoming fast solution providers for their clients.

The IT industry has been moving into Tier-II cities as well. Among the IT landscape, a greater number of firms belongs to enterprise software, fintech, healthtech and adtech category (Fig. 11). It may be observed that the Indian IT industry provides service somewhere at the low-end or middle of the IT value chain. Looking at IT verticals, BFSI (18%), across sectors (17%), healthcare (17%) and next-generation commerce (15%) occupy the dominant share (Fig. 12). As per the NASSCOM's Product Compendia Beta, the concentration of IT firms was found the highest in Bengaluru followed by Delhi NCR, Mumbai, Chennai, Hyderabad and Pune, in that order.[8] All these developments point to a maturing of the IT industry in India and building up of potential to handle high-end technology services.

[8]http://www.productsmade.in/ Accessed June 5, 2016.

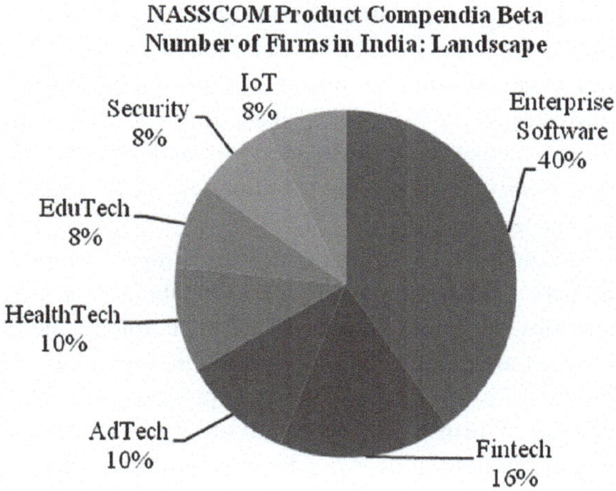

Fig. 11 Firms in India: Landscape. *Source* Drawn on data obtained from http://www.productsmade.in/. *Note* Product Compendia Beta for Landscape refers to digital technologies available as products for digital solutions across sectors

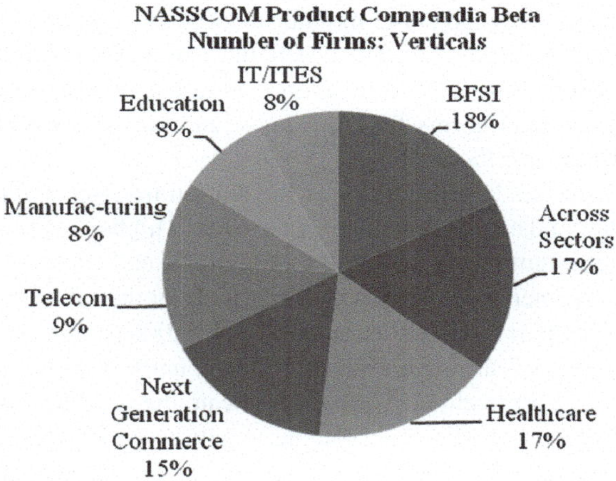

Fig. 12 Firms in India: verticals. *Source* Drawn on data obtained from http://www.productsmade.in/. *Note* Product Compendia Beta for Verticals refers to a particular digital technology available for common problems across sectors

5 Opportunities and Challenges

Digital technologies have unleashed what is being called the Fourth Industrial Revolution. A combination of technological advancements is transforming consumer lives, creating value for the business, and unlocking broader societal benefits at an unprecedented scale. The potential value at stake is estimated at a massive US$ 100 trillion over the next 10 years. In India alone, digitalisation can lead to benefits valued at more than US$ 5 trillion. The IT company Accenture estimated the impact of technological disruptions as follows: Virtual collaboration and talent portals can reduce hiring costs by approximately 10%, cloud-based accounting systems and AI-driven automation can reduce costs by approximately 40%, cloud computing can reduce IT system costs by 25–50%, autonomous transport and sensors for monitoring supply chains can cut costs by 50%, crowdsourcing and AI can improve productivity by 20–40% (Dawar and Lacy 2017). As technological breakthroughs rapidly shift the frontier between the work tasks performed by humans and those performed by machines and algorithms, global labour markets are undergoing major transformations, however, if these transformations are managed wisely, could lead to a new age of good work, good jobs and improved quality of life for all, but if managed poorly, pose the risk of widening skills gaps, greater inequality and broader polarisation (WEF 2018: 9).

Automation has the potential to bring revolutionary changes in the Indian IT industry. Automation, being seen as a labour-replacing technology, could also create new jobs. As, in all likelihood, it may eradicate the need for human intervention in different areas, especially high-volume, repetitive tasks, jobs related to IT support, remote infrastructure, and business processes may be adversely impacted. Additionally, the IT firms find a high rate of labour attrition as a major concern. Therefore, they are switching over to newer technologies that involve limited human intervention. Seeing the potential of IoT, the government is promoting IoT to capitalise on the business opportunities by improving the supply chain, better delivery of services by smart cities and closer monitoring of production lines. For example, to make Andhra Pradesh a hub for IoT by 2020, the state government has been creating 10 IoT hubs by providing land on lease on easy terms, offering relaxed fiscal and administrative procedural norms for companies, and building world-class IT infrastructure (*The Times of India* 2016a).

As the Fourth Industrial Revolution unfolds, companies are seeking to harness new and emerging technologies to reach higher levels of efficiency of production and consumption, expand into new markets, and compete on new products for a global consumer base composed increasingly of digital natives (WEF 2018: 9). According to a report by Great Learning, "Over 50,000 positions in the fields of data science and machine learning are vacant in the country owing to a lack of skilled workforce".[9] As, in all likelihood, it may eradicate the need for human intervention in different areas, especially high-volume, repetitive tasks, jobs related to IT support, remote infrastructure, and business processes may be adversely impacted. Therefore, they are switching over to newer technologies that involve limited human intervention.[10]

[9]http://timesofindia.indiatimes.com/articleshow/66259707.cms?utm_source=contentofinterest&utm_medium=text&utm_campaign=cppst.

[10]This process is described thus: "Digital tools are creating a new informal "gig economy," where workers can combine a number of disconnected tasks to earn their incomes. In many cases, these gig economy platforms have disrupted traditional markets in the 'real world' as well; for example, Uber has confronted taxi unions and regulators in a number of countries, while Airbnb (which allows someone to rent out their residence partly or in entirety) has challenged the hotel industry. Concerns about these platforms include the lack of price floors, little social safety nets, and difficulties in regulating the entry and behaviour of workers, customers, and the platforms themselves. Regulating these platforms has proven to be challenging" (World Bank Group 2015: 7).

6 The Threat of Technological Disruptions

Most of the big IT companies in India are investing heavily in automation of processes in their traditional businesses like BPO, application management and infrastructure management (*The Times of India* 2016b). At this stage, only big IT firms can create tools and platforms for automation in infrastructure, application, testing and BSP service due to their capability in terms of investment, sophisticated technology and business network with multinational corporations. This will have a two-fold impact on employment; firstly, drop in hiring and second, removing some of the existing labour. It has been argued that while all jobs are at risk of automation, it is the "routine" and "predictable" jobs that will be impacted most (Ford 2015: 10). To shift to automation, major IT companies in India are reducing their employee strength in recent times (Fig. 13). As shown in Fig. 14, the headcount of six top IT companies—TCS, Cognizant, Infosys, Wipro, HCL and Tech Mahindra—put together dropped by 4157 in the first six months of 2017–18 compared to an increase of almost

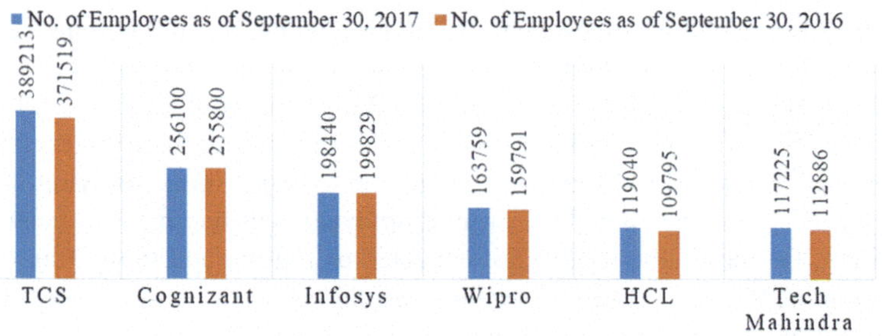

Fig. 13 Employment in major IT-ITES companies in India. *Source* Drawn on data sourced from Das and Phadnis (2017)

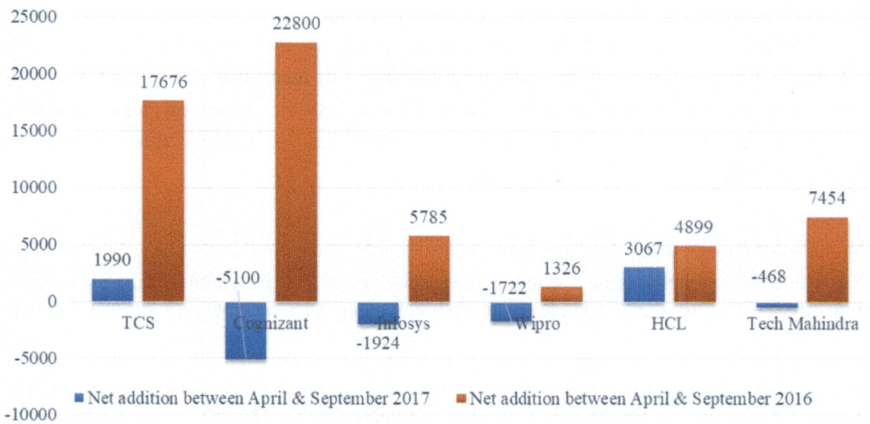

Fig. 14 Impact of automation on jobs in select Indian IT-ITES companies. *Source* Drawn on data sourced from Das and Phadnis (2017)

60,000 during the same period last fiscal year (Das and Phadnis 2017). New sets of skill required for the existing workforce, automated machines replacing labour for repetitive tasks and artificial intelligence are important factors behind this shift in recruitment in the industry.

As the nature of IT, application in various processes would transform, it would seriously impact employment prospects for conventional tasks in different industries. Both the possibilities and limits appear beyond easy comprehension.[11] Google's driverless car would reduce demand for the regular driver of cars. Similarly, repetitive tasks in a factory would be handled by robots in the future, replacing human labour again. Interestingly, the impact of labour-reducing and labour-replacing would be felt more at the bottom of the pyramid of work hierarchy, however, the top management of the companies would be least affected by robotics and smart machines. Technological disruptions such as robotics and machine learning—rather than completely replacing existing occupations and job categories—are likely to substitute specific tasks previously carried out as part of these jobs, freeing workers up to focus on new tasks and leading to rapidly changing core skill sets in these occupations (WEF 2016: 7).

In the absence of any comprehensive database on the manner in which the future of work in this sector would unfold, a recent survey-based study (FICCI et al. 2017: 72) estimated that by 2022 in the Indian IT-BPM sector would have 4.5 million jobs of which while 10–20% would be 'new' jobs (requiring hitherto-unavailable new skills) 60–65% jobs would require 'changes' in existing skills implying upgrading skills. By 2022, no less than 54% of all employees will require significant re- and up-skilling. Of these, about 35% are expected to require additional training of up to six months, 9% will require re-skilling lasting six to 12 months, while 10% will require additional skills training of more than a year (WEF 2018: 11). HfS Research (2016) taking note of the fast progress in the automation and digital technologies predicted that by 2021 demand for low-skilled and routine jobs would drop sharply by 30% globally and the number of loss of such low-end jobs would be around 0.64 million in India. However, new IT jobs in India would grow by 14% to about 0.16 million. Job cuts in Indian IT companies would be around 0.2 million per year in the next three years, due to under-preparedness in adopting newer technologies (Lakshmikanth 2017). Based on the job profiles of their employee base today, nearly 50% of companies expect that automation would lead to some reduction in their full-time workforce by 2022 (WEF 2018: 10).

[11]Regarding the possibilities and limits of new technologies, as these unfold through growing applications, "Opportunities exist to leverage analytics, algorithms, and drones in the near future to protect and potentially expand markets. In the medium to long term, robots and driverless cars will also likely gain adoption although, as with any technology, how they will be deployed will likely evolve over time. Factors affecting the adoption of the new technologies and business models examined in this paper include business profitability; environmental considerations that may accelerate the use the technology that save carbon emission, customary safety and trust concerns regarding new technology, labour issues with crowdsourcing and other models; and regulations governing drones, robots, and driverless cars" (Standard Business Graduate School 2016: 13).

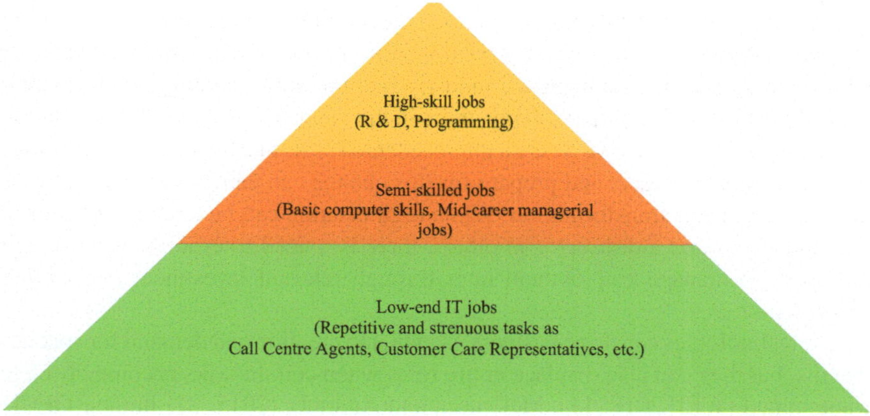

Fig. 15 Risk of job losses due to new technologies at different work hierarchy. *Source* https://www.gsb.stanford.edu/sites/gsb/files/publication-pdf/vcii-publication-technological-disruption-innovation-last-mile-delivery.pdf

Given the nature of employment-skill configuration in the Indian IT industry, as shown in Fig. 16, the greatest and earliest risk of job losses would be in the massive low-end jobs, while the few top-notch professionals might move up in career performance through re-skilling and resilience with alacrity (Fig. 15).

7 Concluding Observations

To make the Indian IT Industry move up the value chain and thereby sustain its growth trajectory, a paradigm shift in the industry's strategy for the software sector is being observed. The focus of the IT industry is on software product development to contribute equitably and significantly along with IT services. The Indian IT industry is passing through a crucial phase of technological disruptions that demands deeper specialisation and constant innovations risking its ability and readiness to deliver quality IT services.

Cloud computing, big data and automation are creating tremendous business opportunities in India but then how to capitalise on such a situation falls in the domain of the stakeholders, including the state. Constant innovation, improving IT infrastructure and removing legal and administrative bottlenecks are the need of the hour for the Indian IT sector to sustain its leadership position and to take anew (Das and Sagara 2017). Though IT exports from India is largely dominated by corporates, there are numerous small firms working on highly technical, innovative and creative projects. Development of mobile applications and platforms for small business units is turning out to be a lucrative business opportunity for small IT firms and individual software developers.

In a joint study of Analytics India Magazine and Great Learning found that the artificial intelligence industry has grown by close to 30% during the financial year 2017–18 to US$ 230 million and the industry is witnessing a shortage of over 4,000 mid and senior-level qualified job positions in the country.[12] Digital transformation has the potential to unlock value at an unprecedented scale and adaptive organisations that understand, embrace, and prepare for this change can gain significant business value as part of this transformation. While digitalisation can be a net job creator in some industries and a destructor in others, there is a need to evaluate and up-skill employees to manage employment rates through relevant investment in enabling infrastructure.

New technologies can drive business growth, job creation and demand for specialist skills, but they can also displace entire roles when certain tasks become obsolete or automated (WEF 2018: 11). McGowan and Andrews (2015: 32) in their OECD Survey of Adult Skills suggested that while differences in skill mismatch across countries are associated with differences in the policy environment in different countries, skill mismatch is lower in countries with well-designed framework conditions that promote efficient reallocation, greater flexibility in wage negotiations and higher participation in lifelong learning as well as better managerial quality.

The Indian IT industry will have to cope with challenges concerning data security, the privacy of individuals, content management and cybercrimes. The lower level of digital literary, unreliable internet connectivity and shortage of power supply are major hindrances before the IT industry in India. It is predicted that India may experience a falling demand in the traditional BPO business, but with the setting up of adequate infrastructure and promoting constant innovations, India could hope to continue to dominate the world in the IT services in the future as well. Creation of relevant opportunities for 'new' jobs would hinge upon the nature and degree of proactive preparedness the state and even the private sector might show. There is a need for a comprehensive 'augmentation strategy', an approach where businesses look to utilise the automation of some job tasks to complement and enhance their human workforces' comparative strengths and, ultimately, to enable and empower employees to extend their full potential (WEF 2018: 11).

For governments and businesses alike, there is a significant opportunity in strengthening cross-sectoral multi-stakeholder collaboration to promote corporate re-skilling and up-skilling among employers in affected countries and regions (WEF 2018: 34). The *National Policy on Software Products* (2016) aims at creating synergies of efforts by the government and industry to create a robust software product industry that would buttress large number of software product start-ups, promote development of an ecosystem encouraging R and D and innovation, open up multitude of opportunities of access to capital and help build and improve domestic demand.

Governments and businesses will need to change profoundly their approach to education, skills and employment, and their approach to working with each other

[12]https://economictimes.indiatimes.com/articleshow/67131803.cms?utm_source=contentofinterest&utm_medium=text&utm_campaign=cppst.

and the governments will need to show bolder leadership in putting through the curricula and labour market regulation changes that are already decades overdue in some economies (WEF 2016: 9). It has been observed that the Digital India initiative of the Government of India has the potential to transform the entire service delivery system accelerating productivity, employment and literacy in areas that are not digitally connected in the country (Goel 2014). Similarly, the Smart City Project, according to NASSCOM, would create a massive business opportunity of US$ 30–40 billion for the IT industry over the next 5–10 years (Srikanth 2015). However, progress on these mega programmes has been sluggish and far from the promises made when these were formally announced.

Acknowledgements We express our sincere gratitude to Dibyendu Maiti (DSE, Delhi) for the opportunity, encouragement and comments in writing this chapter. Towards improving the quality of the paper useful comments, suggestions and technical help were received from Pratap C. Mohanty (IIT, Roorkee), Jaya Prakash Pradhan (CUG, Gandhinagar), Itishree Pattnaik (GIDR, Ahmedabad), Tara Nair (GIDR, Ahmedabad), Fulvio Castellacci (TIK Centre for Technology, Innovation and Culture, University of Oslo, Norway) and Grace Kite (SOAS, London). Detailed comments from Pralok Gupta (Centre for WTO Studies, IIFT, New Delhi) contributed to improving the content and readability of the paper. We are grateful to all of them. The authors remain responsible for any errors and omissions that might remain.

References

Agrawal, S. (2016a). BPOs beware! Chatbots are on their way. *The Times of India*, June 15. Retrieved on June 10, 2016 from http://timesofindia.indiatimes.com/tech/tech-news/BPOs-beware-Chatbots-on-their-way/articleshow/52757547.cms.

Agrawal, S. (2016b). *How chatbots could soon put BPOs out of business*. Retrieved on June 10, 2016 from http://economictimes.indiatimes.com/articleshow/52754634.cms?from=mdr&utm_source=contentofinterest&utm_medium=text&utm_campaign=cppst.

Ahmed, G. (2012). Krugman trade theory and developing economies. *China-USA Business Review, 11*(12), 1557–1564.

Antras, P., & Helpman, E. (2004). Global sourcing. *Journal of Political Economy, 112*(3), 552–580.

Baldwin, R. (2011). Trade and industrialisation after globalisation's 2nd unbundling: How building and joining a supply chain are different and why it matters. *Working Paper 17716*. Cambridge, MA: National Bureau of Economic Research. Retrieved on April 25, 2018 from http://www.nber.org/papers/w17716.

Bhattacharya, B. (2016). Cloud computing: The silver lining for SMEs and start-ups. *PCQUEST*, March 23. Retrieved on November 3, 2017 from http://www.pcquest.com/cloud-computing-the-silver-lining-for-smes-start-ups/.

Cherian, P. (2014, October 31). Mobility and scalability of the public cloud. *Dataquest*, *32*(20), 60.

Das, A., & Phadnis, S. (2017, November 2). Infosys, Wipro's headcount shows the kind of IT jobs will survive. *The Economic Times*. Retrieved on November 3, 2017 from https://economictimes.indiatimes.com/articleshow/61449803.cms?utm_source=contentofinterest&utm_medium=text&utm_campaign=cppst.

Das, K., & Sagara, H. (2017). State and the IT industry in India: An overview. *Economic and Political Weekly, 52*(41), 56–64.

Dawar, S., & Lacy, P. (2017, August 8). Digital disruption: Capitalizing on the 4th Industrial Revolution fuelled by digital technologies. *Live Mint*. Retrieved on April

10, 2018 from https://www.livemint.com/Home-Page/2No24MFhEFWjwj4pNIEMML/Digital-disruption-Capitalizing-on-the-4th-Industrial-Revol.html.
FICCI, NASSCOM & EY. (2017). *Future of jobs in India: A 2022 perspective*. Retrieved on February 28, 2018 from http://www.ey.com/Publication/vwLUAssets/ey-future-of-jobs-in-india/$FILE/ey-future-of-jobs-in-india.pdf.
Ford, M. (2015). *Rise of the robots: Technology and the threat of a jobless future*. New York: Basic Books.
Goel, R. (2014, October 31). Digital India is the need of the hour. *Dataquest, 32*(20), 40–43.
Golub, G. H., & Van Loan, F. C. (1996). *Matrix computations*. Baltimore: The Johns Hopkins University Press.
HfS Research. (2016, July 5). Automation to impact 1.4 million global services jobs by 2021 with India the most affected. Retrieved on March 25, 2018 from https://www.hfsresearch.com/press-releases/automation-to-impact-14-million-global-services-jobs-by-2021-with-india-the-most-affected.
KPMG. (2016). Global IT-BPO outsourcing deals analysis, February. Retrieved on June 8, 2018 from https://assets.kpmg.com/content/dam/kpmg/pdf/2016/03/KPMG-Deal-Tracker-3Q15.pdf.
Kaur, B. (2015). Impact of E-Commerce on E-Retail. *Journal for Studies in Management and Planning, 6*(1). Retrieved on June 8, 2018 from https://edupediapublications.org/journals/index.php/JSMaP/article/view/1548.
Kiran, P. C. (2015, September 15). When Smart Cities meet big data. *Dataquest, 33*(17), 52–53.
Krugman, P. (1979). Increasing returns, monopolistic competition, and international trade. *Journal of International Economics, 9,* 469–479.
Lakshmikanth, K. (2017, May 14). Indian IT firms to layoff up to 2 lakh engineers annually for next 3 years. *Livemint*. Retrieved on April 20, 2018 from https://www.livemint.com/Industry/Y0oIb1D6N1ADZDfq3BUhUM/Indian-IT-firms-to-layoff-up-to-2-lakh-engineers-annually-f.html.
Mani, S. (2014). Emergence of India as the world leader in computer and information services. *Economic and Political Weekly, 49*(49), 51–61.
McGowan, M. A., & Andrews, D. (2015). Skill mismatch and public policy in OECD countries. *The Future of Productivity: Main Background Papers, Economics Department Working Papers No. 1210*, ECO/WKP (2015) 28. https://www.oecd.org/eco/growth/Skill-mismatch-and-public-policy-in-OECD-countries.pdf.
McKinsey Global Institute. (2013). *Disruptive technologies: Advances that will transform life, business, and the global economy*. Retrieved on November 7, 2017 from file:///C:/Users/Lenovo/AppData/Local/Packages/Microsoft.MicrosoftEdge_8wekyb3d8bbwe/TempState/Downloads/MGI_Disruptive_technologies_Full_report_May2013.pdf.
Melitz, M. (2003). The impact of trade on intra-industry reallocations and aggregate industry productivity. *Econometrica, 71*(6), 1695–1725.
Modi, D. (2015, December 23). IoT shall be the next big force to drive mobility. *PCQUEST*, 24–25. Retrieved on November 3, 2017 from http://www.pcquest.com/iot-shall-be-the-next-big-force-to-drive-mobility/.
Nair, E. (2015). The challenge of change. *Dataquest, 33*(13), 82.
NASSCOM. (2017). *The IT-BPM Industry In India 2017: Strategic Review*. Retrieved on June 7, 2018 from https://www.nasscom.in/knowledge-center/publications/it-bpm-industry-india-2017-strategic-review.
NASSCOM. (2018–19). *CEO Survey: 2019–20 Industry Performance: 2018–19 and what lies ahead*. https://www.nasscom.in/sites/default/files/Industry-Performance2018-19-and-what-lies-ahead_0.pdf.
Productivity Commission. (2016). Digital disruption: What do governments need to do? *Commission Research Paper*, Canberra, June. Retrieved on June 7, 2018 from https://www.pc.gov.au/research/completed/digital-disruption/digital-disruption-research-paper.pdf.
Sadagopan, S. (2012, September 13–16). IT in India. *Yojana, 56*.

Sen, A. (2015). Marrying IoT with big data: Not possible without a cloud home. *Dataquest, 33*(13), 78–79.

Shrikanth, G. (2015). A utopia called secured cloud. *Dataquest, 33*(13), 28–31.

Srikanth, R. P. (2015, September 15). Smart cities: An opportunity to transform India. *Dataquest, 33*(17), 8.

Standard Business Graduate School. (2016). Technological disruption and innovation in last-mile delivery. *Stanford Value Chain Innovation Initiative in Collaboration with United States Postal Service Office of Inspector General* GSB.Stanford.Edu/R/Vcii, White Paper, June.

The Times of India. (2016a, March 3). *Andhra cabinet okays internet of things (IoT) policy*. Retrieved on June 10, 2016 from http://timesofindia.indiatimes.com/good-governance/andhra-pradesh/Andhra-cabinet-okays-Internet-of-Things-IoT-olicy/articleshow/51237426.cms?.

The Times of India. (2016b, November 2). *Amid IT layoffs, this could be a reason to cheer*. Retrieved on November 2, 2017 from https://timesofindia.indiatimes.com/business/india-business/amid-it-layoffs-this-could-be-a-reason-to-cheer/articleshow/61459252.cms.

World Bank Group. (2015). The effects of technology on employment and implications for public employment services. *G20 Employment Working Group Meeting Report*, Istanbul, Turkey, May 6–8. Retrieved on June 7, 2018 from http://g20.org.tr/wp-content/uploads/2015/11/The-Effects-of-Technology-on-Employment-and-Implications-for-Public-Employment-Services.pdf.

World Economic Forum (WEF). (2018). *The future of jobs: An insight report*. Centre for New Economy and Society. http://www3.weforum.org/docs/WEF_Future_of_Jobs_2018.pdf.

World Economic Forum (WEF). (2016). The future of jobs employment: Skills and workforce strategy for the fourth industrial revolution. *Global challenge insight report*, Executive Summary, January. http://www3.weforum.org/docs/WEF_FOJ_Executive_Summary_Jobs.pdf.

IT Enabling Indian Firms: The Importance of IT Outsourcing Companies

Grace Kite

Abstract The literature on the role of information technology outsourcing (ITO) only rarely considers purchasers in developing countries. This is an important omission and even more so in India, which has an IT outsourcing industry that is well placed to bring world-class applications of the technology to domestic firms. This chapter assesses the sector's role in India using evidence from econometric analysis covering 10,100 firms over 5 years as well as qualitative responses from 29 in-depth interviews. The econometrics shows that there is a strong positive impact of IT outsourcing on output and productivity, and that the effect is bigger than that achieved by buying hardware and software alone. Comparing with studies from around the world also reveals that the effect of ITO in India is typically larger than firms in developed countries achieve with investments into IT—so that ITO facilitates catching up. The qualitative evidence helps to understand why these strong effects occur. It suggests that ITO companies are engaging in a conscious process of learning in both developed markets and India, and that in doing so, they bring innovations to India and assist in adapting them to the local context.

Keywords Information technology · Outsourcing · Software · Productivity · Catching up · Learning

1 Introduction

Since its emergence in the 1980s, information technology (IT) has proliferated in many industries as firms have transformed and improved their processes using the technology. The vanguard of this wave of technical progress was made up of firms in the developed world, and for developing nations, the prospect of catching up by learning from them is enticing. But doing this successfully is problematic, it depends on the transfer of tacit knowledge that developed country firms have accumulated

---

G. Kite (✉)
Gracious Economics, 4th Floor, 18 St Cross St., London EC1N 8UN, UK
e-mail: grace@graciouseconomics.co.uk

D. Maiti et al. (eds.), *Digitalisation and Development*,
https://doi.org/10.1007/978-981-13-9996-1_5

through years of experimentation and experience; knowledge that in general, these firms do not want to share (Abramovitz 1986; Cohen and Levinthal 1990).[1]

This chapter is concerned with efforts to adopt IT by Indian firms, and the circumstances under which adoption leads to strong increases in productivity. What emerges is that IT outsourcing firms are important. Econometric evidence outlined here demonstrates that their involvement in IT adoption improves outcomes significantly, and shows that unaided investment into IT doesn't generally bring catching up, but an investment with ITO can. The chapter also includes complementary qualitative evidence, which suggests an explanation for this strong productivity effect. At least in some cases, ITO firms with experience of using IT in the developed world have absorbed knowledge on how best to use IT in particular industries. They marshal and repackage this knowledge to re-use it in India and co-create innovations with their Indian clients.

Existing related literature is mainly focussed on developed countries. It includes a great deal of research that quantifies the impact of in-house IT—either at firm or industry level (e.g. Stiroh 2002) or economy-wide level (e.g. Jorgenson et al. 2007)—but very little that quantifies the effect of ITO. There is also a growing evolutionary economics literature that describes the role of knowledge-intensive business services firms, arguing that when outsourced services are knowledge-intensive, they can help to produce and spread innovations (e.g. Muller and Zenker 2001).

This chapter applies ideas from the evolutionary economics literature about learning from outsourcing companies to IT in developing countries. While that literature is predominantly concerned with innovation at the technical frontier, here it is applied to innovation that occurs alongside adaptations of existing IT applications for a new context.

The rest of the chapter begins with a summary of related literature. Then, Sect. 2 briefly outlines econometric evidence on the effect of IT adoption in India with and without ITO. Section 3 describes the role of ITO workers and firms in adapting and co-creating IT innovations, and Sect. 4 concludes.

2 Related Literature

When IT is used well by firms, it brings process improvements, cost savings, and ongoing opportunities to learn and adapt. Firms incorporate the technology by gathering information from all departments into one or more pieces of software and then making them available to all relevant staff (Perez 1985, p. 9). This increases the amount and quality of information available to workers and managers, enabling decisions to be made independently, without managerial assistance (Brynjolfsson and Yang 1996, p. 11). It also opens up the possibility of computerised monitoring of

[1]Certain portions of this chapter draw from the author's previous work, cited at the end of the chapter as Kite (2011, 2013, 2018).

performance. Workers, processes and outcomes can be tracked using the new software so that there is a further saving on supervisory staff, and so that opportunities for improvement can be identified and acted upon quickly (Perez 1985, p. 9; Brynjolffson and Yang 1996, p. 30). Alongside an improved ability to compete and expand, IT brings savings on "processing time", "transaction costs", "inventory costs", and even "material wastage" (Mody and Dahlman 1992, p. 1708).

Given this role for the technology, it is not surprising that the literature which evaluates its impact in developed countries finds significant productivity and output effects. Figures 1, 2 and 3 provide a summary of this research. Figure 1 is a meta-analysis of econometric studies using firm or industry-level data from a variety of developed countries (Stiroh 2002). It plots the output elasticity of IT in 40 econometric models from 20 different studies. The median estimate suggests that doubling the stock of IT capital leads to an impressive 5% increase in output. Figures 2 and 3 together summarise the country-level evidence. Figure 2 shows the number of percentage points of GDP growth attributable to IT in the United States (US). It shows that IT adoption was responsible for a remarkable acceleration in economic growth in the 1990s and that by the end of that decade, IT use was contributing almost 1.4% points of GDP growth per annum. Figure 3 illustrates the share of GDP growth attributable to IT in a selection of other developed countries. It indicates a norm of between 10% and 30% throughout the 1990s.

So far, there are only a few comparable analyses in developing countries. Using firm or industry-level data and econometric analysis, these often find strong effects of IT: Commander et al. (2011) found a 12% increase in productivity for a 100% increase in in-house IT in India and Brazil; Lee et al. (2011) found 15% in China; and, Banga and Goldar (2004) found 13% for purchases of services outsourcing including ITO in Indian manufacturing. This literature provides tentative support for the idea that there is potential for strong productivity effects from IT in developing

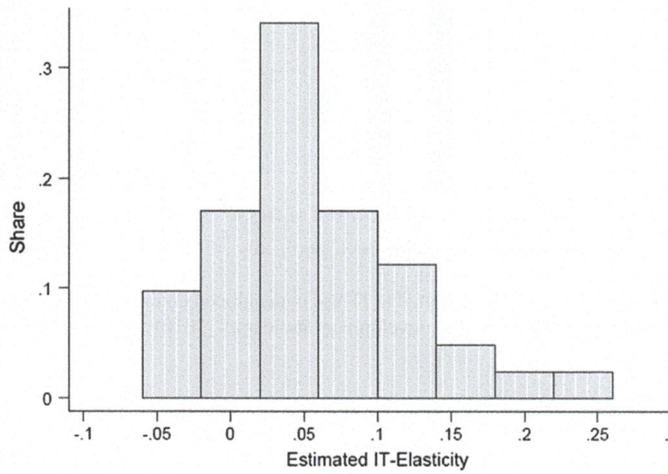

Fig. 1 Histogram of productivity effects in econometric studies. *Source* Stiroh (2002, p. 30)

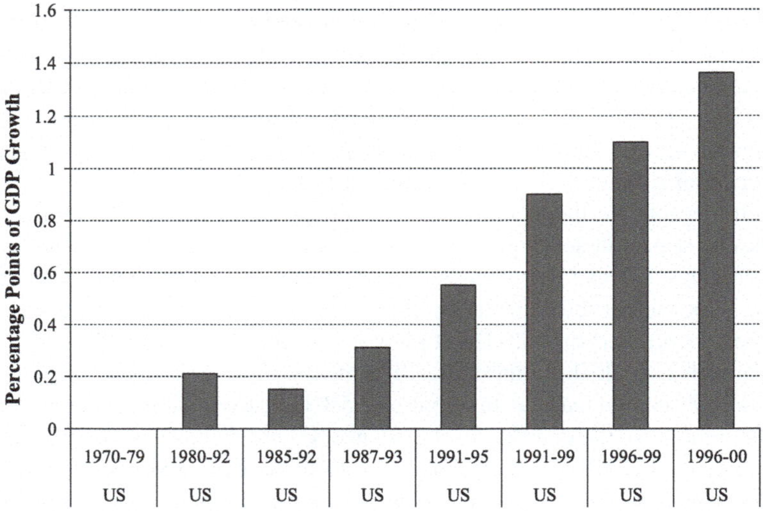

Fig. 2 GDP growth per annum attributed to IT in the US. *Notes* Adapted from Jorgenson et al. (2007, p. 9), International monetary fund (2001, pp. 106–116), Oliner and Sichel (1994), Jorgensen and Stiroh (1995), Sichel (1997), Jeong et al. (2002), Crafts (2001), Daveri (2001), Oliner and Sichel (2000)

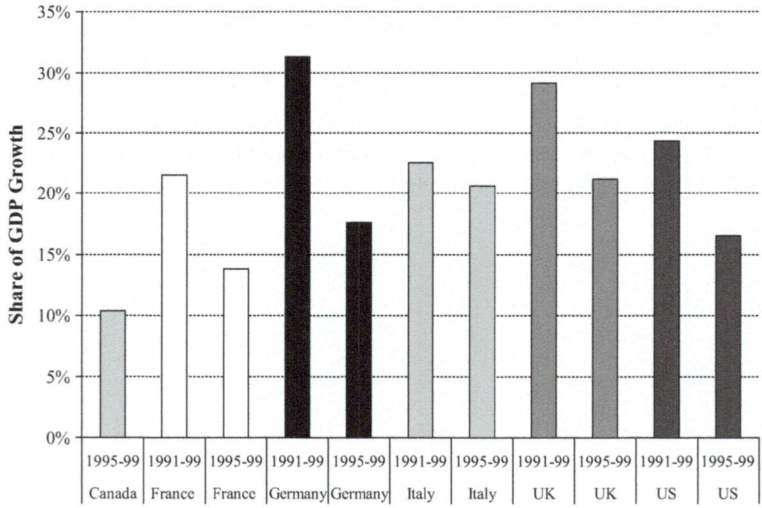

Fig. 3 Share of total GDP growth attributed to IT use in developed countries. *Notes* Adapted from Colecchia (2001), Daveri (2001), World development indicators (2010)

countries. However, none of these studies uses large samples, and for that reason, they are unable to dig into the stories underneath the strong effects and identify the circumstances when IT adoption is particularly successful, or less so.

The literature on knowledge-intensive outsourcing in the developed world is suggestive of a role for outsourcing firms (Guerrieri et al. 2005; den Hertog 2000; Muller and Zenker 2001). The evidence shows that knowledge-intensive services firms have initiated innovation in Germany (Czarnitzki and Spielkamp 2003), Europe, and Canada (Tether and Tajar 2008; Tether and Hipp 2002; Doloreux and Shearmur 2012; Muller and Zenker 2001; Gago and Rubalcaba 2007; Guerrieri et al. 2005; Shearmur and Doloreux 2013; Arvanitis and Loukis 2013). They have also helped to diffuse innovations into Singapore (Thompson and Bhattacherjee 2014). Wood (2005, 2006) has shown that outsourcing firms have supported catching up in backward regions within Europe and argued that they could be critical in supporting catching up in the global south.

3 Empirical Estimates of the Impact of IT Investment in India

This section outlines an empirical analysis that assesses the impact of IT adoption in firms in India and separates out the productivity effect for IT investments made with help from ITO firms. A full and detailed description of this analysis is available in Kite (2018).

The research uses the PROWESS database, published by the Centre for Monitoring the Indian Economy (CMIE 2009), which covers public-sector enterprises and firms registered on India's main stock exchanges. The database includes almost 27,000 observations suitable for the purposes of analysing IT and productivity. These cover 10,100 firms for over 5 years (Fig. 4).

Unfortunately, the PROWESS database reports ITO and other outsourced services together in one metric called "Expenditure on Software and Other Professional Services". This includes expenditure on ITO, as well as all other "expenses reported by a company on external professional services engaged by the company for services other than for audit, consultancy, software development, IT-enabled services, cost audit and legal services" (CMIE 2009). The data does not allow a break down by the different sub-components of this measure. However, the modelling strategy discussed below does mitigate for the most likely type of bias arising from its use.

	2005	2006	2007	2008	Total
Manufacturing	4,908	4,406	3,640	2,284	15,238 (56%)
Finance	1,932	1,695	1,221	676	5,524 (21%)
Services	2,120	1,862	1,425	817	6,224 (23%)
Total	8,960	7,963	6,286	3,777	26,986

Fig. 4 Sample by sector and year. *Source* Author calculations based on CMIE (2009)

Figure 5 shows the extent of ITO by industry. The table ranks industries by their mean annual expenditure on ITO per firm, and it also includes the percent of firms in each industry that undertake ITO. The top ten purchasers of ITO in the table include communications, manufacturing, banking, retail, transport and logistics, and two other categories of services. These industries match very closely with those that have been found to use IT intensively in other developed and less-developed countries (Baily and Lawrence 2001, p. 309; Hanna 1994, p. 40). This does suggest that the majority of the expenditures in the ITO measure are ITO and not other outsourced services.

The methods used to estimate the effect of IT both with and without ITO are well established in the econometric literature on the impact of IT and outsourcing in the developed world (Olsen 2006; Stiroh 2002). This, as well as the large sample size, ensures that the results of the analysis here can be successfully compared to findings in the wider literature. The approach is to use econometrics to estimate the parameters of a production function which includes IT as an input to production alongside ordinary capital and ITO as a factor that can improve total factor productivity.

This relationship is summarised in the expression below. In it, Y is gross output; K stocks of ordinary capital; IT is in-house hardware and software; L is labour; M is

Rank	Sector	ITO spend per firm (Rs. Crore)	% IT outsourcers	ITO spend by all firms (Rs. Crore)	ITO spend by all firms (US$m)
1	Communications	Rs. 34.3	88%	Rs. 1,570.6	$348.5
2	Banks	Rs. 7.0	97%	Rs. 674.3	$149.6
3	Housing Finance	Rs. 3.0	81%	Rs. 74.1	$16.4
4	Misc Services	Rs. 2.5	77%	Rs. 1,232.5	$273.5
5	Chemicals Manufacturing	Rs. 2.3	71%	Rs. 1,552.7	$344.5
6	Computers Manufacturing	Rs. 1.5	71%	Rs. 26.4	$5.9
7	Machines Manufacturing	Rs. 1.5	70%	Rs. 537.9	$119.4
8	Metals Manufacturing	Rs. 1.4	74%	Rs. 466.3	$103.5
9	Transport Manufacturing	Rs. 1.4	68%	Rs. 216.0	$47.9
10	Media and Films	Rs. 1.3	84%	Rs. 107.4	$23.8
11	Hotels	Rs. 1.3	74%	Rs. 104.7	$23.2
12	Financial Brokers	Rs. 1.3	80%	Rs. 65.7	$14.6
13	Consultants	Rs. 1.0	68%	Rs. 87.6	$19.4
14	Misc Finance	Rs. 0.8	49%	Rs. 317.1	$70.4
15	Minerals Manufacturing	Rs. 0.7	64%	Rs. 106.7	$23.7
16	Food Manufacturing	Rs. 0.7	60%	Rs. 247.9	$55.0
17	Misc Manufacturing	Rs. 0.6	70%	Rs. 120.1	$26.7
18	Securities Brokers	Rs. 0.5	45%	Rs. 96.6	$21.4
19	Textiles Manufacturing	Rs. 0.5	69%	Rs. 197.1	$43.7
20	Wholesalers	Rs. 0.4	61%	Rs. 127.7	$28.3

Fig. 5 ITO by sector. *Notes* Annual averages amongst those firms that purchase outsourced SWIS. Monetary values are in constant 2005 rupees or dollars. Total number of observations is 26,986. *Source* Author calculations based on CMIE (2009) and RBI (2009)

intermediate inputs (including materials, energy, and any other purchased inputs to production) and $F(.)$ is the production function which determines how inputs map to output. A is total factor productivity (TFP), a parameter which estimates the efficiency of converting inputs into output, ITO refers to IT outsourcing and OS to other types of outsourcing.

$$Y = A(\mathrm{ITO}, \mathrm{OS})F(K, \mathrm{IT}, L, M)$$

Assuming a Cobb–Douglas functional form for $F(.)$ and taking logs of the resulting expression leads to the expression below. In it, ln(.) is the natural logarithm, the γ's are the elasticities of output to different kinds of outsourcing, and the α's are the elasticities of output to the other inputs. All other elements of the equations are defined as before.

$$\begin{aligned}\ln(Y) = \gamma_{\mathrm{ITO}}\ln(\mathrm{ITO}) + \gamma_{\mathrm{OS}}\ln(\mathrm{OS}) + \alpha_K\ln(K) + \alpha_{\mathrm{IT}}\ln(\mathrm{IT}) + \alpha_L\ln(L)\\ + \alpha_M\ln(M)\end{aligned}$$

Figure 6 shows the econometric results.[2] Column 1 is a benchmark estimate of the production function without ITO, and with in-house IT combined with capital and goods and services outsourcing combined with intermediate inputs. Column 2 splits intermediate inputs to show goods and services outsourcing separately, and column 3 splits in-house IT from ordinary capital. Column 4 incorporates both types of outsourcing and in-house IT separately. Then, column 5 eliminates insignificant variables to give the preferred specification. In both column 4 and column 5, IT and ITO are highly significant. The models indicate that doubling expenditure on IT leads to a 5% increase in real gross output and doubling ITO expenditure leads to a 9% increase in output. The test reported in the bottom row of the table rejects the null hypothesis that the effect of ITO is equal to the effect of in-house IT, in favour of the alternative that ITO has a bigger effect.

All the models in Fig. 6 are estimated using fixed effects because the data has a panel structure. This modelling approach also controls for unobserved firm-specific heterogeneity that might otherwise bias the estimated coefficients. This is an important source of bias when the nature of individual firms can affect both dependent and explanatory variables in ways not fully captured by the data and models. Two pertinent possibilities are the firm's organisational and managerial setup, and its skill profile,[3] because these are factors that affect the efficacy of ITO but can also be productivity-enhancing in their own right (Bresnahan et al. 2002). If these are not

[2]Kite (2018) includes a range of econometric tests and robustness exercises to support these findings. These include a first difference model, a Blundell and Bond (1998) estimate which corrects for production function endogeneity, a test for attrition bias in the sample, and estimates by sector, by public versus privately owned firms and by Indian versus foreign-owned firms.

[3]Unfortunately, PROWESS does not include a measure of firms' skill level, although clearly including such a measure would improve the analysis here. Commander et al. (2011) carried out primary research to create a skills profile variable in their study on IT in Brazil and India, this necessitated using a much smaller sample in their econometric work.

Dependent Variable is log of real output	1	2	3	4	5
Log real capital	0.2076***	0.1990***	0.1895***	0.1766***	0.1825***
	(0.0233)	*(0.0222)*	*(0.0227)*	*(0.0212)*	*(0.0219)*
Log real labour	0.4863***	0.4869***	0.4660***	0.4391***	0.4363***
	(0.0686)	*(0.0654)*	*(0.0644)*	*(0.0587)*	*(0.0610)*
Log real intermediate inputs	0.2827***	0.2719***	0.2900***	0.2758***	0.2832***
	(0.0587)	*(0.0575)*	*(0.0566)*	*(0.0529)*	*(0.0534)*
Log real other outsourcing		0.0897*		0.0667	
		(0.0484)		*(0.0519)*	
Log real in-house IT capital			0.0667***	0.0519***	0.0502***
			(0.0154)	*(0.0147)*	*(0.0147)*
Log real IT outsourcing				0.0868***	0.0951***
				(0.0261)	*(0.0274)*
Constant	Yes	Yes	Yes	Yes	Yes
Year Dummies	Yes	Yes	Yes	Yes	Yes
Sector Dummies	Yes	Yes	Yes	Yes	Yes
N	26,986	26,986	26,986	26,986	26,986
R-squared	71.7%	72.1%	72.3%	73.5%	73.3%
Returns to Scale	0.98	0.96	1.02	0.95	0.95
P-value from test of H0: ITO=in-house IT vs H1: ITO>in-house IT					0.049**

Fig. 6 Econometric Estimates of the effect of IT and ITO in India. *Key* ***means significant at the 0.1% level, **means significant at the 1% level, * means significant at the 5% level. *Notes* Estimated using with cluster-robust standard errors to account for panel data. All equations are weighted using the log of real spending on wages. Robust standard errors are given in parentheses and italics. All variables are in 2005 rupees crore, with 1 crore equivalent to US$221,900 in 2005. Returns to scale are the sum of coefficients for all non-outsourced inputs and should equal 1 under neo-classical assumptions. Where outsourcing or in-house IT is reported separately, they are excluded from intermediate inputs and from the capital, respectively. *Source* Author calculations based on CMIE (2009)

tackled within models—for example, by using fixed effects—their presence could bias the estimates of the effect of ITO.

Fixed effects estimation also controls for the most likely type of bias arising from the use of a composite variable to measure ITO. This bias arises if some subgroups of firms—perhaps exporters or smaller firms—have both higher productivity and a higher proportion of the expenditures measured by the composite variable being ITO. Assuming ITO is more important for output and productivity than the other miscellaneous expenditures included in the measure, this situation would tend to bias the estimated elasticity for ITO upwards. However, as long as the mix of ITO versus other types of expenditures included in the composite variable depends predominantly on the nature of each firm's business, it will mostly vary across firms and will change rarely, or slowly, over time. In this scenario, any bias arising from

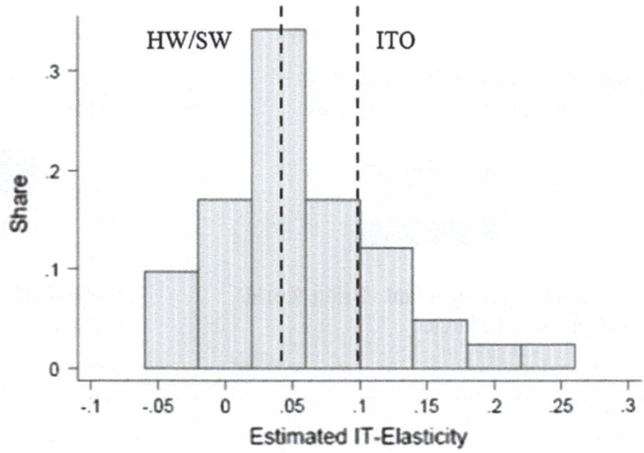

Fig. 7 Econometric estimates of the effect of IT and ITO in India. *Source* Stiroh (2002, p. 30), Author calculations based on CMIE (2009)

the mix of what is in the composite variable will be largely corrected by the inclusion of firm-level fixed effects.

Figure 7 revisits Fig. 1, Stiroh's (2002) meta-analysis of econometric estimates from IT adoption in the developed world, now overlaying the findings from India. It shows that the estimate for IT adoption without support from IT outsourcers is close to the median Stiroh found in US/Europe at 5%. With ITO, the estimate is bigger than Stiroh's median, showing that the productivity effect of ITO in India is bigger than the IT adoption effect in the majority of the developed world studies.

Since Indian firms typically have less experience with IT than their developed country counterparts, the resemblance in the two 5% figures is surprising. It implies that even though IT hardware and software embody innovations, purchasing them for use in-house does not guarantee firms in India a chance to catch up. Instead, they typically only progress at the same rate, remaining behind. On the other hand, if ITO firms are involved, progress can be faster than it is in the US and Europe, and catching up can occur.

4 Why Does ITO Contribute so Much More?

This section adds qualitative detail to the quantitative work. It is based on 29 in-depth interviews with ITO professionals, executives in IT-buying firms and experts, which took place between 8 January 2009 and 4 March 2009 in India. Further description of this research and its findings can be found in Kite (2013).

What emerged from the interviews is that ITO firms based in India both spread knowledge across borders and create innovations as part of a conscious effort to learn. They absorb, create and repackage knowledge as an important part of their strategy for acquiring new clients and so achieving growth. Figure 8 depicts this process. In the right-hand panel, which is concerned with projects in export markets, ITO firms learn how leading firms in a particular industry use IT to benefit their specific

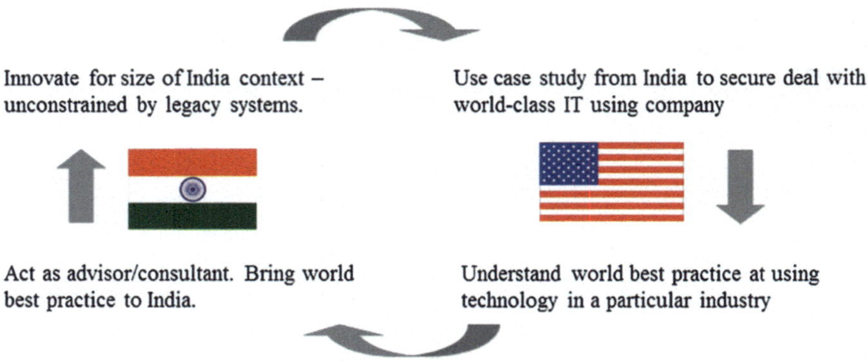

Fig. 8 ITO firms learning the strategy. *Source* Author's summary of in-depth interviews

business. This "domain expertise" is then bought back to India, where clients expect ITO partners to advise on how best to use IT as well as to implement an appropriate IT solution successfully.

ITO workers testified that their work in India, represented by the left-hand panel in Fig. 8, also offers learning. In India, client firms have fewer existing IT systems, and some are setting out on their very first installations. This means that the operation of any new IT is not constrained by pre-existing and technologically out of date "legacy" systems with which the new system must work. According to the ITO professionals, many Indian clients are also more tolerant of trial and error than export clients. These two factors, together with the simple fact of proximity to the ITO firms' staff and base make India an ideal place to trial new technologies for the first time.

Indian client firms purchasing ITO benefit from this process in two ways. First, they gain a partner with both implementation experience and knowledge of industry-specific uses of IT from leading firms in developed countries. Second, they are also able to use the newest technologies because of their status as an ideal test bed for multinational ITO companies' learning needs.

Benefit 1: Domain expertise and implementation experience

In many cases, ITO firms' developed country clients have considerably more experience of how IT can be used successfully because they have been experimenting with technology for considerably longer. When ITO firms bring that knowledge to Indian clients, it presents an important opportunity, as a senior figure in the ITO sector put it:

> We brought in a lot of experiences from our work with British Telecom, from our work with General Electric, our work with all the banks in the world, and now we are saying [to Indian firms], "Look, guys, it's time for you to pull up your socks". Mr Ashama.[4] (interview with the author, 22 January 2009, Delhi)

[4]To protect the identity of interviewees, many of whom are senior professionals in well-known companies, all of their real names have been replaced by pseudonyms.

Indian clients are fully aware that western domain expertise exists in ITO firms and insist on working with ITO companies that can demonstrate past experience with successful companies in their particular industry. Mr. Ekapure explained that Indian clients "are looking for value for money, but it is more about credentials, experience, reference, assets, and methodologies that you bring to the table" (interview with Mr. Ekapure, 27 February 2009, Bangalore). Mr. Falodiya, an SVP in charge of IT purchasing for a large Indian conglomerate concurred. Talking about his own ITO purchases, he said, "We are not only cost-conscious, but we are also heavily quality conscious… it [the IT and servicing we buy] has to be in line with global best practice" (interview with Mr. Falodiya, 13 February 2009, Mumbai).

Mr. Ghosh, an ITO veteran, gave the example of his company's involvement with the National Health Service (NHS) in the United Kingdom. Through several export projects with the NHS, they experienced and solved many of the issues that occur with managing hospitals' and patients' records in a large health service. According to Mr. Ghosh, these experiences were subsequently useful in a sales pitch to healthcare providers in Mumbai, who insisted on finding a partner with relevant experience from the West (interview on 17 February 2009, Mumbai).

But it is not just experience of the challenges that arise in specific sectors that ITO firms bring to India. Implementation of a new IT system can often mean a pervasive restructuring of processes and a great deal of organisational change (Perez 1985, p. 9). According to the interviewees, this kind of restructuring can be difficult, but IT firms with experience in developed countries are aware of both what to do in particular client industries and how to manage the processes:

> Organisation change management can be a serious impediment to the successful implementation of IT programmes. Over the past 20 years, these are issues we have seen in the Western world, and we know how to manage it; we have gone through this cycle. [Interview with Mr Holkar, chief executive officer of an IT and business analytics company, 24 February 2009, Bangalore].

Levina and Ross (2003) label this knowledge of how to manage IT implementation as an "application management competency" and argue using a range of evidence that ITO companies develop very strong capabilities in this area through their experience of doing and being in control of lots of different IT projects with different objectives, in different places, and with different types of clients. Their paper concludes that it is often an important motivation for firms choosing IT outsourcing rather than developing systems in-house, particularly where client firms have little experience with IT.

Benefit 2: Co-creating innovation and innovative adaptations

Along with applying lessons from their experience in developed countries, several of the interviewees made it clear that IT firms working in India need to be able to innovate.

One reason innovation has to take place is the sheer scale of India's landmass. Mr. Ashama gave an example of a project which was to automate the workings of one of India's largest banks. According to him, this project was a "massive challenge" because it involved 3000 branches being linked across the nation. Innovation took place "to make sure backups were safe, for example where there might be floods or other risks," and solutions involving satellite systems not yet in use in the West were deployed. Mr. Deshpande gave another reason why innovations are needed in Indian projects: India is less developed and far more populous than Europe and the United States, therefore IT systems must serve a larger number of customers at a much lower cost. When Mr. Deshpande talked about the innovation that his company undertakes to achieve these aims, it was clear that these considerations compel ITO professionals to get the best from the technology, and as a result, they are both challenging and exciting:

> The number of people in India is just amazing. Ten million transactions a day, 70 million accounts. When you test, when you configure, when you adopt, when you test your product, you really, really gain some wonderful experiences in what I call performance engineering in systems. "How do you get the maximum out of the systems?" [Interview with Mr Deshpande, 17 February 2009, Mumbai]

Mr. Deshpande said that part of the reason undertaking innovation in India is so rewarding is that IT-buying firms in the country are, for the most part, not constrained by the problem of how to accommodate or replace existing, and out-of-date hardware and software. This means that they can implement the latest technology unrestricted. Many of the other IT professionals agreed, saying that Indian SWIS projects allow them to "start from scratch" (interview, Mr. Balakrishnan, 20 February 2009, Pune) and to "use the newest technologies" (interview, Mr. Ghosh, 17 February 2009, Mumbai).

Another factor which makes innovation in domestic contracts easier is the proximity of these projects to client IT companies' headquarters, and thus, their senior and most experienced staff. Mr Jampana, the chief executive officer of a small IT firm which is becoming increasingly focused on the Indian market, said that "it is easier to experiment" in India because it is easier to maintain "management access" and to "monitor and talk about experiments, to see what is working and what isn't" (interview, 1 March 2009, Bangalore). Mr Ashama stressed another benefit of the close proximity with the client: "Tolerance of failure and ability to get a second chance is higher in India because you are nearby", adding that for IT companies with a strong brand and strong credentials, the Indian client is often more patient with experiments, as long as they eventually work (interview, Mr. Ashama, 22 January 2009, Delhi).

Mr. Deshpande worked on ITO for the Bombay Stock Exchange and gave this project as an example to illustrate how innovation in India can produce strong results:

> This is the 3rd biggest stock market in the world… The Bombay stock market does a higher throughput of transactions with 1/3 of infrastructure than the New York Stock Exchange… When the people from NASDAQ came in, we shared our best practices. [Interview with Mr Deshpande, 17 February 2009, Mumbai]

To some extent, the benefit of having a clean sheet upon which to build new IT systems and the willingness to experiment is also available to Indian firms who buy

IT unaided. However, it was clear from the ITO professionals' comments that experimentation with new technologies is a costly and risky affair. The ITO consultants said that they often undertake learning in the domestic market at a cost which exceeds the revenues they collect from the Indian client. This is justified because knowledge of the new technology and a demonstrated ability to use it successfully is valuable in securing lucrative export market contracts using the same technologies. Continuing with the example of the Bombay Stock Exchange, Mr. Deshpande explained:

> Based on that one project (digitising the Bombay Stock Exchange), and it was very complex, and we really worked hard on it, we must have got at least 20–30 projects using that as a case study. It was a big learning experience, but we can proudly say, 'We did it' with customers saying what a wonderful job you'd done.

5 In Conclusion

This chapter has investigated the impact of IT adoption in Indian firms, looking at how the productivity effect differs when firms purchase IT on their own versus when ITO firms aid them. What emerges is that by their experiences with previous projects both in India and abroad, the presence of ITO workers during IT adoption is more likely to bring catching up with western competitors. This is in part because ITO workers have experience of using IT in the United States and Europe and have absorbed knowledge on how best to use the technology in particular industries. It is also because India-based ITO firms invest in innovation in their home market where legacy systems are less of an issue as a way to build case studies that they use to help sell projects abroad. In short, and exactly as predicted by the evolutionary economics literature on knowledge-intensive business services, ITO firms are involved in innovation, adaptation, and spreading knowledge into India.

In India, these findings have an important policy implication. The country is host to a large ITO sector, which has, for several decades, been incentivised to focus on exports. This sector has accumulated a great deal of experience with leading companies in North America and Europe (NASSCOM and Delloite 2008). The finding that ITO offers opportunities for catching up implies that the Indian economy would be much better served if this industry was also incentivised to carry out work in India.

But there are wider implications for IT adoption in firms across the developing world. China, Mexico, Malaysia, the Philippines, Brazil, Thailand and Indonesia all host IT outsourcing sectors involved in providing export services. These countries might well have significant expertise already within their borders and be in a position to incentivise that knowledge being delivered to local firms and sectors.

Acknowledgments With thanks to Simon Commander, Chrisanti Avgerou, Fredrik Tell, Ben Groom, Duo Qin, Arlene Luck and participants at Economics of ICTs (Information and Communication Technologies): Transformation, Digital Divides and Development, Delhi School of Economics 2018.

References

Abramovitz, M. (1986). Catching up, forging ahead, and falling behind. *Journal of Economic History, 46,* 386–406.

Arvanitis, S., & Loukis, E. N. (2013). Outsourcing and firm performance—A comparative study of Swiss and Greek firms. *Industrial and Corporate Change, 22*(3), 771–806.

Baily, N., & Lawrence, R. (2001). Do we have a new e-conomy? The american economic review. *Papers and Proceedings of the Hundred Thirteenth Annual Meeting of the American Economic Association, 91*(2), 308–312.

Banga, R., & Goldar, B. (2004). *Contribution of services to output growth and productivity in Indian manufacturing: Pre and post reforms*. New-Delhi: Indian Council for Research on International Economic Relations.

Blundell, R., & Bond, S. (1998). GMM estimation with persistent panel data: An application to production functions. Institute of Fiscal Studies, Working Paper, no. W99/4

Bresnahan, T., Brynjolfsson, E., & Hitt, L. (2002). Information technology, workplace organization, and the demand for skilled labor: Firm-level evidence. *Quarterly Journal of Economics, 117*(1), 339–376.

Brynjolfsson, E., & Yang, S. (1996). Information technology and productivity: A review of the literature advances in computers. *Academic Press, 43,* 179–214.

CMIE, (2009). *PROWESS database*, November 2009 Available Online: http://www.cmie.com/.

Cohen, W. M., & Levinthal, D. A. (1990). Absorptive capacity: A new perspective on learning and innovation. *Administrative Science Quarterly, 35,* 128–152.

Colecchia, A. (2001). The impact of information and communications technologies on output growth: Issues and preliminary findings. In *OECD directorate for science, technology, and industry working paper no. 11*. Paris: Organization for Economic Cooperation and Development.

Commander, S., Harrison, R., & Menezes-Filho, N. (2011, May). ICT and productivity in developing countries: New firm-level evidence from Brazil and India. *The Review of Economics and Statistics, 93*(2), 528–541.

Crafts, N. (2001). The solow productivity paradox in historical perspective. In *Long-Term Trends in the World Economy-Conference Proceedings*. University of Copenhagen.

Czarnitzki, D., & Spielkamp, A. (2003). Business services in Germany: Bridges for innovation. *The Service Industries Journal, 23*(2), 1–30.

Daveri, F. (2001). *Information technology and growth in Europe*. Unpublished. Parma: University of Parma.

den Hertog, P. (2000). Knowledge-intensive business services as co-producers of innovation. *International Journal of Innovation Management, 4,* 491–528.

Doloreux, D., & Shearmur, R. (2012). Collaboration, information and the geography of innovation in knowledge intensive business services. *Journal of Economic Geography, 12,* 79–105.

Gago, D., & Rubalcaba, L. (2007). Innovation and ICT in service firms: Towards a multidimensional approach for impact assessment, *Journal of Evolutionary Economics, 17*, 25–44.

Guerrieri, P., Maggi B., Meliciani V., & Padoan, P. C. (2005). Technology diffusion, services, and endogenous growth in Europe: Is the lisbon strategy useful? In *IMF working paper WP/05/103*, IMF Washington.

Hanna, N. (1994). Exploring information technology for development: A case study of India. In *World Bank discussion* paper no. 246. Washington DC: The World Bank.

International Monetary Fund, (2001). *World economic outlook: The information technology revolution,* Chap. 3 (pp. 103–142). Available online http://www.imf.org/external/pubs/ft/weo/2001/02/pdf/chapter3.pdf.

Jeong, K., Jeong, H., & Shin, I. (2002). The economic impact of information and communication technology in Korea. In M. Pohjola (Ed.), *Information technology, productivity, and economic growth: International evidence and implications for economic development.* UNU/WIDER studies in development economics, Oxford University Press.

Jorgenson, D., & Stiroh, K. (1995). Computers and growth. *Economics of Innovation and New Technology, 3*(3 & 4), 295–316.

Jorgensen, D., Ho, M., & Stiroh, K. (2007). *A retrospective look at the U.S. productivity growth resurgence* (Federal Reserve Bank of New York Staff Reports No. 277).

Kite, G. (2011). *Linkedin: The software and IT services sector in India's economic development, 1980 to 2011* (PhD thesis). SOAS University of London.

Kite, G. (2013, July 27). *The Indian software and information technology services sector: A teacher to treasure, economic and political weekly, 48*(30).

Kite, G. (2018). A conduit for knowledge? Demonstrating the strength of technology improvements in Indian firms that buy outsourced information technology. *Journal of Evolutionary Economics, 28,* 225–243.

Lee, S., Xiang, J., & Kim, J. (2011). Information technology and productivity: Empirical evidence from the Chinese electronics industry. *Information & Management, 48*(2011), 79–87.

Levina, N., & Ross, J. (2003, September). *MIS Quarterly*, 27(3), 331–364.

Mody, A., & Dahlman, C. (1992). Performance and potential of information technology: An international perspective. *World Development, 20*(12), 1703–1719.

Muller, E., & Zenker, A. (2001). Business services as actors of knowledge transformation: The role of KIBS in regional and national innovation systems. *Research Policy, 30*(9), 1501–1516.

NASSCOM & Delloite. (2008). *Indian IT/ITES industry: Impacting economy and society 2007–08.* Teen Murti Marg, Chanakyapuri, New Delhi 110021, India: NASSCOM foundation. Available online August 1, 2009 http://www.nasscom.in.

Oliner, S. D., & Sichel, D. E. (1994). Computers and output growth revisited: How big is the puzzle? *Brookings Papers on Economic Activity, 1994*(2), 273–334.

Oliner, S. D., & Sichel, D. E. (2000). The resurgence of growth in the late 1990s: Is information technology the story? *Journal of Economic Perspectives, 14,* 3–22.

Olsen. (2006). Productivity impacts of offshoring and outsourcing: A review. STI working paper, OECD, Directorate for Science, Technology and Industry (STI), vol 2006/1.

Perez, C. (1985). Microelectronics, long waves and world structural change: New perspectives for developing countries. *World Development, 13*(3), 441–463.

Reserve Bank of India. (2009). *Handbook of statistics on Indian economy*. Available online December 21, 2009 http://www.rbi.org.in/.

Shearmur, R., & Doloreux, D. (2013). Innovation and knowledge-intensive business service: The contribution of knowledge-intensive business service to innovation in manufacturing establishments. *Economics of Innovation and New Technology, 22,* 751–774.

Sichel, D. (1997). Computers and aggregate economic growth. *Business Economics, 34*(2), 18–24.

Stiroh, K. (2002). *Reassessing the role of IT in the production function: A meta analysis*. Federal Reserve Bank of New York, mimeo.

Tether, & Hipp. (2002). Knowledge intensive, technical and other services: patterns of competitiveness and innovation compared. *Technology Analysis & Strategic Management, 14*(2), 163–182.

Tether, B. S., & Tajar, A. (2008). The organisational-cooperation mode of innovation and its prominence amongst European service firms. *Research Policy, 37*(4), 720–739.

Thompson, S., Teo, A., & Bhattacherjee, A. (2014). Knowledge transfer and utilization in IT outsourcing partnerships: A preliminary model of antecedents and outcomes. *Information & Management, 51,* 177–186.

Wood, P. (2005). A service-informed approach to regional innovation—Or adaptation? *The Service Industries Journal, 25*(4), 429–445.

Wood, P. (2006). The regional significance of knowledge-intensive services in Europe: KISINN and after. *Innovation: The European Journal of Social Science Research, 19*(1), 51–66.

World Bank. (2010). *World development indicators* (2010). Washington, DC: World Bank.

ICT, Access to Finance and Firm Exports: A Cross-Country Study

Prakash Singh and Dibyendu Maiti

Abstract The present study tries to empirically evaluate how information and communication technology (ICT) and access to finance separately and jointly affect the firm export decision. The study uses data from the World Bank Enterprise Survey for two different waves. Empirical results based on the probit model suggest that ICT and access to finance plays an instrumental role in the firm export decision. Although the interaction of ICT and access to finance is insignificant, the indirect effect of ICT on the firm export decision through access to finance still cannot be ruled out as ICT is one of the significant explanatory variables in the simultaneous equation with access to finance as the dependent variable. The direct effect of ICT reduces cost and hence increases the likelihood of export decision. Indirectly, ICT affects export decision through its effect on access to finance and export decision.

1 Introduction

The information and communication technology (ICT)[1] has experienced a significant rise both in the developed and developing countries, and its usage has expanded encompassing both conventional and newer areas.[2] With its expansion, the ongoing interest has been to understand its effect on various domains of the economy and society among researchers and policymakers. In the present study, we intend to

[1] Although there is no perfect definition of ICT, yet it can be broadly considered as the technology which integrates internet, computer (hardware and software) to receive, store, disseminates and transform information (Bresnahan 2010).

[2] Now firms are using data mining to understand consumer behaviour, to predict market size and share.

P. Singh (✉)
Centre for Development Economics, Delhi School of Economics, Delhi, India
e-mail: prakash.archa@gmail.com

D. Maiti
Delhi School of Economics, Delhi, India

D. Maiti et al. (eds.), *Digitalisation and Development*,
https://doi.org/10.1007/978-981-13-9996-1_6

understand how uses of ICT affect firm export market entry decision directly and indirectly through its effect on firm access to finance.[3]

No doubt, the exports benefit industry and state through a reduction of transaction costs and improvement of market competition. The existing literature emphasises that getting into the export market is rewarding for firms, too if they could improve productivity by an improvement in technology. Melitz (2003) suggested that a firm requires additional sunk cost (in terms of market search, transaction cost, product customisation, advertisement, setup and distribution cost etc.) to enter into export market and part of the sunk cost has to be paid up front, and, it is only those firms which can overcome the sunk cost will enter the export market. Hence, only the most productive firms in the industry will take up an export activity, and the rest could not enter due to a shortfall of productivity level. Further, many firms near the productivity threshold could not enter the export market due to inaccessibility to finance (financial constraint). Exporting firms need external financing to meet the sunk cost, and further to raise working capital. Often there is a huge lag in the expenditure and payment received after sales in the export market. Thus, access to finance and firm export market entry decision seems to be strongly correlated.

ICT can potentially help in overcoming the sunk cost by reducing the production cost and improving the productivity and efficiency of the enterprise which finally induces comparative advantage for international trade (Madon 2000; Puri 2007; Walsham 2001; Basu and Ferald 2008; Rangan and Sengul 2009). The other channel through which ICT reduces cost is a drop in marketing cost and an improvement in market search and network establishment (Muto and Yamano 2009). Moreover, ICT use raises allocative efficiency by enabling the business to monitor worker better and thus reduces monitoring cost. It helps in optimising time and resources utilisation by keeping a record of day to day inventories of demand and supply, etc. Further, it helps in matching buyers and sellers by bridging information more readily available and at a very lower cost. For instance, it is very easy and less costly to search for a firm with online access (Freund and Weinhold 2004).

In addition to its direct effect, it is also possible that ICT can positively influence firm export market entry decision by improving their access to finance. It can reduce the information asymmetry and leverage the access to finance and cost of finance (Aminuzzaman et al. 2003; Andonova 2006), by making the financial sector more accessible with lower transaction cost and time. Use of ICT by firms signal transparency to the lenders and thus increases their chance of getting a loan. It reduces information asymmetry between borrower and lenders, which allows banks to reduce potential losses, and eventually leads to an improved lending condition and higher availability of credit. This can further help to increase competition and, hence, reduce the unit cost of lending. It can also improve credit opportunities by allowing access to even distance lenders.

Thus, ICT has potential not only to improve productivity (cost reduction) but also to increase access to finance, and thus can influence the firm export decision (Wang and Li 2017). However, surprisingly, the role of information and commination

[3]With access to finance we mean access to formal finance.

technology (ICT) has not been explored extensively in determining the firm's export decision. There is a complete dearth of studies examining the role of ICT in the firm export decision in association with access to finance.

In this backdrop, the present study attempts to understand the role of ICT in driving the firms' export decision directly and indirectly through its impact on enterprise access to finance. To our best understanding, there exist very few studies examining the role of ICT on the firm export decision. No study is found that analysed its indirect effect on the firm export decision through its impact on access to finance. In this study, firm-level data from the manufacturing and services sectors have been explored to understand the effect of ICT and access to finance on the export decision. Further, to the best of our knowledge, except Clarke (2008), we do not find any empirical study using firm-level data that examined the role of ICT use in the export performance of services firms.

Rest of the paper is organised as follows. Section 2 presents a review of existing literature and Sect. 3.1 deals with data. Discussion on methodology and empirical model has been put in Sect. 3.2. Section 4 put forward summary statistics result and discussion and paper end with conclusion policy recommendation in Sect. 5.

2 Review of Literature

Despite the extensive use and far-reaching effect of ICT uses, the empirical literature examining the role of ICT in firm internationalisation through export market entry is scanty. The evidence of research, although not very conclusive but so far points out that there exists a positive relationship between ICT and firm export decision.

ICT uses improve the chances of the firm entering into export market by reducing the cost through multiple channels. It reduces the time of filing of customs documents, which in turn, likely to improve their exporting chances (Clarke 2008). It helps in reducing cost by establishing direct customer contact and thus bypassing traditional market intermediaries and strengthens before-after sells customer services at a much lower cost (Lohrke et al. 2006). It helps in managing customer relationships better and thus expected to affect firm internationalisation (Morgan-Thomas 2009). It reduces the cost of market-related information acquisition (Borges et al. 2009) and reduces the information friction (Allen 2014) and thereby improving the chances of getting into the export market. It can overcome some of the traditional problems of marketing for internationalising firms (Berthon et al. 1999). Further, it will improve the business environment and interaction between the customer and the seller by deciphering valuable information to both the side with the use of data mining technique, market survey and research techniques (Prasad et al. 2001).

Investment in new technology and exporting activity is complementary (Lileeva and Trefler 2010; Bustos 2011). Thus, ICT would improve firm export market entry decision and intensity. The same was validated when Bennett (1997) suggest that ICT improves firm export sales, but what is more important is how ICT is being used. That determines its effect (Morgan-Thomas and Bridgewater 2004) and requires a combination of online and offline strategy to improve the pay-outs (Sinkovics et al. 2013). One such strategy is the integration of firms' back end online technology with front end functionality (Reuber and Fischer 2011).

As ICT brings down the barrier of location, hence it facilitates services of exporting with the help of the internet (Freund and Weinhold 2002) and the effect is more profound concerning the location (Freund and Weinhold 2004). Thus, internet penetration to geographically remote locations improves export decisions of firms (Clarke and Wallste 2006). It is also observed that better ICT infrastructure improves exports, and the effect is proportional to the quality of infrastructure (Portugal-Perez and Wilson 2012). The firm-level, studies found that firms involved in services export use ICT more intensively (Abramovsy and Griffith 2006; Clarke 2008; Ariu and Mion 2010; Fort 2014).

Clarke (2008) and Ricci and Trionfetti (2012) based on multi-country data, including low and middle-income countries, indicates that firms that use ICT are more probable to export than similar firms that do not. However, there are also studies showing that ICT uses do not seem to be correlated with their extensive intensity, i.e. exporting firms using ICT did not seem to export more than those who do not use it (Clarke 2008). Mathews and Bianchi (2010), in a study for Australian firms, reveals that ICT (measured as websites and e-sales) has a significant and positive impact on the growth of exports. Whereas Bianchi and Mathews (2016) in their study on Chilean firms finds that the effect of ICT on export is positive, but the nature of the effect is indirect through the improved information flows and business relationships. Hagsten and Kotnik (2017) worked on the role of different ICT capabilities on export decision and intensity of European firms and found a positive relationship.

Literature on finance and investment suggest that financial constraint hurts firm investment (Fazzari et al. 1988; Bernanke and Gertler 1990; Clementi and Hopenhayn 2006) and Melitz (2003) suggest that exporting involves sunk cost and only those firm which are able to clear this barrier can be select into the export market. Thus, the financial constraint is strongly linked to a firm export decision (Chaney 2016; Manova 2013). Access to finance improves firm exporting ability by reducing the productivity barrier of entry (Manova 2013). The literature on the role of financial intermediaries suggests that access to finance improves the productivity of the firm, and the managerial decision, and thus helps the firm in entering the export market (Beck 2002).

A firm requires additional financial resources to meet the export market entry, and information asymmetry is the main obstacle, and hence must look for external sources of finance (Moro et al. 2015; Petersen and Rajan 1994). Banks find it difficult and costly to gather the necessary information to access information about the riskiness of the project. Use of ICT helps information dissemination to find less risky and hassle-free projects. This further brings down the geographical proximity of the lender and borrower and makes the information more reliable (Attom 2013). Similarly, Asongu and Moulin (2016) suggest that ICT reduces information asymmetry and hence improves access to finance, although the strength of the effect is not very strong. For firms' entering into the export market, these costs play an important role in their overall expenditure and earnings. Castillo-Merino et al. (2010) found a positive relationship between ICT uses and firm financial constraint. This corroborates the argument made in favour of ICT use and its impact on firm access to finance.

Although, there exists sufficient literature which analyses the role of access to finance on form export decision yet they are not very conclusive. Further, the literature on ICT and the firm export decision is scanty. Whatever is available, is only at the individual country level or industry level. There is no study at the firm level using cross-country data examining how ICT and access to finance jointly affect the firm export decision.

3 Data and Methodology

3.1 Data

To examine the role of ICT and access to finance on firms' export decision empirically, the present study utilises rich enterprise-level dataset provided by the World Bank Enterprise Survey (WBES). WBES offers a multi-country level enterprise survey data taking the responses from managers of the enterprise from the private sector of the economies. The WBES data covers a broad range of indicators to measure the performance, challenges perceived by the enterprise in their respective economy. WBES data comes in two different waves: wave-I and wave-II. In wave-I, firms were surveyed across different countries from 2002 to 2006, and in wave-II, the survey started in the year 2006 till to date. We have combined both the waves' data. All the variables in wave-I and wave-II are not common, so we have taken only those variables which are common across the two waves. The data is apt for the study as it has information on ICT uses at the enterprise level as well as other valuable information, i.e., firms' age, size, ownership, industry, sector, export intensity, access to finance, etc. They are identified as important factors in the existing literature in connection with firms export decision. Information collected in the survey is standardised to maintain comparability of enterprise-level information across the countries. The data is available for a mix of firms ranging from small, medium to large size enterprises.

3.2 Methodology

Firms' export decision in literature is usually derived from their export to sales ratio. Thus, a firms' export decision is unobservable and non-linear variable. Let P_j^* be the firm export to sales ratio and P_j is the unobserved firm export decision variable such that:

$$P_j = \begin{cases} 1 \text{ for } P_j^* > 0 \\ 0 \text{ for } P_j^* = 0 \end{cases}$$

Given that firm export decision (P_j) is a binary variable; we will use a probit model to estimate the determinants of it. This is defined as:

$$P_j = \alpha X_j + \varepsilon_j$$

where, P_j is a binary variable with the value 1 if the firm is engaged in export activities (export to sales share is positive) and 0 otherwise. X_j represents an array of variables affecting the likelihood of firm export decision including industry, country and sector-level attributes and ε_j is the random error term.

According to the new-new trade theory literature, a firm enters into the export market if the profit from the export market is positive otherwise not (Melitz 2003). Now, foreign profit is spent to meet additional variable cost and fixed sunk cost. Thus, all those attributes causing a decrease in the cost will influence the firm export market entry decision. Existing empirical and theoretical studies suggest that firm size, age, productivity and ownership are some of the critical elements which influences enterprise export market entry decision.[4] Additionally, the recent work of Manova (2013) and Muûls (2015) add access to finance as one of the important factor influencing firms' export market entry decision. They argue that firm heterogeneity cannot be completely explained by exogenous productivity differences. Thus, the empirical model for the firm export decision can be written as:

$$\text{export}_i = \alpha_0 + \alpha_1 \text{lage}_i + \alpha_2 \text{size}_i + \alpha_3 \text{foreign}_i + \alpha_4 \text{productivity}_i + \alpha_5 \text{location}_i + \alpha_6 AF_i + \alpha_7 ICT_i + \varepsilon_i \quad (3)$$

where *export* is firm's export decision with values 1 if the export share in sales is positive, otherwise 0. *lage* represents firms age. This is measured as the difference between the year of survey and the year of firm inception in the logarithmic term. Existing literature on covariates of a firm's export market entry decision suggests that the firms' age is positively correlated with their entry decision. It is argued that as firm grow older, it becomes more efficient as it acquires skills, organisational linkages, accumulates knowledge and establishes arm length relationship that makes the older firm self-selected into the export market easily (Roberts and Tybout 1997). Although, there are studies which refute this argument that age influences firm exportability. For example, Ottaviano and Martincus (2011) argue that age and the export decision is not correlated and Alvarez and LÓpez (2005) suggest that there exist a negative relationship between age and firm export decision.

Firm *size* is a categorical variable capturing values 0 for a small firm (<20 workers), 1 for medium-sized firm (20–99 workers) and 2 for large firm (>100 workers). The small size category is the base of comparison for size variable. According to the

[4]See review of literature for variables determining the firm export market entry.

literature on the selection of the firms to the export market, the role of firm size has been well established (Marinov et al. 2008). It suggests that larger firms can make use of their size to attain economies of scale, which reduces their average or marginal costs (Wagner 1995, 2001).[5] Drawing from the argument that in the long run, only the efficient firms survive and grow (Jovanovic 1982; Roberts and Tybout 1997). This suggests that large firms are more productive; hence, their likelihood of entering into the export market is higher. Whereas, Dhanaraj and Beamish (2003) propose that large firm acquire organisational capabilities achieved through their managerial abilities, which enables them to transform their financial and physical resources into competency level and thus help self-selection to export market. Further, hierarchical governance structure allows large firms to realise economies of scale that helps them enter the export market (Majocchi et al. 2005).

Further, *foreign* is a dummy variable reflecting ownership pattern of the enterprise. The variable *foreign* takes value 1 if the share of foreign ownership in the enterprise is more than equal to 10%, otherwise 0. The prior research exhibits that ownership structure also plays an instrumental role in the firm's export market entry decision (Lall 1986; Rasiah 2003; Du and Girma 2007). The theoretical argument in support of the ownership-export decision is that foreign-owned firm gets access to the network and superior knowledge from the parent companies. Further, it is argued that superior governance mechanism, dynamic corporate culture and better resource access also contribute to their higher likelihood of exporting (Filatotchev et al. 2008).

Variable productivity measures the level of productivity of the enterprise and represents the logarithmic value of firms' utilisation capacity. We have taken capacity utilisation as the proxy of productivity. This is typically measured as the change in output at given input due to technological factors and can be measured by a change in efficiency, reallocation of resources of improvement in capacity utilisation. With the use of technology and learning by doing, a firm improves its capacity to utilise the input (i.e. increase in capacity utilisation) that leads to increase in output given input (see Baldwin et al. 2013). Hence, capacity utilisation can be perceived as productivity. Both theoretically and empirically, the role of productivity as an important predictor of the decision to export has been well established (Wagner 2007; Cassiman and Golovko 2011). The explanation for the above observation is that exporting involves an additional sunk cost in the form of the cost associated with the market search, transportation, establishing distribution channels, business networks, customising products for foreign market, etc. (Baldwin 1989; Greenaway et al. 2007). Thus, it is only those productive firm which can overcome these costs will be able to propel themselves to the export market (Roberts and Tybout 1999; Melitz 2003; Das et al. 2007). Moreover, Liu et al. (2008) suggest that higher productivity helps firms in the export market through cost leadership.

AF is a measure of firms' access to finance. It is constructed using information in the questionnaire to report on the percentage of new investment/working capital being finance by sources, such as internal capital, banks (domestic and foreign), and trade credit. The measure of access to finance takes value 1 if more than 50%

[5]It is believed that strong network and bulk buying also helps large firm in reducing trading cost.

of the new investment or working capital of the enterprise is financed by formal sources, otherwise 0. Finally, *ICT* is introduced to measure the effect of the use of the information and communication services on firm self-selecting into the export market. The variable, *ICT*, is constructed from the response to the questionnaire. They are asked whether the enterprise uses email to communicate with suppliers or customers; whether the firm uses a website to communicate with suppliers or customers. If enterprise reply or the response is yes, then the variable *ICT* takes value 1, and, if the answer is no in both the question, it takes value 0.

To control the country, year and industry differences, we have introduced country, year and industry fixed effects in the estimation. Additionally, to make error terms homogeneous, we have used a robust form of probit model. Further, it is possible that firm export decision, ICT adoption and access to finance are endogenously related. As a result, there could be a problem with simultaneity and endogeneity. To tackle this problem, this study uses bi-probit SUR model estimation technique.

4 Result and Discussion

4.1 Preliminary Analysis

Before we get into any formal econometric analysis on how ICT uses and access to finance affect firm export decision, it will be interesting to have a primary understanding of the relationship with simple graphs and summary statistics. Figure 1 presents the preliminary effect of ICT uses on export (number of firms exporting and export intensity) across the countries. Scatter plot with a line of fit and the correlation

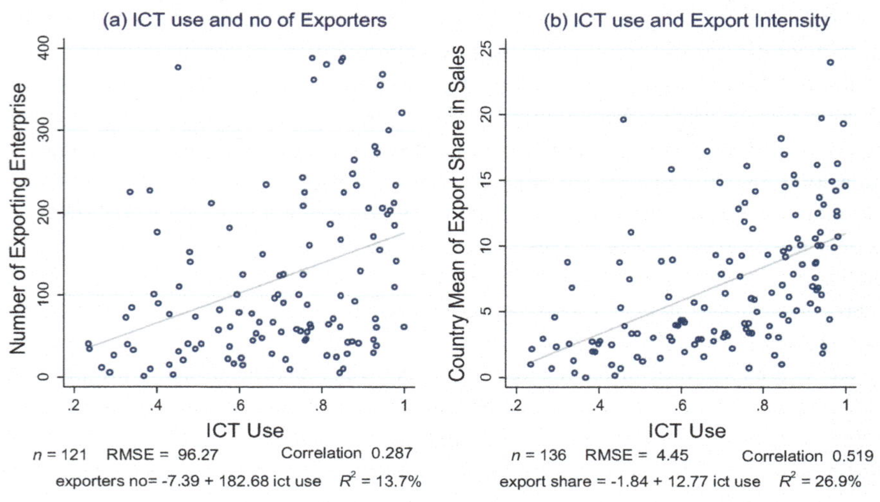

Fig. 1 ICT use and export activity. *Source* Authors calculation based on WEBS wave-I and II data

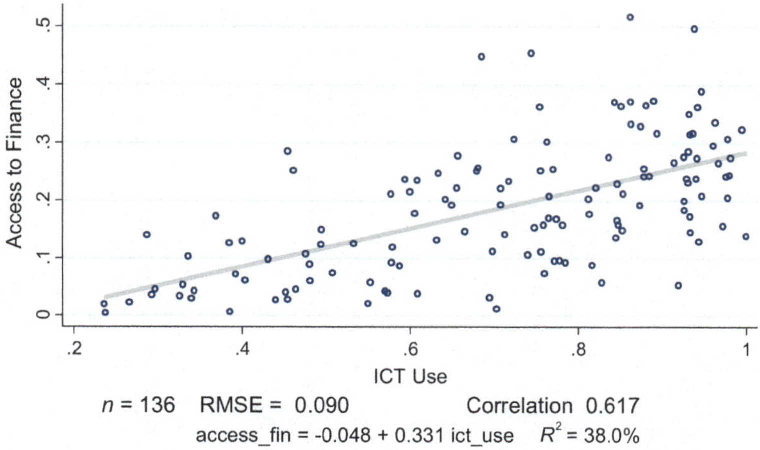

Fig. 2 ICT use and access to finance. *Source* Authors Calculation Based on WBES wave-I and wave-II data

between ICT uses and exporting firms in a country (Fig. 1a) suggest that the higher the use of ICT larger the number of exporting firms. This indicates that with more use of ICT, the number of firms entering into the export market will increase, and thus, it is expected that ICT will positively influence the firm export market entry decision.

Similarly, the ICT uses are positively correlated with export's share in sales (Fig. 1b). This shows that ICT is positively correlated with the higher export market sales of the firm. Thus, more firms will find export activity lucrative and hence would tend to enter more into the export market. Thus, increased use of ICT can boost the number of the firm entering into the export market.

Likewise, to understand how ICT uses affecting access to finance, we used a scatter plot with a fitted line (see Fig. 2). Figure 2 depicts that ICT and access to finance are positively correlated. As the intensity of ICT uses is increasing the level of access to finance is rising. This suggests that higher use of ICT leads to more access to finance at the firm level.

Further, to analyse how firm access is linked to export decision we used a scatter plot of access to finance variable with firms exporting at a country level and also with the mean export share in sales at country level. Figure 3 shows that access to finance and firms exporting is positively linked. Thus, with an increase in access to finance more firm opts for exporting (Fig. 3a). Similarly, with an improvement in access to finance the export share in sales rises (Fig. 3b). This jointly connotes that access to finance influences firm export decision. Overall it appears that ICT has a positive effect on both firm export decision and their access to finance. Further, access to finance improves the firm export entry decision. Thus, it can be argued that ICT influences firm exporting decision directly and indirectly also through improvement in their access to finance.

Table 1 presents a summary statistics of the explanatory variables for the exporter

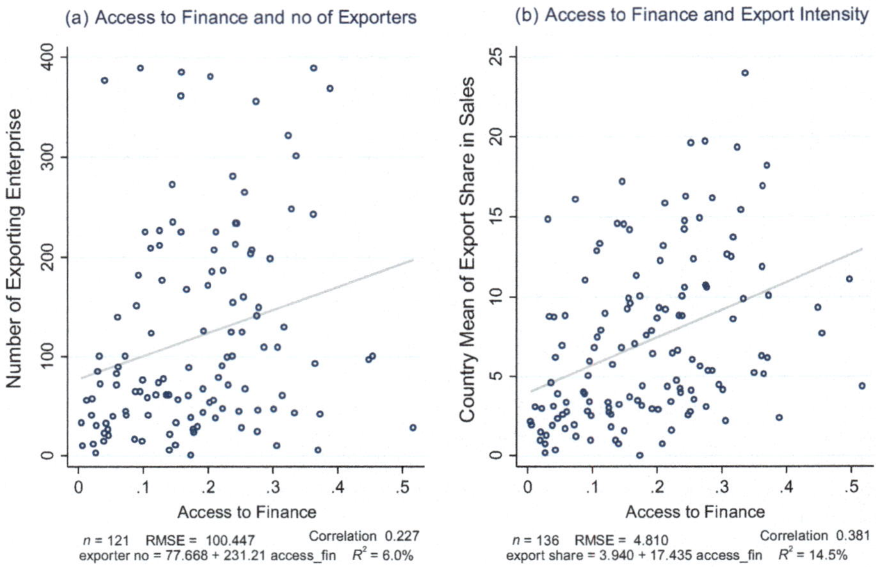

Fig. 3 Access to finance and export activity. *Source* Authors Calculation Based on WBES wave-I and wave-II data

and a non-exporter group of firms. Looking at the mean of firm's age, we see that non-exporters are younger than exporter. Comparison of size across exporter and non-exporter directs that exporting firms are older than non-exporting ones. Capacity utilisation, a proxy of firm productivity across both the groups, is not showing big difference although the exporters are found to be slightly more productive.

Similarly, there is not much difference in terms of locations. Comparison of mean values suggests that foreign-owned firms are more into exporting. Same is true for access to finance variables. Access to finance is higher for the exporting firm group compared to the non-exporting group. We find a similar effect for ICT use for both the groups. Even though for some of the attributes, the difference between exporting and non-exporting firms is not big, but the *t*-test for difference in mean suggests that the differences are statistically significant.

4.2 ICT, Access to Finance and Firm Export Decision

We now move on to empirically evaluate the how ICT uses and access to finance after controlling for other attributes (such as firm age, size, foreign ownership, productivity, location and country, industry and year effect) affect the firm export decision. Estimation results based on probit model are presented in Table 2. Further, Table 2 presents the probit results for the whole sample as well as for manufacturing and

Table 1 Summary statistics

		N	Mean	Standard deviation	Minimum	Maximum	*T*-test
Firm age	Exporter	44345	21.57	21.72	0	1954	−5.278***
	Non-exporter	137,535	16.29	14.66	0	225	(−58.03)
Firm size	Exporter	44,993	2.23	0.77	1	3	−0.636***
	Non-exporter	138,689	1.60	0.71	1	3	(−161.63)
Capacity utilisation	Exporter	35,803	75.84	20.92	0	960	−1.708***
	Non-exporter	78,189	74.13	22.15	0	150	(−12.29)
Location of the firm	Exporter	35,606	0.50	0.50	0	1	−0.0127***
	Non-exporter	109,895	0.49	0.50	0	1	(−4.18)
Foreign ownership	Exporter	44,531	0.23	0.42	0	1	−0.152***
	Non-exporter	138,027	0.07	0.26	0	1	(−91.30)
Access to finance	Exporter	42,295	0.37	0.48	0	1	−0.143***
	Non-exporter	130,432	0.23	0.42	0	1	(−58.72)
ICT use	Exporter	44,125	0.89	0.31	0	1	−0.262***
	Non-exporter	134,789	0.63	0.48	0	1	(−106.96)

Source Authors calculation based on WBES wave-I and II data
Note *, ** and *** indicate $p <= 0.10$, $p <= 0.05$ and $p <= 0.01$, respectively

services firms separately in column 1, 2 and 3, respectively. Similarly, column 4, 5 and 6 present the marginal effect for full sample, manufacturing and services firms.

Regression results put in Table 2 suggest that irrespective of the fact that whether the firm is from manufacturing sector or services, firm age is found to be positively and significantly correlated with their export's market entry decision (see Table 2). Hence, the old firm is more likely to enter the export market. Thus, as suggested in the literature, with the age firm acquires knowledge, and this serves as a sufficient cushion to absorb the sunk cost to get into the export market (Roberts and Tybout 1997; Ottaviano and Martincus 2011; Alvarez and LÓpez 2005).

Concerning the variable productivity, the coefficient of the variable is statistically insignificant irrespective of whether the firm is engaged in manufacturing or service activities. Thus, the productivity of the firm is not linked to its export decision. This result is in contrast to one of the existing studies, which strongly suggest that it is the more productive firm that finds exporting natural (Greenway et al. 2007; Roberts and Tybout 1999; Melitz 2003; Das et al. 2007).

Table 2 ICT, access to finance and firm exportability

Export (direct + indirect > 0)	Probit (coefficient)			Marginal effect		
Age	0.082***	0.089***	0.092***	0.271***	0.278***	0.347***
	(0.007)	(0.008)	(0.021)	(0.023)	(0.024)	(0.079)
Productivity	0.014	0.028	−0.181***	0.076	0.139	−1.292***
	(0.014)	(0.015)	(0.044)	(0.076)	(0.076)	(0.316)
Size (medium)	0.463***	0.532***	0.266***	0.209***	0.236***	0.104***
	(0.014)	(0.016)	(0.036)	(0.006)	(0.007)	(0.014)
Size (large)	1.077***	1.206***	0.417***	0.343***	0.388***	0.092***
	(0.016)	(0.018)	(0.044)	(0.005)	(0.006)	(0.010)
Access to finance	0.139***	0.124***	0.173***	0.055***	0.046***	0.081***
	(0.012)	(0.014)	(0.033)	(0.005)	(0.005)	(0.015)
Location (less than 1 m pop city)	0.029*	0.003	0.188***	0.017*	0.002	0.123***
	(0.013)	(0.014)	(0.033)	(0.008)	(0.008)	(0.021)
Foreign firm	0.653***	0.678***	0.526***	0.093***	0.088***	0.106***
	(0.018)	(0.020)	(0.041)	(0.003)	(0.003)	(0.008)
ICT use	0.675***	0.656***	0.679***	0.608***	0.561***	0.698***
	(0.016)	(0.018)	(0.040)	(0.015)	(0.016)	(0.043)
Constant	−2.237***	−2.506***	−4.546***	–	–	–
	(0.360)	(0.404)	(0.792)			
Pseudo-R^2	0.267	0.273	0.200	–	–	–
Observation	79261	63459	12464			
Wald-chi^2	18745.62	15961.35	8481.073	–	–	–
Year fixed effect	234.27	205.22	235.25			
Industry fixed effect	2463.79	1128.50	302.77	–	–	–
Country fixed effect	4219.06	3851.98	1088.88			

Note *, ** and *** represents significance at 10, 5 and 1% level of significance

The variable size has turned out to be positively correlated with the firm export decision, and the correlation is statistically meaningful. Thus, as the size of the firm increases, it becomes more likely that the firm will be self-selected to export. The result holds for both manufacturing and services sector firms also. It may be possible that with size firm attains efficiency, economies of scale, organisational capabilities, which essentially helps them in absorbing sunk cost needed for export market entry. Consequently, the result is in line with the existing studies (Wagner 1995; 2001; Roberts and Tybout 1999; Dhanaraj and Beamish 2003). Similarly, the coefficient of foreign ownership is found to be positive and statistically significant. This suggests that foreign-owned firm have a higher propensity for exporting compare to the domestic firm. Probably, it is the access to better technology, human resources, a bigger network which enables the foreign-owned firm to get into the export market successfully. The same is substantiated in earlier studies (Lall 1986; Rasiah 2003; Du and Girma 2007).

For our variable of interest, i.e. ICT use and access to finance, we find that the coefficient of the variable ICT use is positive and significant for full sample, manufacturing and services firms separately. They suggest that firms that use ICT are more likely to export irrespective of the sector. The marginal effect of the variable indicates that ICT uses increases the likelihood of exporting by 60%. Thus, the result confirms the findings of the existing studies. Use of ICT helps the firm to not only reduce the cost but also helps in finding a new market and other things at a lower rate and hence firm which uses ICT finds easier to choose to export.

Similarly, concerning access to finance estimation result reveals that the coefficient of the variable access to finance has a positive sign, and it is statistically significant also. Hence, there exists a positive association between firm access to finance and the export decision. Access to finance helps firmly in meeting the requirement of sunk cost and the additional cost of searching the market and thus favours firm export market entry. The result is broadly consistent for the sample of all the firms, manufacturing firms and services firms. Year, country and industry fixed effects are significant, suggesting that firm export decision varies across the country, year and industry.

4.2.1 Issue of Endogeneity

Existing literature suggests that access to finance and the firm export decision is likely to have endogeneity (see, for example, Kumarasamy and Singh 2018). A firm having no access to finance will find it difficult to get into the export market, and those who are not into the export market will have a problem in accessing finance. This suggests that access to finance and firm export are having simultaneity or problem of reverse causation. In the presence of endogeneity, the estimation result does not give a meaningful correlation. Thus, the results presented in Table 2 may not be true. To overcome this problem, we have used SUR bi-probit regressions. We have used a line of credit or overdraft as the additional determinants of firms access to finance.

SUR bi-probit regression result is present in Table 3. The coefficient of the age variable after correcting endogeneity has not changed in terms of sign and statistical meaning. Hence, the result suggests that age plays an instrumental role in the firm export decision. Similarly, the coefficient of the size has remained similar, and it is statistically relevant also. This confirms the vital role of in its export market entry. About the coefficient of the foreign ownership variable, we find that the variable is not only positive but also statistically significant. Thus, the result suggests that foreign-owned firms are more probable to choose to export activity.

Regarding the variable productivity, we find a deviation in the endogeneity corrected result from the normal probit regression result. The coefficient of the variable

Table 3 ICT, access to finance and firm exportability (correcting endogeneity)

Dependent variable export (direct + indirect > 0)	Coefficient	First stage reg	Coefficient	First stage reg	Coefficient	First stage reg
Age	0.067*** (0.007)	−0.007*** (0.002)	0.073*** (0.008)	−0.009*** (0.002)	0.055*** (0.014)	−0.004 (0.003)
Productivity	0.041*** (0.004)	0.007*** (0.001)	0.057*** (0.005)	0.008*** (0.001)	0.018** (0.007)	0.006*** (0.001)
Size (medium)	0.327*** (0.014)	0.029*** (0.003)	0.443*** (0.018)	0.033*** (0.004)	0.163*** (0.024)	0.025*** (0.005)
Size (large)	0.859*** (0.018)	0.069*** (0.004)	1.080*** (0.024)	0.072*** (0.006)	0.324*** (0.034)	0.060*** (0.008)
Access to finance	0.613*** (0.053)		0.627*** (0.062)		0.602*** (0.105)	
Location (less than 1 m pop city)	0.009 (0.013)	−0.033*** (0.003)	0.014 (0.016)	−0.038*** (0.004)	0.033 (0.026)	−0.018*** (0.005)
Foreign firm	0.616*** (0.017)	−0.048*** (0.005)	0.663*** (0.022)	−0.057*** (0.006)	0.566*** (0.030)	−0.036*** (0.007)
ICT use	0.560*** (0.017)	0.019*** (0.003)	0.557*** (0.021)	0.025*** (0.005)	0.452*** (0.031)	0.004 (0.005)
The line of credit or overdraft		0.225*** (0.003)		0.229*** (0.004)		0.212*** (0.005)
Constant	−2.237*** (0.342)	−0.039 (0.085)	−2.693*** (0.436)	−0.041 (0.132)	−5.127 (0.000)	−0.266** (0.093)
Observation	84781		53110		30971	
Wald test of exogeneity $chi^2(1)$	81.37		62.97		19.92	
Country fixed effect	Yes		Yes		Yes	
Industry fixed effect	Yes		Yes		Yes	
Year fixed effect	Yes		Yes		Yes	

Note *, ** and *** represents significance at 10, 5 and 1% level of significance has turned out positive and statistically significant. The positive and significant coefficient of the variable suggests that productivity plays an instrumental role in firm export market entry. After controlling for endogeneity, the result concerning productivity confirms the argument of existing literature that productive firm is more likely to get into the export market. Another deviation is in terms of the coefficient of the variable location. After taking care of endogeneity, location is no longer a significant predictor of the firm export decision.

Result of our main variable is still in line with the argument and makes sense statistically also. The coefficients of both the variables, access to finance, and ICT use, have retained the sign and statistical property. This suggests that access to finance and ICT uses plays a prominent role in firm export market entry.

Further, we have run the SUR probit regression for full sample; manufacturing firm and services firm samples separately for robustness checking, and the sign and statistical property of the coefficients have not changed with the change in the sample. They suggest that the results are robust.

Our next objective is to find how ICT affects firm export decision indirectly. For that, we have used the interaction variable in the probit model. Here, our main interest is to see how access to finance in interaction with ICT is affecting the firm export decision. Additionally, we have also tried to understand whether the indirect effect of ICT also runs through size, ownership and location. The coefficients of all the non-interaction variables continue to have the same sign and statistical property. But if look at the coefficient of the interaction variable, we find that except for large firm the coefficients are not significant. The positive and significant coefficient of the large enterprise reflects that ICT helps more to a large firm in contrast to small and medium firms. Whereas the coefficient for access to finance is insignificant, meaning that ICT is not playing a significant role in firm export decision through its effect on the firm access to finance. Probably this is due to that fact the ICT variable in the data only measures the use of ICT with their business client, whether the firm is using ICT for borrowing purposes is not captured in the variable and also there is no variable which captures the lender's side of the credit.

Overall the result suggests that firm age, size, productivity, foreign ownership, ICT use and access to finance play a significant role in the firm export decision. Thus older firms, large firms, foreign-owned firms; more productive firms will find exporting as a more attractive option. Further, if the firm uses ICT, it has more likelihood of entering the export market. Firms having access to finance will find export market entry easier. Moreover, firm location is also instrumental in the decision to get into the export market (Table 4).

Table 4 ICT, access to finance and firm exportability (interaction effect)

Dependent variable	Export (direct + indirect> 0)			
Age	0.090***	0.089***	0.090***	0.090***
	(0.010)	(0.010)	(0.010)	(0.010)
Productivity	0.001	0.001	0.001	0.002
	(0.018)	(0.018)	(0.018)	(0.018)
Size (medium)	0.486***	0.418***	0.486***	0.485***
	(0.019)	(0.043)	(0.019)	(0.019)
Size (large)	1.157***	0.954***	1.157***	1.156***
	(0.022)	(0.073)	(0.022)	(0.022)
Size (medium) * ICT use		0.087		
		(0.048)		
Size (large) * ICT use		0.226**		
		(0.076)		
Access to finance	0.200**	0.190***	0.191***	0.191***
	(0.061)	(0.018)	(0.018)	(0.018)
Access to finance * ICT use	−0.010			
	(0.064)			
ICT use	0.645***	0.583***	0.665***	0.655***
	(0.027)	(0.034)	(0.032)	(0.026)
Location (less than 1 m pop city)	0.044*	0.044*	0.084*	0.043*
	(0.019)	(0.019)	(0.042)	(0.019)
Location * ICT use			−0.047	
			(0.045)	
Foreign firm	0.693***	0.693***	0.693***	0.812***
	(0.026)	(0.026)	(0.026)	(0.075)
Foreign * ICT use				−0.131
				(0.079)
Constant	−1.529***	−1.474***	−1.546***	−1.541***
	(0.383)	(0.383)	(0.384)	(0.383)
Pseudo-R^2	0.265	0.265	0.265	0.265
Observation	40946	40946	40946	40946
Wald-chi^2	9805.07	9928.752	9805.274	9786.903
Country fixed effect	Yes	Yes	Yes	Yes
Industry fixed effect	Yes	Yes	Yes	Yes
Year fixed effect	Yes	Yes	Yes	Yes

Note *, ** and *** represents significance at 10, 5 and 1% level of significance

5 Conclusion

Over the last two decades, the uses of ICT has increased tremendously, and its uses have touched almost all aspects of life. As it has potentially reduced the cost of operation for enterprise, thus, it is expected that its uses will affect firm export decision positively. Further, it may be possible that ICT affects firm export decision directly by increasing the firm efficient by reducing the cost of production, and it may be possible that it also affects the firm export decision indirectly by improving firm access to finance. The present study endeavours to empirically examine whether it is only the direct channel or also the indirect channel or only it is the indirect channel through which the ICT and the firm export decision are linked. Thus, the study contributes to the existing literature on firm export market entry decision with a new set of empirical evidence on the use of ICT and access to finance on exporting.

To examine these objectives empirically, the study uses WBES wave-I and wave-II data spanning from 2002 to 2016 and enterprise from more than 100 countries. As the dependent variable is dichotomous study uses probit regression model, Further to encompass the problem of endogeneity and simultaneity study uses SUR probit model.

Estimation results based on probit model and SUR probit model reveal that firm export market entry is strongly linked with its ICT uses. Thus, a firm using ICT services are more likely to get into the export market. Consequently, the study confirms the argument provided in the existing literature on the role of ICT in reducing the cost of operation. Further, the effect of ICT use is consistent as the sign, and statistical property did not change with a change in the sample. Similarly, we found that access to finance plays an instrumental role in the firm export decision. Results provide support to the existing argument that access to finance will improve the probability of exporting by allowing the firm to manage sunk cost. Additionally, it may be possible that the external pressure of lenders enables the firm to be more productive and thus increases thus chances of exporting. Although, the indirect effect of ICT through its effect on firm access to finance did not come significantly in the interaction effect regression, yet the presence of indirect effect cannot be ruled out as ICT is a significant variable in the SUR model with access to finance as the dependent variable. Additionally, we find our results are in corroboration of the existing literature on the effect of age, size, productivity, foreign ownership as the important predictor of the firm export decision.

As the estimation results remain the same in terms of sign and size of coefficient with change in sample (manufacturing and services firms separately) results are robust. Further, Results hold even after correcting for endogeneity, validating the robustness of the analysis.

Although the study makes a valuable contribution to the existing literature still, the study has some limitations. First of all, the information on ICT uses is very limited, that binds the scope of the study. To understand the role of ICT clearly, it is important to have a measure of ICT on different dimensions. The WBES data only provides information on the use of email to contact the seller and use of a computer, which will not reveal the entire spectrum of ICT innovations. Further, we believe that if the information on ICT from the lender's side is available, it would have enabled us to examine the inter-linkages of ICT and access to finance more systematically.

Finally, to reap benefit from exporting, the domestic government needs to provide ICT infrastructure widely and at a very cost-effective rate. Further, the policy is needed to strengthen the financial sector so that the firm should have adequate access to finance for their investment needs.

References

Abramovsky, L., & Griffith, R. (2006). Outsourcing and offshoring of business services: How important is ICT? *Journal of the European Economic Association, 4*(2–3), 594–601.

Allen, T. (2014). Information frictions in trade. *Econometrica, 82*(6), 2041–2083.

Alvarez, R., & LÓpez, R. A. (2005). Exporting and performance: Evidence from Chilean plants. *Canadian Journal of Economics, 38*(4), 1384–1400.

Aminuzzaman, S., Baldersheim, H., & Jamil, I. (2003). Talking back! Empowerment and mobile phones in rural Bangladesh: A study of the village phone scheme of Grameen Bank. *Contemporary South Asia, 12*(3), 327–348.

Andonova, V. (2006). Mobile phones the internet and the institutional environment. *Telecommunication Policy, 30*(1), 29–45.

Ariu, A., & Mion, G. (2010). Trade in services: IT and task content. *National Bank of Belgium working paper* (p. 200). Brussels.

Asongu, S. A., & Moulin, B. (2016). The role of ICT in reducing information asymmetry for financial access. *Research in International Business and Finance, 38,* 202–213.

Attom, E. B. (2013). The impact of information communication technology (ICT) on business growth strategies of small and medium-scale enterprises (SMEs) in the Awutu-Senya east municipality of central region of Ghana. *Asian Journal of Business and Management Sciences, 3*(2), 13–28.

Baldwin, R. (1989). Sunk-cost hysteresis. *NBER working paper*, 2911.

Baldwin, J. R., Gu, W., & Yan, B. (2013). Export growth, capacity utilization, and productivity growth: Evidence from the Canadian manufacturing plants. *Review of Income and Wealth, 59*(4), 665–688.

Basu, S., & Fernald, J. (2008). Information and communications technology as a general purpose technology: Evidence from U.S. industry data. *Economic Review* (pp. 1–15). Federal Reserve Bank of San Francisco.

Beck, T. (2002). Financial development and international trade: Is there a link? *Journal of International Economics, 57*(1), 107–131.

Bennett, R. (1997). Export marketing and the internet: Experiences of web site use and perceptions of export barriers among UK businesses. *International Marketing Review, 14*(5), 324–344.

Bernanke, B., & Gertler, M. (1990). Financial fragility and economic performance. *The Quarterly Journal of Economics, 105*(1), 87–114.

Berthon, P., Pitt, L., Katsikeas, C. S., & Berthon, J. P. (1999). Virtual services go international: International services in the marketspace. *Journal of International Marketing, 7*(3), 84–105.

Bianchi, C., & Mathews, S. (2016). Internet marketing and export market growth in Chile. *Journal of Business Research, 69*(2), 426–434.

Borges, M., Hoppen, N., & Luce, F. B. (2009). Information technology impact on market orientation in e-business. *Journal of Business Research, 62*(9), 883–890.

Bresnahan, T. (2010). General purpose technologies. In B. Hall & N. Rosenberg (Eds.), *Handbook of the economics of innovation and technical change*. North-Holland: Elsevier.
Bustos, P. (2011). Trade liberalization, exports, and technology upgrading: Evidence on the impact of MERCOSUR on Argentinean firms. *American Economic Review, 101*(1), 304–340.
Cassiman, B., & Golovko, E. (2011). Innovation and internationalization through exports. *Journal of International Business Studies, 42*(1), 56–75.
Castillo-Merino, D., Vilaseca-Requena, J., & Plana-Erta, D. (2010). Financial constraints for innovative firms: The role of size, industry and ICT uses as determinants of firms' financial structure. In M. D. Lytras., P. Ordonez de Pablos., A. Ziderman A. Roulstone H. Maurer J. B. Imber. (Eds.), *Organizational, business, and technological aspects of the knowledge society. WSKS 2010. Communications in computer and information science* (vol. 112). Berlin, Heidelberg: Springer.
Chaney, T. (2016). Liquidity constrained exporters. *Journal of Economic Dynamics and Control, 72*(C), 141–154.
Clarke, G. R. G. (2008). Has the internet increased exports for firms from low and middle-income countries? *Information Economics and Policy, 20*(1), 16–37.
Clarke, G. R. G., & Wallsten, S. J. (2006). Has the internet increased trade? Developed and developing country evidence. *Economic Inquiry, 44*(3), 465–484.
Clementi, G. L., & Hopenhayn, H. A. (2006). A theory of financing constraints and firm dynamics. *The Quarterly Journal of Economics, 121*(1), 229–265.
Das, S., Roberts, M. J., & Tybout, J. R. (2007). Market entry costs, producer heterogeneity, and export dynamics. *Econometrica, 75*(3), 837–873.
Dhanaraj, C., & Beamish, P. W. (2003). A resource-based approach to the study of export performance. *Journal of Small Business Management, 41*(3), 242–260.
Du, J., & Girma, S. (2007). Finance and firm export in China. *Kyklos, 60*(1), 37–54.
Fazzari, S. M., Hubbard, R. G., & Petersen, B. C. (1988). Financing constraints and corporate investment. *Brookings Papers on Economic Activity, 1988*(1), 141–205.
Filatotchev, I., Stephan, J., & Jindra, B. (2008). Ownership structure, strategic controls and export intensity of foreign-invested firms in transition economies. *Journal of International Business Studies, 39*(7), 1133–1148.
Fort, T. (2014). *Technology and production fragmentation: Domestic versus foreign sourcing*. Hanover, NH: Unpublished paper Tuck School of Business, Dartmouth College.
Freund, C. L., & Weinhold, D. (2004). The effect of the internet on international trade. *Journal of International Economics, 62*(1), 171–189.
Freund, C. L., & Weinhold, D. (2002). The internet and international trade in services. *American Economic Review, 92*(2), 236–240.
Greenaway, D., Guariglia, A., & Kneller, R. (2007). Financial factors and exporting decisions. *Journal of International Economics, 73*(2), 377–395.
Hagsten, E., & Kotnik, P. (2017). ICT as facilitator of internationalisation in small and medium-sized firms. *Small Business Economics, 48*(2), 431–446.
Jovanovic, B. (1982). Selection and the evolution of industry. *Econometrica, 50*(3), 649–670.
Kumarasamy, D., & Singh, P. (2018). Access to finance, financial development and firm ability to export: Experience from Asia-Pacific countries. *Asian Economic Journal, 32*(1), 15–38.
Lall, S. (1986). Technological development and export performance in LDCs: Leading engineering and chemical firms in India. *Weltwirtschaftliches Archiv, 122*(1), 80–91.
Lileeva, & Trefler, D. (2010). Improved access to foreign markets raises plant-level productivity for some plants. *Quarterly Journal of Economics, 125*(3), 1051–1099.
Liu, X., Xiao, W., & Huang, X. (2008). Bounded entrepreneurship and internationalization of indigenous Chinese private-owned firms. *International Business Review, 17*(4), 488–508.
Lohrke, F., Franklin, G., & Frownfelter-Lohrke, C. (2006). The internet as an information conduit: A transaction cost analysis model of US SME internet use. *International Small Business Journal, 24*(2), 159–178.
Madon, S. (2000). The internet and socioeconomic development: Exploring the interaction. *Information Technology and People, 13*(2), 85–101.

Majocchi, A., Bacchiocchi, E., & Mayrhofer, U. (2005). Firm size, business experience and export intensity in SMEs: A longitudinal approach to complex relationships. *International Business Review, 14*(6), 719–738.
Manova, K. (2013). Credit constraints, heterogeneous firms, and international trade. *Review of Economic Studies, 80*(2), 711–744.
Marinov, R., Rocha, N., & DiNino, V. (2008). Trade liberalization and new exporters' size: A test of the heterogeneous firm model. *The BE Journal of Economic Analysis and Policy, 8*(1), 71–79.
Mathews, S. W., & Bianchi, C. (2010). The role of the internet on international market growth of Australian firms: An exploratory study. In *Proceedings of the Australia and New Zealand International Business Academy (ANZIBA) Conference* (pp. 15–17). April 2010, Sydney, Australia.
Melitz, M. J. (2003). The impact of trade on aggregate industry productivity and intra-industry reallocations. *Econometrica, 71*(6), 1695–1725.
Morgan-Thomas, A. (2009). Online activities and export performance of the smaller firm: A capability perspective. *European Journal of International Management, 3*(3), 266–285.
Morgan-Thomas, A., & Bridgewater, S. (2004). Internet and exporting: Determinants of success in virtual export channels. *International Marketing Review, 21*(4/5), 393–408.
Moro, A., Fink, M., & Maresch, D. (2015). Reduction in information asymmetry and credit access for small and medium-sized enterprises. *Journal of Financial Research, 38*(1), 121–143.
Muto, M., & Yamano, T. (2009). The impact of mobile phone coverage expansion on market participation: Panel data evidence from Uganda. *World Development, 37*(12), 1887–1896.
Muûls, M. (2015). Exporters and credit constraints. *Journal of International Economics, 95*(2), 333–343.
Ottaviano, G., & Martincus, C. V. (2011). SMEs in Argentina: Who are the exporters? *Small Business Economics, 37*(3), 341–361.
Petersen, M. A., & Rajan, R. (1994). The benefits of firm creditor relationships: Evidence from small business data. *Journal of Finance, 49*(1), 3–37.
Portugal-Perez, A., & Wilson, J. S. (2012). Export performance and trade facilitation reform: Hard and soft infrastructure. *World Development, 40*(7), 1295–1307.
Prasad, V. K., Ramamurthy, K., & Naidu, G. M. (2001). The influence of internet-marketing integration on marketing competencies and export performance. *Journal of International Marketing, 9*(4), 82–110.
Puri, S. (2007). Integrating scientific with indigenous knowledge: Constructing knowledge alliances for land management in India. *MIS Quarterly, 31*(2), 355–379.
Rangan, S., & Sengul, M. (2009). Information technology and transnational integration: Theory and evidence on the evolution of the modern multinational enterprise. *Journal of International Business Studies, 40*(9), 1496–1514.
Rasiah, R. (2003). Ownership, technology and electronics exports from Malaysia and Thailand. *Journal of Asian Economics, 14*(5), 785–811.
Reuber, A. R., & Fischer, E. (2011). International entrepreneurship in internet-enabled markets. *Journal of Business Venturing, 26*(6), 660–679.
Ricci, L. A., & Trionfetti, F. (2012). Productivity, networks, and export performance: Evidence from a cross-country firm dataset. *Review of International Economics, 20*(3), 552–562.
Roberts, M. J., & Tybout, J. R. (1997). The decision to export in Colombia: An empirical model of entry with sunk costs. *American Economic Review, 87*(4), 545–564.
Roberts, M. J., & Tybout, J. R. (1999). *An empirical model of sunk costs and the decision to export* (November 30, 1999). World Bank Policy Research Working Paper No. 1436.
Sinkovics, N., Sinkovics, R. R., & Jean, R. J. B. (2013). The internet as an alternative path to internationalization? *International Marketing Review, 30*(2), 130–155.
Wagner, J. (1995). Exports, firm size, and firm dynamics. *Small Business Economics, 7*(1), 29–39.
Wagner, J. (2001). A note on the firm size-export relationship. *Small Business Economics, 17*(4), 229–237.
Wagner, J. (2007). Exports and productivity: A survey of the evidence from firm-level data. *World Economy, 30*(1), 60–82.

Walsham, G. (2001). *Making a world of difference: IT in a global context*. USA: Wiley & Sons.
Wang, Y., & Li, J. (2017). ICT's effect on trade: Perspective of comparative advantage. *Economics Letters, 155*, 96–99.

Time Zone Differences and Service Trade

Biswajit Mandal and Alaka Shree Prasad

Abstract The paper explains how service trade has been facilitated because of the availability and development of Information and Communication Technology (ICT). With this, the paper points to the emerging theory of time zone (TZ) differences and trade where time zone difference between two countries evokes service trade given the availability of ICT. A simple 2×2 general equilibrium framework is considered to explain the effect of trade across non-overlapping time zones on factor prices and output. Results show a rise in the wage of skilled labour and a fall in rent. The result is conditional on the assumptions of factor intensity. In the case of output, the sector exploiting the time zone difference is seen to expand while the other contracts. This outcome, however, is independent of the assumption of factor intensity.

Keywords Time zones · Outsourcing · Services · Trade

JEL Classification F1 · F11

1 Introduction

Development in Information and Communication Technology (ICT) has allowed sharing information with any part of the world very quickly and at a negligible cost. Be it an individual or multinational firms, everyone is utilizing the communication network for their benefit. With the development of communication technology, there are also changes in day-to-day life. People are increasingly relying on electronic tools and the internet to accomplish their needs. So, the availability of ICT has expanded the market for both producers and consumers. Now consumers are not restricted

The paper has benefited from the comments received in ICCEM, St. Xavier's College, Kolkata; International Seminar on 'Issues in Sustainable Development in India: Present Problems & Future Perspective', A. K. Dasgupta Centre for Planning and Development, Visva-Bharati University; and Workshop on Economics of ICT, Delhi School of Economics, University of Delhi. This paper is a part of a chapter of the second author's Ph.D. dissertation. The usual disclaimer applies.

B. Mandal · A. S. Prasad (✉)
Department of Economics & Politics, Visva-Bharati University, Santiniketan 731235, India
e-mail: alakashree56@gmail.com

D. Maiti et al. (eds.), *Digitalisation and Development*,
https://doi.org/10.1007/978-981-13-9996-1_7

to avail any good or service from their local suppliers only. Rather they can get connected to a large range of goods or service providers residing in different parts of the globe and order their requirement all through the communication network. Producers, on the other hand, can now contact professionals like architects, software engineers, lawyers, doctors, business consultants, etc. residing at different locations for their assistance in developing or planning a particular project irrespective of whether it is the manufacturing of a good or development of a service or provision of a service. Professionals can share information or trade the demanded service through the internet. Therefore, as Christen (2017) mentions that the requirement of being at the same space and time has been reduced because of the developing technology that aims for seamless exchange of knowledge. Now a variety of services that were considered to be non-tradable a few decades ago are being traded across the world. In Fig. 1, WTO (World Trade Organization) data on services related to ICT and ICT-enabled services have been clubbed together to get an overall estimate of exports using ICT services. The figure shows that ICT-oriented exports have a considerable share in total commercial service exports and we observe an increasing trend of ICT and ICT-enabled services. This reveals that the prevalence of ICT and ICT-enabled trade is growing over time.

One major contributor to the increasing trend of ICT and ICT-enabled service trade is the outsourcing of service provisions activities to different parts of the world to professionals who can provide it most efficiently. Such outsourcing or off-shoring comprises of Information Technology Outsourcing (ITO) which consists of IT consulting, software development and management, network management, etc.;

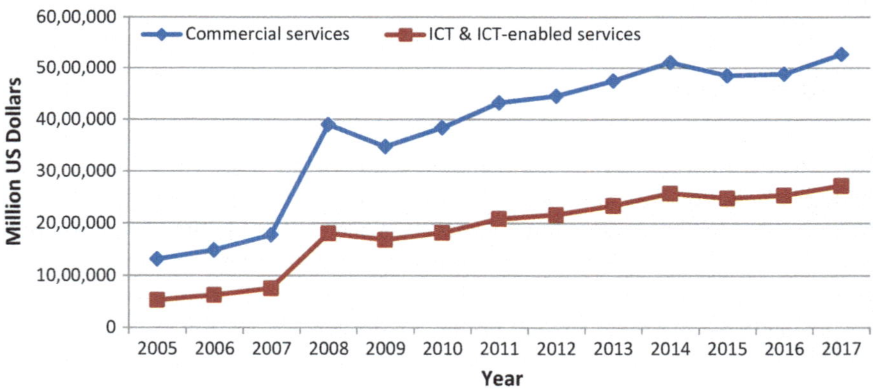

Fig. 1 Export of commercial services and ICT and ICT-enabled services. *Source* World Trade Organization (2019). *Notes* Commercial services include all the service categories of Extended Balance of Payments Services (EBOPS) 2010 except government goods and services not included elsewhere (n.i.e.). ICT and ICT-enabled services include the following categories of commercial services: insurance and pension services, financial services, charges for the use of intellectual property n,.i.e. telecommunications, computer, and information services, other business services and personal, cultural, and recreational services. The choice regarding ICT and ICT-enabled services follows from UNCTAD (2015)

Business Process Outsourcing (BPO) which consists of Finance and Accounting, Marketing and Sales, Supply Chain Management, Training, Call Centres, Document Management, etc.; Knowledge Process Outsourcing (KPO) which includes services like Business consulting, legal services, etc.; and many industry-specific activities (Fernandez-Stark et al. 2011).

Again, outsourcing of service provision activities is mainly done from developed to developing countries like India, Vietnam, Brazil, Ukraine, Philippines, etc. to provide the service in an efficient and economical way. There are many factors that are taken into account while deciding the location to outsource the service. Major among them are factor cost, skills of the labours, transport/communication network, availability of resources, etc. One more factor that can be taken into account while deciding where to outsource is the difference in time zones between the engaged countries. Often the affiliates are located at distant places in some non-overlapping time zones and thus their regular working hours do not match. For example, if we consider the case of India, one of the leading ICT service exporters—second largest according to OECD (2017)—around 60% (as shown in Fig. 2) of its software service export is directed towards USA and Canada, located many hours apart from India.

There are both positive and negative impacts of the difference in time zones of the partner countries. Time Zone (TZ) differences have a significant impact on the trade of services as well as goods. The impact on goods trade is mainly negative because then time zones get associated with the distance between the countries and transaction and transportation cost rises with distance and differences in TZ. However, in the case of services which are traded using ICT, the negative effect owing to huge distance does not arise as it is being traded electronically. Though there may be some interaction problem due to the difference in time zones termed as the synchronization effect by Head et al. (2009) but the same difference in time zone, also helps to continue a task for 24 h without any halt. In this paper, we focus on the effect of round-the-clock work process that is possible when time zones of engaged countries are non-overlapping. For example, services like customer care, data management etc.

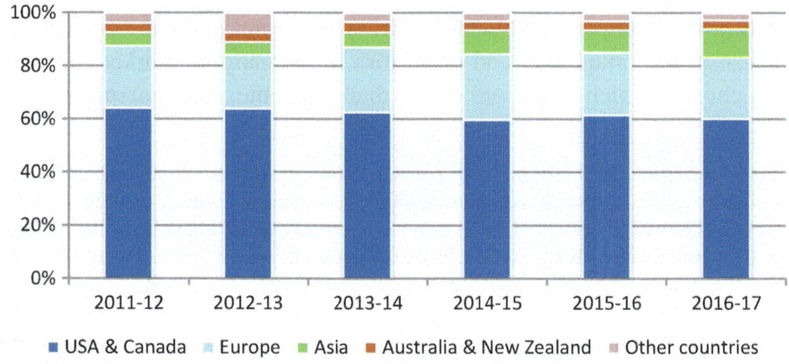

Fig. 2 % share of countries in the total export of software services of India. *Source* Reserve Bank of India (2018), https://www.rbi.org.in/scripts/Pr_DataRelease.aspx?SectionID=364&DateFilter=Year

that need to be provided all the time are divided into teams located in different time zones. When the working hour of one team is finished, the task is delegated to the other team located in a different time zone. Therefore, the task continues though the first group enjoys their leisure time.

Another example can be of a software development process. After completing a certain portion of the process during regular working hours, the semi-finished work is traded to another country located in a different time zone where working hours have just started. At the end of the day, the intermediate service is again traded to the first country for subsequent actions or completion. In this way, the development process goes on continuously without making anyone do overtime or nightshifts.[1] This process of working continuously round the clock is termed as the continuity effect by Head et al. (2009). To examine the effect of time zones on goods and service trade, Head et al. (2009) have used the Eurostat data for 65 countries over the period 1992–2006 and have found a positive effect for both goods and service trade suggesting that continuity effect dominates the synchronization effect. Tomasik (2013) has given empirical evidence on the presence of both synchronization effect and continuity effect. The results showed a dominating synchronization effect for goods trade while for service trade, continuity effect was seen to dominate. Dettmer (2014) also empirically tests continuity effect while estimating the impact of time zone on business and commercial service trade, and merchandise trade. Analyzing data from 27 OECD countries with their respective 226 partner countries for the period ranging from 1999 to 2006, it is shown that there is a positive effect of time zone on services, especially for business service trade, suggesting a stronger continuity effect. The continuity effect becomes more fruitful when time matters in case of production and trade of a good or service. Time indeed plays a very important role in trade and production in this era where technology is developing swiftly and so are the preferences of consumers. New products are being developed every day, and existing products get outmoded quickly; an example of this is mobile handsets and related software (Carmel et al. 2010). Thus, product sales life has become shorter (Afonso et al. 2008). In such cases, delay in production or delivery will make the producers suffer a loss resulting from a lower amount of sales or fall in demand-price. Hummels and Schaur (2013) also point out some evidence where to make transportation quicker and avoid loss from changing market condition, air route was chosen, which was more costly than sea route. The dynamic technology

[1] Gupta (2007) and Gupta and Seshasai (2007) includes some examples, where product development task or service provision is distributed across multiple time zones in order to achieve a 24-h development process. Gupta and Seshasai (2007) mention about an experiment done by the multinational company IBM (International Business Machines Corporation) where they compared two identical teams one located in the same place and one team divided between two groups—one in the US and the other situated in India. It was observed that the non-co-located team took almost half the time for resolving any problem and also provided a 24-h development process because of difference in time zones. Another example is of the Motorola Company. It divided a software development task between six countries and was able to achieve 21.5 h of work where each country worked in their own local working time. Some similar researches that deal with providing round-the-clock service provision using the time zone difference, are Carmel et al. (2010), Taweel and Brereton (2006), Sooraj and Mohapatra (2008), etc.

has increased the expectations of humans and also made them impatient to delays, which were acceptable earlier (Deardorff 2003). So, timely production and delivery have become more important than it was before and if the continuity effect is present, it will help the production to get accomplished early.

Theoretical studies also focus on the advantage of working round the clock. Notable papers on the idea of time zones and service trade are Kikuchi (2006), Marjit (2007), Matsuoka and Fukushima (2010), Kikuchi and Marjit (2010), Kikuchi and Iwasa (2010), Kikuchi and Long (2011), etc. Marjit (2007) proposes time zones as a new factor that can induce trade between the two countries. Even if technology and endowment of the trading countries are the same, the difference in time zones can lead to a beneficial venture. Using a Ricardian framework, it is shown that if two countries located in different time zones vertically integrate the production process, they can attain comparative advantage in the production of the concerned service as compared to the rest of the world. This results from early production through the continuous work process. Marjit (2007) even suggests that if one of the countries does not have the required technology for production, costless transfer of the same will still be beneficial as the two countries get the advantage of being in different time zones. Kikuchi (2006) uses a monopolistic competition model to explain the phenomenon of trade between different time zones. Since separating production between different countries will lead to specialization in a particular task by each country, there will be an increase in productivity. This increase in productivity of workers is explained as a source of the benefit of using the time zone difference in addition to the continuous work process. Kikuchi and Iwasa (2010) also focus on the positive effect of early delivery due to continuous work while analyzing the effect of trade between different firms located in different time zones. Matsuoka and Fukushima (2010) compare the phenomenon of outsourcing to different time zones with production in two shifts—day and night—undertaken domestically. In the case of outsourcing a part of the production, the firm has to incur communication cost. On the other hand, opting for nightshifts also raises the production cost. The rise in cost is because of a disutility that workers face due to nightshifts. In order to compensate for the disutility, nightshift workers are paid a higher wage, which raises the cost. Therefore, it is proposed that a firm will decide to outsource only when the nightshift disutility is more than the communication cost. They point out that in addition to the rise in productivity, the producers can also utilize the day–night wage difference while outsourcing to a different time zone. In this case, nightshift work is done by the dayshift workers of the other country who are paid dayshift wages. According to Kikuchi and Marjit (2010), the difference in dayshift and nightshift wage induces a *periodic intra-industry trade* where a country becomes an importer of services during the night and an exporter of the same during the day. Mandal (2015) using a Cobb–Douglas production function shows timely production, as a result of trading between different time zones, increases the volume of output. With trade, not only the production of the good increases but there is also a rise in the volume of trade—as along with the final product, intermediate inputs are also traded between the trading partners. Papers like Marjit and Mandal (2017), and Kikuchi and Marjit (2011) show the possibility of growth because of lower time for production. Thus, fragmenting production between different time zones allows production to continue for 24 h without any halt which in turn leads to early completion of tasks, rise in productivity, reduction in production costs, rise in output, and growth. It is to be noted here that for exploiting the full benefit of time zone difference the time zones of the trading countries must be non-overlapping, i.e. when the day starts in one country, the night starts in the other, or in case of more than two countries, the working hours should not coincide. For example, if four hours of a day of two partner countries overlap, the maximum time that can be used out of 24 h is 20 h. Therefore, to utilize every hour of the 24 h, the daytime of one country or its working hours should not coincide with the other. Our research focuses on the advantage of reduced time for the production process and aims to show the effect on factor prices and output of the economy. Papers like Kikuchi et al. (2013), Mandal et al. (2018) and Kikuchi and Long (2011) also focus on the effect of trading intermediaries on the factor prices and composition of production but the idea has not been framed in a standard Heckscher–Ohlin framework as depicted by Jones (1965).

The subsequent section describes the model and explains the results. As mentioned earlier, there are many kinds of ICT-enabled service processes, including both intermediates and final product, which can exploit the continuity effect by working in non-overlapping time zones such as customer care services, back-office works, providing legal advice, video-editing, examining medical reports, etc. Here, we focus on the production of service activity. Taking a cue from the software development process where each task (designing, implementation, testing, etc.) is sequentially distributed to different groups of professionals, we assume the development process to be divided into two sequential stages where each stage is completed in one working day or 12 h. Each stage requires the same amount of labour and capital. With only day shifts, the production takes two calendar days. Idle nighttime delays the production. Delay in reaching the market reduces consumers urge to own the product and thus, the demand is low, which makes the producers discount their price. To utilize the nighttime, producers divide the production (software development) task between two countries located in different time zones. The continuity effect helps the product to get developed in less time and increases the value of the product. The paper tries to explore the effect of early production on outputs and factor inputs. The model mainly follows the ideas of Marjit (2007), Mandal (2015), and Matsuoka and Fukushima (2010). The third section provides conclusions. Mathematical calculations and explanations are relegated to the appendices.

2 The Model and Results

Let us assume that there are two identical countries in the world located in non-overlapping time zones, one in the east and the other in the western part of the world. Both of them are small open economies having competitive markets. Each country has two sectors, one producing good (Y) and one producing service (X). Since the countries are small, the price of both the good and service are determined in the rest of the world. To explain the concerned phenomenon, here we focus on only one country. Skilled labour (S) and capital (K) are used as inputs in both sectors. Skilled labour is used intensively in the production of service, while capital is the intensive factor for good production. Both factors are fully employed within the two sectors. We assume one working day consists of 12 working hours, and there is no work during the nighttime. Even markets are closed during the night and open every 24 h. The goods' sector takes one working day to produce one unit, whereas the service sector needs two working days to produce one unit of service. The production of service, therefore, can be divided into two stages, each requiring one working day. Further, each stage requires one unit of skilled labour and one unit of capital which cannot be substituted, or in other words, we assume that the technology that allows the substitution of $S(K)$ for $K(S)$ is not yet developed. Therefore, the two stages will require two units of skilled labour and two units of capital. We assume the cost of trading the service to the consumers to be negligible. Since the competitive situation is assumed, the price of one unit of service (P_X) will be equal to the unit cost of production. However, the price that the producers receive is not the full value of the service but an amount lower than the price. This is because, consumers of the economy are assumed to be sensitive to delays—a tacit assumption in this time of fast-changing technology where a product in high demand today can become obsolete after few days leading to a fall in the satisfaction of owning the particular good. Given that it takes two working days to prepare the service, the consumers can own it after 48 h. As the consumers have to wait for two days to receive the service, the price is discounted by a discount factor δ. The value of the discount factor ranges between 0 and 1. When there is a delay in production, the value of δ is less than 1, and as the time of the service to reach the consumers fall, δ gradually rises to 1.

The cost-price equality of X is given by:

$$2w_S + 2r = \delta P_X$$

where w_S is the wage and r is the rent. The input cost of service production equals the discounted price, where δ is less than one. In other words, we can say that the price of X is distributed among the factors and a part of it goes as compensation for the delay.

On the other hand, the equilibrium condition of Y is given as:

$$a_{SY}w_S + a_{KY}r = P_Y$$

where a_{SY} and a_{KY} are, respectively, the amount of skilled labour and capital used for the production of one unit of Y. Unlike in X, in case of Y the inputs can be substituted at a constant rate. The amount of inputs thus chosen for the production of one unit of Y is to make the cost of production minimum, given the factor prices.

Now producers of service must be willing to acquire a higher value for their output. This can be achieved if they can reduce the time taken to complete the preparation of service. Since it takes two working days within which 24 h of the night time, equivalent to one full working day, is wasted; the service producers will certainly want to utilize the nighttime. There are two options, to either organize work even in the night or outsource the second stage to the other country located in non-overlapping time zone.[2] For organizing nightshift production, available labours should be halved to two groups, one working in day shift and one working in the nightshift. Since the nightshift workers are sacrificing their leisure time, they need to be paid higher than the day shift to compensate for their disutility. The workers who consider that their disutility of nightshift is compensated, choose to work at night while others work in a day. However, it cannot be said that the number of workers who chose to work in day shift will be equal to the number of workers who chose to work in night and since there exist full employment, additional labour cannot be employed (given the wage rate) to equate factors of both the shift. For the current model, it is necessary that there is a one-to-one correspondence with the first-stage and second-stage workers. Therefore, the higher cost of employing labours in the night and the possibility of a shortage of nightshift workers does not encourage the producers to continue production during the night.

The second option is to divide the production process sequentially between two countries with each country producing one 12-h stage. Since the two countries are identical, the number of factors is also the same. Therefore, the requirement that both the stages should employ a same number of labours is also fulfilled. In this case, as the working hours of the two countries are non-overlapping because of opposite time zones, the first stage is completed in the eastern country, and at the end of the day, the intermediate service is traded to the western country where the day of the same calendar date has just begun. The second stage undertakes in the regular working hours of the western country while workers in the eastern country rest in their regular resting time. The phenomenon illustrating both the cases of domestic production and fragmented production is shown in Fig. 3.

As we see from Fig. 3, the two countries are in non-overlapping time zones and their working hours do not overlap; when daylight fades in one country the day of the same calendar date starts in the other. So both the stages are done on the same date, but we get two working days within one 24-h day. The service becomes available to the consumers in 24 h, which earlier took 48 h. Therefore, producing the service in two countries located in opposite time zones helps for early production and the consumers receive it one day early. The discount factor that was attached with the price of the service now rises to 1 and the producers now realize the full value of the service.[3] The rise in the value of the service reflected in the effective price will

[2]Working in nightshifts are motivated by sunk cost of fixed factors. Even if the fixed factors are not utilized in the night, their rent has to be paid (we thank the reviewer for raising the point). So, when producers choose to outsource it means that the opportunity cost of not working in the night is also compensated.

[3]Since we have assumed time zones of the two countries to be such that daytime of one does not coincide with the daytime of the other, all of 24 h can be utilized to work without wasting any time. Therefore, the discount factor attains the value one. If some hours of daytime would have coincided with each other, 24 h of continuous work could not be achieved as one of the teams will have to stay idle during the overlapping hours. This will not allow δ to attain the highest value, 1. This idea follows from Marjit (2007) and Mandal (2015).

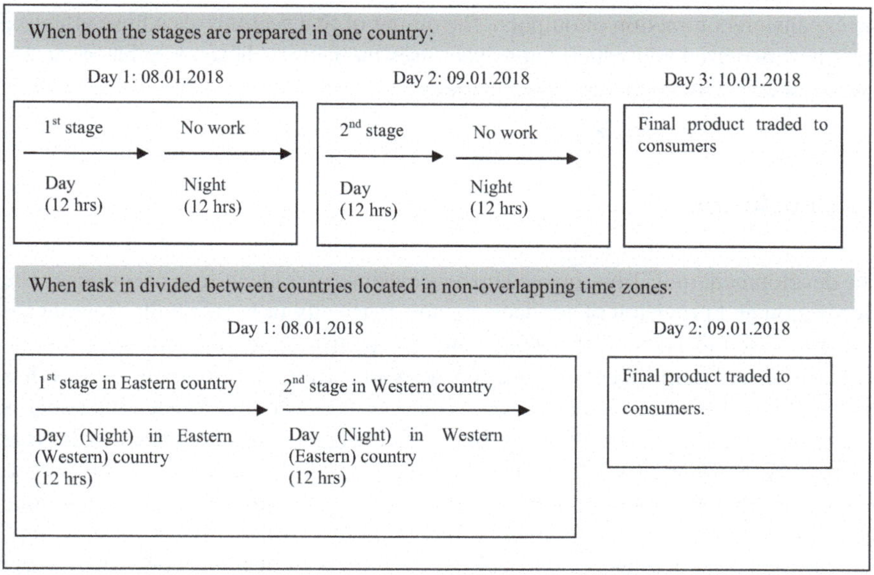

Fig. 3 Domestic production versus production utilizing the time zone difference

have to be appropriated by the factors of production. Higher value of the service thus received by the producers encourages them to raise their output. Raising the output level requires more labour and capital. Therefore, there is an increase in demand for factors in the economy and factor prices rise. Since there is no change in the price of good *Y*, the rise in factor prices will make the existing level of output unviable for *Y* producers. Sector *Y* reduces the level of output. With this, skilled labour and capital are released from *Y* and gets absorbed in *X*. Thus, now, sector *X* can raise its production. It is to be noted here that since good *Y* was capital intensive, more of capital than labour is released in the economy. *X* being *S* intensive, the available *S* is employed, but some *K* remains unemployed. This leads to an excess supply of *K* in the economy lowering its rent.[4] As a result, one of the factors becomes dearer, and one of them is cheaper than the initial situation. *Y* producers can employ more of *K* in order to substitute the work done by *S* with *K* and therefore use less of *S*. The unemployed *K*, therefore, gets employed back in *Y*. The economy returns to a full-employment situation. There is also a slight rise in output of *Y* because of a fall in rent and substitution among factors, but still, it will be less than the initial level.[5]

Therefore, when the service sector opts to produce by utilizing the time zone difference, there is a rise in economy-wide wage and a fall in rent. This effect also depends on the factor intensity condition. If *X* was *K* intensive and *Y* was *S* intensive. *Y* would have released more of *S*, and *X* would have used up more *K*, leading to a rise in rent and fall in wage. However, the factor intensity condition is not significant for

[4]The outcome is similar to the Stolper–Samuelson theorem.

[5]For mathematical arguments, readers are suggested to check appendices at the end of this paper.

the expansion/contraction of outputs. The output of that sector rises whose effective price has increased and which intensively uses the factor whose price has gone up, and the sector with unchanged price shrinks.

3 Conclusion

The development in ICT has opened up new avenues of trade in case of services. The preparation and provision of services are now vertically or horizontally fragmented between different parts of the world, and the intermediate and final services are traded with the help of communication network. Thus, development of ICT has made outsourcing of service activities a common trend. In this respect, the paper is an attempt to highlight the effect of time zone difference as a beneficial factor that needs to be considered while deciding on the location to outsource. Even if cost, technology, the efficacy of performing a task is the same, just the difference in time zones of two countries can prove to be beneficial for trading service. To show this, we construct a model having the Heckscher–Ohlin type of framework where early production is valued more. We find that fragmenting production to a country located in non-overlapping time zone leads to an expansion of the service sector. On the other hand, the sector sharing the same factors with the service sector is seen to contract. Also, the factor that is used intensively in the production of the service gains while the other factor loses.

Appendices

This section elucidates the mathematical calculations and derivations regarding how splitting production between different time zones affects the factor prices and output of the economy. The resultant effect on factor prices is shown in Appendix 1, while Appendix 2 is assigned to illustrate the change in output level. Note that we have focused on the eastern country while analyzing the effects. Since we have assumed both the countries to be identical, the western country will also face the same changes when their service producers decide to outsource to the eastern country. For convenience, all the symbols used in the paper are summarized as follows: X = service; Y = tangible good; S = skilled labour; K = capital; w_S = wage; r = rent; δ = discount factor; P_X = price of X; P_Y = price of Y; a_{ij} = amount of factor i required for the production of one unit of $j\,(i = S, K;\ j = X, Y)$; θ_{ij} = share of i in the price of j; λ_{ij} = employment share of factor i in sector j; σ_Y = elasticity of substitution between S and K in Y.

The basic structure of the model is summarized in the following equations:

$$2w_S + 2r = \delta P_X \tag{1}$$

$$a_{SY}w_S + a_{KY}r = P_Y \quad (2)$$

$$2X + a_{SY}Y = S \quad (3)$$

$$2X + a_{KY}Y = K \quad (4)$$

Equations (1) and (2) show the competitive market equilibrium condition where the cost of producing one unit is equal to the price. Equations (3) and (4) give the skilled labour and capital constraint, respectively. There are four unknowns w_S, r, X and Y and four equations, hence the model is solvable.

Appendix 1

Differentiating both sides of (1) we get,

$$2dw_S + 2dr = P_X d\delta$$

Dividing throughout by P_X and expressing relative change by '^',

$$\frac{dw_S}{w_S}\frac{2w_S}{P_X} + \frac{dr}{r}\frac{2r}{P_X} = \frac{d\delta}{\delta}\frac{\delta P_X}{P_X}$$

$$\hat{w}_S\theta_{SX} + \hat{r}\theta_{KX} = \hat{\delta}\delta \quad (5)$$

Similarly from (2)

$$\hat{w}_S\theta_{SY} + \hat{r}\theta_{KY} = 0 \quad (6)$$

Here $\theta_{ij}(i = S, K; j = X, Y)$ refers to the share of i in the price of j. The symbols follow from Jones (1965, 1971). Equation (5) suggests that change in δ will be absorbed by changes in w_S and r. Since both the sectors use the same factors, the equilibrium condition of sector Y also gets affected. Using (5) and (6) we can solve for the values for the relative change in skilled wage (w_S) and rent (r). The results are as follows:

$$\hat{w}_S = \hat{\delta}\delta\left(\frac{\theta_{KY}}{|\theta|}\right) > 0 \quad (7)$$

$$\hat{r} = (-)\hat{\delta}\delta\left(\frac{\theta_{SY}}{|\theta|}\right) < 0 \quad (8)$$

The denominator $|\theta| = \theta_{SX}\theta_{KY} - \theta_{SY}\theta_{KX}$. Since X is S intensive and Y is K intensive $\theta_{SX} > \theta_{SY}$ and $\theta_{KY} > \theta_{KX}$. Therefore, $|\theta| > 0$ and a positive $\hat{\delta}$ make $\hat{w}_S > 0$ and $\hat{r} < 0$. This implies, an increase in the value of the discount factor due to the utilization of time zone difference results in a rise in skilled wage and a fall in rent when the sector utilizing the time zone difference is skilled labour intensive. The results are similar to what we get from the Stolper–Samuelson theorem, but here the resultant effect is not because of the rise in price but because of the rise in δ. We also find that the relative change in w_S is more than that in r;

$$\hat{w}_S - \hat{r} = \hat{\delta}\delta\left(\frac{\theta_{KY}}{|\theta|}\right) - (-)\hat{\delta}\delta\left(\frac{\theta_{SY}}{|\theta|}\right)$$

$$\text{or, } \hat{w}_S - \hat{r} = \frac{\hat{\delta}\delta}{|\theta|}(\theta_{KY} + \theta_{SY})$$

$$\text{or, } \hat{w}_S - \hat{r} = \frac{\hat{\delta}\delta}{|\theta|} > 0$$

Appendix 2

Since the factor prices have changed, the cost-minimizing blend of inputs can now be changed. However, given our assumptions, the input coefficients of X cannot be changed but it is possible for Y to substitute K with S at a constant rate. The rate at which substitution can take place is given by the elasticity of substitution:

$$\sigma_Y = \frac{\hat{a}_{SY} - \hat{a}_{KY}}{\hat{r} - \hat{w}_S}$$

To find the relative change in the input coefficients, we manipulate the formula of elasticity of substitution as:

$$\hat{a}_{SY} = \hat{a}_{KY} - (\hat{w}_S - \hat{r})\sigma_Y \tag{9}$$

Together with this, we make use of the Envelope theorem

$$\hat{a}_{SY}\theta_{SY} + \hat{a}_{KY}\theta_{KY} = 0$$

$$\Rightarrow \hat{a}_{KY} = -\hat{a}_{SY}\frac{\theta_{SY}}{\theta_{KY}}$$

Substituting the value of $\hat{a}_{KY}$ in (9) and putting the value of $(\hat{w}_S - \hat{r})$ we have

$$\hat{a}_{SY} = (-)\hat{\delta}\delta\frac{\theta_{KY}}{|\theta|}\sigma_Y < 0 \tag{10}$$

Similarly, we get,

$$\hat{a}_{KY} = \hat{\delta}\delta\frac{\theta_{SY}}{|\theta|}\sigma_Y > 0 \tag{11}$$

Thus, there is a rise in the amount of K required per unit of Y and a fall in that of S.

Now, to check the relative change in output, we take total differential of (3) and (4) and express them in the relative change form

$$\lambda_{SX}\widehat{X} + \lambda_{SY}\widehat{Y} + \lambda_{SY}\hat{a}_{SY} = 0$$

$$\lambda_{KX}\widehat{X} + \lambda_{KY}\widehat{Y} + \lambda_{KY}\hat{a}_{KY} = 0$$

Using (10) and (11),

$$\lambda_{SX}\widehat{X} + \lambda_{SY}\widehat{Y} = \lambda_{SY}\hat{\delta}\delta\frac{\theta_{KY}}{|\theta|}\sigma_Y$$

$$\lambda_{KX}\widehat{X} + \lambda_{KY}\widehat{Y} = (-)\lambda_{KY}\hat{\delta}\delta\frac{\theta_{SY}}{|\theta|}\sigma_Y$$

Using Cramer's rule,

$$\widehat{X} = \frac{\delta\hat{\delta}}{|\lambda||\theta|}\lambda_{KY}\lambda_{SY}\sigma_Y > 0$$

$$\widehat{Y} = (-)\frac{\delta\hat{\delta}}{|\lambda||\theta|}(\theta_{SY}\lambda_{SX}\lambda_{KY} + \theta_{KY}\lambda_{KX}\lambda_{SY})\sigma_Y < 0$$

where, $|\lambda| = \lambda_{SX}\lambda_{KY} - \lambda_{KX}\lambda_{SY}$

Thus, utilization of time zone difference for production of service raises service output whereas indicates a contractionary effect on the other sector. This effect is independent of the factor intensity assumption as both $|\lambda|$ and $|\theta|$ have the same sign.

References

Afonso, P., Nunes, M., Paisana, A., & Braga, A. (2008). The influence of time-to-market and target costing in the new product development success. *International Journal of Production Economics, 115*(2), 559–568. https://doi.org/10.1016/j.ijpe.2008.07.003.

Carmel, E., Espinosa, J. A., & Dubinsky, Y. (2010). "Follow the sun" workflow in global software development. *Journal of Management Information Systems, 27*(1), 17–38. https://doi.org/10.2753/MIS0742-1222270102.

Christen, E. (2017). Time zones matter: The impact of distance and time zones on services trade. *The World Economy, 40*(3), 612–631. https://doi.org/10.1111/twec.12326.

Deardorff, A. (2003). Time and trade: The role of time in determining the structure and effects of international trade, with an application to Japan. In R. M. Stern (Ed.), *Japans economic recovery: Commercial policy, monetary policy and corporate governance* (pp. 63–76). UK: Edward Elgar Publishing Limited.

Dettmer, B. (2014). International service transactions: Is time a trade barrier in a connected world? *International Economic Journal, 28*(2). https://doi.org/10.1080/10168737.2013.825305.

Fernandez-Stark, K., Bamber, P., & Gereffi, G. (2011). *The offshore services global value chain: Economic upgrading and workforce development*. Duke University, Center on Globalization, Governance and Competitiveness. Retrieved from https://gvcc.duke.edu/wp-content/uploads/2011-11-11_CGGC_Ex.Summary_Offshore-Services-Global-Value-Chain-1.pdf.

Gupta, A. (2007). Deriving mutual benefits from offshore outsourcing: The 24-hour knowledge factory scenario. *SSRN Electronic Journal*. https://doi.org/10.2139/ssrn.968761.

Gupta, A., & Seshasai, S. (2007). 24-hour knowledge factory: Using internet technology to leverage spatial and temporal separations. *ACM Transactions on Internet Technology, 7*(3), 14. https://doi.org/10.1145/1275505.1275507.

Head, K., Mayer, T., & Ries, J. (2009). How remote is the offshoring threat? *European Economic Review, 53*(4), 429–444. https://doi.org/10.1016/j.euroecorev.2008.08.001.

Hummels, D., & Schaur, G. (2013). Time as a trade barrier. *The American Economic Review, 103*(7), 2935–2959. https://doi.org/10.1257/aer.103.7.2935.

Jones, R. W. (1965). The structure of simple general equilibrium models. *The Journal of Political Economy, 73*(6), 557–572. Retrieved from http://links.jstor.org/sici?sici=0022-3808%28196512%2973%3A6%3C557%3ATSOSGE%3E2.0.CO%3B2-B.

Jones, R. W. (1971). A three-factor model in theory, trade and history. In J. Bhagwati, R. W. Jones, R. A. Mundell, & J. Vanek (Eds.), *Trade, balance of payments and growth* (pp. 3–21). North-Holland: Amsterdam.

Kikuchi, T. (2006). Time zones, outsourcing and patterns of international trade. *Economics Bulletin, 6*, 1–10. Retrieved from http://www.accessecon.com/pubs/EB/2006/Volume6/EB-06F10018A.pdf.

Kikuchi, T., & Iwasa, K. (2010). A simple model of service trade with time zone differences. *International Review of Economics and Finance, 19*(1), 75–80. https://doi.org/10.1016/j.iref.2009.02.004.

Kikuchi, T., & Long, N. V. (2011). Shift working and trade in labor services with time zone differences. *Pacific Economic Review, 16*(5), 553–564. https://doi.org/10.1111/j.1468-0106.2011.00564.x.

Kikuchi, T., & Marjit, S. (2010). *Time zones and periodic intra-industry trade*. (EERI Research Paper Series 08/2010), Economics and Econometrics Research Institute. Retrieved from http://hdl.handle.net/10419/142570.

Kikuchi, T., & Marjit, S. (2011). Growth with time zone differences. *Economic Modelling, 28*(1–2), 637–640. https://doi.org/10.1016/j.econmod.2010.06.006.

Kikuchi, T., Marjit, S., & Mandal, B. (2013). Trade with time zone differences: Factor market implications. *Review of Development Economics, 17*(4), 699–711. https://doi.org/10.1111/rode.12060.

Mandal, B. (2015). Distance, production, virtual trade and growth: A note. *Economics: The Open-Access, Open-Assessment E-Journal, 9*(2015–1), 1–12. Retrieved from http://www.economics-ejournal.org/economics/journalarticles/2015-1.

Mandal, B., Marjit, S., & Nakanishi, N. (2018). Outsourcing, factor prices and skill formation in countries with non-overlapping time zones. *Eurasian Economic Review*. https://doi.org/10.1007/s40822-017-0086-9.

Marjit, S. (2007). Trade theory and the role of time zones. *International Review of Economics and Finance, 16*(2), 153–160. https://doi.org/10.1016/j.iref.2005.08.002.

Marjit, S., & Mandal, B. (2017). Virtual trade between separated time zones and growth. *International Journal of Economic Theory, 13*(2), 171–183. https://doi.org/10.1111/ijet.12123.

Matsuoka, Y., & Fukushima, M. (2010). Time zones, shift working and international outsourcing. *International Review of Economics and Finance, 19*(4), 769–778. https://doi.org/10.1016/j.iref.2010.05.001.

OECD. (2017). *OECD digital economy outlook 2017*. Paris: OECD Publishing. https://doi.org/10.1787/9789264276284-en.

Sooraj, P., & Mohapatra, P. K. J. (2008). Modeling the 24-h software development process. *Strategic Outsourcing: An International Journal, 1*(2), 122–141. https://doi.org/10.1108/17538290810897147.

Reserve Bank of India. (2018). *Survey on computer software & information technology enabled services exports*. Retrieved April 30, 2018, from https://rbi.org.in/Scripts/BS_PressReleaseDisplay.aspx.

Taweel, A., & Brereton, P. (2006). Modelling software development across time zones. *Information and Software Technology, 48*(1), 1–11. https://doi.org/10.1016/j.infsof.2004.02.006.

Tomasik, R. (2013). Time zone-related continuity and synchronization effects on bilateral trade flows. *Review of World Economics, 149,* 321–342. https://doi.org/10.1007/s10290-013-0147-4.

UNCTAD. (2015). *International trade in ICT services and ICT-enabled services: Proposed indicators from the partnership on measuring ICT for development*. United Nations. https://unctad.org/en/PublicationsLibrary/tn_unctad_ict4d03_en.pdf.

World Trade Organization. (2019). *WTO Data*. Retrieved January 22, 2019, from http://data.wto.org/.

Towards One Agricultural Market in India: Does the ICT Help?

Nilabja Ghosh, Mayanglambam Rajeshwor and Parmeet Kumar Vinit

Abstract The current phase of economic reforms in agriculture is oriented to help farmers reach out to a larger all India market in order to fetch the best prices and earn higher incomes. The government has already been relaxing regulations to clean the market of imperfections and improve its efficiency, but moving towards 'one' Indian market has become a more targeted objective of reforms. The paper reviews the fast-changing scenario of institutional reforms and application of ICT as a facilitator of reforms. Empirical analysis with data on pulses reveals a convergence of prices in states towards a national-level price enabled by information flow from major markets but cannot confirm the role of trade in equalizing prices nor the benefit of higher prices reaching the producers. This transition period still shows signs of selective market integration and asymmetrical market responses mostly observed in consuming states.

India's agriculture, now in a new transition, is targeted towards a nationally integrated market (MoA 2013).[1] Market integration can support farmers to take advantage of demand arising in any part of the country for fetching the best prices for their products. It also will help the sector to face the world market as a strong player in the global competition, enabling farmers to adjust their production patterns in line with their comparative advantages. Central to this transformation is not just notional knowledge of reality elsewhere to aid local transactions but also realized trade across the country. Experiences show it is not easy to promote cross-state trade in grains in a large politically diverse country, but what arouses optimism is the advent of communication technology in the wider world that can be used to aid the process in unprecedented ways.

[1]States are encouraged to reform markets in order to provide a barrier-free national market for the benefit of farmers and consumers.

N. Ghosh (✉) · M. Rajeshwor
Institute of Economic Growth, Delhi, India
e-mail: nila@iegindia.org

P. K. Vinit
Agro-Economic Research Centre, Delhi University, Delhi, India

D. Maiti et al. (eds.), *Digitalisation and Development*,
https://doi.org/10.1007/978-981-13-9996-1_8

In the absence of trade and information, any potential market can be seen as composed of smaller fragmented markets with their price signals. Swift transmission of information from one sub-market to another is a precondition for removing market imperfection and attaining an integrated 'one' competitive market where theoretically, any residual price difference persisting post-trade would signify only the transportation ordeals. Larger the geographic extent of the market, greater would be the role of information and brisk trade to sustain its integrity. The process of price equalization is not instantaneous, and the speed of price response to potential demand or supply would depend on the efficiency of the market. Information and communication technology (ICT), which enables exchanges of knowledge, finance and contracts between distant locations, is becoming an integral part of the ongoing transformation of Indian agriculture.

Exploring the criticality of information transmission for an efficient market in a large, federal and geographically diverse country, this paper revisits market transformation in Indian agriculture, tracing the rise, the entry and the assimilation of ICT into India's agricultural markets which have been independently evolving under economic reforms of the time. Application of ICT in agriculture relates to using extraneous and evolving technology, while market reforms relate only to the institutional restructuring of rules and regulations to allow more flexibility of operations. Having discussed the evolution of ICT and its induction in Indian agriculture (Sect. 1), the paper addresses the ongoing reforms which have begun to draw from the ICT options (Sect. 2). Conducted over a historic transition, the study takes a view of the present state of Indian agricultural markets which are anticipated to increasingly become interlinked by trade until they compositely constitute the Indian market. Using alternative quantitative methods, the paper probes how far state markets of India diverge and how strongly they are tied up at this juncture of ICT dynamics (Sect. 3). The market considered is for pulses that have drawn government promotion only during the study period but have historically felt less government interference than other food grains. The study, therefore, has a focus on pulses, specifically two crops gram and arhar.

1 Entry of ICT in the Agricultural Domain of India

Green revolution (GR) amply demonstrated the significance of 'knowledge' as a critical resource with public extension transferring agrarian technology to producers. While it is not surprising that ICT became an important vehicle for extension in the post-GR age, its potentials for marketing is only a growing realization even now. ICT's overtures with agricultural marketing have a short history in India. Entering the realms in the 2000s mostly as trials, ICT picked up steam within agriculture post-2010 when the sector also gained relative emphasis in public policy. Targeting the integration of Indian markets using the power of ICT began as late as 2017.

The world's ICT revolution started in the early nineteenth century when communication was based purely on physical proximity. By the 2000s, disrupted successively by innovations, tools generated in the fields of computer science and telecommunication were found to be converging (Andrews 2013). They were become increasingly smaller, mobile and interactive. ICT and its synergies even at this point are not static. Integrated with another powerful source of data, the satellite it serves in weather forecasting, television broadcasting, radio and Internet communications, and geo-referencing. ICT compliant softwares are helping in timely and accurate collection of socio-economic data for policy-making. Convenience is being offered by 'cloud' for accessing data and software only on demand. Artificial intelligence, machine learning, Internet of things, unmanned aerial technology and financial applications promise to further enrich ICT's capabilities.

Only in 1985, telecommunication became important enough in India to be detached as a separate department.[2] Manufacture of electronic exchanges was initiated in the end 1980s, and years after India's telecom system had begun feeling the need of technology overhauling. Computerization was progressing sluggishly in the 1980s, and Internet was an even slower process, first available to only academic institutions (ERNET), expanding into inter-government uses (Nic.net), and reaching out to the public only in the late 1990s but with slow speed. The vast rural sector and agriculture remained dependent on posts and telegraphs for connectivity creating a digital devide.

For the Indian economy, the decade of the 2000s was transformative when the telecom sector was opened up to the private but regulated competition.[3] The historic broadband policy of 2004 attended to people's growing need for Internet, and the last-minute connectivity became mobile with the auction of 3G spectrum in 2010 by when the simple wireline telephone was already giving way to innovations culminating in the cellular phone and the smartphone converging with other emerging technologies.

Evident in the inflexion in Fig. 1a, telephones changed from a luxury to a necessity in Indian psyche from 2010, as the idea of a phone gave way to the lightweight and multi-purpose mobile phones. Internet subscription was picking up gradually since 2004, but a larger leap was seen in 2014–15, marking the visible beginning of rural connectivity (Fig. 1b). As will be seen later, at that time, the government intent of transforming the rural economy using ICT began to appear as a green shoot for India's development. Rural areas of the country have historically been secluded from the mainstream economy by poor road networks, lack of telecommunications, and above all, by poverty and ignorance. Farmers had very little resources by way of market intelligence to support them in deciding the crops they grew and marketed. Unorganized traders, who were themselves outdated in their practices, served as the main link with other regions and were highly influential in the pricing of products in a region. Their trade coverage was bound by poor infrastructure, scarce information and their inward looking approach complemented by their lack of resources. ICT seemed

[2]To start with, the telegraph (1850) and the formal telephone (1882) only supplemented the postal system of the government which was the core component for long distance communication in India.

[3]Moving telecom away being a government monopoly, the National Telecommunication Policy (NTP) 1994, for the first time, showed respect for private participation and investment as well as for checks on unfair practices to institute and enact the Telecom Regulatory Authority of India (TRAI) in 1997.

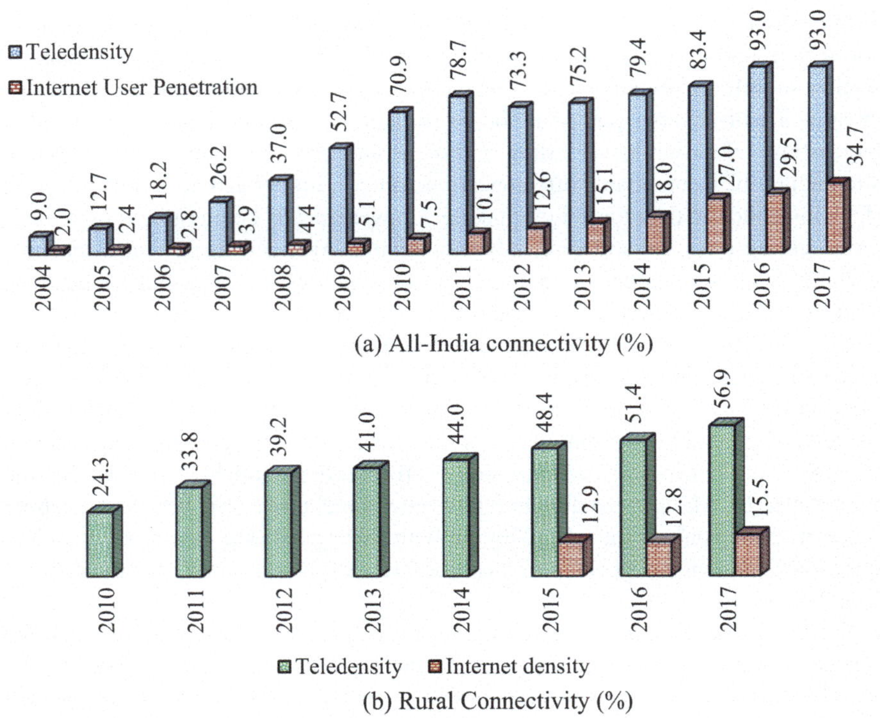

Fig. 1 Communication by telephones and Internet among Indian population. *Note* Internet use is reported by calendar year in all India and other data by financial year. *Source* MoC (2018), FAO, Website

to offer ways to overcome the communicational barriers with equity and symmetry in the new millennium. Unlike in industry, the central and state governments took active role in making this happen.

Tele-density in India rose phenomenally from 9 to 93% between 2004 and 2017 when Internet subscription also increased from 2 to 35% (Fig. 1a). An ICT indicator (share of people with ICT facility) is calculated as the simple average of ICT facilities per hundred population: tele-density wireline and tele-density wireless, Internet subscription broadband, Internet subscription narrowband, wire line and wireless telephones, village public telephones (VPT) and public call office (PCO). While both tele-density and Internet density by wireline as well as public telephones diminished in number between sub-periods 2010–2013 to 2014–2016 balanced by remarkable increases in wireless connections (Table 1), the composite indicator of ICT improved from 12.4 to 17.8%. More remarkably, tele-density in rural areas doubled between 2010 and 2015 in steady growth and despite its late entry, Internet intensity continued increasing after 2015 (Fig. 1b).

The ICT budget for agriculture (DoA&FW, Website) in nominal terms was only Rs. 16 crores in 2004–05, the early stage of ICT in India, but it rose by 16% per annum

Table 1 ICT indicators per 100 population (average)

	Tele-density		Internet density						IT Indicator
Year	Wireline	Wireless	Narrow-band	Broad-band	Wireline	Wireless	VPT*	PCO	
1	2	3	4	5	6	7	8	9	10
2010–11–2013–14	2.60	72.51	4.30	2.09	1.64	15.73	0.07	0.23	12.4
2014–15–2016–17	2.02	83.99	14.36	13.86	1.62	26.60	0.06	0.07	17.8

Note *Per 100 rural population, IT indicator is the simple mean of columns 2–9
Source MoC (2018)

up to the 2010–13 and then by another more moderate 6.4% per annum by 2014–16 (Table 2). Expressed at constant prices (2011–12) the ICT budget in agriculture (Fig. 2) had shot up in after 2004, became depressed up to 2012 and again peaked in 2014 but the real budget remained largely stagnant except for the spurts, but its pattern changed. In 2004–05 highest allocation, 63% was marked under the heading other agricultural programmes (major head) which mainly constituted expenses on marketing and market information (see Table 4). Since then that allocation diminished almost to extinction, but 'other expenditure (Minor)', meant for strengthening the department's capacity continuously gained share up to 2013–14. In the period 2014–16, a substantial share of 41% went to the states as grants in aid. Market intelligence, highlighted in the AMIS efforts of G20, has been identified as an important resource for designing efficient markets (AMIS, Website).

ICT has become a game-changer (Box 1) for agriculture, aimed to reach farmers with timely weather alerts and market information, relief and insurance claims although the effectiveness requires more evaluation. It was supporting data collection and informed policy-making and was monitoring production to avoid a crisis. Qualitative dimensions like user-friendly interface, language compatibility, two-way

Table 2 ICT budget in agriculture sector in India (Rs. Crore)

Year	2004–05	2010–13*	2014–16*
Crop husbandry (Major Head)	1.03	0.47	0.62
Agricultural Economics and Statistics (Minor Head)		0.04	0.02
Other Expenditure (Minor Head)	4.95	36.64	35.40
Other Agricultural Programmes (Major Head)	10.05	1.02	
Grants-in-aid to State Government (Major Head)		1.50	20.38
Other Agricultural Programmes–Marketing Facilities (Minor Head)		0.20	
Total	16.03	38.57	49.42
WPI—All Commodities (2011 – 12 = 1)	0.64	1.03	1.12

Note *Average
Source DoA&FW (Website)

Fig. 2 Agriculture IT budget (2011–12 prices)

query-based communication, use of multiple mediums supported rural penetration of ICT (Shalendra and Sharma 2011) and the Kisan Call Centre served as a useful instruments. Satellite-based monitoring of production, drought assessment and digital money transfer, under trials and pilots in 2000s, showed a success. Now ICT is enabling payment from public funds to target beneficiaries with least diversion through Direct Benifit Transfer (DBT) on subsidiaries of fertilizer, other inputs, support price and welfare payments to bank accounts of farmers. Integration of meteorology, satellite imagery and computer-aided crop modelling in an umbrella multidisciplinary FASAL project, launched in 2006 and further revamped in 2012, was providing an early outlook of production, but ICT use can lead to more frequent and real-time monitoring of crop prices and production than ground-level insights allow. A dynamic Atlas of agricultural markets, designed on the GIS platform (MoA 2013), facilitates both public and private sectors in planning marketing strategies.

Harnessing the advancements in (ICT) a Central Sector Scheme of Agricultural Marketing Information Network (AGMARKNET) was already working since March, 2000 to link important produce markets spread all over the country with the technical support of National Informatics Centre (NIC). The AGMARKNET portal has linkage with futures prices and international price trends available on the FAO website are also accessible through the portal. In 2014–15, allocation was made under Market Research and Information Network (MRIN) to strengthen market linkages and inter-market information with ICT power. Finally, the Union Government's e-NAM starting in 2016 is a major step towards harnessing the power of ICT in Indian agriculture to integrate the fragmented markets. It is a pan-India electronic trading portal which networks the existing regulated mandis (Sect. 2.2) to create a unified national market for agricultural commodities. Moving beyond making marketing data of the country universally available, the platform enables e-trading across the country by all-India electronic-auctioning. To reduce financial and supervisory cost, procurement operation is conducted in pockets, decisions about which are made consultatively between state and Centre to avoid overlaps and exclusions while the ICT enabled trio schemes Jan Dhan, Aadhar and mobile comprehensively called JAM enable payments to be made directly by government to recipient's bank account by DBT.

Box 1: How ICT is usable for Indian Agriculture

Global Positioning System (GPS): A satellite-based navigation system to locate positions, made available for civilian use in the 1980s, can be useful for identifying location for intervention in agriculture.

Global Information System (GIS): is a computerized data storage and retrieval system, used to manage and analyse spatial data relating to crop productivity and agronomic factors.

Remote Sensing (RS) Technique, the science of making an inference from measurements, made at a distance without coming into physical contact. RS has been used for monitoring land use and crop production from the 1980 s but has been more actively used from 2012.

AKASHGANGA, established in 1996 in the private sector, showed that even illiterates or semi-illiterate people can adopt IT-based systems.

E-Chaupal-ITCs launched Agri-Business Division of a private company in June 2000. E-Sagu-ICT based personalized agro-advisory system is being developed since 2004.

ICTs and Farmers' Advisory Service: The online phone-based expert advice service, Kisan Call Centres (KCC), launched by Government of India is available for all within the country since January 2004 with a toll-free telephone number is operational on all days from 6:00 a.m. to 10:00 p.m., KCC—that makes agriculture knowledge available free of cost to the farmers as and when desired.

Decision Support System (DSS): Interactive software-based system intended to help decision-makers to compile useful information from raw data, documents, personal knowledge and/or business models to identify and solve problems and make decisions.

Decision Supportive System for Agro-technology Transfer (DSSAT): A software package integrating the effects of soil, crop phenotype, weather and management options that allow users to ask 'what if' questions.

AGMARKNET: Agricultural Marketing Information Network (AGMARKNET) was launched in March 2000 by the Union Ministry of Agriculture. The Directorate of Marketing and Inspection (DMI), under the Ministry, links around 7000 agricultural wholesale markets in India with the State Agricultural Marketing Boards and Directorates for effective information exchange. This e-governance portal AGMARKNET, implemented by National Informatics Centre (NIC), facilitates generation and transmission of prices, commodity arrival information from agricultural produce markets and web-based dissemination to producers, consumers, traders and policy-makers transparently and quickly.

Market Research and Information Network (MRIN): Under an umbrella scheme ISAM launched in 2014, creation of improved marketing infrastructure, scientific storage and integrated value chains was aimed to be supported by trained personnel in ICT and a strong nationwide information network by which a large number of wholesale markets were planned to be linked using computers, mobile phones and SMS

FASAL: Well-planned programmes for crop acreage and production forecasts (Forecasting Agricultural Output using Space, Agro-meteorology and Land-based Observations) culminated in the establishment of a dedicated Mahalanobis National Crop Forecasting Centre (MNCFC) by Ministry of Agriculture (GoI), for crop inventorying and drought assessment. Advanced methods of remote sensing, meteorology and econometrics are used for forecasting production.

PMFBY: Pradhan Mantri Fasal Bima Yojana is a new crop insurance scheme that was announced by the Government on 13 January 2016. It provides a comprehensive insurance cover to all food, oilseeds and commercial/horticultural crops against the failure of the crop, thus helping in stabilizing the income of the farmers. Availability of past yield data is from General Crop Estimation Survey (GCES) which is important, but modern ICT methods are encouraged for timely collection of data for assessment and release of claims.

e-NAM: National Agriculture Market is an online trading platform for agricultural commodities in India to facilitate farmers, traders and buyers with transparent online trading in commodities. e-NAM is helping in better price discovery with smooth marketing facilities. Launched by Ministry of Agriculture, Government of India on April 2016, the electronic market pilot across India is managed by Small Farmers' Agribusiness Consortium (SFAC) with a technology provider, NFCL's iKisan division. Before it was rolled out nationally, a similar project in the State of Karnataka had proved successful. It also removes the information asymmetry between states and markets within a state.

2 Marketing Reforms and the Application of ICT

Retrospection shows that events of food shortage that still haunt India's memory resulted from failures not just of weather but also of the markets and government strategies.[4] Enquiry committees[5] in colonial and newly independent India rejected free trade as a policy (Kahlon 1991). In the 1960s and 1970s decades, the food market was therefore highly regulated and even nationalized briefly. Even reforms in the larger economy from the 1990s had only meagre outreach to agriculture where government intervention continued. When ICT offered new ways of the transaction, market reforms in agriculture became an easier option. Latecomer in the arena of India's economic reform, agricultural marketing is yet in its early stage. It is probably

[4]Famines at different locations owing to local rainfall failure were a common event from early times resulting in tax waivers, public works and economic relief, three Famine Commissions (1878–1900) having been set up in colonial times owing to pressure. Though irrigation was treated as a solution, failure of the distribution system emerged as a greater concern than production failure at the national level leading to the construction of railways as a mode of transport beyond the cheaper roads and canals but without attacking economic poverty at its root even this large investment had limited effect (Sweeney 2008; Naoroji 1901; Sen 1981). Recent soil findings have suggested that the disastrous famine of 1943 was linked more with government strategies than production losses (Scroll 2019). Government's entrance into the food market for rationing and procuring grains in post-independence times was related to spatial disparities of production and demand and the inadequacy of private traders to bridge the gap.

[5]Food Policy Committee in 1943, the Food grain Procurement Committee (1950), the Food Grain Enquiry Committee (1957) and the Agricultural Prices Commission (APC) (1965).

the most challenging part of economic reforms that are known to be politically sensitive and difficult as they affect various sections in dissimilar ways in the short run and long run.

The Commission for Agricultural Costs and Prices (CACP) formed in 1985 advises the union government on food prices.[6] Minimum support prices (MSP) is offered to ensure that farmers get remunerative returns above the cost of production.[7] India's food policy, designed to achieve food security was executed by Food Corporation of India (FCI), a large central agency established in 1965 (Ghosh and Khasnobis 2008) though the food market remained dualistic as private traders remained free to compete with government agencies. Although MSP was announced for 25 crops (DES, Website), open-ended procurement supported only cereals.

Since 1980 FCI's operations became confined to rice and wheat and National Agricultural Cooperative Marketing Federation (NAFED), founded in 1958 for promoting cooperative marketing among farmers, started operating in perishable items[8] but even then, rice and wheat remained the main beneficiaries of public intervention. The rather unstructured price support scheme (PSS) faced further transition after 2010 when pulses, so long under market forces began to receive protection from the government. To arrest price volatility under international influences, a new central agency called Small Farmers Agri-Business Consortium (SFAC) which, unlike FCI and NAFED also draws on private investment, was established in 1994 (PIB 2017b). NAFED and SFAC are leading the central agencies for procuring of pulses.

Marketing policy, rooted in the findings of the Royal Commission on Agriculture (1928) and continued through the enactment of legislation for Agricultural Produce Marketing (APMC Acts) in states, was meant to protect the interests of the farmers. Prices in regulated (APMC) markets were determined by open auctions, but the regulations of the APMC markets began to appear stifling in the era of reforms (Acharya 2004). The central government in 2002 circulated a model bill in response to which the states began amending their APMC regulations at varied speeds. New players were invited into an even playing field. The reform was also expected to draw investment, modern methods and technology, all of which would reduce the cost of the transaction and product wastage and discover prices transparently. Further, limits and permits for stocking 'essential' commodities were relaxed when the Essential Commodities Act (ECA 1955) was reviewed in 1990 and 2002.

---

[6]Initially, the government announced procurement price (PP) and minimum support prices (MSP) separately for two distinct purposes. Though both were calculated to allow some profit, the PP tended to fall below the prevailing market price, while the guaranteed MSP in principle served as a floor price for the market. Since the early 1970s, only the MSP has been announced, and all the products offered by farmers were guaranteed to be purchased by the government.

[7]The Ministry of Agriculture had been collecting primary information on cost of cultivation since 1970–71 on the recommendation of a Technical Committee.

[8]Besides FCI and NAFED, Cotton Corporation of India (CCI), Jute Corporation of India (JCI) and Central Warehousing Corporation (CWC) are some of the other organizations that help the government procure from farmers.

2.1 A policy shift

The year 2014–15, agro-marketing policy shifted towards farmers' interests. A price stabilization fund (PSF) was set up in 2014–15 under the Department of Agriculture, Cooperation & Famers Welfare (DAC&FW), later transferred to the Department of Consumer Affairs (DOCA) in 2016, to moderate the prices of important agri-horticultural commodities (PIB 2017a). Public support to pulses using PSF was a new development started in 2014 which expectedly would raise prices above what market itself would realize. The AGMARKNET was already in operation since 2000 for linking important agricultural produce markets and the national and state marketing departments. The union budget allocated funds for computers and the necessary software. At the end of 2014, to strengthen this endeavour, an Integrated Scheme for Agricultural Marketing (ISAM) was brought under a single umbrella all Central Sector Schemes aiming to improve the efficiency of marketing, keeping the farmers at the heart of it. It emphasized infrastructure and ICT to expand a market's outreach. The ISAM was a further recognition of the potentials of ICT to form a nationwide information network for speedy collection and dissemination of market information to help timely price realization. Minimum, maximum and modal prices of varieties and qualities transacted were posted. At the start of the XII Plan (2013), 3241, i.e. 45% of the wholesale markets of the country had online facilities, and the ISAM targeted 3700 new markets to be covered through computers, mobiles and SMS facilities.

An intention of doubling farmer's income by the year 2022 was announced in 2015, making it clear that the priority of agricultural policy is shifting from producing more to delivering more to the producer. Empirical evidence of low farm incomes in a growing economy (NABARD 2018) had already been drawing political attention. The Ministry of Agriculture was renamed Ministry of Agriculture and Farmers Welfare in 2015. Rural markets were getting ready for the technology-enabled methods like electronic auctioning, computerized market intelligence, spot and futures markets, mobile 'apps', specialized call centres and anticipated forecasting algorithms (Union Budget on demand forecasting 2018) for demand and price discovery.

2.2 Innovative Reforms 2016–2018

Karnataka government was implementing a unified market platform jointly through a private company ReMS from 2014. It demonstrated how, supported by facilities for grading and standardization, a common platform for a transparent and integrated e-trading mechanism can be successful in expanding the market within and beyond the state for fetching remunerative producer prices. Following the ReMS model, a central sector scheme created a common e-platform at the national level aimed to link 585 selected wholesale markets across the country to which free software and funds for hardware and equipment would be given by the central government.

The electronic trading platform for e-NAM was launched in 2016. The e-NAM, to be monitored intensely, is expected to draw private investment and benefit farmer directly and indirectly with competitiveness, efficiency, lower price spreads and better price realization and to reduce their dependence on MSP, but the success will depend greatly on state cooperation (Chand 2016). The national e-market platform allows transparent sale transactions and price discovery initially only in regulated markets in willing states that have a liberal licensing policy for traders without any precondition of physical presence. Harmonization of quality standards of agricultural produce with infrastructure for assaying (quality testing) is essential for informed bidding by buyers for trade to follow and still proves to be a challenge. Recent data (2019) shows a limited coverage of only 14% farmers under e-NAM (BL 2019).

In the way forward in reforms, PSS imposes a costly administrative burden, leakages of scarce public funds targeted for farmers and possibility of price distortion. An umbrella scheme 'Pradhan Mantri Annadata Aay Sanrakshan Abhiyan or the PM-AASHA' approved in 2018 brought together the conventional procurement scheme and an option of purchase from farmers by private traders against DBT by government. It followed the model 'price deficiency scheme' which was already in operation in Madhya Pradesh. Replacement of actual physical public purchases by the government could over time diminish price and production distortion that MSP implicates and simplify the administration of PSS. In the latest move to secure farmer's welfare, a financial transfer to farmers dissociated from nature or quantity of crop is grown is implemented as a token measure under the Kisan Samman Nidhi Yojana (PM-Kisan) in 2019, similar in spirit to Rythu Bandhu scheme in Telangana. The innovations started in 2016 are rudimentary in development.

2.3 Production and Public Operations in Pulses

Pulses are consumed across the country, but production fell short historically. Gram and arhar are the two dominant crops, accounting for 40 and 20% of India's pulses production, respectively. Production is concentrated towards Maharashtra, Madhya Pradesh and Karnataka in case of arhar and towards Madhya Pradesh, Maharashtra and Rajasthan in case of gram (Table 3), but Gujarat, Uttar Pradesh and Andhra Pradesh are minor producers of arhar and Karnataka, Andhra Pradesh and Uttar Pradesh of gram. Between the two periods, 2010–13 and 2014–16, Madhya Pradesh gained share in both gram and arhar, but Maharashtra lost share in arhar whose production became more spatially concentrated in Madhya Pradesh. More than 1.5 million tonnes of pulses out of the 23 million tonnes produced was procured in 2016–17. Among the agencies procuring gram and arhar, NAFED was by far the largest followed by SFAC. Arhar and gram were prominent items of procurement.

Plots of annual price indices of major producer states show differential behaviour of markets (Fig. 3a, b). Gram price, reaching an upper bound in end 2012, was arrested thereafter but rose steadily subsequently. Arhar, on the contrary, showed plateauing at two levels, but like gram the price in all growing states increased sharply from 2014

Table 3 Production distribution of gram and arhar across states (%) in India

States	Gram		Arhar	
	Period-I	Period-II	Period-I	Period-II
Madhya Pradesh	38.2	41.5	10.1	18.7
Maharashtra	13.4	15.1	32.8	27.1
Rajasthan	16.3	13.3	-	-
Karnataka	7.1	8.1	15.7	15.9
Andhra Pradesh	8.3	6.5	7.7	8.0
Uttar Pradesh	6.9	4.9	10.6	7.0
Jharkhand	-	-	5.0	6.0
Gujarat	-	-	8.6	8.7
Other states	9.8	10.6	9.5	8.6
India (Million Tonnes)	8.57	7.92	2.93	3.41

Note Period-I: 2010–11 to 2013–14, Period-II: 2014–15 to 2016–17. Andhra Pradesh includes Telangana
Source DES (Website)

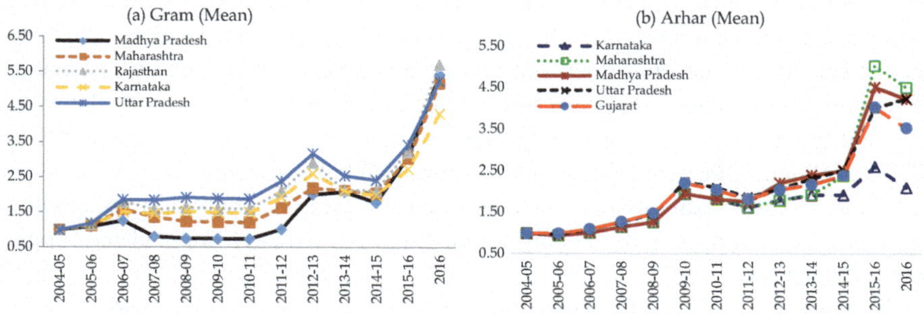

Fig. 3 Movements of mean of annual price indices (base 2004–05) across states 2004–5 to 2016–17

till it reached a crisis point in 2016 when the curve takes an inverted U-shape due to unprecedentedly high production of 4.9 million tonnes against 2.6 million tonnes in 2015–16 followed by imports adding to the stock. The steady decline of producer price thereafter has been a cause of greater concern for the economy.

3 Moving Towards an Integrated Agricultural Market

An idealized 'perfectly competitive' market allows space to numerous agents as buyers (traders) and sellers (farmers) to transact with chosen partners and an open option to enter or leave the trade. Theoretically, the market generates a representative 'one' price, which leaves no super-normal profit. The perfect competition also implies efficiency, which means that the equilibrium price incorporates all possible information (Samuelson 1964). In practice, trade theory (Balassa 1964; Samuelson 1964) has its gaps attributed to quality differences, demand patterns and costs imposed by non-traded goods. Differential market behaviour (Hallak and Schott 2011; Feenstra and Romalis 2014) is also manifested in empirical correspondence between income and price level (Bekker et al. 2012; Melchoir 2016). The geographic ambit of the market bound by roads, ports and trade laws is important for any analysis of markets (Samuelson 1964; Enke 1951; Samuelson 1952; Takayama and Judge 1971). As a concept, market integration is an extension of the theory of general competitive equilibrium to the spatial context where a number of locations are conceived to be tied by trade relations through the law of one price across markets which has been questioned and tested empirically in a broad discourse (Goodwin 1992; Goodwin and Wohlgenant 1990; Crougy-Veyrac et al. 1981).

Influenced by geography, production is seldom found to be distributed with uniformity and even government interventions, constrained by administrative and fiscal constraints, cannot be uniformly dispersed across producing regions. In a free market, integration is essential for preventing localized famines in consuming areas (Ravallion 1986), but when a positive shock is created by PSS in one location, trading responses of surrounding states will convey its benefit across state borders. The large gap between prices that consumers pay and what producers receive has been a matter of concern, but it is also important to note that prices that farmers get for the same commodity can be widely variant among locations (Chatterjee and Kapur 2016). ICT can influence the convergence of markets not only by disseminating price information across wholesale markets swiftly to enable price benchmarking in smaller markets but more importantly, also by stimulating trade to match demand and supply across the nation.

The regulated (APMC) market of India, which served agricultural marketing for decades, was designed with a strong mechanism of price discovery. The economic reforms, by relaxing the entry barriers to traders expanded the options available to farmers to choose their buyers (Ghosh 2013) and reduced the role of the APMC market. As price discovery in the absence of an auction became a challenge, regulated markets, especially the larger ones with numerous transactions in the specific products, continued to provide benchmark prices to others. Thus, despite critical reports, even at the extreme, the regulated APMC market can not be seen as an 'auction mechanism' grounded on competition laws (Reddy and Rajshekhar 2014). The AGMARKNET initiative of the government (see Box 1) was aimed at disseminating price information from relevant wholesale markets so that benchmark prices can be drawn from across India and even international markets. The effectiveness and outreach to farmers and small traders remained limited so long as access to the Internet was scarce.

The year 2014–15 could therefore be seen as a watershed. The MRIN under ISAM (Sects. 1 and 2) was linking wholesale markets with locally accessible information using modern technologies under ICT. The year was a departure also because pulses came under the ambit of PSS. The public policy of PSS is expected to enhance market prices in areas of concentrated procurement. In the short run, procurement can widen price differentials with other producing regions, but at a reasonably longer time scale, so long as private trade flows are uninhibited, PSS, by attracting supplies from other producing areas, can only widen the outreach of public benefit to farmers across the country. The government's intervention in pricing is a distortion in the market, but the PSS of 2014 was a recognition of the distressfully low pulses prices determined in producers' markets. The sharp rise in prices in the producing states with converging tendencies seen in Fig. 3 is a further affirmation of the distress caused by local market forces in the absense of state intervention and the increased role of information networking across the markets where producers sold pulses. Concurrently undertaken public intervention with PSS and ICT linkage will reflect on both price level and their differentials. Analysis of monthly price data at the state level in the whole study period is expected to show enhancement of prices due to procurement in the Sub-Period-II along with increased convergence of state prices owing to ICT-enabled market networking.

3.1 Methodological Approaches

The approach taken to assess market integration is neither unique nor has it been static. Food price differences across countries and within large and heterogeneous counties have been under research lens (Melchior 2016; Deaton and Dupriez 2011; Li and Gibson 2014) to identify border effects (USA and China), convergence of fragmented markets (China, Russia), segmentation (Russia), their implications for poverty (India) and their determinants (India). The bivariate correlation coefficient is another simple quantitative measure of market integration. It has been applied to show that Indian markets tended to be increasingly integrated with the development of roads and aberrations were attributed to price controls in cereals (Cummings 1967; Lele 1967, 1971; Kainth 1982; Gupta 1973; Palaskas and Hariss 1993). However, any observed correlation may be spurious when the price is affected by another traded good (Blyn 1973; Hariss 1979). The role of trade in handling bulky consignments across distances is not explicitly patent in results based on this analysis. An alternative method, hinging on long-run convergence of markets, is to track the spatial variances of prices across markets, but this method too is not spared from criticisms (Hurd 1975; Ravallion 1986). Gini coefficients are computed with the population as weights also to analyse unit values of products, their wholesale and retail prices across states, but price differentials are explained by standard regressions of pooled price data on the state-level and supply-side variables as proxies because interstate trade data is not available, state level and supply side variables are taken as proxies (Melchior 2016). Focus on the role of trade is also placed in examining the effect of highway construction in India (Atkin 2013), which is expected to reduce trading cost. Imports from other states are apprehended to make farmer's income volatile. Compiling micro-data from 308 districts in 19 states over 40 years and 15 major crops, distributions of the mean and variance of prices were plotted at decadal levels for comparison, but structured econometric methods showed that portfolio reallocation across crops helped farmers to minimize risk and amplify gains from trade. Implicitly information proved important in this argument.

A more popular as also evolving procedure is the dynamic bivariate or multivariate regression-based method of measuring price cointegration that allows local dynamic structures to be incorporated in the measurement (Johansen 1988). Using a radial framework with a single central urban market and six satellite markets, Ravallion (1986) identified two highly restricted rice markets in Bangladesh in a period of price turbulences. An important insight gained in this study is the preference for a linear rather than a logarithmic form to allow transport cost to affect price differentials. In one critical application, Gonzalez-Rivera and Helfand (2001) also searched for geographical boundaries of markets in Brazil, attributing any non-exclusion to factors like remoteness, trade reversals and non-stationary transaction costs, but in the same paper (p. 579), statistical limitations of the procedure in large dimensioned data have been cautioned by the authors. Gonzalo and Granger (1995) also isolated an unobserved common factor between two cointegrated variables. In a step ahead of the cointegration analysis, an error correction model (ECM) takes account of the possible reactions of each location to disequilibria elsewhere. The launch of market reforms and methodological advances intensified the applied research interest in the flow of price signals. Application of cointegration analysis and ECM on price data expanded. Johansen method was commonly used to show improvement of spatial integration of wholesale markets for wheat, rice and other products in India (Wilson 2001; Acharya 2004; Kumar and Sharma 2000; Bathla 2008).

3.2 Data and Method Used in This Study

The analyses that follow primarily examine the association of price levels and their movements between pairs of states treated as markets using monthly wholesale data. The sample period starts with 2010 when ICT application entered agriculture marketing (see discussion in Sect. 2) but, limited by access to data at the time of analysis the sample period is truncated at the end of 2016. In reality, the sample period 2010–16 covers a gestation period for the reforms targeting market expansion and is dynamic with the years 2014–15 marked a watershed when policy emphasis in various ways shifted to farmers' welfare. Subsequently, the years 2016 was another watershed when the objective was oriented specifically towards expanding farmers' reach to spatially distant buyers. Given that the sample is a period marked by dynamics in policy and ICT, two sub-periods are compared to track the tendencies in the entire period.

The number of states covered is 10 each for arhar and gram which include both producer and consuming states and Sub-Period-I: 2010:04–2014:03 and Sub-Period-II: 2014:04–2016:12 with 2014 as a break point. The state price is represented as the average of the nominal mandi (wholesale market) prices in the state reported officially (DES, Website, MoA&FW, Various). The time series sample sizes in Sub-Period-I and Sub-Period-II are 48 and 33, respectively, reasonably adequate for time series analysis.

Simple correlation analysis of prices is made for both sub-periods anticipating improved correlation among prices in Sub-Period-II compared to Sub-Period-I as markets get increasing linked by trade. The standard deviation among the prices in any market measures the spread of prices from the mean. To correct for inflation, the deviation is standardized by the mean to get the coefficient of variation (CV) which can be compared and tracked by the two sub-periods. Finally, prices are also analysed by modelling for cointegration and ECM across markets for the two consecutive sub-periods. If non-stationary random variables have a stationary linear combination, the variables are said to be cointegrated in the sense that they have a long-run linear relation. When prices in two markets do not have a long-run linear relation, the markets are not integrated and have their price determination processes as separate markets. Cointegration and ECM are estimated to assess if any pair of markets (states) are integrated by trade and whether the price in one market catches up with a movement in another within a time frame of one month which seems reasonable for a food product that is perishable only in the medium term. The ECM, in its dynamic approach, allows lags in responding to disequilibrium.

First, each price series is subjected to unit root analysis using ADF (augmented Dickey–Fuller) test choosing lags based on AIC (Akaike information criterion) and alternatively the SIC (Bayesian information, Schwarz criterion). An alternative to ADF test is the PP test (Phillips–Perron test) which can be used with Newey–West bandwidth to choose lags. Time trend is considered only if statistically significant. The ADF and PP tests help identify the order of integration $I(k)$ which implies that the kth difference in price data is stationary. If the series is stationary at level, it is $I(0)$ and if the series at the level has a unit root, the first difference is tested and so on. If two series are $I(k)$ and $I(j)$ where orders k and j are not equal, they are not cointegrated. Further cointegration analysis is continued only if the order of integration is the same. Johansen's method is used to find the cointegrating relation and the error correction in prices in a bivariate process between states.

A long-run equilibrium or a cointegrating relation between two price series is given by the equation

$$P_i = \alpha + \beta P_j + \in_i \tag{1}$$

where β the long is run coefficient of adjustment and α is a constant and the error $\in_i$ is stationary, expressed as

$$\epsilon_i = P_i - \alpha - \beta P_j \tag{2}$$

measuring the extent of short-run disequilibrium which stimulates trade flows from market-j to market-i. When $\epsilon_i > 0$ which means that the price in the ith market exceeds the target set by the price in the jth market through the hypothetical long-run cointegrating relation (1), the traders' responses tend to raise the price in market-j and bring down the price in market-i in an equilibrating move in the short run represented by the error correction equation as follows

$$\Delta P_{it} = \theta_i \epsilon_{it-1} + \alpha_{1i}\Delta P_{i_{t-1}} + \alpha_{2i}\Delta P_{i_{t-2}} \cdots + \beta_{1i}\Delta P_{j_{t-1}} + \beta_{2i}\Delta P_{j_{t-2}} \cdots + \varepsilon_t, \tag{3}$$

where

θ_i is treated as the ECM coefficient.

3.3 Have Markets for Pulses Integrated Over Time?

Prices in Maharashtra and Madhya Pradesh, both dominant pulses producers, are consistently low (Tables 5 and 6). Within the sub-periods, temporally the price was relatively stable in the first period in arhar, but in both crops, intra-period variation increased over time. Inflation made prices much higher in the second period, the ordering of states did not always remain consistent and the prices became temporally more unstable in both crops. Comparisons of the prices and their variations based on range, correlation and CV suggest that state prices at levels are converging through it must be admitted that the results do not present robust confirmation. The literature (see Sect. 3.2) is clear about specific flaws in these indicators.

3.4 Prices and Their Interstate Variations

Compared to the sample average, gram prices are low in producing states Madhya Pradesh, Maharashtra and Rajasthan in all of which public procurement is also reported. In Sub-Period-I, gram price is lowest in Madhya Pradesh, but the price is high in Tamil Nadu, Karnataka and Bihar, all-consuming or minor producer states. In Sub-Period-II, the price of gram in the consuming state Tamil Nadu is higher by Rs. 32 than the lowest price state Madhya Pradesh. The range of gram price fell from 148 to 74%, and its CV fell from 26 to 21% from Sub-Period-I to Sub-Period-II. The curve for the CV of state prices of gram (Fig. 4a) showed no convergence to start with, there was a mild rise in 2013 followed by a distinct reversal.

In Sub-Period-I, arhar price is particularly low in major producing states Madhya Pradesh and Maharashtra and also in minor producing states Rajasthan and

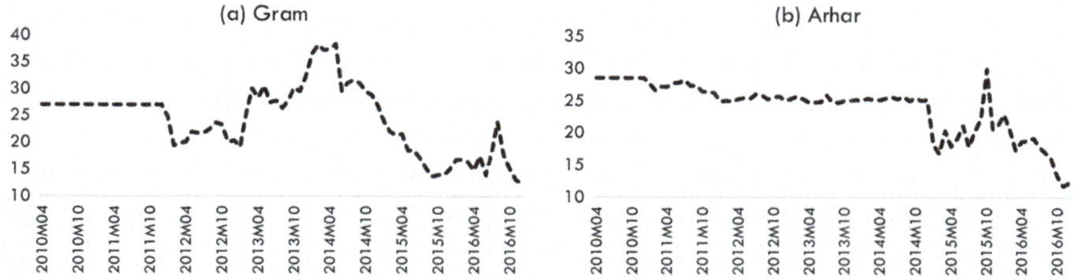

Fig. 4 Tendency of interstate price variation (coefficient of variation %)

Uttar Pradesh but paradoxically, not in Karnataka which also produces the crop, attributable arguably to some extent to quality difference, demand factors related to dietary patterns and probably also to initiation of policy experiments with online marketing (Sect. 2.2). In the second period, Madhya Pradesh, Rajasthan and Maharashtra were still left with relatively low prices. Between the two periods, the interstate range reduced from 113 to 86%, and the CV is less in Sub-Period-II at 23% compared to 27% in the Sub-Period-1. Interstate price variances seem to be static in most of Sub-Period-I, showing some volatility in 2014 but falling mostly in Sub-Period-II (Fig. 4b).

3.5 *Correlation*

If the bivariate correlation coefficient is considered as an indication of integration, Tables 7 and 8 suggest that transmission of price movements has improved in Sub-Period-II over Sub-Period-I for gram, but for arhar the result is mixed. For gram in Sub-Period-I prices in producing states, Maharashtra and Madhya Pradesh have low correlation with states Gujarat, Haryana and Rajasthan despite the proximity and Rajasthan prices are weakly correlated with prices in other two producing states and Tamil Nadu, while Bihar prices have a relatively high correlation with producing states. In Sub-Period-II on the contrary, coefficients are mostly 99–100% except between Bihar and the three major producing states and between Rajasthan and Tamil Nadu. In the case of arhar, correlation of prices with Karnataka actually reduces for all cases except Tamil Nadu and West Bengal. The result may signify that Madhya Pradesh, the major producer integrated into a larger market, unlike Karnataka, where the price clings to its high level.

3.6 *Cointegration and Error Correction Analysis*

Cointegration is indicative of a long-run price relation suggestive of trade. All the price series have a unit root at levels (Table 9), but at first difference, mixed results emerge from alternative methods because choosing lags based on AIC, the ADF tests show non-stationarity in several cases in both sub-periods for gram and only in Sub-Period-II for arhar. Since the second differences prove to be stationary, these price series are deemed to be I(2) in 11 out of the total 42 cases and I(1) in others (Table 10). If these results are accepted, long-run cointegration can be examined only for states with I(1) series and for states with I(2) series separately.

On finer scrutiny, the results are observed to be highly sensitive to the number of lags. AIC and SIC criteria often differ in the indication of model selection, and the literature is not clear on the choice, leaving much to judgment. While SIC is parsimonious, the longer lag structure of a typical AIC-based model can be more representative of the dynamic process of price changes in the different states. The PP test is more robust, and the lags are chosen by the method itself (Newey–West bandwidth). ADF test by choosing lags based on SIC reduces the I(2) to only 2 cases and applying the PP test eliminates them. Assuming all series to be I(1) to allow space to alternative methods, bivariate cointegration tests are conducted though the findings from ADF-AIC methodology suggest some caution in dealing with the results. Seasonality in monthly time series data is a possibility, gram being a rabi crop and arhar being grown in the kharif season. Plots of the monthly prices are not conspicuous for seasonality. Nevertheless, as a trial, the ADF analysis was conducted on prices corrected for seasonality (not reported).[9] The results remained same except that gram price in Gujarat with ADF-AIC method (Table 10) changed from I(2) to I(1) which is assumed in this study anyway based on the other methods. Although AIC is used for model selection, sensitivity test is conducted for varying lags to ensure consistency between AIC and SIC.

When prices between two markets are found to be cointegrated, the two markets are treated as integrated or linked together as a larger market, whereas segmented markets are expected to be not integrated. In both crop cases, profound changes are seen in market pairing (Table 11). More the number of states any producer state is integrated with, larger is its potential market. However, even if two markets are integrated, despite the trade links implied, price transmission may not be mutual or significant in one month. To the extent a producing state remains unresponsive, it serves as an exogenous influence to another consuming or producing state and remains insulated from the benefit coming from consumer demand or public procurement.

Considering price cointegration as a sign of market integration and error correction to be suggestive of the direction of causality and the strength of adjustment to short-term disequilibrium, the two crops differ in price behaviour though producer states in both cases tend to be cointegrated. Gram markets in Maharashtra and Rajasthan, in general, appear to be relatively large sprawling across the country and Rajasthan's arhar market covered as many as five states from different regions. There appears to be a shift in the trading partners of Maharashtra from eastern states to northern and

[9]Admittedly, seasonal adjustment may produce mistaken inference of economic relationship and loss of valuable information, and application of new methods (Franses 1991; Johansen and Schaumburg 1999; Darne 2004) is found in the literature. The analysis in this study also could not correct for seasonality in Sub-Period-II owing to the small size of the sample. Use of monthly data is common in cointegration analysis of agricultural prices (Ahmed and Singla 2017; Shreshtha et al. 2014; Singh et al. 2018).

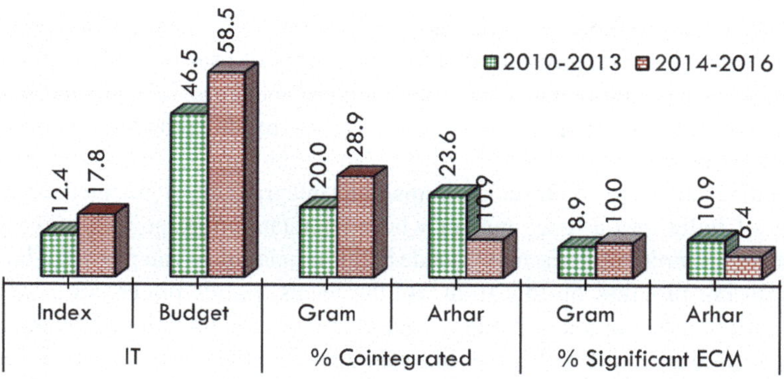

Fig. 5 Change in IT index (%) and budget (Rs. per 100) and market expansion

western neighbours. The ECM coefficient showed limited and mostly asymmetrical responses of gram producing states in Sub-Period-II. In particular, gram price in Maharashtra did not respond to differentials with producing or consuming states, Madhya Pradesh responded only to Maharashtra, while Rajasthan was insulated to price differentials with all other states. Prices in producer states, however, were found to cause price changes in consumer states. Compared to gram, markets for arhar performed poorly in integration and the responses of producer states (Fig. 5). Producing states generally have low prices but some developed integration with consuming states such as Gujarat with West Bengal, Maharashtra with Rajasthan, Madhya Pradesh with Bihar, but in all these cases, the latter showed price responses asymmetrically. Maharashtra, a major producer, did not expand its market and did not respond to price differential though consuming states adjusted prices in response.

4 Conclusion

India's agricultural markets are being reformed to enable farmers to take advantage of market opportunities and earn higher incomes. The direction taken is towards supporting farmers with higher incomes without distorting the market. Currently, the policy emphasis of the central government is moving towards creating a larger national-level market for agro-products beyond state borders so that with improved supply chains farmers fetch best prices for their products. By relaxing regulations and simplifying administration, entry barriers are removed, and new and resourceful trading agents are allowed to enter the market as buyers.

Market reforms implemented by tinkering with institutional rules aim to clear markets of imperfections and expand the market through competitive means but the entry of ICT into the domains of reforms can be expected to facilitate the process at every step by enabling easy financial transfers, forecasting early outlooks of production, monitoring prices and above all by supporting farmers, traders and consumers across the country to transact at efficient prices. A review of the transition process in the new millennium demonstrates that the large array of uses that ICT has found in moving Indian agriculture into a new technology-enabled age. ICT, as a facilitator of reforms, seems to offer a way to transform agriculture into a modern, adaptive and lucrative sector.

A leading objective of current reforms is to integrate the segmented state-level markets of India into a 'one' market where interstate arbitrage will make prices move in line. Empirical assessments made at this crucial stage can provide a baseline for measuring progress on this front. At the levels, pulses prices continue to be widely different across states, but they have come closer with reduced divergence in the 2010–2016 period as indicators like range and coefficient of variation suggest. The year 2014–15 marked by price support on pulses and a large budget on linking markets by information (ICT) started proved to be a departure. Prices of both crops in producing states started rising due to public support, and while dispersions in prices began declining sooner in the case of gram, arhar which is increasingly concentrated in Madhya Pradesh saw price convergence only later in 2015 attributable largely to ICT.

Though mere access to ICT may have helped in price discovery by accessing benchmark prices at major centres elsewhere, which tend to be production centres and large wholesale markets, these methods cannot capture the role of trade in price movements that involve dynamics. The correlation coefficient between prices across markets has not also shown any clear sign in this regard with price movements being contemporaneously even becoming less correlated in the case of arhar, but this indicator says little about trade and causality.

The cointegration and error correction methods, by modelling the price behaviour econometrically accounting for local dynamics and the theory of price adjustment to disequilibrium, show that market coverages are limited and variable in the study period. Even if two markets are integrated, more often, the consuming states responded to price differential with producing states bringing down their prices. With rare exceptions, the producing states were seen to lead the market, largely remaining exogenous. Also, during this time high prices of pulses happened to be the dominant concern of the country, invoking varied policy responses and the market response observed seem to be the fulfilment of the aspiration of the time although arguably it added to farmer's distress. Segmentation was not uniformly observed in the sub-periods though a few pairs of states lost their linkages, but there is no evidence that distances stood in the way of trade.

ICT can be anticipated to support the supply chains with information and operational efficiency, enable government to support farmers without distorting the market and help farmers and traders to expand markets with modern marketing methods defeating the imposed barriers with its own universality. The recent origin of the e-NAM which actually facilitates auctioning and trade on ICT portals across the country has much more to offer but the effects are awaited. Prerequisite to physical goods movements, are however freight pathways bolstered by suitable storage facilities, minimal transaction cost of flow (rules, toll gates, restrictions, harassment etc.). The speed of trading responses is contingent on the presence and readiness of a well equipped, willing and forward looking trading community. Further, the ICT budget for agriculture marketing has not retained its share throughout. In a federal nation despite the Union government's intentions, market expansion and responses are largely outcomes of the political economy reactions and capabilities of states to restrain grain movements across borders. Market exchange is not costless and outdated supply chains can add to unproductive costs associated with trading. The government instituted ICT system for agro-marketing may also have biases towards harnessing information specifically from larger producer markets when similar attention from consumer markets can be more helpful to farmers

Acknowledgements The authors thank Dr. Sangeeta Chakravarty, Institute of Economic Growth, Delhi, for her advice on the empirical analysis.

Appendix

See Tables 4, 5, 6, 7, 8, 9, 10, 11 and 12.

Table 4 ICT budget classification in agriculture sector

Crop Husbandry (Major Head)
Farm Information Bureau (Non-Plan)
Information Support/Management Information System
Agricultural Economics and Statistics (Minor Head)
Commission for Agricultural Costs and Prices
Other Expenditure (Minor Head)
Strengthening of IT and Information Net Work in DAC
Strengthening/Promoting Agricultural Information System
National E-Governance Plan-Agriculture
Other Agricultural Programmes (Major Head)
Marketing Research, Survey and Marketing Information Network
Grants-in-aid to State Government (Major Head)
Crop Husbandry—Other Grants (Minor Head)
Promotion/strengthening of IT in Agriculture
National E-Governance Plan-Agriculture
Other Agricultural Programmes–Marketing Facilities (Minor Head)
Marketing Research, Survey and Marketing Information Network

Table 5 Mean and variations in of wholesale prices (Rs./kg) of gram in India

	Temporal average and variation within states										Spatial average and variation across states	
	BH	GJ	HR	KRN	MH	MP	RJ	TN	UP	WB	Mean	CV
Sub-Period-I												
Mean	37.8	29.4	30.2	38.7	27.4	20.1	29.2	49.8	35.3	36.0	33.4	26
CV	19	26	23	22	26	44	25	28	21	22	23	
Sub-Period-II												
Mean	51.2	46.4	49.1	55.0	49.7	44.8	46.9	77.8	50.2	55.8	52.7	21
CV	29	46	46	36	42	49	45	33	35	38	39	

Note Sub-Period-I: 2010:04 to 2014:03, Sub-Period-II: 2014:04 to 2016:12. Calculations are based on monthly data
Source MoA&FW (various), DES, Website

Table 6 Mean (Rs./kg) and variations (%) in of wholesale prices of arhar in India

	Temporal average and variation within states										Spatial average and variation across states	
	AP	BH	GJ	KRN	MH	MP	RJ	TN	UP	WB	Mean	CV
Sub-Period-I												
Mean	37.6	34.3	52.1	59.5	28.0	30.7	29.4	41.3	35.5	42.9	39.1	27
CV	9	8	8	8	8	15	8	11	10	13	8	
Sub-Period-II												
Mean	67.4	53.2	85.0	73.8	61.3	55.6	45.7	58.9	60.3	64.1	62.5	23
CV	29	22	30	22	37	30	22	18	25	30	25	

Note Sub-Period-I: 2010:04 to 2014:03, Sub-Period-II: 2014:04 to 2016:12. Calculations are based on monthly data
Source MoA&FW (various), DES, Website

Table 7 Correlation of monthly wholesale price of gram

	BR	GJ	HR	KR	MH	MP	RJ	TN	UP	WB
Sub-Period-I										
MH	0.88	0.66	0.69	0.80	1.00	0.80	0.73	0.82	0.80	0.73
MP	0.82	0.65	0.64	0.79	0.80	1.00	0.67	0.90	0.77	0.85
RJ	0.88	0.98	0.99	0.97	0.73	0.67	1.00	0.65	0.92	0.84
Sub-Period II										
MH	0.95	0.98	0.99	0.99	1.00	0.99	0.99	0.96	0.98	0.98
MP	0.95	0.99	0.99	0.99	0.99	1.00	0.99	0.94	0.97	0.99
RJ	0.95	0.98	0.99	0.99	0.99	0.99	1.00	0.95	0.97	0.98

Note Sub-Period-I: 2010:04 to 2014:03, Sub-Period-II: 2014:04 to 2016:12
Source MoA&FW (various), DES, Website

Table 8 Correlation of monthly wholesale price of arhar

	AP	BR	GJ	KR	MH	MP	RJ	TN	UP	WB
Sub-Period-I										
KR	0.89	1.00	0.92	1.00	1.00	0.68	1.00	0.68	0.94	0.63
MH	0.89	1.00	0.92	1.00	1.00	0.68	1.00	0.68	0.94	0.63
MP	0.65	0.68	0.71	0.68	0.68	1.00	0.68	0.64	0.70	0.29
Sub-Period-II										
KR	0.85	0.66	0.82	1.00	0.71	0.78	0.66	0.82	0.61	0.79
MH	0.93	0.95	0.92	0.71	1.00	0.93	0.95	0.88	0.91	0.91
MP	0.93	0.94	0.93	0.78	0.93	1.00	0.94	0.86	0.91	0.93

Note Sub-Period-I: 2010:04 to 2014:03, Sub-Period-II: 2014:04 to 2016:12
Source MoA&FW (various), DES, Website

Table 9 Unit root test of monthly price data

Sub-Period-I					Sub-Period-II			
	Level		First difference		Level		First difference	
	ADF	PP	ADF	PP	ADF	PP	ADF	PP
Gram								
BR	−1.59	−1.48	−4.63	−4.63	1.88	7.01	−1.72[a]	−6.50[a]
GJ	−1.92	−0.13	−2.52	−6.27	−1.24	−2.66	−3.81[a]	−7.49
HR	−1.40	−1.49	−6.31	−6.38	−1.58	−1.43	−5.55[a]	−6.52[a]
KR	−1.73	−1.47	−3.49	−3.43	1.48	3.18	−3.18[a]	−4.53[a]
MH	−3.16	−2.49	−5.89	−9.44	−1.93	−1.70	−3.88	−3.86
MP	−1.62	−1.32	−1.76	−9.22	−1.74	3.09	−6.63[a]	−6.64[a]
RJ	−2.02	−1.45	−2.32	−5.44	−1.58	−1.80	−2.09	−4.74
TN	−1.97	−2.58	−4.34	−5.34	−1.69	−1.76	−4.78	−4.87
UP	−1.57	−1.57	−5.41	−5.49	3.51	3.51	−5.78[a]	−5.81[a]
WB	−1.30	−1.25	−4.63	−5.51	−2.64	−1.67	−3.83[a]	−4.75
Arhar								
AP	−2.38	−2.11	−5.15	−5.08	−1.51	−1.57	−6.25[a]	−6.25[a]
BR	−1.89	−1.65	−5.05	−5.05	−1.84	−1.37	−3.44	−3.38
GJ	−2.78	−2.23	−4.91	−4.88	−1.58	−1.58	−7.77	−7.83
KR	−1.89	−1.65	−5.06	−5.05	−1.53	−1.62	−6.42	−6.43
MH	−1.89	−1.65	−5.06	−5.05	−0.15	−0.19	−5.76[a]	−5.76[a]
MP	−2.40	−2.31	−8.02	−8.07	−2.53	−1.52	−2.10	−8.08
RJ	−1.89	−1.65	−5.06	−5.05	−1.84	−1.37	−1.10	−3.38
TN	−1.97	−1.84	−8.54	−8.53	−1.37	−1.49	−5.47	−5.52
UP	−1.89	−1.74	−6.64	−6.65	−1.39	−1.28	−3.31	−3.28
WB	2.15	−2.17	6.76	−6.77	−0.29	−0.29	−4.92	−4.93

Note Lags are chosen using AIC for ADF test and Newey–West bandwidth for PP test. Sub-Period-I: 2010:04 to 2014:03, Sub-Period-II: 2014:04 to 2016:12

[a]Denotes having time trend

Source MoA&FW (various), DES, Website

Table 10 Order of integration of monthly prices

	Sub-Period-I			Sub-Period-II		
States	ADF–AIC tests	ADF–SIC tests	PP–BK tests	ADF–AIC tests	ADF–SIC tests	PP–BK tests
Gram						
BR	I(1)	I(1)	I(1)	I(2)	I(1)	I(1)
GJ	I(2)	I(1)	I(1)	I(1)	I(1)	I(1)
HR	I(1)	I(1)	I(1)	I(1)	I(1)	I(1)
KR	I(1)	I(1)	I(1)	I(2)	I(2)	I(1)
MH	I(1)	I(1)	I(1)	I(1)	I(1)	I(1)
MP	I(2)	I(1)	I(1)	I(2)	I(1)	I(1)
RJ	I(2)	I(1)	I(1)	I(2)	I(2)	I(1)
TN	I(1)	I(1)	I(1)	I(1)	I(1)	I(1)
UP	I(1)	I(1)	I(1)	I(1)	I(1)	I(1)
WB	I(1)	I(1)	I(1)	I(2)	I(1)	I(1)
Arhar						
AP	I(1)	I(1)	I(1)	I(1)	I(1)	I(1)
BR	I(1)	I(1)	I(1)	I(2)	I(1)	I(1)
GJ	I(1)	I(1)	I(1)	I(1)	I(1)	I(1)
KR	I(1)	I(1)	I(1)	I(1)	I(1)	I(1)
MH	I(1)	I(1)	I(1)	I(1)	I(1)	I(1)
MP	I(1)	I(1)	I(1)	I(2)	I(1)	I(1)
RJ	I(1)	I(1)	I(1)	I(2)	I(1)	I(1)
TN	I(1)	I(1)	I(1)	I(1)	I(1)	I(1)
UP	I(1)	I(1)	I(1)	I(1)	I(1)	I(1)
WB	I(1)	I(1)	I(1)	I(1)	I(1)	I(1)

Note Sub-Period-I: 2010:04 to 2014:03, Sub-Period-II: 2014:04 to 2016:12
Source Based on estimated model

Table 11 Bivariate cointegration analysis of markets integration using monthly wholesale prices

States		Sub-Period-I			Sub-Period-II		
I	J	Lag	AIC	Coeff.	Lag	AIC	Coeff.
Arhar							
AP	BR	1	24.60	−1.17*			–
AP	RJ	1	24.29	−1.36*			–
BR	RJ	1	8.71	−1.16*			–
GJ	BR	5	9.08	−1.52*			–
GJ	RJ	5	9.09	−1.77*			–
GJ	WB			–	5	33.07	−1.52*
KR	AP	1	25.70	−1.48*			–
KR	GJ	5	9.56	−1.14*			–
MH	AP	1	24.19	−0.70*			–
MH	BR			–	5	28.95	−1.93*
MH	GJ	5	8.80	−0.54*			–
MH	RJ	1	8.18	−0.95*	5	28.64	−2.24*
MP	BR			–	1	29.01	−1.39*
MP	TN			–	1	30.74	−1.55*
RJ	KR	1	9.14	−0.49*			–
TN	WB			–	1	31.01	−0.63*
UP	AP	1	25.77	−1.11*			–
UP	GJ	1	25.23	−0.91*			–
Gram							
BR	TN			–	5	30.33	−0.49*
GJ	WB			–	4	29.08	−0.97*
HR	UP			–	5	29.76	−0.93*
KR	WB	5	26.09	−1.19*			–
MH	BR	1	26.30	−0.89*			–
MH	HR			–	1	29.40	−0.89*
MH	KR	1	26.71	−0.74*	2	27.84	−0.95*
MH	MP	5	28.17	−0.83*	1	29.31	−0.89*
MH	RJ			–	2	28.95	−0.94*
MH	WB	3	28.40	−0.92*			–
MP	BR	4	26.42	−1.12*			–
MP	HR			–	1	29.73	−0.97*
MP	RJ			–	1	29.38	−1.12*
MP	WB			–	4	28.89	−0.96*
RJ	BR			–	5	29.34	−0.21

(continued)

Table 11 (continued)

States		Sub-Period-I			Sub-Period-II		
I	J	Lag	AIC	Coeff.	Lag	AIC	Coeff.
RJ	HR	4	24.74	−1.05*	1	28.88	−0.89*
RJ	KR	5	23.90	−0.79*	4	27.57	−0.99*
RJ	WB	5	26.42	−0.91*			–

Note *Significant at 5%. Sub-Period-I: 2010:04 to 2014:03, Sub-Period-II: 2014:04 to 2016:12
Source MoA&FW (various), DES, Website

Table 12 Error correction coefficients (ECM) of monthly prices in the cointegrated pairs of States

States		Sub-Period-I		Sub-Period-II	
I	J	State I	State J	State I	State J
Arhar					
AP	BR	−0.37	0.24*	–	–
AP	RJ	−0.37	0.21*	–	–
BR	RJ	160.56	138.98	–	–
GJ	BR	−104.00	0.51*	–	–
GJ	RJ	−102.85	0.53*	–	–
GJ	WB	–	–	1.91	1.33*
KR	AP	−0.28*	0.25	–	–
KR	GJ	−0.81*	72.11	–	–
MH	AP	−0.28*	0.53	–	–
MH	BR	–	–	0.78	0.49*
MH	GJ	−0.97*	370.37	–	–
MH	RJ	−435.94	−457.52	0.78	0.42*
MP	BR	–	–	−0.55	0.49*
MP	TN	–	–	−0.71*	−0.07
RJ	KR	638.28	1291.94	–	–
TN	WB	–	–	0.14	0.99*
UP	AP	−0.23*	0.40*	–	–
UP	GJ	−0.36*	0.35*	–	–
Gram					
BR	TN	–	–	−0.08	1.00
GJ	WB	–	–	0.26	1.08*

(continued)

Table 12 (continued)

States		Sub-Period-I		Sub-Period-II	
I	J	State I	State J	State I	State J
HR	UP	–	–	−1.04	0.65*
KR	WB	0.19	0.82*	–	–
MH	BR	−0.69*	0.02	–	–
MH	HR	–	–	0.18	1.31*
MH	KR	−0.42*	0.02	0.14	0.87*
MH	MP	−0.08	0.66*	−0.24	0.64*
MH	RJ	–	–	−0.40	0.83
MH	WB	−0.37*	0.36*	–	–
MP	BR	−0.39*	0.01	–	–
MP	HR	–	–	0.38	1.13*
MP	RJ	–	–	−0.49	0.16
MP	WB	–	–	0.19	1.42*
RJ	BR	–	–	0.43	0.12
RJ	HR	−0.11	1.93	0.54	1.36*
RJ	KR	−0.27	0.20	0.77	1.26*
RJ	WB	0.03	0.51*	–	–

Note *Significant at 5%. ECM is standardized in State I. Sub-Period-I: 2010:04 to 2014:03, Sub-Period-II: 2014:04 to 2016:12
Source MoA&FW (various), DES, Website

References

Acharya, S. S. (2004). State of the Indian farmer: A millennium study. Agricultural Marketing, Department of Agricultural and Cooperation, Ministry of Agriculture, and Academic Foundation, New Delhi.

Ahmed, M., & Singla, N. (2017). Market integration and price transmission in major onion markets of India. *Economic Affairs, 62*(3), 405–417.

Andrews, E. (2013). Who invented the internet? *History News*. https://www.history.com/news/who-invented-the-internet.

Atkin, D. (2013). Trade, tastes, and nutrition in India. *American Economic Review, 103*(5), 1629–1663.

Balassa, B. (1964). The purchasing power parity doctrine: A reappraisal. *Journal of Political Economy, 72*(1964), 584–596.

Bathla, S. (2008). Agriculture reforms and market integration: A spatial analysis of food and non-food commodities. *Journal of Social and Economic Development, 10*(2), 196–221.

Bekker, E., Francois, J., & Manchin, M. (2012). Import prices, income and inequality. Vienna Institute for International Economic Studies, Vienna. WIIW Working Paper No. 82, June.

Blyn, G. (1973). Price series correlation as a measure of market integration II. *Indian Journal of Agricultural Economics, 28*(2).

Business Line (BL) (2019). *Just 14% of farmers registered on eNAM platform*. July, 10. https://www.thehindubusinessline.com/economy/agri-business/just-14-of-farmers-registered-on-enam-platform/article28363454.ece.

Chand, R. (2016). E-platform for national agricultural market. *Economic & Political Weekly, 51*(28), 15–18.

Chatterjee, S., & Kapur, D. (2016). Understanding price variation in agricultural commodities in India: MSP, government procurement, and agriculture markets. India Policy Forum, July 12–13, National Council of Applied Economic Research, New Delhi.

Crouhy-Veyrac, L., Crouhy, M., & Melitz, J. (1981). More about the law of one price. *European Economic Review, 18*, 325–344 (North-Holland Publishing Company).

Cummings, W. (1967). *Pricing efficiency in Indian wheat market*. New Delhi: Impact of India.

Darne, O. (2004). Seasonal cointegration for monthly data. *Economics Letters, 82*, 349–356.

Deaton, A., & Dupriez, O. (2011). Spatial price differences within large countries. Working Paper No. 1321, Woodrow Wilson School of Public and International Affairs, Research Program in Development Studies, Princeton University, Princeton NJ, and World Bank, Washington DC.

Directorate of Economics and Statistics (DES) (Website). http://eands.dacnet.nic.in/. Government of India Ministry of Agriculture & Farmers Welfare Department of Agriculture, Cooperation & Farmers Welfare.

Enke, S. (1951). Equilibrium among spatially separated markets: Solution by electronic analogue. *Econometrica, 10*, 40–47.

Feenstra, R., & Romalis, J. (2014). International prices and endogenous quality. *The Quarterly Journal of Economics, 126*(2), 477–527.

Franses, P. H. (1991). Seasonality, nonstationary and the forecasting of monthly time series. *International Journal of Forecasting, 7*, 199–208.

Ghosh, N. (2013). *India's agricultural marketing—Market reforms and the emergence of new channels*. India: Springer.

Ghosh, N., & Guha Khasnobis, B. (2008). Measuring the efficacy of targeted public programmes: Public works programmes in India. In B. Guha Khasnobis, S. S. Acharya, & B. Davis (Eds.), *Food security indicators, measurement, and the impact of trade openness* (ICSSR, UNU-WIDER and FAO). Oxford University Press.

Gonzalez-Rivera, G., & Helfand, S. (2001). The extent, pattern, and degree of market integration: A multivariate approach for the Brazilian rice market. *American Journal of Agricultural Economics, 83*(3), 576–592.

Gonzalo, J., & Granger, C. (1995). Estimation of common long-memory components in cointegrated systems. *Journal of Business and Economic Statistics, 13,* 1–9.
Goodwin, B. K. (1992). Multivariate cointegration tests and the law of one price in international wheat markets. *Review of Agricultural Economics, 14*(1), 117–124.
Goodwin, B. K., Grennes, T. J., & Wohlenant, M. K. (1990). A revised test of the law of one price using rational price expectations. *American Journal of Agricultural Economics*, 682–693.
Gupta, R. P. (1973). *Agricultural prices in a backward economy*. New Delhi: National Publishing House.
Hallak, J. C., & Schott, P. K. (2011). Estimating cross-country differences in product quality. *Quarterly Journal of Economics, 126*, 417–474.
Harriss, B. (1979). There is method in my madness: Or is it vice versa? Measuring agricultural market performance. *Food Research Institute Studies, 17*(2).
Hurd, J. II. (1975). Railways and the expansion of markets in India, 1861–1921. *Explorations in Economic History, 12*(3), 263–288.
Johansen, S. (1988). Statistical analysis of cointegration vectors. *Journal of Economic Dynamics and Control, 12*(2–3), 231–254.
Johansen, S., & Schaumburg, E. (1999). Likelihood analysis of seasonal cointegration. *Journal of Econometrics, 88*, 301–339.
Kahlon, A. S. (1991). Agricultural price policy and terms of trade. In M. L. Dantwala (Ed.), *Indian agricultural development since independence*. New Delhi: Oxford and IBH.
Kainth, G. S. (1982). *Foodgrains marketing system in India—Its structure and performance*. New Delhi: Associated Publishing House.
Kumar, P., & Sharma, R. K. (2000). Market integration and market efficiency of wheat in Haryana. *Indian Journal of Quantitative Economics, 15*(1&2), 90.
Lele, U. J. (1967). Market integration: A study of sorghum prices in western India. *Journal of Farm Economics, 49,* 147–159.
Lele, U. J. (1971). *Food grain marketing in India: Private performance and public policy*. Ithaca, New York: Cornell University Press.
Li, C., & Gibson, J. (2014). Spatial price differences and inequality in the People's Republic of China: Housing market evidence. *Asian Development Review, 31*(1), 92–120.
Melchior, A. (2016). Food price differences across Indian states: Pattern and determinants. NUPI Working paper 869, Norwegian Institute of International Affairs.
Ministry of Agriculture (MoA). (2013). Final report of the Committee of State Ministers Incharge of Agricultural Marketing Reforms. Department of Agriculture and Co-operation, Government of India.
Ministry of Communications (MoC). (2018). Telecom statistics India-2018. Economics Research Unit—Statistics, Department of Telecommunications, Government of India New Delhi.
MoA&FW (Various). *Agricultural statistics at a glance*. Government of India Ministry of Agriculture & Farmers Welfare, Department of Agriculture, Cooperation & Farmers Welfare, Directorate of Economics and Statistics.
MoA&FW (Website). Price support scheme (PSS): The operational guidelines. Ministry of Agriculture and Farmers Welfare, Government of India. http://agricoop.gov.in/sites/default/files/pssguidelines.pdf.
NABARD. (2018). NABARAD All India Rural Financial Inclusion Survey 2016–17. Department of Economic Analysis & Research, Mumbai.
Naoroji, D. (1901). *Poverty and un-British rule in India*. S. Sonnenschein.
Palaskas, T. B., & Harriss White, B. (1993). Testing market integration: New approaches with case material from the West Bengal. Department for Environment, Food and Rural Affairs, FAO.
Press Information Bureau (PIB). (2017a). Price stabilization fund. Government of India Ministry of Consumer Affairs, Food & Public Distribution, 28th March. http://pib.nic.in/newsite/PrintRelease.aspx?relid=160050.

Press Information Bureau (PIB). (2017b). Small farmers agri-business consortium. Government of India, Ministry of Agriculture & Farmers Welfare, 8th August http://pib.nic.in/newsite/mbErel.aspx?relid=169745.

Ravallion, M. (1986). Testing market integration. *American Journal of Agricultural Economics, 68*(1), 102–109.

Reddy, R., & Rajshekhar, M. (2014). Farmers should get access to larger markets to get benefits of APMC reform. *The Economic Times*, January 06.

Samuelson, P. A. (1952). Spatial price equilibrium and linear programming. *American Economic Review, 42,* 283–303.

Samuelson, P. A. (1964). Theoretical notes on trade problems. *The Review of Economic and Statistics, 46*(2), 145–154.

Scroll. (2019). New soil study confirms 1943 Bengal famine was caused by Winston Churchill's policies, not drought. Scroll, March 30. https://scroll.in/article/918373/new-soil-study-confirms-1943-bengal-famine-was-caused-by-winston-churchills-policies-not-drought.

Sen, A. (1981). *Poverty and famines: An essay on entitlement and deprivation.* Oxford: Clarendon Press. https://www.prismaweb.org/nl/wp-content/uploads/2017/06/Poverty-and-famines%E2%94%82Amartya-Sen%E2%94%821981.pdf.

Shalendra, Gummagolmath, K. C., & Sharma, P. (2011). ICT initiatives in Indian agriculture—An overview. *Indian Journal of Agricultural Economics, 66*(3), 489–497.

Shrestha, R. B., Huang, W.-C., & Ghimire, R. (2014). Market price cointegration of tomato: Effects to nepalese farmers. *International Journal of Food and Agricultural Economics (IJFAEC), 2*(2), 1–10 (Alanya Alaaddin Keykubat University, Department of Economics and Finance).

Singh, S., Singh, K. N., Gurang, V., Shekhawat, R. S., Panotra, N., & Singh, A. (2018). Cointegration and causality analysis of Tur (Pigeon pea) in neighboring states. *International Journal of Chemical Studies, 6*(3), 715–719.

Sweeney, S. (2008). Indian railways and famine 1875–1914: Magic wheels and empty stomachs. *The Economic and Business History Society, 26.* http://www.ebhsoc.org/journal/index.php/journal/article/view/13/13.

Takayama, T., & Judge, G. G. (1971). *Spatial and temporal price and allocation models.* North-Holland, Amsterdam: Netherlands Publishing Company.

Wilson, E. J. (2001). Testing agricultural market integration: Further conceptual and empirical considerations using Indian wholesale prices. In S. S. Acharya & D. P. Chaudhary (Eds.), *Indian agricultural policy—At the crossroads* (pp. 213–246). Jaipur, India: Rawat Publications.

World Bank (Website). https://data.worldbank.org/indicator/IT.NET.USER.P2.

Digital Divide and Inequalities

Digital Divide: How India and China Stack Up

Nidhi Tewathia

Abstract India and China are emerging technological powers and are becoming increasingly important players on the global stage in terms of their gross domestic product (GDP) growth and their share in the world economy. This chapter provides a descriptive empirical analysis for country-level comparison of major economic and information and communication technology (ICT) indicators. The ICT diffusion index (ICTDI) has been constructed to identify within-country inequalities in terms of the digital divide across Indian states and Chinese provinces. The descriptive analysis indicates that India is far behind China on fronts like the maturity of the Internet ecosystem, ICT foundations, ease of Internet entrepreneurship, and ICT health. But Internet growth in India has been around three times more than China between the years 2000 and 2017. The constructed ICTDI indicates that Indian states such as Kerala, Maharashtra, Karnataka and Tamil Nadu are more digitalised than Bihar, Chhattisgarh and Madhya Pradesh. In China, the East region is dominant as Beijing, Tianjin, Shanghai and Guangdong show higher ICT diffusion.

Keywords China · Diffusion index · Digital divide · ICT · India

JEL Code O3 · O57 · P51 · R58

1 Introduction

From entertainment to managing the household, digital technologies have changed the way we live. Many people use their phones to board planes and unlock hotel rooms. Doctors and teachers are also available on the Internet. Social media have changed the way individuals communicate. According to Rao (2005), Facebook reached 50 million users' mark in 2 years. The old generation has also started taking an interest in Internet activities, for example, connecting to old friends through Facebook, paying electricity bills and handling their bank transactions. The communication technology revolution has given rise to the app store. Customised mobile

N. Tewathia (✉)
Department of Economics, Gargi College, University of Delhi, New Delhi, Delhi, India
e-mail: tewathian@gmail.com

D. Maiti et al. (eds.), *Digitalisation and Development*,
https://doi.org/10.1007/978-981-13-9996-1_9

apps like Uber and Fasoos provide services to countless sub-segments of consumers with particular needs. Many services and applications are particularly made to suit a mobile lifestyle. Smartwatches and games like Pokémon Go are other applications that are much in demand.

It is evident that international competition in the telecom market has led to innovative business models (where the service is coupled with certain apps leading to the instant provision of goods and services) based on the on-demand economy.[1] Producers are earning higher profits as middlemen are eliminated to a great extent due to the usage of the Internet. We can easily say that the Internet has become an economic activity. Internet manifests itself in two roles. It acts as an integrator and a divider. The flow of education, health and many services, which are traded, takes place across borders; on the other hand, due to disparities in access to the Internet, many are left out of the network. This is simply called the digital divide.

The previous literature has documented many definitions of the *digital divide* and at various levels. Norris (2001) mentions that the term digital divide reached popularity in the mid-1990s as a way to describe the disparities between those who had access to the Internet and those who did not. Song (2008) mentions that as per national telecommunications and information administration (2000), the digital divide was earlier defined as the divide separating 'information haves' and 'information have-nots'. As per Wilhelm (2001), the digital divide is the gap between those who have access to and can effectively use information technologies and those who cannot. Norris (2001) categorises the digital divide along with three distinct aspects. These are the global divide, social divide and democratic divide. According to her, the global divide refers to the difference in access to the Internet between industrialised and developing societies; the social divide concerns the gap between the information-rich and poor in each nation; the democratic divide concerns those who use the Internet for civic participation versus those who are passive consumers of Internet resources. Kaur and Neena (2014) used the digital divide in terms of the global, regional and national divide. The authors understand the national level digital divide mainly as an urban–rural divide. They also acknowledge that there are inter-state differences in access to and usage of information technology within a country.

Globally, the digital divide is manifested in terms of Internet access distribution across nations. Mostly, the Internet is accessible in most economically developed parts of the world (Fig. 1).

There is a large gap between the developed and the developing world. The numbers show that Internet users in developing countries for the year 2017 (41%) have just reached the level of Internet users in the developed world of 2002. Developing countries have low Internet penetration (Table 1), which leads to the denial of access to information and technology, which is web-based.

Apart from known divides such as rural, urban, social and democratic, there are also digital divides based on household income, education, gender, age group, caste,

[1] An on-demand economy is an economy where economic activity is created by digital markets and technology companies to fulfil consumer demand.

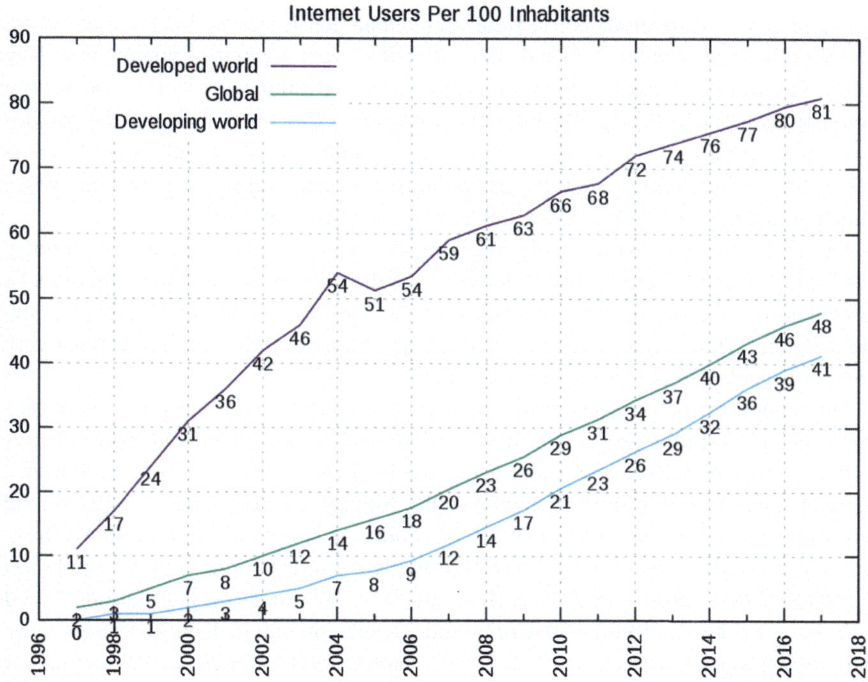

Fig. 1 Internet users per 100 inhabitants (1996–2018). *Source* https://en.wikipedia.org/wiki/Global_Internet_usage

Table 1 Region-wise internet users and penetration rate—2018

Region	Percentage of global internet users (%)	Penetration rate (%)
Asia	49	49
Europe	16.8	85.2
Africa	11	36.1
Latin America/Caribbean	10.4	67.2
North America	8.2	95
Middle East	3.9	64.5
Oceania/Australia	0.7	68.9

Note (1) Figures pertain to June 2018. (2) Penetration rate is the percentage of population of the region that uses Internet
Source Internet World Stats (2018)

class and so on (Katz et al. 2001; Kaur and Neena 2014; Norris 2001; Song 2008). Internet reinforces gender, race and occupational segregation within society (Lindsay 2005). Technological trickle-downs, therefore, are contested. Despite ICTs becoming increasingly affordable and offering applications in a variety of domains, the trickle-down of technology is affected by uneven geographies (Parthasarathy and Aoyama 2017). Social inequalities and geographical disparities lead to the same outcomes (Bosman and Chakraborty 2002; Chakraborty and Bosman 2005).

The ICT revolution is radically affecting the way countries operate. A country with sound ICT infrastructure and delivery has the edge over a country which lacks these. This revolution has brought leverage in two essential commodities, that is, time and distance, which, in terms of business, mean efficiency and cost. It also positively affects research and development in any nation.

This chapter draws a comparative analysis concerning ICT between two major global players—India and China. In recorded history, these countries have always been the most populous countries in the world. In the book 'India's and China's Recent Experience with Reform and Growth', Meghnad Desai, while comparing the two countries, writes that in 1820, they had a combined population over half a billion, and that reached 700 million by 1900. Within the twentieth century, their population had trebled. According to the World Bank, in 2017, 35% of world population resided in these two nations (18.52% in China and 17.89% in India). Both countries were two of the poorest countries as well. These countries were thought of as locations of famine, disease, backwardness and superstition. In the mid-twentieth century, they became independent republics and launched on their development paths, but both suffered devastating famines (Desai 2005).

Within the next 50 years, China and India came to be viewed not as failures but as dynamic modern economies. In 2016, together the two countries accounted for 18.03% of the world's GDP—China 14.98% and India 3.05% (World Bank). Magazines like the Economist write editorials telling the world not to be scared of the huge economic power that China has mustered. Legislators in America feel the pressing need to pass laws that prevent their business houses from outsourcing work to Indian software and telecommunication companies.

This chapter focuses on comparing India and China on the basis of descriptive analysis and explores the within-country digital divide by constructing the ICT diffusion index (ICTDI)[2] for Chinese provinces and Indian states. The chapter has been divided into six sections. Section 1 deals with an introduction to and the background of the concept of the digital divide. Section 2 discusses the methodology to assess the digital divide in Indian states and Chinese provinces. In Sect. 3, an attempt has been made to present the country comparisons with the help of descriptive statistics. Section 4 presents the ICTDI for Indian states and Chinese provinces. Section 5 discusses the problem of the digital divide in the two countries with some suggested policy measures. Section 6 concludes the chapter.

---

[2]Diffusion is the process by which an innovation or idea is communicated through certain channels over time among members of a social system (www.encyclopedia.com).

2 Data and Methodology

For only the purpose of country comparison, data from various sources like the International Telecommunications Union (ITU) and World Bank open data have been used. Data for constructing the diffusion index have been procured from secondary sources, mainly the Handbook of Statistics on Indian Economy by The Reserve Bank of India, reports by the Telecom Regulatory Authority of India (TRAI) and the China Statistical Yearbook. There are two distinct motivations behind this chapter. One is to give a descriptive empirical analysis for country-level comparison of major economic and ICT indicators, while the other is to assess the level of digital divide across Indian states and Chinese provinces by constructing the ICTDI.

Any one indicator of ICT diffusion will not capture the inclusive magnitudes of the digital divide. Hence, it is useful to construct the diffusion index considering several indicators. Previously, studies have considered indicators such as GDP per capita and education as factors determining technology diffusion (Hargittai 1999; Kiiski and Pohojola 2002; Norris 2000). Wong (2002) estimated the divide in eleven Asian countries through ICT diffusion. He considered ownership of computers, main telephone lines, cellular mobile telephones and Internet use. Kaur and Singh (2016) considered various determinants of the digital divide and ICT diffusion along with poverty, education, knowledge divide and electricity consumption. Generally, a mix of adoption indicators and infrastructure indicators has been considered for creating the diffusion index. As per Das (2010), the adoption perception, being a traditional and dominant approach to diffusion studies, concentrates on the method by which adoption occurs. The book by Rogers and Shoemaker (1971), contend that by emphasising the demand side of the problem, it is assumed that the prospect of all individuals adopting technology is equal. Therefore, such a view concentrates on individual features to describe the differences in real-time adoption. In contrast, many studies emphasise the market and infrastructure perspective (Brown 1975; Wong 2002). This perspective focuses on the supply aspect of diffusion in terms of innovations and the conditions which make adoption easy and simple for individuals or households.

Secondary data were not available for the same diffusion indicators for both countries; hence, an attempt has been made to keep the indicators similar, as much as possible. For Indian states, indicators such as teledensity, literacy rate, per capita state domestic product, per capita availability of power, households with computers, households with Internet and wireless subscribers are considered. For Chinese provinces, the following indicators are used: literacy rate, per capita gross regional product, electricity consumption, mobiles owned by households, computers owned by households, penetration rate and Internet users.

The methodology used by Das (2010) has been considered for constructing the index. First, we normalise all the indicators using min-max transformation, and then we compute the index by taking the weighted average of the normalised values derived for each indicator. Normalisation is needed as the indicators are considered to have different measurement units, and it is imperative to bring these indicators to be pure and dimensionless numbers. Normalising also converts the indicators' numeric values into a scale which ranges between 0 and 1 without disturbing their position. The coefficient of variation (CV) of every indicator is considered as the respective weight.[3] More weight has been given to an indicator which has more variance. Though Liu et al. (2017) have considered the same weight for all the normalised indicators to construct the ICT development index (IDI), simple averaging of indicators means equal weight or importance is attached to each indicator, and hence there is the possibility of offsetting the importance of one indicator by another. In other words, the averaging model indicates that the strength of any one of the variables could compensate for the weakness of others, and hence, CV is used as the weight. The constructed composite index sensitises the level of inequality existing in one particular indicator across states/provinces. The index can be written as follows:

$$\text{ICTDI} = \frac{\sum_{i=1}^{n} w_i \cdot \text{NV}_{is}}{\sum_{i=1}^{n} w_i}$$

where w_i is the specified weight assigned to each indicator, i stands for the indicator, NV is the normalised values of each indicator and stands for the state/province.

We have considered 29 Indian states[4] and 31 Chinese provinces for index construction. The index takes values between 0 and 1. It reflects the relative position of each state between the least and best performers at a particular point of time.

3 Country Comparison

India and China are growing more than three times faster than the world average (Dahlman 2007). India has surpassed China in the GDP growth rate (Fig. 2), but GDP per capita in China is much higher (Fig. 3) than in India.[5] The World Bank provides data on capital investment as a percentage of GDP. In the period 2010–2017, India invested more than 30% of its GDP towards capital investment, whereas China invested more than 43% of its GDP.

According to the United States (U.S.) Census Bureau's International Data Base estimates, population growth rates have been consistently higher in India than in China since the early 1970s and will remain so for years to come (Wolf et al. 2011). The one-child policy of China is a probable reason for its high per capita income growth. Soon, India will surpass China to become the world's most populous country.

According to Kochhar (2015), between 2001 and 2011, the share of middle-income Chinese—those making $10.01–$20 a day—jumped from 3 to 18%. In India,

---

[3]Sensitivity was checked considering equal weights also and the results are similar.

[4]Data for Telangana state are not available and hence the state is not included.

[5]Data for descriptive analysis have been collected for the duration 2010–2016 for most of the comparative indicators. Due to data unavailability for the year 2016, the statistics till 2015 are considered for certain indicators.

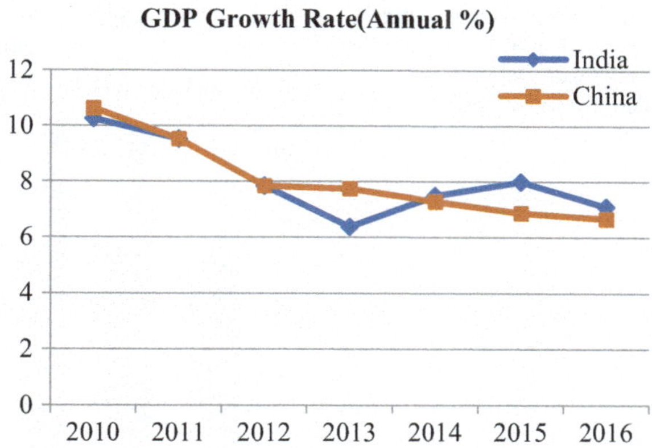

Fig. 2 GDP growth rate. *Source* World Bank Open Data (data.worldbank.org)

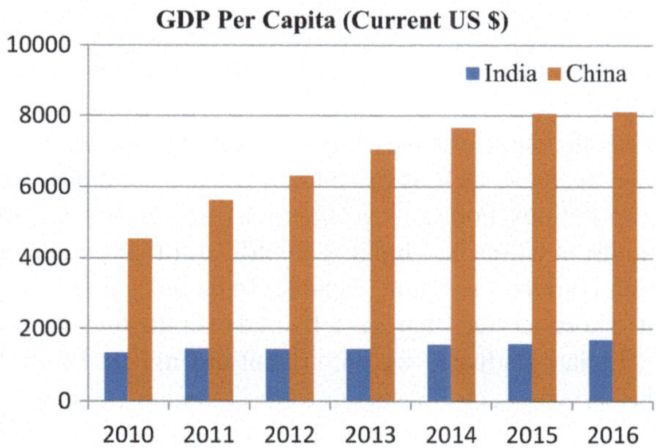

Fig. 3 GDP per capita. *Source* World Bank Open Data (data.worldbank.org)

over the same decade, the middle-class share of the population grew from 1 to 3%. The rapid per capita growth rate in China has helped lift many people out of poverty. As per the World Bank, the poverty headcount ratio at $1.90/day (2011 Purchasing Power Parity) was 21.2 for India and 7.9 for China (as a percentage of the population) for the year 2011.

China has advanced more rapidly than India in improving literacy and overall educational attainment (Dahlman 2007). According to the most recent censuses of the two countries, China's literacy rate is 95.12% (National Bureau of Statistics of China 2016), and India's is 69.3% (Ministry of Home Affairs [MOHA] 2011). It is observed that China has invested very heavily in expanding the higher education system of the country. In China, tertiary enrolment has doubled between 2010 and 2016 (from 24.05 to 48.44%), whereas tertiary enrolment in India has increased from 17.91% to only 26.93% in that period. As per the United Nations, in 2015, China spent 2.07% of GDP on research and development, whereas India spent a mere 0.63% (which includes both private and public spending). Patent applications by Chinese

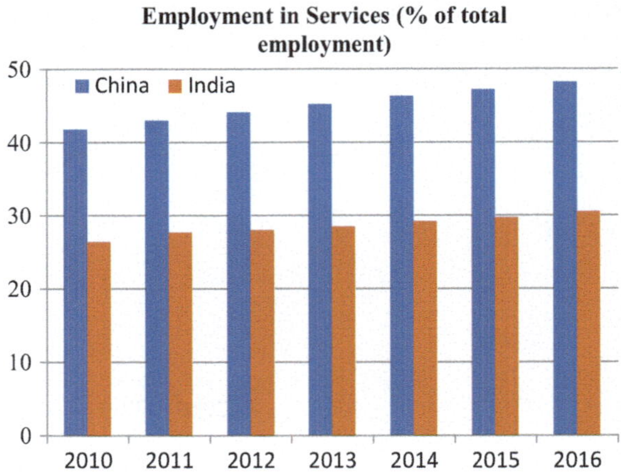

Fig. 4 Employment in the services sector. *Source* World Bank Open Data (data.worldbank.org)

residents numbered 1,204,981 in 2016; the corresponding figure for India was only 13,199.

Both countries have a huge capacity for innovation that is being deployed for their own needs as well as to conduct research and development for many international corporations. Foreign investment in research and development facilities by U.S. companies in China and India is an indicator that graduates from the best institutions of both countries are quite capable. India has gained a reputation as a major source of off-shore services that are delivered over the Internet because we have a large number of Indian graduates who are fluent in English. From 2010 to 2016, employment in the services sector has risen for both nations (Fig. 4).

3.1 Internet Landscape and Usage

Poushter (2017) argues that the number of people online is probably the most basic indicator of a region's progress towards the information era and a digital economy. He writes that since the Pew Research Center began tracking advanced technology adoption in China and India in 2013, the Chinese have consistently reported rates of Internet and smartphone use that are at least triple that of Indians. He also found that the trend has continued through 2016 and contends that the digital divide between the two countries mirrors the differences in their broader economic trajectories.

As per Dean et al. (2012), India is going 'straight to social' (users are adopting social networking quickly as they come online). The annual growth of social media users for the year 2017 was 31% in India against 10% in China (Kemp 2018). The average speed of Internet connection in general and the speed of the Internet on mobile, in particular, are quite low in India (Table 2). Number of web pages served on a mobile phone encourages a consumer to use the mobile phone more. According

Table 2 Internet speed and web traffic statistics (2017)

	Average fixed Internet connection speed[a] (Mbps)	Average mobile Internet connection speed (Mbps)	Share of web traffic by laptop/desktop (%)	Share of web traffic by mobile (%)
China	63.7	32.5	373	61
India	19.7	9.1	20	79

[a]Figures represent average download speed
Source Internet World Stats (2018), Kemp (2018)

to Kemp (2018), the percentage of total web pages served to mobile phones in India was 79, and in China, 61.

The use of mobile phones was non-existent in China and India until about the late 1980s. It (mobile cellular subscriptions—per 100 people) has undergone extreme growth since 1990, growing from nearly 0 to over 104.5 for China and 87.2 for India in 2017 (World Bank). In India, the Internet has grown more than three times as compared to China (Table 3). The per day Internet use of an Indian Internet user,[6] on average, is more than that of a Chinese user. One of the probable reasons for higher per day usage of Internet by Indians, in general, could be low-speed Internet connections in India. In India, an Internet user takes more time to do the same task than a Chinese user. The average number of hours per day spent accessing the Internet via a mobile phone is just marginally higher for China.

Time spent per day on the Internet via mobile is nearly the same in both countries. Access through a laptop/desktop is low across both countries. This could be due to China's Internet censorship, which restricts consumers from using the Internet fully. The mobile revolution has presented users with diverse options of smartphones and apps and carrying a laptop has become an inconvenience for many. Only 15% of the adult population use a laptop or desktop computer in India, but the figure stands at 53% for China (Kemp 2018).

Table 3 Internet users and usage (2017)

	Internet users (% of population)	Share of world Internet users (%)	Internet growth rate (2000–2017)	Time spent per day on Internet (h)	Time spent per day on Internet via mobile (h)	Time spent per day on social media (h)
China	53	21.2	3182.4	6 h 30 m	3 h 26 m	2 h
India	34	13.5	9142.5	7 h 25 m	3 h 23 m	2 h 26 m

Source Kemp (2018), CNNIC (2017)

[6]Internet users are presented as the proportion of people who have access to the Internet at home, work or in public spaces (Kemp 2018).

3.2 Internet Health and Foundation

A study by Gnanasambandam et al. (2012), provided extensive data on the *Internet Foundation Statistics* for 57 countries. These statistics are given for nine indicators (Fig. 5). Scores indicate the percentile rank of the country across the sample. The country with the best-performance receives a score of 100, while the country with the worst performance receives a 0. A comparison of these indicators for India and China shows that both countries have a similar shaped spider web. But China's foundations are better established than India's (the web is bigger for China). The human capital percentile rank of India and China shows a huge difference. Although India stands marginally above China in the area of financial capital, India needs to work upon infrastructure, accessibility and connectedness so that the country does not lag in the digital world. As per the study, only 19% of countries fall below China in terms of Internet accessibility.

Furthermore, the report by Gnanasambandam et al. (2012) assesses the health of a country's Internet ecosystem with the help of three indices (Fig. 6). The first one is the *e3 index* (it measures the current maturity of an Internet ecosystem according to three major drivers: environment, engagement and expenditure); the second is *i4F index* (it measures the strength of the Internet's foundations using the four key foundations—*financial capital*: availability of financing for Internet and ICT companies, *business environment*: country's attractiveness to business due to regulatory and societal effects, *infrastructure*: penetration and quality of Internet-enabling infrastructure and *human capital*: education and research); the third is the *ENE index* (it measures the ease of Internet entrepreneurship, based on three components—*ease of starting a new business*: industry-agnostic view of the overall business ecosystem in a country, *ease of financing a new business*: availability and attractiveness of financing for ICT start-ups as well as the cost of financing a new business and *Internet accessibility*: extent and cost of Internet access for both enterprises and their target consumers).

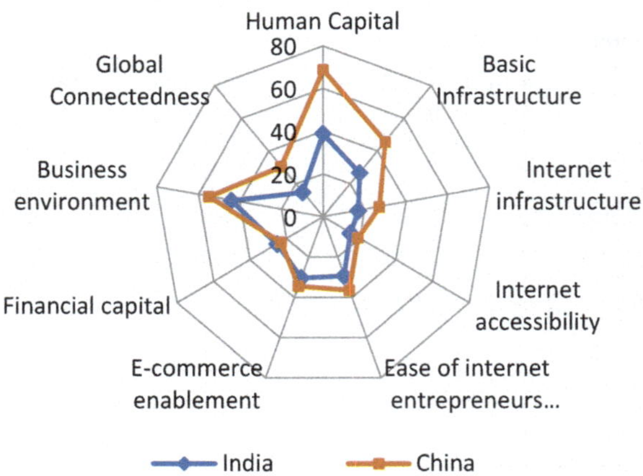

Fig. 5 Internet foundation statistics. *Note* (1) Figures 5 and 6 show the percentile rank. (2) e3 measures Internet ecosystem; i4F measures strength of Internet foundations and; ENE measures ease of Internet entrepreneurship. *Source* Data inputs from Gnanasambandam et al. (2012)

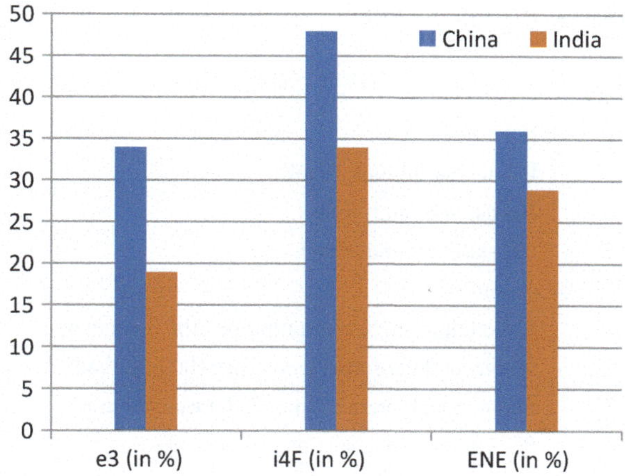

Fig. 6 Internet health and foundation indices. *Note* (1) Figures 5 and 6 show the percentile rank. (2) e3 measures Internet ecosystem; i4F measures strength of Internet foundations and; ENE measures ease of Internet entrepreneurship. *Source* Data inputs from Gnanasambandam et al. (2012)

China has a higher percentile rank than India for all three indices. Among 57 countries, India stands at 49th in the e3 index and 33rd in the i4F index. The report mentions that India is less urbanised than its peer aspiring countries with just 30% of its population living in urban areas. As far as ENE index is concerned, India scores well on the availability of financing opportunities, but much lower on the ease of starting a new business and on Internet accessibility (Gnanasambandam et al. 2012).

Digital technologies also connect government and citizens. In India, ministries such as the Ministry of Finance and the Ministry of Personnel, Public Grievances and Pensions, offer various online services like the provision of tools to file taxes and access to educational services such as school registration, and so on. The most common use of the internet in this area is e-filing of tax returns, which has made filing very convenient for citizens. The time consumed and flexibility and comfort are the major factors which were missing from the earlier system as it required standing in long queues. But the report by Gnanasambandam et al. (2012) shows India lags behind other countries on the e-government development index due to the lack of digital literacy and Internet accessibility; China scores 0.47, whereas India scores 0.38.

Another relevant set of indices is presented by the ITU. The annual ITU report documents the universality of ICTs and the extent of the digital divide between regions and countries through its annual IDI.[7] This index aggregates quantitative indicators for ICT access, ICT use and ICT skills in a large majority of the world's economies (www.itu.int). India's rank in IDI and its sub-indices (Table 4) is low when compared to China's for the year 2016. The maximum difference between the two nations is in the use sub-index.

Nearly 50% of households have a computer in China, whereas only around 14% own a computer in India. When compared with fixed broadband subscriptions, mobile

---

[7]The IDI was developed by ITU in 2008 in response to ITU Member States' request to establish an overall ICT index. It was first presented in the 2009 edition of the Report and has been published annually since then (www.itu.int).

Table 4 ICT indices (2016)

		China	India
Indices and indicators			
1	IDI rank	81	138
2	IDI access sub-index rank	91	129
3	IDI use sub-index rank	67	142
4	IDI skills sub-index rank	92	122
Access indicators			
1	Fixed telephone subscriptions per 100 inhabitants	16.5	2
2	Mobile cellular subscriptions per 100 inhabitants	93.2	78.8
3	International Internet bandwidth bits/s per user	6530	5725
4	Percentage of households with a computer	49.6	14.1
5	Percentage of households with internet	54.2	20
Use indicators			
1	Percentage of individuals using the internet	50.3	26
2	Fixed broadband subscriptions per 100 inhabitants	18.6	1.3
3	Active mobile broadband subscriptions per 100 inhabitants	56	9.4
Skills indicators			
1	Gross enrolment ratio—secondary (%)	96.2	68.9
2	Gross enrolment ratio—tertiary (%)	30.2	23.9
3	Mean years of schooling	7.5	5.4

IDI ICT development index
Note A sample of 175 countries was considered
Source ITU (2016)

broadband subscriptions are higher in both nations. Skills are crucial for the operative use of ICT and are necessary to leverage their complete potential for social and economic progress. The skills' sub-index includes three proxy indicators and seeks to capture capabilities or skills that are important for ICT.[8]

Another index, the Network Readiness Index (NRI), is presented in the Global Information Technology Reports (GITR) annually by the World Economic Forum (2018). For the years 2010–2016, China's NRI is higher than India's, but the index for the two nations has not changed substantially over that period (Fig. 7). On the other hand, ITU's IDI for China has shown a higher increase over the same period. The use index for China shows a significant sharp rise when compared with India's use index (Fig. 8); the difference between the three sub-indices seems to have remained the same over 2010–2016.

According to a report by the Economist Intelligence Unit (2012), Yuanfu Jiang, director of the E-Government Department in the E-Government Research Center

[8]The skills sub-index is given less weight in the computation of the IDI than the other two sub-indices due to the presence of these proxy indicators (www.itu.int).

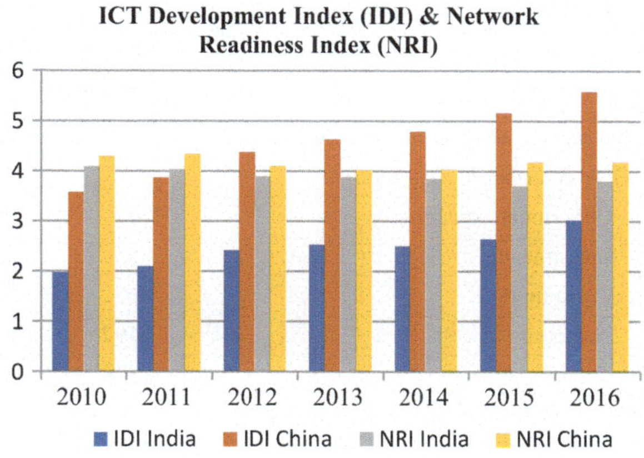

Fig. 7 IDI and NRI. *Source* ITU and GITR reports, various

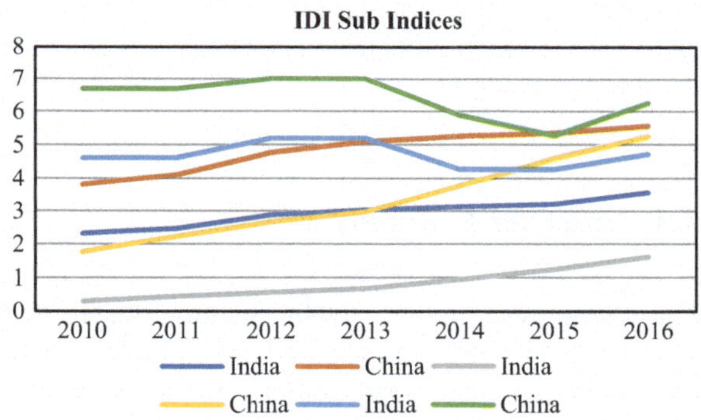

Fig. 8 Sub-indices of the IDI. *Source* ITU reports, various

at the Chinese Academy of Governance, says that the three primary digital divide challenges, i.e. access, skills and content. The government pays a lot of attention to the first two, but not enough attention has been paid to content. For example, rural Chinese farmers can purchase new agricultural products, but there may be a lack of information in the local language on how to use them.[9] Similarly, in India, there are 22 officially recognised languages. The English-speaking population can gain digital literacy much faster than the others. This makes local content the biggest challenge.

In China, as per Tseng and You (2013), only government-approved agencies and businesses are permitted to establish an Internet Interconnecting Network and to licence the operation of Internet service providers at the next tier. All private Internet service providers are licensed through one of these backbone networks and are required to install filters to block undesirable content. In order not to risk having their licences revoked, most of these companies complied with the self-censorship regulation in China (Liang and Lu 2010; MacKinnon 2008). Based on the China Internet Network Information Center (CNNIC) reports, a great loss of search engine usage was found in 2006. But still, China has a lower e-friction index (it assesses 55

[9]Worldwide, 51% of the websites are in English language (Kemp 2018).

Table 5 Internet economy

	China		India	
	2010	2016	2010	2016
Internet economy as a percentage of GDP	5.5	6.9	4.1	5
GDP contribution ($ billion)				
Government spending	12	27	2	11
Investment	55	92	12	32
Consumption	62	321	14	108
Net exports	197	412	41	91
Total	326	852	70	242

Source Dean et al. (2012), Jain et al. (2017)

indicators of friction) when compared to India (Shah et al. 2015). The index comprises factors that can inhibit consumers, businesses and others from fully participating in the Internet economy.

3.3 Internet Economy

The 39th survey report by CNNIC mentions that in 2016, the Internet industry generally moved towards being standardised and value-oriented in China. It has introduced many policies to speed up the orderly and sound development of Internet-based fields and improve the development environment of the Internet. With the growing per capita spending power of Internet users and more per capita consumption in online shopping, online-to-online services and online entertainment, there is a driving effect of online consumption on GDP (CNNIC 2017). As per Kemp (2018), E-commerce penetration[10] was 26% for India and 45% for China. Similarly, M-commerce penetration[11] was 20% for India and 39% for China.

In 2010, the Internet contributed 5.5% of GDP in China (Table 5) and only 4.1% of GDP in India (Dean et al. 2012). The gap between the two nations increased by the year 2016. The table provides information on the impact of the Internet on GDP, which is divided into the categories of government spending, investment, consumption and net exports. Net exports contribute the highest to the GDP in both nations. China and India stand out for their enormous Internet-related exports—China in goods and India in services, which propel their Internet economy rankings toward the top of the charts (Dean et al. 2012).

[10]Percentage of the population who bought something online via any device in the past month as per the survey which was conducted in 2017.

[11]Percentage of the population who bought something online via a phone in the past month as per the survey which was conducted in 2017.

India's ICT service exports are above 40% of total service exports for the whole duration of 2010–2016 (Fig. 9). China lags behind India in the export of services but exports more ICT goods as compared with India (Fig. 10). The Indian information technology (IT) and IT-enabled services industry has become one of the most significant growth catalysts for India. A report by Jain et al. (2017) projects that by 2020, the Internet will contribute 7.5% of GDP in India. Direct employment in the IT sector in India has increased from 2.3 to 3.6 million from 2009–10 to 2015–16, and India's software exports have increased from Rs. 612,144 billion from 2009–10 to 2014–2015 (MeitY 2018).

Fig. 9 ICT service exports. *Source* World Bank Open Data (data.worldbank.org)

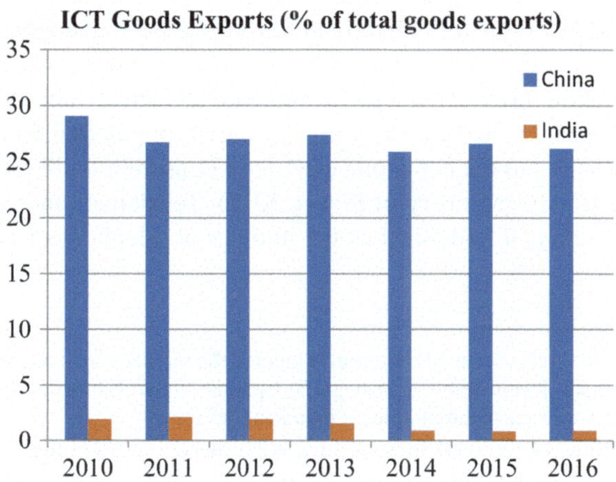

Fig. 10 ICT goods exports. *Source* World Bank Open Data (data.worldbank.org)

4 Digital Divide

After presenting the comparative statistics of both countries, we understand that they are experiencing high levels of growth in the digital sector. Citizens are embracing the digital era at an exponential rate. These economies have started experiencing growth patterns that are dependent on the Internet and allied activities. But there are still some factors that constrain these economies from fully realising the benefits of the digitalised world.

4.1 India

India is a multi-cultural, multi-lingual and multi-religious country with complex socio-economic conditions. A developing country like India faces many issues which curb the development of society. Despite a strong and fast-growing IT industry, access to ICTs remains very low, particularly in rural areas (Rao 2005). At present, India has a population of over 1 billion with 68.84% of it living in villages. The adult literacy rate is around 74.04%, and the female literacy rate is around 65.46% (MOHA 2011). Around 12% of the population speak English, which in absolute numbers is the second largest in the world. Governments have been striving to provide fundamental needs such as food, shelter, clothing and education, which are the top priorities in an impoverished country.

The Government of India took different initiatives in the form of the telecommunication policy in three stages. The first reforms in India started in the 1980s with the mission of better communication.[12] The second phase came in the early 1990s with the New Economic Policy, 1991.[13] The TRAI was established as an independent regulatory body for the telecom sector. The third phase appeared in the late 1990s when the Government of India introduced the New Telecom Policy, 1999.[14] Still, access to technology is constrained by infrastructure parameters such as electricity, IT penetration through personal computers, teledensity and Internet service providers (Rao 2005). In 2016, 84.53% of the Indian population had access to electricity (World Bank) and the per capita electricity consumption in India was around 1075-kW h in 2015–16 (Ministry of Power 2017). Teledensity indicates telecom penetration in a country; it is defined as the number of telephones (wireless and wireline) per 100

[12]Several tailor-made equipment entered the market via private manufacturers. The Videsh Sanchar Nigam Limited and Mahanagar Telephone Nigam Limited were set up under the Government of India, Department of Telecommunication.

[13]It was a landmark in the history of the telecom sector in India. Several value-added services were introduced in addition to the decentralisation of the manufacturing of equipment pertaining to the telecom sector.

[14]The TRAI was endowed with more power. The Bharat Sanchar Nigam Limited was reformed, followed by the introduction of the Internet in the Indian market.

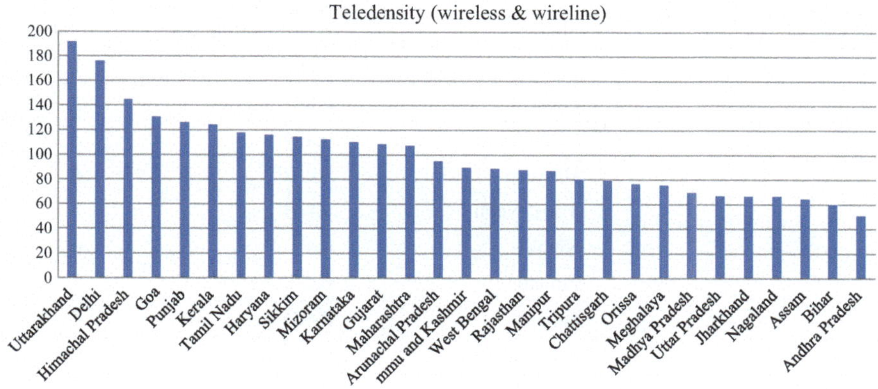

Fig. 11 Teledensity in Indian states (Oct–Dec 2017). *Source* TRAI report (July–Sept 2018)

population. Data by TRAI show that teledensity is maximum in Delhi and the least in Andhra Pradesh (Fig. 11).

A mix of adoption and infrastructure indicators has been carefully considered to construct the ICTDI (Table 6) for Indian states. In the early phases of technology diffusion, income remains a very crucial factor. At that time, the prices of the technologies were higher, and only those with higher income could afford them. Hence, state domestic product per capita has been taken as one of the indicators of ICT diffusion in Indian states. Technology costs are assumed to be the same for all states as we are looking at inter-state diffusion. Such costs would include, for example, monthly telephone subscriptions/costs of a local call/monthly Internet subscriptions. Education plays an important role in adopting the technology. In particular, users of interactive technologies such as the Internet, computer and mobile should be able to access information and in addition, be able to use the access itself. Hence, the literacy rate, as per Census 2011, is considered. To implement, maintain and expand the diffusion process, the development of infrastructure is an important aspect of strategy. Hence, some infrastructural dimensions (teledensity,[15] per capita availability of power) have been considered. To analyse the diffusion of the Internet, the percentage of households with computers, the percentage of households with Internet and total wireless subscribers (in millions) has been considered.

The index only delivers an idea of the state's position concerning the ICT indicators. It does not explain the extent of the inter-state divide between states. The index measures the development of ICT in different states and the differences among states with different levels of ICTs. Overall, the index shows high ICT diffusion variations as the index values dropped from 0.8 to 0.07. The top five performers are Goa, Delhi, Maharashtra, Haryana and Tamil Nadu. The worst five states are Jharkhand, Bihar, Assam, Nagaland and Meghalaya. States such as Kerala, Maharashtra, Karnataka and Tamil Nadu are more digitalised than Bihar, Chhattisgarh and Madhya Pradesh.

[15]Data for all 29 states were not available on a yearly basis, hence the October–December 2017 data have been used from the TRAI report.

Table 6 ICTDI of Indian states

States	ICT diffusion index	Rank
Goa	0.863	1
Delhi	0.839	2
Maharashtra	0.494	3
Haryana	0.453	4
Tamil Nadu	0.433	5
Kerala	0.422	6
Punjab	0.419	7
Gujarat	0.404	8
Karnataka	0.373	9
Himachal Pradesh	0.329	10
Uttarakhand	0.322	11
Sikkim	0.304	12
Uttar Pradesh	0.264	13
Mizoram	0.261	14
West Bengal	0.247	15
Rajasthan	0.221	16
Andhra Pradesh	0.218	17
Jammu and Kashmir	0.217	18
Madhya Pradesh	0.183	19
Chhattisgarh	0.155	20
Orissa	0.152	21
Tripura	0.147	22
Manipur	0.147	23
Arunachal Pradesh	0.141	24
Meghalaya	0.140	25
Nagaland	0.139	26
Assam	0.120	27
Bihar	0.087	28
Jharkhand	0.079	29

Source Author's calculations

4.2 China

Before the 1980s, today's Internet activity was far beyond people's imagination in China. The next two decades dramatically transformed the country. As per Song (2008), information technologies are restructuring China's traditional production and consumption models. As per Harrington (2007), in the early 1990s, the Chinese government acknowledged the need to expand China's ICT infrastructure. China also emphasised the use of ICT for its national economic growth plan. To encourage competition, the government broke up the state-owned telecom monopoly, China Telecom (Song 2008). The Ministry of Information Industry was merged with the restructured Ministry of Post and Telecommunications and the Ministry of Electronics. The government also passed a series of market-opening regulations that allowed freer competition among existing firms and encouraged new entrants into the emerging mobile phone and Internet service provider markets (Song 2008).[16] According to Guthrie (2006), the government also supported partial privatisation of its largest IT firms through listings on foreign stock exchanges.[17] Every major foreign IT firm has a presence in China; for instance, market leaders Cisco and Motorola have identified China as their most important growth market and are in the process of making multi-billion dollar investments there. The penetration of these technologies indicates that the spread of information in China has occurred in dramatic ways throughout the economic reforms (Song 2008).

Administratively, China has been divided into three regions: Eastern, Central and Western. The Eastern region has the highest population density, followed by the Central region, while the West, the most geographically elevated, has the lowest population density (en.wikipedia.org). At present, China has a population of over 1 billion, with 42.04% of the population living in villages. The adult literacy rate was about 95%, and the female literacy rate was about 92.7% in 2010 (World Bank). Less than 1% of the population speak English, which is a very low number. World Bank data shows 100% of the Chinese population has access to electricity.

As is the case across much of the world, younger, more educated and higher income Chinese people are more likely to own a smartphone than their older, less educated and poorer brethren (Poushter 2017). But China faces a severe digital divide problem that exists not only between China and developed countries but also among its regions and social groups (Wensheng 2001). According to Song (2008), the increase in the number of Internet users in the provinces near the very bottom of the hierarchy was quite unimpressive, which indicates that these remote and interior provinces are lagging in technological diffusion. Recent data show that Internet penetration rate is the highest in Beijing (Fig. 12), while Tibet has the highest netizen (one who uses the internet, as a habit) population growth rate for 2015–16. There is a negative correlation of −0.36451, which indicates that the netizen growth rate is low in provinces where Internet penetration is high.

The netizen population growth rate and the Internet penetration rate for Hubei, Jilin, Gansu, Hunan and Shandong provinces (largely Central and Western) are below the national figures. The Eastern region (Fujian, Jiangsu, Zhejiang, Shandong) pos-

---

[16] Internet consultancy and IT-related hardware markets including personal computers and mobile handsets have flourished (Song 2008). The telecommunications sector was given a huge boost by the market-opening moves, which were accompanied by massive public and private investment.

[17] In terms of foreign investment, all the high-tech sectors of the economy, including telecommunications, are among the most active.

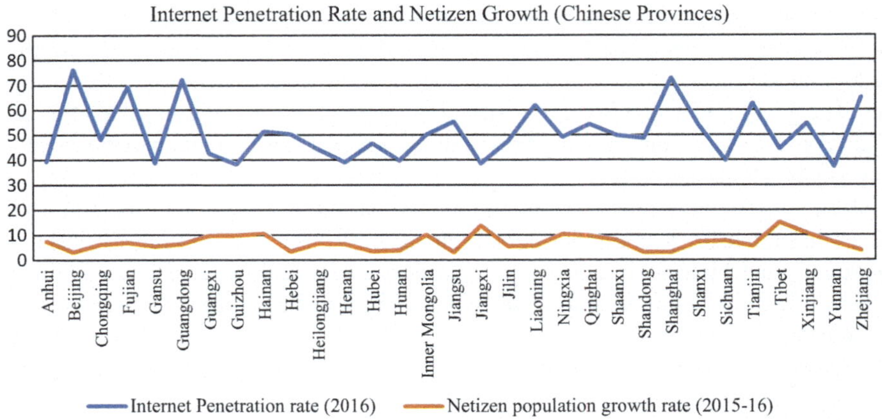

Fig. 12 Internet penetration and netizen population growth rate—Chinese provinces. *Source* Data from CNNIC (2017)

sesses the largest segment of total Internet users, and the Central and Western regions possess the smallest fraction, respectively. There is a significant threat to the less developed regions, particularly in rural and remote areas, of being forced into an ICT-related poverty trap (Wensheng 2001). The situation depicted in Fig. 12 indicates the digital divide among regions in China. Literacy rate, per capita gross regional product, electricity consumption in the province, mobiles owned per 100 households, computers owned per 100 households, Internet penetration rate and Internet users (per 10,000 persons) are taken as the diffusion indicators,[18] which represent adoption and infrastructure indicators.

Based on Table 7, we can say that the variation in diffusion is high in China as well. The index values decrease from 0.7 to 0.06 across provinces. The constructed ICTDI is maximum for Guangdong and minimum for Tibet. Other good performers are Jiangsu, Shanghai, Beijing and Zhejiang, while the ones in bottom five are Gansu, Heilongjiang, Qinghai and Yunnan apart from Tibet.

5 Discussion

One would imagine that we, at present, are living in an Internet bubble.[19] When we look at the data for the two countries, China and India, we find it is true. The annual growth of social media users and per day use of the Internet is higher in India when compared with China. While Internet connection speed and mobile cellular subscriptions in China are higher, mobiles are used for Internet access more than laptops, and Internet access via mobiles is quite high in both nations. IDI, developed

[18]The data for all the indicators are taken from the China Statistical Yearbook 2016.

[19]Massive investment in telecom and IT infrastructure.

Table 7 ICTDI of Chinese provinces

Provinces	ICT diffusion index	Rank
Guangdong	0.738	1
Jiangsu	0.668	2
Shanghai	0.664	3
Beijing	0.624	4
Zhejiang	0.612	5
Shandong	0.554	6
Fujian	0.538	7
Tianjin	0.473	8
Hebei	0.409	9
Liaoning	0.382	10
Henan	0.359	11
Hubei	0.353	12
Guangxi	0.352	13
Inner Mongolia	0.350	14
Hunan	0.335	15
Chongqing	0.326	16
Shaanxi	0.321	17
Shanxi	0.303	18
Sichuan	0.291	19
Xinjiang	0.273	20
Jilin	0.271	21
Anhui	0.269	22
Jiangxi	0.264	23
Ningxia	0.256	24
Hainan	0.241	25
Guizhou	0.216	26
Yunnan	0.211	27
Qinghai	0.188	28
Heilongjiang	0.180	29
Gansu	0.173	30
Tibet	0.068	31

Source Author's calculations

by ITU, strongly indicates that India is behind China in terms of ICT access, use and skill. Gnanasambandam et al. (2012) also assessed the health of a country's Internet ecosystem, through the e3, i4F and ENE indices and it was found that India is way behind China in terms of human capital, basic infrastructure, global connectedness, ease of starting and financing a new business, Internet accessibility and so on. E-commerce and M-commerce penetration too are quite high for China.

One can say that at the country-level, China is reaping the benefits of the digital era much more than India is. But there are within-nation disparities in ICT diffusion, which exist both in China and India. The digital divide has never received top priority in any government agenda. The reason why it has become so important to tackle the digital divide is that the Internet is not only a communication medium but has become a market place as well (Rao 2005). The enormous power which the Internet possesses is bound to change our society forever. The Internet of Things has begun to impact almost every aspect of day-to-day life. Although governments of both nations have successfully broken the state-owned telecom monopoly, there is a lot more to be done than privatising the sector and attracting major IT firms. ICTs are one of the enabling tools to bridge the digital divide.

As per the latest poverty data by the Planning Commission, Indian states with a low ICT diffusion index (Jharkhand, Bihar, Assam, Nagaland and Meghalaya) have relatively higher poverty (in terms of the proportion of the population below the poverty line 2011–12) while states with a high ICT index (Goa, Delhi, Maharashtra, Haryana and Tamil Nadu) have low levels of poverty. We cannot expect the benefits of the opportunities offered by the internet to be harnessed by an individual who is struggling to meet basic daily needs. Such individuals remain disconnected from digital services, and there is a high probability that they will be pushed further into exclusion and poverty. Many other demandside barriers arise out of socio-economic inequalities. India faces a lot of infrastructural constraints too, in addition to the provision of basic amenities to the population. As per the national institution for transforming India Aayog's data on ICT infrastructure in secondary schools in India for the year 2015–16, nearly half of all schools are computer-equipped in the economically richer states such as Gujarat, Tamil Nadu and Maharashtra as compared to poorer states, which also suffer from low enrolment. Most state-led initiatives to address digital inequalities (such as the National Digital Literacy Mission and Digital Indian programmes) have emphasised improving technology access alone, based on the assumption that technology access is the principal issue at hand (DiMaggio et al. 2001; Kvasny 2002).

In the case of China, the statistics indicate that the level of economic development is closely related to Internet access. Internet users also concentrate largely in metropolitan areas (Wensheng 2001). The Western provinces of China (Guangdong, Jiangsu, Shanghai, Beijing, Zhejiang) are at the top of the index, while the eastern provinces lie at the bottom (Gansu, Heilongjiang, Qinghai, Yunnan and Tibet). Liu et al. (2017) also found that regions with the highest ICT penetration levels are distributed along China's eastern coast and the provinces in the west present very low ICT penetration levels. Fong (2009) states in her study that in 2003, the Chinese government pledged to invest 200 million yuan (the US $24.2 million) in narrowing the digital gap between the eastern and western regions (12 provinces and autonomous regions). These provinces largely have a majority of the poorer and rural population, and this fund has been used to purchase computers and install broadband in this area. The author holds the view that the fund is still insufficient to close the gap for rural regions. Besides, issues like the affordability of ICT and literacy need to be resolved for rural areas, in particular. As per Loo and Ngan (2012), local governments in central and western China have taken steps toward more affordable access to ICT. For instance, the government of Sichuan has implemented effective policies to encourage information infrastructure construction and public and private investment in big data, cloud computing, e-commerce, and so on.

It is clear that issues related to the digital divide are cross-cutting and require resolution of several other problems in different sectors. As on date, most of the knowledge present in the global digital pool is in the English language, which is often not understood by the poor of society due to lack of educational avenues. In the case of China and India, there is a huge difference in the percentage of the population which speaks English. The digital content in vernacular languages of non-English-speaking communities is insignificant and is the underprivileged population's first barrier to access to the knowledge pool. Hence, it is more important for China to encourage the development of new digital content and translation of already existing content in vernacular languages.

In addition to the language issue, people need to acquire not only the necessary digital skills but also analogue skills, such as basic literacy and numeracy, to exploit the potential of the Internet (ITU 2016). The adult literacy rate (and female literacy rate) is much greater in China. This leaves a lot to be done in the education sector for India. Various dimensions of the sector, such as public spending (investment) on education, reducing the dropout ratio, and increasing enrolment ratios (tertiary enrolment in particular) need a reformatory approach. This would help bring more and more people online.

All the dimensions of the digital divide in China and India warrant thorough and ongoing research that will be able to elaborate further on the causes and social and economic implications of the growth of the Internet and its diffusion (Song 2008). Analysis at the micro-level may also provide a detailed picture of the factors that are detrimental to ICT adoption. However, it is a well-known fact that there is data constraint on ICT indicators for developing countries and within countries. Studies on the inter-state digital divide in India and China are scant due to deficiency of data on ICT indicators. There are also no existing comparative studies of India and China; hence, this chapter attempted to give a descriptive comparison of the two nations and their within-county digital divide with the help of ICTDI. In the case of India, inter-state data on Internet users and computer users are not available on a time series basis. The available data are either aggregated at the level of states or centrally administered municipalities. Future research can only explore information flows if data exist. As per Song (2008), data at the urban and firm levels and data of intercity interactions via the Internet can help reveal the way specific metropolises or regional networks and individual firms adapt to and exploit the opportunities offered by the Internet.

6 Conclusion

The chapter broadly focused on the country-level comparison of ICT diffusion and its manifestation in various sectors in China and India. Construction of ICTDI made it possible to identify the level of ICT diffusion across Indian states and Chinese provinces. The digital divide has been observed globally and has now become a worldwide concern. The challenge is to expand the ICT issue beyond the isolated economic viewpoint and investigate its roots causes. Just as socio-economic divides have always been part of human history, digital divides are likely to remain for a long time across individuals and countries. Such a divide presents the threat of economic exclusion and hence, the creation of ICT infrastructure is suggested. A well-planned thrust to technology will lessen the digital divide in both China and India. To respond to future challenges associated with the digital divide, a proactive approach to implementing smarter policies is imperative. There is a requirement for systematic and collaborative efforts by both the government and industry not only in technology but also in efforts directed to socio-economic structures around technology.

Acknowledgements I wish to thank Dr. Ganesh Manjhi for granting me his precious time for discussing my work, amidst his busy schedule. His inputs provided a concrete direction to my ideas. I would also like to thank the detailed review by the discussant, Prof. Fulvio Castellacci, at the two-day international workshop on 'The Economics of ICT' held in February 2018, Delhi. However, I am solely responsible for all the remaining errors and inadequacies.

Appendix

Definitions (Source: www.itu.int and www.data.worldbank.org).

Economic growth (GDP) %: The percent change in GDP in a particular quarter from the same quarter in the previous year using constant prices.

Percentage of world population: The population share of a particular country is measured as its population as a percent of the total world population in a given year. The total population is based on the de facto definition of population, which counts all residents regardless of legal status or citizenship—except for refugees not permanently settled in the country of asylum, who are generally considered part of the population of their country of origin. The values are mid-year estimates.

Internet users: The internet users are presented as the percent of people who have access to the Internet at home, at work or in public spaces. **Definition**: Internet users are individuals who have used the Internet (from any location) in the last 3 months. The Internet can be used via a computer, mobile phone, personal digital assistant, games machine, digital TV and so on.

Fixed broadband Internet subscribers, per 100 people: Fixed broadband subscriptions refer to fixed subscriptions to high-speed access to the public Internet (a TCP/IP connection), at downstream speeds equal to, or greater than, 256 kbit/s. This includes cable modem, DSL, fibre-to-the-home/building, other fixed (wired)-broadband subscriptions, satellite broadband and terrestrial fixed wireless broadband. This total is measured irrespective of the method of payment. It excludes subscriptions that have access to data communications (including the Internet) via mobile-cellular networks. It should include fixed WiMAX and any other fixed wireless technologies. It includes both residential subscriptions and subscriptions for organisations.

Mobile phone subscribers, per 100 people: Mobile cellular telephone subscriptions are subscriptions to a public mobile telephone service that provide access to the PSTN using cellular technology. The indicator includes (and is split into) the number of post-paid subscriptions and the number of active prepaid accounts (i.e. those that have been used during the last 3 months). The indicator applies to all mobile cellular subscriptions that offer voice communication. It excludes subscriptions via data cards or USB modems, subscriptions to public mobile data services, private trunked mobile radio, telepoint, radio paging and telemetry services.

International Internet bandwidth: International Internet bandwidth is the sum of the capacity of all Internet exchanges offering international bandwidth measured in bits per second (bits/s).

Literacy rate: Adult literacy rate is the percentage of people aged 15 years and above who can both read and write with understanding a short simple statement about their everyday life.

References

Bosman, M. M., & Chakraborty, J. (2002). Regional variations in on-line job search trends: Does race (still) matter? In *Papers and Proceedings of the Applied Geography Conferences* (Vol. 25, pp. 350–358).

Brown, L. A. (1975). The market and infrastructure context of adoption: A spatial perspective on the diffusion of innovation. *Economic Geography, 51*(3), 185–216. https://doi.org/10.2307/143117.

Chakraborty, J., & Bosman, M. M. (2005). Measuring the digital divide in the United States: Race, income, and personal computer ownership. *The Professional Geographer, 57*, 395–410. https://doi.org/10.1111/j.0033-0124.2005.00486.x.

China Internet Network Information Centre. (2017). *The 39th statistical report on internet development in China*. https://cnnic.com.cn. Accessed January 1, 2019.

Dahlman, C. J. (2007). China and India: Emerging technological powers. *Issues in Science and Technology, XXIII*(3). http://issues.org/dahlman/. Accessed October 21, 2017.

Das, B. (2010). *Diffusion of information and communication technology across Indian states and its determinants: An empirical analysis*. https://pdfs.semanticscholar.org/2c24/e1f8439d5bc68fac2b96f5467b9536f13ec8.pdf. Accessed November 24, 2018.

Dean, D., Digrande, S., Field, D., Lundmark, A., O'Day, J., Pineda, P., & Zwillenberg, P. (2012). *The connecting world: The internet economy in the G-20*. Boston Consulting Group. http://image-src.bcg.com/Images/The_Internet_Economy_G-20_tcm9-106842.pdf. Accessed July 22, 2017.

Desai, M. (2005). India and China: An essay in comparative political economy. In W. Tseng & D. Cowen (Eds.), *India's and China's recent experience with reform and growth* (pp. 1–22). New York: Palgrave Macmillan.

DiMaggio, P., Hargittai, E., Neuman, W. R., & Robinson, J. P. (2001). Social implication of the internet. *Annual Review of Sociology, 27A,* 307–336.

Economist Intelligence Unit. (2012). *Smart policies to close the digital divide—Best practices from around the world.* http://unpan1.un.org/intradoc/groups/public/documents/un-dpadm/unpan049753.pdf. Accessed August 15, 2017.

Fong, M. W. L. (2009). Digital divide between urban and rural regions in China. *The Electronic Journal on Information Systems in Developing Countries, 36,* 1–12. www.ejisdc.com. Accessed February 24, 2019.

Gnanasambandam, C., Madgavkar, A., Kaka, N., Manyika, J., Chui, M., Bughin, J, & Gomes, M. (2012). *Online and upcoming: The internet's impact on India.* McKinsey & Company. https://www.mckinsey.com/~/media/mckinsey/dotcom/client_service/high%20tech/pdfs/online_and_upcoming_the_internets_impact_on_india.ashx. Accessed July 22, 2017.

Guthrie, D. (2006). *China and globalization: The social, economic, and political transformation of Chinese society.* New York and London: Routledge.

Hargittai, E. (1999). Weaving the western web: Explaining differences in internet connectivity among OECD countries. *Telecommunications Policy, 23,* 701–718.

Harrington, J. (2007). *The digital divide: Lessons from the People's Republic of China.* http://www.greennation.com/chidigi.pdf. December 12, 2007.

International Telecommunication Union. (2016). *Measuring the information society report.* https://www.itu.int/en/ITU-D/Statistics/Pages/publications/mis2016.aspx. Accessed October 15, 2017.

Internet World Stats. (2018). *Internet usage statistics.* http://www.internetworldstats.com/stats.htm. Accessed October 22, 2018.

Jain, N., Bhalla, K., Roy, P. K., & Mittal, A. (2017). *The $250 billion digital volcano: Dormant no more.* Mumbai, India: Boston Consulting Group. https://media-publications.bcg.com/BCG-TiE-Digital-Volcano-Apr2017.pdf. Accessed October 28, 2017.

Katz, J. E., Rice, R. E., & Aspden, P. (2001). The internet, 1995-2000: Access, civic involvement, and social interaction. *American Behavioral Scientist, 45,* 405–419.

Kaur, K., & Neena. (2014). Pattern of inter-state digital divide in India. *Economic Affairs, 59.* https://doi.org/10.5958/0976-4666.2014.00006.0.

Kaur, K., & Singh, J. (2016). ICT diffusion and digital divide in India: Implications for economic policies. *Pacific Business Review International, 1,* 1–9.

Kemp, S. (2018). *Digital in 2018.* We are Social and Hootsuite. https://digitalreport.wearesocial.com/. Accessed February 20, 2019.

Kiiski, S., & Pohojola, M. (2002). Cross-country diffusion of the internet. *Information Economics and Policy, 14,* 297–310.

Kochhar, R. (2015). *China's middle class surges, while India's lags behind.* https://www.pewresearch.org/fact-tank/2015/07/15/china-india-middle-class/. Accessed June 7, 2019.

Kvasny, L. (2002). *Problematizing the digital divide: Cultural and social reproduction in a community technology initiative* (Unpublished doctoral dissertation). Georgia State University, Atlanta, GA.

Liang, B., & Lu, H. (2010). Internet development, censorship, and cybercrimes in China. *Journal of Contemporary Criminal Justice, 26*(1), 103–120.

Lindsay, C. (2005). Employability, services for unemployed job seekers and the digital divide. *Urban Studies, 42,* 325–339.

List of Regions of China. https://en.wikipedia.org/wiki/List_of_regions_of_China, Accessed on April 2, 2018.

Liu, H., Fang, C., & Sun, S. (2017). Digital inequality in provincial China. *Environment and Planning A, 49,* 2179–2182.

Loo, B., & Ngan, L. (2012). Developing mobile telecommunications to narrow digital divide in developing countries? Some lessons from China. *Telecommunications Policy, 36*(10–11), 888–900.

MacKinnon, R. (2008). Flatter world and thicker walls? Blogs, censorship and civic discourse in China. *Public Choice, 134,* 31–46.

Ministry of Electronics and Information Technology (MeitY). (2018). *Electronics and information technology annual reports (various)*, India. https://meity.gov.in. Accessed March 2, 2018.

Ministry of Home Affairs, Office of the Registrar General & Census Commissioner. (2011). *India: Census of India*. www.censusindia.gov.in. Accessed October 22, 2017.

Ministry of Power. (2017). *Central electricity authority report*, India. http://www.cea.nic.in/reports/annual/annualreports/annual_report-2018.pdf. Accessed March 2, 2019.

National Bureau of Statistics of China. (2016). *China statistical yearbook 2016*. Beijing, China. http://www.stats.gov.cn/tjsj/ndsj/2016/indexeh.htm. Accessed 2 March 2018.

National Telecommunications and Information Administration. (2000). *Falling through the net: Towards digital inclusion*. Washington, DC: Department of Commerce. https://www.ntia.doc.gov/report/2000/falling-through-net-toward-digital-inclusion. Accessed October 21, 2017.

Norris, P. (2000). The global divide: Information poverty and internet access worldwide. In *Internet Conference at the International Political Science World Congress*, August 2000, Quebec City. https://sites.hks.harvard.edu/fs/pnorris/Acrobat/IPSA2000.PDF. March 2, 2018.

Norris, P. (2001). *Digital divide: Civic engagement, information poverty and the Internet in democratic societies*. New York, NY: Cambridge University Press.

Parthasarathy, B., & Aoyama, Y. (2017). Deploying ICTs for development: An evolutionary perspective. *Information Technologies & International Development (Special Section), 13,* 157–170.

Poushter, J. (2017). *China outpaces India in internet access, smartphone ownership*. http://www.pewresearch.org/fact-tank/2017/03/16/china-outpaces-india-in-internet-access-smartphone-ownership/. Accessed October 21, 2017.

Rao, S. S. (2005). Bridging digital divide: Efforts in India. *Telematics and Informatics, 22,* 361–375.

Rogers, E. M., & Shoemaker, F. F. (1971). *Communication of innovation: A cross-cultural approach* (2nd ed.). New York, NY: The Free Press.

Shah, A., Jain, N., & Bajpai, S. (2015, January). *India@Digital, Bharat creating a $200 billion internet economy*. India: Boston Consulting Group and Internet and Mobile Association of India. https://timedotcom.files.wordpress.com/2015/04/file180687.pdf. Accessed October 24, 2017.

Song, W. (2008). Development of the internet and digital divide in China: A spatial analysis. *Intercultural Communication Studies, VXII*(3). https://web.uri.edu/iaics/files/03-Wei-Song.pdf. Accessed April 4, 2018.

Telecom Regulatory Authority of India. (2018). *The Indian telecom services performance indicators*, October–December 2017, Delhi. https://main.trai.gov.in/release-publication/reports/performance-indicators-reports. Accessed March 2, 2019.

Tseng, S. F., & You, Y. C. (2013). The digital divide in China, Hongkong and Taiwan. In M. Ragnedda & G. W. Muschert (Eds.), *The digital divide* (1st ed., pp. 134–146). London and New York, NY: Routledge Taylor and Francis Group.

Wensheng, W. (2001). *Bridging the digital divide inside China*. https://www.researchgate.net/…/228908087_Bridging_the_digital_divide_inside_China. Accessed April 4, 2018.

Wilhelm, A. G. (2001). They threw me a computer… but what I really needed was a life preserver. *First Monday, 6*(4). https://firstmonday.org/ojs/index.php/fm/article/view/844/753. Accessed April 2, 2018.

Wolf, C., Dalal, S., DaVanzo, J., Larson, E. V., Akhmedjonov, A., Dogo, H., et al. (2011). Population trends in China and India: Demographic dividend or demographic drag? In *China and India, 2025A comparative assessment* (pp. 7–29). RAND Corporation. https://www.rand.org/content/dam/rand/pubs/monographs/2011/RAND_MG1009.pdf. Accessed February 19, 2019.

Wong, P. K. (2002). ICT production and diffusion in Asia: Digital dividends or digital divide? *Information Economics and Policy, 14,* 167–187.

World Bank. World Bank data. Retrieved from http://data.worldbank.org. Accessed October 24, December 2018.
World Economic Forum. (2018). *Global information technology reports*. https://www.weforum.org/reports?page=6. Accessed March 7, 2018.

Is India Digitally Divided? Identifying the Determinants of ICT Diffusion at the Household Level

Pratap C. Mohanty

Abstract This paper shows that poor digital connectivity undermines the socio-economic development in rural India and finds out various socio-economic factors responsible for the wide difference in ICT diffusion, using household-level nationally representative database of NFHS (National Family Health Survey)-III round (2005–6), NFHS-IV (2015–16) round and DLHS (District Level Household Survey) 2007–8. The probit regression with marginal effect and reference category methods are applied to derive the socio-economic factors explaining the ICT diffusion. A pooled probit regression method is further applied to check the robustness of the results. The results suggest that the gap in access to ICTs between rural and urban areas has been widened during the period from 2007 to 2016. The access to ICT innovations and the levels of socio-economic development have been found highly correlated with the extent of the digital divide in India. More emphasis should be given on human development (like education, health), income generation schemes in rural areas, improvement of infrastructural facilities, strategies to narrow down the information gaps and other social barriers will improve the access to the ICTs.

Keywords ICT · Socio-economic disparities · Policy implications

JEL Code O33 · O35

1 Introduction

Information and Communication Technology (ICT) contains a great level of potentialities in transforming the economy. But, economic and social backwardness create additional hindrance for the poor to access ICT and thus do not allow to take the benefit of ICT applications. In other words, ICT cannot break the 'vicious circle of poverty' unless a major parallel development takes place. This is because rural India still lacks many basic infrastructures, education income opportunities, etc. It is therefore important to understand the issues of ICT diffusion with an emphasis on

P. C. Mohanty (✉)
Indian Institute of Technology Roorkee, Roorkee, India
e-mail: pratapfhs@iitr.ac.in

D. Maiti et al. (eds.), *Digitalisation and Development*,
https://doi.org/10.1007/978-981-13-9996-1_10

identifying the extent of digital divide and factors limiting the access of ICTs among rural and people in the backward areas of the Indian economy.

A host of literature defines digital divide as a result of inequalities persisting in the society over the access and use of ICTs, specifically access to the internet (Castells 2002). This has emerged as a bigger concern since the early 1990s owing to the rising trend of access to computers and the internet (Eastin et al. 2015). The wealth created in India from the ICT boom benefits the relatively wealthy and educated people more while the trickle-down effects to the poor and uneducated section of people are dubious, and the statistics show mixed evidence (Kambhampati 2002). However, Cecchini and Scott (2003) summarize a range of ICT-based applications that helped poverty reduction in rural India.

It is argued that location and density are two important factors behind internet penetration. The existing literature on USA data identified urban biasness in internet diffusion (Augereau and Greenstein 2001; Forman et al. 2005; Downes and Greenstein 2007). The extent of complementarity, as well as substitutability between cities and internet use, are highlighted by Forman et al. (2005) using the firm's data of the USA. They also confer the results that large cities adopt internet technology faster than small cities or rural areas. The study of Downes and Greenstein (2007) highlights evidence of increasing availability of local online content and show that local availability in large cities is higher than rural areas. Hence, *digital future proofing* has become imperative as part of the present telecommunication policy. Without this, there will be an increasingly entrenched urban–rural divide (Philip et al. 2017; Salemink et al. 2017).

It is argued that effective ICT use through computerized health information systems is seen as a key prerequisite for improved health care delivery and better implementation of health programmes. Telecentres are the instruments of ICT which have been recognized to bridge the digital divide for the poor (Reilly and Gómez 2001), provide them with access to information and better freedom of choice.

ICT leads to increasing concentration of economic activities and thereby raises inequalities (Deursen et al. 2017; Salemink et al. 2017; Gaspar and Glaeser 1998). These studies emphasize the availability of population; digital infrastructure which leads in the compoundness and sequentiality (Deursen et al. 2017) of digital inequalities, especially in rural areas (Salemink et al. 2017). There are two reasons why ICT may lead to an increase in concentration. First, the increase in the size or population density of a location may increase the marginal benefit from electronic communication (Gaspar and Glaeser 1998). This states that improvement in electronic communication increases the prevalence of face-to-face meetings, thereby increasing the value of locating in cities. Moreover, an increase in the size of the population adds the availability of complementary products and services that facilitate the net benefits of ICT investment.

The problem of the digital divide is more acute for the developing countries like India (Servon 2008). Some studies (Singh 2008; Dasgupta et al. 2001) looked at the problems of the digital divide in the Indian context and observed that the digital divide is significant between urban and rural areas of India. A strand of literature identifies the factors which affect the digital divide, but no identification is made for the individual heterogeneities (Van Deursen et al. 2017).

The existing literature contains very limited information in tapping the digital divide at the household level. The empirical estimations in the existing literature are dealt largely on the aggregate or macro context. The growth of the economy does not truly represent the existing inequalities in access to ICT. Developing countries and India, in particular, are poised with many developmental challenges. Further, these countries have huge heterogeneities at the individual level, specially in access to basic facilities like education, health and information, etc.

The primary objective of this paper is to map the availability of ICTs and their use at the household level in India. The focus here is to highlight the gaps in access to ICTs, specially between rural and urban areas. This study also investigates the relevant factors which limit the households in accessing ICTs.

This paper structures into five sub-sections. Section 2 maps the extent of availability and use of ICT. This highlights gaps in ICT use among rural and urban areas. Section 3 discusses the model specifications to identify individual heterogeneities. Section 4 includes the results based on the marginal effect and interaction effects with respect to their reference category using probit regression model and also checks the robustness of the results using pooled data. This section identifies relevant factors which restrict the access to ICTs. Based on the descriptive analysis and regression results, Sect. 5 concludes with suggestions.

The analysis is developed with the help of latest household level nationally representative database of NFHS (National Family Health Survey)-III round (2005–06), NFHS-IV (2015–16) round and DLHS (District Level Household Survey) 2007–8. The individual and household files are considered for the analysis.

2 Mapping of ICT Access in India

There are several dimensions to the digital divide, as mentioned in the literature. The divide in the pattern of ICT diffusion is explained with the help of the availability of data. For some indicators like the density of ICT devices like telephone, internet and personal computers are collected from TRAI's (Telecom Regulatory Authority of India) reports of various years. The household-level or unit-level digital divide is emphasized throughout the sections by computing and estimating from the household-level survey data of NFHS 2005–6, NFHS 2015–16 and DLHS 2007–8.

2.1 Teledensity in India

The diffusion of the telephone is very widespread. The data on telephone availability and their use are composed of both wireline and wireless telephone. Due to the

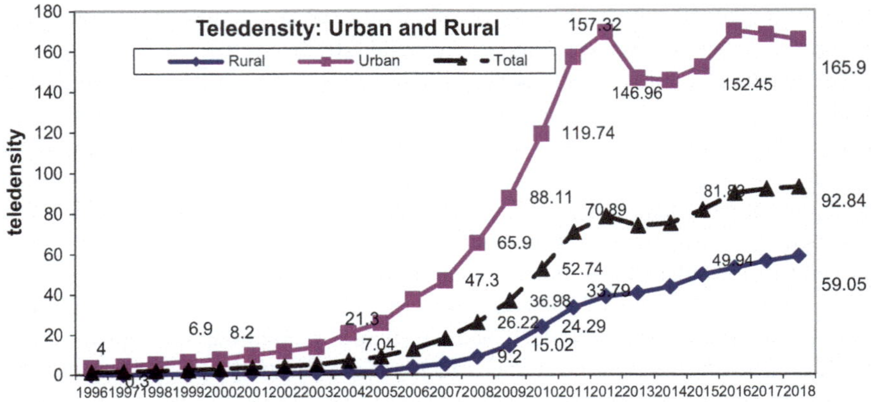

Fig. 1 Teledensity in urban and rural areas in India. *Source* TRAI Reports of various years

evolution of the cellular phone, the spread of subscribers has been unparalleled. Teledensity was measured as several subscribers per 100 people (ITU 1998).[1] Till March 2018, as per the TRAI reports, teledensity has been accentuated to 92.84 per 100 persons of which urban teledensity stands at 165.9 and rural teledensity is of only 59.05 (Fig. 1). The broadband subscribers were 99.2 million till March 2015. It is noticed that this spiral development has been initiated from 1999 to 2000 due to a number of policy facilitations. However, the major impetus in the diffusion process has been since 2001 following the implementation of India's National Telecommunication Policy (NTP), 1999.[2]

2.2 *Rural–Urban Divide*

The rural–urban teledensity divide is explained in Fig. 1. The urban teledensity has reached to 157.3 in 2011 as compared to only 33.8 in rural areas as per the census 2011 data. This is validated with the TRAI reports as presented in Fig. 1. The rate of growth is very fast in urban areas. Therefore, the gap has been persisting and widening. Moreover, the favourable policies on telephone infrastructure development are indeed confined to urban areas.

However, the growth of teledensity in recent years has been sluggish. As per the latest reports of TRAI, the urban teledensity is 165.9, and rural teledensity is 59.05. The urban teledensity is much higher than the rural teledensity. The rural teledensity is also very less than the national average (92.84 in 2018).

[1]This benchmark level of teledensity has been adopted from the International Telecommunication Union (ITU) report on 'Methodological note on the choice of teledensity bands'.

[2]NTP 1999 included these objectives: Making affordable and effective communication as part of the goal of telecom policy, universal service to all including uncovered areas, better R&D, transparency in spectrum management, etc.

The teledensity of India is decomposed by place and types of devices and presented in Figs. 1 and 2, respectively. Given the availability of data over time, Fig. 1 covers the teledensity data from 1996 to 2018 and Fig. 2 contains the density of ICT devices from 1990 to 2017. Following the NTP, 1999, the major change has been observed since 2001. The rural teledensity as on 31st March 2010 was 24.3 increased to 33.8 at the end of March 2011, as compared to the urban teledensity of 119.8 in 2010 and 157.3 in 2011. However, the growth rate of subscribers in rural areas during the year was higher at 40.6% compared to 34.1% in urban areas (Fig. 1). The urban teledensity was more than three times the rural areas in 2018. These figures suggest that the gap of teledensity between the urban and rural areas is rising.

The density of ICT devices is presented in Fig. 2. The holding of the internet, landline and mobile telephone are expressed per 100 persons. In contrast to the growth of mobile/wireless telephone, there has been a reverse growth of landline telephone since the same period. While the mobile telephone subscribers were 87.3 per 100 persons, the landline connections were only 1.7 per 100 persons in 2017. In contrast to the rapid growth in the voice segment, the growth in the internet and broadband connections were modest. The growth of internet subscribers has been slightly better since 1999 but still below the level of many countries in the world. The density of internet users reached to 18 per 100 persons in December 2014 from 15.1 in 2013. The slow growth of the Internet and broadband connection were predominantly due to the use of digital subscriber line (DSL) technologies over copper pairs, which were limited in number and also due to less geographical spread.

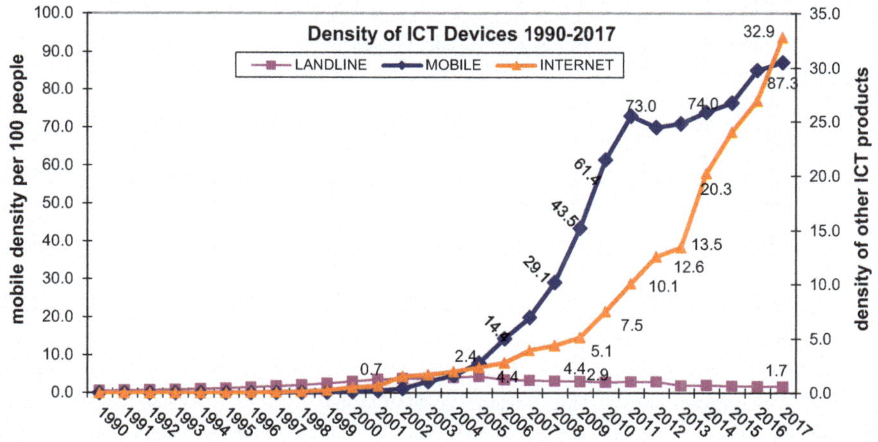

Fig. 2 Density of ICT devices in India. *Source* TRAI reports of various years

2.3 The Density of All ICT Devices

ICT diffusion is better understood through each device by their geographical and locational distributions. Table 1 presents household-level holding of various ICT devices by percentage. States like Odisha, Bihar, Jharkhand and Chhattisgarh etc. are among the bottom five states using ICT devices. Likewise, all other percentages, Table 1 can be interpreted accordingly. Table 1 presents the figures for the top and bottom five states using different ICT devices like radio, TV, telephone and computer. They are also compared to the All India average.

The information contained in Tables 2 and 3 is on exposure to ICT devices using NFHS-III (2005–06) and IV (2015–16) respectively. The quality of ICT access is understood better when the information of the individuals regarding the frequency of ICT use is available. These tables highlight the gaps across socio-economic characteristics. The socio-economic characteristics are age, place of residence, education, marital status, religion, caste and standard of living (proxied by wealth index). The figures mentioned in these tables are well indicative. The gaps are also observed between male and female for each of the background characteristics. 'Reading a newspaper or magazine at least once a week' varies by age and sex: higher the age, lesser the access. Male are more exposed to ICT devices than female across different categories.

Table 1 Household-level holding of various ICT devices (in percent)

	Radio		TV		Telephone		Computer	
Top five states	Jammu & Kashmir	66.32	Manipur	84.11	Delh	79.82	Goa	21.84
	Manipur	62.81	Goa	82.21	Goa	75.52	Delhi	18.83
	Kerala	42.01	Odisha	78.43	Kerala	72.13	Kerala	7.90
	Arunachal Pradesh	40.53	Andhra Pradesh	71.33	Punjab	69.72	Punjab	5.61
	Mizoram	37.32	Kerala	71.32	Himachal Pradesh	60.81	Mizoram	4.20
	India	**26.32**		**29.14**		**36.81**		**2.60**
Bottom five states	Madhya Pradesh	19.01	Gujarat	29.42	Meghalaya	20.71	Odisha	1.41
	Chhattisgarh	16.91	Uttarakhand	26.44	Odisha	18.71	Chhattisgarh	1.32
	Odisha	16.80	Assam	25.81	Jharkhand	18.60	Jharkhand	1.21
	Gujarat	16.14	Uttar Pradesh	19.63	Bihar	18.04	Uttar Pradesh	1.04
	Andhra Pradesh	11.24	Punjab	11.82	Chhattisgarh	14.03	Bihar	0.52

Source Computed from DLHS-III—household profile
Note Figures are in percentage of ICT access out of total household in each state

Table 2 Exposure to ICT (percentage of men and women of age 15–49) in 2005–06

Background characteristics	Read a newspaper or magazine at least once a week		Watch television at least once a week		Listens to radio at least once a week		Not regularly exposed to any media	
	Female	Male	Female	Male	Female	Male	Female	Male
Age								
15–19	28.63	55.71	59.44	71.24	34.31	48.81	28.51	11.81
20–24	25.52	57.71	58.01	69.52	30.91	48.80	31.30	12.22
25–29	21.92	54.92	54.50	65.41	26.90	45.41	35.70	15.54
30–34	20.51	53.13	52.60	60.80	26.60	41.80	37.81	20.14
35–39	19.61	49.11	51.70	57.52	25.82	40.90	38.31	24.21
40–44	19.40	48.01	51.43	54.31	26.24	39.41	38.90	26.34
45–49	18.52	47.72	52.82	54.70	25.90	39.71	38.54	25.72
Residence								
Urban	41.62	69.40	82.00	83.90	31.70	45.32	12.60	6.22
Rural	13.73	43.63	41.90	51.23	27.31	43.70	45.40	25.33
Education								
No education	0.22	1.63	29.41	31.80	18.14	30.61	60.31	48.81
<5 years complete	6.12	17.90	51.70	47.90	28.50	40.80	36.54	29.81

(continued)

Table 2 (continued)

Background characteristics	Read a newspaper or magazine at least once a week		Watch television at least once a week		Listens to radio at least once a week		Not regularly exposed to any media	
	Female	Male	Female	Male	Female	Male	Female	Male
5–7 years complete	19.12	45.20	62.80	59.52	30.60	42.04	25.34	18.91
8–9 years complete	36.14	65.50	72.14	68.71	37.71	48.61	16.34	10.40
10–11 years complete	52.91	79.61	82.50	78.61	39.71	49.00	7.90	5.30
12 or more complete	74.20	91.50	90.90	85.40	42.90	52.31	3.01	2.01
Marital status								
Never married	40.61	62.01	70.81	74.71	38.50	49.62	18.90	9.80
Currently married	18.71	48.24	51.20	56.80	26.40	41.22	38.41	22.90
Widowed/divorced/separated/deserted	12.40	35.70	47.44	45.02	23.41	41.34	43.90	33.40
Religion								
Hindu	22.70	53.80	55.62	63.34	29.14	44.71	34.41	18.00
Muslim	18.02	45.02	45.51	57.20	27.33	43.70	41.70	21.71
Christian	40.20	60.14	68.61	71.90	30.50	43.01	20.30	13.33
Sikh	33.00	56.01	80.42	84.01	20.20	32.31	16.01	10.71
Buddhist/Neo-Buddhist	30.30	61.10	66.23	70.40	32.00	43.20	26.50	15.52
Jain	76.71	95.51	90.11	90.42	37.50	46.14	3.14	0

(continued)

Table 2 (continued)

Background characteristics	Read a newspaper or magazine at least once a week		Watch television at least once a week		Listens to radio at least once a week		Not regularly exposed to any media	
	Female	Male	Female	Male	Female	Male	Female	Male
Other	9.03	21.50	22.22	30.42	16.70	34.81	68.01	46.50
Caste/tribe								
SC	15.61	45.13	50.61	59.52	26.51	43.81	38.90	21.11
ST	10.01	29.51	30.33	39.52	20.90	36.32	57.40	37.80
OBC	19.90	54.11	53.12	63.11	28.12	46.20	36.82	17.40
Other	33.90	62.31	66.01	71.11	32.82	44.20	24.14	13.01
Wealth index								
Lowest	2.01	17.11	13.90	24.50	16.34	34.40	73.71	49.31
Second	5.50	33.32	29.60	40.50	24.31	43.31	55.14	29.41
Middle	12.31	48.70	51.90	61.12	29.70	46.50	34.90	16.01
Fourth	27.01	65.31	75.33	79.81	33.60	48.24	16.22	6.71
Highest	59.71	84.81	92.51	93.11	36.84	46.14	3.90	1.70

Source Computed from the NFHS-III (2005–06) individual and household file

Table 3 Exposure to ICT (percentage of men and women of age 15–49) in 2015–16

Background characteristics	Reads a newspaper or magazine at least once a week		Watch television at least once a week		Listens to radio at least once a week		Not regularly exposed to any media	
	Female	Male	Female	Male	Female	Male	Female	Male
Age								
15–19	32.52	54.82	70.81	78.51	11.50	20.52	23.51	12.83
20–24	30.32	58.50	73.62	79.20	11.25	20.71	22.32	11.62
25–29	27.31	57.40	72.44	79.90	10.44	20.61	24.24	12.44
30–34	25.51	55.30	70.91	78.45	10.11	20.80	25.91	14.11
35–39	23.33	51.71	69.91	76.16	10.12	20.80	27.04	16.21
40–44	21.83	52.04	69.23	75.45	10.28	21.25	27.81	17.22
45–49	19.11	48.81	68.74	74.14	9.77	20.20	28.43	18.71
Residence								
Urban	43.41	66.80	89.04	89.41	14.22	24.82	8.28	5.60
Rural	17.51	46.90	61.51	70.41	8.61	18.19	34.29	19.71
Education								
No education	0.51	4.53	46.80	51.60	6.50	16.11	50.52	41.71
<5 years complete	4.52	14.64	64.50	65.60	7.40	15.74	32.44	27.42

(continued)

Table 3 (continued)

Background characteristics	Reads a newspaper or magazine at least once a week		Watch television at least once a week		Listens to radio at least once a week		Not regularly exposed to any media	
	Female	Male	Female	Male	Female	Male	Female	Male
5–7 years complete	14.92	34.94	72.34	72.32	8.25	17.33	24.18	19.60
8–9 years complete	26.23	52.44	75.81	76.61	10.02	19.20	19.49	13.81
10–11 years complete	42.63	69.62	85.24	85.52	12.92	22.41	10.50	6.52
12 or more complete	63.14	84.81	90.11	89.30	17.01	25.10	5.82	3.19
Marital status								
Never married	40.61	60.61	76.21	81.54	13.61	21.92	18.41	10.25
Currently married	22.74	51.01	69.71	75.52	9.71	20.00	27.08	16.70
Widowed/divorced/separated/deserted	15.93	37.04	67.24	61.60	8.91	16.80	29.72	29.12
Religion								
Hindu	26.43	55.11	71.91	77.82	10.71	20.42	24.61	14.45
Muslim	22.04	48.42	61.51	73.42	10.22	22.79	33.17	16.15
Christian	42.34	64.72	81.12	85.21	11.81	23.27	15.25	9.36
Sikh	38.91	54.02	93.04	90.61	5.20	6.90	5.81	6.81
Buddhist/Neo-Buddhist	34.31	61.42	83.31	84.42	12.11	29.65	12.90	9.12
Jain	64.22	84.71	94.50	97.50	17.90	24.12	4.32	0.22

(continued)

Table 3 (continued)

Background characteristics	Reads a newspaper or magazine at least once a week		Watch television at least once a week		Listens to radio at least once a week		Not regularly exposed to any media	
	Female	Male	Female	Male	Female	Male	Female	Male
Other	12.32	39.52	47.14	62.23	6.67	18.34	49.42	26.17
Caste/tribe								
SC	19.91	48.83	69.80	76.61	9.70	20.42	26.60	15.64
ST	14.31	35.42	55.34	63.71	8.27	17.61	40.81	27.80
OBC	26.02	56.32	70.34	76.62	10.15	20.60	25.90	14.44
Other	36.91	62.12	78.90	84.62	12.82	21.81	17.30	9.00
Wealth index								
Lowest	4.51	21.31	23.80	36.21	6.42	15.66	70.60	47.81
Second	9.61	37.82	56.41	64.90	7.90	18.28	38.41	22.50
Middle	18.51	51.52	80.40	84.04	9.81	20.08	15.91	8.70
Fourth	34.14	66.12	90.82	91.41	11.80	23.18	6.63	3.80
Highest	60.71	80.81	95.50	95.31	16.07	24.24	2.42	1.81

Source Computed from the NFHS-IV (2015–16) individual and household file

In all indicators, access to ICT by female is much lesser than the male. This change has been very minimal for over ten years. The role of education indeed matters a lot. The location of the respondent influences the extent of access to ICT. There are 6.22% urban residents who don't regularly expose to any media in 2005–06. This is reduced to 5.6% in 2015–16. The rural residents who do not have regular exposure to any ICT devices are 25.33% in 2005–06 as compared to 19.71% in 2015–16. This indicates the fact that rural areas are catching up to the urban areas in terms of access to any media devices. Similarly, significant changes are noted in the case of the standard of living, caste.

3 Model Specification

ICT access and diffusion were modelled using Epidemic and Bass models. These models do not figure the individual characteristics. These models also do not explicitly model the adoption decisions of individual users, nor do they allow for differences in the costs and benefits of adoption by different members of the population. As a result, these models omit many important aspects of economic behaviour. Later models, including the *Probit model*, explicitly include these elements.

Probit model emphasizes population heterogeneity, thus is considered for the analysis here. This model based on the information utility theory, which is affected by a number of unobservable utility index called a *latent variable* that is determined by many explanatory variables. Thus, larger, the value of the latent variable, greater is the probability of accessing ICT devices. The probit model is specified as per the variables and the nature of the data. The Kernel density function of the error distribution is estimated which approximates to a normal density function. The dependent variable is binary with value 0 and 1.

$$I_i = \alpha + \beta_1 X_1 + \beta_2 X_2 + \cdots$$

With the assumption of normality, the probability that I_i* is less than or equal to the threshold limit that be computed from the standardized normal CDF[3] as:

[3]Normal CDF: if a variable X follows with mean μ and variance σ^2, its Normal PDF is

$$f(X) = \frac{1}{\sqrt{2\sigma^2\pi}} e^{-(X-\mu)^2/2\sigma^2}$$

and its CDF is

$$F(X) = \int_{-\infty}^{X_0} \frac{1}{\sqrt{2\sigma^2\pi}} e^{-(X-\mu)^2/2\sigma^2}$$

where X_0 is some specific value of X.

$$P_i = P(Y = 1|X) = P(I_i* \leq I_i) = P(Z_i = \alpha + \beta_1 X_1 + \beta_2 X_2 + \beta_3 X_3 + \cdots)$$
$$= F(\alpha + \beta_1 X_1 + \beta_2 X_2 + \beta_3 X_3 + \cdots)$$

where $P(Y = 1|X)$ means the probability of using ICT given all the above explanatory variables.

To get the information utility index, I_i, and α, β_i

$$I_i = F^{-1}(I_i) = F^{-1}(P_i) = \alpha + \beta_1 X_1 + \beta_2 X_2 + \beta_3 X_3 + \cdots$$

4 Results

The probit estimates confirm the idea that socio-economic factors indeed affect the probability of having an ICT device. The probability estimate is derived here for three devices telephone (mobile + landline), TV and Radio as per the availability in the NFHS data set in both the rounds. Some of the variables are considered as categorical like newspaper (0 = not at all, 1 < once a week, 2 = at least once a week, 3 = every day), education level, age group and de facto residence (categorized as 1: capital, 2: small city, 3: town and 4: countryside). The variable 'electricity access' is a dummy.

The variables such as caste, wealth, newspaper, electricity, education and place of residence influence the access of telephone significantly (Tables 4 and 8). The probability of having a TV is significantly explained by marital status, wealth, reading the newspaper, member of the households, electricity, level of education, age group. For access to Radio, variables like caste, the standard of living, although some of the variables are significant (caste, newspaper, level of education, and age group, etc.). Some of the coefficients mislead the standard theoretical arguments of the probability of diffusion. This can further be verified with the help of marginal effect analysis. The pseudo R^2 and the overall level of significance are very good. The standard error is closed to zero for most of the coefficients (Table 5).

4.1 Effect of Reference Category

The interaction effect of probit analysis justifies the argument of having ICT asset given other covariates. The probability of holding a computer as a function of caste is quite unclear to understand. But it is easier to understand how people belong to General category possesses a computer as compared to the reference category, i.e. SC. Similarly, between OBC and SC or ST, SC, etc. In this variable, ST, OBC and General category people have the probability of holding a computer is positive and

Table 4 Probit regression with marginal effects using NFHS 2005–06

	Model 1 (Telephone)		Model 2 (TV)		Model 3 (Radio)	
	β	dy/dx	β	dy/dx	β	dy/dx
Caste	0.039* [0.01]	0.009* [0.00]	−0.013 [0.01]	−0.003 [0.00]	0.030* [0.01]	0.012* [0.00]
Occupation	−0.000 [0.00]	−0.000 [0.00]	−0.000 [0.00]	−0.000 [0.00]	−0.002* [0.00]	−0.001* [0.00]
Marital status	−0.002 [0.09]	−0.001 [0.02]	−0.203* [0.07]	−0.053* [0.02]	−0.234* [0.06]	−0.093* [0.02]
Wealth index[a]	0.000* [0.00]	0.000* [0.00]	0.000* [0.00]	0.000* [0.00]	0.000* [0.00]	0.000* [0.00]
Newspaper#	0.087* [0.01]	0.021* [0.00]	−0.065* [0.01]	−0.017* [0.00]	0.076* [0.01]	0.030* [0.00]
HH members	0.064* [0.00]	0.015* [0.00]	0.044* [0.00]	0.012* [0.00]	0.031* [0.00]	0.012* 0.00]
Electricity#	0.898* [0.03]	0.215* [0.00]	0.671* [0.03]	0.176* [0.00]	0.386* [0.01]	0.153* [0.00]
Education level	0.131* [0.03]	0.031* [0.01]	0.093* [0.02]	0.024* [0.00]	−0.012 [0.02]	−0.005 [0.01]
Residence	0.408* [0.04]	0.097* [0.01]	0.041 [0.04]	0.011 [0.01]	0.399* [0.03]	0.158* [0.01]
Age group	0.007 [0.01]	0.002 [0.00]	−0.069* [0.01]	−0.018* [0.00]	0.041* [0.01]	0.016* [0.00]
Constant	−3.561* [0.21]		−0.098 [0.16]		−1.246* [0.12]	
Number of observation	29,134		29,139		29,132	
Prob > chi^2	0		0		0	
Pseudo R^2	0.5435		0.4224		0.1602	

Source Computed from NFHS-III, 2005–06 individual and household file
Note #Dummy; *$p < 0.01$, **$p < 0.05$, ***$p < 0.10$; SE is in the brackets
HH: Household, Edn: education, dy/dx: marginal effect, MFX: marginal effect probit regression, MFX_C: MFX computer, similarly for others
[a]This is derived using Principal Component Analysis method. PCA is applied to various indicators of household expenditure. The original variables are transformed into smaller set of variables which explain most of the variance. It constructs out of a set of variables, Z_j's$(j = 1, 2, \ldots, k)$ new variables (PC_i) called 'Principal Components', which are linear combinations of the Z's (NFHS-3 and 4). The construction of these indices are explained as follows

$$PC_1 = a_{11}Z_1 + \cdots + a_{1n}Z_n$$
$$PC_2 = a_{21}Z_1 + \cdots + a_{2n}Z_n$$
$$\ldots$$
$$PC_m = a_{m1}Z_1 + \cdots + a_{mn}Z_n$$

'a's are the factor loadings. Here, as the maximum possible variance is captured by the first PC. The study considers factor loadings correspond to the first PC to get the index.

Table 5 Probit regression with marginal effects using NFHS-2015–16

	Model 4 (Telephone)		Model 5 (TV)		Model 6 (Radio)	
	β	dy/dx	β	dy/dx	β	dy/dx
Caste	0.094* [0.01]	0.031* [0.00]	−0.025* [0.01]	−0.006* [0.00]	0.229* [0.01]	0.045* [0.00]
Occupation	0.002* [0.00]	0.001* [0.00]	0.001** [0.00]	0.000** [0.00]	0.000 [0.00]	0.000 [0.00]
Marital status	0.285* [0.01]	0.113* [0.00]	0.021* [0.01]	0.005* [0.00]	−0.086* [0.01]	−0.017* [0.00]
Wealth index	0.253* [0.01]	0.101* [0.00]	0.822* [0.01]	0.205* [0.00]	0.132* [0.00]	0.026* [0.00]
Newspaper#	0.125* [0.01]	0.041* [0.00]	−0.010 0.01]	−0.003 [0.00]	0.068* [0.01]	0.014* [0.00]
HH members	−0.051* [0.00]	−0.024* [0.00]	−0.001 [0.00]	0.000 [0.00]	0.027* [0.00]	0.005* [0.00]
Electricity#	−0.137* [0.02]	−0.051* [0.01]	1.110* [0.02]	0.276* [0.00]	0.562* [0.01]	0.111* [0.00]
Edn level	0.344* [0.01]	0.131* [0.00]	0.093* [0.01]	0.023* [0.00]	0.031* [0.01]	0.006* [0.00]
Residence	−0.071* [0.01]	−0.021* [0.00]	0.008 [0.01]	0.002 [0.00]	0.199* [0.01]	0.039* [0.00]
Age group	0.050* [0.00]	0.012* [0.00]	0.023* [0.00]	0.006* [0.00]	0.033* [0.00]	0.007* [0.00]
Constant	−94.858* [5.99]		21.716* [7.15]		−229.559* [6.21]	
Number of observation	117,719		121,850		121,850	
Prob > chi^2	0.00		0.00		0.00	
Pseudo R^2	0.1788		0.4592		0.2097	

Source Computed from NFHS-IV, 2015–16 individual and household file
Note #Dummy; *$p < 0.01$, **$p < 0.05$, ***$p < 0.10$; SE is in the brackets
HH: Household, Edn: education, dy/dx: marginal effect, MFX: marginal effect probit regression, MFX_C: MFX computer, similarly for others

also significant at 1% level. The reverse trend is followed in the case of TV use (Table 6).

Married as compared to unmarried has lesser probability of holding computers, telephone and radio but just the reverse in case of TV.

The economic status of the individual is also explained through the standard of living. This paper considers the wealth index as a proxy of the standard of living. The wealth index is derived using Principal Component Analysis (PCA) method, which is the weighted average of many variables on expenditure incurred by the household. This is an ordinal variable. The wealth index is further categorized as poorest, poorer, middle, rich and richest. With the order of a higher degree of wealth

Table 6 Probit regression with interaction effect of reference category

	Model 7		Model 8		Model 9		Model 10	
	Computer	(Std. Err.)	Telephone	(Std. Err.)	TV	(Std. Err.)	Radio	(Std. Err.)
Caste: SC®								
ST	0.39*	0.08	−0.08**	0.04	−0.42*	0.03	0.02	0.02
OBC	0.20*	0.07	0.13*	0.03	−0.11*	0.02	0.05*	0.02
Gen	0.34*	0.07	0.18*	0.03	−0.15*	0.02	0.08*	0.02
DK			0.27	0.17	−0.06	0.12	−0.07	0.11
Married: never®								
Current	−0.23	0.44	−0.49***	0.28	0.79*	0.26	−0.01	0.20
Past	−0.14	0.45	−0.50***	0.29	0.57**	0.27	−0.16	0.20
Wealth: poorest®								
Poorer	3.15*	0.27	3.90		0.64*	0.03	0.58*	0.03
Middle	3.57		4.50*	0.08	1.15*	0.03	0.98*	0.03
Rich	3.95*	0.11	5.31*	0.07	1.85*	0.04	1.24*	0.03
Richest	4.87*	0.10	6.54*	0.08	2.91*	0.04	1.56*	0.03
News paper: no®								
Once a week	0.13**	0.06	0.13*	0.03	−0.02	0.02	0.12*	0.02
At least once	0.21*	0.06	0.23*	0.03	−0.04	0.03	0.19*	0.02
Everyday	0.47*	0.06	0.46*	0.03	−0.07***	0.04	0.29*	0.03
Electricity: no®								
Yes	0.52***	0.29	0.25*	0.06	0.70*	0.02	−0.26*	0.02
Education: no®								
Primary	0.06	0.10	0.02	0.04	0.13*	0.02	0.05**	0.02
Secondary	0.01	0.08	0.16*	0.04	0.20*	0.02	−0.01	0.02
Higher	0.68*	0.09	0.57*	0.04	0.49*	0.05	0.18*	0.03
Residence: capital®								
Small city	−0.08	0.05	0.12*	0.04	−0.04	0.04	−0.17*	0.03
Town	−0.09**	0.04	0.19*	0.03	0.01	0.03	−0.02	0.02
Countryside	−0.20*	0.05	0.63*	0.03	−0.07*	0.02	0.31*	0.02
Age: 15–19®								
20–24	−0.21***	0.12	0.01	0.06	0.03	0.04	−0.01	0.03
25–29	−0.20	0.12	0.01	0.06	−0.02	0.04	−0.02	0.03
30–34	−0.16	0.12	0.03	0.07	−0.11*	0.04	0.04	0.03
35–39	−0.13	0.13	0.06	0.07	−0.12*	0.04	0.09**	0.04
40–44	0.01	0.17	0.20***	0.10	−0.13**	0.06	0.10***	0.05
45–49			0.15	0.21	−0.11	0.12	0.17***	0.09
Constant	−6.91*	0.54	−7.08*	0.30	−2.65*	0.27	−1.55*	0.20
Number of obs.	46,060		46,060		46,071		46,059	
Prob > chi^2	0		0		0		0	
Pseudo R^2	0.4341		0.4341		0.4319		0.0959	

Source Computed from NFHS-III individual and household file
$*p < 0.01$, $**p < 0.05$, $***p < 0.10$
®Is the reference category

index, the probability of all ICT holdings increase, and almost all are significant at 1% level as the unit change in the wealth index. Thus, wealth is a very important predictor of ICT diffusion.

The frequency of reading newspaper has been considered to be an important medium for better access to information. They are reading the newspaper as a variable categorized as 'not reading at all', 'once a week', 'at least once' and 'every day'. For the diffusion of computer, telephone and radio are increasingly positive across groups that confirm newspaper as an important indicator, except for the diffusion of TV. The coefficients of other categories in the newspaper group are negative as compared to people who don't read the newspaper at all. People who watch TV may not feel necessary to go to read the newspaper for further information.

Households having electricity possess more ICT devices than in case of radio access which doesn't necessarily require electricity. Education as a factor clarifies the understanding that with the increase in the level of education, the probability increases and most of the coefficients are significant. Thus, education plays an important part in ICT content.

Place of resident matters for the diffusion of the computer a lot. As already argued in the literature that network effect, agglomeration does matter much. This is because the spread of computer and internet requires huge entry cost. The supporting infrastructure for this also possible if the number of users is more.

Age matters for the young age to use more of ICT devices except for the use of radio. The newly developed devices attract more of young age people than the old as evident from this result. The results in this table are very appropriate and robust as the average coefficient is strongly significant (prob > chi^2 approximate to zero) and the pseudo R^2 is closed to 0.5 except for radio.

4.2 Robustness Check

To check the robustness of the model and the variables which influence the use of ICT, we develop a pooled data of 10 years period using NFHS-III and IV. The pooled regression results also support our previous regression results in identifying the relevant variables for policy analysis (Tables 7 and 9).

5 Conclusion

The ICT access over time has been uneven, and changes therein are also significant as observed across socio-economic characteristics in India. The access to ICT in certain indicators of rural areas are catching up. The analysis using the latest rounds of NFHS data assures the differences. Theoretical arguments also support these empirical findings. The existing literature addresses various dimensions of the divide in accessing ICT between rich and poor.

Table 7 Pooled probit regression with marginal effects

	Model 7 (Telephone)		Model 8 (TV)		Model 9 (Radio)	
	β	dy/dx	β	dy/dx	β	dy/dx
Caste	−0.314* [0.00]	−0.098* [0.00]	−0.235* [0.00]	−0.086* [0.00]	0.319* [0.01]	0.103* [0.00]
Occupation	0.004* [0.00]	0.001* [0.00]	0.002* [0.00]	0.001* [0.00]	0.001 [0.00]	0.000 [0.00]
Marital status	0.128* [0.01]	0.040* [0.00]	−0.023* [0.01]	−0.008* [0.00]	−0.100* [0.01]	−0.032* [0.00]
Wealth index	0.341* [0.00]	0.106* [0.00]	0.711* [0.00]	0.259* [0.00]	0.310* [0.00]	0.100* [0.00]
Newspaper#	0.128* [0.00]	0.040* [0.00]	−0.013* [0.00]	−0.005* [0.00]	0.094* [0.00]	0.030* [0.00]
HH members	0.006* [0.00]	0.002* [0.00]	0.026* [0.00]	0.010* [0.00]	0.022* [0.00]	0.007* [0.00]
Electricity#	0.236* [0.01]	0.069* [0.00]	0.956* [0.01]	0.366* [0.00]	−0.273* [0.00]	−0.093* [0.00]
Edn level	0.337* [0.00]	0.105* [0.00]	0.149* [0.00]	0.054* [0.00]	−0.013* [0.00]	−0.004* [0.00]
Residence	0.171* [0.01]	0.053* [0.00]	−0.061* [0.01]	−0.022* [0.00]	0.211* [0.01]	0.068* [0.00]
Age group	0.080* [0.00]	0.025* [0.00]	0.041* [0.00]	0.015* [0.00]	0.025* [0.00]	0.008* [0.00]
Constant	−2.661* [0.02]		−2.642* [0.02]		−2.665* [0.02]	
Number of observations	343,647		343,647		343,647	
Prob > chi^2	0.00		0.00		0.00	
Pseudo R^2	0.2244		0.4324		0.1222	

Source Computed from using a pooled data of NFHS 2004–5 and 2015–16
Note #Dummy; *$p < 0.01$, **$p < 0.05$, ***$p < 0.10$; SE is in the brackets
HH: Household, Edn: education, MFX: marginal effect probit regression, MFX_C: MFX computer, similarly for others

The results of probit regression with marginal effect for each device indicate that caste, size of the household, occupation, marriage and location of the household significantly affect the use of ICT devices. The role of education is also important. The interaction effect also confirms the conclusion that place and inherent network effect, sex, education, age (young age), occupation and caste are the dominant factors of ICT diffusion in India.

Table 8 Variable descriptions

Variable	Type	Obs.	Mean	Std. Dev.	Min	Max
Agegroup	Categorical	123,691	3.468	1.900	1	7
Location	Dummy	123,691	1.541	0.498	1	2
Education	Categorical	123,691	1.323	1.033	0	3
Electricity	Dummy	123,691	1.082	1.334	0	1
Radio	Dummy	123,691	0.679	1.444	0	1
Television	Dummy	123,691	0.883	1.404	0	1
HHmembers	Numeric	123,691	6.006	2.951	1	35
Telephone	Dummy	123,691	0.515	1.455	0	1
Newspaper	Categorical	123,691	0.930	1.164	0	3
Wealth index	Categorical	123,691	3.500	1.356	1	5
Married	Categorical	123,691	0.800	0.503	0	2
Occupation	Numerical	123,691	82.785	34.098	1	20
Caste	Categorical	118,987	2.537	0.850	1	4

Source Computed from NFHS-IV

The urban–rural divide is increasing primarily due to negligible ICT coverage in rural areas as compared to urban areas and policies must ensure rural teledensity to ensure the access faster. This is going to be possible when rural growth is mobile and competition-driven, like in urban areas. At present, there is less rural mobile coverage, and the growth is majorly PSU (public sector undertaking) driven. Unless it is competition-driven, growth will continue to be stagnant, but this has to be followed with caution.

The analysis in this paper further suggests that the gap between rural and urban is very high. The major effort may be considered to transform the local spoken and written languages into a universally used set of computer codes, fonts, and so on. This will act as an instrument of better information. The second need is for operating systems and useful software that is relevant to, and that speaks to the needs of the local people. This could be ascertained by the so-called 'generic' software which helps the rural people to know the application quickly.

Acknowledgements Some of the contents of this paper were presented at the Paris 2017: Econworld conference in 2017, Paris. This paper was not submitted for publication elsewhere. I am the sole author of this paper. The revised version of this paper was also presented at the two-day workshop on 'Economics of ICTs: Transformation, Digital Divides and Development' at the Delhi School of Economics (22–23 Feb. 2018).

Table 9 Variable description of Pooled regression model

Variable	Type	Obs.	Mean	Std. Dev.	Min	Max
Agegroup	Categorical	699,686	3.609	1.955	1	7
Location	Dummy	699,686	1.707	0.455	1	2
Education	Categorical	699,686	1.426	1.017	0	3
Electricity	Dummy	699,686	1.087	1.113	0	1
Radio	Dummy	699,686	0.319	1.246	0	1
Caste	Categorical	697,461	1.259	0.661	1	4
HHmembers	Numerical	699,686	5.790	2.657	1	41
Newspaper	Categorical	699,686	0.752	1.073	0	3
Wealth index	Categorical	699,686	2.979	1.387	1	5
Occupation	Numerical	122,351	2.684	10.614	1	20
Telephone	Dummy	118,215	0.463	0.499	0	1

Source Computed from the pooled data of NFHS-III and IV

Appendix

References

Augereau, A., & Greenstein, S. (2001). The need for speed in emerging communications markets: Upgrades to advanced technology at Internet Service Providers. *International Journal of Industrial Organization, 19*(7), 1085–1102.

Castells, M. (2002). *The Internet galaxy: Reflections on the Internet, business, and society*. Oxford: Oxford University Press on Demand.

Cecchini, S., & Scott, C. (2003). Can information and communications technology applications contribute to poverty reduction? Lessons from rural India. *Information Technology for Development, 10*(2), 73–84.

Dasgupta, S., Lall, S., & Wheeler, D. (2001). *Policy reform, economic growth, and the digital divide: An econometric analysis* (Vol. 2567). World Bank Publications.

Downes, T., & Greenstein, S. (2007). Understanding why universal service obligations may be unnecessary: The private development of local Internet access markets. *Journal of Urban Economics, 62*(1), 2–26.

Eastin, M. S., Cicchirillo, V., & Mabry, A. (2015). Extending the digital divide conversation: Examining the knowledge gap through media expectancies. *Journal of Broadcasting & Electronic Media, 59*(3), 416–437.

Forman, C., Goldfarb, A., & Greenstein, S. (2005). *Technology adoption in and out of major urban areas: When do internal firm resources matter most?* (No. w11642). National Bureau of Economic Research.

Gaspar, J., & Glaeser, E. L. (1998). Information technology and the future of cities. *Journal of Urban Economics, 43*(1), 136–156.

ITU. (1998). Methodological note on the choice of teledensity band. https://www.itu.int/osg/spu/intset/focus/bands.pdf. Accessed July 20, 2017.

Kambhampati, U. S. (2002). The software industry and development: The case of India. *Progress in Development Studies, 2*(1), 23–45.

Philip, L., Cottrill, C., Farrington, J., Williams, F., & Ashmore, F. (2017). The digital divide: Patterns, policy and scenarios for connecting the 'final few' in rural communities across Great Britain. *Journal of Rural Studies, 54,* 386–398.

Reilly, K., & Gómez, R. (2001). Comparing approaches: Telecentre evaluation experiences in Asia and Latin America. *The Electronic Journal of Information Systems in Developing Countries, 4*(1), 1–17.

Salemink, K., Strijker, D., & Bosworth, G. (2017). Rural development in the digital age: A systematic literature review on unequal ICT availability, adoption, and use in rural areas. *Journal of Rural Studies, 54,* 360–371.

Servon, L. J. (2008). *Bridging the digital divide: Technology, community and public policy*. London: Wiley.

Singh, N. (2008). Transaction costs, information technology and development. *Indian Growth and Development Review, 1*(2), 212–236.

Van Deursen, A. J., Helsper, E., Eynon, R., & Van Dijk, J. A. (2017). The compoundness and sequentiality of digital inequality. *International Journal of Communication, 11,* 452–473.

Effect of ICT on the Performance of Indian States in Terms of Human Development Indices

Chiranjib Neogi

Abstract The differences among the states in terms of Human Development Index (HDI) can be an outcome of the performance of the regional governments. The components of HDI can be taken as services produced by the state governments while some variables like tax collection of states, population, etc. can be considered as inputs of the states. The differences in the capacity of states in the utilization of grants and revenue of the states are important determinants in explaining the disparities among the states. The objective of the central government is to go for balanced development of different regions. The ICT is expected to improve social indicators like performances in health, education, etc., by effective utilization of social expenditure by states, and can potentially reduce the regional disparity in India. Identifying some services as output produced by some inputs in the different state governments in India, we rank the states according to their performances using Data Envelope Analysis (DEA). We have further estimated the target output that a state government should emphasize for its overall development. We have identified that the ICT, defined as a composite of teledensity, internet and mobile use, has been a responsible factor for the variation of performance of the state governments in terms of improvement of social indicators.

JEL Classification H0 · H11 · O40 · O47

1 Introduction

Unlike many European and East-Asian countries, India is a vast country with her heterogeneous population in terms of cast creed and culture, and availability of natural resources. Also, there is a wide variation in topographical character in different regions. All these characters differentiate the level of development across the states of India. The objective of the government is to build an egalitarian society, coupled with the balanced development of different regions. Government interventions were

---

C. Neogi (✉)
Guest Faculty, Department of Economics, West Bengal State University, B-10/244, Kalyani, West Bengal 741235, India
e-mail: cneogi@yahoo.co.uk

D. Maiti et al. (eds.), *Digitalisation and Development*,
https://doi.org/10.1007/978-981-13-9996-1_11

envisaged to prevent the lopsided development of the states. The level of development of states is likely to be the consequence of a complex set of historical, cultural, and sociological factors of the states in a federal setting. However, the difference in the capacity of the utilization of grants and revenue by the states is the most important for explaining the disparities among the states. Therefore, to understand the difference in the development of states, the relative performance of states given resources should be measured. Whether The ICT helps them to improve performance and leads them to converse are the issues of our interest in this paper. In most of the conventional studies on regional imbalances, the assessment of inequality in India is undertaken based on statistical indices of GDP as a given norm. However, the comparative disadvantage of the regions should be studied in terms of some socio-economic profiles based on the Human Development Index. This has not been viewed yet in the literature.

It has generally been observed that a state is underdeveloped because of its poor natural resources, weak institutions and the social environment is not conducive for generating enough economic activity. However, some states are developed by efficiently managing limited resources. The basic question is that what policies a less developed state should take to catch up with the fast-growing states and whether ICT is helping to do so. To understand the issues of the factors behind the difference of growth among states and what could be the possible way out in narrowing the development gap among the states it will be necessary to discuss the variations of some indicators across states over the last couple of decades in detail. Recognizing the need for equitable growth to flow over all sections of the population, the 'inclusive growth' is the major thrust of The Eleventh Five-Year Plan (2007–12). It has been understood that the benefits of growth have not reached all parts of the country equitably.

The ranking of the regions in terms of the degree of development has been a major study area in the development literature. Regions are considered as economic areas because the harmonious development of all the regions is essential for economic progress and sustainable development of a country like India. The ranking of the regions is considered in terms of the development of some social and economic indicators given the available resources of a region. There are different ways to identify the rank of a region in a multi-criteria development model. In this study, we use the Data Envelopment Analysis (DEA) to rank the regions based on the efficient use of available resources of the regions. Here, regions are considered as the administrative area defined as a state. The characteristics of these states are diverse, and the degree of development varies widely among these states.

Several authors have studied the impact of Information and Communication Technology (ICT) in economic growth during the last few decades. However, the effect of ICT on social indicators like performances in health, education, etc. is comparatively less discussed, particularly in the context of regional disparity of a country. Some social indicators, like health or education, can be identified as service produced by the regional government using some inputs, including the investment in ICTs. It can be argued that difference in availability of ICT divides the society digitally due to the difference in the information available to those who have access to internet or broadband facilities. Rural areas and poor section of the population have less accessibility of internet facility and/or computer facility for which these sections of the society have to face the problem of asymmetric information in every sphere of activity. It has been argued that the strategic approach of using ICT is followed by many governments to strengthen the performance of its public sector in providing high-quality public services to its citizens and businesses. Efforts are made by introducing e-governance to boost the efficiency and effectiveness of the public sector through coordination across various levels of government. However, empirical analyses of the effect of ICT on the efficiency of state governments in India have not been found in recent years. In this study, empirical analysis has been made to find the effect of ICT on the efficiency of various state governments in India.

The objective of this study is twofold. First, the comparative positions of the states in terms of HDI are identified, and the effects of ICT on the components of HDI are investigated. Second, the efficiency of state governments in terms of economic and social development to the society given resources of the states and the factors affecting the efficiency are investigated empirically using Data Envelopment Analysis.

The paper is organized in the following way. In Sect. 2, a brief literature survey has been done on regional disparities among the states and on the relationship between human development and ICT. In Sect. 3, a detailed measure of different socio-economic characters is done, and the position of some selected states in terms of those characteristics is observed over the last few decades and their relationship with ICT. In Sect. 4, we discuss the data and methodology of DEA and advantages of the use of different measures of Productivity Indices. Section 5 deals with empirical analysis of efficiency of state and discusses the factors including ICT behind the variation of efficiencies of states over the period of study. Finally, some concluding remarks are made in Sect. 6.

2 Literature Review

Hirschman (1973) in an article argued that in an early stage of development inequalities of income among different groups of people and different regions of a country increases but the deprived section of the population would expect that over time the disparities become narrow and the benefit of growth ultimately reach to them. However, if this will not happen, then a catastrophic situation may occur in the country concerned. He also argued that everyone expects that the situation will improve and his or her turn will come in due course which Hirschman termed and "Tunnel effect". As long as the tunnel effect lasts, everybody feels better off, both those who have become richer and those who have not. Thus, during this period, a lopsided growth may be preferred from an egalitarian distribution by all member of society. However, inequality of income or development for a considerably long period may bring social and political disturbances in the region.

It has been observed in many studies that the on-going economic reforms since 1991 with liberalization and deregulation policies as their central pieces seem to have further widened the regional disparities during the early phase of liberalization

(Marjit and Mitra 1996; Ghosh et al. 1998). In a recent article, Bash et al. (2015) have undertaken an exercise to understand the regional backwardness in India over the last few decades. The state-level analysis of this study concludes that there is no sign of absolute convergence of per capita income over the last few plan periods while the study found a convergence of HDI during the same period. The district-level analysis suggests that districts are polarized in terms of different development criteria during the last few decades. It also suggests that the most intense forms of poverty and deprivation getting increasingly concentrated within backward communities of India. In another study by Dash (2014) investigation are done to find the influence of government intervention in terms of the size of public expenditure in the reduction of interstate disparities over the last three decades. An empirical investigation is done to find the link between policy interventions of the governments, measured through decentralization policies and income differences across the Indian states. It was suggested in the study that there is a positive relationship between increasing both central and local government expenditure and reduction in disparity among the states. Kumar et al. (2014) made an elaborate study on the regional disparities among the states over last few decades and have argued for more inclusive growth. The study found that there is no remarkable change in the relative position of the states in terms of various Human development indicators.

Mundle et al. (2016), in their paper, analyzed the efficiency of public spending. They argued that the outcome of public expenditure covered all long-term effects of public programmes in terms of the welfare of the society and stressed the importance of studying efficiency and effectiveness of public spending. Among the many suggestions, they suggested the use of information and communication technology (ICT) as an effective tool to improve the efficiency of government. Sustainable growth is one of the main preconditions of economic development that enhance the well-being of society. GDP is the most common criteria of development. However, development is considered as a process that changes in the quality of life, empowerment, enhancing basic capabilities, equality, and poverty reduction (Pieterse 2001). Information and knowledge base of an economy is always important for human development. The microelectronics based information and communication technologies (ICTs), with all its consequences has the ability to (i) create organizational forms (ii) the infrastructure and the rapidity of processing information, transforming it into knowledge and (iii) using these transformations into knowledge to make actual changes in the production system. Freedom to access information through ICT generates human capital and thus enhances the quality of life. The information and communication technology is important not only because it increases the ability of society to generate and produce more, but also it changes the social conditions and the conditions of stability.

The process of globalization depends on three conditions. First, the *technological infrastructure* (or ICT) that allows for a global information system without border. Second, an *organizational form or networking* that allows for greater efficiency and greater capacity to manage information and communication on a global scale. Thirdly, *an institutional condition* is the way that opens up the connection between different states at the global level so that the networks can articulate activities across countries. Development based on modern information technology should focus on the freedom to access information where ICT enhances development by influencing a change in the quality of life through the innovation and diffusion of human-oriented technologies.

In modern society, the whole planet is interconnected to get access to any valuable resources or information by a computer network. Productivity growth of any economy can be linked to the relationship between strong networking, and human resources increase productivity, which leads to economic growth by diffusing information and knowledge. Knowledge and information have been important in production not only for high-tech industries but by using better information in the traditional industries like tourism, agriculture and even fish farming the physical output or service can be improved. Information and communication technology also have a varied impact on both middle and higher education. The less developed countries tapping into global networks can get access to improved knowledge that develops primary and secondary education without having their quality. Also, higher education systems can have enough knowledge and research by connecting the global networks of research. It is observed that access to communication is directly correlated not only to economic growth but also to a reduction of poverty.

Good governance states ability to manage effectively the transition to development, which is conditional on the implementation of good policies. These policies aim to promote democracy, reduce corruption, increase transparency, and expand human capabilities. There is an indication that e-government implementation would lead to better governance in the way that government agencies and institutions with greater access to various ICTs promote the reorganization of governments' internal and external information flows over the Internet. The lack of appropriate incentives and a weak property rights structure are responsible for state failure that leads to underdevelopment (North 1981). Development of laggard regions is a complex political process, with fast-changing institutional structures and rapid capital accumulation of other regions. For a less developed state, technology should be introduced to order the state functioning according to a precise model to move towards the neoclassical ideal state model. Such process entails the re-alignment of its functions and relationships not only internally, but also with outside markets. It is found that the models inscribed in the ICT based government will ultimately deliver economic and social development.

3 Data

Data for this study has been collected from both government and non-government organizations. Population and demographic related data are collected primarily from the data published from Census of India. The decadal data of population figures are collected from the Census of India publications. However, data for the mid-year population are collected from the publications of the Ministry of Statistics and Programme Implementation (MOSPI) and Planning Commission and Office of the

Registrar General of India, Ministry of Home Affairs. Values of Per Capita Net State Domestic Product (PCNSDP) is collected from two sources, namely, Reserve Bank of India publications and Website of Niti Yaog Government of India. Figures for Life expectancy at birth are collected from Census of India and Government of India websites. Similarly, state-wise figures for literacy have been collected from the Census of India and the Government of India websites. The basic source of data for various components of Information and Communication Technology are collected from the Telecom Regulatory Authority of India (TRAI), Government of India. The basic source of state-wise figures on poverty is the Planning Commission of India and NSSO. Data on state-wise tax revenue are taken from the publications of Reserve Bank of India. Data on state-wise police personnel and crime record have been collected from Indiastat website. However, their basic sources are different organizations of India Government.

4 Status of States in Terms of Some Socio-economic Index

Since the inception of the planning process in India in the 1950s, a major issue of the economic policy was to foster 'balanced' development among the states. The policy of 'freight-equalization' and subsidies to industries in backward regions were the basic policies towards harmonious progress of the nation. It has been argued that in the long run, the 'crowding out' effects may have a negative impact on further development, and, the role of market forces tends to increase rather than decrease the inequalities between the competing regions. The enriched regions, with natural geographic scopes for ports, roads, good soil conditions, may gain a 'competitive advantage' (Myrdal 1958; Porter 1990).

Human Development Reports, developed by the United Nations Development Programme (UNDP), is the well-accepted method of measuring the HDI that includes life expectancy at birth, adult literacy; gross enrolment in primary, secondary, and tertiary education, and gross domestic product per capita. This index allows for a ranking of countries to provide quick feedback to policymakers. The *National Human Development Report 2001* prepared by the Planning Commission uses somewhat different indicators but follows a similar approach. The value of these indices lies in their simplicity and the focus on a limited number of variables. In a diverse country like India, only HDI cannot reflect the livelihood status of the population. "It would be a great mistake to concentrate on the Human Development Index. These are useful indicators in rough and ready work: but the real merit of the human development approach lies in the plural attention it brings to bear on development evaluation, not in the aggregative measures it presents as an aid to diverse statistics." Sen (2000).

Here we will discuss our method of calculation of HDI in India and the status of each state according to the composite HDI index and according to its components. Planning commission of India uses to estimate the HDI of some discrete years and rank the states according to those indices.

Enlarging People's choices is one of the basic purposes of the human development process. It focuses on three essential components: a long and healthy life, knowledge, and "access to resources needed for a decent standard of living" because, "if these essential choices are not available, many other opportunities remain inaccessible." (UNDP 1990). It is argued that in many societies, GNP can increase while human well-being is not achieved, and there are other factors which influence the actual well-being of the societies. On the other hand, better nutrition and health service, a better access of knowledge, better working conditions, better cultural environment, and security against violence are some of the factors which influence the human development apart from the higher income of society.

It is recognized that disparities in development across the states have been the major issue for adopting planning process in India since independence. During the last few decades of planned development in India, private investment has also been encouraged through public policies besides massive government investment in backward regions. Achievements were not often commensurate with these efforts from both public and private levels to reduce regional disparities in India. As a result, a considerable level of regional disparities is found still today. It has been found in many studies (Ghosh et al. 1998) that the on-going economic reforms since 1991 with stabilization and deregulation policies as their central themes seem to have further widened the regional disparities. The income disparity among the states can be visualized from the increasing values of coefficient of variations of PCNSDP over the years (the values are 0.385, 0.449 and 0.450 for the years 2001, 2011 and 2015, respectively). The seriousness of the emerging acute regional imbalances has not yet received the public attention it deserves.

The main concern of the Government of India is despite various measures taken to reduce the poverty level and other socio-economic disparities there is a wide disparity of the values of those indicators among the states. Some states are lagging far behind the other high growth states in terms of many social and economic indicators. The basic question that emerged was what policies a less developed state would take to catch up with the fast-growing states. Let us discuss some issues on the factors behind the difference of growth among states and what could be the possible way out in narrowing the development gap among the states. Recognizing the need to make growth 'more inclusive' in terms of benefits of growth flowing to all sections of population 'inclusive growth' is the major thrust of The Eleventh Five-Year Plan (2007–12). It has been understood that the benefits of growth have not reached all parts of the country equitably. In contrast to the conventional results of the developed countries, Indian states have been diverging over the period. However, the role of planning through the disbursement of development funds across the states is an essential process for holistic development (Ghosh et al. 1998). Several papers were published in different national and international journals on the issue of convergence in India. However, the conclusions of those papers regarding growth and convergence are not unidirectional. The national character of most of the developed countries, particularly the small countries are homogeneous in terms of their economic and social indicators. On the contrary, the national character of India in terms of her population, geography, culture and economy is diverse. Thus, this heterogeneity is also reflected in the economic and social development of different regions in India. The basic issue of planning in India is to foster 'balanced' regional development with active support for industrialization in backward regions as well as through minimizing interregional disparities in costs and prices. Harmonious progress of the nation through 'freight-equalization' and subsidies to industries in backward regions is one of the policies of the Government of India. But the disparity of all-round development among the states is still a major concern of the policy personnel.

Let us first review the latest positions of the states in terms of some major indicators. If we do not consider the figures of Union Territories the Census of 2011 tells us that population density of the states varies from 17 persons per square kilometre in Arunachal Pradesh to 1102 in Bihar, which indicates a wide variety of demographic character of Indian states. In terms of literacy rate, Kerala is the most advanced states with 93.3% literate population while the figure of Bihar is only 67%. According to the Human Development Report of India 2011, the infrastructural Development Index (IDI) shows a wide variation among the states. Values of the IDI in the states like Bihar, Orissa, Assam, MP and Rajasthan are cradled around 88. While the States like Punjab and Kerala, the figure is above 150. It is found from the values of HDI and the values of IDI that there is a correlation between these two values. However, there are some states with high IDI but low HDI and vice versa. But the figures of inequality indicate that many states with high IDI and HDI have a very high value of inequality. For example, Tamil Nadu with a very high value of IDI (149.3) shows 22.9% of the people are below the poverty line while Rajasthan with the lowest value of IDI (75.9) have only 18.7% of population below the poverty line.

We will now discuss the inequalities in some social indicators and HDI across the regions of India as we have already discussed that we follow the UNDP definition of HDI, where we have considered three basic components, namely, health, education and income. First, we will discuss the disparities among the states regarding these three aspects. Table 1 shows the actual values of life expectancy at birth and the corresponding index calculated using the method developed by UNDP.

In some cases, we have taken some fixed values instead of the minimum value of an indicator. In this case, we have taken 25 years as the minimum value of life expectancy at birth. The mean values show that there is an increasing trend of life expectancy at birth in India, and there are large variations in the values. However, this disparity is scaling down over the period.

Table 9 (in Appendix) indicates that health index indicates that Kerala was always on top during the whole period. Some of the states like Haryana, Himachal Pradesh, Maharashtra and Punjab are in the upper rung of the ladder. It has been observed that there is an overall growth of all the states of health index during this period. The similar index was constructed for education and income for the construction of the Human Development Index.

It is observed from Table 10 that the position of Kerala is always on top in literacy index. The trend of literacy index is improving over time, and the variation among the states is decreasing over time. However, the literacy level of Uttar Pradesh, Rajasthan and Bihar are not impressive compared to the other states.

Next, we consider the income index of the states over the period under consideration. We have taken the PCNSDP data from Reserve Bank of India data source. It is observed in Table 11 that there are wide variances in the values of PCNSDP index among the states. Maharashtra is always on the top of the list. Some states like Haryana, Karnataka, Tamil Nadu and Punjab are in the upper rung of the list. On the other hand, Orissa, Bihar, Assam and Uttar Pradesh fall in the lower rung of the table.

For calculation of HDI of the states, we relied on the simple HDI indices using (i) weighted linear combination of this index and (ii) geometric mean of these indices. There is hardly any difference of values of HDI using the arithmetic mean and the geometric mean of the states. Also, the ranks of the states are almost similar for both the indices. The state-wise figures in Tables 1 and 2 indicate that Kerala, Punjab, Haryana and Gujarat maintained high ranks in Human Development over the last four decades. On the other hand, Andhra Pradesh, Assam, Bihar, Rajasthan and Uttar Pradesh were in the lower rung of the table of HDI over these years. So there is a marked difference in the performance among the states in terms of human

Table 1 HDI of some major states for three different years

State	HDI index (arithmetic mean)			HDI index (geometric mean)		
	2000–01	2010–11	2014–15	2000–01	2010–11	2014–15
Andhra Pradesh	0.6492	0.7104	0.7163	0.6483	0.7098	0.7157
Assam	0.4954	0.5676	0.5857	0.4699	0.5420	0.5633
Bihar	0.0401	0.5561	0.5846	0.3294	0.5288	0.5669
Gujarat	0.7146	0.8050	0.8108	0.7116	0.8025	0.8073
Haryana	0.7619	0.8038	0.8107	0.7537	0.7999	0.8057
Himachal Pradesh	0.7134	0.7605	0.7676	0.7125	0.7603	0.7675
Karnataka	0.6934	0.7371	0.7529	0.6924	0.7369	0.7527
Kerala	0.7864	0.8295	0.8408	0.7779	0.8249	0.8373
Maharashtra	0.8224	0.8203	0.8688	0.8128	0.8061	0.8638
Madhya Pradesh	0.5331	0.6407	0.6379	0.5251	0.6286	0.6348
Orissa	0.5121	0.6261	0.6337	0.4940	0.6185	0.6241
Punjab	0.8026	0.7782	0.7903	0.7940	0.7777	0.7898
Rajasthan	0.5775	0.6487	0.6693	0.5759	0.6458	0.6684
Tamil Nadu	0.7385	0.7886	0.8148	0.7371	0.7876	0.8133
Uttar Pradesh	0.5018	0.5838	0.5954	0.4911	0.5673	0.5834
West Bengal	0.6628	0.7516	0.7656	0.6626	0.7515	0.7656

Source Author

Table 2 Ranks of the states according to HDI for three different years

State	HDI index (arithmetic mean)			HDI index (geometric mean)		
	HDI 2001	HDI 2011	HDI 2015	HDI 2001	HDI 2011	HDI 2015
Andhra Pradesh	10	10	10	10	10	10
Assam	15	15	15	15	15	16
Bihar	16	16	16	16	16	15
Gujarat	6	3	4	7	3	4
Haryana	4	4	5	4	4	5
Himachal Pradesh	7	7	7	6	7	7
Karnataka	8	9	9	8	9	9
Kerala	3	1	2	3	1	2
Madhya Pradesh	12	12	12	12	12	12
Maharashtra	1	2	1	1	2	1
Orissa	13	13	13	13	13	13
Punjab	2	6	6	2	6	6
Rajasthan	11	11	11	11	11	11
Tamil Nadu	5	5	3	5	5	3
Uttar Pradesh	14	14	14	14	14	14
West Bengal	9	8	8	9	8	8

development over this period of study as we have said earlier that there are some qualitative differences in terms of topology, culture and socio-economic structure of the states. In the next section, we have calculated the efficiencies of these states in terms of some socio-economic indicators and tried to understand the reasons for differences in the performance (Figs. 1, 2, 3 and 4).

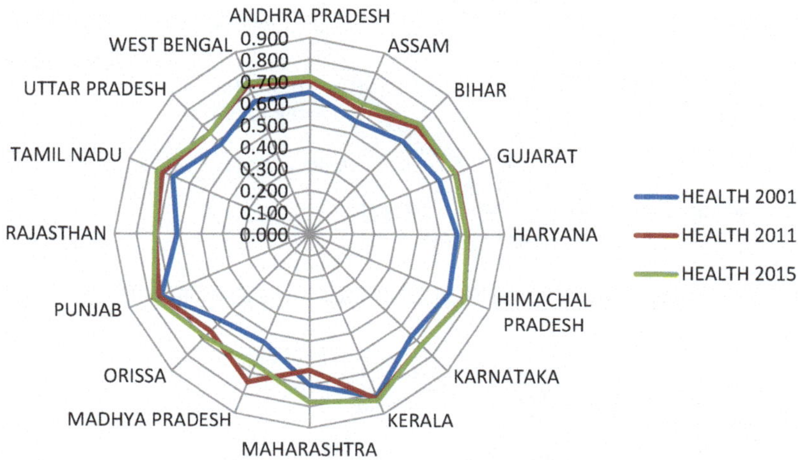

Fig. 1 Comparative position of health indices of states over the period 2001–2015

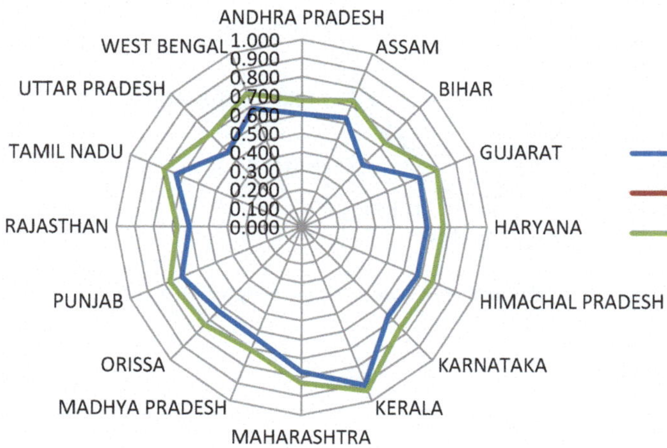

Fig. 2 Comparative position of literacy indices of states over the period 2001–2015

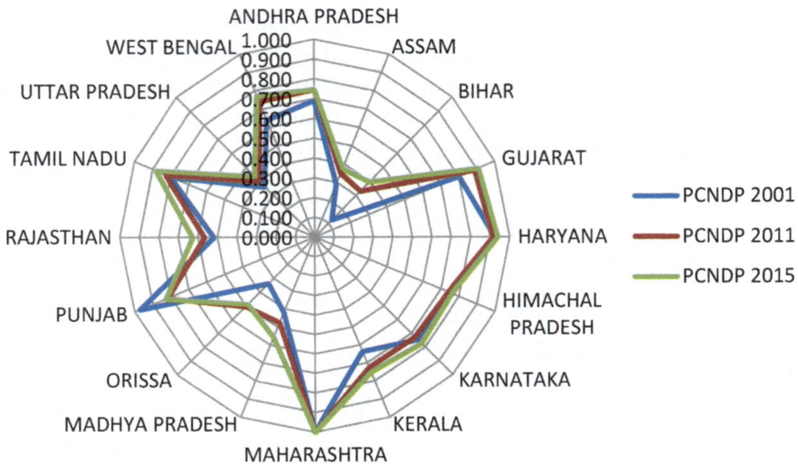

Fig. 3 Comparative position of PCNSDP indices of states over the period 2001–2015

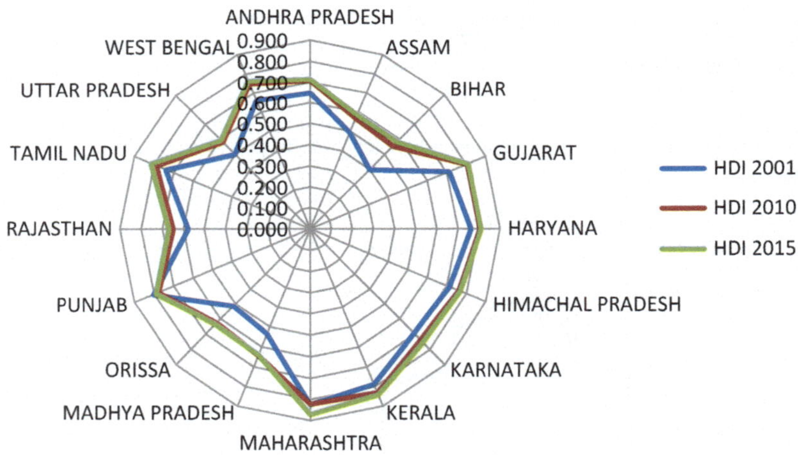

Fig. 4 Comparative position of HDI indices of states over the period 2001–2015

5 ICT and HDI

Several authors have studied the impact of Information and Communication Technology (ICT) in the economic growth of countries during the last few decades. A group of studies relating to ICT deals with the effect of IT industries on the growth of any country or regions. Also, some studies examine the effect of IT industries on the efficiencies of regions of a country. However, the effect of ICT on social indicators like performances in health, education, etc. is comparatively less discussed, particularly in the context of regional disparity of a country. The difference in the availability of ICT divides the society digitally due to the difference in the information available to those who have access to internet or broadband facilities. Rural areas and poor section of the population have less accessibility of internet facility and computer facility for which these sections of the society have to face the problem of asymmetric information in every sphere of activity. In this section, we will try to understand the issue of performance of Indian states in terms of social and economic indicators and the impact of ICT availability index on those indicators.

The analysis of this section faces severe problem due to non-availability of consistent data throughout this study. Data on ICT in India was very scanty, and there is no data from any authentic source on internet and computer use before the year 2000. During the year 2000 around TRAI use to provide information on the use of the phone (both land and mobile), use of computer and internet in India, etc. Data on different components of ICT are available in the portal of TRAI and other sources. However, the data on different components of ICT varies from time to time. Naturally, during the early phase, data were available for only limited items of ICT and only recently data on various components are available from various sources, including TRAI. So, we have collected data on each component of ICT for three different years 2001, 2011 and 2015.

Based on these data, we have tried to find out the availability index of each component of ICT (Table 3). However, there are data on some similar items available for any particular year, and we have considered only those items which are uncorrelated. From the indexes of these items, we have constructed two indexes.

1. Simple ICT availability index of states where weights for each component are equal.
2. Indexes are also computed using Principal Component Analysis (PCA) where weights are calculated using "varimax" method.

The components of ICT for different years are the followings:

2001

- State-wise Number of Internet Subscribers in India
- State-wise Teledensity in Rural Areas of India
- State-wise Teledensity in Urban Areas of India
- State-wise Teledensity in India-Total

2010

- State-wise Teledensity in Rural Areas of India
- State-wise Teledensity in Urban Areas of India
- State-wise Teledensity in India-Total
- Percent of households with internet
- Percent of households with landline

Table 3 ICT index of some major states for three different years

State	2010		2011		2015	
	ICT index	PCA ICT	ICT index	PCA ICT	ICT index	ICT PCA
Andhra Pradesh	0.355	−0.269	0.297	−0.242	0.342	−0.441
Assam	0.300	−0.461	0.137	−0.165	0.145	−0.604
Bihar	0.252	−1.186	0.124	−0.940	0.046	−1.723
Gujarat	0.331	0.050	0.298	−0.346	0.437	0.437
Haryana	0.335	0.159	0.488	0.167	0.328	0.426
Himachal Pradesh	0.583	2.754	0.749	−0.534	0.835	0.429
Karnataka	0.354	0.136	0.410	1.046	0.496	0.513
Kerala	0.614	1.181	0.733	2.766	0.697	1.272
Maharashtra	0.509	0.496	0.423	1.017	0.436	0.416
Madhya Pradesh	0.133	−0.794	0.092	−0.758	0.133	−0.717
Orissa	0.271	−0.669	0.105	−1.064	0.153	−1.203
Punjab	0.409	0.885	0.524	0.774	0.611	1.733
Rajasthan	0.240	−0.558	0.259	−0.933	0.291	−0.433
Tamil Nadu	0.280	0.177	0.412	0.229	0.585	1.377
Uttar Pradesh	0.086	−1.070	0.215	−0.698	0.093	−1.338
West Bengal	0.232	−0.830	0.207	−0.320	0.262	−0.141

- Percent of households with mobile
- Percent of households with internet computer
- Percent of households without internet computer
- Wireline teledensity Rural
- Wireline teledensity Urban
- Wireless teledensity Rural
- Wireless teledensity Urban

2015

- Teledensity Rural
- Teledensity Urban
- Teledensity Total
- Percent of households with Internet
- Percent of households with Landline
- Percent of households with Mobile
- Percent of households with Computer with Net
- Percent of households with Computer without Net
- Wireline teledensity Rural
- Wireline teledensity Urban
- Wireless teledensity Rural
- Wireless teledensity Urban

Next, we tried to find out the relation of these indexes with different components of socio-economic indicators. These relationships are tested using a simple correlation between variables and corresponding values of t-test.

From Table 4 it is found that Kerala, Himachal Pradesh, Maharashtra and Punjab are much ahead of the other states in terms of availability of ICT. While the states like Bihar, West Bengal, and Orissa are laggard states in terms of ICT availability. There are not many changes in ranks of the states in these three periods except a few like West Bengal and Haryana who manage to improve their position in recent years (Figs. 5 and 6).

Table 5 of correlation coefficients shows that most of the socio-economic indicators have a high correlation with the components of ICT indexes and the ICT index. We can summarise the results of different years as follows.
In the year 2001 the following points are observed:

(i) Teledensity (Total) Index has high correlations with the components of Human development indicators indexes and HDI.
(ii) Correlation of Urban Teledensity index with the components of Human development indicators indexes and HDI are lower compared to that of Rural.
(iii) ICT index has high correlations with the components of Human development indicators indexes and HDI, and maximum correlation is with Health Index.

In the year 2011, the observation is as follows:

Table 4 Ranks of the states according to ICT index for three different years

State	2010		2011		2015	
	ICT index rank	ICT index rank	ICT index rank	ICT index rank	ICT index rank	ICT index rank
Andhra Pradesh	5	9	9	9	9	9
Assam	9	10	13	13	13	13
Bihar	12	16	14	14	14	14
Gujarat	8	8	8	8	8	8
Haryana	7	6	4	4	4	4
Himachal Pradesh	2	1	1	1	1	1
Karnataka	6	7	7	7	7	7
Kerala	1	2	2	2	2	2
Madhya Pradesh	15	13	16	16	16	16
Maharashtra	3	4	5	5	5	5
Orissa	11	12	15	15	15	15
Punjab	4	3	3	3	3	3
Rajasthan	13	11	10	10	10	10
Tamil Nadu	10	5	6	6	6	6
Uttar Pradesh	16	15	11	11	11	11
West Bengal	14	14	12	12	12	12

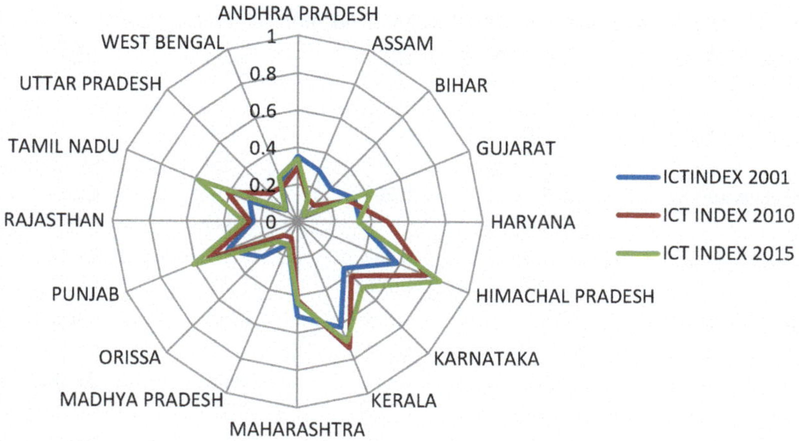

Fig. 5 Comparative position of ICT indices of states over the period 2001–2015

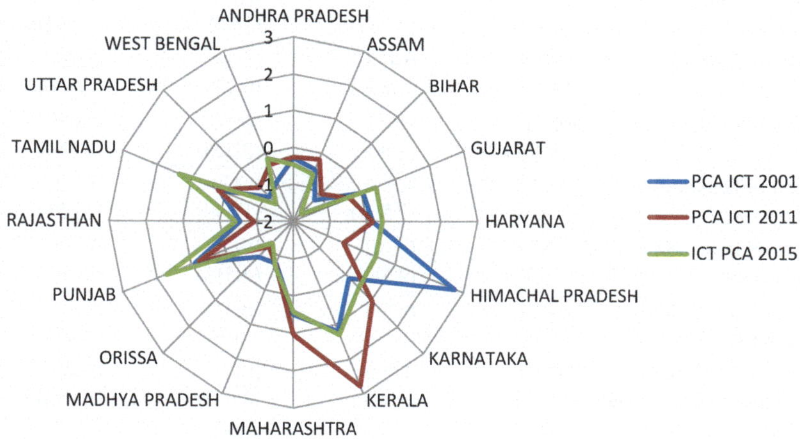

Fig. 6 Comparative position of PCA ICT indices of states over the period 2001–2015

(i) Teledensity (Total) Index has high correlations with the components of Human development indicators indexes and HDI.
(ii) Urban Teledensity has no significant correlation with the components of Human development indicators indexes and HDI.
(iii) Per cent of Households with mobile has no significant correlation with the components of Human development indicators indexes and HDI.
(iv) Computer with the Internet has a significant correlation with Literacy Index.
(v) ICT index has high correlations with the components of Human development indicators indexes and HDI, and maximum correlation is with Health Index.

Table 5 Correlation of components of HDI with ICT (a) 2001, (b) 2011, (c) 2015

ICT components index	PCNDP	Health	Literacy	HDI
(a)				
Internet subscriber	0.644 (3.15)	0.477 (2.03)	0.551 (2.47)	0.659 (3.28)
Teledensity total	0.849 (6.03)	0.904 (7.92)	0.807 (5.11)	0.940 (10.33)
Teledensity rural	0.449 (1.88)	0.847 (5.98)	0.706 (3.73)	0.634 (3.07)
Teledensity urban	0.662 (3.30)	0.629 (3.03)	0.492 (2.12)	0.685 (3.52)
ICT index	0.547 (2.45)	0.811 (5.19)	0.683 (3.49)	0.688 (3.55)
PCA ICT index	0.613 (2.90)	0.716 (3.84)	0.597 (2.79)	0.694 (3.61)
(b)				
Teledensity Rural	0.742 (4.138)	0.594 (2.765)	0.609 (2.87)	0.809 (5.164)
Teledensity Urban	0.100 (0.377)	0.438 (1.821)	0.191 (0.729)	0.206 (0.786)
Teledensity Total	0.812 (5.204)	0.613 (2.901)	0.664 (3.323)	0.879 (6.884)
Percent of house hold with internet	0.229 (0.882)	0.564 (2.554)	0.339 (1.349)	0.361 (1.451)
Percent of house hold with landline	0.510 (2.217)	0.610 (2.884)	0.770 (4.513)	0.684 (3.507)
Percent of house hold with mobile	0.450 (1.885)	0.220 (0.844)	-0.027 (-0.103)	0.364 (1.464)
Percent of house hold having computer with net	0.778 (4.633)	0.399 (1.629)	0.778 (4.639)	0.842 (5.830)
Percent of house hold having computer without net	0.331 (1.313)	0.259 (1.005)	0.601 (2.816)	0.443 (1.850)
Wireline teledensity Rural	0.325 (1.285)	0.713 (3.807)	0.761 (4.393)	0.566 (2.571)
Wireline teledensity Urban	0.638 (3.103)	0.544 (2.428)	0.764 (4.433)	0.764 (4.428)
Wireless teledensity Rural	0.756 (4.324)	0.524 (2.304)	0.544 (2.428)	0.791 (4.833)
Wireless teledensity Urban	0.040 (0.149)	0.400 (1.628)	0.160 (0.606)	0.146 (0.553)

(continued)

Table 5 (continued)

ICT components index	PCNDP	Health	Literacy	HDI
ICT index	0.621 (2.968)	0.645 (3.157)	0.700 (3.459)	0.749 (4.232)
PCA ICT index	0.500 (2.161)	0.440 (1.832)	0.830 (5.566)	0.6 (3.2801)
(c)				
Teledensity Rural	0.712 (5.394)	0.685 (4.825)	0.5174 (2.644)	0.7396 (6.109)
Teledensity Urban	0.061 (0.228)	0.432 (1.988)	0.161 (0.619)	0.159 (0.609)
Teledensity Total	0.782 (7.528)	0.765 (6.887)	0.584 (3.315)	0.819 (9.290)
Wireless Teledensity Rural	0.711 (5.380)	0.641 (4.068)	0.464 (2.212)	0.718 (5.550)
Wireless Teledensity Urban	0.035 (0.133)	0.407 (1.825)	0.133 (0.508)	0.130 (0.494)
Wireless Teledensity Total	0.776 (7.295)	0.739 (6.095)	0.546 (2.911)	0.801 (8.343)
Wline Teledensity Rural	0.287 (1.169)	0.745 (6.267	0.781 (7.504)	0.523 (2.698)
Wline Teledensity Urban	0.619 (3.753)	0.783 (7.568)	0.723 (5.668)	0.744 (6.244)
WirelineTeledensity Total	0.625 (3.839)	0.839 (10.603)	0.854 (11.796)	0.791 (7.902)
Internet per 100 pop Rural	0.616 (3.712)	0.748 (6.357)	0.618 (3.743	0.710 (5.357)
Internet per 100 pop Urban	0.175 (0.675)	0.544 (2.888)	0.343 (1.454)	0.302 (1.244)
Internet per 100 population Total	0.778 (7.390)	0.818 (9.250)	0.712 (5.408)	0.857 (12.121)
Mobile subscriber	0.545 (2.906)	0.606 (3.580)	0.428 (1.959)	0.589 (3.376)
Mobile with internet	0.5936 (3.429)	0.686 (4.854)	0.714 (5.443)	0.707 (5.296)
%Schools with Computer	0.715 (5.483)	0.627 (3.864)	0.595 (3.445)	0.751 (6.448
ICT index	0.674 (4.614)	0.823 (9.519	0.672 (4.581)	0.776 (7.310)
ICT PCA index	0.784 (7.621)	0.756 (6.608)	0.743 (6.203)	0.858 (12.177)

In the year 2015 the points to be noted are as follows:

(i) Teledensity (Total) Index has high correlations with the components of Human development indicators indexes and HDI.
(ii) Urban Teledensity has no significant correlation with the components of HDI and HDI.
(iii) Correlation of the components of HDI and HDI with Wireline urban Teledensity has higher correlation compared to Wireless urban Teledensity.
(iv) Internet in rural households has high correlation while the Internet in urban households has no significant correlation with the components of HDI and HDI.
(v) Index of Schools with Computers Index has a significant correlation with the components of HDI and HDI.
(vi) ICT index has high correlations with the components of Human development indicators indexes and HDI, and maximum correlation is with Health Index.

From all these observations, we can argue that there is a positive association of Information and Communication Technology with most of the socio-economic indicators. Interestingly, from the above result, it can be said that the use of mobile and wireless teledensity has no or very little effect on the social and economic development.

6 Efficiency of Major Sixteen States in India

It has been observed from the earlier section that there are some imbalances among the regions in terms of socio-economic conditions of the states in India. The efficiency of states usually measures in terms of level or growth of per capita net state domestic product as output and some economic variables as inputs. However, there are some studies where some socio-economic factors are taken to find out the efficiency of states. Here in this study, we concentrate on the measure of efficiency in terms of some social and economic indicators as output and some infrastructural variables and resource components of the states. We have estimated the efficiencies using Data Envelopment Analysis (DEA). We measure an output-oriented non-radial DEA model for estimating the efficiency scores of the states. In a standard radial model, the basic difficulty is that all inputs are contracted or all outputs are expanded by the same proportion.

The assessment of comparative efficiency of regions is done using the principles of Data Envelopment Analysis (DEA) developed originally by Farrell (1957) and estimated values of efficiency by Charnes et al. (1978). DEA models are based on three fundamental components, namely the selection of DEA model, Decision-Making Units (DMU) and the definition of input-output systems. First, we will discuss the DEA model we have adapted for this analysis. Next, we will discuss the selection of variables and the selection of States as DMU before we proceed for the empirical part of the paper.

6.1 Non-radial Measures of Technical Efficiency

The radial output-oriented DEA measure of technical efficiency does not reflect any unutilized potential for increasing outputs. On the other hand, a non-radial output-oriented measure does include all potential increases in any component of the output bundle. Färe and Lovell (1978) introduced the output-oriented, *non-radial* measure of technical efficiency.

In any radial DEA model, the problem of slacks arises since all outputs are expanded or all inputs are contracted by the same proportion. In non-radial DEA approach, the outputs are allowed to increase or the inputs are allowed to decrease at different rates. One simplest approach is non-radial DEA which is an additive variant of the DEA model. In an output-oriented additive DEA model, the idea is to maximize the total slacks in all outputs that exist in the observed input-output bundles. Similarly, in an input-oriented model, the basic problem is to maximize the total slacks in inputs (Ray and Neogi 2007).

Let us consider an m-element output vector y, and an n-element input vector x. The output-oriented slack based model for the VRS technology can be written as

$$\max S = \sum\nolimits_k S_k^+$$

$$\text{s.t.} \sum_j \lambda_j y_{kj} + S_k^+ = y_{k0}; \quad (k = 1, 2, \ldots, m)$$

$$\sum_j \lambda_j x_{ij} \leq x_{i0}; \quad (i = 1, 2, \ldots, n)$$

$$\lambda_j \geq 0; \quad (j = 1, 2, \ldots., N); \; S_k^+ \geq 0; \quad (k = 1, 2, \ldots, m)$$

$$\sum_j \lambda_j = 1$$

Naturally, output slack is not possible at the projected bundle

$$y^* = y^0 + S_*^+.$$

where $S_*^+ = \left(S_{1*}^+, S_{2*}^+, \ldots, S_{m*}^+\right)$ is obtained from the optimal solution of the radial DEA model. Output set y^* is the point in the efficient subset of the output isoquant of x^0 that is the farthest from y^0.

6.2 *Estimation of Efficiencies of the States*

6.2.1 Selection of Variables

The concept of devolution of funds from the centre is based on the needs of individual regions to be given funds for improving their socio-economic profile. According to this definition, a region will be comparatively disadvantaged if there is another region with a similar economic and infrastructural profile that delivers higher levels of social and economic values. The process will yield targets of comparative disadvantage that cover a wide spectrum of socio-economic activity within each region. The achievement of these targets can be facilitated using the funds allocated by some objectives. DMU is considered here as different states that perform uniform functions to pursue their objectives, integrate regional administrative and statistical territorial structures. We have already discussed the socio-economic structure of the sixteen states we have considered.

The input–output process in a regional analysis is made of components that reflect the attributes of socio-economic development within each geographical area under consideration. The basic objective of this paper is to rank the states in order of the efficient utilization of revenue and other assets of the states for providing the social and economic services to the citizens of the states. Since the performance of the states is evaluated based on socio-economic development, the selection of the variables as inputs and outputs are difficult in the sense which outputs are to be considered as output and inputs. On this background, we have selected the following variables as input and output variable. We have taken the basic human development indicators like PCNSDP, Literacy and Life expectancy as outputs of the states. Also, we include some development indicators like Employment, Percentage of people having access to safe drinking water, Percentage of people above the poverty level and Per capita Electricity consumption. A less developed state, in general, has low economic activity and poor industrialization. Naturally, the per capita electricity consumption will be low of those states. The inputs are Population, Total central grant and Own tax revenue and Number educational Institutions. We have taken Number educational Institutions since a state with the higher educational facility (Infrastructure) may have a higher literacy rate.

6.2.2 Empirical Estimation

Based on these input and output vectors, we have estimated the non-radial efficiency of the states. As we have said that efficiencies are estimated using a non-radial VRS model. We have found efficiencies for three-time points 2001, 2011 and 2015. Table 6 describes the year wise efficiencies of the major 16 states in India. It has been found that five states out of the sixteen are efficient throughout the years we have studied. The states are namely, Haryana, Himachal Pradesh, Kerala, Maharashtra and Punjab. Gujarat and Tamil Nadu become efficient in the years 2011 and 2015. Bihar is

Table 6 Non-radial efficiencies of the states

States/year	Efficiency		
	2001	2011	2015
Andhra Pradesh	0.74	0.81	0.80
Assam	0.45	0.36	1.00
Bihar	0.29	0.23	0.36
Gujarat	0.88	1.00	1.00
Haryana	1.00	1.00	1.00
Himachal Pradesh	1.00	1.00	1.00
Karnataka	0.79	0.85	0.74
Kerala	1.00	1.00	1.00
Madhya Pradesh	0.54	0.56	0.63
Maharashtra	1.00	1.00	1.00
Orissa	0.56	0.63	1.00
Punjab	1.00	1.00	1.00
Rajasthan	0.59	0.67	0.70
Tamil Nadu	0.93	1.00	1.00
Uttar Pradesh	0.44	0.49	0.52
West Bengal	0.61	0.71	0.70
Average efficiency	0.74	0.81	0.80

efficient for the year 2001 while Assam and Madhya Pradesh were efficient in 2015. The average efficiency of 2001 is higher than in the year 2011, but it increases in the year 2015. The efficient states like Haryana, Himachal Pradesh, Kerala, Maharashtra, Punjab, Andhra Pradesh, Gujarat and Tamil Nadu also have very high HDI index. However, the only state Bihar which is found to be efficient is not corroborated with its HDI. Some states like West Bengal, Orissa, Rajasthan, Madhya Pradesh and Uttar Pradesh are in the middle range of efficiency which is around 0.5.

In this section, the percentage of output that could be increased within the given capacity of the states in terms of input possessed by the states is discussed. In the year 2001 (Table 7a) Assam, Bihar, Madhya Pradesh, Rajasthan, Orissa and Uttar Pradesh could increase their PCNSDP more than 100%. Andhra Pradesh and West Bengal could increase their PCNSDP by more than 50%. The deficiencies of Indicator 'Above Poverty Level' are not very high for almost all the state except Orissa, Assam and Madhya Pradesh. The percentages of deficiencies of states in terms of per capita electricity consumption are very high for almost all the states except the efficient states along with Gujarat and Tamil Nadu. The employment scenario is also not impressive for Madhya Pradesh, Orissa and Uttar Pradesh.

Table 7b gives the percentage of deficiencies of states in terms of concerned variables for the year 2011. In terms of percentage of deficiencies of PCNSDP the

Table 7 Percentage of deficiency (a) 2001, (b) 2011, (c) 2015

States	PCNSDP 1980–81 base	Employment (%)	Literacy (%)	Life expectancy (years)	APL (%)	Per capita electricity consumes (in KWH)	Population access safe drinking water (%)
(a)							
Andhra Pradesh	55.72	27.41	13.97	7.87	11.41	110.21	21.85
Assam	127.31	10.26	17.56	14.76	45.01	596.03	53.88
Bihar	211.41	128.03	56.73	9.90	61.83	1237.84	5.97
Gujarat	29.50	4.33	0.00	8.16	9.09	26.90	14.72
Haryana	0.00	0.00	0.00	0.00	0.00	0.00	0.00
Himachal Pradesh	0.00	0.00	0.00	0.00	0.00	0.00	0.00
Karnataka	41.12	0.00	4.40	6.02	17.27	105.89	14.88
Kerala	0.00	0.00	0.00	0.00	0.00	0.00	0.00
Madhya Pradesh	140.40	79.08	8.64	20.39	49.98	247.89	42.69
Maharashtra	0.00	0.00	0.00	0.00	0.00	0.00	0.00
Orissa	116.68	101.39	18.12	13.83	75.52	189.47	41.74
Punjab	0.00	0.00	0.00	0.00	0.00	0.00	0.00
Rajasthan	105.25	58.10	14.12	12.11	10.76	239.39	43.11
Tamil Nadu	15.26	0.00	0.00	4.01	17.86	12.82	5.69
Uttar Pradesh	161.85	161.76	21.43	15.91	36.30	477.24	11.16
West Bengal	68.36	21.01	0.62	7.20	28.58	314.24	10.28

(continued)

Table 7 (continued)

States	PCNSDP 1980–81 base	Employment (%)	Literacy (%)	Life expectancy (years)	APL (%)	Per capita electricity consumes (in KWH)	Population access safe drinking water (%)
(b)							
Andhra Pradesh	0.00	117.61	23.53	1.92	1.03	12.74	3.28
Assam	162.81	30.43	11.82	9.35	35.08	944.66	35.71
Bihar	163.29	1152.82	33.11	2.09	38.73	908.50	0.00
Gujarat	0.00	0.00	0.00	0.00	0.00	0.00	0.00
Haryana	0.00	0.00	0.00	0.00	0.00	0.00	0.00
Himachal Pradesh	0.00	0.00	0.00	0.00	0.00	0.00	0.00
Karnataka	47.00	0.00	5.74	0.32	7.16	59.28	2.41
Kerala	0.00	0.00	0.00	0.00	0.00	0.00	0.00
Madhya Pradesh	86.05	287.58	19.45	7.37	34.51	85.24	20.13
Maharashtra	0.00	0.00	0.00	0.00	0.00	0.00	0.00
Orissa	94.84	200.03	13.54	7.00	34.44	35.17	22.50
Punjab	0.00	0.00	0.00	0.00	0.00	0.00	0.00
Rajasthan	83.46	168.43	25.06	1.91	4.92	38.19	16.49
Tamil Nadu	0.00	0.00	0.00	0.00	0.00	0.00	0.00
Uttar Pradesh	136.50	313.45	18.65	8.17	3.53	243.97	0.00
West Bengal	16.70	39.98	0.64	0.00	14.68	209.75	5.31

(continued)

Table 7 (continued)

States	PCNSDP 1980–81 base	Employment (%)	Literacy (%)	Life expectancy (years)	APL (%)	Per capita electricity consumes (in KWH)	Population access safe drinking water (%)
(c)							
Andhra Pradesh	21.12	33.37	14.47	3.82	29.94	0.00	74.20
Assam	0.00	0.00	0.00	0.00	0.00	0.00	0.00
Bihar	314.26	1.75	23.43	1.20	71.65	34.55	811.90
Gujarat	0.00	0.00	0.00	0.00	0.00	0.00	0.00
Haryana	0.00	0.00	0.00	0.00	0.00	0.00	0.00
Himachal Pradesh	0.00	0.00	0.00	0.00	0.00	0.00	0.00
Karnataka	47.13	0.00	4.31	0.93	123.75	8.93	55.50
Kerala	0.00	0.00	0.00	0.00	0.00	0.00	0.00
Madhya Pradesh	184.57	18.02	12.56	7.06	0.84	21.98	158.92
Maharashtra	0.00	0.00	0.00	0.00	0.00	0.00	0.00
Orissa	0.00	0.00	0.00	0.00	0.00	0.00	0.00
Punjab	0.00	0.00	0.00	0.00	0.00	0.00	0.00
Rajasthan	158.67	0.00	19.37	3.28	68.47	0.14	47.40
Tamil Nadu	0.00	0.00	0.00	0.00	0.00	0.00	0.00
Uttar Pradesh	267.69	26.34	15.29	7.10	0.52	18.14	319.32
West Bengal	30.74	0.00	3.79	0.00	100.65	10.45	150.28

states Assam, Bihar and Uttar Pradesh could increase their PCNSDP more than 100%.

The percentage of deficiency in terms of employment is very high for almost all the states except West Bengal and Assam. In this year we again find many states like Assam, Bihar, Uttar Pradesh and West Bengal have the scope of improvement in the power sector. One interesting point is that there is not much scope of improvement of literacy rate and life expectancy of the inefficient states.

Table 7c gives the percentage of deficiencies of states in terms of concerned variables for the year 2015. In terms of percentage of deficiencies of PCNSDP, the states Bihar, Rajasthan and Uttar Pradesh could increase their PCNSDP more than 100%. The percentage of deficiency in terms of employment, Literacy, Life expectancy and Electricity consumption the deficiencies are negligible for most of the states. In this year we again find many states like Assam, Bihar, Uttar Pradesh and West Bengal have made a significant improvement in the power sector. In terms of Access to Safe Drinking Water states like Bihar, Uttar Pradesh and West Bengal lie far behind the optimum values.

Thus there is a wide variation among the states in terms of provision of services to the people of the states and terms of some developmental characteristics of the states. In the next section, attempts have been made to find out the factors responsible for this variation.

6.3 Explanation of Variance of Efficiencies Among States

It is discussed in Sect. 2 that ICT can reorganize and restructure working methods of the sectors in which it is used. It offers generic advantages of efficiency gains, through the dissemination of knowledge and information that help faster knowledge accumulation, in support of the specific purposes for which it is used. E-governance, which is an essential part of ICT requires an entirely new attitude in the managing of government activities and public administration. A cooperative interaction between citizens and public administration is considered as an important determinant for successful implementation of processes based on "single portals" and "one-stop shops" models to achieve administrative efficiency and procedural simplicity. ICT is supposed to bring about gains in efficiency of service delivery and reduce internal coordination costs (Ciborra et al. 2005). Thus besides other factors level of development of ICT in a state is an essential factor for explaining the efficiency variation of states.

In this section, we discuss the factor behind the variation of efficiencies among states. We have selected a few variables which indicate the differences in the character of each state. Since the efficiencies lie between zero and one, Tobit regression methods are used to find out the factors for the variation of efficiencies. Police per population is considered as one of the factors since law and order is a major problem behind the smooth functioning of any government and thus lowering the efficiency of the state. Next, two ICT indicators which are considered as important forces to explaining the variation of efficiency of state are taken in the analysis. The result of

Table 8 Factor behind variations in efficiency (panel tobit model)

Dependent variable: efficiency-non-radial	Model I	Model II	Model III
Pop-per-police	−0.341** (−2.89)	−0.290* (−1.99)	−0.421** (−3.12)
E-readiness index rank	0.104** (3.52)		0.109** (3.09)
ICT index (equal weights)	0.805** (2.97)		
ICT index (PCA method)		0.244** (3.27)	0.100 (1.53)
Constant	0.516	1.153	0.845
Log likelihood	−0.421	−7.707	−3.792
Obs:	48	48	48

Note Values within parenthesis represent Z statistics
*indicates significant at 10% level and **indicates significant at 5% level

first panel Tobit regression taking different combinations of independent variables given in Table 8 shows that some factors like (i) Police personnel per lack population, (ii) E-readiness Rank and (iii) ICT indices (both with equal weight and PCA) are found statistically significant in explaining the variation of efficiency of states.

7 Concluding Remarks

It has been observed that there are wide differences among the states of India in terms of Human Development indexes. These differences are found in some basic characteristics like income, literacy and health. These differences could be ascribed to the poor natural resources of the regions, population density, and regional or state administration. It has been observed that a state is underdeveloped because of its poor natural resources, and the social environment is not conducive for generating enough economic activity. But we can also think of the opposite story where the states with poor natural resources become developed while the states with rich natural resources have not developed to that extent. Thus, the achievement of the states can be linked with the efficient management of resources of the states. In this backdrop, we tried to estimate the components of Human Development of the states and tried to explain the reason for these differences. Some of the states like Kerala, Maharashtra, Gujarat, Himachal Pradesh and Punjab are much better compared to the other states of India. We have found the rank of the states in terms of efficiency using non-radial DEA where the outputs are some socio-economic indicators and inputs are the revenue of the states, Central grants, Roads and population of the states. Based on our results, we have estimated the percentage of deficiencies of achieving the targets of these socio-economic indicators, where targets are based on their peer groups which can give some indication of the lacuna of the states in performing better from the present scenarios. Also, we have found some factors responsible for the variation of efficiency of states. Besides the significant role of ICT, it has been found that E-readiness of the states in terms of the rank of E-readiness index has a significant positive effect and provision of keeping law and order of the state in terms of strength of police personnel have a positive effect on the efficiency of the states.

Appendix

See Tables 9, 10 and 11.

Table 9 Life expectancy of states of India and health index

States	Actual values			Health index		
	2001–05	2006–10	2010–14	2001–05	2006–10	2010–14
AP	64.1	67.4	68.5	0.652	0.707	0.724
Assam	58.7	62.2	63.9	0.562	0.620	0.649
Bihar	61.4	66.9	68.1	0.607	0.698	0.718
Gujarat	63.9	69	68.7	0.648	0.733	0.728
Haryana	65.9	68.8	68.6	0.682	0.730	0.727
HP	67	71.5	71.6	0.700	0.775	0.777
Karnataka	65.1	68.8	68.8	0.668	0.730	0.731
Kerala	73.9	74.5	74.9	0.815	0.825	0.832
Maharashtra	66.9	62.9	71.6	0.698	0.632	0.777
MP	57.7	69.5	64.2	0.545	0.742	0.653
Orissa	59.2	63.5	65.8	0.570	0.642	0.681
Punjab	69.4	70	71.6	0.740	0.750	0.777
Rajasthan	61.7	67.6	67.7	0.612	0.710	0.712
Tamil Nadu	66	69.1	70.6	0.683	0.735	0.760
UP	59.8	64.2	64.1	0.580	0.653	0.652
West Bengal	64.6	69.5	70.2	0.660	0.742	0.753
Mean	64.08	67.84	68.69	0.651	0.714	0.728
Standard deviation	4.28	3.29	3.10	0.071	0.055	0.052

Source Author

Table 10 Literacy of states of India and literacy index

States	Actual values		Literacy index	
	2001	2011	2001	2011
AP	60.47	67.66	0.666	0.721
Assam	63.25	73.18	0.696	0.779
Bihar	47	63.82	0.517	0.680
Gujarat	69.14	79.31	0.761	0.845
Haryana	67.91	76.64	0.747	0.816
HP	67.91	76.64	0.747	0.816
Karnataka	66.64	75.6	0.733	0.805
Kerala	90.86	93.91	1.000	1.000
Maharashtra	76.88	82.91	0.846	0.883
MP	63.74	70.63	0.702	0.752
Orissa	63.08	73.45	0.694	0.782
Punjab	69.65	76.68	0.767	0.817
Rajasthan	60.41	67.06	0.665	0.714
Tamil Nadu	73.45	80.33	0.808	0.855
UP	56.27	69.72	0.619	0.742
West Bengal	68.64	77.08	0.755	0.821
Mean	66.58	75.29	0.733	0.802
Standard deviation	9.53	7.18	0.105	0.076

Source Author

Table 11 PCNSDP of states of India and income index

States	Actual value			PCNSDP index		
	2000–01	2010–11	2014–15	2000–01	2010–11	2014–15
Andhra Pradesh	3054	5864	6513	0.691	0.748	0.748
Assam	1624	2321	2599	0.292	0.351	0.377
Bihar	1247	2220	2736	0.125	0.332	0.398
Gujarat	3650	8141	9757	0.804	0.889	0.911
Haryana	4419	8660	10455	0.925	0.915	0.939
Himachal Pradesh	3410	5757	6700	0.761	0.740	0.759
Karnataka	3326	5560	6920	0.745	0.725	0.772
Kerala	2797	5550	6562	0.636	0.724	0.751
Maharashtra	4977	10563	12157	1.000	1.000	1.000
Madhya Pradesh	1978	3094	4039	0.417	0.474	0.555
Orissa	1739	3303	3409	0.335	0.502	0.486
Punjab	4756	6904	7930	0.971	0.818	0.827
Rajasthan	2317	3831	4809	0.517	0.566	0.625
Tamil Nadu	3614	7059	9059	0.798	0.827	0.881
Uttar Pradesh	1816	2608	3016	0.363	0.401	0.437
West Bengal	2825	5788	6937	0.642	0.742	0.773
Mean	2972	5452	6475	0.626	0.672	0.702
Standard deviation	1143.275	2447.77	2912.576	0.261	0.208	0.200

Source Author

References

Bash, S., Chawla, A., & Shah, M. (2015). Regional disparities in India: A moving frontier. *Economic and Political Weekly, 1*(1), 44–52.
Charnes, A., Cooper, W. W., & Rhodes, E. (1978). Measuring the efficiency of decision making units. *European Journal of Operational Research, 6,* 429–444.
Ciborra, C., & Navarra, D. D. (2005). Good governance, development theory, and aid policy: Risks and challenges of e-government in Jordan. *Information Technology for Development, 11*(2), 141–159.
Dash, B. B. (2014). Regional income disparity and government intervention in India: Evidence from sub-national data. *South Asia Economic Journal, 15*(2), 281–314.
Färe, R., & Lovell, C. A. K. (1978). Measuring the technical efficiency of production. *Journal of Economic Theory, 19*(1), 50–62.
Farrell, M. J. (1957). The measurement of productive efficiency. *Journal of the Royal Statistical Society, 120,* 253–281.
Ghosh, B., Marjit, S., & Neogi, C. (1998). Economic growth and regional divergence in India. *Economic and Political Weekly, 33*(26), 1623–1630.
Hirschman., A. O., & Rothschild, M. (1973). The changing tolerance for income inequality in the course of economic development. *The Quarterly Journal of Economics, 87*(4), 544–566.
Kumar, M., & Kumar, R. (2014). Regional disparities in human development in India. *International Research Journal of Commerce Arts and Science, 4*(3), 788–798.
Mitra, S., & Marjit, S. (1996). Convergence in regional growth rates-indian research agenda. *Economic and Political Weekly, 31*(33), 2239–2242.
Mundle, S., Chowdhury S., & Sikdar, S. (2016). Governance performance of Indian states changes between 2001–02 and 2011–12. *Economic and Political Weekly, 51*(36), 55–64.
Myrdal, G. (1958). Value in social theory. In P. Streeten (Ed.), *A selection of essays on methodology*. London: Routledge and Keegan Paul.
North, D. C. (1981). *Structure and change in economic history* (p. 1981). New York: W.W. Norton.
Pieterse, J. N. (2001). *Development theory: deconstructions/reconstructions*. Sage Publication.
Porter Michael E. (1990). *The competitive advantage of nations*. Harvard Business Review.
Ray, S. C., & Neogi, C. (2007). *Non radial measure of efficiency in Indian textile industry: An analysis of unit-level data*. University of Connecticut Working Paper, No. 2007–38.
Sen, A. (2000). *Development as freedom*. OUP.
United Nations Development Programme. (1990). *Human development report*. Oxford University Press.

ICT Users and Socio-Economic Effects

ICTs and Effectiveness of Governance: A Cross-Country Study

Anubha Agarwal and Dibyendu Maiti

Abstract This paper investigates the impact of innovations in ICTs on the effectiveness of governance using cross-country unbalanced panel data for the period from 1996 to 2017. With the ability of information storing, sharing and automation, ICT innovation can improve governance by enriching the governmental information infrastructure, presenting opportunities for better decision-making, encouraging proactive government-citizen interaction and increasing public accountability. At the same time, the increasing trend of the digital divide, cyber-crime, loss of privacy, unemployment and inequality put pressure on the ability of a state to govern effectively. The resultant effect of ICTs on the effectiveness of governance depends on the relative strength of the two forces. We find that improvement in ICT leads to a rise in the effectiveness of governance and control corruptions subject to the efficacy of the judicial system and the rule of law, and the presence of a better rule of law strengthens the favourable impact of ICT on governance.

1 Introduction

With the growing ability to store and share information through continuous innovations, information and communication technologies (ICTs) influence not only the level of individual activities but also affect operation and coordination among the agents belonging to an institution, organization and state. This seems to have improved the market functioning, reduced distortions and minimized information asymmetries and thus resulted in the rise of economic systems that are the key to economic development. On the other hand, ICTs raise the risks of unemployment, inequality, cyber-crime, lead to loss of privacy and a thriving digital divide, which essentially could dent a state's ability to effective governance and control corruptions. In this light, this paper attempts to investigate whether ICTs have successfully

A. Agarwal (✉)
University of Toronto, Toronto, Canada
e-mail: anubhaagarwal2605@gmail.com

D. Maiti
Delhi School of Economics, New Delhi, India

D. Maiti et al. (eds.), *Digitalisation and Development*,
https://doi.org/10.1007/978-981-13-9996-1_12

improved the efficiency of governance and control of corruptions across countries. If so, what is the extent of this effect?

After the recent financial crisis, the states are increasingly concerned about their fiscal discipline to avoid the risk of fiscal indebtedness. Montes et al. (2018) take a look at the reforms undertaken by countries for the effectiveness of government policies and the improvement of fiscal transparency. They analyse two channels to study the efforts made by countries to improve fiscal transparency and the effect of fiscal transparency on government effectiveness and spending efficiency. The first channel works indirectly through public debt. The second channel works directly through the transparency of government effectiveness and government spending efficiency as resource allocation and accountability is enhanced by transparency. Using panel data for a sample of 82 countries (14 developed and 68 developing) for 2006–2014, they compare the scores of fiscal transparency and find that efforts for improving fiscal transparency were made by approximately 80% of the countries. Their results show that fiscal transparency plays a role in reducing public debt and improving the efficiency of government spending and effectiveness of government. Application of ICTs plays a primal role behind this, and most of the developing countries are pursuing digitalization to improve fiscal performance.

In the recent past, there has been a spurt in the growth of ICTs. This was seen as being an engine propelling the growth of businesses, productivity rise and increasing transparency in major sectors of the economies. In general, ICT affects human activities by saving time required for various tasks, creating new activities and services (such as monitoring location, robotics, artificial intelligence, energy informatics, Apps and the Internet of things), enhances social interaction by increasing access to new and improved communication and enables to process and store information in a much more systematic and rapid manner (Castellacci and Tveito 2018). Today, ICT has become a keystone of everyday life, with people increasingly relying on electronic devices for most of their clerical as well as routine works. Due to the presence of such functions, the ICT innovation gives rise to a massive expansion in the set of goods and services continuously required for governance and monitoring, one of them being the increasing use of e-governance, that applies ICTs for carrying out the functions and achieving the results of governance. At the same time, ICT innovations have also brought new challenges and risks to employment opportunities, semi-skilled workers, individual rights as well as work-life balances, privacy, security and raised cyber-crime. It is also evident that the rate of absorption and access to ICTs substantially vary across individuals, income and age groups, rural–urban divisions, sectors and regions, which seem to have created a 'digital divide' in the modern society (Connolly et al. 2017). IT literacy is an important factor in digital divide research, which essentially depends on individual attitude and interest, socio-economic characteristics and public structure (Ferro et al. 2011; Philip et al. 2017). The rising impediments of these kinds would force individuals to find ways to manipulate the system. Therefore, it is important to investigate the net effect of ICTs on the level of effectiveness of governance.

Economists have always been concerned with the determinants of growth and development. Governance and institutions have become detrimental factors over the years. For example, Barro (1998) studies a panel of 100 countries from 1960 to 1990, and his study supports the idea of conditional convergence. Lower inflation, lower fertility, lower government consumption, higher initial schooling and life expectancy, lower inflation and improved trade, including better implementation of the rule of law help accelerate the growth rate for a given level of per capita GDP. Since then, a large amount of economic literature has also focused on the positive effects of better institutions and governance that go beyond the rules of laws. Lin and Nugent (1995) define institutions broadly as '*a set of humanly devised behavioural rules that govern and shape the interactions of human beings, in part by helping them to form expectations of what other people will do*'. Institutions such as economic freedom, well-specified property rights, quality of government and the rule of law are shown to have a bearing on economic performance (Barro and Sala-i-Martin 1997; Dawson 1998; Knack 1996). As a result, Hausmann et al. (2008) recommend alleviating the most binding constraints and hence producing the biggest bang for the reform buck. Rodrik (2000) focuses on the importance of institutions such as property rights, regulations limiting fraud and corruption, institutions that reduce risks and effective implementation of the rule of law, especially in poor and developing countries. Robinson et al. (2005) also argue that good economic institutions consist of an interrelated cluster of things including enforcement of property rights for a broad section of society to give the incentive to invest, equality of opportunity, equality before the law and transparency in government functioning. Rodrik et al. (2004) find that the quality of institutions is the most important factor in determining income levels. Incomes are directly but weakly affected by measures of geography after controlling for institutions. These measures of geography have strong indirect effects due to their effects on institutional quality. Égert (2016) studies the ability of better institutions to augment the positive effects of R&D spending on multi-factor productivity (MFP) and finds that variations in labour market regulations, institutions and barriers to trade and investment can explain variations in MFP across nations to a large extent.

Note that scholars have interpreted governance differently and focused on various specific components within the broad governance affecting economic growth. These characteristics can be divided into two broad types, and they could be mutually exclusive. One canvases regulatory dimensions (like taxation, financial and labour market rigidities), which specify exact legal orders and instructions. The other one encompasses dimensions that affect the degree of enforcement and implementation of these laws effectively in practice. Essentially, they are not the same but represent two separate things (Maiti and Bhattacharyya 2019). The former represents the rule of law, and the latter shows the level of governance effectiveness or effective implementation of those laws since the mere existence of laws does not matter much unless they are implemented effectively. We are interested in investigating the effect of ICT on the effectiveness of governance only in this paper.

In light of the importance of institutions in affecting growth and development outcomes, and the recent spurt in information and communication technologies (ICTs), research has also focused on indirect effects of ICTs on growth through betterment in institutions and governance. Governance, or how governments mobilize resources and spend them on the citizens is a very important determinant of the overall growth and well-being of societies. According to the IMF's book 'Digital Revolutions in Public Finance,' fiscal policy has a great impact on all citizens, and digitization promises to reshape fiscal policy by transforming governance. The growth in ICT affects the ability of governments to collect, process, share and act on information, hence expanding their ability to design better policy for tax and expenditure, administration, compliance, delivery of public services, social programs, etc. In addition to having access to better data, governments now have avenues for better data storage and tracking of information through digitalization, linking records between various departments, more efficient ways of tax collection, etc., that can greatly enhance the possibilities for governance. The authors also note that each nation must recognize the risks and challenges in tapping these spurts in ICT by taking care of the institutional and capacity constraints, privacy concerns, fraud, and evasion: practices that limit the beneficial impact of ICT in governance and fiscal policy management. In this context, various attempts have been made worldwide to improve the delivery of government services through attempts to digitalize them.

Since both, rule of laws and governance effectiveness, significantly influence growth, scholars have taken a keen interest in identifying strategies to raise their levels. In this scenario, information and communication technologies (ICTs) have received greater attention due to their ability to improve institutional quality. The growth in ICTs is known to increase inclusivity and development prospects as it has been shown that countries with a high level of digital transformation have lower levels of corruption, hence leading to better delivery of services and increased efficiency. Technology diffusion and digital transformation are supposed to increase public awareness and information levels, hence increase detection risks, leading to lower corruption and better governance. There is growing evidence of such stories, and da Silva et al. (2018) have provided a comprehensive survey about it. Odendaal (2003) also found favourable effects in the context of urban and environmental development in South Africa.

Liu et al. (2018) introduce the Internet Plus Government (IPG), a new government initiative emerging in the last decade. They conduct analyses on research articles published in e-governance areas to note how the new ICTs have been adopted in the IPG initiative and study the interaction between ICTs and governance. They find that IPG initiative has strengthened the government information infrastructure and provided opportunities for better decision-making and pro-active government-citizen interaction.

Martin and Goggin (2016) analyse how Australia's 2015 Digital Transformations initiative, based on the British Gov.uk program, attends to international benchmarks for gender equality and empowerment in ICT policy. This study is undertaken in the context that digital government strategies espouse user-centric design and citizen participation, but it is unclear how they explicitly address the needs of women, who are significant users of health, social welfare and aged-care services. Callen and Long (2015) study the links between weak institutions, political networks and election fraud during the 2010 parliamentary election in Afghanistan. They find evidence of aggregation fraud in favour of candidates connected to election officials.

There was a reduction in election materials' thefts by about 60% and vote counts for connected candidates by about 25% after the introduction of a new monitoring technology. The results show how technology can reduce political corruption and improve opportunities for better governance.

Jha and Sarangi (2017) show that social media and ICTs serves for social mobilization and citizen empowerment and some evidence of the Internet and Facebook penetration having a sizable and negative impact on corruption. There are also examples of the positive impact that some ICT interventions have had on the perception of corruption.

Sabbagh et al. (2012) also study the impact of digitization on government effectiveness using the transparency of governmental activities, provisioning of public education and the delivery of e-government services. They conclude that greater digitization increases public participation and gives them more insight into government policies. It also enhances the government's ability to disseminate information and deliver basic government services and leads to a society being more transparent.

Shim and Eom (2009) examine the argument that ICT and social capital serve as major factors in limiting corruption, hence improving governance. Their statistical analysis using panel datasets reveals that even though the relationship between social capital and ICT was inconclusive, both ICT and social capital were effective tools for reducing corruption. According to them, ICT reduces the need to monitor corrupt behaviour, hence reducing unnecessary human intervention in government work processes. Also, a higher level of social capital is likely to make the citizens more involved in the political decision-making process and increase the chances of corrupt public employees to be exposed. Pina et al. (2007) assess the extent to which ICTs enable better accountability in public bureaucracies through e-governance initiatives through an empirical study in the USA, Canada, Australia, New Zealand and 15 EU countries. Their analysis shows that both the context and characteristics of public administration styles influence the developments and changes in financial accountability levels and the application of ICTs to the public sector fits well into any kind of public administration style since it does not entail major changes in the style of the government–citizen relationship

Hence, research has shown that ICT can contribute towards better governance and government effectiveness by enriching the governmental information infrastructure, presenting opportunities for better decision-making, encouraging pro-active government–citizen interaction and increasing public accountability. Increasing use of ICT has also been shown to limit corruption by digitizing payments for services rendered, reducing the need to monitor corrupt behaviour, reducing unnecessary human intervention in government work processes and increasing the likelihood of fraud detection. The prevalence of e-government services can make systems more transparent and allow easy dissemination of information for effective governance. It should be noted that growth in ICT leads to increased access to goods and services and opens up new avenues for communication and information dissemination. Although ICT can lead to better governance, which can positively affect growth and development outcomes, it can also negatively affect governance by encouraging corruption and fraud. The possible negative effects of ICT gain more importance in developing nations that do not have proper institutions and systems to take care of the negative effects of ICTs.

There has not been much focus on the negative effects of ICTs in the literature, especially in the context of its effects on governance and institutional development, leading to a gap when it comes to our understanding of how ICT can hamper institutions and governance, thus limiting growth and developmental outcomes. There is often a misplaced emphasis on solely strengthening the functioning of ICT as it has been shown to affect governance positively.

A study conducted by World Bank (2015) documented that problems of petty corruption and poor services in the Dominican Republic, Nigeria and Pakistan have been reduced with the help of citizen feedback systems. Digital technologies have helped reduce absenteeism, but they have not significantly improved service provider management in government bureaucracies. Some evidence from Bangladesh indicates that digitalisation can be effective in addressing petty corruption involving street-level bureaucrats, but less so for dealing with grand corruption involving higher-level officials (Baniamin 2015). Scholars are also highlighting that the relationship has not been monotonic. It depends on government infrastructure, trust and motive. For example, Lee et al. (2019) focus on the importance of public trust in the government, as this encourages citizens to seek assistance and health risk information from the government.

According to the literature, the effect of digitalisation on the effectiveness of governance and corruption has been ambiguous. We argue that ICT in itself may not be enough to improve governance outcomes and reduce corruption unless it is supported by a well-defined system of institutions such as the effective rule of law and judiciary. The critical constraints that manifest themselves in the form of bad institutional quality can hamper the positive effects of ICT on governance. While the digitalization improves governance effectiveness and control corruptions directly, but its adverse effect on employment and privacy can limit its efficacy. The resultant effect depends on the relative strength of these two forces. To investigate this, we now use panel data for major countries and study some variables related to governance and ICT to substantiate our claim. Hence, the empirical and econometric analysis of the relationship between ICT and effective governance using panel data for major countries during 1996–2017 is presented in the next section. This is followed by the results and related discussion. The last section provides concluding observations.

2 Data and Analysis

The Worldwide Governance Indicators (WGI) dataset for measures of governance and institutional quality and World Development Indicators (WDI) dataset for other variables are used for the following analysis. The Freedom House Organization panel datasets on civil liberties (CL) and political rights (PR) are used as proxies measuring the extent of freedom and political scenarios in the respective countries.

Human Development Index data (wherever used) is obtained from the United Nations Development Programme (UNDP).

The WGI dataset covers more than 200 countries and territories and measures six dimensions of governance and institutional quality from 1996: government effectiveness, control of corruption, political stability and absence of violence/terrorism, voice and accountability, regulatory quality and rule of law. These aggregate indicators are made using many underlying variables in various existing data sources and governance surveys (Kaufmann et al. 2010). The WDI dataset is a collection of development indicators from various officially recognized international sources and provides country-wise estimates of various variables. Data on relevant indicators of ICTs and other variables from WDI (and education index from HDI dataset) was combined with the governance indicators from WGI and CL, PR variables from Freedom House Organization for the following analysis.

As is observed, developing nations suffer from a lack of governance efficacy and control of corruption that limit their potential growth and development. In spite of these problems, some developing countries are performing well in terms of their growth rate during the last two decades. BRICS countries (Brazil, Russia, India, China and South Africa) are great examples. In general, there has been a notable variation in the level of government effectiveness and control of corruption across these nations (see Fig. 1). As far as the level of government effectiveness is concerned, there has been a general improvement during the last 4–5 years for all the comparators, except South Africa, which was performing far above the others until the recent years. India and China showed lower than average values during the later 1990s but an improvement up to 2007, followed by deceleration until a recent year. The

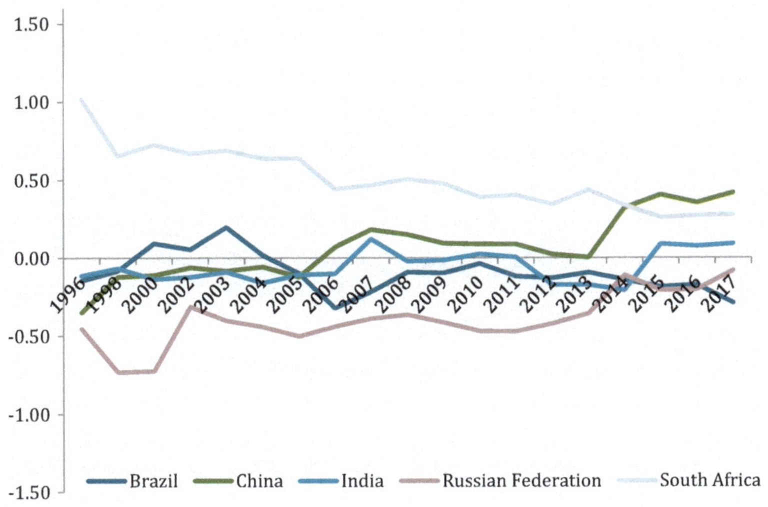

Fig. 1 Government effectiveness index in major developing nations: 1996–2017. *Source* WGI, World Bank

performance accounts for improvement from 2014 onwards. However, one cannot be sure whether it is due to digitalisation.

Similarly, the control of corruption shows a general improvement in most of the countries except Brazil in the recent years (Fig. 2). China and India also demonstrate a similar pattern. Brazil and South Africa, who were doing better during the 1990s, did not show much improvement. In summary, there have been mixed experiences in terms of the effectiveness of governance and control of corruption among the BRICS nations. Although a sign of general improvement can be traced in the recent years, growth in ICT may not be the factor responsible for this trend.

To visualize the tentative relationships, governance variables have been plotted against the ICT variable across all the countries. A variable measuring the level of ICT in a country (ict_var) was created using four ICT variables (fixed broadband subscriptions per 100, fixed telephone subscriptions per 100, mobile cellular subscriptions per 100 and secure internet servers per million) from the WDI dataset. All the four variables were normalized using respective global minimum and maximum values, and then a weighted average (giving equal weights to each of the four variables) was taken to finally get the variable depicting ICT (ict_var). We use 'control of corruption' (controlofcorr) and 'government effectiveness' (gvteff) as indicators of the level of governance in each nation (from the WGI dataset).

Figure 3 shows a positive relationship between the ICT variable and control of corruption, while Fig. 4 shows a positive relationship between the ICT variable and government effectiveness across the panel of countries for the respective period. These observations are in line with the literature, which shows that digitalization is

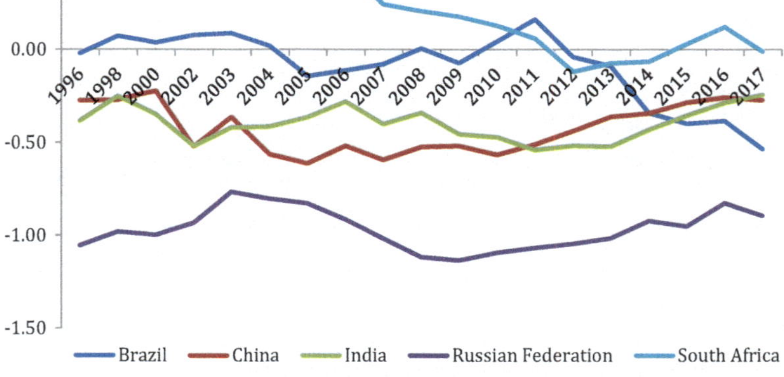

Fig. 2 Control of corruption index in major developing countries: 1996–2017. *Source* WGI, World Bank

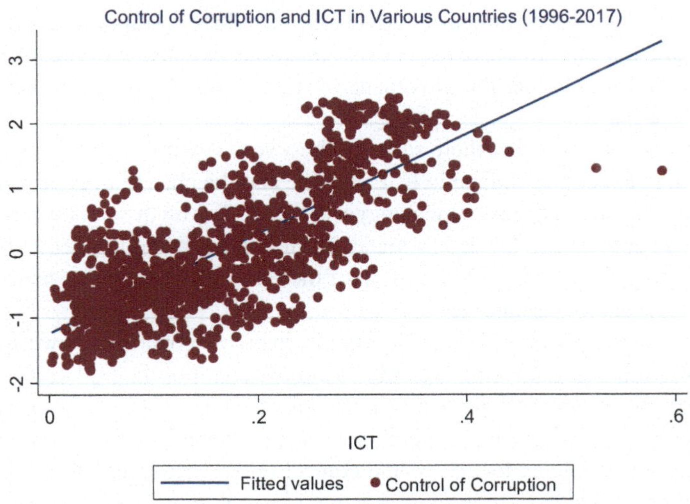

Fig. 3 Digitalization and control of corruption across countries. *Source* Authors' Calculations (WDI and WGI Data, World Bank)

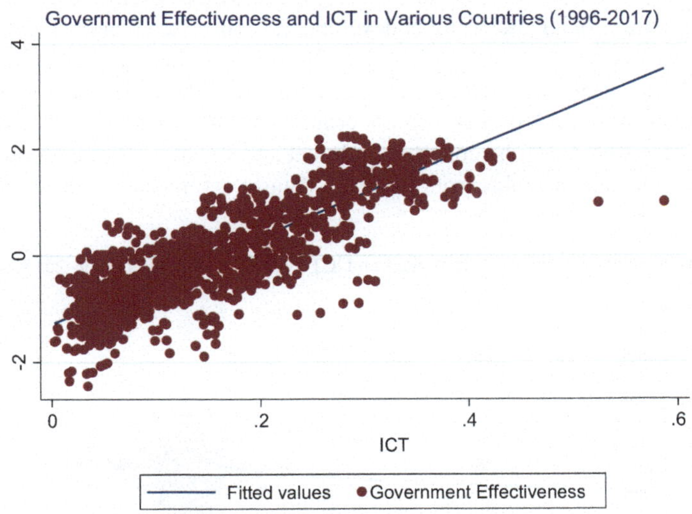

Fig. 4 Digitalization and government effectiveness across countries. *Source* Authors' Calculations (WDI and WGI Data, World Bank)

supposed to improve government effectiveness and reduce corruption (hence increase control of corruption). To delve deeper into this issue, we also plot the difference in values of ICT variable and the governance variables for our panel of countries for the respective period.

Figures 5 and 6 show that there seems to be a very slight positive or insignificant relationship between the change in ICT variable and the change in governance indicators across these countries, which suggests that ICT growth might not be driving the change in governance levels in some countries. Thus, an econometric exercise is undertaken to get a deeper understanding of the relation between the growth in ICT and governance across countries.

To show the effect of ICTs on the effectiveness of governance, we first run a set of regression using the variables that are most common in explaining the level of effective governance. These are baseline regressions. Then, ICT variables and their interaction terms have been added in the same regressions. However, one needs to address the possible endogeneity and control other factors affecting them in the regression model. Hence, we rely on instrument variable and dynamic panel model for this purpose.

Rontos et al. (2015) undertake a global analysis to study the determinants of governance quality and find that they can be classified into three broad categories: indicators of economic, social and political development. They find that the cross-country variation in governance can be attributed to differences in the range of political freedom and the level of social development in addition to the difference in countries' level of economic development. We undertake a similar exercise and first regress indicators of governance on economic, political and social development indicators. We use the relevant variables from the WGI dataset estimated by the World Bank.

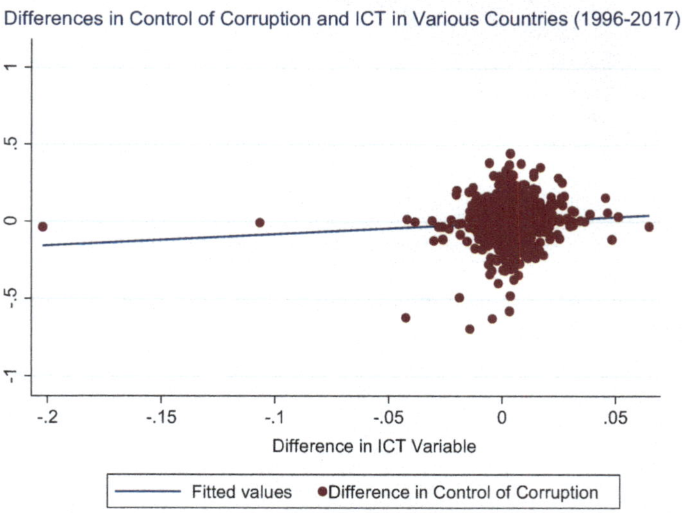

Fig. 5 Change in digitalization and control of corruption. *Source* Authors' Calculations (WDI and WGI Data, World Bank)

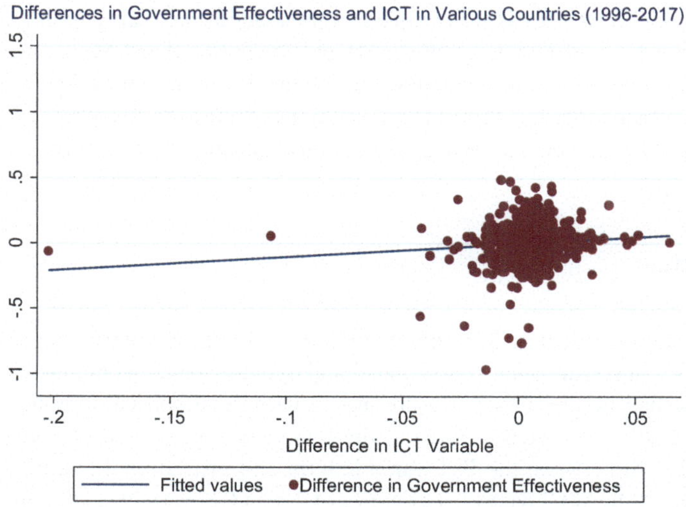

Fig. 6 Change in digitalization and government effectiveness. *Source* Authors' Calculations (WDI and WGI Data, World Bank)

The values of these indicators lie between −2.5 and 2.5, with higher values corresponding to better governance and institutional quality. We limit ourselves to the WGI indicators measuring 'control of corruption' and 'government effectiveness' as proxies for governance, as we want to focus on the ability of ICT to affect countries' effectiveness of governance and level of corruption. The econometric study focuses on three strands of the governance literature: the economic, political and social. The economic strand is captured by the gross domestic income per capita in constant 2010 US $.

The political strand is captured by variables measuring the range of political rights and the extent of civil liberties (measured separately by two indices, each taking values from 1 to 7 where lower values correspond to more civil liberties or more political rights). Countries and territories with a rating of 1 on the PR index enjoy many political rights like free and fair elections, whereas those with a rating of 7 have few or no political rights because of severe government oppression. Countries and territories with a rating of 1 on the CL index enjoy many of civil liberties, like freedom of expression, education, assembly and religion, whereas those with a rating of 7 have few or no civil liberties.

The social strand is measured using the Human Development Index that takes into account the average achievements by a country in providing a decent standard of living, a long and healthy life and access to knowledge. Since GDP per capita is already used as a variable for the standard of living in the regression equations, education index and life expectancy are considered in place of HDI to avoid correlation between the explanatory variables in the regression equations.

In addition to capturing the indicators for economic, political and social development as done in the literature so far, we also capture income inequality using Gini index from the WDI data as we believe that the level of inequality within a country should affect the government effectiveness and corruption there. More unequal societies are expected to be more corrupt, and we test this expectation by including an indicator for inequality in some of the regression equations for the panel of countries having major developed and developing countries from 1996 to 2017.

3 Results

To investigate the effect of ICTs on the effectiveness of governance, some baseline regressions will be run using simple panel and dynamic panel techniques first. After doing these baseline exercises that are in line with the empirical literature, we add the ICT variable (weighted average of the four indicators described above) and an interaction term between the ICT variable term and institutional quality shown by 'rule of law' in the WGI dataset. Two types of dependent variables are used—governance effectiveness and control of corruptions in the regression, and the results are presented separately.

Table 1 has the results of regressing 'control of corruption' (controlofcorr) on various economic, social and political indicators using fixed effect panel regression in column 2, instrumental variables for GDP per capita in columns 1 and 3 and dynamic panel regression using lagged value of the dependent variable (L.controlofcorr) and GDP per capita (L.gdp_capita) as instruments in column 4. GDP per capita is used as the economic development indicator, civil liberties (cl) or political rights (pr) are used as the political development indicators, and education index (edu_index) and life expectancy (life_expctncy) are used as social development indicators.

As expected, GDP per capita, education index and life expectancy are positively and significantly related to control of corruption. Civil liberties and political rights have the expected negative signs and are significant (Similar results are obtained when PR index is used instead of CL index in the regression equations). In the case where HDI is used as a measure of social development, GDP per capita, education index and life expectancy are dropped. We obtain the expected signs on HDI and CL/PR variables. Gini index is insignificant, signifying that income inequality is not statistically significant in explaining the control of corruption. Thus, economic, political and social development indicators have the expected effects on the control of corruption.

Table 2 has the results of regressing 'government effectiveness' (gvtefff) on various economic, social and political indicators using fixed effect panel regression in column 2, instrumental variables (for GDP per capita) in columns 1 and 3 and dynamic panel regression using lagged value of the dependent variable (L.gvteff) and GDP per capita (L.gdp_capita) as instruments in column 4. GDP per capita is used as the economic development indicator, civil liberties (cl) or political rights (pr) are used as the political development indicators, and education index (edu_index) and life expectancy (life_expctncy) are used as social development indicators.

Table 1 Factors affecting control of corruption—Baseline results

	(1)	(2)	(3)	(4)
Variables	controlofcorr	controlofcorr	controlofcorr	controlofcorr
gdp_capita	2.84e − 05***		2.73e − 05***	3.61e − 06
	(6.81e − 07)		(1.02e − 06)	(3.70e − 06)
edu_index	0.547***		0.546***	0.148
	(0.0981)		(0.169)	(0.131)
life_expctncy	0.00974***		0.00306	−0.00345
	(0.00181)		(0.00338)	(0.00295)
Cl	−0.199***	−0.0769***	−0.235***	−0.00689
	(0.00690)	(0.00890)	(0.0153)	(0.00570)
HDI		0.685***		
		(0.108)		
Gini			−0.00184	
			(0.00207)	
L.controlofcorr				0.969***
				(0.0187)
L.gdp_capita				−2.79e − 06
				(3.67e − 06)
Constant	−0.540***	−0.147	0.0481	0.166
	(0.105)	(0.103)	(0.259)	(0.141)
Observations	2,600	2,499	913	2,087
R-squared	0.767		0.799	
No. of countries		137		151

Standard errors in parentheses
***$p < 0.01$, **$p < 0.05$, *$p < 0.1$

As expected, GDP per capita, education index and life expectancy are positively and significantly related to government effectiveness. Civil liberties and political rights have the expected negative signs and are significant (Similar results are obtained when CL index is used instead of PR index in the regression equations). In the case where HDI is used as a measure of social development, GDP per capita, education index and life expectancy are dropped. We obtain the expected signs on HDI and CL/PR variables. Gini index is also significant and negative as expected (larger values of the index signify more inequality, hence leading to less government effectiveness). Hence, we obtain all the expected results for determinants of governance.

We now add the ICT variable and interaction terms (depicting the interaction of ICT with institutional quality) to our baseline results to measure the effect of ICT on the effectiveness of governance as measured by ‘control of corruption’ and ‘government effectiveness’.

Table 2 Factors affecting government effectiveness—Baseline results

	(1)	(2)	(3)	(4)
Variables	gvteff	gvteff	gvteff	gvteff
L.gvteff				0.861***
				(0.0430)
gdp_capita	2.39e − 05***		2.20e − 05***	3.23e − 06
	(6.33e − 07)		(9.14e − 07)	(5.44e − 06)
L.gdp_capita				−1.25e − 06
				(5.44e − 06)
edu_index	1.010***		1.030***	0.608***
	(0.0901)		(0.150)	(0.212)
life_expctncy	0.0166***		0.00989***	−0.00245
	(0.00169)		(0.00309)	(0.00554)
Pr	−0.134***	−0.0413***	−0.157***	−0.0146
	(0.00519)	(0.00644)	(0.0109)	(0.0264)
Gini			−0.00420**	0.000960
			(0.00192)	(0.00293)
HDI		1.096***		
		(0.109)		
Constant	−1.482***	−0.543***	−0.792***	−0.220
	(0.0951)	(0.0932)	(0.232)	(0.420)
Observations	2,598	2,497	913	801
R-squared	0.781		0.805	
No. of countries		137		129

Standard errors in parentheses
***$p < 0.01$, **$p < 0.05$, *$p < 0.1$

Table 3 shows the results of regressing 'control of corruption' (controlofcorr) on the ICT variable (ict_var) and various control variables using instrumental variables for GDP per capita to take care of endogeneity problem. Instruments include all control variables and one period lag for GDP per capita. The instrumental variables used here could be subject to criticism. One period lag may work perfectly. Also, there could be possible endogeneity with other variables.

As expected, GDP per capita, life expectancy and education index are positively and significantly related to control of corruption for most specifications. Civil liberties and political rights have the expected negative signs (greater values of these indices mean less civil liberties/political rights, which should transform to lesser control of corruption, as observed) and are significant. Gini index is observed to be insignificant in most specifications and has the unexpected sign in some specifications, also reducing the number of observations due to paucity of data. Adding the ICT variable makes the indicators for social development insignificant. To measure

Table 3 Effect of ICT on control of corruption—2SLS regression results

	(1)	(2)	(3)	(4)	(5)	(6)
Variables	controlofcorr	controlofcorr	controlofcorr	controlofcorr	controlofcorr	controlofcorr
gdp_capita	2.46e − 05***	2.53e − 05***	2.53e − 05***	2.57e − 05***	1.26e − 06	1.62e − 06
	(1.61e − 06)	(1.66e − 06)	(1.21e − 06)	(1.60e − 06)	(1.65e − 06)	(1.67e − 06)
edu_index	0.00756	0.188	0.282		0.726***	0.689***
	(0.328)	(0.337)	(0.188)		(0.234)	(0.236)
life_expctncy	−0.00736	−0.00540	0.00958***	−0.00270	0.00720	0.00624
	(0.00684)	(0.00706)	(0.00365)	(0.00670)	(0.00492)	(0.00492)
Gini	0.000473	5.64e − 05		0.00252	0.00874***	0.00825***
	(0.00358)	(0.00376)		(0.00349)	(0.00263)	(0.00258)
Cl	−0.220***					−0.0260
	(0.0244)					(0.0201)
ict_var	2.530***	2.902***	1.663***	3.250***	0.603	0.571
	(0.701)	(0.719)	(0.389)	(0.575)	(0.510)	(0.509)
Pr		−0.143***	−0.141***	−0.128***	−0.00765	
		(0.0196)	(0.00908)	(0.0182)	(0.0151)	
Ict_ruleoflaw					3.261***	3.189***
					(0.161)	(0.167)
Constant	0.593	−0.0202	−0.881***	−0.318	−1.659***	−1.470***
	(0.507)	(0.508)	(0.219)	(0.475)	(0.360)	(0.377)
Observations	381	381	1,016	404	381	381
R-squared	0.819	0.807	0.769	0.809	0.908	0.908

Standard errors in parentheses
***$p < 0.01$, **$p < 0.05$, *$p < 0.1$

the effect of institutional quality in the presence of ICT in governance variables, we add an interaction term between ICT variable and 'rule of law' (ict_ruleoflaw).

As is evident from the table, ict_ruleoflaw has a significant positive impact on the control of corruption, hence supporting our claim that ICT can reduce corruption in the presence of supporting institutions and better institutional quality (as captured by the 'rule of law' index). In the presence of this interaction term, the ICT variable becomes insignificant, indicating that ICT in itself may not lead to better governance unless the right institutional quality augments it. Even though these results tell us something beyond the conventional literature, some signs are unexpected; hence, we also estimate the same equation using dynamic panel data estimation (Table 5).

Table 4 shows the results of regressing 'government effectiveness' (gvteff) on the ICT variable (ict_var) and various control variables using instrumental variables for GDP per capita to take care of the endogeneity problem. Instruments include all control variables and one period lag for GDP per capita.

As expected, GDP per capita, life expectancy and education index are positively and significantly related to government effectiveness for most specifications. Civil liberties and political rights have the expected negative signs (greater values of these

Table 4 Effect of ICT on government effectiveness—2SLS regression results

	(1)	(2)	(3)	(4)	(5)
Variables	gvteff	gvteff	gvteff	gvteff	gvteff
gdp_capita	1.69e − 05***	1.71e − 05***	1.67e − 05***	−1.15e − 06	−1.48e − 06
	(1.35e − 06)	(1.35e − 06)	(1.03e − 06)	(1.24e − 06)	(1.42e − 06)
edu_index	0.670**	0.803***	0.618***	0.747***	1.219***
	(0.275)	(0.274)	(0.160)	(0.135)	(0.201)
life_expctncy	0.00990*	0.00991*	0.0168***	0.0230***	0.0196***
	(0.00574)	(0.00574)	(0.00309)	(0.00263)	(0.00421)
Cl	−0.181***				
	(0.0205)				
ict_var	1.931***	2.100***	2.779***	1.470***	0.324
	(0.588)	(0.585)	(0.330)	(0.285)	(0.436)
Gini	0.000586	−0.000998			0.00571**
	(0.00300)	(0.00306)			(0.00225)
Pr		−0.139***	−0.0978***	−0.0355***	−0.0350***
		(0.0159)	(0.00770)	(0.00718)	(0.0129)
ict_ruleoflaw				2.394***	2.518***
				(0.118)	(0.138)
Constant	−0.963**	−1.181***	−1.816***	−2.337***	−2.446***
	(0.425)	(0.413)	(0.186)	(0.159)	(0.308)
Observations	381	381	1,016	1,016	381
R-squared	0.840	0.839	0.816	0.869	0.915

Standard errors in parentheses
***$p < 0.01$, **$p < 0.05$, *$p < 0.1$

indices mean less civil liberties/political rights, which should transform to lesser government effectiveness, as observed) and are significant. Gini index is observed to be insignificant in most specifications and has the unexpected sign in some specifications, also reducing the number of observations due to paucity of data.

To measure the effect of institutional quality in the presence of ICT in governance variables, we add an interaction term between ICT variable and 'rule of law' (ict_ruleoflaw). As is evident from the table, ict_ruleoflaw has a significant positive impact on government effectiveness, hence supporting our claim that ICT can improve governance more in the presence of supporting institutions and better institutional quality (as captured by the 'rule of law' index). In the presence of this interaction term, the ICT variable becomes insignificant in one specification, indicating that ICT in itself may not lead to better governance unless the right institutional quality augments it. Even though these results tell us something beyond the conventional literature, some signs are unexpected; hence, we also estimate the same equation using dynamic panel data estimation (Table 6).

Table 5 shows the results of regressing 'control of corruption' (controlofcorr) on the ICT variable (ict_var) and various control variables using dynamic panel data estimation. Instruments include one period lag for GDP per capita.

As expected, GDP per capita and education index are positively and significantly related to control of corruption for most specifications, though life expectancy has the unexpected sign in some cases. Civil liberties and political rights have the expected negative signs (greater values of these indices mean less civil liberties/political rights, which should transform to lesser control of corruption, as observed) and are significant. Gini index is observed to be insignificant, also reducing the number of observations due to the paucity of data. The ICT variable is negative wherever it is

Table 5 Effect of ICT on control of corruption—Dynamic panel regression results

	(1)	(2)	(3)	(4)	(5)
Variables	controlofcorr	controlofcorr	controlofcorr	controlofcorr	controlofcorr
gdp_capita	9.71e − 06***	1.00e − 05***	2.48e − 05***	−1.01e − 05***	4.54e − 06**
	(9.20e − 07)	(9.68e − 07)	(1.11e − 06)	(1.27e − 06)	(2.10e − 06)
edu_index	5.272***	4.677***	4.805***	0.615**	1.423***
	(0.180)	(0.187)	(0.225)	(0.250)	(0.371)
life_expctncy	−0.00474	0.0148**	−0.0702***	0.0701***	−0.0432***
	(0.00573)	(0.00602)	(0.00882)	(0.00603)	(0.00873)
Cl	−0.239***				
	(0.0111)				
ict_var	−1.377***	−1.536***	0.253	−2.959***	0.185
	(0.393)	(0.416)	(0.574)	(0.385)	(0.546)
Pr		−0.202***	−0.139***	−0.00975	−0.0492[a]
		(0.0109)	(0.0306)	(0.0132)	(0.0302)
Gini			−0.00227		−0.00306
			(0.00276)		(0.00263)
ict_ruleoflaw				4.383***	3.213***
				(0.197)	(0.288)
Constant	−1.986***	−3.125***	2.101***	−5.101***	2.220***
	(0.362)	(0.372)	(0.720)	(0.351)	(0.685)
Observations	1,018	1,018	381	1,018	381
No. of countries	152	152	106	152	106

Standard errors in parentheses
***$p < 0.01$, **$p < 0.05$, *$p < 0.1$
[a]significant at 11%

significant, indicating that ICT in itself may not lead to better governance unless the right institutional quality augments it. To measure the effect of institutional quality in the presence of ICT in governance variables, we add an interaction term between ICT variable and 'rule of law' (ict_ruleoflaw). As is evident from the table, ict_ruleoflaw has a significant positive impact on the control of corruption, hence supporting our claim that ICT can reduce corruption in the presence of supporting institutions and better institutional quality (as captured by the 'rule of law' index). This is an important result as it captures the inefficacy of ICT/digitalization alone to reduce corruption without the necessary institutional set-ups.

Table 6 shows the results of regressing 'government effectiveness' (gvteff) on the ICT variable (ict_var) and various control variables using dynamic panel data estimation. Instruments include one period lag for GDP per capita.

Table 6 Effect of ICT on government effectiveness—Dynamic panel regression results

	(1)	(2)	(3)	(4)	(5)
Variables	gvteff	gvteff	gvteff	gvteff	gvteff
gdp_capita	2.70e − 06***	3.21e − 06***	1.16e − 05***	−2.10e − 05***	−1.06e − 05***
	(9.82e − 07)	(1.07e − 06)	(1.26e − 06)	(1.41e − 06)	(2.33e − 06)
edu_index	5.173***	4.456***	3.264***	−0.285	−0.143
	(0.192)	(0.207)	(0.257)	(0.303)	(0.410)
life_expctncy	−0.00609	0.0172***	−0.0420***	0.0810***	0.00155
	(0.00613)	(0.00666)	(0.0101)	(0.00708)	(0.00891)
CI	−0.288***			−0.0280*	−0.157***
	(0.0119)			(0.0162)	(0.0345)
ict_var	−0.412	−0.553	1.319**	−2.328***	0.682
	(0.420)	(0.460)	(0.655)	(0.418)	(0.589)
Pr		−0.237***	−0.295***		
		(0.0120)	(0.0349)		
Gini			−0.00329		−0.00273
			(0.00315)		(0.00300)
ict_ruleoflaw				5.189***	3.526***
				(0.225)	(0.325)
Constant	−1.636***	−3.030***	1.800**	−5.193***	0.588
	(0.386)	(0.412)	(0.821)	(0.408)	(0.672)
Observations	1,018	1,018	381	1,018	381
No. of countries	152	152	106	152	106

Standard errors in parentheses
***$p < 0.01$, **$p < 0.05$, *$p < 0.1$

As expected, GDP per capita, life expectancy and education index are positively and significantly related to government effectiveness for most specifications. Civil liberties and political rights have the expected negative signs (greater values of these indices mean less civil liberties/political rights, which should transform to more government effectiveness, as observed) and are significant. Gini index is observed to be insignificant, also reducing the number of observations due to the paucity of data. The effect of ICT variable is not obvious when it is significant, indicating that ICT may not lead to better governance unless it is augmented by the right institutional quality.

To measure the effect of institutional quality in the presence of ICT in governance variables, we add an interaction term between ICT variable and 'rule of law' (ict_ruleoflaw). As is evident from the table, the interaction effect between ICT and rule of laws (i.e., ict_ruleoflaw) has a significant positive impact on government effectiveness, hence supporting our claim that ICT can improve governance in the presence of supporting institutions and better institutional quality (as captured by the 'rule of law' index). This is an important result as it captures the inefficacy of ICT/digitalization alone to improve governance without the necessary institutional set-ups. We did not find suitable instruments to further check the robustness of the regression results in the unbalanced dataset. This is a limitation of the study.

4 Discussion

The preceding analysis shows how the effects of ICTs on governance could be limited in the absence of supporting institutions that can augment the positive effect of growth in ICTs on effective governance and control of corruption. Even though ICTs have shown to have various positive impacts on growth, development and governance, the massive expansion in ICTs has also initiated the discussion around privacy issues, theft, fraud, etc., that limit its positive impacts. The growth in ICT provides increased benefits for governance, but it also leads to increased opportunity for corruption, as the incentive of increased access to information is not weighed by the disincentive of the possibility of getting caught. Many governmental digital initiatives taken to enhance governance have been criticised as being counterproductive due to increased corruption with the onset of digitalization that concentrates power in a few hands. One such initiative is the biometric identity system or Aadhaar system in India.

The Aadhaar system has also led to increased opportunities for corruption. Evidence from an arid village in Jharkhand shows the misery of families who were deprived of subsidized food from the vast public distribution system due to their ration cards not being linked to their biometric-based personal identification numbers. Villagers trying to get their ration cards linked to Aadhaar either had to shell out days of family earnings to bribe the government officers at the offices or face rejection and the risk of having no food for many more days of the month. Even though the government had made the linkage mandatory to avoid leakages and digitalize the process, a lot of people faced more hardships in getting access to food, hence hampering their well-being despite a well-functioning digital set-up. This evidence is a case in point, supporting the previous analysis that shows how the absence of the right institutional set-up can hamper the positive effects of digitalization on governance and provision of government services.

Second, technological developments allow individuals to participate in modern society without leaving electronic traces or 'electronic footprints,' thus compromising their privacy since they can be easily stored, copied and searched through for an indefinite period. The EPTA report on ICT and Privacy in Europe recognizes privacy as an important democratic right. It discusses e-government and e-health, two other fields of public interest where the use of ICTs may conflict with privacy. The report mentions that a balance needs to be made between conflicting societal values and rights, and it is through this channel that ICT mostly affects privacy.

It is evident that ICT hurts employment, specifically unskilled workers, through the application of automation and artificial intelligence. Increased unemployment would put additional pressure on the regulatory system of a particular country.

Bhattacharya and Mukherjee (2019) study the aspects of ICT, which can reduce the length of red tape. They find that the support for ICT reform that can enhance the provision of public service delivery is expected to be lower in countries having long periods of red tape and corruption. Commander et al. (2011) also investigate the effect of the institutional and policy environment of a region or state on ICT capital investment and productivity using Indian firm data. They find that poorer infrastructure quality and labour market policy is associated with lower ICT adoption, thus throwing light at the connection between the overall level of institutional quality and ICT growth.

All this evidence supports our econometric analysis showing that mere focus on ICT expansion without efforts to bridge any gaps in institutional quality and supporting institutions is bound to be insufficient in improving the effectiveness of governance. The presence of better institutions can strengthen the favourable impact of ICT in governance and hence it is very important to streamline the overall institutional quality including an effective judicial system and other enforcement mechanisms to ensure that the benefits of ICT growth can percolate to all sections of society through better governance.

5 Conclusion

This study investigates the effect of ICT on the effectiveness of governance using cross-country unbalanced panel data for the period from 1996 to 2017 with the help of fixed effect and dynamic panel regressions. However, there is scope to improve the econometric results with the help of more level of analysis.

This paper shows how the effect of ICT expansion is significantly favourable. The institutional quality is better and how a mere focus on the expansion of ICTs is bound to be ineffectual in improving the effectiveness of governance and control of corruption. We have shown how ICT expansion may not be sufficient in itself to improve government effectiveness and reduce corruption. ICT improves the government directly. But, the increased unemployment, inequality and cyber-crime originated with more ICT exposure weaken the ability of governance effectively. As a result, the effect of ICT is found to be favourable if the legal system is effective. Other, the net effect happens to be quite weak. We recommend that the stakeholders should focus on the benefits that can come with focusing on reform in the judiciary system.

Acknowledgements We are thankful to Fulvio Castellacci for giving useful comments on the previous draft. We are also thankful to NUPI for facilitating this research as a part of the research grant received from RCN (project grant no. 247921). Usual disclaimers apply.

References

Baniamin, H. M. (2015). *Controlling corruption through e-governance: Case evidence from Bangladesh*. U4 Brief; http://www.u4.no/publications/controllingcorruption-through-e-governance-case-evidencefrom-bangladesh/.

Barro, R. J., & Sala-i-Martin, X. (1997). Technological diffusion, convergence and growth. *Journal of Economic Growth, 2*(1), 1–26.

Barro, R. J. (1998). *Determinants of economic growth: A cross-country empirical study*. MIT Press Books, The MIT Press, 1st ed., Vol. 1, No. 0262522543, April.

Bhattacharya, P., & Mukherjee, V. (2019). Red Tape, corruption and ICT in Maiti, D. C.

Biswas, S. (2018, March 27). Aadhaar: Is India's biometric ID scheme hurting the poor?. *BBC News*. Retrieved from https://www.bbc.com/news/world-asia-india-43207964.

Bütschi, D., Cope, D., Sandsgaard, J., Cas, J., Klüver, L., Vouilloz, N., et al. (2006). ICT and Privacy in Europe. Experiences from technology assessment of ICT and Privacy in seven different European countries. Final report October 16, 2006, European Parliamentary Technology Assessment network (EPTA). http://hw.oeaw.ac.at/ita-projektbericht.

Callen, M., & Long, J. D. (2015). Institutional corruption and election fraud: Evidence from a field experiment in Afghanistan. *American Economic Review, 105*(1), 354–381.

Castellacci, Fulvio, & Tveito, Vegard. (2018). Internet use and well-being: A survey and a theoretical framework. *Research Policy, 47*(1), 308–325.

Commander, S., Harrison, R., & Menezes-Filho, N. (2011, May). ICT and productivity in developing countries: New firm-level evidence from Brazil and India. *The Review of Economics and Statistics, 93*(2), 528–541.

Connolly, M., Lee, C., & Tan, R. (2017). The digital divide and other economic considerations for network neutrality. *Review of Industrial Organization, 50*(4), 537 554.

da Silva, M. B. D., dos Santos, A. M., dos Santos Soares, M., do Nascimento, R. P. C., & Nunes, I. D. (2018) A survey on adoption good practices for ICT governance at enhanced organizations. In: Latifi, S. (Eds.), *Information technology—New generations*. Advances in Intelligent Systems and Computing (Vol. 738). Cham: Springer.

Dawson, J. W. (1998). Institutions, investment, and growth: New cross-country and panel data evidence. *Economic Inquiry, 36*, 603–619. https://doi.org/10.1111/j.1465-7295.1998.tb01739.x.

Égert, Balázs. (2016). Regulation, institutions, and productivity: New macroeconomic evidence from OECD countries. *American Economic Review, 106*(5), 109–113.

Ferro, E, Helbig, N. C., & Gil-Garciac, J. R. (2011). The role of IT literacy in defining digital divide policy needs. *Government Information Quarterly, 28*(1), 3–10.

Hausmann, R., Rodrik, D., & Velasco, A. (2008). Growth diagnostics. The Washington consensus reconsidered: Towards a new global governance.
International Monetary Fund. (2017). *Digital revolutions in public finance*. USA. https://doi.org/10.5089/9781484315224.071 Web.
Jha, C. K., & Sarangi, S. (2017). Social media, internet, and corruption. *Information Economics and Policy, 39,* 42.
Kaufmann, D., Kraay, A., & Mastruzzi, M. (2010). The worldwide governance indicators: Methodology and analytical issues. *Hague Journal on the Rule of Law, 3*(2), 220–246 (June 2011). https://doi.org/10.1017/S1876404511200046.
Knack, S. (1996, June). Institutions and the convergence hypothesis: The cross-national evidence. *Public Choice, 87*(3–4), 207–228.
Lee, T., Park, H., & Lee, J. (2019). Collaborative accountability for sustainable public health: A Korean perspective on the effective use of ICT-based health risk communication. *Government Information Quarterly, 36*(2), 226–236.
Liu, S. M., Pan, L., & Chen, X. (2018). *Citation analysis of innovative ICT and advances of governance (2008–17)*. arXiv:1801.05916 [cs.SI].
Maiti, D., & Bhattacharyya, C. (2019). Informality, enforcement and growth. *Economic Modelling*. ISSN 0264-9993. https://doi.org/10.1016/j.econmod.2019.04.015. (http://www.sciencedirect.com/science/article/pii/S0264999318309325).
Martin, F., & Goggin, G. (2016). Digital transformations?: Gendering the end user in digital government policy. *Journal of Information Policy, 6,* 436–459. https://doi.org/10.5325/jinfopoli.6.2016.0436.
Montes, G. C., & Bastos, J. C. A., & de Oliveira, A. J. (2018). Fiscal transparency, government effectiveness and government spending efficiency: Some international evidence based on panel data approach. *Economic Modelling, 79*(C), 211–225.
Odendaal, N. (2003). Information and communication technology and local governance: Understanding the difference between cities in developed and emerging economies. *Computers, Environment and Urban Systems, 27*(6), 585–607. https://doi.org/10.1016/S0198-9715(03)00016-4.
Philip, L., Cottrill, C., Farrington, J., Williams, F., & Ashmore, F. (2017). The digital divide: Patterns, policy and scenarios for connecting the 'final few' in rural communities across Great Britain. *Journal of Rural Studies, 54,* 386–398.
Pina, Vicente, Torres, Lourdes, & Acerete, Basilio. (2007). Are ICTs promoting government accountability?: A comparative analysis of e-governance developments in 19 OECD countries. *Critical Perspectives on Accounting, 18,* 583–602. https://doi.org/10.1016/j.cpa.2006.01.012.
Robinson, James A., Acemoglu, Daron, & Johnson, Simon. (2005). Institutions as a fundamental cause of long-run growth. *Handbook of Economic Growth, 1A,* 386–472.
Rodrik, Dani. (2000). Institutions for high-quality growth: What they are and how to acquire them. *Studies in Comparative International Development, 35*(3), 3–31.
Rodrik, D., Subramanian, A., & Trebbi, F. (2004). Institutions rule: The primacy of institutions over geography and integration in economic development. *Journal of Economic Growth, 9,* 131. https://doi.org/10.1023/B:JOEG.0000031425.72248.85.
Rontos, K., Syrmali, M. E., & Vavouras, I. (2015). The determinants of governance: A global analysis. *International Journal of Latest Trends in Finance and Economic Sciences, 5*(2), 868–877.
Sabbagh, K., Friedrich, R., El-Darwiche, B., Singh, M., Ganediwalla, S., & Katz, R. (2012). *Maximizing the impact of digitization*. The global information technology report 2012, World Economic Forum.
Shim, D. C., & Eom, T. H. (2009). Anticorruption effects of information communication and technology (ICT) and social capital. *International Review of Administrative Sciences, 75*(1), 99–116. https://doi.org/10.1177/0020852308099508.

The World Bank. (2015). *Enabling citizen-driven improvement of public services: Leveraging technology to strengthen accountability in Nigerian healthcare*. http://reboot.org/wordpress/wpcontent/uploads/2015/03/Enabling-Citizen-DrivenImprovement-of-Public-Services_2015.pdf.

Yifu Lin, J., & Nugent, J. B. (1995). Institutions and economic development. In H. Chenery & T. N. Srinivasan (Eds.), *Handbook of development economics* (1st ed., Vol. 3, Chap. 38, pp. 2301–2370). Elsevier.

Red Tape, Corruption and ICT

Poulomi Bhattacharya and Vivekananda Mukherjee

Abstract This chapter focuses on that aspect of ICT which reduces the length of red tape and analyses the desirability of introduction of ICT from the stakeholders' perspective. In a theoretical model, we show that the support for such a reform depends on the stakeholders' profile, the nature of the public good/service and the initial length of red tape. The implementation of ICT in delivery of public goods/services may create demand for an honest regime. However, paradoxically, the support for ICT reform is expected to be lower in countries marred with long red tape and entrenched corruption. The chapter also provides empirical support for the theoretical results.

Keywords Corruption · Red tape · Screening · ICT

JEL Classification D73 · O38

1 Introduction

Information and communication technologies (ICTs) are usually considered as an antidote to the problems related to 'red tape' and corruption in public administration. It not only reduces the length of red tape by speeding up the administrative procedures but also minimizes the scope of interaction between the prospective recipient of public goods/services and the corrupt officials. This chapter focuses on that aspect of ICT, which reduces the length of red tape and analyses the desirability of the introduction of ICT from the stakeholders' perspective. In a theoretical model, we show that the support for such a reform depends on the stakeholders' profile, the nature of the

The earlier versions of the paper were presented at the DSE Workshop on 'ICTs: Transformation, Digital Divides and Development'. The helpful comments from Fulvio Castellacci and Dibyendu Maiti are acknowledged. The usual disclaimer applies.

P. Bhattacharya · V. Mukherjee (✉)
Department of Economics, Jadavpur University, Kolkata, India
e-mail: mukherjeevivek@hotmail.com

P. Bhattacharya
e-mail: poulomi.ju.eco@gmail.com

D. Maiti et al. (eds.), *Digitalisation and Development*,
https://doi.org/10.1007/978-981-13-9996-1_13

public good/service and the initial length of red tape. The implementation of ICT in the delivery of public goods/services may create demand for an honest regime. However, surprisingly, the support for ICT reform is expected to be lower in countries marred with long red tape and entrenched corruption. The chapter also provides empirical support for the theoretical results.

Since public goods are delivered with a specific social objective and are funded by public money, its provision involves a careful screening process at the governmental level. The complexity of the screening process like the number of stages involved, the time taken between the application and delivery of the good sometimes is referred to as 'red tape' in the administration. The length of 'red tape' for delivery of a public good/service depends on the efficiency of the administration. The more efficient administration is likely to have a shorter length of 'red tape'. The existence of 'red tape', on the other hand, opens for the possibility of corruption in the administration as bribes are paid to speed up the process. Sometimes, the corrupt officials deliberately lengthen the 'red tape' to make the bribe option more attractive to the applicants.[1] This is a phenomenon particularly observed in countries with persistent corruption, such as the developing countries of the world. The ICTs can interfere with this phenomenon by increasing the speed with which screening is done and assuring time-bound delivery of the services. It may also minimize the interaction between the corrupt officials and the applicants, but the later remain out of the scope of this chapter.

In developing countries like India, the introduction of ICT, in recent times, has been able to reduce the time to process applications and get services done from few days or months to few minutes, reduced information secrecy and reduced the intensity of giving speed money (Bussell 2012; Bhatnagar 2003). The studies on the implementation of ICTs reveal that it has not been successful in all the states and across all the schemes in India. It has not always been successful in other countries as well. Moreover, in countries like India, where the introduction of ICT is widely held as successful,[2] corruption has shown an increasing trend over the last decade.[3] Therefore, the question arises, what are conditions for the success of ICT in the reduction of red tape and corruption in developing countries known for their red tape and corruption? The chapter explores the answer to this question.

The structure of the chapter is as follows: Sect. 2 briefly reviews the literature on red tape and corruption, the role of ICT in red tape and the effect of ICT (e-governance) on corruption. Section 3 presents the theoretical model. Section 4 provides empirical support to the theoretical hypotheses. Section 5 concludes.

[1] See Banerjee (1997), Saha (2001) and Guriev (2004) on this.

[2] Look at the lauding of India on this count in the Global Competitiveness Report (GCR), 2017–18 (Schwab 2017).

[3] India has slipped a few places in the recent edition of Corruption Perception Index (Transparency International 2018).

2 Literature Review

In a recent paper, Raj et al. (2018) compare the data from Doing Business Report (World Bank 2014a) and Enterprise Survey Report (World Bank 2014b), respectively, on *de jure* number of days and de facto number of days required for starting a business in Indian states and find that the de facto numbers are much smaller than the *de jure* numbers. The gap between the two numbers shows the existence of wide-spread 'deal-making' corruption in the state administration circumventing the 'red tape'. The existing literature in economics deals with different aspects of 'red tape'. A class of papers like Banerjee (1997), Saha (2001), Guriev (2004), Fredriksson (2014) tries to explain the length of red tape. Banerjee (1997) shows why the red tape is likely to be longer in developing countries vis-à-vis developed countries. Saha (2001) shows the way the length of red tape depends on the waiting costs of the recipients of the transfer of the targeted benefits programme. Guriev (2004) derives the socially optimum level of red tape and explains why in the absence of proper incentive, the officials may create excessive red tape. Fredriksson (2014) investigates the role of intermediaries in red tape and corruption. He shows that inclusion of intermediaries in bureaucracy leads to a long red tape than in exclusion of it and a consequent fall in social welfare. Ahlin and Bose (2007) explore the effect of bureaucratic competition in a model of red tape. In this paper, unlike Banerjee (1997), Saha (2001), Guriev (2004), Fredriksson (2014), the length of red tape is exogenously fixed by technological factors. It also does not deal either with the bureaucratic competition or with intermediaries. Instead, it looks at the demand side of corruption in the presence of 'red tape'. It first tries to explain under what kind of situation the applicants for the delivery of public good would like to pay a bribe and would prefer persistence of a corrupt system to an honest system. Then, it tries to derive implications for the introduction of ICT in such a set-up.

To deter corruption and deal-making in red tape, e-governance (ICT-enabled red tape) was introduced. E-governance is aimed at reducing misallocations and time cost while screening individuals through red tape. MukabetaMaumbe et al. (2008) explain that for the developing countries, the implementation of ICT becomes a second priority as that requires first the elimination of illiteracy, poverty and unemployment thus having the undesired impact of ICT on preventing corruption. Koutrakou (2006) particularly mentioned that the success of e-government initiatives would be in terms of improved citizen–government interaction. Twinomurinzi and Ghartey-Tagoe (2011) with case studies on e-government initiatives from Asia, Africa and South America identified three underlying factors for the successful implementation of ICT in red tape as strong political leadership for anticorruption, active community participation and available funding for the creation of dedicated ICT systems that target corruption. Bussell (2012) in her book about the implementation of ICT in India, supports the fact that political elites have a huge influence on the implementation of ICT. The book analysing a relation between political corruption and e-governance reports that the e-choupal programme succeeded in the below-average corruption states like Himachal Pradesh, Chhattisgarh and Andhra Pradesh but failed in relatively above-average corruption states like Orissa and Haryana. Mimbi and Bankole (2016) find that the extent to which ICT can efficiently increase voice and accountability, the rule of law and government effectiveness in BRICS countries is low and varies greatly among these countries.

Bussell (2012) in her survey of the e-choupal program (establishment of information kiosk and application centres for receiving public services) implemented by various state governments in India around 2006 for time-bound, corruption-free delivery of public services reports that a section of beneficiaries preferred status-quo. While it is apparent that the corrupt officials would oppose e-choupal programme as it puts a bound on the length of red tape and eliminates the interface between the applicants and the officials, it was puzzling why the applicants wanted persistence of corruption. Reddick et al. (2012) found a similar result from a study in Egypt that people preferred not availing the offline provision of services over the online provision. Banerjee et al. (2016) and Muralidharan et al. (2016) through their surveys in Indian states of Bihar and Andhra Pradesh, respectively, claim that fund transfers through e-channels in National Rural Employment Guarantee Programme (NREGA) was successful in reducing leakages and hence corruption. Ali and Gasmi (2017) show that e-governance is generally negatively related to corruption, but there may exist a threshold level of ICT above which it can curb corruption. The theoretical model presented in the next section attempts to find a logical regularity behind the empirical findings mentioned above.

3 The Model

Let us consider a government that provides a public good/service among the applicants for free[4] in a way that social welfare is maximized. There are two types of applicants in the economy: 'deserving' and 'undeserving'. The 'deserving' applicants derive higher benefit $\beta > 0$ from the possession of the good than the 'undeserving' applicants who derive a benefit of $g > 0$; $\beta > g$. The social welfare is higher too if a deserving applicant gets the good in lieu of an undeserving applicant. Therefore, the government with its objective of social welfare maximization wants the good to be allocated to the deserving applicants alone. However, the identity of an applicant is private information to her, which is revealed only through a screening process organized by the government. The screening process starts with the submission of credentials to an official in period 1, and the eligibility of the applicant is revealed at period 2. If the applicant turns out to be 'deserving', the good is delivered free. An applicant who turns out to be 'undeserving' is denied. We assume the bureaucracy is 'monopoly' in the sense that the delivery of the good is done by the same official

[4]Examples would be delivery of free food, hospital beds for people below the poverty line etc.

in period 2 who has checked the credential of the applicant in period 1.[5] The length of 'red tape' is defined as the time taken between the checking of the credentials and the delivery of the good. The better is the screening technology, less time is taken for delivery of the good; the lower is the length of the red tape. The existence of the red tape turns out to be costly for an applicant. The higher is the time elapsed before the delivery of the good, the lower is the effective benefit derived from the good. If $\beta > 0$ represents the benefit that was supposed to be received by a 'deserving' applicant from the delivery of the public good without delay, with delay, she receives only $\delta\beta < \beta$. The parameter $\delta \in (0, 1)$ stands for the length of the red tape in the sense that the longer is the red tape, the lower is the value of δ. With no red tape $\delta = 1$. A more efficient bureaucracy has a higher value of δ. The application of ICT reduces the length of red tape by reducing the screening time.

In an honest bureaucracy with a length of the red tape of δ, a deserving applicant receives a payoff of $\delta\beta$. An undeserving applicant does not receive the good; therefore, it receives a payoff of zero. Thus, the expected payoff of a deserving applicant in an honest regime is:

$$U_d^h = \delta\beta. \tag{1}$$

The expected payoff of an undeserving applicant is:

$$U_u^h = 0. \tag{2}$$

In a corrupt bureaucracy, we assume, it is common knowledge that ρ proportion of the officials are honest, but the rest are corrupt. But an applicant does not know which official is corrupt before she meets one. A corrupt official, independent of the type of the applicant, transfers the good to an applicant only in exchange for a bribe. This can happen in either in period 1 or period 2 of the application process. If a bribe is charged, we assume, the amount of bribe is determined as the entire amount of bribe surplus lying with an applicant.[6] For simplification, we also assume that the applicants have sufficient ability to meet the bribe demand and their outside option of zero.[7] Now let us discuss the determination of bribes and other payoffs in a corrupt equilibrium.

First, consider the corrupt official's behaviour in period 2 of the application process. We discuss his behaviour in period 1 later as his behaviour in period 1 depends on his expectation about the period 2 outcome. In period 2, it may be recalled that the type of applicant is revealed through the 'red tape'. So, the corrupt official knows whether the applicant who has come to receive the good is a 'deserving' one or not.

[5]In a competitive bureaucracy, these two tasks are done by two different officials. An analysis of a competitive bureaucracy remains as our future research agenda.

[6]Alternatively, the amount of bribe could also be determined through Nash bargaining where the corrupt official would share the bribe surplus with the applicant. But with alternative bribe conventions, the results would remain unchanged.

[7]In a companion paper, we relax this assumption of the model.

In the presence of red tape, the corrupt official knows that by receiving the good, the deserving applicant would have a payoff of $\delta\beta$ and the undeserving applicant would have a payoff of δg. Since the outside option of each type of applicants is zero, their payoffs also define their bribable surplus. Therefore, the corrupt official as bribe charges $\delta\beta$ to a deserving applicant and δg to an undeserving applicant for delivery of the good. While for a deserving applicant, the bribe incidence would be a situation of extortion, for an undeserving applicant, it would be a situation of collusion. Notice that because of the corruption in period 2 both types of applicants leave with the good but with zero net payoffs.

Let us now discuss the possibility of bribery in period 1 of the application process. Now the corrupt official offers the good to the applicants who have come for submitting the credentials at period 1 in period 1 itself without any delay, in exchange of a bribe.[8] The bribe rate depends on the bribe surplus lying with the applicants at this period. What is the amount of bribe surplus lying with the two types of applicants at period 1? First, let us look at the case of a deserving applicant. By receiving the good immediately at period 1, she knows that she can skirt the red tape and enjoy a payoff of β. But if she rejects the bribe offer and waits for the good to be delivered in period 2, since the bureaucracy is a monopoly, she knows that the good will be delivered by the same corrupt official at period 2 and in that case, she will surely be extorted to receive a net payoff of zero in period 2. So, her bribable surplus in period 1 is calculated as $(\beta - 0) = \beta$. Now let us look at the case of the undeserving applicant. By similar logic as applied for the deserving applicants, her bribable surplus at period 1 is calculated as $(g - 0) = g$. If the corrupt official could identify the types of the applicants in period 1, he would charge β as a bribe to a deserving applicant and g to an undeserving applicant. But since the type of applicant gets revealed only at the end of period 2, the corrupt official does not have the information to differentiate a deserving applicant from an undeserving one. However, we assume, it is common knowledge that α proportion of the applicants is deserving and $(1 - \alpha)$ proportion is undeserving. So, the corrupt official knows that the applicant whom he meets in period 1 for checking credentials is a deserving applicant with probability α and is an undeserving applicant with probability $(1 - \alpha)$. Therefore, he also knows that since $\beta > g$ if he offers a bribe rate of β to the applicants for avoiding the red tape, with probability α the offer will be accepted; and with probability $(1 - \alpha)$ the offer will be rejected. Only the deserving applicants will agree to pay the bribe. An undeserving applicant will reject the offer and wait for the period 2 interaction when she receives the good by paying δg. So, this bribe offer is exclusionary in nature. If the corrupt official is risk-neutral, he calculates his expected payoff from the offer of the exclusionary bribe rate of β as $[\alpha\beta + (1 - \alpha) \cdot \delta g]$. Similarly, he knows that on the offering of a bribe rate of g his expected payoff is g since both types of applicants are expected to accept the bribe offer in period 1 itself. So, this bribe offer is

[8] Ideally, an official detected of such a practice will be liable to punishment. However, to keep things simple here, we assume that the expected punishment is zero, which can be relaxed in an extended version of the model. But it is also true that the expected punishment for the corrupt officials is close to zero in many countries, especially in the developing part of the world.

pooling in nature. The corrupt official will offer an exclusionary bribe if and only if $\alpha\beta + (1-\alpha)\cdot\delta g > g$ which implies $\alpha > \frac{g-\delta g}{\beta-\delta g} = \alpha^*$, i.e. if and only if the proportion of deserving applicants in the economy exceeds a critical threshold value of α^*. Otherwise, a pooling bribe will be offered.

Let us summarize the equilibrium in a corrupt regime as discussed above. In an economy where $\alpha > \alpha^*$, if a corrupt official is met, an exclusionary bribe is offered at the stage of checking credentials (in period 1) for skirting the red tape of length δ; only the deserving applicants accept such an offer, the undeserving applicants wait through the length of red tape for getting the good in period 2 only; both receive a payoff of zero as the entire bribe surplus gets extracted in the process. If an honest official is met in period 1, a deserving applicant receives the good at the end of period 2 with a discounted payoff of $\delta\beta$. However, if an honest official is met in period 1, an undeserving applicant does not receive the good. Therefore, the expected payoff of a deserving applicant in a corrupt regime is:

$$U_d^E = \rho\delta\beta + (1-\rho)(\beta-\beta). \tag{3}$$

Similarly, the expected payoff of an undeserving applicant in this regime is:

$$U_u^E = \rho\cdot 0 + (1-\rho)0 = 0. \tag{4}$$

In an economy where $\alpha \leq \alpha^*$, if a corrupt official is met, a pooling bribe is offered at the stage of checking credentials which are readily accepted by both types of applicants for skirting the red tape; a deserving applicant receives a payoff of $(\beta - g) > 0$ and an undeserving applicant receives a payoff of zero. Therefore, the expected payoff of a deserving applicant in such a case is:

$$U_d^P = \rho\delta\beta + (1-\rho)(\beta-g) \tag{5}$$

Similarly, the expected payoff of an undeserving applicant, in this case, is calculated as:

$$U_u^P = \rho\cdot 0 + (1-\rho)\cdot(g-g) = 0. \tag{6}$$

Observe that though the possibility of extortion is there, in neither of the economies, extortion is an equilibrium outcome. The deserving applicants are the ones who readily collude at the stage of submission of credentials itself and avoid the red tape. The undeserving applicants also collude but suffer the red tape in an economy where the proportion of deserving applicants is above the threshold. It is imperative that the corrupt official would always like the corrupt regime to persist, which is apparent in the preceding analysis as well. The corrupt officials enjoy a positive payoff in a corrupt regime compared to zero in an honest regime. What about the applicants? Do they prefer a corrupt regime to persist, or long for honesty to prevail? The model provides an interesting answer to this question.

First, consider the case of undeserving applicants. In an honest regime, they do not receive the good and their payoff is zero. In a corrupt regime, if $\alpha > \alpha^*$ and if a corrupt official is met, they endure the red tape to receive the good in period 2. But their entire bribe surplus gets extracted in period 2 bribery and they receive a payoff of zero. On the other hand, if $\alpha \leq \alpha^*$ and a corrupt official is met, they pay the collusive bribe at period 1 itself and receives the good without a wait but receives a net payoff of zero. If an honest official is met, even in a corrupt regime, their payoff is zero. So, the undeserving applicants must be indifferent between a corrupt regime and an honest regime. Next, let us consider the case of the deserving applicants. In an honest regime, they receive the good for free at the end of period 2 and enjoy a payoff of $\delta\beta$. In a corrupt regime, if $\alpha > \alpha^*$ and a corrupt official is met, they pay a collusive bribe for avoiding red tape, but the exclusionary bribe rate extracts their entire surplus so that they end up with a net payoff of zero. If an honest official is met, their payoff is zero. So, in an economy where $\alpha > \alpha^*$, the deserving applicants would always vote for an honest system over a corrupt system. If $\alpha \leq \alpha^*$ and a corrupt official is met, they again enter a collusive bribery and avoid the red tape; but the pooling bribe rate being low enjoy a positive payoff of $(\beta - g)$. Therefore, now they prefer a corrupt regime to an honest regime if and only if $\beta - g > \delta\beta$ or $\delta < 1 - \frac{g}{\beta} = \delta^*$, i.e. the length of the red tape is long enough. If the length of the red tape is below the threshold value of δ^*, they would not mind waiting in an honest regime.

The implications of the above analysis in terms of preference towards corruption in red tape can be illustrated in Fig. 1, where the horizontal and vertical axis represents the values of $\delta \in (0, 1)$ and $\alpha \in (0, 1)$, respectively. In the presence of red tape, at all the (δ, α) combinations in the unit square, 'speed money' is paid in a corrupt bureaucracy. But it is not that at all the combinations of (δ, α) 'speed money' and corruption is a preferred option for the applicants. Some of the applicants, if asked about their preference over a corrupt regime vis-à-vis an honest regime will vote for

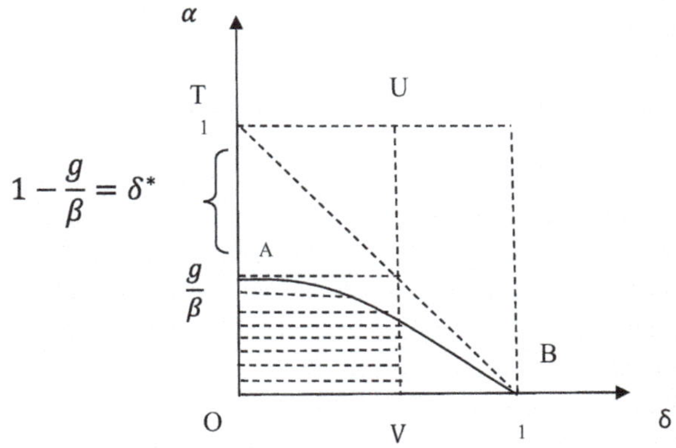

Fig. 1 Preference towards corruption and its existence under red tape

an honest regime, and if their preference prevails, corruption would not exist in an economy even in the presence of red tape.

The curve AB in the above figure represents $\alpha^* = \frac{g-\delta g}{\beta-\delta g}$. Since for all $\alpha > \alpha^*$, the exclusionary contract is offered by the corrupt official at the time of checking credentials, in Fig. 1, at all the points above AB curve in the unit square, the deserving applicants prefer an honest regime to a corrupt regime and if they are supported by the undeserving applicants who are indifferent between the two regimes, corruption would not exist in red tape. From the above analysis, it implies if the preference of the deserving applicants prevails, corruption is preferred and exists in red tape at the combinations of α and δ such that $\alpha \leq \alpha^*$ and $\delta < \delta^*$. In Fig. 1, the length AT $= 1 - \frac{g}{\beta} = \delta^* =$ length TU $=$ length OV. Therefore, the vertical line UV represents δ^* which is independent of α and the shaded area AOV represents the combinations of α and δ for which corruption in red tape would exist. For the (δ, α) combinations in AOV, no one complains about the existing corruption in the economy.

Notice that the shape of the area AOV depends on $\frac{g}{\beta}$, i.e. the ratio of benefits accrued to an undeserving applicant vis-à-vis a deserving applicant from the public good/service which is being distributed. As $\frac{g}{\beta} \to 1$, i.e. there is not much difference in benefits accrued to the two types of applicants, the AB curve becomes steeper as A moves to T, δ^* falls and the UV line shifts in the inward direction to the vertical axis as V moves to O. The opposite happens if $\frac{g}{\beta} \to 0$, i.e. there is a sharp difference between the benefit accrued to a deserving applicant vis-à-vis an undeserving applicant. These two extreme cases are represented in Fig. 2.

The above analysis shows that in the presence of red tape and corruption, both types of applicants would participate in collusive bribery for avoiding the red tape, which is empirically supported by Raj et al. (2018). However, the undeserving applicants would never complain about the existence of a corrupt regime. It is the deserving applicants who would complain about the existence of corruption under two different situations: (i) if the number of deserving applicants is above the threshold, i.e. $\alpha > \alpha^*$; and (ii) if the number of deserving applicants is below the threshold, i.e. $\alpha \leq \alpha^*$ but the length of the red tape is short enough, i.e. $\delta \geq \delta^*$. The result is

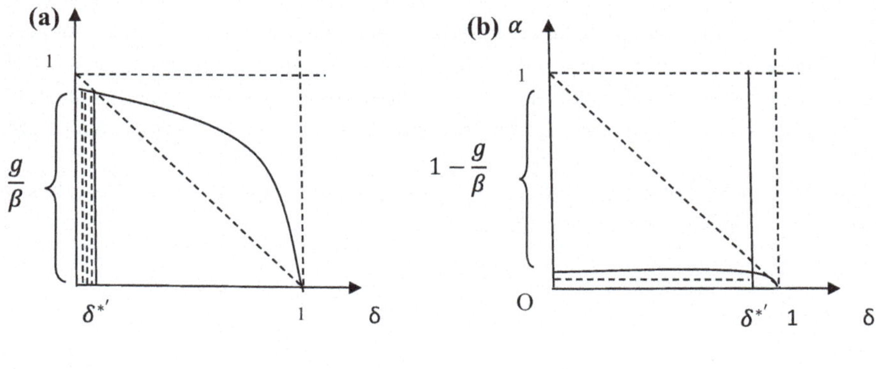

Fig. 2 **a** Extreme case I: $\frac{g}{\beta} \to 1$. **b** Extreme case II: $\frac{g}{\beta} \to 0$

interesting because it helps us to understand the responses from the individuals in the survey conducted by Bussell (2012) and from the firms as part of surveys like World Economic Forum Executive Opinion survey 2017–18 (GCR, 2017–18) and Enterprise Survey Report (World Bank 2014b) about red-tape-related corruption in economies. For example, consider the case of the Enterprise Survey Report (World Bank 2014b). The survey reports that 35.8% of firms in India, consider corruption as a major obstacle in doing business. If $\alpha > \alpha^*$, the result of the theoretical model suggests that the firms complaining about corruption are essentially the deserving applicants for delivery of the firm-specific public good/service. But India being a less developed country, if we accept it is most likely to be the case that $\alpha \leq \alpha^*$, the theoretical prediction of the model suggests it must be the case $\delta \geq \delta^*$, i.e. the length of the red tape is not long enough in the country. If the second possibility is true, in the case of distributing firm-specific public goods/services, shortening of the length of red tape further through the introduction of ICTs is not expected to reduce corruption. What is really needed for solving the problem of corruption is the creation of a political system where the preference of the deserving applicants complaining about corruption prevails. However, if the length of red tape is too long to start with such that $\delta < \delta^*$, shortening of red tape through ICT and time-bound delivery of services can create a possibility that the threshold is crossed, and the deserving applicants start complaining about corruption. Similarly, for delivery of individual/household-specific public goods, the finding of Bussell (2012) that in some of the Indian states, the individuals preferred the corrupt system of good public delivery to ICTs which can also be explained through our model. Our model suggests that it must be the case in such situations it was $\alpha \leq \alpha^*$ and the length of the red tape was long enough, i.e. it was $\delta < \delta^*$ so that the deserving applicants preferred the corrupt system to the ICTs. The introduction of ICTs was not sufficient in shortening the length of the prevailing red tape such that the direction of inequality reverses to $\delta \geq \delta^*$. This explains why for individual/household public goods delivery, the introduction of ICTs was not successful in some states of India, but it was successful in some other states. The extreme situations presented in Fig. 2a suggest that if the difference in the payoff of the deserving and undeserving applicants is not much, i.e. $\frac{g}{\beta} \to 1$ the success of ICT and time-bound delivery of public services in the creation of demand for an honest regime is more imminent. However, extreme situations presented in Fig. 2b suggest that if the difference in the payoff of the deserving and undeserving applicants is not much, i.e. $\frac{g}{\beta} \to 0$, the ICT and the time-bound delivery of public services are less likely to be successful in solving the problem of corruption in the presence of red tape.

In the section below, we provide limited empirical support of the hypotheses thrown above from cross-country data.

4 Empirical Evidence

The hypotheses derived in the theoretical model about the role of ICT in generating support for an honest regime is tested in this section by use of the data on firms' responses at different countries as given in World Bank Enterprise Survey (WBES), 2006–18 about desirability of an honest regime at the respective countries and the cross-country index of e-governance published in UN E-government Survey (2004–2016). We test for the following hypotheses:

H1: The ICT creates demand for an honest regime.
H2: The longer is the red-tape the less successful is ICT in creating demand for an honest regime.

In WBES (2006–18), the firms are asked to express their opinion about the extent to which they think corruption is an obstacle for doing business against five different options[9]: (i) no obstacle (0), (ii) minor obstacle (1), (iii) moderate obstacle (2), (iv) major obstacle (3) and (v) severe obstacle (4). Since all the corruption indices show the developing countries are entrenched in corruption,[10] for the developing countries we have considered in our study, we interpret the response of the firms to this question as their desirability of an honest regime in the following way: a response of 'no obstacle' is interpreted as 'the firm is comfortable with the current regime with existing corruption' and a response of 'severe obstacle' is interpreted as 'the firm is extremely uncomfortable about the existing corrupt regime and looks for a change towards an honest regime'. The intermediate responses are interpreted as the desirability of change towards an honest regime in increasing order. Looking at the responses of the firms in each of the countries, we derive the median response of each of the countries as the respective countries' desirability towards an honest regime. The higher is the value of the median; the more is the desirability towards an honest regime in the country. We call this variable 'PFH' in our study[11] and check how PFH responds to ICT and red tape in the country.

The UN E-government Survey (2004–2016) provides for cross-country e-government index (EGI), which we interpret as data on the level of implementation of ICT in a country. EGI combines the indices of online services, telecommunication infrastructure and human capital stock of the countries. The higher values of EGI would imply greater penetration of ICT in the countries. The variable 'red tape' stands for the extent of red tape prevailing in a country and is constructed from WBES database as the median response of firms in each country regarding the proportion of time they spend in a year for getting through administrative processes. The higher value of the variable means more red tape in the country.

It is not that the data is available for all the countries for all the years. Depending on the availability of data, we construct an unbalanced panel of 19 developing countries

[9]WBES (2006–18) attaches scores for respective responses which are given in parenthesis against each option.

[10]See Svensson (2005).

[11]PFH stands for preference for honest regime.

over the period 2006–2018 for analysis. The list of the countries is given in Table 1 in the appendix. We have also provided the Corruption Perception Index rank of these countries in the table (Transparency International 2018). In the Index, the least corrupt country of the World receives the rank of 1. So, the countries taken in our study are moderate to severely corrupt countries in the World with a minimum rank of 27 (Chile) and the maximum rank of 170 (Burundi). We have also mentioned in the table the number of firms surveyed in these countries as part of WBES. The regression that we run is:

$$\mathrm{PFH}_{it} = \beta_0 + \beta_1 \mathrm{ICT}_{it} + \beta_2 \left(\mathrm{ICT}_{it} * \mathrm{Red\ Tape}_{it}\right) + \beta_3 t + a_i + \epsilon_{it}$$

where i stands for countries and t stands for a year. For H1 to hold, β_1 must be positive. For H2 to hold β_2 must be negative. We control for the variation of time and the country-specific fixed effect in the regression.

The summary statistics of the variables are given in Table 2.

Table 1 List of countries with their corruption rank and number of firms surveyed

Country	Continent	Corruption rank (corruption perception index)	Number of firms surveyed
Botswana	Africa	34	606
Burundi	Africa	170	424
Angola	Africa	165	727
Lao PDR	Asia	132	597
Dominican Republic	Central America	129	709
El Salvador	Central America	105	1739
Guatemala	Central America	144	1093
Honduras	Central America	132	1111
Nicaragua	Central America	152	1111
Panama	Central America	93	953
Argentina	South America	85	2071
Bolivia	South America	132	955
Chile	South America	27	2012
Colombia	South America	99	1909
Ecuador	South America	114	1008
Paraguay	South America	132	964
Peru	South America	105	1616
Uruguay	South America	70	1180
Venezuela	South America	168	805

Source WBES (2006–2018), Transparency International (2018)

Table 2 Descriptive statistics

Variable		Mean	Std. dev.	Min	Max	Observation
PFH	Overall	2.11	1.06	0	4	41
	Between		0.76	1	3.5	19
	Within		0.76	0.61	3.61	2.16
ICT	Overall	0.43	0.12	0.15	0.68	41
	Between		0.11	0.19	0.63	19
	Within		0.03	0.36	0.49	2.16
Red Tape	Overall	0.15	0.14	0	9.8	41
	Between		0.09	0.0075	0.3875	19
	Within		0.10	0.12	0.43	2.16

Table 1 shows that in the panel of countries on average, the firms report moderate desirability for an honest regime. The penetration of ICT had been moderate in these countries throughout study, the average value of EGI standing at 0.43. As the firms on average spend only 15% of their time in a year towards administrative procedures, the extent of red tape is also not very high in these countries. Since the ICT data do not match year-wise for the countries, we take the first year of ICT data as the starting year and the subsequent years are interpreted accordingly. For ICT, we have two to three observations per country. The result of the fixed effect panel regression is presented in Table 3.

Table 3 Regression result

Independent variable	Coefficients
ICT	12.79** (5.50)
ICT * Red Tape	−4.20** (1.68)
t	−0.16 (0.30)
Constant	−2.79 (2.08)
Prob > *F*	0.06

'*', '**' and '***' denotes significance at 10%, 5% and 1%, respectively. The values of robust standard errors are given in the parenthesis

The regression result shows the expected sign. The implantation of ICT increases the desirability of an honest regime. The result is significant at 5% level. Notice also that the impact is likely to be weaker in countries with longer red tape. The variable (ICT * Red Tape) has an expected negative sign. But it is found to be significant at the 10% level.

5 Discussion and Conclusions

The chapter studies the interaction between red tape, corruption and introduction of ICTs in the delivery of public goods and services. The chapter develops a theoretical model for the study and empirically tests its predictions. The model first defines two types of individuals in an economy: the individuals who are targeted by the government for the delivery of the public good and the individuals who are not. Since the type of individual, whether she is deserving or not is her private information, the government screens the applicants by checking their credentials. The screening process takes a certain time to establish the type of the individual, which is defined as 'red tape' in the model. However, the good loses some of its value because of the red tape. The longer is the length of the red tape; the higher is the loss. A corrupt official independent of the type of applicant takes a bribe for delivery of the good. The ICT promises to shorten the length of the red tape.

The results of the model show that although all types of applicant pay speed money in the presence of red tape, it is not that everyone prefers a corrupt regime to an honest regime. The undeserving applicants never complain about a corrupt regime. But the deserving applicants complain about the corrupt regime in two types of situations: if the proportion of deserving applicants is high enough and if the proportion of deserving applicants is low, but the length of the red tape is not long enough in the presence of a too long a red tape no one complaints about corruption. The introduction of ICT by shortening the length of red tape may increase support for an honest regime if the red tape is not long enough and if the gap between the two types of applicants' payoff is not large enough. The empirical analysis with cross-country data shows that the theoretical apprehensions hold good as the ICT increases demand for an honest regime in general, but it reduces the demand for an honest regime and therefore the implementation of further ICT reform in countries with longer red tapes.

The results explain why the introduction of ICT has not been successful in many corrupt economies and some of them, preference for a corrupt regime has been found. One limitation of the empirical study is that although the theoretical model predicts, the deserving firms would prefer honest regime under the shorter length of red tape, due to lack of sufficient data about the nature of the firms, we are unable to test it. The future extension of this work involves finding out the effect of the ability to pay of the stakeholders and the strength of the legal system on the scope of ICT.

Appendix

See Table 1.

References

Ahlin, C., & Bose, P. (2007). Bribery, inefficiency, and bureaucratic delay. *Journal of Development Economics, 84*(1), 465–486. https://doi.org/10.1016/j.jdeveco.2005.12.002.

Ali, M. S. B., & Gasmi, A. (2017). Does ICT diffusion matter for corruption? An economic development perspective. *Telematics and Informatics*. https://doi.org/10.1016/j.tele.2017.06.008.

Banerjee, A. (1997). A theory of misgovernance. *Quarterly Journal of Economics, 112*(4), 1289–1332.

Banerjee, A., Duflo, E., Imbert, C., Mathew, S., & Pande, R. (2016). *E-governance, accountability and leakage in public programs: Experimental evidence from a financial management reform in India* (Working Paper 22803). National Bureau of Economic Research, Inc.

Bhatnagar, S. (2003). *Transparency and corruption: Does E-government help?* Retrieved from: http://unpan1.un.org/intradoc/groups/public/documents/unpan/unpan035963.pdf.

Bussell, J. (2012). *Corruption and reform in India: Public services in the digital age*. New Delhi: Cambridge University Press.

Fredriksson, A. (2014). Bureaucracy intermediaries, corruption and red tape. *Journal of Development Economics, 108,* 256–273.

Guriev, S. (2004). Red tape and corruption. *Journal of Development Economics, 73*(2), 489–504.

Koutrakou, V. N. (2006). The Greek e-government. *Journal of E-government*, *3*(2), 75–98. https://doi.org/10.1300/j399v03n02_05.

Mimbi, L., & Bankole, F. O. (2016). ICT and public service value creation in Africa: Efficiency assessment using DEA approach. In *Proceeding of the 27th Australian Conference on Information System*, Sydney, Australia.

MukabetaMaumbe, B., Owei, V., & Alexander, H. (2008). Questioning the pace and pathway of e-government development in Africa: A case study of South Africa's Cape Gateway project. *Government Information Quarterly, 25*(4), 757–777.

Muralidharan, K., Niehaus, P., & Sukhtankar, S. (2016). Building state capacity: Evidence from biometric smartcards in India. *American Economic Review, 106*(10), 2895–2929.

Raj, R., Sen, K., & Kar, S. (2018). *De Jure rules meet De facto deals: The political economy of business-state relations in Indian states*. Paper Presented at ICAS-MP Workshop on Political Economy of India, CSSS, Kolkata, 11–12 January, 2018.

Reddick, C. G., Abdelsalam, H. M. E., & Elkadi, H. A. (2012). Channel choice and the digital divide in e-government: The case of Egypt. *Information Technology for development, 18*(3), 226–246.

Saha, B. (2001). Red tape, incentive bribe and the provision of subsidy. *Journal of Development Economics, 65*(1), 113–133.

Schwab, K. (2017). *Global competitiveness report 2017–18*. World Economic Forum, Geneva, Switzerland. Retrieved from https://www.weforum.org/reports/the-global-competitiveness-report-2017-2018.

Svensson, J. (2005). Eight questions about corruption. *Journal of Economic Perspective, 19*(3), 19–42.

Transparency International. (2018). *Corruption perception index*. Retrieved from https://www.transparency.org.

Twinomurinzi, H., & Ghartey-Tagoe, K. B. (2011). Corruption in developing countries and ICT: The urgent need for work systems to precede E-government. In *Proceedings of the 11th International Conference on Social Implications of Computer in Developing countries*, Kathmandu, Nepal.

UN E-Government Survey. (2004). *UN E-government knowledgebase*. Retrieved from https://publicadministration.un.org/egovkb/en-us/Reports/UN-E-Government-Survey-2004.

UN E-Government Survey. (2008). *UN E-government knowledgebase*. Retrieved from https://publicadministration.un.org/egovkb/en-us/Reports/UN-E-Government-Survey-2008.

UN E-Government Survey. (2010). *UN E-government Knowledgebase*. Retrieved from https://publicadministration.un.org/egovkb/en-us/Reports/UN-E-Government-Survey-2010.

UN E-Government Survey. (2012). *UN E-government knowledgebase*. Retrieved from https://publicadministration.un.org/egovkb/en-us/Reports/UN-E-Government-Survey-2012.

UN E-Government Survey. (2014). UN E-government Knowledgebase. Retrieved from https://publicadministration.un.org/egovkb/en-us/Reports/UN-E-Government-Survey-2014.
UN E-Government Survey. (2016). UN E-government Knowledgebase. Retrieved from https://publicadministration.un.org/egovkb/en-us/Reports/UN-E-Government-Survey-2016.
World Bank. (2014a). *Doing business report 2014*. Retrieved from: http://www.doingbusiness.org.
World Bank. (2014b). *Enterprise survey report*. Retrieved from: http://www.enterprisesurveys.org.
World Bank. (2018). *Enterprise survey 2006–18*. Retrieved from: http://www.enterprisesurveys.org.

Role of Technology in Governance and Development: The Case of *e-Uparjan* in Madhya Pradesh

Satyendra Nath Mishra and Kushankur Dey

Abstract This study explored the interlinkages between the attributes of technology, governance and development. The *e-Uparjan* is a case of digital inclusion and synchronisation of activities of stakeholders like farmers, designate procurement agencies, technology providers, financial institutions and state administrative agencies. A single case study approach is adopted to understand the technology-enabled procurement system at the micro-level. Field observations expanded the scope of understanding of the context and potential implications of the procurement system to associated stakeholders. The study conjectures that faster and real-time information flow along with the decision nodes can plug in fund leakage, reduce transaction costs and mitigate rent-seeking behaviour of actors along the value chain. It is proposed that the improvisation with a low-cost information and communication technology (ICT) can have potential to streamline procurement operations and secure farmers' pay-off in a time-bound manner through direct benefit transfer under the price support scheme. The *e-Uparjan* appears to have improved operational efficiency of collection, warehousing and optimising transportation network for food grains procurement and distribution. The *e-Uparjan* offers fresh insights on social policy making as network processes that requires an adequate understanding of social realities, seamless synchronisation of involved stakeholders and aspects of public procurement policies.

Keywords Technology · Governance · Development · *e-Uparjan*

JEL Code H19 · H77 · O33 · Z18

This paper is expanded version of Working Paper (XSRM-WPS-1) of Xavier University Bhubaneswar. Authors acknowledge the comments shared by the audience of University Dialogue Series (UDS; dated 09th September 2016) at Xavier University Bhubaneswar and at two day workshop on 'Economics of ICTs: Transformation, Digital Divide, and Development' at Delhi School of Economics (22–23 February 2018).

S. N. Mishra (✉)
School of Rural Management, Xavier University Bhubaneswar, Puri, India
e-mail: saty.nm@gmail.com

K. Dey
Indian Institute of Management Bodh Gaya, Bodh Gaya, India

D. Maiti et al. (eds.), *Digitalisation and Development*,
https://doi.org/10.1007/978-981-13-9996-1_14

1 Introduction

Food grains procurement and distribution in India has been an epicentre of debate and discussions in policy circles (Narayanan 2015; Ganesh et al. 2007). The Food Corporation India (FCI) was established in 1965 (under the Food Corporation Act 1964) with the primary duty to undertake the purchase, storage, movement, transport, distribution and sales of food grains and other foodstuffs (FCI 1964). The offtake of food grains under the public distribution system (PDS) enhanced the scope of procurement under the minimum support price (MSP) scheme. MSP has a twin effect on the producer and market functioning. First, producers can avoid distress sales just after the harvest. Second, because of high political intervention with a national interest in food grains procurement, the market is not allowed to dictate the prices of essential commodities covered under MSP (Chand 2017). However, it is reported that only 20% farmers in India have received the benefits of the price support scheme, about 25% of the farmers was aware of the MSP at all India level. In 2012–13, only about 19% farmers knew of the FCI and 75% did not sell to procurement agencies (Singh 2012).

The failure or ill-equipped procurement and distribution system can be attributed to the socio-political tensions between the state-centre, minimal deployment of procurement officials on the field and conflict of interests between FCI, state procurement agencies and milling agents, among others.[1] Sekher et al. (2017) conducted a process mapping analysis of six Indian states on PDS opined that the reforms brought in PDS are attributed to coverage expansion, technology adoption and decentralising procurement. This improvisation in PDS, procuring cereals or pulses from farmers at MSP either from designated agricultural markets or APMCs remains a herculean task for FCI or state-level procurement agencies due to exorbitant transaction costs and lack of aggregation at the farm gate (Krishnamurthy 2012a). The concentration of private traders, corporate involvement in trading and role of the state agencies as a mere spectator in food grains management has made the procurement system rather ineffective and inefficient, and governance issues have been central to this fragile system (Chand 2012).

In the backdrop of several process bottlenecks in food grains management, the Government of India (GoI) initiated the decentralised procurement scheme (DPS) in 1997–98. Under DPS, the state agencies participated in MSP-based procurement. The state's Food and Civil Supply Corporation (F&CSC) and State Marketing Federation (MARKFED) got empowered to participate and oversee the operation. This was done to enhance the efficiency of procurement of food grains (based on local requirement), PDS, and to benefit the local farmers under MSP[2] (Krishnamurthy 2012b).

In spite of these improvisations in food grains management, the procurement remained an area of concern in policy circles (Chand 2012, 2017) that calls for an investigation of a few research questions, like (i) can the dual participation of centre-state agencies in MSP-driven food grains management will improve public

[1] Based on field-based observation of second author.

[2] Accessed from http://dfpd.nic.in/decentralized-procurement.htm, dated 06 April 2018.

procurement operations? (ii) Is there any role of information and communications technologies (ICT) in systematising the food grains procurement? (iii) Can ICT-based intervention impact the farmer participation in the state adopted price support scheme (i.e. MSP)? At the core of these question is an exploration of the role of ICT-based technology intervention in addressing the challenges of governance and development in public procurement. To address the above questions, we used a single case study approach of ICT-based intervention in food grains management—*e-Uparjan*[3]—in Madhya Pradesh (MP).

The chapter is organised as follows. Section 2 covers the review of literature in ICTs, governance and development. Section 3 discusses the relevance of price support scheme and elucidates some existing models in-vogue in food grains procurement. Section 4 briefs the *e-Uparjan* model as part of ICT-intervention, and Sect. 5 explores the linkages between the attributes of technology, governance and development in the context of food grains procurement through *e-Uparjan* in MP. Section 6 discusses the potential challenges of the *e-Uparjan*. Section 7 offers a discussion and potential future research questions in the light of technology's criticality in governance and development.

2 Literature Review

The innovation in technological paradigm has the potential to enhance productivity, employment and access to services in the varied field of the economy (Dosi 1982; Freeman et al. 1982, 2001). This technology-based paradigm has potential to play an important role in the growth of the economy, welfare services for public, improving the effectiveness of services, improvement in production and changing the institutional arrangements (Castellacci 2006; Ramnath and Assisi 2018). It may be noted that when a technology-based solution is scaled up to address the social challenges at the national, regional or international level, then state policy and agencies play a critical role to achieve the desired objectives. Hudson's (2006) work on telecommunication for development in rural areas addresses some issues and challenges. The initial studies in India on the potential of ICT to address the developmental challenges also substantiated this point (Thomas 2005).

In this background, the social experiment of *e-Uparjan* is an interface between affordable and accessible—ICT—technological development and proactive role of the state policy environment. This interface needs to be supported by flexible and adaptive administrative structures with the intervention of appropriate technology (Gluckman 2016). Fukuyama (2013) proposed two important dimensions of governance, viz. capacity and autonomy. Capacity consists of both resources and the degree of professionalisation of bureaucratic staff. On the other hand, autonomy refers to how the principal political issues mandates to the bureaucrats who act as an agent. On these counts, we explored the appropriateness of ICT-based technological

[3]The English translation of word *Uparjan* is procurement.

intervention and potential flexibility of governance dimensions of state administration to address the developmental challenges of farmers on account of food grains procurement.

3 Price Support Scheme and Food grains Procurement

To protect farmers from distress sales, the approach can be wider adoption of price support scheme that covers the costs of cultivation at the nominal price level, gunny bag charges, transportation and opportunity costs for family labour if deployed and other incidentals. Recently, GoI proposed a comprehensive cost model (covers three definitions of production cost, viz. A2,[4] FL[5] and C2[6]) covering all explicit and implicit costs of production that subsume the existing calculation of MSP.[7] The MSP is announced by the GoI at the onset of procurement season every year, viz. *kharif* and *rabi* marketing seasons. Commission for Agricultural Costs and Prices calculates MSP and GoI declare it for 22 commodities in the year 2017–18.[8]

The FCI at the centre and F&CSC at the state level play an instrumental role in food grains procurement. The functional convergence for food grains procurement must create an efficient system of procurement and processing (milling) through milling agreement with millers at the state level. This operation helps to maintain buffer stock in the central pool and offtake for PDS at the state level. To facilitate all these, the Central Warehousing Corporations offer an operational storage capacity of 100.02 lakh metric ton (in January 2018) across 433 warehouses.[9] The state agencies are also involved in buffer stock management, food grains offtake for PDS and regulating fair price shops.

In 2015, a high-powered committee set-up by the GoI recommended that private warehousing and logistics companies should be involved in food grains stocking and movement of under-price support scheme (Kumar 2015). This has kick-started the dual participation of public and private agencies and extended the benefits of price support scheme in parts of Bihar, Odisha, West Bengal, eastern Uttar Pradesh, Assam, etc.[10] The private agencies (like NCML, NBHC, Star Agri., Origo Commodities, etc.) have deployed manpower, notified purchase centres, constructed storage facilities and improved payment mechanism for farmers. The private-public-partnership

---

[4]A2 costs cover all paid-out expenses (cash and kind), incurred by farmers on seeds, fertilisers, chemicals, hired labour, fuel, irrigation, etc.

[5]FL covers imputed value of family labour.

[6]C2 cover costs are more comprehensive, accounting for the rentals and interest forgone on owned land and fixed capital assets, respectively, on top of A2 + FL.

[7]Accessed from https://indianexpress.com/article/india/the-cost-plug-50-percent-swaminathan-formula-mirage-agriculture-sector-minimum-support-price-4715922/, dated 08 February 2019.

[8]Accessed from http://farmer.gov.in/mspstatements.aspx, dated 10 March 2018.

[9]Accessed from http://dfpd.nic.in/storage-intro.htm, dated 10 April 2018.

[10]Accessed from http://pib.nic.in/newsite/PrintRelease.aspx?relid=114860, dated 06 April 2018.

(PPP) model appears to be accountable to beneficiaries through improved governance in procurement, storage and transportation and fund management. For example, the National Collateral Management Services Limited (NCML) adopted pay order format to MSP operation in Odisha in 2005–06 *kharif* and *rabi* marketing calendar year.[11] In addition to the above steps, the ICT-based e-procurement offers cost-effective and real-time interactive platform between farmers and state agencies for efficient and accurate food grains procurement, transportation, stocking and distribution. *e-Uparjan* (electronic procurement) is one such step taken forward by the government of MP to provide time-bound services to farmers and streamline the paddy and wheat procurement.

4 Role of Technology—ICT—and Genesis of *e-Uparjan*

The role of technology to address socio-economic challenges has received considerable attention and debate in recent times. This has generated renewed interest among professionals and policy makers to address the problem of rural India, especially to achieve the sustainable development goals (Rajvanshi 2016; TIFAC 2015). Development through techno-economic intervention can bring about change in two ways. First, where the social structure is made to change based on the imposed techno-economic intervention. This is often slow and socially resistive. The second option is designing the techno-economic intervention as per the requirement of existing social challenges. This is not often adopted by research institutions or pushed by policy makers due to the specificity of techno-economic intervention (Perez 1985; Massey 2016; Mishra 2013, 2014; Warschauer 2003).

In this background, this section explores how this dilemma can be addressed, drawing inputs from a social experiment of *e-Uparjan* implemented in MP in 2010–11. The improvisation using a low-cost ICT and administrative flexibility has played a critical role to streamline the procurement operations and secure farmer pay-off under MSP. *e-Uparjan* addresses the challenges faced by the farmers and food grains procurement agencies during *rabi* and *kharif* season. Importance of ICT for effective governance and development has been reiterated time and again (Anonymous 1935; Mathur and Neurath 1959; UNESCO 1967; Warschauer 2003; Navarra and Cornford 2005). This has been recently advocated unequivocally by the scientists (Swaminathan and Keswan 2016), policy makers (GoI 2013; TIFAC 2015) and Prime Minister of India Narendra Modi (Modi 2015, 2016; Pulakkat 2015).

The precursor to the *e-Uparjan* initiative was a law and order situation that arose in 2010 at food grains procurement centre—*mandi* (Agriculture Produce Market Committee (APMC)—in Harda district of MP due to bumper production (NITI Aayog 2015). To address the unrest among farmers and manage operational activities of procurement at the *mandi*, the district administration took the initiative to include farmers under digital governance system of MSP-based procurement. The registered

[11] Based on field-based observation of second author.

farmers were linked to cellular-based short message service (SMS) for information dissemination and communication. The information about the date and venue of procurement was shared with farmers four days in advance. This initiative has reduced the chaos and improved the *mandi's* functioning. In *rabi* season of 2011, Shivraj Singh Chouhan, the then Chief Minister of MP rolled out this initiative in the state as *e-Uparjan* with several facilitative features. The objective of *e-Uparjan* is to create an efficient system of food grains procurement, management and to protect the farmer's interest by providing maximum coverage under MSP (NITI Aayog 2015).

5 Linkages Explored: Technology, Governance and Development

With a brief description of the electronic procurement system, an attempt had been made to explore the potential linkages of attributes of technology in facilitating the governance process to address the developmental challenges (see Figs. 1 and 2).[12]

In 2011, for implementing *e-Uparjan*, the National Informatics Centre (NIC) had developed software based on Dot-NET platform having two modules—offline and online—in the Hindi language. This mainframe architecture is acting as the backbone for information collection and dissemination. The offline module is located at the *e-Uparjan Kendra*[13]of the block and district that collects information on following features, viz. (i) farmer's registration details, (ii) processes of buying and selling of food grains, (iii) scheduling of daily storage capacity and procurement status based on SMS details, (iv) reporting of direct money transfer to farmers account, (v) gunny bag management, (vi) transport management, (vii) storage management and (viii) information regarding agriculture loan and recovery of registered farmers. The online module facilitates farmer registration and verification of shared information. Also, it provides area-wise information through SMS for scheduling of procurement, the opening of new procurement centres, updates on crop loss due to natural disaster and real-time update to farmers about MSP payment (NITI Aayog 2015). The online module also helps in generating standardised dashboard reports shared at various layers as part of management information system (MIS) that facilitate in planning and forecasting of food grains management for upstream actors (see Fig. 2).

At the *e-Uparjan* platform, the cooperative society (Primary Agriculture Cooperative Society—PACS) hires data entry operator and [bike]runners to maintain the real-time flow of information during the procurement season. Data entry operators are deputed at online *Kendra* for updating information regularly. Runners are deployed across offline *Kendra* (having no internet connectivity/access). The *Kendra* where electricity was an issue, the solar panel had been set up. The information collected

[12]In Fig. 1, we have deliberately not used directional arrow. This is because our purpose is to explore functional attributes of technology, governance and development, rather than examining causality.

[13]*Kendra* in Hindi language means centre.

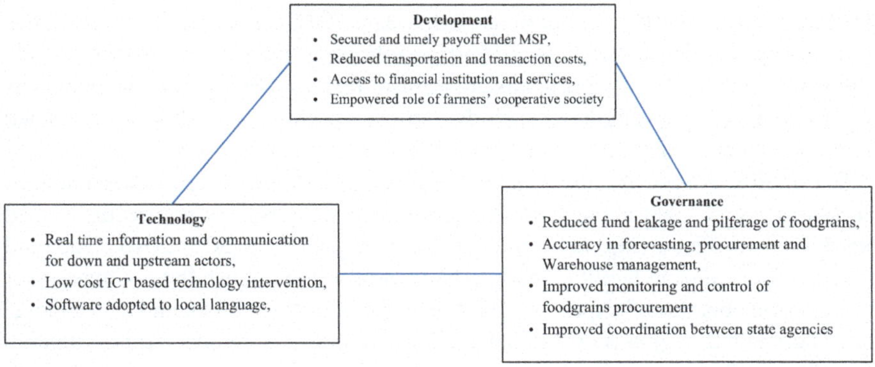

Fig. 1 Schema of interlinkage between the attributes of technology, governance and development. *Source* Authors contribution

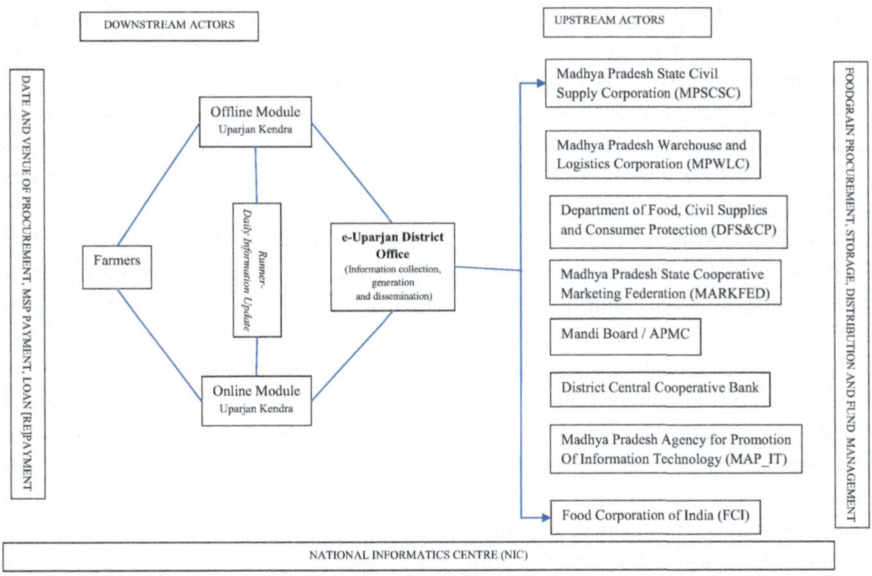

Fig. 2 Functional linkages and activities of *e-Uparjan* actors. *Source* Authors contribution

at the offline module is synchronised with an online module in the evening, with the information update provided by [bike]runners. The operator and [bike]runner is being updated with the latest changes in hardware and software modules. This is done at the start of *rabi* and *kharif* season on a regular basis and organised by Madhya Pradesh State Civil Supply Corporation (MPSCSC) in collaboration with NIC and district administration. NIC has 24 × 7 grievance redressal cell for troubleshooting that registered more than one lakh complaints at the end of 2015. The troubleshooting is facilitated by the quick response team of nearest NIC office, who are contacted by the runner and data entry operator of respective *Kendra* (NITI Aayog 2015; NIC n.d.). For capacity building of officials, *e-Uparjan* follows a 'train-the-trainer' approach. In this, first state and district officials are trained, followed by training the personals of participating organisations at each district. The training workshop is conducted by the district administration at the start of the procurement season.

To establish *e-Uparjan* infrastructure at block and district level, Government of MP (GoMP) had spent about INR 76/- crore (INR 22/- crore of non-recurring and INR 54/- crore of recurring) in five procurement seasons (from 2012/2015). The fund was used for acquiring facilities such as hardware, software, installation, manpower and covering operational expenses. The *e-Uparjan Kendra* at block and district level was set up with the support of PACS that is involved in procurement. Approximately 250 lakh metric tonne of food grains (paddy and wheat) had been procured under *e-Uparjan* with overhead costs of less than INR 2/- per quintal. Under MSP regime, INR 36,089/- crore had been transferred to the participant farmers' bank account. In five procurement seasons (from 2012 to 2015) about 64% of registered farmers participated in MSP-based operation. On average, each farmer had done 1.38 transactions at *Kendra* and was paid approximately INR 96200/- on food grains sales (Sa 2014; DFCS&CP 2015). About 2900 *Kendra* was set up during *rabi* season across 40 districts. During *kharif* season about 1130, *Kendra* was set up across 50 districts. *e-Uparjan* had accounted for some 17 lakh registered farmers (NITI Aayog 2015; Sa 2014). During *rabi* season, *Kendra* functioning was facilitated by 708 [bike]runners and 2830 data entry operators. On a daily average basis, about 12,834 farmers sold their produce during *rabi* season. In *kharif* season, about 199 runners and 1130 data entry operators facilitated procurement. On average, about 4,250 farmers sold their produce on a daily basis during *kharif* season (GoMP n.d.).

The access to real-time information is an instrumental factor for downstream and upstream actors (see Fig. 2) at the *e-Uparjan* platform. Farmers receive the date and venue of procurement four days in advance. This facilitates farmers to manage transport cost and time of travel from farm to *Kendra*. At *Kendra,* this reduces the time interface for unloading of food grains. Farmers receive on the spot receipt and SMS-based information about food grains offloaded and MSP to be paid. The MSP get transferred to the farmers account within one week, and information is shared through SMS. These arrangements reduced the transaction costs for all concern actors and possible fund leakage. This is evident from the first-hand account shared by one such farmer:

> Earlier, local traders used to pay lower prices even for good quality produce, so farmers used to suffer losses. The fact that we would bring the produce to the *mandi* would go against us. We were forced to sell the produce at whatever price was offered to us in the open market rather than wait for *Mandi*. We would not get any receipts nor would be know how much produce had we sold. Now the produce is sold transparently and we get our money on time. The system is checked by the highest officials, and there is no way in which corruption can happen. We are very happy with this system. (NITI Aayog 2015: 134)

NIC runs a call centre to report farmer grievances to concern department/official for redressal within a time-bound manner. *e-Uparjan* provides a platform for loan repayment to the farmer. For upstream actors (see Fig. 2), the *e-Uparjan* network provides a standardised report for effective management of food grains procurement, storage and distribution. Procurement centre receives apriori information about a possible number of farmers and food grains to be procured on a specified date. This facilitates unloading and bagging of food grains at *Kendra*. The access to real-time information about storage space in warehouse expedites the planning for transportation facility from the *Kendra* within and between districts. The information generated at the *Kendra* about collection helps in monitoring the food grains movement from specified *Kendra* to warehouses. This node to node access and dissemination of information on a real-time basis reduces the chances of leakage and malpractices. The storage capacity of state-run warehouses is updated regularly that maintains the proper distribution, storage and movement of food grains well in advance.

6 Addressing Potential Challenges

Farmers' intent and actual participation to avail this service, share [accurate] information and grievances redressal are critical to run this platform effectively. This requires active involvement and support of farmers. The state government had started information, education and communication (IEC) strategy, which was piloted in the Harda district. Also, the regular awareness campaign has been conducted during procurement season through television, radio and newspapers, about the programme activities and potential benefit to farmers (NITI Aayog 2015). The authenticated database of farmers and its regular update helps DFCS&CP to accurately forecast the procurement, which further aids in transportation and storage arrangements. Thus, it facilitates the decision-making process for different actors along food grains procurement value chains.

However, the initiative seems to have faced some inroads as it is scaled up to the entire state. As state government provides a bonus to its farmers, it has attracted farmers from bordering states. To overcome this bottleneck, DFCS&CP cross-checks 10% of farmers verified by the *patwari*[14] (NITI Aayog 2015). However, this does not make the initiative full proof measure due to the scale of operation and involvement of diverse and discursive groups of actors. In addition, the implementation has faced challenges which are beyond the mandate of programme design, such as electricity and internet connectivity; road and rail linkage; and deployment of skilled human resources at a remote location. The *e-Uparjan* operation is encountering systemic problems like lack of basic infrastructure and existing bottleneck in the value chain of food grains procurement (Krishnamurthy 2012a, b), rather than the design of the initiative per se. This draws a parallel with other studies (Warschauer 2003) that the

[14] *Patwari* is the state appointed personal who maintains the land and tax record of the village.

technology alone cannot solve a set of problems faced by [rural] people unless they are able to participate and make their choices (Stewart 2000).

7 Discussions and Future Questions

e-Uparjan offers fresh insights on social policy making as a network process that requires an adequate understanding of social realities. On two important dimensions of governance—capacity and autonomy—the *e-Uparjan* has re-engineered the decision support system of the government as far as food grains procurement is concerned. The initiative has shown a way forward on how multiple state agencies can work in unison to address the challenges of governance and development.

The upstream value chain comprising of processors to customers is captive and controlled by few actors and stringent state regulations (Gereffi et al. 2005). On the other hand, downstream value chain from farmer/farm to procurement centre is relational and controlled by intermediaries, such as *āṛhatiyā* [15] and commission agents (Singh and Bhogal 2015). This is due to limited options available to the farmers for a better market and scale problem of their fragmented operational holdings (Singh 2012). In other words, small and medium farmers are more susceptible to distress sales and market failures, and thus, they need to be protected through effective governance under the aegis of the state. It is noted that the decentralised food grains procurement system in India has been facing challenges for not followed any stringent regulation to maintain transparency in a multitude of transactions between procuring agencies and farmers. The system effectuating the transaction process is often devoid of integrity. Eventually, the lack of integrity affects transaction governance (Mishra 2016; Williamson 1979) and arrests the flow of information between the actors of the procurement system (Mishra 2016; Gereffi et al. 2005).

The e-Uparjan platform has created an open, interdependent and a critical feedback loop with real-time information flow on food grains management between farmers and state agencies across various layers and nodes of decision-making. *e-Uparjan* provides information about food grains procurement, fund transfer, the fund received, material issued, material moved and MSP payments across different decision nodes. The real-time information flow can play a crucial role for upstream actors in planning, monitoring, warehouse management, material flow, transportation, information on farmer's loan and remove the operational bottleneck in the system. The mandate of sharing updated and real-time information with different actors, across various activity nodes, has the potential to plug in the fund leakage, reduce transaction cost and mitigate the rent-seeking behaviour of state actors.

As advocated by Swaminathan and Keswan (2016), it is high time to explore and extend the role of technology to address the challenges in downstream and upstream value chain governance for evergreen revolution. However, whether the

[15] In English, the nearby word would be agent, broker or jobber.

perceived role of technology has been instrumental in improving the governance and attaining development, necessitates an incisive understanding of the techno-economic intervention in the given setting and outcomes of that intervention.

References

Anonymous. (1935). A scheme of broadcast development for India. *Current Science, 3*(9), 393–395.

Castellacci, F. (2006). Innovation, diffusion and catching up in the fifth long wave. *Futures, 38*(7), 841–863.

Chand, R. (2012). Development policies and agricultural markets. *Economic and Political Weekly, 47*(52), 53–63.

Chand, R. (2017). Doubling farmers' income-rationale, strategy, prospects, and action plan. NITI Policy Paper No 1, 2017, NITI Aayog, Government of India, New Delhi.

DFCS&CP. (2015). *e-Uparjan: Computerization of food grain procurement system in Madhya Pradesh*. Accessed from http://www.mmp.cips.org.in/documents/Workshops/2015/19-21_Jan/20th/e-Uparjan-Computerization_of_Food_Grain_Procurement_System_in_Madhya_Pradesh.pdf, dated May 17, 2016.

Dosi, G. (1982). Technological paradigms and technological trajectories: A suggested interpretation of the determinants and directions of technical change. *Research Policy, 11*(3), 147–162.

FCI (1964). The Food Corporations Act 1964. Accessed from http://fci.gov.in/pdf/The_Food_Corporation_Act.pdf, on April 09, 2018.

Freeman, C., Clark, J., & Soete, L. (1982). *Unemployment and technical innovation: a study of long waves and economic development*. Burns & Oates.

Freeman, C., Louçã, F., & Louçã, F. (2001). *As time goes by: from the industrial revolutions to the information revolution*. New Delhi: Oxford University Press.

Fukuyama, F. (2013). What is governance? *Governance, 26*(3), 347–368.

Ganesh-Kumar, A., Gulati, A., & Cummings, R. J. (2007). *Food grains policy and management in India: Responding to today's challenges and opportunities*. Mumbai and Washington DC: Indira Gandhi Institute of Development Research and IFPRI.

Gereffi, G., Humphrey, J., & Sturgeon, T. (2005). The governance of global value chains. *Review of International Political Economy, 12*(1), 78–104.

Gluckman, P. (2016). The Science-policy interface. *Science, 353*(6303), 969. https://doi.org/10.1126/science.aai8837.

GoI. (2013). *Science, technology and innovation policy 2013*. New Delhi: Ministry of Science and Technology.

GoMP. (n.d.). *e-Uparjan updates*. Accessed form http://mpsc.mp.nic.in/csms/mpeuparjan/Home.aspx/#thumb. Dated August 4, 2016.

Hudson, H. E. (2006). *From rural village to global village: Telecommunications for development in the information age*. London: Lawrence Erlbaum Associates Inc, Publishers.

Krishnamurthy, M. (2012a). All in the name of farmers. *Business Line* [Dated 2 January 2012]. Accessed from http://www.thehindubusinessline.com/opinion/all-in-the-name-of-the-farmer/article2769198.ece, dated September 5, 2016.

Krishnamurthy, M. (2012b). The changing dynamics of public procurement in Madhya Pradesh: States of wheat. *Economic and Political Weekly, 47*(52), 72–83.

Kumar, S. (2015). *Report of the high-level committee on reorienting the role and restricting of Food Corporation of India*. New Delhi: GoI.

Massey, G. (2016). *Ways of social change-making sense of modern times* (p. 391). New Delhi: Sage.

Mathur, J. C., & Neurath, P. (1959). *An Indian Experiment in farm radio forums*. Paris: UNESCO.

Mishra, S. N. (2013). Issues before evolving energy cooperative: Field note from Leh, India. *International Journal of Rural Management, 9*(2), 209–216.

Mishra, S. N. (2014). Reflections on science in service of a symbiotic society. *Current Science, 107*(11), 1787–1789.

Mishra, S. N. (2016). *Policy implementation and dynamics of operational level institutions: Case studies of jatropha based biofuel policy in Chhattisgarh, India*. [FPRM Thesis] Anand: Institute of Rural Management.

Modi, N. (2015). *PM's address at special session of National Meet on Promoting Space Technology based Tools and Applications in Governance and Development*. Accessed from www.narendramodi.in/pm-s-address-at-special-session-of-national-meet-on-promoting-space-technology-based-tools-and-applications-in-governance-and-development-291184, dated June 8, 2016.

Modi, N. (2016). Question and Answer session at town hall meet on 06 August 2016. Accessed from http://www.narendramodi.in/excerpts-of-pm-s-interaction-at-the-town-hall-marking-two-years-of-mygov-511355, dated August 11, 2016.

Narayanan, S. (2015). Food security in India: The imperative and its challenges. *Asia and The Pacific Policy Studies, 2*(1), 197–209.

Navarra, D. D., & Cornford, T. (2005). ICT, innovation and public management: Governance, models and alternatives for egovernment infrastructures. In *ECIS 2005 Proceedings*. Accessed from http://workspace.unpan.org/sites/Internet/Documents/UNPAN93556.pdf on June 3, 2016.

NIC. (n.d). *National Informatics Center—Khandawa*. Accessed from http://khandwa.nic.in/nic_files/NIC-khandwa.pdf on August 17, 2016.

NITI Aayog. (2015). *Social sector service delivery-good practices resource book*. New Delhi: Government of India.

Perez, C. (1985). Microelectronics, long waves and world structural change: New perspectives for developing countries. *World Development, 13*(3), 441–463.

Pulakkat, H. (2015). *How PM Narendra Modi wants science to fuel development*. Accessed from http://economictimes.indiatimes.com/news/science/how-pm-narendra-modi-wants-science-to-fuel-development/articleshow/48892070.cms, dated June 8, 2016.

Rajvanshi, A. K. (2016). Roadmap for rural India. *Current Science, 111*(1), 39–43.

Ramnath, M. S., & Assisi, C. (2018). *The Aadhar effect-why the world's largest identity project matters* (p. 291). New Delhi: OUP.

Sa, A. D. (2014). *e-Uparjan: Using IT for streamlining the foodgrain procurement system in Madhya Pradesh*. Accessed from http://www.cips.org.in/documents/2014/UPAAM_Workshop/Shri_Anthony_de_Sa.pdf, on May 18, 2016.

Sekher, M., Parasuraman, S., Pritchard, B., Kumar, S. S., & Rai, R. K. (2017). Empowering people to power the public distribution system: A process mapping analysis of six India states. *Economic and Political Weekly, 52*(51), 97–107.

Singh, S. (2012). New markets for smallholders in India: Exclusion, policy and mechanisms. *Economic and Political Weekly, 47*(52), 95–105.

Singh, S., & Bhogal, S. (2015). Commission agent system. *Economic and Political Weekly, 50*(45), 57–62.

Stewart, A. (2000). Social inclusion: An introduction. In P. Askonas & A. Stewart (Eds.), *Social inclusion: Possibilities and tensions* (pp. 1–16). Houndmills, England: Macmillan.

Swaminathan, M. S., & Kesavan, P. C. (2016). Achieving the sustainable development goals. *Current Science, 110*(2), 127–128.

Thomas, J. J. (2005). Informational development in rural areas: Some evidence from Andhra Pradesh and Kerala. In G. Parayil (Ed.), Political economy and informational capitalism in India: Digital divide, development and equity. New York: Palgrave Macmillam.

TIFAC. (2015). *Technology vision 2035*. New Delhi: Department of Science and Technology-Government of India.

UNESCO. (1967). *New educational media in action: Case studies for planners-I* (pp. 104–134). Paris: UNESCO.

Warschauer, M. (2003). *Technology and social inclusion: Rethinking the digital divide*. Massachusetts: The MIT Press.
Williamson, O. E. (1979). Transaction-cost economics: The governance of contractual relations. *The Journal of Law and Economics, 22,* 233–261.

ICT, Gender, and the Labor Market: A Cross-Country Analysis

Sigrid Valberg

Abstract Information and communication technologies (ICTs) have changed societies all over the world through the way we interact and the way we live. By increasing efficiency and information, lowering transaction costs and creating jobs, ICTs have also changed the way we work. ICTs are presumed to especially beneficial for women, who traditionally have been limited from working by time and mobility constraints. Previous studies have been conducted on a microlevel, but few attempts have been made to systematically investigate the relationship between ICTs, female employment and development on the macrolevel. This chapter investigates whether ICTs have an impact on gender equality in the labor market and are among the first to investigate the global trends. Using panel data analysis for 156 countries from the period 1991–2014, this chapter argues that ICTs contribute positively to narrowing the gender gap in labor market participation, mainly due to increased female labor force participation. However, the impact is lower in developing countries, suggesting that ICT is not necessarily a leapfrogging strategy, many are hoping for in terms of female labor force participation and a more gender-equal labor market.

1 Introduction

Information and communication technologies (ICTs) such as mobile phones and the Internet have spread faster than any previous technology. Today, more households in developing countries have access to a mobile phone than to electricity and clean water. The number of internet users globally has tripled during the last decade, from 1 billion users in 2005 to 3.2 billion users in 2015 (World Bank 2016a). The increase in access to digital technologies brings more choice and greater convenience for most people. International organizations such as the UN and the World Bank are promoting ICTs as a poverty reduction strategy, with the additional benefit of empowering women.

S. Valberg (✉)
Norwegian Ministry of Education and Research, Norwegian Institute of International Affairs, University of Oslo, Oslo, Norway
e-mail: sigrid.valberg@gmail.com

D. Maiti et al. (eds.), *Digitalisation and Development*,
https://doi.org/10.1007/978-981-13-9996-1_15

A whole branch of literature is dedicated to the links between ICTs and poverty reduction. However, little is known about ICTs impact on gender identities.

This chapter investigates whether ICT contributes to women's economic empowerment through increased female labor force participation and thereby a more gender-equal labor market. By increasing information, lowering transaction costs and creating new jobs, ICTs are likely to influence the labor market. This is presumably especially beneficial for women, who have traditionally been limited from working by time and mobility constraints.

Several empirical studies have been conducted based on natural experiments and household surveys, but few attempts have been made to examine systematically the gender aspect of the relation between ICTs and labor participation outcomes.

This chapter has a cross-country and comparative approach and is among the first to investigate the *global* trends and impact of ICTs in the labor market. The ambition of this chapter is to shed light on ICTs impact on gender equality in the labor market and to examine whether effects differ with technologies as well as the level of development.

To investigate this further, a panel data analysis is conducted, studying how ICTs might have influenced gender equality in the labor market globally from 1991–2014. Using macrodata from the World Development Indicators on ICTs, share of internet users and mobile phone subscribers, in addition to female and male labor force participation, this relationship is investigated for 156 countries. The aim is to address the following questions:

(1) What is the impact of ICTs on gender equality in the labor market?
(2) How does the effect of ICTs differ between levels of economic development?

The gender component of ICTs potentially reveals important information for both decision makers and academics. First, understanding whether ICTs affect men and women differently could potentially improve the implementation of ICTs for decision makers that seek to increase women's participation in the economy. Second, *if* ICTs successfully include women in the market economy, increased female labor force participation could potentially involve important contributions to GDP and welfare. Last, increasing access to income possibilities could give women in developing countries more economic freedom and independence.

The main findings from this chapter support the argument that ICTs contribute positively to narrowing the gender gap in labor market participation, mainly driven by increased female labor force participation. Although the results are positive, the effects are not as high as expected, considering the priorities and prospects ICTs have gotten in the international development agenda. A one-unit increase in the Internet per 100 inhabitants increases the female-to-male labor force participation ratio with 0.04% points. A one-unit increase in mobile phones increases the ratio with 0.02% points. One of the most important findings from this chapter is that the effect of ICTs in low-income countries for participation rates is almost non-existing. ICTs have even hurt gender equality in the latest years. The general decrease in the gender gap in these countries is not due to an increased amount of females joining the labor market, but rather a decrease in males, potentially caused by a displacement of jobs due to the new technology. This suggests that technology investments are not a 'shortcut' for development and women's economic empowerment as such and that ICTs should be a complement to economic and social reforms in developing countries. It seems like basic skills, health and infrastructure are needed to enable countries, in general, and women in particular, to take advantage of digital technologies.'

This chapter proceeds as follows: Sect. 2 presents existing theories and previous empirical findings. Section 3 presents the data and empirical strategy. Section 4 present the results, test their robustness and discusses the findings, and Sect. 5 concludes.

2 How Can ICTs Increase Female Labor Force Participation?

Gender-specific patterns of labor force participation exist all around the world. Women tend to have lower participation rates than males, reflecting the role of care work and home production traditionally ascribed to women. However, international labor market trends since the 1990s show that female labor force participation has increased, while male participation has fallen (Gillard et al. 2008). Many factors are likely to have influenced this development; better health, lower fertility rates, increased female enrollment rates in school and improved infrastructure, such as ICT.

Labor market outcomes for both females and males are likely to be affected by ICTs. As women tend to be more constrained by transaction costs and lack of information than men, benefits will possibly be higher for them (Uteng 2011). Remoteness and isolation supposedly have a higher impact on female's opportunities to earnings than males. ICTs make time and distance less important in organizing business and production, making it easier to combine work with household responsibilities. Several empirical studies have recently been conducted both for developed and developing countries. They have all found that ICTs increase labor force participation, especially for females. In the literature, several potential channels are identified for ICTs contribution to increased female labor force participation. These are listed in Fig. 1. It is, however, important to emphasize these may not be the only channels affecting labor market outcomes for women.

2.1 Information

ICTs increase information, and can potentially reduce structural constraints, improve job search—and matching and reduce discrimination in the labor market. Even though women are disadvantaged in the use of ICT due to their unfavorable conditions in employment, education, and income, they still tend to make better use of

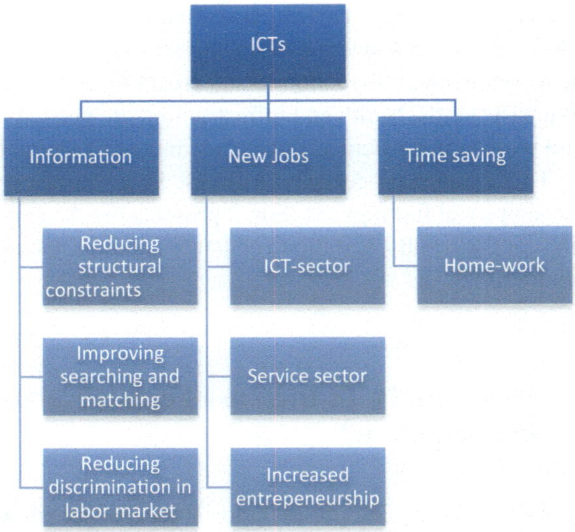

Fig. 1 Channels of ICTs impact

digital technologies than men do. Women use ICTs as a channel for training and education, while men tend to use ICTs for entertainment purposes (Hilbert 2011). ICT can accordingly be a tangible opportunity to tackle longstanding challenges of gender inequalities and structural constraints, including access to employment, income, education and health services (Hilbert 2011).

Digital technologies are expected to facilitate searching, matching, and information sharing between economic agents, such as employees and employers, by providing individuals with more information (World Bank 2016a). Online platforms for job matching exist both internationally and locally and provide valuable information for possible employees and employers (World Bank 2016a, p. 113). In developing countries, online job platforms are challenged by having up-to-date vacancies and reaching low-skilled workers. Despite this, these platforms increase information about jobs and are potentially lowering search costs, especially for women. Lower search costs are explained as one of the main reasons for the increase in female employment in rural South Africa by a rollout of a mobile network (Klonner and Nolen 2008).

Discrimination can potentially be a reason why female participation is lower than male in many countries. Three general sources of labor market discrimination are often modeled in labor economics, all explained by lack of information; personal prejudice, statistical prejudgment, and presence of noncompetitive forces in the labor market (Ehrenberg and Smith 2012, p. 411). Mobile phones and the Internet can, however, erase asymmetric information and mitigate labor market discrimination. Increased information potentially allows men and women to view each other from a different perspective, which over time will change mindsets (Nath 2001, p. 327). ICTs provide women with an opportunity to overcome unfavorable starting conditions. According to Hilbert (2011), females are already using ICTs to fight these longstanding inequalities.

2.2 *New Jobs*

New jobs that are suitable for women have been important in increasing female labor force participation. The ICT sector provides direct opportunities, but in developing countries, this sector is still relatively small (World Bank 2016b, p. 14).[1] With ICT, the content of work has changed in favor of females, not requiring the physical strength as traditional industry jobs. In both Germany and the US, more of workplaces using ICTs explain the increase of female employees the past decades (Black and Spitz-Oener 2007). Similar changes have also taken place in Brazil, Mexico, and Thailand (World Bank 2016a, p. 109). Job growth in the service sector is enabled by ICTs. For developing countries, this is often related to outsourcing. Export-oriented information processing such as call centers, banking, insurance, and bookkeeping are all examples of jobs that today are held mostly by women (Gillard et al. 2008, p. 269). Recruitment to the service sector, such as call centers, raises young women's career aspirations leading them to enroll in computer and English training courses, and delay their marriage and childbearing (Jensen 2012). In addition, the aspirations of jobs also led to a significant increase in school enrollment, also for girls.

Additionally, when lowering information barriers and costs, ICTs shifts production to home-based workers with locations more distant from the main commercial units. ICTs facilitate gathering and transmission of prices and information, potentially increasing flexibility in where and when economic activities can occur. Thus, new forms for market platforms have developed in e-commerce and sharing economy. In China, investments in rural infrastructure, in recent years, have started to pay off: now four out of ten online shop owners in Alibaba, the dominant Chinese e-commerce platform, are females (World Bank 2016a, p. 109).

2.3 *Time-Saving*

Lastly, time-saving in home production is also enhancing female labor supply. A study from the US, based on household surveys from 2003–2009, finds that for married women accessing the Internet, labor force participation increases by 4.1% points (Dettling 2017). This increase is explained by time-saving in household production and increased telework.

[1] Employing 1% on average, in addition to 1% in ICT maintenance.

2.4 Developed and Developing Countries

A well-known hypothesis emerged in the 1960s to explain why female labor force participation differed with the level of development: the U-feminization hypothesis. The U-shape indicates that female labor force participation falls during the initial period moving from agriculture to industrialization and rises once a certain level of development is reached. In the agricultural phase, incomes are low, and women are mostly contributing to farms. The fall in female participation is due to the income effect; industrialization is more labor-intensive and more male than female input is demanded (Goldin 1994). In the post-industrial phase, female labor supply increases with the development of ICTs and the service sector.

The development of female labor force participation in today's advanced economies could be explained by the U-shape, but the U-hypothesis has not been able to explain the observed variation in female labor force participation from 1980–2005 (Gaddis and Klasen 2011). Thus, the U-hypothesis seems to have little relevance for today's developing countries. One reason is that the process of development no longer needs to pass the industrial phase, but countries can move straight from agriculture to an information economy. This has happened, for example, in Cambodian villages, and has been beneficial for women (Fong 2009, p. 3708). This development could be an example of leapfrogging.

Leapfrogging means to accelerate development by skipping intermediate technologies. Mobile phones have, for example, enabled countries to skip the expensive fixed-line infrastructure and move directly to wireless technologies. In countries with bad roads and few trains, mobile phones have additionally been a substitute for traveling. Developing countries have been latecomers in the ICT revolution, but gearing up their utilization of ICTs, they potentially have the same technological opportunities as developed countries (Fong 2009, p. 3707). The possibility of achieving economic growth and women empowerment through advanced and less costly technology seems attractive to developing countries and might provide 'shortcuts' in development. Benefits from leapfrogging are potentially high, but critics believe ICT investments compete with the provision of necessities for the poor (Fong 2009, p. 3707). The technology in itself is not expected to solve problems, but the availability of ICTs is seen as a prerequisite for economic and social development.

2.5 The Context of This Chapter

As noted above, the majority of empirical studies on ICTs impact on female participation in the labor market have been based on natural experiments and household surveys. They are all consistent with the view that ICTs contribute positively to female labor force participation. A general concern regarding these studies is external validity. The comparability of results across countries has often been a challenge due to differences in the definitions of the variables. Research at the global level is rather scarce. The most extensive comparative study is a panel study examining 48 African countries from 1990 to 2014, investigating the impact of ICTs on female labor force participation (Efobi et al. 2016). By utilizing similar data on ICTs and female labor force participation as in this chapter, but with a different set of controls, Efobi et al., find that higher penetration of ICTs increases female economic participation (2016).[2] The effects were increasing in magnitude from mobile phones to the Internet.

This chapter extends the literature by studying the effects of ICTs on gender equality in the labor market at the global level. A global study overcomes the concern of external validity, making the results comparable across countries. This study also aims to draw some conclusions on whether the effect of ICTs will differ between levels of development.

3 Empirical Investigation

To study how ICTs affect gender equality in the labor market, a panel data analysis is undertaken using annual data for 156 countries during the 24 years between 1991 and 2014.[3]

3.1 Data

The data are from the World Development Indicators (WDI) by the World Bank. Internet and mobile phones are relatively new technologies; consequently, the data before 1991 is rather scarce.[4] The regressors of interest are internet users (per 100 inhabitants) and mobile subscriptions (per 100 inhabitants). Due to the high correlation between the Internet and mobile phones, they are used as independent variables in separate regressions. Telecommunication operators have traditionally been the main source of ICT data on subscriptions, and accordingly, these data are considered precise. Estimates for the Internet and mobile users give a general idea of the presence of ICT across countries but does not specify *who* has access.[5]

The main outcome of interest is the *ratio* of female-to-male participation in the labor force. The reason for studying the ratio as the dependent variable rather than

[2]Efobi et al. controls for trade liberalization, GDP per capita, FDI and level of democracy.

[3]The countries included in the analysis are listed in Appendix 1.

[4]Preferably, I would run the analysis for the most recent years after 2014, but the available data on labor force participation does not go further and naturally limits the analysis to 2014.

[5]A more precise measure would, of course, be the share of households or individuals, preferably disaggregated by sex, with access to ICTs. Data on household access is unfortunately only accessible from the latest years' World Bank household surveys from a limited amount of countries. Data on ICT use disaggregated by sex is limited and only reported by 31 countries for 2011 and 2014 (ITU 2016).

Table 1 Summary statistics

Variables	(1)	(2)	(3)	(4)	(5)	(6)
	Obs.	Mean	SD	Min	Max	Source
Internet	3,952	20.13	25.73	0	98.20	WDI
Mobile	4,538	43.00	49.93	0	324.4	WDI
GDP per capita	4,085	9,552	15,296	64.81	116,613	WDI
Total population	4,643	3.404e+07	1.278e+08	95,304	1.371e+09	WDI
Trade as % of GDP	4,264	86.34	53.51	0.0210	531.7	WDI
Fertility rate	4,457	3.243	1.731	0.827	8.459	WDI
Total unemployment	4,176	8.918	6.307	0.100	39.30	WDI
Average years of schooling (interpolated)	3,993	7.218	3.091	0.300	13.10	UNDP
Female/male ratio total labor force (%)	4,464	67.65	20.30	12.33	108.1	WDI
% Christians (interpolated)	4,292	52.52	37.18	0	98.98	CoWP
% Jews (interpolated)	4,292	0.528	5.871	0	82.05	CoWP
% Muslims (interpolated)	4,292	26.36	36.55	0	100	CoWP
% Buddhists (interpolated)	4,292	4.448	16.41	0	96.69	CoWP
% Hindus (interpolated)	4,292	2.426	10.15	0	81.34	CoWP

the relative change in female versus male labor force participation is to examine the overall effect on gender equality in the labor market. An increased female participation rate will not improve gender equality if the male participation rate increases with the same relative size. However, in an alternative model, female and male participation rates will be regressed separately as dependent variables, to investigate further what drives the change in ratio. Data on labor force activity are expressed as the percentage of females and males, 15 years and older, that are economically active. These data include both employed and unemployed. Data are obtained from the World Bank database and consist of both nationally reported and imputed data.

The analysis also includes a set of country-level control variables. These variables and their sources are described in Table 1. GDP per capita, total population, trade as percent of GDP, and unemployment rate are all included as controls.[6] The fertility rate is also controlled for, as it is an important determinant of female labor force participation.

Education affects individuals' decision to participate in the labor market, depending on the income and the substitution effect. To control for education, a measure of

[6]A natural log transformation was applied to GDP and population because the distribution was skewed in all samples.

average years of schooling is included, using data from UNDP database.[7] Lastly, the analysis controls for religion gathered from The Correlates of War Project (CoWP 2017).[8] Religious norms might add important information, in addition to country-fixed effects, on conservative views on traditional gender roles, which might affect female labor force participation.

To distinguish the effect of ICTs between countries of different income levels, an interaction variable between a baseline level of GDP per capita at the 1991 level, and the Internet or mobile phones is created. GDP_{1991} per capita is logged due to skewness.[9] For countries that did not have reported values of GDP per capita in 1991, the first GDP-value reported, was extrapolated to increase the number of observations.[10]

3.2 *Econometric Specification*

With panel estimation, time-invariant country-specific unobservable effects are controlled for and capture unobserved heterogeneity that causes the bias in an ordinary OLS regression. Based on the analytical structure presented above, this empirical framework will depart from the following dynamic relationships for the Internet and mobile phones, respectively:

$$\begin{aligned}\text{Female/Male Ratio}_{it} = \beta_0 + \beta_1(\text{Internet})_{it} + \gamma\big((\log)\text{GDPpc}_{1991} * \text{Internet}_{it}\big) \\ + \sum \beta_n X_{n,i,t} + \tau(\text{years})_t + \alpha(\text{countries})_i + \epsilon_{it} \quad (1)\end{aligned}$$

[7]The data are collected every fifth year until 2005, and annually the following years. The education level in a population tends to change very slowly, and to enable the maximum number of observations included in the regression samples, a linear interpolation procedure was conducted to fill in the missing observations (Chen 2004, p. 17). Average years of schooling are used because WDI data for enrollment disaggregated by sex lacks observations.

[8]Data provide information of percentage religious people, Christian, Muslim, Jewish, Buddhist, or Hindu beliefs and are available for each country every half-decade from 1945–2010. As the level of religious population changes slowly, I have conducted a linear interpolation to increase the number of the observations. After conducting a linear interpolation, the observations increased from 854 to 4,292. While the last observations from CoWP are from 2010, the same percentage is assigned to the last four years, to not lose too many observations.

[9]The ICT variables were considered logged, but as more than 25% of the all values for both the Internet and mobiles were lower than 1 users/subscriptions per 100 inhabitants this was not pursued. Log variables of ICTs would lead to negative logs, not capturing the percentage changes in a good way nor benefiting the interpretation of the model. Accordingly, I will use a non-logged interaction of the Internet/mobiles*log of GDP percapita level in 1991 as the interaction term.

[10]A total of 20 countries missed GDP per capita values from 1991, the average lag in reporting is 5.8 years. Some countries, Afghanistan, Iraq, Myanmar, Montenegro, Somalia, Sao Tome and Principe and Timor Leste, did not report GDP per capita until 9–13 years after the baseline year. This could lead to biased results. However, the rest of the countries had their first GDP per capita observations from 1 to 4 years after baseline. These are typically post-Soviet and post-Yugoslavian countries.

$$\text{Female/Male Ratio}_{it} = \beta_0 + \beta_1(\text{Mobile})_{it} + (\log)\text{GDPpc}_{1991} * \text{Mobile}_{it} + \sum \beta_n X_{n,i,t} + \tau(\text{years})_t + \alpha(\text{countries})_i + \epsilon_{it} \quad (2)$$

The coefficients of interest are β_1 and γ, measuring the marginal impact of the Internet and mobiles to the female/male ratio of labor force participation. $X_{n,i,t}$, is a matrix of n variables controlling for the logarithm of GDP per capita, logarithm of population, schooling, unemployment, fertility rate, trade of GDP and religion. τ is the vector of time-fixed effects, α the country-fixed effects, and ϵ the error term capturing all other omitted factors and measurement errors.

3.3 Threats to Internal Validity

The nature of a panel analysis involves a risk of internal validity. The main threats to internal validity in this study are potentially omitted variable bias (OVB), measurement error and reverse causality. The following section will briefly discuss how these might affect the results.

Changing attitudes toward women and increased gender equality is difficult to capture in a model and may represent omitted variable bias. Some variation might be captured, controlling for GDP per capita, as GDP and gender equality is considered closely correlated and mutually reinforcing (Dollar and Gatti 1999). Nevertheless, improved gender equality in a society could be explained by other factors such as female representation, political reforms, or change in national and regional laws. Such changes are not constant over time and accordingly not captured by the country-fixed effects. A law change in favor of women's rights could potentially be influential for gender equality in the labor market. Change in laws, reforms and representation could lead to an upward bias in the analysis, meaning an overestimation of the results.

In the analysis, there is additionally a possibility for a downward bias of the estimates. In many countries, females are less likely to use ICTs than males, known as the gender digital divide. The ICT data used in this study challenges the analysis by not being disaggregated by gender but is a general estimate of ICT penetration in a country. Consequently, an increase in the share of the Internet or mobile users will, for many countries, imply that the increase in ICT use is higher for males than for females, leading to a downward bias of the results. The actual estimate of ICTs impact on female labor force participation could supposedly be higher if the gender digital divide were accounted for in the model.

Another potential threat is measurement errors. The World Bank performs a strict data selection of the WDIs to ensure comparability of data across time and countries. However, estimates of women in the labor force are often hard to compare between countries. The demographic, social, legal, and cultural norms and trends often determine whether women's activities are regarded as economic, and these might vary between countries. Another potential challenge is that the data neither provide information about intensive versus extensive work. Additionally, ICTs might bring on new labor market agreements such as online freelancing. Traditional labor force surveys are poorly equipped to track these new developments and might accordingly not capture all forms of employment (Katz and Krueger 2016).

Lastly, reverse or simultaneous causality could also pose a threat to the validity of the results. In this analysis, it is implicitly assumed that ICTs affect labor force participation rates. However, the opposite could be argued; participation rates influence the share of ICT users—the more females are participating in the labor force, the higher the demand for mobile phones and the Internet. Working females would raise their earnings and their possibility to consume, including consumption of digital technologies. Working women could feel the need to be connected and online, to easier coordinate family and work life, and consequently, demand more ICTs.

Establishing causality of ICTs to gender equality in the labor force is extremely difficult. A common method in the literature to deal with this is to use lagged variables in the regression, but in practice, this rarely solves the endogeneity problem. The data on ICTs have been considered lagged by one year, but it remains unclear whether there is a lag effect from ICTs, and if so, how many periods the lag should be (Minges 2015, p. 12) I therefore choose not to lag the variables in the main analysis, but rather test the data with one-year lags as a robustness check. As neither an IV-regression or a randomized experiment are feasible for this study, the direction of causality will be supported with evidence from the literature.

Several studies have by their experimental design and statistical methods, found evidence of the direction of causality. One of the most thorough studies argues causality of the relation ICT and development, was presented as a response to the lack of studies investigating causality (Chew et al. 2011). Utilizing data from a multistage probability survey, ICTs impact on business growth by women micro-entrepreneurs in India were tested with structural equation modelling. Chew et al. finds a weak, but statistically significant, causal relationship between ICTs and increased female businesses.

In addition to this comprehensive study, there are examples of empirical studies conducted, suggesting a causal direction from ICTs to female participation. Based on household studies Dettling (2011, 2017), used an IV-approach to study the effect of internet use on female labor supply and advocates a causal impact. The 2SLS estimates suggest a causal link from the Internet to increased female participation. Similarly, Klonner and Nolen (2008) use instrumental variables in their mobile phone study from rural South Africa, allowing them to argue for a causal effect from mobile phones to employment. These findings corroborate the causal direction expected and support the hypothesis.

4 Results

The following section will present the results. First, the findings from the main regressions, studying the effect of ICTs on the gender ratio, will be presented. Secondly, an analysis was run to examine whether the effects of ICTs potentially differed between time-periods, as the technological revolution involving lower-income countries mostly evolved during the last decade. Thirdly, analyses were run to find whether increased female or male participation drove the results from the ratio. Lastly, robustness tests are briefly presented.

4.1 Main Regressions

The regressions are run with both OLS and fixed-effect models and presented in Table 2. Table 2 shows, when including the interaction term, that the effect of ICTs on the labor market gender ratio is increasing with level of development. The results from OLS are more than double in size than from the fixed effects model, column (3) and (6). The total, marginal effect on the participation ratio of ICTs, are presented in Tables 3 and 4.

Looking at the fixed effects without the interaction term, (2) and (5), ICTs seem to have a significant positive effect of β_1 to the participation ratio of females to males. β_1 is interpreted as the effect at the ratio of a one-unit increase in ICTs; resulting in a 0.065% point increase in the participation ratio for the Internet and 0.032 for mobiles. The effect is largest for the Internet, similar to the findings from Efobi et al. (2016).

The control variables are as expected: increasing the gender ratio in population growth, unemployment and fertility rate, and decreasing the ratio with GDP, fertility rate and religion. *R*-squared is high when adding country and year fixed effects, implying that time and country effects account for much of the variation in the dependent variable.

Table 3 presents the marginal effects from the Internet, calculated by interpreting the coefficients β_1 and γ together from the fixed-effect model, column (3).[11]

Column (1), Table 3, shows that the total, aggregate effect of a one-unit increase in the Internet users per 100 inhabitants, increases the ratio of female-to-male participation by 0.044% points. A one-unit increase in the Internet users per 100, will, therefore, increase the global mean ratio from 63.17 to 63.21.[12] Columns (2)–(5) present the marginal effects, respectively, in low-income, low-middle-income, upper-middle-income and high-income countries, based on the World Bank's definitions of income status from the baseline of 1991.[13] Internet has a positive, significant effect on all income levels, but clearly the effect increases with a country's income level and is more than three times as high in high-income countries as in low income.

---

[11] STATA command; margins, dyd*x*.

[12] In 1991, the global mean ratio was 63.17.

[13] According to the World Bank classifications; Low-income countries with GNI per capita on less than $1025: Low-middle-income countries have GNI per capita between $1,026 and $4,035; upper-middle-income countries have GNI per capita between $4,036 and $12,475; high-income countries are those with a GNI per capita of $12,476 or more. The GNI level of 1991 is used to classify the countries. For those countries without GNI from 1991, the closest observation was used.

Table 2 Results from main regression

Variables	(1) Internet OLS	(2) Internet FE w/o/interaction	(3) Internet FE w/interaction	(4) Mobile OLS	(5) Mobile FE w/o/interaction	(6) Mobile FE w/interaction
Internet	−0.155**	0.0650***	−0.0436			
	(0.0646)	(0.00773)	(0.0280)			
Internet*GDPpc$_{1991}$(log)	0.0405***		0.0115***			
	(0.00702)		(0.00305)			
Mobile				−0.0681***	0.0322***	−0.0908***
				(0.0263)	(0.00400)	(0.0116)
Mobile*GDPpc$_{1991}$(log)				0.0206***		0.0144***
				(0.00335)		(0.00139)
GDP per capita (log)	−5.302***	−2.603***	−2.137***	−5.139***	−2.934***	−1.798***
	(0.317)	(0.306)	(0.341)	(0.318)	(0.282)	(0.306)
Total population (log)	−1.151***	4.737***	3.843***	−0.926***	4.937***	3.728***
	(0.184)	(0.838)	(0.880)	(0.184)	(0.793)	(0.808)
Total unemployment	−0.314***	0.0835***	0.0765***	−0.376***	0.156***	0.123***
	(0.0482)	(0.0294)	(0.0291)	(0.0460)	(0.0300)	(0.0287)
Fertility rate	2.261***	−1.829***	−2.116***	2.491***	−0.207	−1.548***
	(0.314)	(0.623)	(0.636)	(0.301)	(0.421)	(0.465)
Trade as %-of GDP	−0.0323***	−0.00240	−0.00190	−0.0350***	−8.03e−05	−0.000395
	(0.00608)	(0.00390)	(0.00384)	(0.00611)	(0.00368)	(0.00336)
Avg. years of schooling	1.215***	0.927***	0.897***	1.578***	0.663***	0.263
	(0.168)	(0.198)	(0.200)	(0.163)	(0.182)	(0.183)

(continued)

Table 2 (continued)

Variables	(1)	(2)	(3)	(4)	(5)	(6)
	Internet OLS	Internet FE w/o/interaction	Internet FE w/interaction	Mobile OLS	Mobile FE w/o/interaction	Mobile FE w/interaction
% Christian population	−0.260***	−0.0594***	−0.0528***	−0.283***	−0.0849***	−0.0446***
	(0.0193)	(0.0153)	(0.0155)	(0.0187)	(0.0152)	(0.0145)
% Muslim population	−0.527***	−0.142***	−0.146***	−0.555***	−0.143***	−0.137***
	(0.0185)	(0.0413)	(0.0415)	(0.0179)	(0.0359)	(0.0355)
% Jewish population	−0.120***	−0.503***	−0.545***	−0.181***	−0.551***	−0.440***
	(0.0416)	(0.114)	(0.117)	(0.0423)	(0.101)	(0.0974)
% Buddhist population	−0.190***	−0.0481*	−0.0378	−0.214***	−0.0771***	−0.0720***
	(0.0254)	(0.0271)	(0.0273)	(0.0249)	(0.0217)	(0.0221)
% Hindu population	−0.461***	−0.420***	−0.433***	−0.490***	−0.311***	−0.370***
	(0.0280)	(0.0633)	(0.0644)	(0.0276)	(0.0528)	(0.0548)
Observations	2,955	2,955	2,955	3,270	3,270	3,270
Number of countries	156	156	156	156	156	156
Country FE	NO	YES	YES	NO	YES	YES
Year FE	NO	YES	YES	NO	YES	YES
R-squared	0.486	0.981	0.981	0.478	0.979	0.980
Adj. *R*-squared	0.484	0.980	0.980	0.476	0.977	0.979

Standard errors in parentheses. Dependent variable; ratio of female-to-male labor force participation
***$p < 0.01$, **$p < 0.05$, *$p < 0.1$

Table 3 Marginal effects of the Internet by income level

Variables	(1)	(2)	(3)	(4)	(5)
	Total effect	Low income	Low-middle income	Upper-middle-income	High income
Internet	0.0437***	0.0252**	0.0437***	0.0593***	0.0715***
	(0.00834)	(0.0114)	(0.00834)	(0.00745)	(0.00827)
Number of countries	156	66	49	17	24
Observations	2,955	1,114	945	343	553

Standard errors in parentheses
*** $p < 0.01$, ** $p < 0.05$, * $p < 0.1$

Table 4 Marginal effects of mobile phones by income level

Variables	(1)	(2)	(3)	(4)	(5)
	Total effect	Low income	Low-middle income	Upper-middle income	High income
Mobile	0.0178***	−0.00438	0.0187***	0.0382***	0.0536***
	(0.00398)	(0.00470)	(0.00397)	(0.00426)	(0.00501)
Number of countries	156	66	49	17	24
Observations	3,270	1,291	1,037	380	562

Standard errors in parentheses
*** $p < 0.01$, ** $p < 0.05$, * $p < 0.1$

Table 4 presents similar effects on mobile phones. The marginal, total effect of mobiles on the gender ratio of labor force participation, is less than half than the Internet. A one-unit increase in mobile phones per 100 inhabitants increases the gender ratio with 0.02% points. Distinguishing the impact by income status, the effect increases with income level. In low-income countries, mobile phones do not have any significant effect, but the effect appears in low-middle-income countries from which it increases with the level of GDP. A possible explanation of why mobiles have a higher effect in developed countries could be that smartphones are more widespread than 'traditional' mobile phones. However, with the data available, it will not allow me to investigate this further.

ICTs, in general, are positive for gender equality in the labor market, with a higher effect for the Internet than for mobile phones. The effect of ICTs is increasing with the countries' level of economic development. The effects are highest in developed/high-income countries, while the effect is more modest in developing countries. These results reveal that the optimism of ICT as a catalyst for gender equality in developing countries could be questioned.

4.2 Female Versus Male Participation Rates

ICTs are expected to provide opportunities *both* for females and for males in the labor market. The dependent variable from the main analysis was the ratio of females to males participating in the labor force. This captures the relative change in gender equality in the labor market. To test what is driving the change in ratio, two separate regressions are run with, respectively, female and male participation as outcome variables. The regression results are presented in Appendix 2.

The increase in aggregate gender ratio from the Internet, presented in Table 3, is driven by increased female labor force participation, in addition to a decrease in male participation rates. Possible explanations for the lower male participation could be that new technology substitute jobs traditionally held by males, or that the increase of working females would displace males from their previous jobs. The increase in women's participation from the Internet is significant in all countries except in low income. The increase in the gender ratio in low-income countries from Table 3 is accordingly mainly explained by a decrease in male participation. The general effect is increasing with income level and is highest in developed countries, but results are still low. For example, in Norway, a one-unit increase in the Internet users per 100 inhabitants would increase the female participation rate by 0.05% points.[14] This is an increase in the female participation rate from 48.77 (1991 level) to 48.82, meaning 678 more females joins the labor force. Male participation in low- and low-middle-income countries is significantly decreasing, but ICTs have no significant effect on men in developed countries.

The impact of mobile phones, on the other hand, is significant and positive for both sexes but with a higher aggregate effect for females. The positive effect for both sexes, as opposed to the Internet, explains why the gender ratio is lower for mobile phones than the Internet (Table 4), as the Internet did not increase male participation. Differing between income statuses, mobile phones in low-income countries have a positive, significant effect for both sexes, but a higher effect for males than for females. Mobiles have less impact on males the higher a country's GDP per capita is. The results for females are the opposite; mobile phones increase labor force participation more, the higher GDP per capita.

4.3 A Growing Digital Divide?

Evidence from the data suggests that ICTs in developing countries did not start spreading considerably until the beginning of the year 2000. To check whether the results would differ, regressions for two different time-periods, 1991–2005 and 2005–2014, were run. Limiting the time-period to these years might change the results, especially for developing countries.

[14]Which in 1991 would mean an increase of 42,000 internet users, increase in 0,05 is for high-income countries.

Regressing the two different time-periods separately reveals interesting results. For the Internet, the aggregate effect on female-to-male participation is positive and significant the first time-period, 1991–2005, but not significant from 2005 to 2014. Disaggregating the effects by income statuses, the Internet had an approximately equal marginal effect across all countries regardless of income status from 1991 to 2005. A one-unit increase in the Internet users increased the ratio by 0.05% points. From 2005 to 2014, low-income countries experienced a significant *decrease* in the ratio of female-to-male labor force participation from a one-unit increase in the Internet users. The marginal effect in high-income countries did not change much from the first time-period.[15] These results suggest that the digital divide of ICT use between countries has been evolving from 2005 and onwards, where developed countries seem to have adapted to benefit from the opportunities of ICT while developing countries are lagging in this regard.

Running similar tests for mobile phones, they had a positive effect on the female-to-male ratio for most countries from 1991 to 2005, with the highest effect in high-income countries. For 2005–2014, the aggregate, global impact of mobiles decreases the gender ratio by 0.01% points. This is explained by a negative, significant effect for mobile phones in low- and low-middle-income countries, and no effect for more developed countries. Accordingly, mobiles do no longer seem to improve gender equality in the labor market and seemed to be most important in the early years of ICTs. Results are presented in Appendix 4.

4.4 Robustness Checks

The overall effect from the results is that ICT improves gender equality in the labor market with a higher effect for the Internet than mobiles. To test the robustness of these findings, additional tests were conducted.

First, the robustness of the control variables was tested. Urbanization ratio was used as a control variable, rather than GDP per capita as a measurement of development, providing robust results. The validity of the education control, average years of schooling, was confirmed by replacing the variable with the ratio female-to-male enrollment in primary and secondary education. Total enrollment in tertiary education was also tested and added as a control. Lastly, infrastructure control was added: electricity consumption. All tests supported the robustness of the results. The World Bank data on education, disaggregated by gender, was not included as control variables in the main regression due to the limited amount of observations. Neither was electricity consumption for the same reason. A regression using lagged ICT variables was also run, still providing robust results.

Another test conducted to test robustness was to omit outliers, to see whether this would influence the findings. By winsorizing the data, setting the outliers to the first

[15]For high-income countries, the ratio significantly increase by 0,045% points.

1%- and the last 99%-percentile replacing the smallest and largest values with the observations closest to them, the results are still robust.[16]

5 Conclusions and Policy Implications

In line with previous literature, ICT seems to be a positive contribution to gender equality in the labor market, mainly explained by increased female participation. In the international development debate, policy makers are optimistic of ICTs contributions to development, poverty reduction and women's economic empowerment. This is reflected among others in UNs Sustainable Development Goals (SDGs). Recalling some of the microstudies based on household surveys, improvements in opportunities for females were substantial because of ICTs.

Interestingly, the considerable effect of ICT in most microstudies seems to vanish when utilizing macrodata as in this analysis. Even though impact from ICTs in this study is positive, it is low. The female-to-male ratio in labor market participation is increasing by 0.04% points for the Internet and 0.02 for mobile phones on the aggregate level.

It is most certainly hard to quantify what is a 'high effect' and what the expected impact of ICT should be for gender equality. Nevertheless, comparing the effects of ICTs with the coefficients of education from the same regressions, an additional year of education seems to have a much higher impact on gender equality in the labor market than a one-unit increase in ICTs. Other economic and social investments, such as education, might accordingly be more beneficial for gender equality than ICT.

Another interesting result from this chapter is how the effect of ICT differs with the level of development. In low-income countries, ICTs do not have any effect in increasing female labor force participation, while these technologies demonstrate a higher impact the more developed a country is. Recalling the U-hypothesis, the U-shape should be mitigated when the development process moved straight from agriculture to the information economy, as a leapfrogging strategy. According to this theory, it should be expected an increase in female labor force participation in low-income countries. This, however, is not present in the results here. The positive effect of the gender ratio in low-income countries is caused by a decrease in male participation, not by inducing more females to work. These results bring important policy implications to the international development debate, suggesting that ICTs may not be the catalyst empowering women in developing countries that policy makers are hoping for. It seems like a country must have a certain level of development, in order to take advantage of ICTs opportunities for empowering women.

[16]The marginal effect of the Internet after winsorizing is significant at 0.0427 (compared to 0.0437 in main regression) and for mobile, the marginal effect is significant at 0.0188 (compared to 0.0178 in main regression).

In general, it seems like developing countries not have geared up in their capabilities to sufficiently harness their technology investments. This argument would be in line with recent findings from the Asian Development Bank (2017, p. xix), that economies priorities different infrastructure as they develop. Low-income countries would rather invest in water, electricity, and sanitation before investing in ICTs. Investments in ICTs become more important in the later stages of development. Lack of investments in ICT infrastructure the latest years could explain why the marginal effects from ICTs were approximately equal across countries before 2005 but developed a digital divide in impact from 2005 to 2014.

In the light of these results, ICTs as a potential leapfrogging strategy for developing countries could, therefore, be questioned. Even though ICTs represent possibilities for shortcuts in communication and information, this does not automatically spill over in other parts of life, such as working life.

A possible problem with this study is that gender-specific data on the use of ICT are not available. This is not necessarily a problem in high-income countries, where the digital divide rarely exists, and females and males use ICTs at an equal level. The gender digital divide might, however, be of substantial impact in countries where females have lower access to ICTs than males, which is often the case in low-income countries. This could lead to downward bias of the results, meaning that they potentially are at the lower bound. The results could potentially be different if the ICT data were disaggregated by sex. Some countries have recently started reporting sex-disaggregated data on ICT use. Future research may, therefore, be able to give a more precise estimation of correlation of female access and female employment.

Another challenge is that opportunities from ICTs for females in developing countries may be in a too early stage to be captured by these regressions. Large spillover effects from ICTs to female labor participation might not yet be present in the limited period considered in this chapter.

ICTs have with no doubt contributed to transforming people's private and professional lives, both for females and males. It has led to more efficient markets, lower transaction costs, and easier access to information. To fully take advantage of the opportunities of ICTs for gender equality, the results suggest that it is necessary with a certain level of development, including basic infrastructure, education, and health. It is therefore important to complement technology investments with economic and social reforms to get the maximum benefits from digital technologies and eventually, a more gender-equal labor market.

Appendix 1: List of Countries

Low income	Low-middle	Upper-middle	High income
Afghanistan	Algeria	Argentina	Australia
Albania	Azerbaijan	Bahrain	Austria
Angola	Belarus	Barbados	Belgium
Armenia	Belize	Croatia	Brunei Darussalam
Bangladesh	Botswana	Cyprus	Canada
Benin	Brazil	Gabon	Denmark
Bhutan	Bulgaria	Greece	Finland
Bolivia	Chile	Israel	France
Bosnia and Herzegovina	Colombia	Kuwait	Germany
Burkina Faso	Costa Rica	Libya	Iceland
Burundi	Cuba	Malta	Ireland
Cambodia	Czech Republic	New Zealand	Italy
Cameroon	Dominican Republic	Oman	Japan
Cape Verde	Ecuador	Portugal	Luxembourg
Central African Republic	Estonia	Saudi Arabia	Netherlands
Chad	Fiji	Slovenia	Norway
China	Georgia	Trinidad and Tobago	Qatar
Comoros	Hungary		Singapore
Cote d'Ivoire	Iraq		Spain
El Salvador	Jamaica		Sweden
Equatorial Guinea	Jordan		Switzerland
Eritrea	Kazakhstan		United Arab Emirates
Ethiopia	Latvia		UK
Ghana	Lebanon		USA
Guatemala	Lithuania		
Guinea	Malaysia		
Guinea-Bissau	Maldives		
Guyana	Mauritius		
Haiti	Mexico		
Honduras	Mongolia		

(continued)

(continued)

Low income	Low-middle	Upper-middle	High income
India	Montenegro		
Indonesia	Morocco		
Kenya	Namibia		
Kyrgyzstan	Panama		
Laos	Peru		
Liberia	Romania		
Madagascar	Russia		
Malawi	Serbia		
Mali	Slovakia		
Mauritania	South Africa		
Moldova, Republic of	Suriname		
Mozambique	Swaziland		
Myanmar	Thailand		
Nepal	Tunisia		
Nicaragua	Turkey		
Niger	Ukraine		
Nigeria	Uruguay		
Pakistan			
Papua New Guinea			
Philippines			
Rwanda			
Senegal			
Sierra Leone			
Solomon Islands			
Sri Lanka			
Sudan			
Syrian Arab Republic			
Tajikistan			
Tanzania			
Togo			
Turkmenistan			
Uganda			
Uzbekistan			
Vietnam			
Zambia			
Zimbabwe			

Appendix 2: Female Versus Male Participation Rates

See Tables 5 and 6.

Appendix 3: Female Versus Male Participation

See Tables 7 and 8.

Appendix 4: 1991–2005 and 2005–2014 Regressions

See Tables 9, 10 and 11.

Table 5 Female versus male labor force participation rate

Variables	(1)	(2)	(3)	(4)
	Females	Males	Females	Males
Internet	−0.0572**	−0.0809***		
	(0.0255)	(0.0167)		
Internet*(log)GDPpc$_{1991}$	0.0109***	0.00839***		
	(0.00277)	(0.00177)		
Mobile			−0.0425***	0.0198**
			(0.0108)	(0.00876)
Mobile*(log)GDPpc$_{1991}$			0.00841***	−0.00144
			(0.00126)	(0.000969)
Total population (log)	−1.651***	0.312	−1.752***	−0.291
	(0.331)	(0.206)	(0.292)	(0.207)
Total unemployment	7.888***	6.100***	8.186***	6.718***
	(0.812)	(0.587)	(0.743)	(0.592)
Fertility rate	−0.0302	−0.0815***	0.0198	−0.0689***
	(0.0266)	(0.0185)	(0.0256)	(0.0191)
Urban population	−1.004*	1.341***	−0.461	1.376***

(continued)

Table 5 (continued)

Variables	(1)	(2)	(3)	(4)
	Females	Males	Females	Males
	(0.529)	(0.189)	(0.376)	(0.168)
Trade as %-of GDP	−0.000776	0.00237	−0.000681	0.000326
	(0.00306)	(0.00180)	(0.00265)	(0.00175)
Avg. years of schooling	0.161	−0.725***	−0.335**	−0.763***
	(0.169)	(0.0962)	(0.152)	(0.106)
% Christians	0.00726	0.0544***	−0.000269	0.0340***
	(0.0156)	(0.0116)	(0.0134)	(0.0108)
% Muslims	−0.152***	−0.00240	−0.165***	−0.0388*
	(0.0366)	(0.0240)	(0.0290)	(0.0229)
% Jews	−0.260	−0.0124	−0.178	0.000196
	(0.183)	(0.208)	(0.196)	(0.219)
% Buddhists	−0.0560**	−0.0128	−0.0775***	0.00372
	(0.0234)	(0.0150)	(0.0174)	(0.0114)
% Hindus	−0.420***	−0.0695**	−0.398***	−0.124***
	(0.0532)	(0.0305)	(0.0453)	(0.0352)
Constant	−46.26***	−27.71***	−50.70***	−31.37***
	(12.81)	(9.154)	(11.66)	(9.046)
Observations	2,955	2,955	3,270	3,270
Country FE	YES	YES	YES	YES
Year FE	YES	YES	YES	YES
R-squared	0.975	0.962	0.974	0.956
Adj. *R*-squared	0.973	0.959	0.972	0.953

Robust standard errors in parentheses, $^{***}p < 0.01$, $^{**}p < 0.05$, $^{*}p < 0.1$

Table 6 Female versus male participation rates: marginal effects from ICTs

Variables	(1)	(2)	(3)	(4)
	Females	Males	Females	Males
Internet	0.0259***	−0.0171***		
	(0.00738)	(0.00468)		
Mobile			0.0209***	0.00897***
			(0.00361)	(0.00239)
Observations	2,955	2,955	3,270	3,270

Table 7 Marginal effects of the Internet: income status and sex

Variables	(1)	(2)	(3)	(4)	(5)	(6)	(7)	(8)
	Low-income females	Low-middle females	Upper-middle females	High-income females	Low-income males	Low-middle males	Upper-middle males	High-income males
Internet	0.00821	0.0259***	0.0407***	0.0523***	−0.0307***	−0.0171***	−0.00574	0.00319
	(0.0104)	(0.00738)	(0.00642)	(0.00712)	(0.00680)	(0.00468)	(0.00375)	(0.00401)
Observations	1,114	945	343	553	1,114	945	343	553

Table 8 Marginal effects of mobiles: income status and sex

Variables	(1)	(2)	(3)	(4)	(5)	(6)	(7)	(8)
	Low-income females	Low-middle females	Upper-middle females	High-income females	Low-income males	Low-middle males	Upper-middle males	High-income males
Mobile	0.00790*	0.0213***	0.0327***	0.0417***	0.0112***	0.00889***	0.00694***	0.00539**
	(0.00444)	(0.00359)	(0.00367)	(0.00424)	(0.00340)	(0.00236)	(0.00207)	(0.00238)
Observations	1,291	1,037	380	562	1,291	1,037	380	562

Table 9 Total marginal effects: mobile and the Internet 1991–2005 and 2005–2014

Variables	(1)	(2)	(3)	(4)
	Internet 1991–2005	Internet 2005–2014	Mobile 1991–2005	Mobile 2005–2014
Internet	0.0553***	−0.000953		
	(0.0156)	(0.00644)		
Mobile			0.0276**	−0.0109***
			(0.0120)	(0.00292)
Observations	1,603	1,499	1,911	1,509

Standard errors in parentheses
***$p < 0.01$, **$p < 0.05$, *$p < 0.1$

Table 10 Marginal effects of the Internet, differed between income levels

Variables	(1)	(2)	(3)	(4)	(5)	(6)	(7)	(8)
	Low income 1991–2005	Low-middle 1991–2005	Upper-middle 1991–2005	High income 1991–2005	Low income 2005–2014	Low-middle 2005–2014	Upper-middle 2005–2014	High income 2005–2014
Internet	0.0554**	0.0553***	0.0552***	0.0551***	−0.0279***	0.00105	0.0256***	0.0451***
	(0.0255)	(0.0161)	(0.0103)	(0.00986)	(0.00815)	(0.00647)	(0.00858)	(0.0115)
Observations	563	510	193	337	611	481	167	240

Standard errors in parentheses
***$p < 0.01$, **$p < 0.05$, *$p < 0.1$

Table 11 Marginal effects of mobile, differed between income levels

Variables	(1)	(2)	(3)	(4)	(5)	(6)	(7)	(8)
	Low income 1991–2005	Low-middle 1991–2005	Upper-middle 1991–2005	High income 1991–2005	Low income 2005–2014	Low-middle 2005–2014	Upper-middle 2005–2014	High income 2005–2014
Mobile	0.00683	0.0278**	0.0455***	0.0596***	−0.0175***	−0.0103***	−0.00423	0.000612
	(0.0175)	(0.0120)	(0.00832)	(0.00720)	(0.00351)	(0.00293)	(0.00376)	(0.00491)
Observations	734	601	230	346	618	484	167	240

Standard errors in parentheses
***$p < 0.01$, **$p < 0.05$, *$p < 0.1$

References

Asian Development Bank. (2017). *Asian development outlook. Transcending the middle income challenge.* http://dx.doi.org/10.22617/FLS178632-3.

Black, S., & Spitz-Oener, A. (2007). Explaining women's success: Technological change and the skill content women's work. *The Review of Economics and Statistics, 92*(1), 187–194. https://doi.org/10.1162/rest.2009.11761.

Chen, D. (2004). Gender equality and economic development: The role for information and communication technologies. In *World Bank Policy Research Working Paper No. 3285.* Retrieved from https://ssrn.com/abstract=610329.

Chew, H., Levy, E. M., & Ilavarasan, V. (2011). The limited impact of ICTs on microenterprise growth: A study of businesses owned by women in urban India. *Information Technologies and International Development, 7*(4), 1–16. Retrieved from http://itidjournal.org/itid/article/view/788.

Correlates of War. (2017). *World religion data.* Retrieved from http://www.correlatesofwar.org/data-sets/world-religion-data.

Dettling, L. (2011). *Opting back in: Home internet use and female labor supply.* Working Paper, Department of Economics, University of Maryland, College Park, MD. Retrieved from www.sole-jole.org/12378.pdf.

Dettling, L. (2017). Broadband in the labor market: The impact of residential high-speed internet on married women's labor force participation. *ILR Review, 70*(2), 451–482. https://doi.org/10.1177/0019793916644721.

Dollar, D., & Gatti, R. (1999). Gender inequality, income, and growth: Are good times good for women? Policy Research Report on Gender and Development. *Policy research report on gender and development working paper series; no. 1.* Washington, D.C. The World Bank. Retrieved from http://documents.worldbank.org/curated/en/251801468765040122/Gender-inequality-income-and-growth-are-good-times-good-for-women.

Efobi, U., Tanankem, B., & Asongu, S. (2016). Technological advancement and the evolving gender identities: A focus on the level of female economic participation in Sub-Saharan Africa. In *African Governance and Development Institute, WP/16/045.* Retrieved from https://ssrn.com/abstract=2885739.

Ehrenberg, R., & Smith, R. (2012). *Modern labor economics* (11th ed.). USA: Pearson Education.

Fong, M. (2009). Technology leapfrogging for developing countries. In *Encyclopedia of Information Science and Technology* (2nd ed., pp. 3707–3713). https://doi.org/10.4018/978-1-60566-026-4.ch591.

Gaddis, I., & Klasen, S. (2011). Economic development, structural change and women's labor force participation. In *EconStor, courant research centre: Poverty, equity and growth.* Discussion Papers, No. 71. Retrieved from https://www.econstor.eu/handle/10419/90566.

Gillard, H., Howcroft, D., Mitev, N., & Richardson, H. (2008). "Missing women": Gender, ICTs and the shaping of the global economy. *Information Technology for Development, 14*(4), 262–279. https://doi.org/10.1002/itdj.20098.

Goldin, C. (1994). The U-shaped female labor function in economic development and economic theory. In T. P. Schultz (Ed.), *Investment in women's human capital and economic development.* Chicago: University of Chicago Press. https://doi.org/10.3386/w4707.

Hilbert, M. (2011). Digital gender divide or technologically empowered women in developing countries? A typical case of lies, damned lies and statistics. *Women's Studies International Forum,* 34(6). Retrieved from https://papers.ssrn.com/sol3/papers.cfm?abstract_id=2039116.

ITU. (2016). *International telecommunication union, statistics.* Retrieved from http://www.itu.int/en/ITU-D/Statistics/Pages/stat/default.aspx.

Jensen, R. (2012). Do labor market opportunities affect young women's work and family decisions? Experimental evidence from India. *Quarterly Journal of Economics, 127,* 753–792. https://doi.org/10.1093/qje/qjs002.

Katz, L., & Krueger, A. (2016). The rise and nature of alternative work arrangements in the United States, 1995–2015. *NBER Working Paper No. 22667*. https://doi.org/10.3386/w22667.

Klonner, S., & Nolen, P. (2008). Does ICT benefit the poor? Evidence from South-Africa. *University of Essex–mimeo*. Retrieved from https://ideas.repec.org/p/zbw/gdec10/56.html.

Minges, M. (2015). Exploring the relationship between broadband and economic growth. In *World bank background paper, digital dividends*. Retrieved from http://pubdocs.worldbank.org/en/391452529895999/WDR16-BP-Exploring-the-Relationship-between-Broadband-and-Economic-Growth-Minges.pdf.

Nath, V. (2001). Empowerment and governance through information and communication technologies: Women's perspective. *The International Information and Library Review, 33*(4), 317–339. https://doi.org/10.1006/iirl.2001.0175.

Uteng, T. P. (2011). Gender and mobility in the developing world. *Background paper, World Bank Development Report 2012*. Retrieved from http://siteresources.worldbank.org/INTWDR2012/Resources/7778105-1299699968583/7786210-1322671773271/uteng.pdf.

World Bank. (2016a). *World Development Report 2016: Digital dividends*. Washington, DC: World Bank. https://doi.org/10.1596/978-1-4648-0671-1.

World Bank. (2016b). *Data description, female labor force participation*. Retrieved from http://data.worldbank.org/indicator/SL.TLF.CACT.FE.ZS.

ICT Exposure and Its Relationship with Academic Self-efficacy and Achievement of Adolescent Students: The Field-Level Study in India and Fiji

Susmita Mandal

Abstract Today, children and adolescents are more interested in spending time on ICT applications such as playing video games, using mobile, computer and Internet, and watching TV by sacrificing learning and extracurricular activity. The present study investigates whether time devoted to ICT applications adversely affects academic self-efficacy and achievement of adolescent students in two developing countries, India and Fiji. The study developed a structured questionnaire to capture the proposed variables such as level (time spent) of ICT exposure, academic self-efficacy and achievement into a quantitative framework. A survey collected relevant information for these variables from 873 adolescent students of the tenth class standard from 16 schools selected in rural and urban areas in India and Fiji. Cronbach's alpha test was used to assess the reliability of the instrument before principal component analysis (PCA) was employed to construct a suitable index of academic self-efficacy. Statistical analyses such as ANOVA and regression methods were followed to establish various relationships among the variables. The results suggested that ICT exposure improves academic self-efficacy and achievement of adolescent students, but at a low rate and up to a certain limit of time (3 h/day) spending.

1 Introduction

Today, children and adolescents are more exposed to ICT applications and innovations and are interested in spending time for this that helps knowledge acquisition, socialization and recreation. This may also have an implication on their physical and mental health (e.g. Thomee et al. 2011). The growing digital innovation has brought various applications to enhance knowledge and competency. By playing video games, using Internet, TV and electronic media, students can increase their knowledge, planning ability as well as resource management, problem-solving and logical power (Head and Eisenberg 2009). At the same time, this has brought substantial changes in adolescent behaviour. By misusing it, they sacrifice their extracurricu-

S. Mandal (✉)
University of the South Pacific, Suva, Fiji
e-mail: susmitammaiti@gmail.com

D. Maiti et al. (eds.), *Digitalisation and Development*,
https://doi.org/10.1007/978-981-13-9996-1_16

lar and learning activities as well as are becoming more moody and distracted (Panahi 2015). These are not conducive for their development. This has serious implication among the youth of a future generation, when mental and psychological disorders, such as schizophrenia, depressive psychosis, organic brain syndrome and substance use, are increasing among the adolescents in recent time (Shah et al. 2005). It draws attention among scholars to investigate the resultant impact of ICT exposure on the overall development of adolescents in recent years.

ICT, mainly through internet applications, become a useful and integrated part of human life. It includes a wide-ranging variation of devices such as smartphones, computers, TV, and a variety of other applications like gaming, social networking and communication tools, etc. These applications could improve efficiency in daily activities. Adolescents use this technology in a huge amount compared to other age groups. They prefer to spend more time online than that of adults by engaging in gaming, chatting, instant messaging and other new forms of electronic communication (Montgomery 2000). During this transitional period from childhood dependence to independence and social acceptance, the children want to enjoy unlimited freedom and separation from parents and adults. Hence, they become excited to be engaged in ICT applications, which serve as regular sources of careful answers and information. Therefore, the obvious purpose of ICT use among young generation would be to gather information for enhancing knowledge. Adolescents, who have a positive attitude towards ICT application, use them to improve learning (Mbah 2010). Moreover, they are very much eager to maintain interpersonal relationships at this stage and hence, are attracted to ICT as a medium that provides the huge facility to maintain interaction with a lot of people for social and emotional support. Therefore, the adolescent in the present generation prefers to use ICT extensively for various reasons. Now, the question is: can it improve their academic performance?

In a developing country, parents and teachers are concerned about their children's academic development very much so that they could secure a job in future. In many cases, they encourage more to use ICT for gathering information as well as to make the children smarter in technology. Of course, this is the positive application of ICT. On the other hand, the parents allow their children also to be engaged more in the video computer game as the children are very much eager to be involved in this activity. This may lead to overuse and overdependence on ICT applications, which can take away their attention from other competing jobs and activities. Then, the parents get frustrated and often cannot control them to stay away from that type of sedentary activity. Such overuse can damage their efficacy level. Now, the questions are to what extent do the adolescents remain engaged in ICT? Does this engagement diminish or improve adolescents' academic aspects such as academic self-efficacy and achievement? The present study attempts to address these issues taking sample observations from two typically developing societies, India and Fiji.

Adolescence is the most important period of life for overall development. Fluctuations occurring in this transitional period can drive adolescents to suffer increasingly from various mental and physical problems. Moreover, in a complex traditional society with high poverty, unemployment and health hazards, adolescents face problems and challenges in their daily lives and suffer from various mental disorders; in reaction, they sometimes commit to high-risk activities (Merikangas et al. 2010; CDC 2009). Therefore, children in this period must be encouraged not only to get success in their academic area, but also to build their mental health with sufficient level of academic self-efficacy. This will help them to perform better in the academic area successfully as well as succeed in future challenging circumstances. A rise in the level of self-efficacy in the academic area helps them to overcome various adversities, setbacks, frustrations, inequities and inefficiencies that adolescents face in the ever-changing socioeconomic environment, particularly in developing countries like India.

By playing video games, using the Internet, TV and electronic media, the students can learn to follow instruction, develop hand–eye coordination and fine motor skills and get various information. They can increase their knowledge, planning ability as well as the power of resource management, problem-solving and reasoning (Head and Eisenberg 2009). These qualities also increase their ability to manage multitasks. But, there is another side of a coin. Children playing more violent video games show more aggressive thoughts, feelings and behaviour, and less pro-social behaviour (Anderson and Bushman 2001). In a prospective analysis, Thomee et al. (2011) showed a positive association of *overuse of mobile phone* with stress, sleep disturbances and symptoms of depression for both men and women *among young adult*. Moreover, it has been critical challenges related to adolescents' exploration of the Internet for information accusation. Several studies indicate that adolescents do not have so much ability to recognize the relevance of information saved by such search engines and do not know which sites are authentic (Hansen et al. 2003; Skinner et al. 2003). Therefore, they become misguided by some information.

The effect of ICT exposure on mental health and academic aspects has been still debatable and controversial. Therefore, whether ICT exposure affects adolescent students' academic self-efficacy and performance is a serious issue in the modern age. Does ICT used by the students affect their academic self-efficacy and performance in adolescent period? These issues are still under-researched. It continues to motivate the researchers to undertake this type of research in different ways under various socioeconomic contexts. The present research addresses these issues and proposes to investigate the effect of ICT exposure on academic self-efficacy and performance of adolescent in typical developing societies like India and Fiji.

Therefore, the current study seeks to meet the following research objectives:

(1) To study the level of ICT exposure among the adolescent students across country and gender
(2) To study the effect of ICT exposure on academic self-efficacy and performance of adolescent students

2 Literature Review

This section presents three related current research areas:

(i) Adolescent development, described in Sect. 2.1
(ii) Self-efficacy and its impact on achievement, discussed in Sect. 2.2
(iii) Usage of ICT in the adolescent period and its role on self-efficacy and academic achievement, outlined in Sect. 2.3

2.1 Adolescent Development

Adolescence is the most important period of human life with substantial mental, physical and cognitive developments. The term *adolescence* comes from the Latin verb *adolescere* (to grow to maturity). This stage carries a lot of physiological, psychological and social changes, depending upon various socioeconomic and other environmental factors. Therefore, a child experiences revolutionary changes in this transitional period from childhood to adolescence (Chauhan 2009). It is inherently a stage of "*storm and stress*" (Hall 1904), a "*period of identity-formation*" (Erikson and Erikson 1997). Rogers (1969) defined adolescence as '*a process rather than a period, a process of achieving the attitudes and beliefs needed for effective participation in the society*' (Chauhan 2009). Piaget (1966) described it as '*the age of great ideals and the beginning of theories as well as the time of simple adaptation to reality*'. The adolescents face a range of problems due to the various changes during the onset of puberty. Puberty is identified as the age of progression from a phase of reproductive immaturity to complete competence. During this period, a child wants to be independent and needs substantial adjustment to the physical, mental and social changes that differentiate mature behaviour from those of infantile. Due to these versatile characteristics, an adolescent should follow proper guidance and nurturing to build a better and healthier future.

Theory of adolescent development

It is essential to understand the adolescent developmental process properly for guiding and carefully nurturing them. There are lots of theories that have been evolved in different aspects of adolescent development. However, the current study includes only a few theories that are related to specific aspects of their development, such as theories of personality (Hall's theory, Freud's psychosexual development theory and Erik Erikson's psychosocial development theory), theory of social learning (Bandura's theory) and theory of cognitive development (Piaget's theory) (Ausubel 2002).

Hall's theory is well known as the original one of '*a scientific study of adolescence*'. According to Hall (1904), an individual's psychological development is influenced by both genetic and social characteristics. He explained the adolescent period as a period of '*storm and stress*', full of inconsistency, quick changes in mood and emotion. Therefore, it is defined as an unstable period of human life.

Here, it should be noted that today some of the psychologists do not agree with Hall's view that adolescence, in general, is a stage of '*storm and stress*'. According to

Bandura (1964), adolescents may execute the role of a rebel if society represents this period as a period of radical tension, rebellion, volatility and carelessness. Bandura says this as a 'self-fulfilling prophecy'. The behaviour of an adolescent is very much affected by the social and traditional setting (Atwater 1992). Bandura, a leading social learning theorist, observed that adolescents' academic activities and behaviour are substantially influenced by observational learning as well as cognitive variables like abilities, programming schemes, ambitions, ethics and self-regulatory systems (self-monitoring and motivation).

Sigmund Freud focused on the unconscious, the interpretation of dreams, the id, ego and superego. These various features are described in his psychosexual development theory (Freud 1962; Pearce 2009; Levesque 2011). The five phases in this theory are oral, anal, phallic, latent and genital. According to this theory, children's unconscious sexual desires are repressed in the latency stage (6–11 years). Most of them like to play and make friendships with the same sex. Then, in the genital stage (adolescence) that is awakened due to puberty, teens feel attraction to the opposite sex. This stage persists throughout adulthood and maintains a balance between all areas of life. According to Freud, personality depends on the ability to deal with id, ego and superego in the formative years of life. The id is the biological and subconscious part of human personality. This emphasizes immediate satisfaction of instinctive appetite, impulse and need. Ego is psychosocial and controls the demands of the id as well as helps the individual to adapt to reality. On the other hand, superego is social that emphasizes the moral values of society. This theoretical perspective explains that the sexual conflict in the adolescent period produces an anxiety that results in the development of a variety of defence mechanisms like suppression and self-discipline for coping with stress. From this, it is clear that Freud ignored the significance of sociocultural influences. Still, some features of his theory are foundations for understanding human behaviour (The-Pennsylvania-Child-Welfare-Training-Program 2005).

According to Erikson (1968), there is a series of internal conflicts, named as '*crisis*', throughout the developmental stages. The crisis in the adolescent period is named as the crisis of identity versus identity of confusion. It signifies the struggle to develop self-identity. Like Freud, Erikson believes that adolescence is a period of stress and confusion originating from an identity crisis (The Pennsylvania Child Welfare Training Program 2005; Steinberg and Morris 2001).

Jean Piaget is one of the most eminent and powerful child development psychologists. Piaget described five types of cognitive development during the adolescent period, i.e. (1) formal operations, (2) hypothetic-deductive reasoning, (3) propositional thought, (4) the imaginary audience and (5) the personal fable.

Formal operations: According to Piaget, the child experiences revolutionary changes in his/her cognitive development during his/her adolescent period. In this period, the youths can move from the boundaries of concrete mental operations and acquire the ability to think more abstract concepts like algebra and science, more immaterial concepts like '*justice*' and '*poverty*' and also the effect of these immaterial concepts. Piaget terms this ability as '*formal operations*'.

Hypothetic-deductive reasoning: Moreover, children in this adolescent stage develop more scientific and logical standing in the way of problem-solving. Piaget terms this ability as '*hypothetic-deductive reasoning*'. With this ability, children can identify various variables in logical ways that help them to formulate hypotheses and to reflect on possibilities.

Propositional thought: According to Piaget, youths in this period can develop another complicated thought process, named as '*propositional thought*'. With this thought process, children can decide whether a testimonial is fully logical or not.

The imaginary audience: The teens in this age group not only develop a more scientific and logical thinking process but also improve their ability for observation and interpretation. By observing others' behaviours, words, remarks and appearance, they are now able to interpret this information and can come to conclusions or reasonable guesses about the thinking, wanting, needing or feeling of that persons. Therefore, the children also begin to ask questions about the thinking of other people about them. According to Piaget, all these factors combine to generate the '*imaginary audience*'. Because of this, sometimes the adolescents might believe by mistake that everybody around them is observing, judging and inspecting their every movement. As a result, sometimes, they become painfully self-conscious. Thus, the '*imaginary audience*' originates due to the interrelationship among intellectual, emotional and social development.

The personal fable: Because of developing the capability to practise abstract thought and strong observational ability, adolescents become more sensitive to people's requirements. They may think themselves exceptionally unique and different from anyone else in the world. This is identified as '*personal fable*' by Piaget. Due to this '*personal fable*', a person can think of himself/herself as superior, cleverer or stronger than others. They may experience some shocking moments as sometimes they might take harmful risks by overestimating their capacities. On the other hand, some children may feel themselves as less clever, feebler and more mediocre than others. This kind of personal fable may lead them to feel unhappy, frustrated and isolated.

Though Jean Piaget's theory has greatly helped us to advance our knowledge and understanding of cognitive development during the adolescent period, new research modifies some aspects of his theory. Modern research shows that everybody does not necessarily pass through the phase of Piaget's formal operations, i.e. the capability to think conceptually (Keating 1979; Cole 1996).

Hence, an individual experiences a substantial change in both physical structure and behavioural characteristics during his/her adolescence. Therefore, they should be nurtured in a proper way for their sound development. As well as it is very important to develop their sufficient level of self-efficacy so that they can motivate themselves in a proper designated level.

2.2 Self-efficacy and Its Impact on Achievement

In the adolescent period, a sufficient level of self-efficacy in the academic area is needed to take the challenge with the ever-changing world successfully, to struggle for future development and employment and to reduce high-risk activities. This section discusses the contribution of self-efficacy mainly in academic performance.

Self-efficacy here refers to one's belief about one's capability to learn or perform a behaviour at a designated level (Bandura 1986, 1993a, 1994, 1997). A person with high efficacy in his/her capability in any area will be able to deal with difficulties and challenging tasks without avoiding them for fear of failing. It increases his/her inherent curiosity and profound attention in that activity. As a result, he/she acquires skill in that particular activity or area. The person can choose a set of difficult aims or objectives and recover quickly, even after failure or setback (Bandura 1994). Similarly, academic self-efficacy is concerned with one's belief about one's capability in academic activity. Students, who have beliefs about their skill and performance in learning activity as well as for making effective use of self-regulatory learning strategies such as organizing their work and managing their time, are more likely to have higher academic self-efficacy as well as an achievement (Usher and Pajares 2008).

Contribution of self-efficacy

According to Bandura (1993a), perceived self-efficacy contributes to cognitive growth and performance. It is related to four main systems such as cognitive, motivational, affective and selection processes. It contributes to academic development. Therefore, the students' efficacy belief to manage their academic activity and be expert in that area supports them to establish aspiration and incentive level, as well as achievements in the academic area.

Self-efficacy in social cognitive theory

In this perspective, to explain the importance of self-efficacy in human life as well as in the adolescent period, it must be mentioned that self-efficacy has a significant role as an element within the theoretical structure of Bandura's social cognitive theory. According to this theory, human nature is the product of the interaction between environmental characteristics and a person's thinking processes like inner merits and self-beliefs (Bandura 1986, 2001).

There is a large volume of recent literature that discusses the involvement of self-efficacy in various aspects of life and academic outcome. Some of these will be described here for understanding the dynamics. Engels et al. (2005) studied the relationship between self-efficacy, emotional adjustment and smoking addiction in early adolescents. They took a sample of 1,861 students aged 12–13 years from 11 secondary schools in the Netherlands. A series of questionnaires were used to capture the above three variables for the study. Cross-sectional and short-term longitudinal analysis showed almost the same result: that more depressive mood, lower self-esteem and self-efficacy are associated with the increased level of smoking.

Mahyuddin et al. (2006) examined the association between students' self-efficacy in the English language and their achievement in that subject. As a sample, the study has taken 1,146 students from various secondary schools in Malaysia. A self-efficacy scale was administered to all the students. The result indicated that there was a positive correlation ($r = 0.48$, $p = 0.001$) between self-efficacy and achievement in the English language.

In a similar study, Caprara et al. (2008) investigated the effect of self-efficacy for self-regulated learning on the academic outcome as well as its role in the possibility of continuing formal education in school. They used a sample of 412 Italian students aged 12–22 years. The result of statistical analysis revealed that self-efficacy of the students was positively associated with their achievement in junior high school. But, there was a significant deterioration in self-regulatory efficacy of the students due to their shifting from junior to senior high school. However, the lesser deterioration in self-regulatory efficacy indicated better senior high school achievement and the possibility of continuing high school education.

Thijs and Verkuyten (2008) carried out an interesting and slightly dissimilar investigation on the relationship of peer ill-treatment and academic outcome, and the function of academic self-efficacy in this regard. The study has taken 1,895 grade 6 students from 108 schools in the USA. The result found that peer ill-treatment was negatively associated with academic outcome through decreasing academic self-efficacy of the students. Therefore, ill-treated students had low academic self-efficacy because they used to underestimate themselves as less capable and thereby, performed academically less well.

2.3 Usage of ICT in the Adolescent Period and Its Role in Cognitive Development and Academic Achievement

This section turns our attention to discuss the usage of ICT in the adolescent period and its role on their behaviour, cognitive development and academic area.

With remarkable development in cognitive ability, adolescents prefer ICT applications very much to satisfy their versatile needs. Research studies (Montgomery 2000; Monetti et al. 2011) show that they use this technology extensively in comparison to any other age group. This is the transitional period from childhood dependence to independence and social acceptance. Thereby, during this period, they want to get unlimited freedom. These make them excited to practice ICT as a regular source to enjoy boundless freedom. On the other hand, they develop more scientific and logical standing in the way of problem-solving and want to get an immediate answer to a question. Therefore, they become very much attracted to ICT to get an instant answer and information by using it. Moreover, adolescents are willing to maintain interpersonal relationships at this stage. In modern complicated society, parents are very much worried about children's safety and security, and cannot allow them to interact with new people easily. Therefore, adolescents choose the option of using ICT as a medium that provides them with various opportunities to maintain interaction easily with a lot of people for social and emotional support. Nowadays, communication channels through the Internet are gradually increasing. Internet mailbox, short message, chat rooms, weblogs and online games all are the social relationship ways between peoples (Montgomery 2000). Adolescents like to engage in these activities desperately and thereby, can find their self-identity.

Some studies in the literature show the role of ICT on various aspects, including the academic area of the children using that. Bavelier et al. (2011), showed that video games increase students' quick thinking for making fast analysis and decisions. Therefore, by playing these games, students can develop their reading and math skills. The study of the Appalachia Educational Laboratory shows that children with the attention-deficit disorder can improve their reading scores through increasing their concentration level by playing Dance Revolution (as cited in Jain and Shakher 2014). According to the study conducted at the Michigan State University, Technology Project and playing video game develops students' creativity. Moreover, the Internet and other ICT like mobile phone short message service (SMS) give the students opportunities to use interactive technologies. In this way, they can increase their skills and information assimilation (Marsch et al. 2006). The preventive substance use interventions through the Internet have been presented with relative success in developed countries (Marsch et al. 2006; Pahwa and Schoech 2008; Bosworth et al. 1994). It is seen that Canadian adolescents used information technology for academic purpose as well as interactions with friends, social concerns, specific medical conditions, body image and nutrition, violence and personal safety, and sexual health (Skinner et al. 2003). On the other hand, children, who play more violent video games, are observed to show more aggressive thoughts, feelings and behaviour, and less pro-social behaviour (Anderson and Bushman 2001). It is also seen that there is a positive association of *overuse of mobile phone* with stress, sleep disturbances and symptoms of depression for both men and women *among young adult* (Thomee et al. 2011). Moreover, adolescents do not have so much capability and knowledge to justify about the importance of information saved by searching the internet as well as do not know which sites are authentic (Hansen et al. 2003; Skinner et al. 2003). Therefore, they become misguided by some information.

There are some other studies that focus on the contribution of ICT mainly in the academic area. Researcher Goddard (1998) found a strong positive correlation between students' achievement and ICT integration. According to Bandura (1993b), teachers also develop a strong sense of self-efficacy if they are prepared to teach technology. The study of Basri et al. (2018) showed that ICT adoption improves students' performance. On the other hand, Marcino (2018) studied the implementation of ICT as a curriculum resource and academic test performance of disabled students. The findings of the study revealed no significant contribution of ICT for students' English language arts (ELA) and mathematics score.

Most of the studies in the literature have focused on cognitive and mental aspects in a developed country, and the effect of ICT exposure on these has been still debatable and controversial. Some studies concentrate on academic performance, but the impact of ICT exposure on this performance is not clear. There is hardly a research study in the interface of ICT exposure and academic self-efficacy in literature.

Within this backdrop, it is important to identify the gaps in contemporary research on this issue.

(i) The effect of ICT exposure on behavioural, cognitive and academic development, in particular, is yet understudied about the problems of the developing world.
(ii) Though some research studies have investigated the influence of ICT exposure on an academic outcome, the impact is not clear.
(iii) Hardly research study to date has shown the effect of ICT exposure on academic self-efficacy.

Based on the research gaps, the current study proposes to test the following hypotheses empirically. The level of ICT exposure would vary among adolescent students because this exposure may depend on the economic condition and culture of a country. ICT exposure may have a positive effect on academic self-efficacy and performance of adolescent students, as it helps them to increase their planning ability as well as the power of resource management, problem-solving and reasoning. Besides, ICT exposure increases students' active participation that can develop their self-efficacy and thereby, improves performance. Then, after a certain limit of ICT exposure, it may have an adverse implication on their academic outcome because overuse of such applications increases sedentary activity, and attention deficit and diversion from the academic activity.

3 Method

The results of the existing research studies are influenced by the methods used, as well as the samples. Still, there are controversial and debatable opinions among the people and researchers regarding ICT uses and the various characteristics of adolescents, mainly in their academic area. Therefore, it motivates the researchers to continuously undertake this type of research in different ways under various socioeconomic contexts. Within this background, the current research study is an attempt to identify the impact of ICT exposure on adolescent students' academic self-efficacy and performance.

3.1 Participants

With limited scope and opportunity, the Indian field survey has been conducted during 2013–2014 within urban, semi-urban and rural areas in the district of Midnapur, which is located 70 km from Kolkata, West Bengal. Similarly, Suva (urban) and Rakiraki (rural) were chosen for the sample survey in Fiji during the same period.

In total, ten schools from India and six schools from Fiji were selected randomly at the region level. The Indian sample includes 435 adolescent students from the 10th standard (aged 14–17 years), of whom 245 are girls and the remaining 190, boys. Similarly, the Fijian sample size is 438 adolescent students, consisting of 252 girls and 186 boys.

3.2 Instrumentation

The research instruments used to measure the level of ICT exposure, academic self-efficacy and achievement are presented below:

3.2.1 ICT Exposure

ICT exposure is the most important and focused variable in this study. The study has utilized a self-recall and report measurement instrument to assess students' exposure in ICT. It consists of questions relating to students' engagement or time spent on playing video/computer games, using the Internet, computer and mobile at school as well as at home in the previous seven days. The study excluded the time spent on watching TV. The total time spent on ICT has been calculated by adding these two types of time spent on it, such as at school and home every day.

3.2.2 Academic Self-efficacy (ASE)

The study has constructed an academic self-efficacy scale based on Bandura (2006) and modified by Thomas (2013) for assessing students' self-efficacy level in the academic area in three different ways:

(i) The first part includes general academic self-efficacy in which the questions are on the students' confidence level in general learning. It contains four questions such as, '*in general, how confident are you in your abilities in learning*?'
(ii) The second part includes academic skill self-efficacy in which the students have been asked to identify their confidence level in various academic subjects such as mathematics, science, language and social studies.
(iii) The third part is self-efficacy for self-regulated learning. The study assumed that students, who have the belief about themselves for using self-regulatory learning strategies effectively, such as organizing their work and managing their time, have higher academic self-efficacy (Usher and Pajares 2008). This part contains ten questions in which the students were asked how they plan, organize and concentrate on their learning activities in different situations, e.g. when there are other interesting things to do or when there are various problems.

The answers of the students for each part under academic self-efficacy have been captured on a 10-point scale, '0' representing '*not at all*' and '10', '*very often*'. The higher the value means the greater will be the ASE value (see Table 8 in Appendix 1).

3.2.3 Academic Achievement (AA)

This is the outcome of students' academic activity to accomplish academic goals. Here, the study has measured the academic achievement of the students as the marks (average percentage) obtained by the students in various common school subjects such as Mathematics, Science, Biology, Agriculture, Mother tongue, English, History, Geography, Social Studies and Home Economics. The students were asked to complete the table with marks obtained in relevant subjects. Academic achievement has been taken from what students' reported as well as from schools' annual records. The average percentage of scores combining all subjects has, for this analysis, been considered as students' academic achievement. The study has also calculated achievement in science, as well as arts, subject separately.

3.3 Procedure

After collecting the required data, the questions have been combined to construct a unique index to represent each variable. In order to do this for a psychological variable like academic self-efficacy, Cronbach's alpha test (Cortina 1993) was applied to examine the reliability of the instrument and then, an index has been constructed to combine them by using proper weights of the questions derived from the method of principal component analysis (PCA) (Lindman and Sellin 2011; Vyas and Kumaranayake 2006).

After indexation, regression analysis has been used to examine the effect of ICT exposure on academic self-efficacy and achievement (Keller 2013).

4 Data Analysis

4.1 Level of ICT Exposure

According to Table 1, the highest proportion of students (52.87%) does not engage at all in ICT in India. Then, gradually, students' share decreases in the higher levels. But, in Fiji, the highest number of students (26.94%) engages in ICT among 30 min-1 h every day. Here, the students' share increases in the higher level up to 30 min-1 h and then, it decreases gradually. Across both countries together, the maximum students

Table 1 Level of ICT by sample distribution

Range of ICT (time)	Total (%)	India (%)	Fiji (%)	India/boy (%)	India/girl (%)	Fiji/boy (%)	Fiji/girl (%)
0	35.51	52.87	18.26	40.00	62.86	10.75	23.81
0–30 min	29.21	32.87	25.57	39.47	27.76	19.89	29.76
30 min–1 h	16.61	6.21	26.94	9.47	3.67	30.65	24.21
1 h–1 h 30 min	7.45	3.45	11.42	5.26	2.04	12.90	10.32
1 h 30 min–2 h	4.24	1.61	6.85	2.63	0.82	9.68	4.76
2 h–2 h 30 min	2.41	1.15	3.65	1.58	0.82	6.99	1.19
2 h 30 min–3 h	2.52	1.15	3.88	1.05	1.22	5.91	2.38
3 h–3 h 30 min	0.46	0.00	0.91	0.00	0.00	2.15	0.00
3 h 30 min–4 h	0.57	0.23	0.91	0.53	0.00	0.54	1.19
4 h–4h 30 min	0.34	0.00	0.68	0.00	0.00	0.54	0.79
4 h 30 min–5 h	0.23	0.23	0.23	0.00	0.41	0.00	0.40
>5 h	0.46	0.23	0.68	0.00	0.41	0.00	1.19

Note min—minutes; h—hour
Source Author's calculation, field survey

(35.51%) do not engage in ICT. Then, students' share decreases gradually in the higher levels. In both countries separately, girls are less involved in ICT than that of boys. As per both distributions (such as Kernel and normal distribution) of the sample students against ICT exposure, the largest share of students has the ICT exposure level within 0–30 min (see Fig. 1) that supports Table 1.

4.2 Level of ICT Exposure by Country

ANOVA of the level of ICT exposure has been undertaken between two countries to find whether there is any significant difference in ICT exposure level between the two countries. The derived F-statistics for the total sample (with $p = 0.00$ in Table 2) suggests that ICT exposure levels across countries are significantly different from each other. It is observed that the mean value of ICT exposure (0.27 h or 16.44 min) for India has been consistently lower than that (0.89 h or 53.34 min) for Fiji. Here, it should be noted that the mean value of ICT exposure for overall sample students is 0.58 h, i.e. almost 35 min every day.

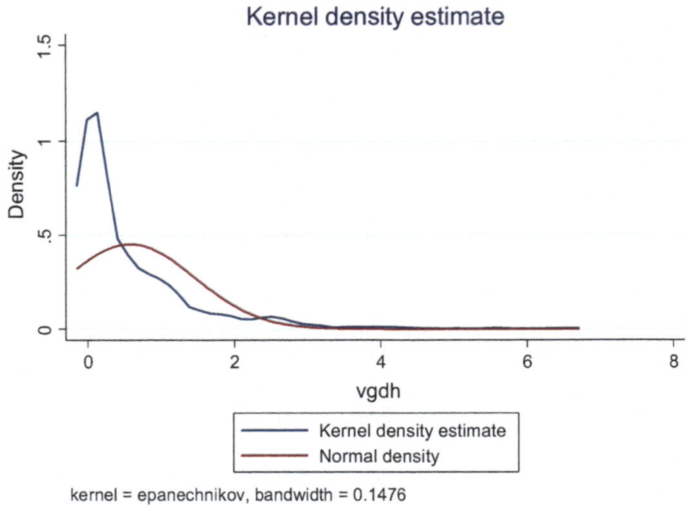

Fig. 1 Kernel density distribution of ICT exposure

Table 2 Summary statistics and ANOVA of the level of ICT exposure by country

Summary statistics					
Country	Mean	Std. Dev.	Freq.		
India	0.27	0.630	435		
Fiji	0.89	0.984	438		
Total	0.58	0.882	873		
ANOVA					
Source	Df	SS	MS	*F*	*p*
Between groups	1	82.619	82.619	120.73	0.00
Within groups	871	596.032	0.684		
Total	872	678.650	0.778		

Note Bartlett's test for equal variances ($chi^2(1) = 83.680$, $p = 0.00$)
Source Author's calculation, field survey

4.3 Level of ICT Exposure by Gender

ANOVA of the level of ICT exposure has been undertaken between gender for the two countries together and each country separately. F-statistics for the total sample ($p = 0.00$ in Table 3) and each country separately ($p = 0.02$ and 0.00 in Table 4) suggest that ICT exposure levels across gender are significantly different from each other. It is observed that the mean value of ICT exposure level for girls is 0.49 h or 29.4 min for overall sample students (see Table 3), whereas it is 0.21 h or 12.6 min in India and 0.76 h or 45.6 min in Fiji (see Table 4). Similarly, boys' mean ICT exposure

Table 3 Summary statistics and ANOVA of the level of ICT exposure by gender combining two countries

Summary statistics					
Gender	Mean	Std. Dev.	Freq.		
Girls	0.49	0.895	497		
Boys	0.71	0.850	376		
Total	0.58	0.882	873		
ANOVA					
Source	Df	SS	MS	*F*	*p*
Between groups	1	10.292	10.292	13.41	0.00
Within groups	871	668.358	0.767		
Total	872	678.650	0.778		

Note Bartlett's test for equal variances $chi^2(1) = 1.124$, $p = 0.00$
Source Author's calculation, field survey

Table 4 Summary statistics and ANOVA of the level of ICT exposure by gender in two countries separately

India	*Summary statistics*					
	Gender	Mean	Std. Dev.	Freq.		
	Girls	0.21	0.639	245		
	Boys	0.35	0.612	190		
	Total	0.27	0.630	435		
	ANOVA					
	Source	Df	SS	MS	*F*	*p*
	Between groups	1	2.079	2.079	5.28	0.02
	Within groups	433	170.368	0.393		
	Total	434	172.447	0.397		
Fiji	*Summary statistics*					
	Gender	Mean	Std. Dev.	Freq.		
	Girls	0.76	1.020	252		
	Boys	1.07	0.906	186		
	Total	0.89	0.985	438		
	ANOVA					
	Source	Df	SS	MS	*F*	*p*
	Between groups	1	10.581	10.581	11.17	0.00
	Within groups	436	413.004	0.947		
	Total	437	423.584	0.969		

Note Bartlett's test for equal variances ($chi^2(1) = 0.3974$, $p = 0.02$ for India; $chi^2(1) = 2.943$, $p = 0.00$ for Fiji)
Source Author's calculation, field survey

level for overall sample students is 0.71 h or 42.6 min (see Table 3), whereas it is 0.35 h or 21 min and 1.07 h or 64.2 min in India and Fiji, respectively (see Table 4). Therefore, girls' ICT exposure levels have been consistently lower than that of boys for both cases.

4.4 Academic Self-efficacy (ASE)

At first, the reliability test for the questionnaire on ASE has been undertaken. It is observed that the signs of all questions are positive and intertest correlations are high enough. The overall Cronbach's alpha combining all questions is 0.881, and it is beyond the critical value of 0.7 (see Appendix 1). So, it indicates that the questions are reliable to explain the variable sufficiently.

Then, the principal component method has been applied. It provides separate and appropriate scores against all questions towards various uncorrelated dimensions. The most significant dimension (component 1) with the maximum eigenvalue 25.553 and 34.9% of the total variance (the largest variation) of the variables has been considered. Note that all coefficients for component 1 are statistically significant and the probability value of chi-square suggests that the coefficients are significantly different from each other (see Appendix 1). Hence, they are combined linearly for index formation with weights. The shared value of each coefficient is used concerning the total value of all coefficients so that the sum of the weight will be exactly equal to one.

$$\text{level of academic self-efficacy} = \frac{\sum_{i=1}^{16} \omega_i asei}{\sum_{i=1}^{16} \omega_i} \quad (1)$$

where ω_i is the coefficient of the i-th variable (question) found in component 1.

As per both distributions such as Kernel distribution and normal distribution of the sample students against ASE, the largest share of students has the ASE level above mid-value, i.e. above 7 (see Fig. 2).

4.5 Academic Achievement (AA)

The study has considered the average percentage of scores combining all subjects (such as Mathematics, Science, Biology, Agriculture, Mother language, English, History, Geography, Social studies and Home economics) as a proxy of overall academic achievement. Moreover, the study has also calculated the average percentage of the scores for all science subjects and all arts subjects separately to get their relationship with ICT exposure also.

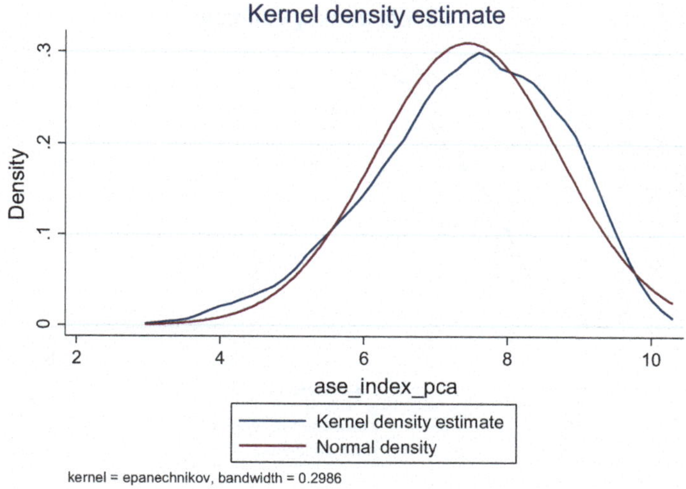

Fig. 2 Kernel density distribution of academic self-efficacy (ASE). *Source* Author's calculation, field survey

The distributions of the level of overall academic achievement, as well as achievement in science and arts of the sample students, have been plotted in Figs. 3, 4 and 5, respectively. As per two distributions (normal and Kernel plots), the highest density of the sample students falls more or less around 60–70 for all cases. Therefore, the

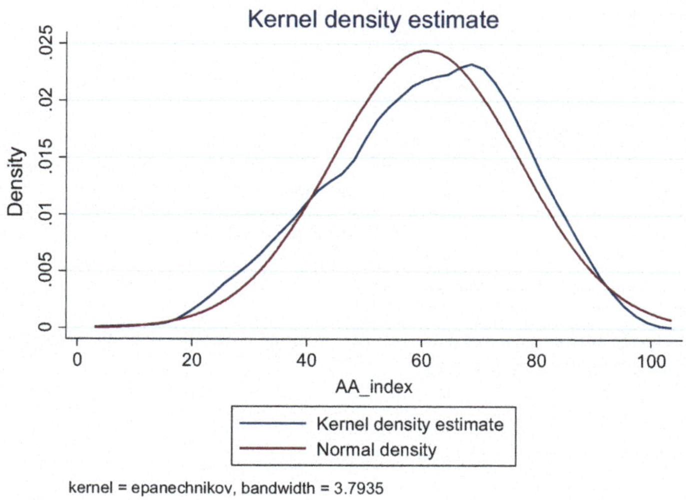

Fig. 3 Estimated Kernel and normal density function of the index of academic achievement. *Source* Author's calculation, field survey

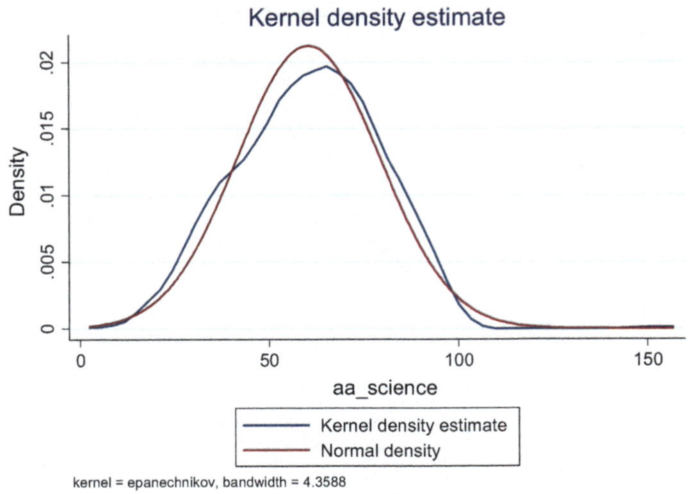

Fig. 4 Estimated Kernel and normal density function of the index of academic achievement in science. *Source* Author's calculation, field survey

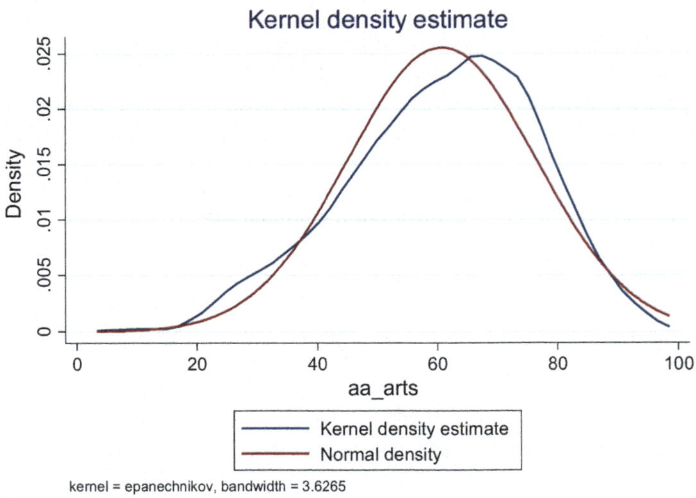

Fig. 5 Estimated Kernel and normal density function of the index of academic achievement in arts. *Source* Author's calculation, field survey

highest share of students has been found to obtain an overall academic achievement as well as achievement in science and arts beyond the middle level.

4.6 Effect of ICT Exposure on Academic Self-efficacy (ASE) and Achievement (AA)

The study examined the relationship of ICT exposure with academic self-efficacy (ASE), overall academic achievement (AA), and science (SA) and arts (ARA) achievement separately. Here, ASE, AA, SA and ARA were regressed on ICT separately along with other sociocultural factors such as gender, learning activities, musical and cultural engagement, and household activities. As the level of ICT exposure is found significantly different between the two countries, the study did not take the country dummy as a separate variable. Interaction effects of the country dummy with ICT exposure have been considered to investigate the differential impacts on ASE, AA, SA and ARA. Similarly, the school effect has been controlled in two out of four cases for robustness checking. The regression results on four outcome variables separately have been presented in Tables 5, 6, 7 and 8. From all the tables, it is seen that the regression coefficients of ICT exposure on students' ASE, AA, SA and ARA have been positive. But, the relationships with the interaction have not been statistically significant in all four cases. It is significant and positive in some cases, meaning that the overall effects of ICT exposure on ASE, AA, SA and ARA are positive but quite weak.

The coefficients of square terms of ICT exposure for all the variables are seen to be negative. It means that ASE, AA, SA and ARA are increasing with ICT exposure, but at a decreasing rate. These academic aspects increase with the level of ICT, reach to the highest peak and then start declining. In other words, beyond the highest peak, greater ICT exposure might work adversely on the level of ASE, AA, SA and ARA. The highest peaks for all the variables are more or less at 3 h/day (see Fig. 6). The estimated values have been plotted against ICT exposure in order to show the highest peak. It can be described that ICT exposure increases their ability of effective planning and active participation as well as the power of resource management, problem-solving and reasoning up to 3 h/day. As a result, students can improve their academic self-efficacy and performance within this limit. At the same time, ICT exposure also has an adverse effect on their self-efficacy and performance due to increased sedentary activity, and attention deficit and diversion from the academic activity. Thus, the combined effects of positive and negative of ICT exposure on ASE, AA, SA and ARA have been quite weak. With the increased exposure, negative effect starts dominating. Thereby, their efficacy level, as well as performance, deteriorates gradually.

Moreover, there is no significant difference in academic self-efficacy across gender. But, academic achievement is significantly different across gender in some cases. Therefore, more or less, boys' academic achievement is significantly greater than that

Table 5 Regression results of academic self-efficacy on the level of ICT combining both countries

Variables	Academic self-efficacy			
ICT exposure	0.217*	0.050	0.235	0.392*
	(0.113)	(0.115)	(0.203)	(0.206)
(ICT exposure)^2	−0.044	−0.007*	−0.059	−0.063
	(0.027)	(0.027)	(0.05)	(0.056)
ICT exposure * country	–	–	−0.021	−0.515**
			(0.219)	(0.244)
(ICT exposure)^2 * country	–	–	0.018	0.084
			(0.063)	(0.064)
Boy	−0.044	−0.125	−0.045	−0.117
	(0.090)	(0.101)	(0.090)	(0.1)
Share of time spent on household works	−0.845*	−1.276***	−0.851*	−1.334***
	(0.470)	(0.472)	(0.471)	(0.472)
Share of time spent on learning activities	−0.478	1.157**	−0.462	1.227**
	(0.383)	(0.520)	(0.410)	(0.52)
Share of time spent on music, singing and drawing	0.939*	0.781	0.983*	0.656
	(0.552)	(0.543)	(0.563)	(0.552)
Constant	7.536***	7.434***	7.529***	7.303***
	(0.153)	(0.266)	(0.159)	(0.271)
School effect	No	Yes	No	Yes
Observations	873	873	873	873
R-squared	0.016	0.120	0.016	0.126

Note Standard errors in parentheses
***$p < 0.01$, **$p < 0.05$, *$p < 0.1$
Source Author's calculation, field survey

of girls. Moreover, the result of an interaction effect of the country dummy with ICT exposure on academic self-efficacy was found as negative. So, in Fiji, ICT exposure decreases students' academic self-efficacy significantly. There is no significant difference in academic achievement for the interaction effect of the country dummy with ICT exposure.

5 Results and Discussion

The growing health and behavioural hazards in the adolescent period could be the results of the greater exposure of ICT. Because the adolescents do not know how to restrain themselves and hence, are engaged within it more by sacrificing their time from physical as well as an academic activity. In many cases, parents and

Table 6 Regression results of academic achievement on the level of ICT combining both countries

Variables	Academic achievement			
ICT exposure	4.000***	1.600	2.479**	2.319
	(1.378)	(1.161)	(2.450)	(2.087)
(ICT exposure)^2	−0.797**	−0.286	−1.458	−0.741
	(0.332)	(0.273)	(0.690)	(0.571)
ICT exposure * country			2.266	−0.786
			(2.650)	(2.472)
(ICT exposure)^2 * country			0.756	0.542
			(0.759)	(0.649)
Boy	6.148***	0.762	6.179***	0.756
	(1.099)	(1.019)	(1.094)	(1.020)
Share of time spent on household works	25.739***	19.430***	26.864***	19.473***
	(5.727)	(4.769)	(5.701)	(4.778)
Share of time spent on learning activities	−10.819**	25.044***	−6.682	24.653***
	(4.668)	(5.248)	(4.956)	(5.264)
Share of time spent on music, singing and drawing	19.078***	9.285*	22.709***	10.578*
	(6.735)	(5.478)	(6.807)	(5.590)
Constant	60.852***	66.384***	59.413***	66.405***
	(1.866)	(2.682)	(1.929)	(2.742)
Control of school	No	Yes	No	Yes
Observations	873	873	873	873
R-squared	0.093	0.444	0.107	0.445

Note Standard errors in parentheses
***$p < 0.01$, **$p < 0.05$, *$p < 0.1$
Source Author's calculation, field survey

teachers are frustrated to restrain their children from these activities. The current study investigated the possible influence of ICT exposure on academic self-efficacy and achievement of adolescent students in two typical developing societies, India and Fiji. The results from the data analysis and discussion can be summarized as follows. Firstly, on average, the sample students engage in ICT exposure almost 35 min every day. This engagement is 16.44 min in India and 53.34 min in Fiji. There is a significant difference in ICT exposure levels across the country. Fiji is more developed than India. Naturally, students are more exposed to ICT there rather than India.

Secondly, it is observed that girls are engaged in ICT exposure consistently at a lower level than that of boys. This could be related to the persistent discriminatory attitude towards the girl child in a traditional society so that they are less exposed and get less facility for these electronic devices.

Table 7 Regression results of science achievement on the level of ICT combining both countries

Variables	Science achievement			
ICT exposure	3.128**	0.892	2.714	0.592
	−1.569	−1.346	−2.803	−2.42
(ICT exposure)^2	−0.712*	−0.193	−1.429*	−0.225
	−0.378	−0.316	−0.79	−0.662
ICT exposure * country			0.761	0.52
			−3.032	−2.867
(ICT exposure)^2 * country			0.847	0.015
			−0.868	−0.752
Boy	9.238***	2.383**	9.236***	2.371**
	−1.252	−1.181	−1.252	−1.183
Share of time spent on household works	−31.511***	−22.784***	−32.287***	−22.715***
	−6.525	−5.527	−6.523	−5.541
Share of time spent on learning activities	−7.584	25.519***	−4.943	25.329***
	−5.318	−6.082	−5.67	−6.105
Share of time spent on music, singing and drawing	23.693***	13.309**	26.742***	13.793**
	−7.672	−6.348	−7.788	−6.484
Constant	58.951***	71.321***	57.992***	71.507***
	−2.126	−3.108	−2.207	−3.18
Control of school	No	Yes	No	Yes
Observations	873	873	873	873
R-squared	0.109	0.435	0.115	0.435

Note Standard errors in parentheses
***$p < 0.01$, **$p < 0.05$, *$p < 0.1$
Source Author's calculation, field survey

Thirdly, boys' all academic achievements (overall as well as science and arts) are significantly greater than that of girls. This may be due also to gender inequality continuing still in traditional societies.

Finally, ICT exposure increases the level of academic self-efficacy, overall academic achievement as well as achievement in science and arts, but at a low and decreasing rate. It supports our hypothesis that usage of ICT increases students' knowledge, planning ability as well as the power of resource management, problem-solving and reasoning (Head and Eisenberg 2009) and thereby, it develops their academic self-efficacy and achievement. This finding supports the study of Basri et al. (2018). Here, these academic aspects are rising with the increased level of ICT exposure, and they reach the highest peak approximately at 3 h/day ICT exposure. Beyond that level of ICT exposure, academic self-efficacy and achievements start to decline. Because overuse and addiction of ICT divert their attention and time from academic and other non-sedentary activities. In this way, the negative effect of

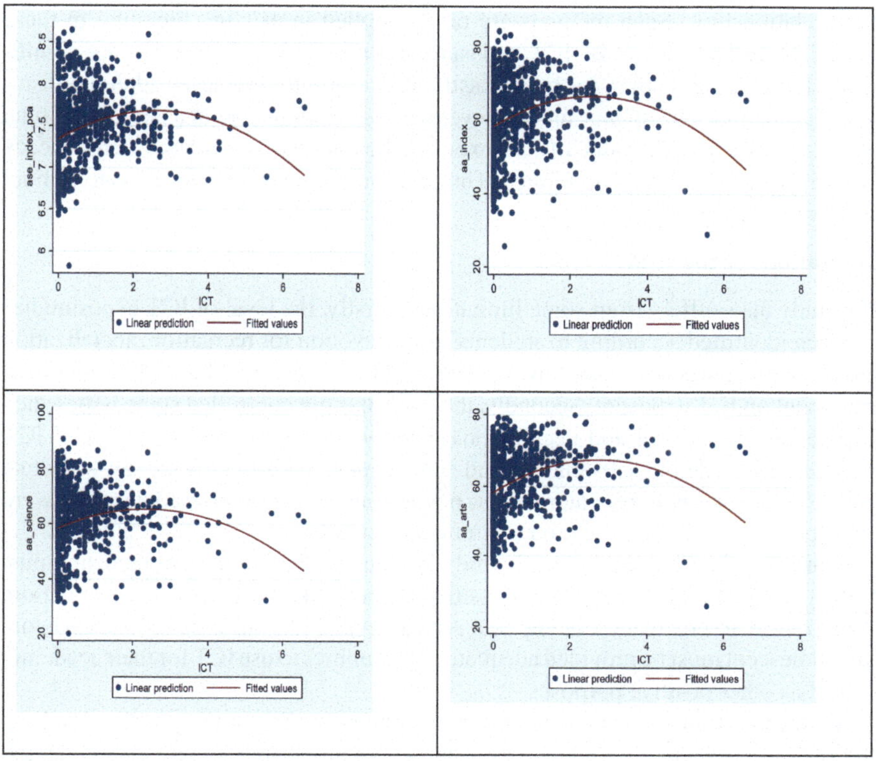

Fig. 6 Estimated outcome values against ICT exposure

ICT exposure starts dominating. These factors have an adverse implication on their academic area. Therefore, the present study is distinct from contemporary literature by identifying the extent of the relationships between ICT exposure and academic aspects.

6 Concluding Remarks

The present study investigated the effect of ICT on academic self-efficacy and achievement of adolescent students in two developing countries like India and Fiji. The results suggested that ICT engagement has a weak but positive impact on academic self-efficacy and achievement of adolescent students up to a certain limit of time spending. The study highlights how ICT exposure affects academic benefits during the adolescent period. The methodological framework applied for the study is quantitative. The quantitative answers on an ordinal scale of the questions for academic self-efficacy are used for indexation applying PCA, after undertaking the reliability test. Moreover, ANOVA and regression techniques have been applied to draw relationships. Such methods are rarely applied in existing literature in these areas. The average levels of ICT exposure and academic achievement are significantly lower for girls than for boys. Lastly, ICT exposure increases adolescent students' academic self-efficacy and achievement significantly, but at a decreasing rate. We find out the critical value of ICT exposure beyond which students' self-efficacy and performance will be deteriorated. Thus, it develops people's consciousness about the adverse effect of ICT exposure.

Limitations of the study

The study also suffers from some limitations. Firstly, the level of ICT exposure has not been identified according to students' time devotion for recreation, socialization and academic purposes separately. Here the students were asked to report their total time spent on ICT exposure. Secondly, the study has not controlled some issues such as parental educational and occupational level while examining the effect of ICT exposure on academic self-efficacy and achievement. Thirdly, the survey was done from 2013 to 14 when free Internet was not available, and thereby, adolescents were not exposed to ICT for recreation unlimitedly like today.

Remarks: The present research study concludes that adolescent students must be encouraged to use the ICT for a positive purpose like for gathering information, socialization and recreation but up to a certain level under the parents' supervision. Girl adolescent must be provided adequate opportunities to use ICT for their academic as well as other positive purposes.

An implication for school health: Since the study found the positive implication of ICT exposure on academic aspects, school authorities should encourage the students towards this activity and place ICT in their curriculum with due care and emphasis to maintain students' knowledge.

Human Subjects Approval Statement

The study undertook clearances from all relevant authorities to conduct the survey.

Acknowledgements The paper is based on my Ph.D. thesis. I acknowledge the support provided by the University of the South Pacific, Fiji, for conducting the research and financial assistance. The usual disclaimer applies.

Appendix 1

Table 8 Questionnaire and results of Cronbach's α test and PCA for ASE

Question	Alpha[a]	PCA coefficient[b]
1. In general, how confident are you in your abilities in learning?	0.874	0.194***
2. How confident are you that you will do well in learning?	0.873	0.204***
3. How confident are you that you can learn all the subjects?	0.875	0.212***
4. How confident are you that you will get an A (or Above 75%) in all subjects this year?	0.873	0.245***
5. How confident are you that you can perform successfully in science subject?	0.871	0.175***
6. How confident are you that you can perform successfully in Arts subject?	0.872	0.179***
7. How well can you finish your homework assignments by deadlines?	0.873	0.260***
8. How well can you perform your study when there are other interesting things to do?	0.878	0.253***
9. How well can you concentrate on school subjects during class?	0.874	0.218***
10. How well can you take good notes during class instruction?	0.877	0.238***
11. How well can you use the library/internet to get information for class assignments?	0.881	0.346***
12. How well can you plan your schoolwork for the day?	0.876	0.273***
13. How well can you organize your schoolwork?	0.871	0.294***
14. How well can you remember information presented in class and textbooks?	0.871	0.269***
15. How well can you arrange a place to study without distractions?	0.874	0.295***
16. How well can you get yourself to do school work?	0.874	0.277***
	Overall alpha = 0.881	

[a]Shows the Cronbach's α coefficient for the test if the particular item in the row is eliminated
[b]Derived from PCA [Rho = 0.349; SE(Rho) = 0.011
LR test for independence ($chi^2(120) = 4254.95$, $p = 0.00$)
LR test for sphericity ($chi^2(135) = 5233.55$, $p = 0.00$)
$Chi^2(17)$ test for equality of estimated coefficients = 38.09, $p = 0.002$]
*$p < 0.10$, **$p < 0.05$ and ***$p < 0.01$
Source Author's calculation, field survey

References

Anderson, C. A., & Bushman, B. J. (2001). Effects of violent video games on aggressive behaviour, aggressive cognition, aggressive affect, physiological arousal, and prosocial behaviour: A meta-analytic review of the scientific literature. *Psychological Science, 12,* 353–359.

Atwater, E. (1992). *Adolescence* (3rd ed.). NJ: Prentice Hall: Englewood Cliffs.

Ausubel, D. P. (2002). *Theory and problems of adolescent development.* Lincoln, USA: Writers Club Press.

Bandura, A. (1964). The stormy decade: Fact or fiction? *Psychology in the Schools, 1,* 224–231.

Bandura, A. (1986). *Social foundations of thought and action: A social cognitive theory*. NJ: Prentice Hall.

Bandura, A. (1993a). Perceived self-efficacy in cognitive development and functioning. *Educational Psychologist, 28*(2), 117–148.

Bandura, A. (1993b). *Social learning theory*. Englewood Cliffs, NJ: Prentice-Hall.

Bandura, A. (1994). Self-efficacy. *Encyclopedia of human behaviour, 4*(1), 71–81.

Bandura, A. (1997). *Self-efficacy: The exercise of control: Macmillan*. New York: Freeman.

Bandura, A. (2001). Social cognitive theory: An agentic perspective. *Annual Review Psychologists, 52,* 1–26.

Bandura, A. (2006). Guide for constructing self-efficacy scales. In F. Pajares & T. Urdan (Eds.), *Self-efficacy beliefs of adolescents* (pp. 307–337). Charlotte, United States: Information Age Publishing.

Bavelier, D., Green, C. S., Han, D. H., Renshaw, P. F., Merzenich, M. M., & Gentile, D. A. (2011). Brains on videogames. *Nature Reviews Neuroscience, 12,* 763–768.

Basri, W. S., Alandejani, J. A., & Almadani, F. M. (2018). ICT adoption impact on students' academic performance: Evidence from Saudi universities. *Education Research International,* 1240197.

Bosworth, K., Gustafson, D. H., & Hawkins, R. P. (1994). The BARN system: Use and impact of adolescent health promotion via computer. *Computers in Human Behavior, 10*(4), 467–482.

Caprara, G. V., Fida, R., Vecchione, M., Del Bove, G., Vecchio, G. M., Barbaranelli, C., et al. (2008). Longitudinal analysis of the role of perceived self-efficacy for self-regulated learning in academic continuance and achievement. *Journal of Educational Psychology, 100*(3), 525–534.

CDC. (2009). *Web-based injury statistics query and reporting system (WISQARS)*. Washington, D.C., USA: National Center for Injury Prevention and Control.

Chauhan, S. S. (2009). *Advanced educational psychology*. New Delhi: Vikas Publishing House Pvt. Ltd.

Cole, M. (1996). *Cultural psychology: A once and future discipline*. Cambridge: Harvard University Press.

Cortina, J. M. (1993). What is coefficient alpha? An examination of theory and applications. *Journal of Applied Psychology, 78,* 98–104.

Engels, R. C. M. E., Hale, W. W., III, Noom, M., & Vries, H. D. (2005). Self-efficacy and emotional adjustment as precursors of smoking in early adolescence. *Substance Use and Misuse, 40,* 1883–1893.

Erikson, E. (1968). *Identity: Youth and crisis*. New York: Norton.

Erikson, E., & Erikson, J. (1997). *The Life cycle completed*. New York: Norton.

Freud, S. (1962). *Three essays on the theory of sexuality, trans. James Strachey.* New York: Basic Books.

Goddard, C. (1998). *Semantic analysis: A practical introduction: New York*. NY: Oxford University Press.

Hall, G. S. (1904). *Adolescence: Its psychology and its relation to physiology, anthropology, sociology, sex, crime, religion, and education.* NJ: Prentice-Hall: Englewood Cliffs.

Hansen, D. L., Derry, H. A., Resnick, P. J., & Richardson, C. R. (2003). Adolescents searching for health information on the internet: An observational study. *Journal of Medical Internet Research, 5*(4), 25.

Head, A. J., & Eisenberg, M. B. (2009). Lessons learned: How college students seek information in the digital age. Project Information Literacy First Year Report with Student Survey Findings, University of Washington's Information School. Retrieved on January 22, 2015, from http://projectinfolit.org/images/pdfs/pil_fall2009_finalv_yr1_12_2009v2.pdf.

Jain, S., & Shakher, C. (2014). Statistical study of video game effects on children. *International Journal of New Trends in Arts, Sports and Science*. 3(1).

Keating, D. P. (1979). Toward a multivariate life-span theory of intelligence. *Intellectual development beyond childhood.* San Francisco: Jossey-Bass.

Keller, G. (2013). *Statistics for management and economics* (7th ed.). s.l.: Brooks/Cole.

Levesque, R. J. (2011). *Encyclopedia of adolescence* (Vol. 1–2). New York: Springer.

Lindman, C., & Sellin, J. (2011). *Measuring human development: The use of principal component analysis in creating an environmental index.* Uppsala University. Retrieved from www.diva-portal.org/smash/get/diva2:464378/FULLTEXT03.

Marcino, P. (2018). Impact of information and communication technology on academic achievement for exceptional student education inclusion students. Walden Dissertations and Doctoral Studies http://scholarworks.waldenu.edu/dissertations.

Marsch, L. A., Bickel, W. K., & Badger, G. J. (2006). Applying computer technology to substance abuse prevention science: Results of a preliminary examination. *Journal of Child and Adolescent Substance Abuse, 16*(2), 69–94.

Mahyuddin, R., Elias, H., Cheong, L., & Muhamad, M. (2006). The relationship between students' self efficacy and their English language achievement. *Jurnal Pendidik dan Pendidikan, 21,* 61–71.

Mbah, T. B. (2010). The impact of ICT on students' study habits. *Journal of Science and Technology Education Research, 1*(5), 107–110.

Merikangas, K. R., He, J. P., Burstein, M., Swanson, S. A., Avenevoli, S., Cui, L. B. C., et al. (2010). Lifetime prevalence of mental disorders in U.S. adolescents. *Journal of the American Academy of Child and Adolescent Psychiatry, 49*(10), 980–989.

Monetti, D. M., Whatley, M. A., Hinkle, K. T., Cunningham, T., Breneiser, J. E., & Kisling, R. (2011). A factor analytic study of the internet usage scale. *Journal of Research in Education, 21*(2), 14–23.

Montgomery, K. (2000). Youth and digital media: A policy research agenda. *Journal of Adolescent Health, 27*(2), 61–68.

Pahwa, B., & Schoech, D. (2008). Issues in the evaluation of an online prevention exercise. *Journal of Technology in Human Services, 26*(2/4), 259–281.

Panahi, S. (2015). Impact of modernization on development of adolescent: The media, culture, technology. *Unique Journal of Pharmaceutical and Biological Sciences*, ISSN 2347-3614.

Pearce, P. (2009). *Psychoanalytic/psychodynamic developmental theories*. S.l.: McGraw-Hill Education.

Piaget, J. (1966). *The origin of intelligence in children*. New York: International Universities Press Inc.

Rogers, D. (1969). *Studies in adolescence: A book of readings in adolescent development. II.* New York: Macmillan.

Shah, B., Parhee, R., Kumar, N., Khanna, T., & Singh, R. (2005). *Mental health research in India.* New Delhi: Indian Council of Medical Research.

Skinner, H., Biscope, S., Poland, B., & Goldberg, E. (2003). How adolescents use technology for health information: Implications for health professionals from focus group studies. *Journal of Medical Internet Research, 5*(4), 32.

Steinberg, L., & Morris, A. S. (2001). Adolescent development. *Annual Review Psychologists, 52,* 83–110.

The-Pennsylvania-Child-Welfare-Training-Program. (2005). *Child and adolescent development.* S .l., Mechanicsburg: University of Pittsburg.

Thijs, J.T., & Verkuyten, M. (2008). Peer victimization and academic achievement in a multiethnic sample: The role of perceived academic self-efficacy. *Journal of Educational Psychology, 100*(4), 754–764.

Thomas, M. K.-K. (2013). *Predicting students' confidence: How teacher feedback and other sources influence self-efficacy in mathematics classrooms*. S.l.: The University of Kentucky.

Thomee, S., Harenstam, A., & Hagberg, M. (2011). Mobile phone use and stress, sleep disturbances, and symptoms of depression among young adults—A prospective cohort study. *BMC Public Health, 11,* 66. https://doi.org/10.1186/1471-2458-11-66.

Usher, E. L., & Pajares, F. (2008). Self-efficacy for self-regulated learning: A validation study. *Educational and Psychological Measurement, 68,* 443–463.

Vyas, S., & Kumaranayake, L. (2006). Constructing socio-economic status indices: How to use principal components analysis. *Health policy and planning, 21*(6), 459–468.

Index

D. Maiti et al. (eds.), *Digitalisation and Development*,
https://doi.org/10.1007/978-981-13-9996-1

The manufacturer's authorised representative in the EU is Springer Nature Customer Service Centre GmbH, Europaplatz 3, 69115 Heidelberg, Germany. If you have any concerns regarding our products, please contact ProductSafety@springernature.com

Printed and bound by CPI Group (UK) Ltd, Croydon, CR0 4YY
25/09/2026
02222884-0009